Contemporary Authors®
Autobiography Series

ISSN 0748-0636

Contemporary Authors

Autobiography Series

Joyce Nakamura
Editor

Sheryl Ciccarelli
Motoko Fujishiro Huthwaite
Associate Editors

volume **30**

GALE

DETROIT · LONDON

Contents

Preface   vii
Acknowledgments   xi

Preface

A Unique Collection of Essays

Each volume in the *Contemporary Authors Autobiography Series (CAAS)* presents an original collection of autobiographical essays written especially for the series by noted writers.

CA Autobiography Series is designed to be a meeting place for writers and readers—a place where writers can present themselves, on their own terms, to their audience; and a place where general readers, students of contemporary literature, teachers and librarians, even aspiring writers can become better acquainted with familiar authors and meet others for the first time.

This is an opportunity for writers who may never write a full-length autobiography to let their readers know how they see themselves and their work, what brought them to this time and place.

Even for those authors who have already published full-length autobiographies, there is the opportunity in *CAAS* to bring their readers "up to date" or perhaps to take a different approach in the essay format. In some instances, previously published material may be reprinted or expanded upon; this fact is always noted at the end of such an essay. Individually, the essays in this series can enhance the reader's understanding of a writer's work; collectively, they are lessons in the creative process and in the discovery of its roots.

CAAS makes no attempt to give a comprehensive overview of authors and their works. That outlook is already well represented in biographies, reviews, and critiques published in a wide variety of sources. Instead, *CAAS* complements that perspective and presents what no other ongoing reference source does: the view of contemporary writers that is shaped by their own choice of materials and their own manner of storytelling.

Who Is Covered?

Like its parent series, *Contemporary Authors,* the *CA Autobiography Series* sets out to meet the needs and interests of a wide range of readers. Each volume includes essays by writers in all genres whose work is being read today. We consider it extraordinary that so many busy authors from throughout the world are able to interrupt their existing writing, teaching, speaking, traveling, and other schedules to converge on a given deadline for any one volume. So it is not always possible that all genres can be equally and uniformly represented from volume to volume, although we strive to include writers working in a variety of categories, including fiction, nonfiction, and poetry. As only a few writers specialize in a single area, the breadth of writings by authors in this volume also encompasses drama, translation, and criticism as well as work for movies, television, radio, newspapers, and journals.

What Each Essay Includes

Authors who contribute to *CAAS* are invited to write a "mini-autobiography" of approximately 10,000 words. In order to give the writer's imagination free rein, we suggest no guidelines or pattern for the essay.

We only ask that each writer tell his or her story in the manner and to the extent that feels most natural and appropriate. In addition, writers are asked to supply a selection of personal photographs showing themselves at various ages, as well as important people and special moments in their lives. Our contributors have responded generously, sharing with us some of their most treasured mementoes. The result is a special blend of text and photographs that will attract even the casual browser. Other features include:

Bibliography at the end of each essay, listing book-length works in chronological order of publication. Each bibliography in this volume was compiled by members of the *CAAS* editorial staff and submitted to the author for review.

Cumulative index in each volume, which cites all the essayists in the series as well as the subjects presented in the essays: personal names, titles of works, geographical names, schools of writing, etc. To ensure ease of use for these cumulating references, the name of the essayist is given before the volume and page number(s) for every reference that appears in more than one essay. In the following example, the entry in the index allows the user to identify the essay writers by name:

> Auden, W.H.
> Allen **6**:18, 24
> Ashby **6**:36, 39
> Bowles **1**:86
> etc.

For references that appear in only one essay, the volume and page number(s) are given but the name of the essayist is omitted. For example:

> Stieglitz, Alfred **1**:104, 109, 110

CAAS is something more than the sum of its individual essays. At many points the essays touch common ground, and from these intersections emerge new patterns of information and impressions. The index is an important guide to these interconnections.

For Additional Information

For detailed information on awards won, adaptations of works, critical reviews of works, and more, readers are encouraged to consult Gale's *Contemporary Authors* cumulative index for authors' listings in other Gale sources. These include, among others, *Contemporary Authors, Contemporary Authors New Revision Series, Dictionary of Literary Biography,* and *Contemporary Literary Criticism*. For autobiographical entries written by children and young adult authors, see *Something about the Author Autobiography Series*.

Special Thanks

We wish to acknowledge our special gratitude to each of the authors in this volume.

They all have been most kind and cooperative in contributing not only their talents but their enthusiasm and encouragement to this project.

Contact the Editor

We encourage our readers to explore the whole *CAAS* series. Please write and tell us if we can make *CAAS* more helpful to you. Direct your comments and suggestions to the editor:

MAIL: Editor, *Contemporary Authors Autobiography Series*
Gale Research
27500 Drake Road
Farmington Hills, MI 48331-3535

TELEPHONE: (800) 347-GALE

FAX: (248) 699-8065

Acknowledgments

Grateful acknowledgment is made to those publishers, photographers, and artists whose works appear with these authors' essays.

Photographs/Art

Maria Espinosa: p. 85, Valrie Massey; p. 101, Michael E. Bry.

Ronald Johnson: pp. 115, 121, Jonathan Williams.

James Martone: p. 138, Lissa McLaughlin.

David Miller: pp. 141, 150, 152, John Levy; pp. 142, 149, Beverly Miller; p. 145, George Murray; p. 155, Leslie Buchnan; p. 156, David Menzies.

James Scully: p. 201, Mondo Jud Hart; pp. 217, 222, George Amabile; p. 230, Judy Doyle; p. 234, Gail Schickele.

Lewis Shiner: p. 237, Viki Blaylock; p. 248, Melissa Mia Hall; p. 253, R. P. Alberts.

Jennifer Stone: p. 264, James Abresch; p. 268, Jane Scherr; p. 271, Ann Namura.

Keith Waldrop: p. 275, Maxine Goddard; p. 285, Walt Odets.

Rosmarie Waldrop: p. 297, Renate von Mangoldt; p. 303, Heinz Puppe; p. 304, Claude Royet-Journaud; p. 308, Michèle Cohen; p. 310, Joseph Guglielmi; p. 311, Keith Waldrop.

Text

Lisa Alther: Essay "Border States" first appeared in the anthology *Bloodroot: Reflections on Place by Appalachian Women Writers,* edited by Joyce Dyer. Copyright © 1998 by University of Kentucky Press. Reprinted with permission of University of Kentucky Press.

Mimi Albert

1940-

CHANGELING

Mimi Albert

New York

Origins

I was born Anna Cohen on a Thursday late in June, in the Brooklyn Jewish Hospital in Brooklyn, New York. Roses were blooming. World War II had recently begun. Apart from these facts, which are indisputable, any knowledge of my birth is as fragile as a web. Suspended upon it, between my birthday itself and my adoption six months later, are only two ephemeral traces. The first is the name of the adoption agency sponsored by an important Jewish judge, which handled my adoption; the second, that of a foster home or orphanage where I was kept for an unspecified period of time. The agency still exists, but the orphanage has vanished. I have no real memory of my life there, but I've always been oddly relaxed in hospitals, and I'm convinced that this is why.

Why, too, I feel so comfortable with mysteries, with unknown forces. I've always believed that the word "changeling" applied to me; also, the word "bastard."

And yes, I have tried to find my parents and to discover my origins. And no, I haven't succeeded. New York State believes in closed adoptions and birth records as hermetic as the grave. My past is as hidden as my future. I've lived with these questions since childhood. They no longer frighten me.

Early Influences

Some mystics believe that we choose our families before we're born. If that's true, why on earth would I have chosen the Ginsbergs? Was it out of some desire for self-destruction, or some need to test myself, to challenge my own strength?

Or even to atone, perhaps, for having had it too easy in a past life?

When they first set eyes on me, Jack and Judith Ginsberg were already middle-aged. Having survived the Great Depression and come out far worse than they had started, they were unhappy in their careers, within themselves, and in their marriage. It's hard for me to believe that anyone would think they'd be capable of raising a child.

But of course, to the naked eye they appeared an ordinary couple, a schoolteacher and his wife, a legal stenographer. Short on cash, perhaps, but long on art and culture. Who was to know that Judith was an insatiable shopper and that Jack had the temper of a rabid dog, or that the one thing they both did really well was to suffer? They had been excellently schooled in suffering during the misery of their respective childhoods and through the deprivation and compromise they experienced as they came of age, married, and watched their own parents lose virtually everything—livelihood, sanity, life.

My adoptive mother's family, the Rochesters, were Russian Jews, escapees from the pogroms and unrelenting poverty within the ghettos of the Pale of Settlement. They waited, in this promised land America, for new variations on the old theme. Instead, prosperity hounded them; the world around them refused to collapse. My maternal grandmother, Rose, was one of their few rebels—a revolutionary activist at fifteen, she was arrested in Odessa during the uprisings of 1905 and was subsequently rescued from hanging by my grandfather, Joseph, already a man of means. After marrying her and fathering two children, Joseph brought her entire family—Rose herself, their firstborn children (my mother and my uncle Max), Rose's four unmarried sisters, and her aged and ailing parents—to a relatively comfortable life in New York City. Then he had the canny prowess to invest in Brooklyn real estate rather than stocks and bonds, and managed to retain his wealth even when everyone else was jumping out of windows after the crash of 1929.

Befuddled by his success, his family contrived, instead, to implode. First, Rose's rebelliousness developed into paranoia; shock treatment was administered to her in an enormous mental hospital in Queens. She never fully recovered, either from her illness or from its cure. Her eldest son Max was next: he had a breakdown in his middle years, and died in the same institution long after his mother had been released. And finally, my adoptive mother, Judith, after threatening to do so during the entire course of my childhood and adolescence, committed suicide at the age of fifty-nine. I had just turned twenty-one; my father had died of a heart attack two years before. There were only two grandchildren, one cousin and myself, and by our teens we were both already

considered failures at the random and terrifying navigation of our lives.

The Rochesters have always reminded me of the old Russian folktale about the man who goes down to the cellar and sees that a scythe has gotten wedged in the ceiling. "Voy voy," he moans. "Any minute now it's going to come crashing out of the ceiling and split my skull." Instead of doing anything about it, he sits down to watch the scythe for the rest of the night, drink vodka, and speculate about how close he is to death. After a few hours the whole family comes down to the cellar to join him, one by one. There they sit, bemoaning the fact that eventually the scythe is going to crash down out of the ceiling and leave them widowed, orphaned, or dead. Eventually they all die of starvation.

My adoptive father's family, Vienna-born (or so they said—my mother always called them "Galitzianer," a Jewish curse), was so rich that his parents had more servants than children. Nonetheless, both of these parents, Minna and Abraham, died young of various diseases, and I was named for them, following the Jewish custom of naming a newborn child for dead ancestors. Jack, my father, and his five brothers and sisters had been raised in a huge brick mansion on Brooklyn's Pitkin Avenue when it was still considered elegant, the Champs-Elysées of its borough. But from early childhood Jack had been chosen as the scapegoat son, marked for intellectuality and concomitant poverty. He failed, however, even to turn into an intellectual, and ended by teaching sixth grade in a neighborhood that went rapidly from poor to poorer. Given all that, he was still the only one of the four sons who was decent enough to support his downtrodden father after the family wealth was lost in the aforementioned crash. The others, who didn't lift a finger, became millionaires to a man and very occasionally descended upon us (at my mother's insistent invitation) from their Gatsbyesque mansions on Long Island, to which we were never invited. They drove enormous Cadillacs and draped their svelte wives in mink and large, ugly, glistening gems.

But when my mother died, the poorest of them all, they clamored for her furniture and art.

My father was, I think, the next-to-youngest son. He was also the first to die. Every morning of his adult life he went into the bathroom and threw up his breakfast because he didn't want to go to his horrible job. He went anyway. The New York Board of Education lured him with the promise of a pension that would ease and succor his old age. Unlike his own father, he reasoned (as he stared into the bowl), he would never die a pauper in the street.

But he died eight years before retirement, at the age of fifty-seven, and didn't live to see a penny of his pension.

Why did they adopt me? To care for them, I think. To salvage what was left of their marriage. To entertain them. To give meaning to their lives.

Tasks too monumental for a six-month-old. On the face revealed in my first baby photographs there glimmers some vague and dismal awareness of that burden. For all I know, I've never really put the burden down—but I've never killed myself to earn a pension, either.

Early Art

For obvious reasons, I have an abiding curiosity about the impact of heredity and environment on the human psyche, and of course I wonder whether any of my genetic ancestors were artists, actors, or intellectuals. Perhaps, like a beautiful blue-eyed Roumanian friend of mine, I have a grandmother who was really a gypsy, and this could account for my nomadic streak and my mysticism, as it accounts for hers. In any case, I did grow up in a household filled with art and music, with literature and with love for the theater, and it could be said that both of my adoptive parents were artists in their own ways.

True to form, however, they were also both failures at their respective forms of art, which they practiced only surreptitiously and after they had made every effort to conform to as many of the conventional demands of their lives as they could stand. In short, they were closet artists, and all the efforts and pains they took for their art were likewise closeted. As my father often insisted to me, art was irrelevant; it had no relation to what he called "the world of reality," belonging merely to "the world of dreams."

A misfit from childhood, he himself had wanted to work at only one thing. He loved gardens. As a boy he planted shrubs and flowers in the backyard of the family mansion, but his efforts extracted either ridicule or wrath

"*My parents on their brief honeymoon somewhere in Massachusetts. A few years later, they drove across the country, and my mother fell in love with northern California, where I ended up spending half my adult life —long after her death.*"

from his authoritative father, sickly mother, and burgeoning, competitive, materialistic brothers and sisters. He grew up handsome and athletic, but he was nonetheless a timid, inhibited young man, who longed to study at Cornell University in Ithaca, New York, which at that time had one of the few departments in landscape architecture and decorative horticulture in America. But going to Cornell would have meant leaving his father's strictly kosher and Orthodox Jewish home, and for that reason was entirely proscribed. Instead, Jack was forced to go to rabbinical school, where he learned to speak and read a fluent, mellifluous Hebrew, so that he was often invited to teach at various Jewish Sunday schools and to officiate at traditional family seders and ceremonies. But this training also made him so miserable that he turned into a hidden, resentful agnostic, who never set foot in a synagogue if he didn't have to.

Failing to become a rabbi, he was next compelled to study law. "Every Jewish family," said Abraham, his father, "should have in it one good lawyer." Until he lost his money in 1929, finding a place for his misfit son Jack was the major burden of his life.

So my father was set to be the "good lawyer." He went to the New York University law school and obtained a law degree, which I discovered in an old bureau drawer years after he died. There was a problem, though (as usual). He couldn't pass the Bar exam. He tried and failed three times; after the third, his pretty fiancée returned his diamond-studded fraternity pin. At last the depression of the 1930s rescued him, because the only job he could possibly have found anyway during that dark time was teaching school, which he did for the rest of his life. Nonetheless, in deference to his own artistic talent and creativity, he also opened a tiny gardening business on the side, for which the entire family continued to ridicule him, including my mother, Judith, whom, by then, he had met and married.

"You are the most interesting woman I ever met," he wrote to her in an early love letter. He came to court her in the family limousine, faded but regal, with tiny bud vases at the two side windows and a seat in front for the chauffeur. There was no more chauffeur; the vases were empty and the upholstery was torn. Nonetheless, she was impressed; and, because at the age of twenty-seven she was considered by her family an irredeemable spinster, her younger sister having married years before, she quickly accepted his proposal. Within six weeks they had eloped to Massachusetts, where they so inflamed each other's senses (she later informed me), that he dropped his inhibitions—and his pants—in public for the first and only time in his life. They were almost arrested for cavorting naked by a stream.

But when they returned to Brooklyn, their brief, unprecedented happiness ended. "You married *her?"* his older sisters screamed when Jack waltzed his new bride through the door of the family home (now fallen into disarray) on Pitkin Avenue. "How could you *do* such a thing? She isn't even pretty!"

Interesting as hell but not very pretty, and painfully aware of it, Judith, my mother, was a self-styled Greenwich Village bohemian who got herself up in flapper clothes and trailing beads. Once her own father had acquired wealth, when she was in her teens, she studied art and the piano, gaining considerable proficiency in both. When I was a child she used to sing me a ragtime blues that she wrote herself, and the house was hung with her richly textured paintings, all of which were stolen by her relatives after her death. But she, too, had no confidence. She dated actors and other artistic men, but none of them ever wanted to marry her. She never sold a painting, never even tried to get a job in commercial art. And when she was chosen to give a recital at the piano, at the famous Henry Street settlement house in Manhattan, she raised a huge blister on her thumb and stayed home with a fever instead.

Probably the ultimate failure for both of them was that they weren't even able to conceive a child. Each blamed the other. Judith confessed to me that she'd been born with two sets of reproductive organs, but said that the fault was nonetheless Jack's; his sperm was weak. They tried for seven years before she decided to do something about it. She went to work for the Judge Stephen S. Wise Adoption Agency. Applying herself with zeal for a change, she became the personal secretary of the judge's daughter, Shirley Wise, who ran the agency, and convinced her that she and Jack would make exceptional parents despite their relative poverty. For the first time in her life, persistence paid off, which might have taught her something—except she was too busy being triumphant. I was awarded to the Ginsbergs, a curly-headed prize, and in an early photograph she's holding me aloft between her hands like a trophy cup.

She and Jack set out on the road of parenthood by infusing me with every half-baked dream of which they were capable. Jack dashed out to Coney Island and made a little recording in an arcade, which you could do in those days, telling me that he looked forward to the day when the letters Ph.D. would follow my name. Mimi Ginsberg, Ph.D. I remember listening to these words of prophecy a few years later, and thinking quietly, in my six-year-old words, "Never gonna happen, man." As soon as I was able to walk and talk, my mother spent her Saturday afternoons dragging me to every art lesson, music appreciation lesson, singing lesson, dance lesson, and elocution lesson she could find in the city of New York. She had been forced to name me for those two prosaic upholders of the traditional and stuffy, Minna and Abraham Ginsberg, but she compensated for this by adding her own touch of bohemian wit. Mimi was the name she chose after listening to the opera *La Boheme* a number of times, and even reading the book on which it was based, Murger's *Bohemians of the Latin Quarter*. That she was naming me for a sixteen-year-old milliner-turned-prostitute who died of tuberculosis before she was barely out of childhood never fazed her. And the name Abraham she twisted into my euphonious middle moniker, Abriel, which nobody in Brooklyn could pronounce but her. She liked that.

I enjoyed my first opera *(Carmen)* at six, my second *(Madame Butterfly)* at eight. I grew up listening to her play Chopin, Brahms, and Bach on the piano, and spent my own tortured moments before its ivory keyboard, learning (at my mother's hands) that I myself had no talent to play. My father taught me to read (from something called *The Little Brownie Books)* when I was four. By the time I got to elementary school my reading level was too far beyond the other kids' to be classified. On the other hand, I could not do math. It took me thirty years to discover that I had a learning disability.

I was a thoroughly artistic child, and also thoroughly disagreeable. Somewhere in the middle of childhood, having become a little radio actress by winning a starring role on a New York City public radio program, I lost most, or all, of my friends. I couldn't spend too much time with other children anyway, because all weekends and most afternoons were taken up with lessons. I had no athletic training or ability whatever; only in my rebellious early teens did I teach myself to hit a ball and run with it, accomplishments which, it turned out, I enjoyed. But in childhood I grew fat and had frequent tantrums. I was often sick and spent hours listening to soap operas on the radio or drawing sticklike figures of people, mainly women with waist-length, wavy hair and big breasts. My sixth-grade teacher, observing me dreaming over these productions instead of applying myself to more important matters, like geography or math, said harshly, "Mimi, if you had any talent for art at all I wouldn't mind you drawing in class. I don't mind Bob drawing, for example, because his work is good at least, but your drawings are nothing but scribbles."

What she didn't realize was that my scribbles were really vehicles for the stories I was telling

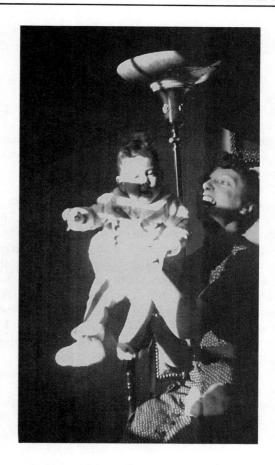

"She held me aloft like a trophy cup: my mother, holding me, soon after I had been adopted," Brooklyn, New York, 1941

myself about my stick figures. Even at eight, nine, ten, I invented (or imitated) the sagas of people who did remarkable things—they went from rags to riches and back again, they became luminously famous but personally complicated Hollywood movie stars or French ballet dancers, and they (very importantly) frequently stayed up all night and ate grand, erotic dinners at midnight at good restaurants in bad company. It's true that Bob was a budding cartoonist and became near-famous when he grew up. But my teacher was wrong—my stick drawings weren't worthless, either.

It's just that what I became was a novelist.

Perhaps all the lessons, the art, the theater, the singing, the literature—perhaps they weren't the only stimuli that contributed to this, however. Because in some ways, art is the response of the human organism to irritation, even to pain. And I was being taught to suffer by my parents, both so gifted, so proficient at the art.

At the same time as they coddled me, spoiled me, took me to a number of different private schools for art and piano and singing and elocution and acting and dance, gave me books at four and made me speak as if I'd been raised on Sutton Place rather than East Flatbush, Brooklyn, and dressed me up like a little puppet—at the same time, they were abusing me.

The two people whom I'd been taught to love beat me frequently and violently. They slammed me across the face when I made a mistake; they brandished belts or coat hangers when and if I said something they didn't like or accidentally woke them up at night; they scratched me and tried to push me down the stairs. There were other kinds of abuse as well: sexual molestation that was so thoroughly hidden and denied it took me years to acknowledge it, and verbal attacks that followed excessive praise like chasers. When they weren't calling me a genius they were telling me that I was "innately bad," "ungrateful," "a little bastard."

What was I to believe?

The Ginsbergs, to do them justice, had both been raised with the precept "spare the rod and spoil the child." And indeed, I was a rebellious child. I went my own way. I was difficult. They believed that corporal punishment would curb my disobedience and build my character. But even now, when I hear people defending the practice of hitting children, my blood begins to rise. There are too many other ways of putting a point across, of teaching; and there's always the danger of physical force getting out of control.

In the manner of all battered children, I felt, first of all, that I was to blame for the abuse: that no matter what I did, how much I achieved, I could never completely win my parents' love; and then, that I was totally alone: that no one could possibly know or understand my plight, that no one would ever listen to me. (What greater stimulus is there to write, to make oneself heard, as if—at last—one might be listened to?)

But years later, after they both had died and been laid to rest in a cemetery plot in Mount Hebron Cemetery in Queens, I ran into one of our Flatbush neighbors while I was teaching at Brooklyn College. It was in the college gymnasium during registration week; the neigh-

bor, apparently at the college to register for some course, caught sight of me and ran over, calling my name.

"Mimmie!" she called me, in her Brooklyn accent (although my mother always corrected people—"Her name is MeeMee," she'd enjoin, obstreperously, until I was so embarrassed I didn't care what my name was anyway).

"Mimmie Ginsberg! What are you doing here?"

"I'm not Mimi Ginsberg any more," I responded. "My name is Mimi Albert now." My last name had changed through marriage and divorce, but I didn't think it was necessary to tell her that. "And I'm here because I teach here. English."

The woman smiled. "You're a professor?"

"Well, an instructor, anyway. I teach English and creative writing. I'm a writer."

Her smile was infectious and I smiled back. Then she did something extraordinary. She touched my hand.

Mimi, age three, riding a tricycle in front of the house owned by her grandparents, Brooklyn, 1943

"I always knew," she said softly. "I always knew you'd be all right." She touched me again before she went away.

And I thought suddenly, *so someone must have heard us, after all.* Someone must have known about it. This woman. Maybe some of the other neighbors. They must have heard my parents screaming. They must have heard me cry.

My mother made much of my weekend education at the Neighborhood Playhouse school for children. The acting school for adults was run by Sanford Meisner, one of the most eminent drama coaches of his time. Meisner, however, didn't think it was appropriate for children to learn how to act; instead we were instructed in modern dance by members of Martha Graham's troupe, and taught to pronounce our words in the correct Eastern Standard style by soft-spoken, genteel instructors of speech, most of whom had been actors at one time or another.

My mother's typical Saturday outfit consisted of a tight-waisted woolen suit garnished with rows of pearl necklaces and gold bracelets, a diamond-and-ruby wedding band, a huge pink-gold watch, a scarf consisting of three extremely dead stone martens hungrily grasping one another with their tiny, wired jaws, and some insane concoction of a hat with fruit and veils. Once she wore a pair of enormous rabbit ears that stuck straight up in the air like antennae, so incongruous that I laughed out loud when I saw the hat, enraging her for a week. She wore this get-up everywhere when we went out together, even to classes at the Jefferson School, a hotbed of culture-ridden Marxism in which she claimed to be seriously interested, despite her obvious addiction to shopping.

She wore it, too, when she befriended one of my dance teachers at the Neighborhood Playhouse, a woman so different from herself that even then I couldn't imagine what they had in common. Marjorie was still beautiful and young when we met her. She had dark curly hair, wore no makeup, and dressed with the uncluttered simplicity typical of modern dancers. But perhaps she and my mother came to care for one another because Marjorie, too, was familiar with pain.

With her husband and several little children, she lived in an empty white apartment in Sheepshead Bay. They had almost no furniture. Just beds, maybe a sofa, and an old black upright piano on one side of the room.

Marjorie's husband sat off in a room of his own, dark and silent, looking as if he'd just gotten up from sleep. His face was long and narrow and a heavy five o'clock shadow lined his cheeks, above which his eyes, half-closed, were a vivid, scary blue. When we were invited into that apartment one bright afternoon in late spring, my mother slid a glance sideways at me, as if in warning.

"Maybe he's drunk," I thought, with the pseudosophistication of a New York eleven-year-old who thought she knew about such things. Nobody ever told me, then or later, that this man was already world-famous, and that what was wrong with him had nothing to do with alcohol. His name was Woody Guthrie, and years later I discovered that the pain which he and Marjorie shared was called Huntington's chorea, a hereditary, degenerative disease which eventually left him totally helpless before he died, and which may already have been passed down to any one of the children with whom I played that afternoon—one of whom, indeed, was his son Arlo, later to become famous in his own right. (He was the eldest. I remember helping Marjorie put a Band-aid on his finger.)

I recall that day most vividly, however, because it ended with what turned out to be a great honor. Because Woody finally came out of his room and sat down at the piano. He played with an amazing zest, and for a few moments it seemed as if none of our sorrows existed. The women laughed. We children danced barefoot in the sun that poured into the room from the many windows. Even my mother, who had put her hat down on the piano, was not offended when he lifted it up and put it on his own head, so that its veils and cherries dangled into his eyes.

I didn't really know this either. That I was already becoming an artist. With an artist's arrogance and independence and an artist's secret turmoil. The misery and violence of my parents ate into my life like battery acid. Worst of all, what they told me—before, during, and after the hours of abuse—was that they loved me more than anyone else on earth would ever love me, and that I would never be able to trust anyone beside themselves.

By the age of ten I had a serious eating disorder (which went untreated, as such things were unheard of at that time), was under the spell of an intense and major depression (which was also unheard of in children), and had already made one suicide attempt, which I dutifully reported at school but for which I received no help. By the age of fifteen, having lived for five more years with all three maladies, I ran away from home, then attempted suicide with even more determination, and was threatened, both by the officials in my high school and by my parents, with incarceration—which I managed to avoid, God knows how.

And by sixteen, I was a thief, a beggar, and living in the streets.

It's no wonder to me that for the past ten years or so I've been working with emotionally ruined children.

Nor that all my books (so far) have been about rebellion, about what happens to young people when they step out of the accustomed order and venture alone into the darkness of a way they try to make themselves.

The Way to India

My Theatrical Career

Surrounded by so much destruction and self-destruction—my parents' abuse, my father's early and lethal heart condition, my mother's suicide attempts, the mental illness that was like a plague infecting the members of the Rochester family, and the judgmental callousness and sanctioned greed of the Ginsbergs—I developed an early sense of the limitations of human life. I remember worrying myself sleepless about The Bomb when I was barely out of fifth grade, having been taught to "Take cover!" under one of the flimsy plywood desks in my classroom. (What, I wondered even then, would such a desk have covered anyway?) At ten, my most pervasive thought was, "If I become a famous actress by the time I'm twenty, then it'll be okay to die."

By the age of twenty, however, I no longer wanted to be a famous actress. This decision offered me the possibility of a longer life.

My career in the theater began when radio station WNYC offered the starring role of an eight-year-old in a new series to every eligible child in the New York City school system. The radio show was called "All in the Family" (no relation to the later television hit), and was broadcast to public school classrooms throughout the city on Wednesday afternoons.

I auditioned, was chosen as a finalist, and won the part. The character I played, ironically, was called Anna, my preadoption name, and when Judith learned this she went into a kind of thrall, as if it had been predestined and I was going to turn into the next Shirley Temple or Margaret O'Brien, give or take a few pounds. But acting on the air took an enormous amount of time and energy, and succeeded only in alienating me from all my friends and classmates; in order to play Anna I was excused from school on Wednesday afternoons, when the rest of the children in New York were chained to their desks and forced to listen to me. But it was also an enormous amount of fun.

As I grew up, however, the tasks of acting became more and more onerous. After the early years at the Neighborhood Playhouse, I was accepted into the School of Performing Arts only to learn that I had to struggle not to be "kicked out," as many young performers were, dumped back into the stew of Midwood High in Brooklyn, the very battleground which had earlier spawned Woody Allen. It turned out that the mavens at Performing Arts didn't think I was a very good actress. They said I "thought too much" to successfully assimilate the Stanislavski method, which was the kind of acting, the only kind, being taught at that time. This dubious label was bestowed on me when I was thirteen years old, and, not having sufficient strength to respond to it with any kind of resilience, spent wretched hours weeping in the shower so my parents wouldn't hear and become even more aggravated with me than they already were.

Performing Arts ultimately kept me on because (apparently) my scholastic record brought them honor, but I was never considered one of their more promising drama students. I remember one teacher in particular, a gigantic woman who wore a kind of round tin breastplate in her hair which made her look like a cookie jar, and who particularly disliked my acting style, or lack of it. Whenever I had a class with her I followed my father's pattern (like the obedient daughter I still was) and spent the morning throwing up.

True to my renegade form, however, I ended up being the only student in my senior class to land a professional acting part. I understud-

*"My mother painting in the country, with my father sitting behind her.
The little girl isn't me, but a friend named Nancy," about 1949.*

ied the part of a twelve-year-old Puerto Rican girl in a play called *Me, Candido!* and struggled through my one performance a week with a bludgeoning persistence, if not grace. The play continued off Broadway (in the Greenwich Mews, then a very good theater) for almost two years.

After which, equally spurred by other stimuli, I decided I didn't really want to be an actress.

I Begin to Write

My desire to be a writer, however, was something very different. The art of writing came to me not as something to achieve externally but as something which in itself exalted and healed my life. I had always written; my stick figures had given way to little stories, and my first major work, at eight or nine, was a biographical novel about Beethoven, the story of whose battered childhood had so moved me

that I insisted on learning some of his simpler pieces for the piano. These I practiced for the rest of my brief musical career under a tiny plaster bust of his stormy face and wild, wind-driven hair.

The real spirit of writing never came to me, though, until I was nineteen years old, living alone in a cold-water flat in a then-unfashionable section of the Upper East Side. Having flunked out of City College, I had just begun to study anthropology and philosophy at Hunter, a few blocks from where I lived.

Apart from these studies, which I loved, my life was as grim as my sixteen-dollar-a-month walk-up. There was no heat, no stove, and no bathtub in that place; I had to bathe in the sink and cook on a hot plate. I couldn't afford a telephone. To make things worse, I felt hunted. Men, and occasionally women, tried to break into my room through the flimsy front door or the fire escape window; they followed me in from the street and offered me money for sexual favors. I invariably refused, not necessarily out of virtue, but because I was too fastidious—the idea of touching someone I didn't really like filled me with nausea.

I began to turn to writing whenever I felt overwhelmed by loneliness and cold. Sometimes there was no money for food, and once the electricity was turned off because I couldn't pay the bill. One day I came home from visiting my mother, who had recently been widowed and was already sliding into her ultimate depression. Her misery as usual exacerbated mine and my apartment offered no comfort. There was no one to call, even if I'd had a telephone. Drinking made me sick to my stomach; I didn't use drugs; I had neither a television set nor a radio; and there was nothing in the house to eat. So I sat down at my ancient IBM typewriter and began to work on the pedestrian and boring novel I had begun, about some people in the small town where my parents and I had vacationed several years before.

My inspiration for this piece of drivel was the most popular novel of the time, the best-selling *Peyton Place*. I reasoned that if, like Grace Metalious, *Peyton Place's* unlikely author, I too could write a best-seller, my life might get a little better. I might meet respectful and remarkable men. I might even get my picture in the paper. At the very least, I might earn enough money to rent an apartment with a kitchen, central heating, and a bathtub.

But that day, for the first time, something happened.

I never expected it to happen, but once it did, my life changed. It was both damnable and marvelous—like all ruling passions, almost as much a curse as a blessing. I was writing the description of a sunset. My words caught fire. An energy filled me and whirled me around. I was possessed. A voice came. I sang on the page. I danced.

Now, many years later, I can't expect the same thing to happen each time I sit down to write. In fact, it happens only rarely, if at all. I've become a craftsperson, patient and calm; I look at every page as a structure that will eventually be taken down and then rebuilt again, perhaps five or ten more times, before it's done. But at that moment the sensation was altogether new. I had no method or technique. I didn't even know that the name for this was *voice*. Nor did it matter. When I sat down to reread what I had written it seemed intensely alive,

intensely real. It was probably intensely imitative; I was reading William Faulkner's novels at the time, and had fallen in love with his syntax, if not his subject matter. But still. I felt as if I'd created something precious, and that I'd never be the same again.

By the age of thirty I had written a novel called *The Second Story Man,* published by the Fiction Collective in 1975, in which I had transformed my childhood persona into two women, a dependent victim named Anna who eventually emerges from her first affair with a victorious sense of self, and an independent rebel named Mary, who eventually becomes a victim. *The Second Story Man* was originally written as my master's thesis when I was getting my master of fine arts degree at Columbia University, during which period I lived as a kind of princess in a six-room apartment on West End Avenue with tiled and parquet floors, a kitchen equipped with every gourmet fixture, a book-lined study of my own, and a very deep, old-fashioned, luxurious bathtub in which I spent as much time as I wanted. The apartment was filled with bright modern fabrics and beautiful antiques, and I had a rich young college professor husband who took me on extended European vacations and bought me designer dresses and eighteenth-century ruby rings.

Which was what it took to teach me that I could be just as miserable having money, status, and luxury as being hungry and cold.

At Columbia I studied with a man whom I considered one of the last great American masters, Edward Dahlberg. I had come across his autobiography, *Because I Was Flesh,* several years before, excerpted in a literary magazine called *Big Table* (also the first to publish excerpts of William Burroughs's *Naked Lunch*), and then later, completed, in a Philadelphia bookstore. Attracted by the title, I read on and was mesmerized. A self-instructed stylist, influenced by the Elizabethans and the Victorian literati rather than by any of his contemporaries, Dahlberg described himself as a Kansas City Jew, a picaresque anti-hero, and the illegitimate son of a psychotically erratic mother. How could I resist? When a new M.F.A. program was announced at Columbia University with Dahlberg's name on the masthead, I was one of the first to apply and one of the few to be accepted.

It was a mixed blessing. Dahlberg, then styled "the father of the Beats" because of his influence on poet Robert Creeley and some of

Creeley's peers, was a powerful, eccentric teacher. Because of his unpopular teaching methods— he frequently intruded on his students' lives, and he almost never gave praise—Dahlberg was quickly refused tenure by the Columbia administration and was dismissed as of the following academic year. At that point he decided to avoid the campus altogether, meeting those of us who were still left in the class in his cluttered apartment on Rivington Street on Manhattan's Lower East Side. Later, he kicked his alcoholic fifth wife out of the house and had a passionate affair with the only woman beside myself still left in the class. She was Native American, with a flashy, marvelous talent.

Dahlberg was almost eighty at the time. The new girlfriend was fifty years younger.

All this happened during the spring of 1968. Suddenly, the campus was closed down by the student strike. Students and faculty alike were outraged by Columbia's reputation as a Harlem slumlord, as well as by the university's involvement in the Vietnam War. Ironically, it was then that I learned, for the first time in my life, to speak up for my beliefs if not necessarily on my own behalf. I had long been deeply moved by the issues surrounding racism and poverty in America, and had demonstrated against the Vietnam War from its beginning. Now I discovered a new eloquence and was elected representative from the School of the Arts to the Columbia Strike Committee. One of my fellow students, a young man who hung out with the SDS, wanted to turn Dahlberg's dismissal into a *cause célèbre*, but it never caught on. Eventually, the strike was broken, Dahlberg left the university, and the Native American woman dropped out of Columbia (and eventually out of Dahlberg's life, when the wife came back), and was never heard from again.

But I stayed on because I wanted—I needed—to get my master's degree. It was time for me to escape my husband's financial domination and start my own teaching career. The following year, the seminar in the novel was run by an ambitious young writer named Richard M. Elman, from whom I actually learned a great deal. I revised one of my stories roughly sixteen times under Elman's guidance, and he helped me get it published in *The Transatlantic Review*. I wrote the first draft of *The Second Story Man* and was granted an M.F.A.

Writing had been my private passion for years. Now I was becoming a writer.

The Seventies

In my early thirties, having left my husband and our six-room uptown apartment complete with expensive antiques and affectionate cats, I returned to the Lower East Side of Manhattan, scene of my teenage escapades, and eventually bought a large co-op apartment in an old brownstone on St. Mark's Place. At that time, St. Mark's Place was, and probably now still is, one of the most interesting streets in the city; it was then home to a famous poet (Auden), a good bookstore, and more glitzy hairdressers and Indian clothing stores than I could count.

For the first time in my life I found myself in sync with my own era. It was the lavish and exuberant seventies, and the sexual revolution was in full swing. New forms of birth control had changed the shape of destiny for most of us, and people were beginning, only beginning, to recognize and realize the many possibilities of living lives which were determined by choice rather than by biology or conditioning.

Although I had missed the famous festival itself, the spirit of Woodstock lingered over the landscape of New York like smoke. Ram Dass had published his first books about spiritual awakening, *Be Here Now* and *The Only Dance There Is,* and had transformed himself from a Harvard psychologist interested in the drug-induced potentials of the human mind into a spiritual teacher, a guru, running around the country dressed in Indian *kurtas* and teaching us all to "live in the present," according to the teachings of his own guru, Neem Karuli Baba. The Tibetan Buddhist teacher, Chogyam Rinpoche Trungpa, caused a sensation with his first book, *Cutting Through Spiritual Materialism,* and thousands of poets, artists, and good-looking young wannabes began to yearn for the meditative life, especially in beautiful places like Vermont and Colorado, and especially if they could still also drink and party and dance in the rain as they'd already done at numerous rock concerts in the sixties. Like Ram Dass, Allen Ginsberg also went to India and returned to chant his poems while playing the harmonium, rocking back and forth over his huge beard like a genuinely enlightened sage. The hard-edged fashions of the sixties gave way to yards of flowing and delicate fabrics. The hard edges of our lives flowed away with the rivers of cloth.

In the summer of 1973, on vacation from my job at Brooklyn College, I was living quietly in a cabin in upstate New York. I was writing a novel about a failed marriage and a woman discovering herself through pain. *The Second Story Man* hadn't yet been published, but I was publishing stories in literary journals and articles in the feminist press. The cabin, owned by my lover at the time, was beside a fast-moving river and several miles from the aforementioned Woodstock. Our cabin had no bathtub—which may sound familiarly grim, but which no longer bothered me as I now liked the adventure of bathing in the river, and could take plenty of baths at home in the city. One day, however, I went to a friend's house to take a shower. His house was a converted nineteenth-century schoolhouse with enormous rooms and high ceilings, and he was always inviting people to come and live there, hopefully for a fee since he had no other visible means of support. In one of those rooms, that day, was a very tall, thin, frail man, with dark skin and radiant eyes. Draped in a shawl, he was leaning on the arm of an attractive dark-haired woman, who led him through the room as if he were an invalid.

"This is the Doctor, Dr. R. P. Kaushik," my friend informed me. I looked at the couple and smiled. And it seemed to me that the man looked back at me and said to his companion, "I like that woman."

No doubt this was only an illusion, but the sense of encompassing warmth stayed with me. Dr. Kaushik looked at my lover and myself and began to talk about his mother and father, who had quarrelled all their lives but had died in the same few minutes, which in India is considered a sign of true love. I smiled. I had no intention of dying in the same few minutes as my lover, with whom there was no real commitment, no sense of lasting relationship. I had just come out of a marriage which had felt like prison. To the Doctor, a rather traditional-looking Indian man, I said nothing of this, however. And when he invited us to come to one of the talks he was giving in a nearby church, I consented eagerly.

We found out later that he had recently had a serious heart attack but had recovered, and was now in this country for the first time, at the invitation of a man who had met him in India, a Yale professor.

Gurus and Indian teachers were coming to America in droves at that point, usually responding to invitations from people who had met them in India and were impressed, possibly

Dr. Rajeshwar Prasad Kaushik, about 1973

wanting to be future disciples. Drawn by the incipient sense I had had since childhood, that there was another life which breathed beneath the surface of the life I led and perceived, I had begun to search, very uncertainly, for a way to discover it.

Drugs had offered me a kind of answer. I've recently published a novel, *Skirts,* which explores this theme; like the protagonist in the novel, I had once been in love with a man for whom drugs were an avenue into awareness. It soon became clear to me, however, as it does to the woman in my book, that drugs eventually rule—and then destroy—both the body and the soul.

I had also been deeply moved by the great teaching stories of the Zen and Sufi traditions, but had failed to find a master with whom I could connect. And I was thoroughly turned off by ceremonies in which friends of mine chanted to some guru's old shoes, or sat at the feet of an elderly, bearded gentleman who told them what kind of light they were going to see as they became progressively more enlightened, through the mantras he was going teach them (for a fee, of course. Beginners saw red lights, more experienced meditators saw blue, but only the truly enlightened saw white).

The Doctor, Dr. R. P. Kaushik, wasn't like any of these. His teachings had no name, although later, in order to fulfill the requirements of the government of India to run a nonprofit organization, he ended up calling the loosely knit group of people who surrounded him the Darshan Yoga Society. The people of Darshan Yoga—no more than a few hundred or so throughout the world—weren't exactly "members" of a yoga society; we were just people who kept coming to hear the Doctor speak, first in India and then in England and Italy and the East and West coasts of the United States. We were people of all ages, backgrounds, and nationalities, who all too often discovered that our lives had been changed through our contact with him.

A group of young Europeans and Americans had met him in India, moved into his household, and never left. Some of them eventually formed communal households in upstate New York, in Florida, in San Francisco (which I eventually joined), and finally in rural Sonoma County. The Doctor used a method of inquiry and self-observation similar to that employed by the Indian philosopher and teacher Jiddah Krishnamurti, and spoke of a mitigating energy, as Krishnamurti did, rather than naming a particular state of being or a deity.

Darshan Yoga

Dr. Kaushik was an M.D. who had practiced medicine in a small town in northern India for many years. Turning his back on the conventions of his society, he had chosen his own wife, had married and had three sons. But this "unarranged" marriage had turned out to be deeply unhappy, and he questioned his own choices. Similarly, he had become involved in politics and ran for office as a Marxist, motivated by his compassion for India's incredibly poor masses—but he was disillusioned by communism after the Chinese brutally invaded Tibet. All his ventures—in politics, in medicine, in humanitarian service, and in his personal life—ended by failing to meet his expectations. After studying Sanskrit and the Vedic holy books

of his own Brahmanic tradition, he had experienced what he called a "cosmic romance," but even that had ultimately proved empty and false for him, and he entered a period of absolute despair.

"[It was] . . . brought home to me that this cosmic consciousness is not the absolute truth," he said later. "It collapsed; and I was absolutely washed out, beaten."

Entering, at that point, a kind of desperate, choiceless state, an utter giving up of all his dreams and desires, he began to experience something altogether new. It was, he said, a great feeling of expansion, of light and joy inside and outside himself, for which there was no reason, no explanation.

"[I realized that] this light or understanding can come to a sinner," he said, "while to a saint it might not come. . . . It is not based upon some method or technique, nor on good works or a meritorious nature; it just comes."

Dr. Kaushik may have said this during the first talk to which he invited me; it was taken from a transcription of his talks in the seventies. The point is, though, that I never heard it. I decided to drive, with two of my friends, to the Woodstock church hall in which he was speaking, but we arrived late and missed the lecture. So we rushed to the house where he was staying with friends, and found a scene typical of the seventies: women wearing dresses made of flowered Indian bedspreads, people playing tambourines and chanting.

I'm embarrassed to say that on that steamy August night I was decked out in a skimpy pair of hot pants (made of suede! The Doctor, like most Brahmans, was a total vegetarian) and a teeny-weeny itsy-bitsy bright red halter top. In this faintly ridiculous get-up I went, after what seemed a long period of waiting, to say goodnight to him and to thank him for his invitation. One of my friends had sat at his feet for about an hour, with his eyes closed and his arms around the Doctor's ankles. Pretty dramatic stuff, I thought, with my usual skepticism—after all, I was still that New York youngster, all grown up and thinned out. And then the Doctor put his hands out to me to say goodbye, and it no longer mattered what I thought.

I wish I could say now, from the vantage point of the twenty-four years that have since passed, that I fully understand what happened to me that night. It helps to read Dr. Kaushik's words—"Whatever this energy is, there is no cause for it. . . . This light or understanding can come to a sinner, while to a saint it might not come . . . "—or to be told that he must have raised my *kundalini*, the sleeping serpent which, according to Hindu psychology, waits to be awakened at the base of the human spine, and which can open all the energy centers, the *chakras*, within the body as it rises.

Perhaps it's just that, in his own expanding awareness of inner light and joy, the Doctor was able to impart it to others, and thus it came to me. Nor has it ever left, at least not for very long; this energy has remained at the center of my life ever since, and, like the joy which came to me when writing, it, too, has been both a blessing and a kind of holy curse.

That night, touched by him for the first time, I can remember nothing in the room but light, and a sense of the electricity coming out of his hands and into mine. I felt as though something were breaking around myself, falling away, as if I had lived inside a plaster cast all my life and suddenly I was set free, naked, without a skin.

I must have spent hours sitting with him like that; I lost all sense of hunger or fatigue, all sense of time. Finally, when everybody else was half-asleep, my friends, faintly amused by my behavior, led me home. I couldn't drive. I sat awake all night. When I returned to see him after a terrified, astounded week during which I barely ate or slept and could not speak to anyone, he looked up at me wearily and asked, "What is it that you want from me?"

"Oh, nothing," I said politely, my childhood manners coming to the fore. I had also changed my clothes, and now wore a covered-up dress.

"Not true," he answered flatly. "You had an experience with me and you want it to happen again. But if I let it happen again you would probably become my slave and follow me anywhere, and I don't want any slaves. So it will not happen again. And besides, you made it happen yourself, anyway. Whatever happened to you, you did it to yourself."

Within three years my novel *The Second Story Man* was published, and to my amazement it was praised in numerous critical reviews. One reviewer called it "a superb dance performance." In the *New York Times Book Review*, it was described as "perfectly written." I was asked to speak and read and possibly teach in a dozen places. But suddenly, instead of basking in the upsurge of respect and critical acknowledgment that I thought I'd been craving all along, all I wanted, perversely, was to go and live in one of Dr. Kaushik's households.

I became exhausted. The conflict of my sudden craving to leave New York, to change my plans for a career, a life, were enervating, impossibly frightening. I took baby steps: stopped smoking, became a vegetarian, vacated my apartment, sold most of my things, and finally went to live first in Connecticut, then in San Francisco, then in rural northern California, and finally, for a single, vivid, poignant year, in India.

And I wish I could say, from the vantage point of twenty-four years, how much better my life has become. How much better I am as a person. That I have purified both my mind and my body, through the years I spent in the household in California (and what an experience that was, as we all "inquired" about everything we did, every bite of food we took, every word we said—even about going to the bathroom!) and then with Dr. Kaushik in northern India, for that one year before he died suddenly of a second heart attack. I wish I could say that I have never again been depressed or angry or had to go on a diet or eaten meat. That I have put rage and ambition and suffering and blame all behind me, like a backpack that has gotten too heavy to carry.

But it wouldn't be true.

What I did put down was a life encumbered by the accumulated griefs and possessions and residue of my birth and my childhood and my parents' marriage and my own first marriage. The time I spent in India changed my perspective about what poverty was, or wealth. About what I could need or want for a comfortable life. I returned from India stripped down, bare of possessions and weight and even of any expectations beside the desire to return there again, which was made impossible by the Doctor's death. A few years later, however, I went and got married again, acquiring new accumulations and new problems. And when that marriage ended precipitously and badly, I lapsed into a self-pitying rage that lasted for years.

Still. This energy remains in my life, like a laser cutting through the fog of my own desires and fears. Despite the fact that I'm no saint, that I'm ambitious, that I sometimes feel

"A view of the Himalayas, near the house in which we lived with the doctor. The house is still available to all of us who lived there, and I hope to go back one day," Dalhousie, India, 1981.

envious or angry or sad and all the terrifying and confused emotions that I felt before.

Except for one.

My mother's legacy has dissipated. Along with the rings and bracelets of hers that I gave away, the emptied safe deposit box once filled with her pearls and amethysts and jade, is the heritage of her ultimate depression, her suicide. I have an innate belief that no matter what befalls me, I may kick and rage for a while, but I'll survive. And then there is this indelible sense of energy, the same energy which I felt the first night I touched the Doctor, and which grew stronger and stronger as I moved to rural California and then to India. It is now a buzzing, living light which propels me through my life, which stays within myself and guides me. As the Doctor said in a later talk, "No difficulty can arise outside unless there is a difficulty inside. And therefore, if I can deal with the difficulty inside, the outside difficulty disappears. The inside and the outside are the same. There is no separation between them."

I Live In Berkeley Now

A Country Life

Both before and after my year in India, I lived in Sonoma County, in the wine and redwood country north of San Francisco. I had driven up there with some of the women in our San Francisco household, and we'd found, at a reasonable rent, a ramshackle Santa Rosa house that had once been a care home for the elderly. We fixed it up and settled there, and some of the Darshan Yoga people stayed in that house for many years after the Doctor died and I had left, improving the property and eventually selling it at a considerable profit.

I found a job at the local community college, teaching creative writing to disabled adults, and although the work didn't present me with the intellectual stimulation or challenge of my previous college teaching, it called upon faculties of patience, understanding, and compassion

"My tiny Berkeley cottage, under the branches of a beautiful plum tree. My dog and cat are in the foreground," 1995

that were beginning to seem just as important. Homesick for India's sense of teeming struggle and spiritual resonance, I discovered that in the midst of affluent, compulsively clean and self-indulgent California there was a subculture of people who were figuratively and sometimes even literally starving. I had always enjoyed college teaching—teaching creative writing enabled me to allow students, and myself with them, to reach out of themselves, or deeply within themselves, to discover and explore new capacities.

In India, however, I had learned to give massage, even to be a kind of minor healer, and I treasured those new abilities as if they were more precious than anything I had learned or done before. I considered for a while giving up writing in order to go back to school to obtain a license to dispense legitimate massage and herbal medicine. However, it gradually became clear to me that it was writing, not healing, which had illuminated and focused my life from the age of nineteen. It seemed to me that the only real spirituality was that which

extended itself into one's own, everyday life, rather than removing one from it. I realized, too, that there were many ways of giving and many ways of healing oneself and others. If I was to be a healer, I finally understood, I would do so as a writer and as a teacher of writing.

Within a few months of Dr. Kaushik's death, I was asked by a friend, the poet Lyn Lifshin, to contribute to *Lips Unsealed,* an anthology of women's memoirs which she was compiling. For the first time since my return, I took out the enormous diary I had kept in India and began to turn it into a book. The finished product, which I called "Go to Calcutta," hasn't yet been published except in increments: one excerpt in Lyn's anthology; another in *The House on Via Gombito,* an anthology of women's travel memoirs published by Two Rivers Press in Minnesota; another in the review *Women's Studies* at Queens College; another in the *Sonoma Mandala,* published at Sonoma State University, where I was teaching at the time. But working on the book put me back into the habit of writing for publication again, and by the time I had finished it, I knew that I would continue to be a writer, and that I would continue to teach.

I also wanted to live surrounded by the lush landscapes and gentle climates of Sonoma County, particularly in the area near the Russian River. The literary scene there was very limited, but I still wasn't sure whether I wanted to participate in a competitive scene again, certainly not one with the intensity of New York's. I came to love the hills, forests, and beaches; I knew that I had been happier there, and in India, than I had ever been in my life.

I first drafted the novel *Skirts,* which is set in the littered slums and tenements of New York City, while living in a tiny cottage under the dappled light of the redwood trees in a town called Camp Meeker, one of the last logging towns in Sonoma County. I had only a wood stove for heat, and as I conjured images of city streets and crowded bars, I hauled in my own wood out of the rain and learned to bank an all-night fire. Later, I finished the novel in a series of similar places in which I lived until I met the man whom I eventually married; together we went to live in a beautiful house in the redwoods on a hill overlooking the Russian River, a few miles from the Pacific. It was idyllic.

I published parts of my memoir about India. I worked on *Skirts.* I participated in the

Russian River Writers' Guild, and gave readings. I joined PEN American Center West, in Berkeley, and became friendly with a number of Berkeley writers. Eventually I became cochairperson of PEN West's Freedom to Write Committee, and hosted events in Berkeley and San Francisco. In 1987 my story "Some Human Beings" won several awards and was published both in America and Europe. It felt as if my career was finally taking off again.

Earning a living was difficult in our rural paradise, however. For a while I worked as a typesetter for a small newspaper; I continued to teach at the community college, at Sonoma State University, and in a program called the Creative Living Center, which was a kind of support system for outpatients in the mental health system in Sonoma County. But funds were cut back; the tendency of corporate greed and disregard of the disadvantaged had already begun in full force by the mid-eighties, and programs that catered to unusual, physically or mentally challenged people, had the lowest priority of any in the California system.

Eventually, now living in a suburban town near Sonoma State University, where I still taught, I found a job teaching in a state mental institution; at this writing, I teach there still, although many programs there are being cut as well. *Skirts* was accepted for publication by Baskerville Publishers in Dallas, Texas, and I began my next novel, *Through Black Seas,* which is set in a huge mental hospital in New York and in Russia at the dawn of the Russian Revolution. And when a friend asked me to move into her beautiful, tiny backyard cottage in a walled garden in Berkeley, I eagerly agreed.

There Is No End

It's a wonderful thing to be a novelist.

You find the voice with which to tell your book; the story roils out of you, again and again as you polish and revise it. Then finally, you know the end. There is an end. What will happen on the day after this ending doesn't matter. You leave your readers guessing. You leave yourself thinking about it as well. You know (perhaps) what your characters are going to say and do when they get out of bed on the morning after the book has ended. You can hear them say it, see them do it. You know that everything may continue to work out as they hoped

Mimi Albert, at home with her cat, Marilyn, Berkeley, 1997

or planned, that they will live together or alone happily ever after, or that their dreams will fail and they'll be crushed. But it doesn't matter. You've written that final line.

How can there be a final line here?

I've just finished another draft of *Through Black Seas,* which is not really like any book I've written before. It was mostly written at my desk in the Berkeley cottage in which I live now, on the other side of French doors facing a quiet garden. I've sat at this desk through four steamy summers and four long, damp, cool, northern Californian winters, during which the rain beat down onto my two skylights, comforting me as I wrote.

My grandmother is in this book, with her stormy revolutionist past, and my sour Rochester grandfather with his hefty income and his miserable disposition. And in some scenes, there's my mother as she described herself to me as a young girl: awkward, skinny, unloved, the oldest of five children, miserable, lonely. Destined for suffering and failure. The early life of the suicide. Except in my book she's transformed into a woman who discovers her own beauty just in time, who loves and marries a handsome and successful man and is loved in return; a woman who doesn't die alone, as my mother did, in a dark house with too many sleeping pills in her system.

Which is better? The glossed-over fiction or the ugly truth? No value judgments here. This is the mother in my book, not the mother in my life.

But it's a wonderful thing indeed to be a novelist.

This isn't fiction so there is no ending. If I could shape reality the way I can shape fiction (Dr. Kaushik said we could; these are powers which I have obviously not perfected), I would give myself a ripe old age, a happy old age. Plenty of time for writing novels and for meditating, under the beautiful Tibetan *thanka* my second husband gave me, although I'm not a Tibetan Buddhist (or any other kind of Buddhist), just a woman who perceives energy coming through the air and from within. Who's able to say, "I don't know what it is," but who welcomes it. Who can shape fiction but not reality. Not yet.

I would give myself loving companions, some recognition for my work, time for friendship and for solitude. Money enough to live without worry, to travel, and to share with the people I love. Very importantly, health.

And yet perhaps Dr. Kaushik was wrong. He believed that he could shape reality, make himself well, heal completely from his first heart attack. The truth is, he was younger than my adoptive father when he died. So perhaps none of us can say exactly what will happen to us, or possibly even what we really want.

The novel *Through Black Seas* represents a synthesis of all the things I've ever been and experienced and known; the family ties and traditions of my childhood, the rage and rebelliousness of my youth. Most of all, the spiritual homecoming of my middle years.

Acceptance. Not passive acceptance, but a fusion of all my lives.

BIBLIOGRAPHY

Fiction:

The Second Story Man, Fiction Collective, 1975.

Skirts, Baskerville Publishers, 1994.

Through Black Seas, forthcoming.

Other:

The Small Singer (stories and poetry collection), Shameless Hussy Press, 1975.

Contributor to anthologies such as *A Different Beat: Early Writing by Women of the Beat Generation; Anthology of the Fiction Collective; A Stone's Throw; The Book of Monologues; Statements 2: New Fiction;* "Go to Calcutta" (memoir), in *The House on Via Gombito, Lips Unsealed: Confidences from Contemporary Women Writers* (edited by Lynn Lifshin), *Sonoma Mandala,* and *Women's Studies.* Albert's short fiction and nonfiction have appeared in *Alt Fur Damerne Magazine, Caprice Literary Journal, Ceilidh Literary Quarterly, Crazyquilt Literary Quarterly, Playgirl,* and *Southern Lights.* She has also contributed books reviews and articles to such periodicals as the *American Book Review, The Journal of the California Alliance for the Mentally Ill, Metro Magazine, Poetry Flash, The San Francisco Chronicle, San Francisco Review,* and *The Yoga Journal.*

Lisa Alther

1944-

BORDER STATES

Lisa Alther

When she. was ninety-six, Hattie Elizabeth Vanover Reed, my paternal grandmother, would put on a stylish silk suit
with a skirt to her knees, nylons and two-inch
heels, costume jewelry, and full-battle makeup
whenever visitors were expected at her nursing
home in Kingsport, Tennessee. Right to the end,
she maintained her standards for a Virginia lady.

I remember my grandmother best presiding over Sunday dinners in the nightclub that
she'd bought from a bootlegger and remod-

eled into her home. An open-air deck, where
patrons had once drunk moonshine, ran the
length of the living room, overlooking the slow-
drifting Holston River, often frothy with waste
from the Tennessee Eastman plant upriver. She
dug a lily pond in the former parking lot, stock-
ing it with goldfish that soon became bloated
from the saltines we grandchildren crumbled
for them. Behind the pond she planted mag-
nolia trees. The first time I stuck my nose into
one of those creamy blossoms, I refused to remove it. Seeing what was possible in the realm
of scent, I didn't want to breathe ordinary air
anymore, especially not the air of our town,
which was sticky with fumes from the Mead
paper mill.

My grandmother's Sunday dinner was a ritual
as inescapable as Sunday school. But my three
brothers and I often delayed it by racing to
the stone wall that overlooked the valley out
back, to count the cars making up a train snaking
past down below. The northbound trains, bulging with the trunks of primordial poplars,
dribbled chunks of coal down the tracks, whereas
the southbound trains flaunted cockscombs of
shiny new-model autos.

After the caboose vanished around the bend,
my grandfather sometimes teed up by the fish
pond and drove his golfball to the ninth green
of the course across the river. He watched the
ball climb, arc and fall, longing to row the
boat tethered by the riverbank across to the
far shore to continue his game. He had been
a semiprofessional left-handed baseball pitcher
in his youth, and his golf scores as a senior
citizen were in the low 70's.

Instead of plunging down the cliff to freedom, though, my grandfather strolled inside and
sat down at the gleaming faux-Sheraton table,
backed by wallpaper featuring a mural of
hoopskirted belles flouncing around the por-
tico of a Southern mansion. Wearing a mono-

*"My grandfather, William Henry Reed,
as a young man"*

grammed silk shirt, he listened in silence as my grandmother regaled my father with the fiery future that awaited those who turned their backs on the Southern Baptist Church in order to attend the Episcopal Church up the street with their misled Yankee brides. Silver platters of fried chicken, shelly beans, Parker House rolls, and molded Jello salad circulated, as my brothers and I disputed the number of tiny silver fruits on the handles of the Francis I flatwear.

My grandparents grew up at the end of the nineteenth century on farms in the coalfields of southwest Virginia. Both were middle children of eight siblings. My grandmother's mother died of pneumonia when my grandmother was thirteen. My grandfather's father died of pneumonia and his mother of gall bladder disease before he was six. He was raised in his older sister's household. Like an episode from Dickens,

the relative who served as executor sold off his parents' farm in 1888 and squandered the proceeds. When my grandfather was twelve, he ran away from his sister's, hiking eighty miles across the mountains into Kentucky to join an older brother.

Both my grandparents trained as teachers in Clintwood and Big Stone Gap, Virginia. Second cousins, they first met when she became his student. After their marriage she persuaded him to pursue his dream of becoming a doctor, a dream no doubt fostered by his watching helplessly as his parents died. He attended the University of Louisville, hopping southbound freight trains to see his wife. The next year he won a scholarship to the Medical College of Virginia in Richmond. My grandmother sold cosmetics in a department store, then taught at a reform school for girls, once fighting off some attacking students with her hat pin. During the summers he sold pots door-to-door and worked as a logger. His final year at school he tended Confederate veterans at the Robert E. Lee Soldiers' Home.

Returning to Clintwood, my grandfather kept a stable of six horses to convey him to patients in the remote hollows. He owned the first car in the county, until it lurched out of control and bounced down a mountainside on its hard rubber tires, crashing into a creek.

When my father was five, my grandparents moved to Kingsport, Tennessee, a new town being established in the Holston Valley to accommodate industry from the North seeking non-unionized labor. My grandfather opened the town's first hospital, while my grandmother oversaw construction of a large neo-Georgian house on the street where the Yankee plant managers were building their houses. (She later gave this house to my father upon his return from World War II with his pregnant wife and two small children, of whom I was the younger).

One day my grandmother decided the masons were building a brick wall in the backyard incorrectly, so she took over. As she slapped mortar on a brick, a mason said, "Excuse me, ma'am, but you can't build a wall like that." My grandmother looked up at him and said, "Sir, not only can I, I am."

Although my grandmother had enough drive to run several factories, such roles weren't open to women. So she was soon running the social life of Kingsport instead, attending a tea, luncheon, bridge game, or club meeting nearly every day. Her favorite group was the Virginia Club. To belong, one had to have been born in Virginia. At their meetings, the members, whom my grandmother referred to as "those fine Colonial ladies," mused about the superiority of Virginia over Tennessee. It was not unheard of for members to cross the nearby state line when they went into labor so their infants could be born Virginians. By the time I knew her, my grandmother was not just a Virginian, she was a Tidewater Virginian whose Cavalier forebears had received land grants from James I.

Meanwhile, I was being groomed as a Virginia belle (even though I was born in Tennessee), attending cooking classes, sewing classes, and weekly sessions of charm school at the local department store. I learned to set a table, plan a menu, arrange flowers, dress, walk, sit, and make myself up. I also learned to waltz, and when I was sixteen, I was presented as a debutante, wearing a white strapless Scarlett O'Hara gown, with kid gloves to my biceps, which bulged unbellelike from years of football with the neighborhood boys. My boyfriend, Harold, and I waltzed in intricate patterns with the other Symphony Belles and their dates to the "Champagne Waltz." (Then we drove in his father's finned yellow Buick to our favorite parking spot and struggled like the Laocoon to free me from my hoops.)

All my life I have longed to belong to some group, so as to escape the lonely task of self-definition. The closest I ever came was in high school when the Queen Teens invited me to join. Finally I knew who I was: I was a Q.T. We were said to be more trashy than the Sub Debs or the Devilish Debs, and to give better parties.

This hard-won self-knowledge evaporated, however, when I arrived at college near Boston during the civil rights years. No one up there had ever heard of the Queen Teens, and when they did, they laughed. I was summoned to the Wellesley gym, stripped down to my underwear, and photographed in profile, like a police lineup. Fortunately, the carriage I had learned by strutting around the Kingsport department store with textbooks on my head got me exempted from Remedial Posture. I was conscripted into Fundamentals of Movement, however, in which I learned how to sit down

in an MG without flashing too much thigh. I was also given a speech test. Thanks to my Yankee mother's childhood coaching on how to pronounce "cow" in one syllable, I passed. Nevertheless, at dinner one night a hallmate observed, "It's so amusing to hear you say something intelligent in that Southern accent of yours." After the murder of the three civil rights workers in Mississippi, a woman from across the hall barged into my room to announce, "You Southerners make me sick!"

I was astonished because, until then, I'd rarely thought of myself as a Southerner. To the contrary, I'd always been teased on the playground because my mother was a Yankee and my pronunciation of "cow" was so weird. And I had assumed that every young woman in America was forced to waltz in hoopskirts. Since

"My grandmother, Hattie Elizabeth Reed, as a young women"

East Tennessee is mountainous, it had hosted few plantations or slaves. And when Tennessee seceded from the Union, East Tennessee tried to secede from Tennessee. My father's great grandfather was a sergeant in the Union army. My grandmother's great uncle lost an arm fighting for the Union at the battle of Cranesnest River. Several forebears moved from southwest Virginia to Kentucky to avoid fighting for the Confederacy. To say nothing of my mother's ancestors in New York, or of her lullabies, which included a Union battle hymn called "Sherman's Dashing Yankee Boys."

But it was also true that other forebears fought for the Confederacy, one dying of measles shortly after enlisting in the Virginia Infantry. And Sullivan County, where I lived, had been prepared to secede from East Tennessee if East Tennessee seceded from the Union. As children, my brothers, neighbors and I played War between the States, giving each other transfusions with lengths of string from bottles of water dyed red with food coloring. Most of us owned gray cardboard Confederate Army caps, and no one wanted to be a Yankee, so this fate usually befell the youngest children.

In sum, I was one baffled college freshman, accepted because my Appalachian origins (of which I was unaware) appealed to the missionary instincts of the admissions committee but now expected to transform myself into something called "the Wellesley Girl." After a bout of mononucleosis that allowed me to sulk in the infirmary for a month, I decided to sort out my confusion by writing a short story. Little did I know that this in itself marked me as a Southerner. As Flannery O'Connor once wrote, "The Southerner knows he can do more justice to reality by telling a story than he can by discussing problems or proposing abstractions. . . . It's actually his way of reasoning and dealing with experience." But when I had one of my characters say, "Law, honey, where'd you get that hat at?" my writing professor informed me that real people didn't talk that way. This was the first time I'd ever realized that the people I'd grown up among weren't real.

It takes a long time to figure out who you are, and it often takes leaving a place behind to recognize how it has shaped you. As Sarah Orne Jewett wrote Willa Cather, "One must know the world *so well* before one can know the parish." After college I moved to

Vermont and wrote my first novel, *Kinflicks*. Predictably, it concerns a young woman who grows up in Tennessee, goes to college near Boston, and moves to Vermont. And during the funk that always follows publication for me, I started wondering why, if my grandmother loved Virginia so much, she'd moved to Tennessee, why she rarely went back, why we hardly ever met our Virginia relatives.

I asked my father. He explained that once when he was visiting kin near Clintwood, his uncle Cas invited him to go fishing. "Fishing" consisted of sitting on a creek bank all afternoon drinking white lightning. When it was time to go home, Cas lit some sticks of dynamite and tossed them into the water, then collected the fish that landed onshore. When my father told him that was against the law, he said, "Son, over here I am the law." My father also described my grandfather's being chased on horseback by an armed thug for defending a cousin during a knife fight. He packed a .38 special for several years afterwards. My father speculated that his parents had left southwest Virginia as much to escape the alcoholism and violence as to try their luck in a new boom town.

The next time I was home, I went to see my grandmother's aunt, Ura Grizzle, who at 103 seemed close to death. She lay in her bed at her daughter's house, eyes closed, face copper against the white pillow, hair pulled back to reveal a broad forehead and high cheekbones, looking like the Cherokee she used to say she was. Discovering it was unfashionable to be Indian, she later denied it. I, however, was from a generation for whom ethnicity of any sort seemed exotic, so I asked about her Cherokee forebears. Even though her daughter assured me she was awake, her eyes and lips remained shut.

Next I went to southwest Virginia on my own, driving in two hours a distance that used to take my grandparents twelve. I could tell this trip upset my grandmother, but she said nothing. She felt well-bred people should communicate like bats, via ultrasonic squeaks. I was eating lunch at a cafeteria in Clintwood when the participants in a trial at the nearby courthouse came in. The waitress told me that a couple had had a son who became a high school football star. He ran into a goalpost, broke his neck, and was buried in the local churchyard. Now his parents were divorcing, and his mother

"The school in Clintwood, Virginia, where my grandmother taught to put my grandfather through medical school"

was moving fifty miles away. Wanting to take her son along, she was suing for custody. As I buttered my cornbread, I first understood the origins of the black humor that had recently made *Kinflicks* successful. It was a regional trait, I realized, based on the assumption that human behavior is so bizarre that the only recourse is to laugh.

Later I returned to East Tennessee to research an article on snakehandling for the *New York Times*. My doctor-father used to tell us at the dinner table about snakehandlers who turned up in the emergency room. Some died and some didn't. What I found in the backwoods frame churches were farmers, truck drivers, car mechanics—people for whom the fondling of copperheads was their only excitement. The famous mountain feuds, over such issues as who left the gate open so the hogs got out, had entertained their forebears similarly. Might it have also been rural monotony that propelled

my grandparents out of southwest Virginia? I wondered.

At this point my Appalachian relatives began to become real to me, despite my writing professor's assurances that they weren't. Because I had grown up in an industrial town in a river valley surrounded by amiable carpetbaggers rather than in a mountain cove, I had failed to grasp the fact that I, too, was Appalachian. For the first time, I began to ponder the caricatures in the funny papers and on television—L'il Abner, Snuffy Smith, the cast of Hee Haw, the Beverly Hillbillies, the Waltons. The Waltons evoked nostalgia; the others, contemptuous amusement. Yet, beneath surface differences, the Appalachians I knew were similar to the Bostonians and Vermonters I'd kept company with since leaving home. The language of the heart, it seemed to me, was universal. At least that had always been the guiding impulse behind my writing.

Still reflecting upon why the rest of the nation would need to view Appalachians as quaint or venal hillbillies, I moved to England. The Vietnam War was just ending, and many of my British friends were leftists, so I received frequent lectures on American imperialism, for which I was apparently a running dog. I was bewildered because I had never thought of myself as an American. I was just getting used to myself as a Southerner and an Appalachian.

As usual, I plunged into a novel as a way to organize my confusion. The question I posed was why, if you have several people coming of age in the same environment, do some leave and others stay? Why did certain fish decide to crawl out on dry land? Why, in other words, did my grandparents leave Virginia? And why did I leave the Tennessee river valley they bequeathed me? The resulting novel, *Original Sins,* features five characters growing up in a small East Tennessee town. Three leave and two stay. After 592 pages, I came to the banal conclusion that the ones who left did so because they didn't fit in.

Applying to my story the Marxist analysis I'd absorbed from my left-wing British friends, I further understood that other Americans needed to see Appalachians as ignorant hillbillies in order not to feel guilty for having plundered our timber and coal, wrecked our environment, and exploited our labor. Victors always portray the vanquished in unflattering terms in order to rationalize their own brutality. At the same time, it occurred to me that perhaps their guilt wasn't really necessary, since the fore-

"My grandmother (left) in Egypt with my Latin teacher, on one of her round-the-world trips," about 1960

bears of most Appalachians stole their land from the Cherokees, the Cherokees having stolen it from the Copena, the Copena from the Hopewells, the Hopewells from the Mound Builders, and so on back to the dawn of our greedy species.

Tired of being attacked in London for being an American when I was attacked in Boston for not being one, I returned to Vermont to lick my ethnic wounds and write my third novel. *Other Women* concerns the interaction between a therapist and her client, a lesbian mother and nurse who is trying to comprehend the violence in the world. Since therapy was nearly as popular as polio when I was growing up in Tennessee, I suspected after publication that I had now disqualified myself as both a Southerner and an Appalachian. To make matters worse, Southern and Appalachian women were known for standing by their men, single-handedly harvesting crops and raising children, sewing dresses from flour sacks and planting petunias in diesel tires, even as their men drank, caroused, and knocked them senseless. I had seen the "accidents" resulting from this ethos several times while working at the hospital as a candy striper during high school. By writing about a woman who preferred to stand by another woman, one who treated her with tenderness, it was likely that I had now doubly disqualified myself from my natal groups.

During my subsequent creative drought, I first began to suspect that, in my northward flight toward freedom, I hadn't really left home. The Vermont house I was living in was a brick Georgian identical to the one my grandmother had constructed in Kingsport in 1926, except that mine was built in 1803. The foothills around me were similar to those I had roamed as a child. Vermonters, although more reticent than East Tennesseeans, had the same droll affability. Some had the same unfortunate tendency to assault their women when they were having a bad day. The accent was different, but the grammar "mistakes" were the same. I could just as easily hear "I ain't never seen nobody like you" in Vermont as in Tennessee.

Vermont, I realized, was merely the northern end of the Appalachians, which was why I felt so much at home. The entire mountain range had been settled by Anglo-Saxons and Celts. The ballads, clogging, speech patterns, black humor, and Calvinism were nearly identical all along its length, apart from local variations based on contributions from different ethnic groups, particularly the Cherokees in the south and the French Canadians in Vermont. Modern civilization had disrupted this mountain culture in the mid-Atlantic states, but it still existed at either extremity. To paraphrase Pogo, I had met the enemy, and they were us.

In the grip of this insight, I wrote my fourth novel, *Bedrock*, which features a Vermont village full of eccentrics, composites of people and situations I had known in both Tennessee and Vermont. And although I had lived in Vermont for twenty-five years by then and had several eighteenth-century ancestors buried in the Rockingham, Vermont, churchyard, a Boston reviewer maintained I had no right to satirize Vermonters since I was a Southerner.

Having finally recognized, accepted, and stitched the Appalachian patch into the crazy quilt of myself, imagine my dismay as I was reading a book by a self-professed Melungeon and realized that he was a third cousin I'd never met. The Melungeons are a group of some twenty thousand people living in the region where East Tennessee, southwest Virginia, southeastern Kentucky, and northwestern North Carolina join. Several hundred thousand people outside this area are thought to have Melungeon ancestry without knowing it. The first Anglo-Saxon settlers to arrive, in the last half of the eighteenth century, found the olive-skinned ancestors of present-day Melungeons already living there, in European-style houses.

When I was a child, babysitters used to threaten us with abduction by six-fingered Melungeons who reputedly lived in trees on the ridges ringing town. Although Melungeons always maintained that they were Portuguese, researchers claimed they were "tri-racial isolates," resulting from intermarriage among Native Americans, escaped slaves, and mountain whites. Considered "free persons of color," they were pushed off their land, denied the vote, and prohibited from marrying whites or attending their schools.

Recent genetic, cross-cultural, linguistic, historical, and medical evidence reported in my newfound cousin's book suggest that they may, in fact, be partly Portuguese and Turkish. Some maintain that their progenitors were explorers, missionaries, colonists, and soldiers from several Spanish towns and forts known to have existed in the southeast in the late sixteenth century, in addition to several hundred Turkish sailors believed to have been dumped on the Carolina coast after a failed attempt to establish a colony in Cuba. Some historians have proposed that these groups may have merged with each other and with Native American tribes over several generations, gradually being forced onto inaccessible mountain ridges by the Anglo-Saxon settlers, who were intolerant of their darker skins and covetous of their rich bottomland.

If my cousin's calculations are valid, each of my grandparents would have been about a quarter Melungeon. Was this the missing link? I wondered. Whether "tri-racial isolates" or Portuguese-Turkish-Native American hybrids or both, might my grandparents have left Virginia because they were targets for discrimination? Did they want a fresh start among people who didn't know them? Could this be why my grandmother was so uncommunicative about her relatives?

These new speculations sent me into a frenzy of family research, which I won't detail since people's genealogies are almost as tedious as their vacation slides. Suffice it to say that I was succumbing to a family obsession. My mother's grandmother was national genealogist for the Daughters of the American Revolution and documented eleven lines of her family that came to America before 1650. Another Virginia cousin has published a book trailing one branch of my grandmother's family, the Vanovers, back to seventeenth-century Holland.

I would be inclined now to agree with the adage "Ignorance is bliss." I soon discovered that both sides of my family have been in this country for twelve generations, the Cherokees and perhaps the Melungeons for longer. Yet I had studied Buddhism, and all I wanted was to be here now. What was I to do with all these snarled roots? It seemed I was English, Scottish, Irish, Scots-Irish, French, Alsatian, German, Dutch, and Cherokee. If my Melungeon cousin was correct about our shared ancestors, I was also whatever mix that that entailed. My ancestors' faiths had been Primitive Baptist, Huguenot, Dunkard, Church of England, Congregational, Puritan, Dutch Reformed, Jewish. The men had been soldiers, sailors, privateers, carpenters, paupers, coopers, weavers, syphilitics, millers, preachers, drug addicts, tavern keepers, suicides, farmers, doctors, debtors, coal miners, lawyers, draft dodgers, teachers. Except

for a couple of suffragists, a midwife, and a breeder of championship chickens, the women died leaving no trace but their children. Despite my heroic efforts at self-definition, I now knew that my genes constituted their own private Balkans. I felt deep nostalgia for the days when I had been a Queen Teen and identity had seemed a simple issue of not being a Sub Deb or a Devilish Deb.

My fifth novel, *Five Minutes in Heaven,* became an attempt to unite these scattered beads of mercury—urban and rural, northern and Southern and Appalachian, American and European. My main character grows up in East Tennessee, lives in New York City as a young woman, then moves to Paris. Experiencing these cultural differences, she comes to understand that love in its highest sense is the only force that can override the conflicts and violence that such surface variations incite. A couple of reviewers demanded to know why an American would want to write about France.

At the moment I am in the process of establishing my United Nations within. As my model, I have selected that early Appalachian existentialist Hattie Elizabeth Vanover Reed. Almost everything I know about creating fic-

Hattie Elizabeth Reed, 1958

tion is a legacy from her. Faced with the void, or with a reality too grim or too complicated to endure, she simply decided that she was a Tidewater lady, and then turned herself into one. After she finished the brick wall behind her Georgian house (a wall still intact after seventy-five years), the architect stopped by to admire it. She replied, "Why, thank you, sir. I know that my wall will stand, because I have studied Thomas Jefferson's walls at the University of Virginia."

This essay originally appeared in the anthology *Bloodroot: Reflections on Place by Appalachian Women Writers,* edited by Joyce Dyer, University of Kentucky Press, 1998.

BIBLIOGRAPHY

Novels:

Kinflicks, Knopf, 1976.

Original Sins, Knopf, 1981.

Other Women, Knopf, 1984.

Five Minutes in Heaven, Dutton, 1995.

Bedrock, Plume, 1996.

Author of introduction to *A Good Man Is Hard to Find,* by Flannery O'Connor, Women's Press, 1980; contributor of short story, "Termites," to *Homewords,* edited by Douglas Paschell and Alice Swanson. Contributor of articles and stories to national magazines, including *Vogue, Cosmopolitan, Natural History, New Society, Yankee, Vermont Freeman, New Englander, New York Times Magazine,* and *New York Times Book Review.*

Alison Anderson

1950-

Alison Anderson

Elements of time, colored by memory, become paintings. You can paint a life, try to give it form or content. You look at patterns, synchronicities; you imagine the discarded images—what might have been—questions of choice, or fate. Your life is no longer linear, but hangs before you like pictures in a museum: glimpsed, studied, observed. You can try to make sense of it in its museum form: yes, the characters portrayed are often the same—is there a story here, a plot?

But why, always, the writer's obsession to shape, explain, order? A writer's life has its own disor-dered logic: certain signs, often slow to emerge. Hidden by elements of time, revealed by memory. Images form, at best a story, at least an identity.

Sofia, Bulgaria, Summer 1978

I sit talking with the woman in her apartment, Komplex Lenin. She is my friend's mother: she has a soft, sweet face, wears her treacle-colored hair in an old-fashioned chignon. I call her Mama Vesse, which is what her grandchildren call her. I would like to think of her as a motherly character in my life; my own mother died eleven years ago.

She is telling me she always reads the letters I send to her daughter Christina. She enjoys these letters, a voice from the West, what she or her daughter might have written if they had lived elsewhere. She tells me I will be a writer some day. I laugh, disbelieve her, plead laziness and incompetence. She shakes her head at me, insisting.

Haskovo, Bulgaria, March 1975

All evening they have entertained me but I cannot stay. We will all get in trouble with the authorities: they have tried, and failed, to get me a certificate of lodging that would allow me to visit "legally." Haskovo is a sensitive area, too near the Turkish border. So I will tell the officers at the border, should they ask, that I was at a party until three in the morning.

The party is small: my friend Krasimira, who has driven with me all the way from Switzerland, where we both live and study, and her cousins, and a handful of neighbors. One of the neighbors, an elegant woman with dark hair and gypsy eyes, reads my fortune in the filigree pattern left by the coffee in the bottom of my cup. *There are darkly handsome men here, who will help you; you will pass this way often.*

On the way to the border I think of what she has foretold. I am alone on this dark March-frosted road, until I see in the rearview mirror the dim shape of an old bus. It follows me, ghostly, without headlamps; I light the way in my small Volkswagen. It does not occur to me to be afraid: I am too young, and this is an adventure which nothing will spoil. But I feel a nervousness of not belonging, as if a strange warning has been beamed from the extinguished headlamps. A gypsy curse, perhaps, of wandering, belonging nowhere, searching.

At the Turkish border I encounter a group of darkly handsome Iranian students, homeward bound in their British-registered Mercedes and Rovers. They invite me to Teheran; I cannot, I say, I am meeting friends in Greece after four days in Istanbul. They invite me instead to convoy with them as far as my friends' house in Istanbul.

One year old, Orient Point, New York, 1951

I feel strangely protected now when I look in the rearview mirror, but this protection too is a constant reminder that I do not belong: a woman travelling alone.

Dogubayazit, Turkish-Iranian border, July 1986

We are camping on a hillside overlooking the mosque of Ali Pasha. In the valley to the east, the sand hills of Iran. I am with my English husband of six months and my seven-year-old daughter, Amy. Alan and I have been sick with some form of food poisoning—the pastirma we bought in Kayseri? the heat-curdled Irish Cream?—and we lie beneath an awning I have rigged with an old sarong from the car to the tent. The heat is metallic, crushing.

Amy plays with the Turkish children in the house behind us. They have goats, dogs, cats, sheep, hens, rabbits. She is not afraid of not understanding their language; they find a language of play. For a short while longer there will be no question of belonging.

When did I cease to belong? Was it in second grade, in New Haven, Connecticut, when I was sent to an exclusive private school that I immediately hated? Where I was the smallest, and skinniest, and smartest, and had a last name that rhymed with "dope?" Was it when a freckle-faced redhead named Ellen Jenkins punched me in the stomach on the playground, as if to make me physically aware of my exclusion?

One day I went up to the teacher and said, "I hate you." As if she were somehow responsible, as if she could take the blame.

Mazamet, France, Spring 1960

There is a strange and wonderful smell in this place. A smell of gutters or a stagnant river, repellant yet sweet at the same time. My mother and I are staying for a month with my older sister Mary Anna, who was married two years ago to a Swiss pastor she met in New Haven. Mazamet is his first parish. They have an infant son, Christopher. I am very proud to be an aunt at the age of nine. My sister scolds me when I drop a pebble from the window to the top of his pram in the courtyard three floors below. Yet I knew it would not hurt him; my aim is good, for dropping pebbles on prams.

I eat my first yoghurts, rich and creamy with berry flavors. I play with the children from the apartment downstairs, the Cadier family. My mother tells me with a conspiratorial tone that they are Catholic: that is why there are twelve children. We play cards, I learn their names, but I am often frightened by their language, in which they can hide and tease. My sister teaches me some card game words, *c'est à toi, gagné, bataille.* She buys me an elementary school history book that I find endlessly fascinating with its pictures of Charlemagne, Joan of Arc, the Revolution and its guillotine. I am frustrated that I cannot read the text; I want to know everything.

There is a hill we climb to a crumbling medieval ruin, a castle called Hautpoul. I am drawn to its decay, its ancient stones: this is perhaps the first thing I have found in the outside world which fascinates and absorbs me. Until now I have always sought to escape from the real world, from classmates and adults, by entering an alternative world, in play with dolls, or in reading.

They take me to Carcassonne, a whole medieval walled city, intact. It is beautiful, but too close to a world of fairy tales, for beautiful princesses. I prefer the broken grandeur of Hautpoul: its inexplicable demise, its haunted abandonment.

Mazamet, France, September 1986

We drive through, so quickly, stopping only at a bakery for some croissants. We have spent the last four months driving through quickly, from the north of England to the Turkish-Iranian border and back. What are we fleeing from? We drive through France with the urgency of refugees, looking for a place to settle. My French has been fluent since I moved to Switzerland at the age of sixteen; now my husband wants to learn French, and it seems sensible to find work in a place we like so that he can fulfill this project.

I tell him I was here when I was nine years old. He does not seem to care; rather, he resents my memories. The miles through Greece, through Bulgaria, were planted with memories like land mines; I never knew when one might explode, spoil the day, destroy the illusion of newlywed happiness. That dinner in the Plaka, at the foot of the Acropolis? Or the conversations with Christina and her husband in their flat in Sofia? I have learned to bury the past, deeper, to where it cannot hurt us. It lies buried beneath Yugoslavia, Hungary, Poland, places we had planned to visit but did not, so raw was our anger with each other.

So now I do not look for Hautpoul as we drive through Mazamet, do not tell Alan about the Cadier family and the card games and the taste of yoghurt and the smell of the river. We go to Carcassonne, mingle, lose ourselves among the crowds of tourists. A fire-eater performing in a medieval square fascinates my daughter.

New Haven, Connecticut, 1964

I am in a private girls' school, where I am a good student. I have been elected president of the ninth-grade class. I am not popular, merely neutral and respected. This is the first and last time I will hold office. Student council meetings seem, already, to be subtly political, a place for back-patting and showing off. I am bored by the tedium of it, but I do the job, without enthusiasm.

My English teacher is an older white-haired woman, tall and gaunt, with an accent from elsewhere, perhaps British, and a stern, fair smile. We read *Romeo and Juliet, Julius Caesar,* the Romantic poets. She likes me, encourages me, begs me to cut my bangs so she can see my face. She gives me in exchange the words to hide behind.

On certain days—perhaps it has something to do with the weather—there is a smell from the gutters which reminds me of Mazamet.

Lausanne, Switzerland, 1969

This teacher is old and jowled and white-haired, and he does not have our respect. With the others in the class—all girls—we knit under the desks during his lectures. He drones; it is rumored that he has given the same lectures for fifty years, and he still has a strong Swiss-German accent.

But in the drone there is a music, a faint melody I strain to hear, perhaps alone of all the busily knitting students. He is teaching us Russian history: the princes of Muscovy, Ivan the Terrible, Boris Godunov. There is something wild and exotic and dangerous here. A classmate, aware of my interest, gives me a book of stories, in English, by Aleksandr Pushkin. It is a lovely book, illustrated, bound in red leather with gold leaf: her father works for the printer who made the book, and they don't read English. I have never heard of Pushkin before, have grown up on a steady diet of F. Scott Fitzgerald and John Steinbeck. I take the book home, read "The Captain's Daughter," "Dubrovsky." I borrow Russian operas from the library, *Boris Godunov, Evgeni Onegin, Prince Igor.* I read Tolstoy and Turgenev. I study Russian from an old textbook with yellowing Soviet paper. I try not to look at the photographs of Lenin, of smiling girls in kerchiefs on the seats of tractors, of cheering Pioneer children. The Soviet Union frightens as much as Russia fascinates.

Thomasville, North Carolina, 1961

We are spending a year in the town where my father grew up. I love it here. We live in a log cabin by a pond; there are fields with horses, forests to explore. My classmates adopt me, even with my Yankee accent, which I quickly lose. We have a club, with dreadful initiation ceremonies involving blindfolds and cold spaghetti. I dance the twist, go to my first boy-girl birthday party, where spin the bottle replaces pin the tail on the donkey. I even kiss a boy.

I have a new red dictionary for school. There is a word I want to look up, because I hear it often, on the radio, at school, and I don't know what it means, really. It sounds like a disease, a plague, and people who have it should be exterminated, I understand. It is evil.

I am so afraid of the word that I close the dictionary without looking. *Communism.*

Moscow, July 1972

We are in the green belt an hour from Moscow via metro, bus, hydrofoil, still within the limits of where I am allowed to travel. It is very warm; summer is generous here. We walk through green, fragrant fields; we stop and eat raw peas. There is a village, Aksakovo, with a derelict church. My friends are Sasha, Alyosha, Natasha; I stopped attending Russian class after my first week, after we met at an ice-cream stand. They are art students; they teach me Russian, they teach me something else, too, an incomparable art for living. Simplicity, humor, their melancholy tenderness. They have a guitar; we make a fire, eat a picnic of hot stew, drink insane quantities of vodka and *samogon.* We sleep in the field by the river under a thick canvas tarp. It is the hottest summer they can remember; peat-soil forests burn out of control.

They teach me gypsy songs and poems by Sergei Esenin. *(Do svidanya, drug moi, do svidanya . . .)* They take me to the circus; they take me to see Rublev's icons; they teach me the painting of Russia. The Tretyakov gallery becomes a place of recurring, familiar breathlessness. They take me to visit an old aunt who lives in an isba without running water or electricity. She fetches her water with a bucket slung over a pole; she remembers the tsar, she still admires Stalin, because he defeated the Germans. She makes us tea from a real samovar, using coals.

The warm summer evenings, vodka-lengthened; there is some mischief here too, and furtive lovemaking, and at night the Italian students sing sweet, melancholy songs outside the windows of the dormitory, like lullabies.

Moscow, July 1976

The two summers merge, four years apart, yet divided irretrievably by time, weather, age. It is as cold and wet now as it was hot then. Our dorm and classes are miles from the center of town on a vast showplace campus for third-world students. Sasha is married now; when his wife is at work he takes me on picnics with their small daughter to parks where berries and mushrooms grow. He is, curiously, unemployed. We fall in love and nourish our sadness like a rare flower. *"Nye grusti, Alisonchik,"* he says often. Don't be sad. Yet he is the one who will stay behind.

I will forget him too quickly. I will return to Greece, where I now live, teaching Russian to Bulgarian diplomats' children who speak it better than I do; on the island of Samos I will listen to Russian folk songs for a time, then I will meet another man. I will forget Sasha as I must forget him: how much of the intensity of that short, melancholy love came from its finiteness, the knowledge that it could not follow me, that there could be no letters or phone calls? The double walls of his marriage and his country.

Athens, June 1978

In a friend's guest room, the small test tube, the purple unbroken circle, telling me I am pregnant. I am neither ecstatic nor upset; perhaps bemused, wondering at this strange new turn my life has taken. I am not married, but the father, Antoni, the soldier I met on Samos with whom I have lived on and off for two years—tempestuously, impossibly—has always said he would marry me if I were pregnant. A Catholic Greek from the island of Syros: for him, fertility in a woman is all.

I have a sense of something coming to an end. This wild freedom to wander across Europe in search of love or belonging: perhaps I will find a place now, with this man and this child and this country that too is like a lover. But first I must travel again, one last time.

Zlatni Piassatsi, Bulgaria, July 1978

Christina has two children now; my child is a whisper in my belly, hardly disturbing me in my thoughts or body. With her husband Zdravko we have bounced across potholed roads

With her parents, aboard the Queen Mary, *June 1963*

The author in Leningrad, 1973

to the seaside to join her in the town she has flown to with the children. They are small and querulous and she keeps a strict regime.

On a day of clouds I escape the claustrophobia of family and come alone to the deserted beach. I sit on the cold sand and write to my sister that she is, at last, about to become an aunt. I am nervous, eager for her approval; I am not married, nor am I sure I will be.

A small bird approaches, hopping across the sand. I stretch out my hand and the bird submits to my caress, confidently. This softness, the tiny head so light that pressure is meaningless. It seems a good omen.

Kaiafa, Peloponnese, August 1978

I am sitting alone in the dunes where Donald and I have been camping. Donald is the friend who will never be a lover: there is a freedom in our friendship which is at times more wonderful than love. I will ask him one day to marry me, mostly in jest, but I cannot think of another man I have liked more. We spend long hours at tavernas drinking Amstel or retsina and talking about love and Greeks and the meaning of life; we spend equally long hours in companionable silence, reading, sunbathing, sleeping chastely side by side, often on the beach. I tell him he looks like the wild man of Borneo when he emerges from his sleeping bag in the morning.

Now I sit alone and watch the turquoise-mirrored sunset, and I feel the child inside me for the first time, not yet moving but as a presence, an incredibly strong force, an incredible source of strength and well-being to me. I know, too—a premonition—that when I return to Syros it will be finished with Antoni, that I will raise this child alone, that I may have to leave Greece altogether. If I am to stay here, I hope the child will be a boy; but already I am wishing, in a deeper, truer place, for a girl.

Kaiafa, Peloponnese, April 1986

We have two tents pitched among the pines by the railroad track. Gypsies have stolen my gold-framed eyeglasses; the Greek air force shaves the tops of trees with its fighter jets. We clean the beach of garbage—toxic cans meant for burial at sea wash up here to poison the villagers. It is Greek Easter but, somnolent and marriage-tense, we miss it. Chernobyl is spreading its cloud over us but we do not know that either; we have not seen a paper or heard the news since we arrived a week ago. We fight constantly, dark, brooding arguments. Sometimes, brief reprieves, we laugh and hold each other as we wash our dishes in the sand, in the polluted Ionian Sea. I should be happy, married at last at thirty-five. And this man loves me. Dare I even think that I miss Donald; and the sunset-hued symbiosis with my daughter, begun here eight years ago, has been broken by a man's neediness, by my own greed for his attention. Other things are born here with the secret spreading cloud: guilt, resentment, a terrible self-censorship which will deny the past.

Only now the writer retrieves the past; makes it whole, gives it life again. What we do to ourselves, to others, in the name of love. A belief system, a dogma, becoming tyrannical, in oneself, in the loved one, when one loves so badly. Writing is still years away from this beach at Kaiafa, but the need is slowly nourished, the answer to one's loneliness not always to be found in other people.

Marina Vallarta, Puerto Vallarta, Mexico, July 1993

Alan has gone away for two weeks, helping deliver a boat to San Diego. I wake early, pick up the spiral notebook that has become a friend, a lover. I have begun work on a novel: my third attempt, but this time feels different. Is it because I am away from California, where we have lived for the last five years, and its overbearing influence, or is it because I feel myself to be on the edge of my marriage and there is such freedom in the space between the seed of the story and the pen on the page?

The novel will be published, though of course I cannot know that now, cannot believe that the early morning dreams in Mexico will change my view of my place in the world, give me at last a curious sense of belonging. The novel will suffer as strange a fate as that of its heroine, Amelia Earhart; in publication I will lose innocence even where I gain identity. There is an intangible happiness in that innocence, like this life in Mexico, soon to vanish forever: palm fronds dipped in sunlight, distant strains of a mariachi band at sunset, first raindrops bringing a burning chill as they wake me where I lie, my face to the stars, beneath the open hatch of the sailboat that brought me to this place of dreams.

Off the Coast of Monterey, California, November 1992

America is electing a new president but we have left behind all sense of belonging to a land-bound society with its laws and choices. Our thirty-foot ketch, *Little Bit,* is our citadel, our only rampart against nature. Now we lie trembling on the floorboards, listening in fear to the rising, swelling waves as they bear down on our small wooden boat like shells upon a besieged city; we do not know if one of those huge waves will seize a decisive moment, cause the boat to founder, taking with it our dreams, perhaps our lives. I try to pray; I hold Alan's hand; I hear the cockpit fill yet again, feel the boat skewer in the trough as she tries to keep her balance, hove-to with her wind-taught jib. There is nothing to be done but wait, cruelty made tangible in time beyond measurement, a space of fear, death whispering in the wings, life hovering in our shivering prayers. My daughter sleeps on, unaware, with the curious faith children have in their parents; the cat, closer to the elements, mews pitifully when we look at her.

Thirty-six hours later we struggle into Monterey harbor, survival-high, sleep-deprived. All day we have heard voices, choruses, strange celestial radios as we beat up past Big Sur to return to civilization. The harbormaster laughs incredulously when we ask who won the presidential election; he fails to understand the existence of parallel worlds.

Anderson on her twenty-fifth birthday, with her sister and brother-in-law, Mary Anna and Clement Barbey

Lausanne, Switzerland, December 1981–January 1982

I draw closer to the hospital bed. He takes my hand, places my fingers against his upper arm. Metastasis, he says, with a kind of pride, because it is all he can do, to thumb his nose at the disease—or is it to provoke me, because he senses my fear of death? The nodules on his arm are the size of cherries; he knows they will kill him a month from now; he knows this.

He is my brother-in-law, the jovial, severe, life-loving and larger-than-life Swiss pastor who, together with my sister, has looked after me since my mother died, with fury, humor, compassion beyond all call of family duty. When I was seventeen and impossible, ringed by a self-absorption as unbroken as a wall of mirrors, he dared, only son of an autocratic, aristocratic Swiss family, to slap my face, shattering the barrier between myself and others, allowing me entry into a life where sharing was possible, where happiness could be sought and found in a mirrored exchange.

Now the characteristic color is gone from his cheeks; he looks so much older than fifty. He both fights and accepts the disease, and has been on national television to talk about cancer, about knowledge and acceptance, about the need for honesty. I cannot believe he will die; I want to say to him, to my sister, to myself, that the doctors will save him, that there are miracles. I have been raised in a culture that both refuses and trivializes death: now he

shows me another, perhaps the first, truth. He is stubborn, defiant in his acceptance, impatient of tears or grief.

On the morning of his death, they call me; his sister Sylvie greets me at the house. I do not know yet that he has already died. When Sylvie says, *C'est fini,* I do not at first understand what she means, because I do not want to understand. Only the weeping, the embracing, the silence tell me what was too hard to put into words. I go into the bedroom: perhaps I touch his hand, defiance in the midst of my fear. Perhaps I merely whisper, *Au revoir,* and feel shame: all the things he has done for me, and I have never known how to show my gratitude.

All morning I sit with my niece and nephew in a sort of silly stupor; we play cards, giggle disrespectfully. They cannot believe their father has died. Yet in our horrible laughter there is a kind of nervous release, a submission like that of fractious children to things too serious for them to understand. My daughter, two years old at the time, questions his absence. *Il est où, Clem?* she will ask, repeatedly. I do not remember what we tell her, how long it will be before she understands, or his face leaves her unformed memory.

Vaison-la-Romaine, France, Summer 1981

A dust-warm road leads through a grove of Mediterranean pines. Into a bright patch my small daughter runs, her sturdy brown legs coaxing sunlight. I stay behind in shade, and watch: her long brown hair braided and coiled above her cheeks, her little face a tease to beauty, to human tenderness before small, young lives. I feel a suffusion of light and love within me, despite shade, as if the promise of Kaiafa were ripening to burst in this perfect light. This perfect life.

Vaison-la-Romaine, France, Summer 1994

In the silent, unmoving portions of the warm days she is, I know, reading my unpublished novel, the one I began in Mexico. My older sister, longtime figure of authority, role model, successful wife, mother, journalist, author, career woman, writing teacher. Her children are grown, have children of their own; long-widowed she does not fear solitude, spends weeks at a time in her house in the deserted Provençal countryside, writing, reading, gardening, preparing perfect little meals. I admire her, have sometimes feared her; now she is reading my novel.

It is a slow thing, the building of an audience, the only mark of a writer's career. First, there is the immediate family: my husband, who has said he likes the book, has given some good criticism—would he dare to give negative criticism? Now my second reader, my sometimes brutally honest sister, will give her professional point of view.

She does not gush or enthuse, states calmly what she likes, what works less. Thinks I might get it published, but cannot really judge the American market. Neither of us can imagine that a year from now she will be exclaiming to friends how her *petite soeur* has found a major New York publisher; or that two years from now she will listen to my tales of publishing lunches and the glib false promises made by editors, agents, publishers, and publicists, will commiserate that my audience—now in the thousands—is easily swayed by marketing forces beyond an author's control, forces that have nothing to do with talent or honesty or even perseverance.

But this is in the future. In this warm innocent summer of 1994 she reads my novel while I knit and dream and absorb the smells and colors and light. I cannot write here; Provence is too lovely. I need opposition, deprivation, struggle, in order to write.

San Francisco, 1988

The office is shining, luxurious, expensive, typical of many such offices, but I have never worked in an office before. I have no window, no view; from his office the president sees the Bay Bridge, Alcatraz, Coit Tower, the Golden Gate.

They pay me well to answer phones, open mail, greet the people who arrive hasty and nervous—artists, doctors, teachers—to plead for funds from the legacy of a billionaire. And, in between, I am bored and unhappy. My life has not prepared me for this: five years studying French and Russian literature in Lausanne, two years of translation studies in Geneva. Nearly ten years of teaching English as a second language in Greece, Switzerland, and France. But my diplomas are not recognized in the United States, my resume is too bizarre (Russian? Greece?), and I have been lucky to get even this job, because my former headmistress in New Haven is the mother of one of the program officers.

I cannot keep doing this all my life; I shall go mad.

I will teach myself to use the computer. Slowly, when no one is looking, I begin to fill it with words: a translation, then a detective thriller I make up to placate my screaming brain.

Over the years I will become expert at juggling the need to survive (rent, food, books, and music) with my brain's allergy to boredom. My words will fill many computers in San Francisco during lulls and lunchtime—stealthily, like children playing hide-and-seek. It is also my way of protesting against a society so relentlessly rooted in work. I will weave successive drafts of translations and novels—my best pleasure, ultimately my best work—into the hours I sacrifice to schools, corporations, insurance companies, law offices, medical associations, even foreign consulates.

Sometimes I like to think we are numerous in our subversive activities, writers and poets of the switched screens, the hidden windows. Like revolutionaries plotting our liberation into creativity.

Lausanne, October 1970

I am about to start university. I am sitting in a small café across the street from the old building where my first classes will be held. This is the old town; the shadow of the cathedral spire falls upon the classrooms, spearing us with history.

I am unaware of a dark-haired young woman watching me—I am writing something in a notebook, chronicling my romantic, hormonal longings, no doubt; she is fascinated by the ease with which I sit alone, in my own space, using my time for myself. I will never know whether this is an American faculty (particularly where women are concerned), some legacy of my strong, widowed grandmother, or some determination on the part of my university professor father that his daughters would be different. So this young woman watches me, and will tell me, much much later, how my quiet self-sufficiency impresses her. She is from Bulgaria; she feels her way nervously into the West, for so many reasons, not least of all that she is also a woman on her own.

Later, when we first meet in Russian class, she will astound us, beginners all, with her fluency; she confuses the professor, who doesn't quite know what to do with her. I am sorry when she leaves the class—she is exotic, intriguing (perhaps the next best thing to a real Russian, I might be thinking)—then pleased when I meet her again in my English class. Her English is even better than her Russian. she is drawn to me, the only American, as I am to her; we find friendship in this complementary opposition to the world where we grew up, in which we have often felt uncomfortable.

Karloukovo, Bulgaria, September 1974

Christina has been married for four months; her husband Zdravko is a doctor in this deserted village, where the only industry is a psychiatric hospital.

The sun bakes the brown hills into a ceramic landscape, parched and dusty, unglazed. We spend our time talking, there is always so much to talk about. So much laughter here, too: the hardship of the regime breeds a special humor, for survival. Christina and Zdravko have a pet hedgehog, whose name is Esh. He eats lettuce; we eat green peppers charred and stuffed with eggs and feta cheese. I meet Ivan Grinin, one of the patients; he sings to me in French, proudly, all the French he knows: *Tombe la neige, tu ne viendras pas ce soir.*

In the balmy evenings we go to the river; Christina catches fish by merely looking at the water, it seems. Zdravko is shamed by his failure to catch anything; he is a large curly-haired man with an awkward toddler's gait and the perpetual melancholy of a Slavic opera singer.

One evening they take me in the fading light to the dog hole. We gather stones on our way; it is a dark well where stray dogs were thrown, years ago; in blindness they breed and feed on each other or what the villagers happen to throw them in jest. We toss our stones into the pit; they resonate, meters into the earth, until the pitiful barking begins, a hollow, mournful plea.

How memories—places in particular—stay with us. *One day I will write an entire book based upon an afternoon's chance visit in a dusty Bulgarian village. Life and words circling, spirals deepening as we understand. Growing older, too, we can weave fate with words, stitching the incidents of the past together, until the tapestry forms the image. The unseen dogs; our astonished faces; the fiction that arose, years later. Finding metaphors in our own lives.*

Bansko, Bulgaria, January 1996

The cold is sharp and shining as a knife blade. Icicles hang from eaves and branches and the snow sparkles with a visual intensity, crystals crisping drily in my nostrils, my lungs. I cannot remember such cold. It makes me miserable and yet, because I am in a strange place of still worse, relentless misery, the cold adds to my martyrdom and thereby offers a curious relief, vindication, distraction.

Christina and her children have gone to the ski slopes, where the exercise will keep them warm. They are so healthy and active it puts me to shame; I have not skied since 1973, when an accident on the slopes left me scarred and wary. I envy the ease with which my friend can use and challenge her body, but have learned, for the most part, to place my own challenges elsewhere.

But today every step is a challenge: I have been ill, and there is the cold, the apathy and depression which have caused me to lose twenty pounds in a month. My marriage has come to a sudden, brutal end: I have been pushed off a cliff into a void of feeling, of future, of belonging. I hardly know at times why I am here except to try to gain some strength: because Christina has also known this terrible state, and is proof that it does not last; because this journey might be a way of going back to the past, of re-creating certain links severed by marriage: independence, a fruitful solitude, the company of friends, the distraction of travel. For a month I have been peddling my misery all over Europe, to friends who will listen, commiserate, offer hope. But even hope flirts with me, sharpens cruelty; the break is not clean and my refusal to accept, my stubborn grasp on hope intensify the blackness, like this unrelenting cold.

I am walking through the small town, each step a penance, dutiful. I must get out, defy this misery. Somewhere, a church bell has begun to ring, a deep, hoarse Slavic tolling, otherworldly. I turn, try to orient myself to the source of the ringing, pick my way carefully over frozen, slippery earth. In the distance is the bell tower; I can see the bells swinging. I follow the sound and it spreads through me, growing louder, a call and a promise.

I find the church behind its high wall and enter the darkness. The void of sentiment is suddenly, inexplicably filled with the deep tolling, the comforting darkness of the church, its flickering candles, the stern and questioning faces of the icons. The cold, the longing, the ache have crystallized into something else, a promise of renewed possibility, a return to life. I light candles, obey a foolish ritual I have repeated many times, of bartering the light for the restoration of my marriage.

But the essential is not there: it is in what happened when the music of the bell shattered the cold clear sky. Something both final and initial, like a call from life itself, a restoration to faith, a reassurance that life would look after me.

In Bansko I will begin to write again. If I cannot ski, and can barely read—my thoughts too vivid and intrusive—then I must write. For weeks I have appeased misery by chronicling it in a diary, but in Bansko I will resume work on a novel. It will be a flawed, unhappy draft, but it will be like a daily call to prayer, a safe, strong ritual.

The Aegean, Lent 1977

The ferry is crowded with Greeks headed to their islands for Easter. I am on my way to Syros to see my boyfriend, and am lucky to find a seat. I settle in, pull out a magazine in French.

Next to me a young Greek woman sits reading a newspaper. We have not exchanged greetings, but now she sees my magazine and asks me if I am French. In her voice is the respectful and wishful curiosity of those who have their own reasons for hoping you are this, or that, and if you meet their expectations, hoping that something of you will rub off on them.

I have my complicated answer ready, because this has happened before: no, I'm not French, I'm American, but I live in Switzerland, in the French-speaking part. Everything held in that little word *but*: an apology, a justification, perhaps even my own secret wish that I were Swiss or French? No, I am only American, I seem to be saying, *signomi*, excuse me;

for Vietnam is still an open wound, the Greeks blame the CIA for the seven years of military dictatorship which have only recently ended, and they want the U.S. bases out of the country.

The girl gets up from her seat, leaves without saying a thing. Her departure from her precious seat indicates the degree of her indignation. I am shocked: I have been given an identity, through a lens of misperception, that I have not chosen.

I never became Swiss, despite sixteen years spent there; I did not marry the Greek father of my daughter (nationality would have been automatic, there), nor did I become British, because we did not live in England. The Swiss think I'm Swiss, the French think I'm French, Americans often think I'm Canadian.

Nationality confers identity through the eyes of the beholder, I have learned. And when you are not what people expect, you confuse them, disturb them in their easy tribal notions of where you belong. My early experience of not belonging, even in such a vast and diverse country, has stayed with me through most of my life. I have found roots in my uprooted-

Epidaros, Greece, August 1978

Daughter, Amelia ("Amy"), Vaison-la-Romaine, France, summer 1981

ness, my gypsy restlessness; I have found belonging in language.

Thomasville, North Carolina, Summer 1961

I don't think I like my life very much. A place of heat and boredom and grown-ups smoking and drinking too much and never having any time for me, unless I beg and wheedle for them to take me to the toy store, buy some new clothes for my dolls, or a new Black Stallion book.

I've found a secret way to escape my life. I invite new friends to visit at night, in the pages of my spiral notebooks. They are sisters, orphans, and they run a riding stable and have adventures on horseback. Horses are so much nicer than people. You always think something bad is going to happen to the sisters—that they'll get hurt, or won't win the blue ribbon at the horse show—but it never does. They have won-

derful lives, and they take me with them. Even though I'm not really a very good rider, and I'm a little bit afraid of horses, with them I ride well and I'm never afraid.

Sifnos, Greece, Spring 1978

They sell lovely hardback notebooks here. You can imagine the Greek schoolchildren using them for their history classes. Pericles, Thermopylae, the Trojan War. Or learning Homer, better still. Writing verse in their looping Greek handwriting.

I am trying, in this rooftop room rattled by wind, circled by sunlight, to be worthy of this notebook. I stare at the blue lines, the brown binding, the classical Greek warrior with his helmet, and wait. Surely I have so many stories to tell—where then is inspiration? Why this silence, only the rattling wind, the occasional braying of a mule? Or my reading: can't that help? I read good books now, Margaret Drabble, Doris Lessing, Kazantzakis. The place, too, is so exceptionally beautiful, the most Cycladic of all Greek islands, unspoiled and vibrant with light and the harsh poetry of its villages lace-draped over the terraced hillsides.

But I cannot write. I stopped writing long ago, in school in Lausanne. Wrote only what had to be written: wrenching last-minute Sunday afternoon dissertations on *Phèdre,* on Rousseau. Or the final obligation, the long thesis devoted to Boris Pasternak for my degree. I've written nothing since, except effusions in diaries. I don't know why I think that because I am in a rooftop room in a medieval Greek village I should "be a writer."

The wind drops, silence settles.

New Haven, Connecticut, Summer 1967

My father has forbidden my brother Tony to come to the house to see either me or our mother. *Goddamn it, Tony, I'll disinherit you if you come anywhere near here.* I have never seen such foolish anger. Nor do I know what my brother has done to deserve this.

He is seven years older than I am. He is a student and wants to be a writer. He has already lived in Paris and Vienna. He sends us *Le Nouvel Observateur* (I read the funny page) and one year he sent us a Sachertorte in the mail: it was in a wooden box with "Sacher" in big letters, a strange cake with a thick chocolate crust like a shell, cracked and crazed by shipping but with the rich inner flavor of elsewhere intact.

I have my driver's license so I lie and take my parents' car to the place where Tony is staying. We go on long secret drives and he tells me what music to listen to (Mahler, Fauré), and what books to read. He talks to me about France, about Gustave Flaubert and Jean-Paul Sartre, but mostly it's over my head, I'm not that interested, but I like being with him. There is a passion, an intelligence here that I find nowhere else. And we are defying our father.

We drive past places he has loved: the house where he grew up (I was too young to remember), the houses of friends, temples to mischief and first kisses. He speaks so vividly that I am moved to tears. He is a strange interruption in my adolescent life of Rolling Stone concerts and Yale mixers and the catty chatter of teen-

age girls. He seems to speak from a place that is grand and noble and true.

Like a priest he confers a blessing on me. *You're going to be a writer someday, Ali.* His words, later echoed by others, puzzle but go deep. There they will remain, buried but not forgotten, working their way slowly to the surface. Through the distractions of travel, the constraints of work and marriage, the peaceful completion of motherhood. Searching, still, for the heat-filled intensity of those summer afternoons, the sense of something vibrant, essential, true.

Mykonos, Greece, February 1996

My landlady brings me stews and spanakopita and sweet pickled fruit. Because it is winter, and tourists are rare. Her name is Maria and she dresses in black; she seems to have an instinctive understanding of this peculiar solitude of mine, despite the difference in our age and culture.

I am here to write. I spend most of the day in the cold dim room, with its view on a stark hillside of flat-roofed white houses and dovecotes. I will finish the first draft of the novel I resumed in Bansko a month ago. The mornings are the best time, when I make a frothy nescafé, the way Donald and I used to (first beating the powder with the sugar and a teaspoon of water into a paste), and eat thick honey-laced yoghurt. In this way I find small emblems of continuity, even if the rest, what I took for both an immediate and lasting reality, has been broken.

In the afternoon I walk to the windmills, sit and look out over the Aegean—cold, wind-shirred—in the direction of Syros, where my daughter's father lives, where I lived briefly.

The ferry called there on its way to Mykonos. The city of Ermoupolis spread like vestments over a king's knees (the Catholic church on one hilltop, the Orthodox on the other) and bathed in an apricot light between two rainstorms. And in this vision was my life coming full circle: when I had last seen this harbor one life was ending, another beginning, as I left Greece behind to return to Switzerland to have my child. Now my daughter has grown up. I wondered, briefly, if I should leave the ferry here, at Syros, and look for her father. But there was something in that apricot light, those houses peaceful in the winter air, that did not want to be disturbed. This generous view from the deck of the ferry was all that was needed, for now. A crystallization of time, sharp and brilliant, trenchant.

I am joined at the windmill by an elderly man, burly and bearded, with thick glasses. He wears the fisherman's cap, carries heavy amber worry beads. We exchange greetings, then he asks the requisite, *Apo pou eisai?* This typical Greek curiosity, wanting right away to know where I am from, my perceptible identity; this curiosity with which they will play, entering exchange. I feel confessional and tell him my current circumstances, my past life in Greece, briefly, with humor and a certain honesty. He could be my father. But I am not really surprised when, after some time, he offers to give me a *filaki*, a little kiss. I laugh and decline, gracefully, with a wealth of excuses. He wants to console me, he says.

He tells me his name is Zorba. I don't for a minute believe it is his real name; Zorba was from Macedonia. But like Zorba he has an image of himself which has not changed in fifty years: the young Greek god who seduces women, preferably blondes. The Swedes, he sighs, ah the Swedes. Don't I want to take his picture, he urges. Don't worry, I tell him, I'll take your picture, with words. I'll write about you. But it's not the same, he protests; he has been in many films, too. The women love him.

And yes, I do love talking with him, admitting the strange magic of this encounter in the winter Cycladic light, the sun low on the water, a millennial chill in the air that breathes of a past before tourism, before Swedish girls and bared skin. Zorba is ingenuous, even in his old age. And he has the curiously Greek gift, or facility, of making even the most trivial concerns seem like a subject worthy of philosophy, an intense interest in and understanding of the present moment. I wonder if he has a wife and children somewhere; I wonder at the curious Mykoniotis society, warped by the easy money and easy sex. That he has had to invent an identity for himself, undoubtedly for display only around foreign women, and to impress his mates, but how much of it lingers in his real life?

He invites me to join him later, here at the windmills. He'll bring a bottle of ouzo, and should he bring some condoms?

By now I am cold, and just vaguely annoyed. I enjoy talking with him, that's it. But the essential has been said; he no longer seems terribly funny, only sad, undignified. I wonder if I would feel the same if he were indeed twenty or thirty years younger. Our different solitudes have no common ground, no place where they might have met, to offer comfort.

Mill Valley, California, August 1996

He is holding my published book in his hands. He turns it over, opens it, looks at the photograph on the dust jacket. Closes it again and traces the letters on the cover with his finger. Then he looks at me mischievously and says my name, slowly, mysteriously, enunciating with his heavy Slavic accent.

I had not shown him the novel; he did not know I was a writer. He is the refugee, and yet for weeks he has been my refuge, my way of finding myself again, of finding reality in the midst of the curious false excitement of publication, readings, reviews, radio interviews, celebration parties. His life is simple to a point of barrenness, with all that he has lost, and yet he is generous with his time, with his heart.

With friends, including Christina from Bulgaria (far right), Switzerland, 1982

Why have I shown him the book? Why break the spell? Because we have been so close, and I felt it was dishonest not to? Because in any true connection with other people we must bring all of who we are, even if, slowly, those realities destroy connection?

He says my name again; I say his, in the same slow, teasing way. A same number of syllables. He restores this other, still new, identity to me. I cannot restore his. We change.

Trondheim, Norway, July 1971

The gray dawn that is, in fact, an absence of night. Time set on its ear, without darkness to order sleep. I am marching through the lush countryside by the fjord, it might be two or three in the morning. I am not sleepy, it is still light, so where is habit, or sense? Besides, this moment contains more than an abnormal light: deeper within me an answering darkness has begun to spread. I do not want to believe it, do not want to believe the words I heard. I see him still, back in his bedroom—the small wooden hut with its grass roof—rocking back and forth with a curious inner keening, telling me No, he had begun to love me but could not leave the girl he was with, could not hurt her; and his family and friends, his social group, what would they think?

He is my stepbrother, the son of the tall, giving divorcee my widowed father met in Spain. We have known each other for perhaps a month. This is the first time for me that the wild hope of love has spread so rapidly, like a bushfire. I walk through the pewter light, through the tall grass by the fjord, oblivious, careless, perhaps somewhat drunk on alcohol or the bitter chemicals of disappointment. Suddenly the ground opens up before me and I slide downwards, land sitting up in a deep trench, stunned and silly, laughing, crying, grateful to nature for a diversion. Is it really so easy to survive? I had thought the heart was everything.

What will be a lifetime of falling into holes, when I thought I could see. Men leaving for other women, men bound to other women or to their own sense of freedom. I have been looking, no doubt, in the wrong place, under an illusion that love would be its own light.

This Norwegian man will nevertheless remain my friend. He will marry the girl and divorce quickly;

With Amy in San Francisco, 1988

he will visit me in Samos when I am not free. He will marry again; our daughters will share a fever at a New Year's Eve party. He had dreams of travelling overland to Tibet when I first knew him, he taught me a mantra. Now he has worked for the same multinational corporation for over twenty years. His wife is a banker. They live in a big fine house overlooking the Oslofjord, full of lovely antiques. Somewhere I still have the handpainted wooden plates his mother gave me; he has the Seth Thomas clock that used to sit in the living room when I was a child.

He sends photos sometimes, at Christmas. His hairline recedes gently; his daughters grow.

Does he remember coming to me in the small kitchen of his mother's house, where I was sitting at the table, and suddenly putting his hands on my shoulders, telling me he was falling in love with me? And I had been silent, told him nothing, because I thought, already, that it was hopeless. That first touch, his hands on my shoulders, and the grey light framed still in the window, promise of dawn or of darkness.

Somewhere, in an attic or storage room, there are diaries, long unread. Telling how I would visit him, later, at his father's house, and bring fresh strawberries from the market. How when he was not looking I wrote messages to him in his copy of For Whom the Bell Tolls. How I gave him this love unconditionally, even when I knew he would not

*With husband, Alan Anderson, Puerto Vallarta,
spring 1993*

*return it. Somewhere, there are diaries: perhaps it is
in this recording that I began, really, to write.*

Trondheim, Norway, Christmas 1973

I creep into the room of the Esso Motor
Hotel where my father has moved in his drunken
anger, and begin to go through his things, dis-
tastefully. He is probably in the bar, which avoids
a confrontation. I feel like a thief, but I am
reclaiming what is mine.

In his briefcase, no longer used for anything else, I find what I am looking for: the
bottle of Veuve-Clicquot I had bought at the
duty-free as a present for my stepmother. In
his anger and drunkenness he was still lucid
enough to go off with all the potable alcohol
in the house.

I drive back to my stepmother's house, deliver my trophy. She tells me, wearily, that I
shouldn't have bothered. Later he will call me
a thief, tell me I betrayed him, threaten to
disinherit me. There are scenes, nasty, ugly, like
the ones I remember from childhood.

Only for that first brief summer with its
love and undying light: he wanted to remake
his life, for this sweet, unsuspecting woman; he
stopped drinking altogether and became a man
who might be someone's father, charming, witty,
sensible. I cannot write the words to describe
the man who was not a father.

He will die four months from now, ravaged
by the disease he had created in his loneli-

ness. I will learn the news in the London underground, at a station telephone where I call
the friend I am staying with. Instead of telling
me where we will meet for drinks, she will tell
me my sister called from Switzerland with bad
news.

*The white bathroom tiles of the Green Park Sta-
tion, the crush of commuters, the old British callboxes
where you frantically pushed the 10p pieces in at
the pipping sound. Not as a decor to grief: I did
not cry, but welcomed the anonymity of the crowd.
Not grief but a sad relief, an awareness of suffering
quelled, of a lost battle ended.*

Arkadi, Crete, April 1975

On this hill, in this church of sand-frail
stone, in 1866, hundreds of men and women
and children sought refuge from the Sultan's
armies. Rather than be captured, when defeat
was imminent, the Greeks died by their own
hand, igniting the explosives stored in the neighboring powder magazine.

Greece is a country of ghosts, where the
past is neither distant nor crystallized. I have
been learning this on my journey from the
Turkish border, across to Corfu, down to Athens, and on to Crete. I am on my own again,
after two weeks with fellow students from
Lausanne. On my way I have visited grander,
more ancient sites: Meteora, Dodoni, Delphi,
the Acropolis. But here I am totally alone, the
only tourist staying in one of the two rooms
in the small taverna. And nowhere else has history
seemed so close, as if the women's voices were
still keening with the wind against the mountain. I sit on the hillside overlooking the valley, the shrine at my back. The sun is setting,
trailing a sharp wind and a dreary chill of winter.
I should be sad, or nervous, to be travelling
alone, but here at last on this hillside I can
feel the throb of the land, hear the whisper of
myths. I have never been so exposed in my
sheltered, fortunate life; and yet this solitude
brings with it a sudden gift, a raw, tear-bright
intensity of feeling, of receptivity and communication, not unlike love.

Sofia, Bulgaria, December 1996

The walls are stripped, the floors are bare
and marked, all the furniture is gone but it is

the same room. A gray loam of time and decrepitude sticks to windowsills and doorframes, kitchen counters, the inside of drawers and cupboards. Outside the windows snow is falling.

I sit stitching old sheets together over a mattress, to protect it from dust when it will be placed into storage. The task seems endless—there are two mattresses to do—as if with each stitch I must draw myself up on thread that is ten years long, from a dark place of hurt and memory. defiled. Life has come unstitched, and I sit here ridiculously with my huge needle, counting inches in my strange task.

Yet it is the same room, and there are whispers of other memories, and there is grief and sadness. This is Mama Vesse's bedroom, in the now renamed Komplex Yavorov, where I sat with her in the summer eighteen years ago. She has died after a long spell of cancer, untreated due to the lack of facilities, because what treatment there is goes to the young. I find it hard to imagine her in this gloom, this decrepitude; I remember a woman still young and vibrant, girlish as she explained to me how she had travelled recently—under communism—to Switzerland to have a beauty mark removed.

Perhaps I think of that conversation we had that summer, perhaps I don't, so absorbed am I in my present misery. Perhaps I am thinking that it is pointless to be a writer now, if it only brings such unhappiness. (There are friends, psychologists among them, who have pointed to the relevant coincidence of my professional success and my husband's betrayal.) Perhaps what matters at this moment is that because I want my husband back, am I prepared to give up writing? Is real life, with love, not more important? Would I have sacrificed the novel to keep him, if such things were possible?

Pictures in a museum: glimpsed, studied, observed. Rooms toured, in an arbitrary fashion, in varying directions, sometimes the left side first, sometimes the right, and when there is no way out on the far side, clockwise or anti-clockwise?

And what of all the paintings not shown?

For all that, a pattern emerges. Certain images which remain, echoing vibrations of memory. Moments whose significance is grasped only years later.

Now I look at the woman stitching sheets over a mattress in a snow-silent room and imagine another, unpainted picture. Imagine Mama Vesse sitting there with her, what she might have said, shaking her head in confirmation: "You see, you are a writer now, and that is something no one can take away from you. That is who you are."

BIBLIOGRAPHY

Fiction:

Hidden Latitudes, Scribner, 1996.

Translations:

Olivier de Kersauson, *The Sea Never Changes,* Sheridan House, 1992.

H. H. The Dalai Lama, *Beyond Dogma,* North Atlantic Books, 1996.

Louise Longo, *Let Me Survive,* Sheridan House, 1996.

Catherine David, *The Beauty of Gesture,* North Atlantic Books, 1996.

J. M. G. LeClézio, *Onitsha,* University of Nebraska Press, 1997.

Guy Beining

1938-

Guy Beining, Rockport, Massachusetts, 1990

I AM OF FOUR VOICES: XIT, XON, XOR, & XUS. IN TOTAL THEY REPRESENT XITONORUS, MY COMPLETE MYSTICAL BEING. THOUGH SHAKEN & FEEBLE AT TIMES, IT HAS QUARTERED MY SOUL & SUBSTANCE WELL.

I have often cursed myself, in a low voice, "you bastard of the winds." I curse the prick of that bardic voice that haunts the poet's head, that disrupts one from taking a so-called normal path in this gambit, shell game that is the monetary pinch of life. It is as if I am looking away from myself in order to save myself, but I do ask again and again how I can carve the word to fit my head. It is this fitting and refitting that carries one into other regions and other bodies of work, and in the suit of language one wrestles with that form. Then there are times when one feels as if one were at the foot of a bad dream, and all the shamanistic tricks cannot break the curse. The visions become thicker and harder to edge out of, and sleep becomes a light, annoying gauze. To write becomes the dominant push, and there are periods when it is easy to lose balance with all else.

Now, I sit here feeling brain dead with the task of putting my literary wanderings into some order, for orderly I am not. It is also strange for me to write "I" anymore, because when I started my most ambitious work, *Stoma*, in 1978, I swore off using I in my poetry, being at that point so disillusioned with the enormous glut of confessional poets who threw all their aches and pains onto the pavement of the page. I also had fallen into that trap. One's writing should not evolve around the ego. As I have already mentioned, the creative process is a bit of a curse that one must appease in writing as well as one can in order to survive with the consciousness of that enigmatic curse.

I feel that everybody's life eventually becomes a map or chart of places and mindsets that make up the character lens as one progresses, as you can see on the chart representing my character lens.

XIT: TINKERING WITH JAWLINE OF OCEAN, ANOTHER CALIBER MISSED, GOING INTO NORTH SEA & THE GNAWING BEGINNINGS OF WAR

The oddity of being born exactly fifty years after T. S. Eliot shovels no great debris onto my beginnings, but being born in the Chelsea section of London gets me closer to the fly ointment. September 26, 1938, was not a particularly bewitching time, being in the thresholds of war; the sky held dark boulders for clouds. But this is all an abbreviated summary, a corpse thumbed in bad light. Weeds enter weeds and wisdom is divided. The earth was shaved once again.

XUS: THOSE CAVES, BEFORE PLATO & ACTS OF BANISHMENT, WITHIN THE POET'S HEAD, SET SO FAR BACK

I was told by my mother that the boat after us on the way to Norway from London was blown up. From Norway we headed for the U.S.A. and landed in New York City in May 1940. Neither this nor my first two years in N.Y.C. left much of an impression on me. I vaguely remember my father trying out a camp stove on the toilet seat, and how it was soon engulfed in flames. Even dimmer is my recollection of accidentally stabbing my brother in the leg with a pair of scissors. Clearing a bit from the dark negatives of that time was our summer stays in Kent, Connecticut. My father, the navigator of those trips, was originally from Norway, and my mother grew up in Russia. She had been of the aristocracy, so had to flee Saint Petersburg in 1917. This is all detailed

in a book she had published in the fifties via Dodd-Mead. My brother like myself was born in London and is two and a half years my senior.

The small summer place my parents built in 1942 was on the perimeters of Macedonia State Park. Our neighbor, roughly several hundred wooded yards away, was Emily Hopson, a person whom I still call up now and then to this day. The open field that the house stood on was surrounded by woods, and there was a brook far in the back of the house that was always in the shade, and a brook, much closer, in the front that wandered thru open meadows.

XIT: I SEPARATE STICKS INTO A CLEARING OF THOUGHTS

Roaming thru the woods in Kent was my first memorable venture into nature, and for the rest of my life I would continue to balance city and country living. Kent is like passing thru a picture postcard. The region is surrounded by mountains and has the Housatonic River passing thru it. It is a place of damp voices and tiger lily embankments. Birds punctuate all sounds and movements. That is why when my wife Anna and I pass thru Kent on our way up to the Berkshires I always get a warm sensation about the town, which has changed remarkably little except for the fact that I now could not afford to live there. In 1944 my parents sold the little house and we went off to California. Looking back it seems that my parents got the urge to move on almost every presidential election year. In 1944 and again in 1948 we went to California, and I distinctly remember the chant "we want Ike" coming from the car radio as we headed to Florida for the first time in 1952. Our trip to California in 1944 was not that memorable. I vaguely remember meeting Aldous Huxley and Anita Luce, but I more dramatically remember a girl of about my age, and how we would run thru an endless poinsettia field. I also recall FDR dying while we were out there. After his death the days seemed to consist of very gray, spotty slides of fractured events.

XIT: INCANDESCENT FORM OF LUNAR MOTH, JUGGLES SHADOWS ON WHITE RECTANGULAR PORCH. LIGHT FROM A WINDOW SCOOPS UP A SECTION OF LAWN.

CHARACTER LENS

PERIOD: 1938-1950 **METALLIC SPHERE:** COPPER MACHINE	**PERIOD:** 1951-1959 **METALLIC SPHERE:** NICKEL MACHINE
RESIDENCES: London NYC Kent, CT Hollywood Kent, CT Pear Blossoms, CA Kent, CT **PSYCHE:** in patches of light	**RESIDENCES:** Ashford, CT Jupiter, FL Gainesville, FL **PSYCHE:** in patches of shade
MENTAL LANDMARKS: brook, sticks, stones, pigiron pit	**MENTAL LANDMARKS:** bed, sandbars
ETYMA **VOICE:** XIT	**VOICE:** XON MAGMA
VOICE: XOR	**VOICE:** XUS
PERIOD: 1960-1977 **METALLIC SPHERE:** SILVER MACHINE	**PERIOD:** 1978- **METALLIC SPHERE:** GOLD MACHINE
RESIDENCES: NYC Germany NYC Brooklyn **PSYCHE:** in shallow shade into all shadows	**RESIDENCES:** Queens Mill River, MA Queens Rockport, MA Queens **PSYCHE:** I rise to light again
MENTAL LANDMARKS: barracks banks bars	**MENTAL LANDMARKS:** glass doors fields ocean
DRAMA	STOMA

The four periods cover childhood, adolescence, early manhood, and middle age. Each lists residences where the author lived, associations (such as the brook of his childhood), and illustrate that he is the sum of all these parts: the four voices of Xit, Xon, Xor, and Xus.

Father, Gunnar Beining, 1958

We returned to Kent late in 1945 and my parents bought another place, this one less remote and right on Route 7, where they opened their first antique shop. It was peaceful and that is why, perhaps, those years until 1948 passed without much excitement. Coming home from school I can recall stretching out on the floor listening to *Hop Harrigan, Terry and the Pirates, Sky King, Superman,* and *Tom Mix.* Much later in the evening I would tune in to *The Lone Ranger.* But the weekend shows intrigued me even more. Programs like *Gangbusters, The F.B.I.,* and *The Fat Man.* To this day, radio occupies more of my time than TV.

XIT: MY RIGHT EYE, WITH THE TIRED STRESS OF SOME WHITE MULE, CANNOT FIND RANGE IN A DAISY FIELD, SUCH A LAZY FIELD OF VISION

Kent is surrounded by mountains, so in the summer thunderstorms seemed to last forever, bouncing off one rock face onto another, but this latest house seemed less vulnerable to these storms. Slate ledges protruded along edges of the porch creating the perfect terrain for me to play with my tin soldiers. There was a cluster of locust trees coming down a hill in back of the house, which we naturally called Locust Hill, and on very hot summer nights my brother

and I would sleep in hammocks at the very top of it. Thunderstorms often had us tumbling down this hill for cover in the house. I remember gathering sticks in the far reaches of this hill and I would play numerous games with them, treating them as magical objects. Perhaps, after seeing a man scout for water spots once with a divining rod, the power of a stick impressed me. If you walked over this hill and roamed a bit, you would come across the railroad tracks and past that a little further you would find the Housatonic River, a body of water that intrigued me greatly. A bit down from us and the town dump was an abandoned pig iron pit.

Starting with my father's shop there were a few more antique shops leading up to and thru the Berkshires on Route 7. Now there is an endless string of them and most of them don't sell antiques. I remember well a lady who also sold old buttons on the side. I shaped this memory into a prose poem which appears in a collection *Too Far to Hear, Part II,* via Standing Stone Press, published August '97. That whole work focused on my days in Kent and later Ashford where we moved in June 1950, just days before the Korean War began, but before that we were to visit California once again. In the fall of 1948 my parents rented their house to an insipid looking middle-aged woman with a head of terribly stained black hair. Her pale arms seemed to dangle by her sides. She would have made a great Dick Tracy character. I recall when we returned in the spring that my mother let out a shriek when she discovered giant pee spots in her mattress. We found out later that she was an alcoholic, and we also uncovered burn marks, from her cigarette smoking, on some of the furniture. We were lucky our house stood up to her drinking sprees. In that second trip to California we went by car, minus my brother Paul, who insisted on staying on in Kent and lived for the duration of the trip with a country doctor who also took in wayward boys.

XIT: A RAKISH FIGURE HOBBLES THRU PENNY-COLORED LEAVES AND LEAVES DUSK TWIRLING. XUS: THERE IS NO POINT TO DIRECTION IF YOU CAN'T BOARD YOURSELF.

My father had bought an old 1930s limousine, just before the trip, at a good price, but it soon turned into a disaster, breaking down on the Pennsylvania Turnpike. We stayed for a good week waiting for parts in a nice little town by the name of Summerset, Pennsylvania. Truman beat Dewey while we were there. Going by car this time we saw a lot more of the countryside. Once we finally got out of Summerset it became a wondrous trip.

At the tail end of our time in California we stayed with friends in Pear Blossom. It was an isolated area in the desert. There we took long, brown walks thru a landscape that made you feel as if you were walking on a treadmill. When we left California, probably in early February, we naturally took the southern route home. It took us over two days just to cross Texas. I remember seeing the signs Kent, but Kent, Texas, was a far cry from Kent, Connecticut. It could have been Dodge City in the frontier days, being so distant and desolate. I recall spotting a one-armed Indian when I was walking down the main street. His shadow cast a timeless piece of clockwork.

We stayed in Past Christian, a small Mississippi town on the Gulf for about a month. My parents must have been charmed by the region, because for a while they were even considering it as a prospective area to live in. The Poor Boy bread was crisp, and spending my mornings crabbing on the piers was enjoyable.

Mother, Tasha Beining, 1948

XIT: IN WAVES OF LEAVES AN ANT CLIMBS SUN-SPOTS.
XON: AN ANT SAW A FOOT COME DOWN IN FRAMES AS AN ETERNITY SLIPPED.
XIT: BIRDS DUST OFF THEIR SONGS, UNFOLDING WATER SPOUT.
XON: LIGHTNING BUG IN CUPPED HAND VIEWS BLOOD DANCE.

It was nearly April when we returned to Kent. I entered the sixth grade in September 1949. It turned out to be a worthwhile grade-school year. My teacher was Mr. Clark and he showed an interest in the arts. I wrote my first little stories in his class. My pencil would eke out a few words for some time after that year with him.

In June 1950 we moved to Ashford, Connecticut. This new home was to be another antique shop, and indeed the house had a grand history, having been built in 1740. It was known as the Hammond House. However, when we arrived there, it was a dilapidated farm house with an attic filled to the rafters with bats. My brother and I actually made bats out of left-over pieces of wood and spent hours taking batting practice at those elusive creatures. It was not long before my parents restored the place.

XIT: THE TEACHER SMEARS GRAYNESS OF CHALK & BOARD AS I COAT MYSELF WITH POWDERED BRUISES OF WORDS.
XON: I HAD ARRESTED MYSELF IN BED AND LATER OUT OF THE COCOON I SAW THE MYSTERY OF THE BLACKBOARD BEFORE IT WAS ERASED.
XOR: ALL THE BLACKBOARDS HAD CRASHED & SPREAD OUT INTO THE FLICKERING NIGHT.
XUS: NOW I TAKE THE BLACKBOARD & CARVE OUT A VISUAL LANGUAGE.

In the fall I went to school in what must have been the last wooden school house in

Connecticut. The sixth, seventh, and eighth grades were all lumped together. I must mention here that in the 1940s an optometrist had discovered that I had a lazy right eye. I was told that I had to wear a patch over my left eye in order to mobilize the right one. I ended up rarely wearing it, and only when I joined the army did I finally get glasses, so in this crowded classroom the blackboard was a blur and that whole school year was a maze.

Around my thirteenth birthday, in September 1951, I was diagnosed as having rheumatic fever. I was laid up in bed for two and a half years. A closer introspection of my surroundings began . . . The i within the eye poured forth.

XON: ALL THE WAY TO THE WOODEN SIDE OF THE BED NETTLES PIERCE STARS TRICKLING THRU THE MASK OF NIGHT.
XON: VIEWING THE SKY FROM WITHIN CREATES A NEW COUNT TO A FABLED EXISTENCE.
XOR: A THIRSTY FLY IS STUCK TO AN ICE CUBE AND WATCHES ITS MIRRORED SHADOW BECOME FATHOMLESS.
XUS: A PIECE OF GOLD IS SLAPPED AT AS A GOLDFINCH JUGGLES LIGHT: AT THAT MOMENT PARADISE IS PIERCED.
XUS: BLUE-BLOOMED WIND BLOWS THRU EAR OF MORNING GLORY.

In 1974 The Bellevue Press printed my *Concrete Dream CCXV* in their Post Card Series:

as a child
I ate pies
in the dark
and watched bees swarm
only to sink into my own lichen-moss bed
with cloaks of bats
around my head.
I once found
a wide tree
& with a key
I locked myself in.

This poem really bridges the period from Kent to Ashford. The first eight lines cover the latter period & the last four lines are of my earlier time in Kent.

It was in the spring of 1954 that I finally walked outside again. My mother and I took a walk deep into the woods, by way of an old dirt sawmill road, which vanished at times, due

to an overgrowth of weeds. Later that same day I wrote a poem about the experience, and though I had felt faint and two and a half years had disappeared, much like portions of that road, I considered that the earth was a part of me once again. Up and down thru goldenrod, skirting junipers, I would walk back and forth, making a hard path in the field; talking out my first steps into poetry. I said to myself that I would wear the shoes of the flying horse and land in fire of water.

From 1954 until 1957 I took correspondence courses via the University of Indiana and got enough high school credits in the three years to enter the University of Florida at Gainesville in the spring semester of '58. The following spring I took a writing course with Barry Spacks. He was just a bit older than the class itself and was filled with enormous poetic energy. In the fall of 1959 I took an advanced writing class with Andrew Lytle, a formidable scholar who had been a part of the Agrarian School that included Tate, Penn Warren, and Caroline Gordon, and he had taught Flannery O'Connor, one of my favorite authors at the time. He was a *Sewanee Review* man, yet the atmosphere at Gainesville was not that of the Old South. Harry Crews, having just returned from the military, was a part of the group. He was older and much wiser, making the classes often just dialogues between Lytle and himself. I had become hooked on the Southern tradition, reading Faulkner, Welty, Porter, and O'Connor with great relish. The first little germ in my writing career was going to be fiction and steeped in the Southern mode.

Nineteen-sixty was indeed a pivotal year for me. I hitchhiked out of Gainesville early on a bright Saturday in early January and made it to my parents' place in New Smyrna Beach, Florida, the next afternoon. I dropped my small bag of possessions in the house and went out on the beach where I found them strolling. They took my sudden move quite well, though I'm sure they wondered what the hell my next step was going to bring. In early March I rode back up North with them. Two weeks later I was in New York City, where Robert B. Hale, an old friend of my parents, helped me out no end by finding me free lodging in the top room of a brownstone owned by Russell Lynes and his wife. Not long before my arrival, their son, who was in the army, went overseas, and they were kind enough to let me stay there. A year later I was to be stationed in Germany, and one of my duties at the APO was to weed out the cards of soldiers who had served in the area and had since returned home. I plucked the card bearing the name of the soldier who had made that room available to me. I had heard about Russell Lynes and his *Taste-Maker* book, besides the one on highbrow, low-brow, and middlebrow, and knew that he was the editor of *Harper's Magazine*. I saw very little of him, and would pass their elegant quarters on the way up to my room, and often would hear voices; every once in a while Mrs. Lynes would shout out a friendly hello. One evening on my way up the stairs, Mr. Lynes invited me in for a drink. In those days when you spoke of poets the name T. S. Eliot always came up, and so we discussed his merits for a while. I enjoyed cummings more than Eliot, but if I had only known that there was a Charles Olson around and that his first Maximus book had come out that year. It took me another seven years to blindly pick up the book in a secondhand store, and many more years before I saw the importance of his Gloucester Epic. I now think how far poetry has come.

Again in 1960 my life took a dramatic turn. After working most of the summer in an office adding up vouchers, I quit and went to New Orleans, where I hoped to find that chemistry of the Old South once again, but I soon ran out of money which prompted me on my twenty-second birthday, 9/26/60, to join the army. I took basic training at Fort Jackson, South Carolina, and on the day after Fasching, Ash Wednesday, I arrived in Wurzburg, Germany, where I stayed for the duration of my military stint. When I got a chance I would start working on a novel I had titled "To Belie the Day." I did only about fifty pages of work on it until my release from the army in September 1963.

My parents came up North to meet with me and we got together at Emily Hopson's house in Kent, where old memories were refreshed. Fall, which is a magical time for me, was just beginning and my favorite team, the Dodgers, were getting ready to play the dreaded Yankees in the World Series. A week or so later the Series began and I watched the games at the home of a cousin of Emily's, Myra Hopson. She must have been in her eighties by then, and was tall, lean, and spry. She was still active in her vegetable garden. There was a lake on her property where, in a log cabin, Dr. Dooley stayed. This is where my brother lived for the period of my family's second visit to California. The Dodgers swept the Series and the leaves began to look as if they were being dipped in bronze; details of the woods sharpened under brilliant, cobalt skies. I distinctly remember reading *The Collected Short Stories of William Faulkner* during that period. In my head I was training myself to be a novelist and short story writer, though poetry was a deeper link to my psyche. The idyllic weeks in the country ended and I set off for New York City. In a short time I got a job in a bank where I stayed, except for one break, until the spring of 1974. This began my dark phase, in a period of literary indecisions.

"With my brother (left)," 1947

XOR: IT WOULD TAKE A LOT OF PEGS TO KEEP THE TENT OVER MY HEAD, TO KEEP ME SAFE IN THAT ZONE WHERE THE POET BREATHES LONG & DARKLY.

XOR: WOODENLY HE WORKS HIS WHISTLE IN THISTLES & THORNS; HE ONCE A HORN PLAYER, A SAYER OF SOUNDS.

XON: THE CREATIVE HIVE GROWS AS YOU DEVELOP SUBTLETIES & TRY TO TIP THE BEES, WINGS INTO THE GOLDEN LIGHT WHERE PASSAGES BREAK THE CATACOMBS OF THOUGHT.

XON: ROWS & ROWS OF THE SAME DREAM MAKE LIVING A PRETENSE.

The opening chapter to "Belie the Day" was printed in the literary magazine *The Rebel* in December 1964. This gave me encouragement, but working every day at the bank became a heavy weight. I continued working on the novel and played around with my poetry. I was handling it awkwardly and it annoyed me no end. I was really just trying to discover my own style and approach. What poetic path I would take was still in the air.

I completed "To Belie the Day" in the last month or so of 1965, on the beach in Jupiter, Florida, while separated from my first wife. I did the final half of the book in that short period of time, and I thought that I had finally found my niche. It was almost romantic, seated under a cabana on the beach writing furiously. Back in New York City I submitted the novel to Atheneum Press in early 1966. An editor there was quite taken by it, but after over half a year of wrangling, the book was finally turned down. I had no patience and, unlike most novelists who would keep submitting, I basically bailed out, and this episode more then anything else pushed me into poetry.

My first poem to find print was a piece called "Comfort." I am quoting it here simply to show how far away I was from developing my own rhythm.

> The Ming pottery was on the mantel
>   piece,
> Outside, the sleet chipped away at the
>   window panes.
> The red Ming cup looked warm;
> The green one was forest full.
> The fireplace threw flames of curling light
> Upon the candle stems and silver spoons.
> Outside, gray branches shook in space.

It was published in the spring issue of *Nexus,* a San Francisco-based magazine. It was crafted to the point of being wooden. The piece draws heavily on my days in Ashford, Connecticut. I carved the mantelpiece and two Ming cups right out of our drawing room and pasted them to the page. I had not been ignited by the expansiveness of poetry and so would write on and off in other mediums. For a time I was absorbed in churning out one-act plays. This floundering about lasted until 1970. After that

Beining, just before entering the University of Florida, 1958

I churned out poetry incessantly. The three-year period from 1972-1974 was actually my most successful time in being accepted by literary magazines. In that short stretch roughly one thousand poems were accepted by several hundred different journals. I had some stability in being anchored in a brownstone in Park Slope, Brooklyn, and still holding down my job. In the spring of 1974 though, I left the bank and with a little savings took six months off. I began by writing *The Ogden Diary*. The opening date in the diary was April and approximates the actual beginning of the piece. It took five years for Zahir Press to publish the book. I don't know if I learned to become more patient in these matters, but in writing so much poetry something was always being accepted, and that is what kept me going. Let me note at this point a problem I have in covering my writing career. I must have appeared, over the years, in five hundred different literary magazines, and over one thousand issues, with between two and three thousand poems seeing print. I will quote from just a few of these issues and concentrate more on the various poetry books that have been published. And too, there must be over three thousand poems which will never see the light of day. In *The Ogden Diary* I wrote for April 13, 1974:

a spot of light
no bigger than a leaf
develops slowly
in what must be the beginning
of day.

Ogden, who is trapped in a cellar, finally is rescued but in the hospital goes into a coma. He is a character who will linger for a long time in my work.

I will not go into my psyche of this period, but I was quite a tortured soul and was very self-destructive. I remember in July of '73 when I lost a manuscript of poetry entitled "Discovery." The following week in a blind fury I wrote another group of poems to replace the lost ones. I called them "Lost in Discovery," and they became another series for me. In the early seventies I began to write poems in such series. It was a good way of keeping track of them, and secondly, I was getting tired of creating all those individual titles. I wrote some three hundred "Ruins" poems, several hundred "Discovery" poems, over one hundred "Sweet Miss Misery" poems, and so on, but my most important series I believe was the "Concrete Dreams" poems, which reached one thousand in number. I must have thought enough of them, for in 1977 I rewrote four hundred of the best ones and titled this latest effort "Concrete Dreams Rebuilt."

In 1976 my first chapbook came out, entitled *Razor with No Obligation.* Included in the text are three Ogden poems, which continued his saga. There were also some "Ruins" poems and "Discovery" poems represented. I would label most of these poems from 1970 through 1975 as surface pieces. They were written in a frenzy and came close to being automatic writing. In most cases they lacked depth, but there were exceptions; for example, I just happen to have come across a short "Ruins" poem that appeared in *River Bottom,* an issue that came out in the autumn of 1975, which goes:

stoop low
in the chariot
the party said.
the furnace has your necklace,
no beads in bed,
& in the mare's smooth eyes
your shadow is being carried away.

About the same time *Razor* came out, a chapbook entitled *Manhattan Spiritual* appeared.

Twenty-two poems of my work and the same number by Paul Grillo made up the book. I picked the poems from a huge batch of individually titled pieces. They are of the frantic/surface category. Some money changed hands in this publishing venture, so unlike all my other books, it borders on self-publishing. That same year I wrote a forty-plus page manuscript which contained unusually long lines. It came out as "New York City Landscape" in a special issue of *NRG* in 1978. It revealed how the city was taking its toll on me.

XOR: SILENCE AS IF A CARVED EAR TOO BROAD TO HEAR.
XOR: THE FOOL FELL FULL FORWARD ON THE SPOT, DOTTING A MEDLEY.
XUS: FAR IN BACK OF THE HEAD A TINY TIN CUP CATCHES A DROP OF WATER & IT EXPLODES UPWARD, HOT & SILVER: IT HARDENS IN SPACE BETWEEN KNOWLEDGE & ACCEPTANCE.
XUS: DISRUPT THE MORAL MAP & RUSTY HINGES OF HISTORY FOR AMATORY IS SPENT WHILE THE RECTORY IN THE WRITER'S HEAD IS REDRESSED.

In 1976 I was smoothing the rough edges of my writing and was pushing away from the various series for a short period. I wrote *The Raw-Robed Few* between mid-May and mid-June. It consists of seventy-two individual poems. The first ten poems introduce the members of the raw-robed few. This is where my first thoughts concerning Xit, Xon, Xor, and Xus came to fruition. These members, though, represent the very darkest side of these mythical characters. In the last fifteen pages of the book Ogden reappears, increasing the stakes surrounding his pathetic existence. Since that time I have read a bit of Beckett and believe that Ogden would feel very much at home in his landscape. One of my favorite poems in the collection is "Sauna," which was also printed as part of a broadside collection by Swamp Press.

will hand this paper
as a towel dripping words
your shaven head as toltec
ablaze by blanketed bed
& modern totem
a talipot to fan the skin
steam rolling up sleeve by tap.
the earth pig sits on screen of leaves

nether air to wean the skull
cloudberry squashed in the fist
cracking the hiss of pores.

The collection was published by Applezaba Press in 1982.

I was still in turmoil in 1977, but was beginning to develop a subtler style, that is, I was putting more distance between me and the reader, making the thinking process more important when approaching the work. The series "Artism" is a good example of this. Two sections are placed on the page and several voices echo and reecho various thoughts. I further developed this process in a later version of the "Lost in Discovery" pieces. A group from both these series appeared in the anthology *Contents under Pressure,* a portable gallery of Visual and Verbal Art from Moonlight Publications which came out in 1981. Examples from both works follow:

exhibition #60
ARTISM

SPECULUM: my parched teeth
a mole gnaws   fall
between the   to another shore.
knowledge of   i watch the prophets
light & dark,   pick the wings
the pin-holes   of gulls.
in his skull   the chewing sound
hears the move-   of the sun
ments of worms.   drops me as a nest.

a thematic comment: lost in discovery
    offerings
                              #67

in the mad box
with the literary breath
he sank into
paradiso
measured by the
larger body of his
cantos.

pound/his rustic joints
to ground, hearing his
cantos drop.
this pound with voice
round as a hound on the make
o some bucolic bolshevik
might call him a fake.
his tempered lips were cold
in the rose of may

only to pick april in eliot
as he combed the river of his
hair thru dark centuries
& replanted an eatable language.

paradiso became
one step out-
side
the hall.

The mechanism was in place for turning poetic language a bit on its side and prodding it with sharp tongue, as if words had become knives eating into the fabric of sound. I have always felt that you have to keep exploring further as you continue writing, and therefore I consider myself an experimental writer first and foremost. In my less inventive poems of the early seventies it was easier for me to get published, but that really is not the driving force behind writing. It is rather to hit new ground, new terrain, and it is also a mental exercise, where you keep pushing the mind in order to turn the scope of what you see in order to create a new approach. If things are going right, you can dance with the words, go in circles and chant to the stone droppings of their sounds as the vault unlocks in your head, becoming the Universe, and the ride is high over the

"A self-portrait in Prospect Park, Brooklyn, New York," about 1976

last blue scrap of light, yet you can also fear the movement of the words that can become a pattern that could drum out a life sentence of mediocrity.

In 1977 I wrote a string of long poems, five of which were later published as full poetry books or chapbooks. The first of these was *City Shingles,* which actually came out the same year it was written. It was published by La-Bas and was the first chapbook of their series edited by Douglas Messerli, now well known for his Sun & Moon Press. It consisted of fifteen pieces, and once again I roared about the mania of city life. I will quote here the briefest of these pieces:

> *II*
> all the bakers
> return with white hands
> the summer chemistry is
> at night
> sweat pins in ear
> welts on skin,
> the city is a body without shine.

All the other works I did that year dealt with nature in one way or another. The next book that came from that year combined two poetic works, "Backroads" and "Artism." The first work was twenty-five pages in length, and "Artism" ran from one thru forty-five. I have mentioned the duel voice of this work already. In "Backroads" I reflected on a nostalgic view of my country days. It is of a muffled time. "all the apples / so heavy that they / bury sound." Looking over the text I see an almost haiku-like pattern throughout it. The sentences are short yet sharp, such as "blackbirds / are frantic / for a place / to burn / their tails." And, "the smell from / the river / puts a belly / in the wind." Again, "thru skin of / blossoms / the white / white country yard."

The next long poems that I wrote in 1977 and that saw print in book form were portions of three works: "The Claw inside the Cage," "Preambles," and "Putting a New Boundary on the Page." The chapbook was titled *A New Boundary* and was published by Woodrose Editions in 1980. "The Claw" was an elusive piece that ran twenty-seven pages and contained a mystery within a mystery. "Preambles" on the other hand was a robber of sleep, a purple stamp over drunken nights. On the last page these lines: "tendrils in quilt / of song / the wind

parked / inside the wooded / slope / now down / down / the moon discs / in boilerroom of / stars—." The complete fifteen pages of "Putting a New Boundary on the Page" appears in the book. Again I handle in the cursed corner of Mystic the dilemma of nature versus the juggling act of Man in his artificial surroundings. I mention that "history is a wet book / of mud." Later to write: "flat stones / pick the pulse of water / & are the ears / of rocks / & they of mountains / these sleeping stones / the ribs of creation." And bringing it further: "the spokes / as skin of the sun / blanket of the sun / uniform of the sun." Man always, due to ego, forgets to put himself in his proper place, which is far down the road. Humility, especially in this consumer society, has been lost.

Gegenschein accepted *Ice Rescue Station,* the next long poem from 1977, but first I must discuss its editor, Phil Smith. I have not been mentioning all the editors involved in my work because most of them I have never gotten to know personally. I did finally meet a few of them at the annual New York City Small Press Book fairs, but they quickly passed into their own good nights. Phil, on the other hand, became a good friend. Our initial connection was through his magazine. He had taken some poems of mine while he was in Bowling Green in the early seventies. A few years later he came to New York City where he is originally from. We met and developed a vague but consistent friendship. In 1980 he published *Ice Rescue Station* as part of his Notbooks series. Phil in his Dada sphere—that is, he accepts whatever you decide to sent him—this has baffled me more than anything.

One day in the mid-seventies I took a picture of myself standing by a sign in Prospect Park which read ICE RESCUE STATION. The sign had always intrigued me and no doubt inspired the chapbook. The rhythm of this text is on the same level as "Backroads," as you can see from the following quotes: "ice trails / wings / & the secret blood / of birds / & the air space / within their bones." "a sickness / as still / as the moon." "thistles wake up / with the beard of ice / & will forget to bloom / & prick the hand." And so goes the massacre of ice, with Nature winning again.

Hugh Fox of Ghostdance Press has published three chapbooks of my work over the years. The first book, *Waiting for the Soothsayer,* represents the final long poem printed from 1977. It is also probably the most complex, but as you have no doubt noticed in handling my work, I don't play the part of critic or analyzer. I will leave that to better qualified people such as Hugh Fox, who in his book *The Ghost Dance Anthology,* via Whitston Publishing Company, which came out late in 1994, covered this poem succinctly. The opening lines to the piece really set things up: "it is summer & the chants / are longer / the hills higher. / inside the house that no longer / stands is a wooden rocker / in milky sunlight. / each movement of the rocker / is an eclipse." And below the text a second voice: "each word doesn't / drop / or matter / each coat of flowers / showered out." In the peak of summer the vegetation closes in and adds several heads to a hill, such as Locust Hill of my past in Kent. Nothing of that time exists now; however, an inanimate object such as a rocker still measures time the same way. The text is concerned with time, as is obvious, judging by its title; it also is a mystical pun on Beckett and his *Waiting for Godot.* But before Godot there was the Magi, the Soothsayer and I journey with the Aztec and their time, but I flicker (and here is the spirit, the will of the poet) back to Kent when I was lounging on the hammock. With a poet there is never straight pain, or precisely marked remembrances, for the slight slip is most important. In this fifteen-page work I wandered all over the terrain and jostled time.

I believe that I wrote *Small Sessions of the Inner Spirit,* and published it, in 1980. The book is about the size of a large postage stamp and was uniquely put together by Ed Rayher. The opening lines start off the layers of silence within the small piece: "lying onto / another ear / it hears / the window open."

In October I gave my first reading in a remote bar, somewhere beyond Flushing, Queens. It was one of my rare visits to that borough. Half a year later it would be my home base. One of the poems I read was "Circulation #7," which I wrote on my way to the reading and which described the scenery on my way there. This "Circulation" series was stronger than any of the earlier ones. First of all the pieces were more connected and secondly more thought out. There were some 110 in number, and were accepted for publication a few years later but never saw print. This has happened more than half a dozen times in my writing career, but

it's an understandable situation since most small presses don't make any money on their efforts.

XIT: A GLOW BELOW MERIDIAN IN A PERIMETER OF SWEAT.
XON: FINI, GRINNING INTO GIN WITH ISINGLASS CHIN IN A SINGING PIN OF LIGHT.
XOR: A SILENT WISH SPRINGS UP THRU THE BORDERS OF MY HEAD. IN SUCH BLUENESS EVERYTHING SEEMS MARGINAL.
XUS: MY SKIN IS WHERE I LEFT IT PINNED TO MY SILENCE.

I finished the "Circulation" poems in the early part of 1978 and right away began another sequence entitled "Rebirth." This was an apt title since I was going thru a sort of rebirth in my private life. Coinciding with the writing of this new work, I noticed a young lady working on the banking floor below me, where I was an auditor, one of those nibbling mice of numerical infamy. I sat on the balcony totally askew in my work watching this damsel with dark hair and thin frame. She fascinated me, and when I finally audited her head teller's cash we finally got to meet. There was as much mysticism in her eyes, dark and forested, as in the poems I was beginning. So, "Rebirth" was a merging of love and spirit tangled in the deepest nightfall. The name itself, Anna Primavera, sings out like the silver bells attached to a troubadour crossing Northern Italy in the twelfth century. She also became a stabilizing force. Though at times, in the beginning, my Baudelairian madness took me mid-stream, I soon straightened out along her shore. I moved in with Anna in July. She lived in Woodside, Queens, where I saw snips of the country in some of its streets. Almost right away I began my first series of collages based on numerous photographs I had taken of myself in various parts of the city. In a way I was shedding my past. Between the photos that I pasted to the page, I scrawled quick thoughts on the images. The pictures covered a four-year period, from 1975 into 1978. I wanted to put my past into a neat pile and go on from there. In the beginning of September I began my long, all-encompassing work, *Stoma.* I believe that there are other works written after *Stoma* (which is still a continuous work) that are better written, portions of *Beige Copy* for example, but in *Stoma* I also rewrote and incorporated some of my earlier works such as "Ruins," "Discovery," "Circulation," "Rebirth," and so on. Therefore, *Stoma* tries to mend much of my pre-1978 material. I was starting afresh with this mammoth cantus. I set up a ratio of stoma pieces per page, and it ended up being one and a half stomas per page, and after completing over thirteen hundred pages of the work I had two thousand stoma pieces. I also decided on having twenty-five-page sections, and in each one of these parts a general theme was developed. Late in 1984 Red Ozier Press in conjunction with students from the New School printed, in hand-set type, with a cover and end papers hand-made by Susan Anderson at Dieu Donne Press, a chapbook which contained eight stomas from section I of the work. The first stoma goes: "it is the peeling from / bodies / sunlight the only probe / the nerve will tell. / ivy print barely green / summer long into cabins / closing into damp apple / smell / & drowning of buggy-eyed dragonflies." And in Stoma 12, a deep shadow is cast on the Western world's notion of Africa: "ashanti / palm vine / stool of gold

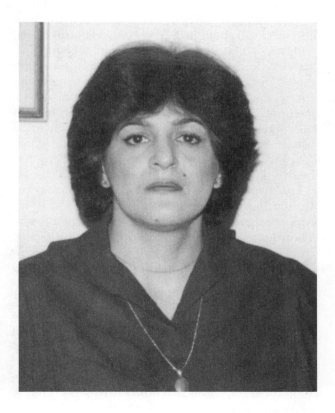

"My wife, Anna, in our apartment," 1982

/ we need a clearer window / turning head away / from doll / unable to make it folly." And on the last two lines of the final poem of this selection: "why not rather fly than touch / the question?" which really hands the reins to modern man who is quick to put in place the spectacular rather than to merely answer a simple question.

About seven weeks into *Stoma,* Anna's mother died. This was an enormous tragedy for her and therefore for me. I transformed the terribly heavy atmosphere surrounding the funeral in Stoma 101 and 102 which appeared in the 1983 issue of *Croton Review.* Short quotes from these poems follow: "the heart moves / to what town? / frost fights for / some life / in a cow's / lung / nothing is lifted." And, "anna, dark flowers / tally / the print / from your hair." And from 102: "10/23/78 & it must be 75 degrees / by noon / bees rage in appetite of / flowers / breaking this quiet leg / of sleep." I no doubt wrote this many days after the fact for I was in no mood at the time to voice opinions. This demonstrates how *Stoma* engulfed my whole thought process.

This first part of *Stoma* was also covered by *American Poetry Confronts the 1990s,* published by Black Tie Press, 1991. It contains twelve poems. In Stoma 23 I write: "the ward of better poets / is in exile / not holding to the skirt of a university. / kindling again in / boilerroom / to bypass the square design of fireplace / in exactitude of flames." And in Stoma 81: "shame to that shaman / under vacuumed rugs / the earth of marigolds breaking / thru his tongue."

In the winter of 1979 I found myself doodling on napkins in a bar. It was as if my right hand finally woke up artistically. I remember in that turnabout year of 1960 when I was in New York City, Bob Hale had invited me to sit in on one of his anatomy classes he gave at the Art Students League. He had told me to try my hand at drawing. My head at the time was on a totally different plane, and so I didn't pursue any art classes, yet nearly twenty years later my hand wanted to draw, and I got very excited by this impulse. Within another year I would start to paint. That fall I had a reading at the Veridian Gallery on Fifty-seventh street. I spotted Bob Hale in a Chock Full O'Nuts restaurant on the corner of Sixth Avenue and handed him a copy of *Backroads and Artism.* It was the last time that I was to see him.

XUS: STOMA, IT BLOOMS OUT, IT DANCES AROUND KNOB OF TIT & IRIS OF EYE: PORTIONS OUT A FIT WITHIN FIXTURE, CHURNING EARTH INTO A CAST UNSETTLED.

XOR: STOMA SITS IN ME AND POKES AT MUD & MYTH; OPENS A PASSAGE, A MOUTH, A CELL WITHIN A CELL & CORKS ORIGIN.

XIT: ONE MUST STEAL THE WORM WITHIN THE WORD THAT HAS ROTTED SO LONG IN THE HOLLOW TREE.

XON: EOPLE BARK AT ME BUT THERE IS NO CLASP WORTH ASKING FOR. THE PASSAGE LEANS INTO THE CLEARING; THE PASTURE WITH A TINT OF GREEN READIES ITSELF FOR A NEW LANGUAGE.

The *Wisconsin Review,* Vol. 14, no. 1, which came out in 1982, featured my work from *Stoma* written in 1979 and 1980. It also contained

Acrylic painting entitled "Xitonorus,"
the complete myth, 1997

some of my photographs and a couple of my Persona Collages. Since I was now painting, my work also was becoming more visual. In Stoma 407 I say "the beginning of the thought / now a blur / or touched over canvas / hearing golden tub fill w/water / in shape of buddha / light budding / stitched to membrane." And in Stoma 623: "it is in destroying / fixtures / piling / rock / up against / pg. / it is not what is normal / but what is precisely you." And finally in Stoma 400: "blind crows of a pencilled out dawn / were the rings / of dead minstrels."

In April of '79 I began section VIII of *Stoma* (pages 176-200; numbers 263-300), which was printed in *Pigiron* #8 in December 1980. I rallied around the theme of the pig and took snips from earlier "Discovery" poems, using a slightly pop art style. For example in Stoma 264: "reading sunset / of minnie & mickey swimming out from / wharf / smoking last AD / fire of mauve days." From Stoma 268: "in cloud & stars / we await the corruptible / pig." And lastly in Stoma 291: "the pig closed the curtains / loud splashing sounds came / from the tub / was he or I passing / the white rose of dante?"

In the early '80s I was beginning to show my art work, though they were rare occurrences, and my collage work was being accepted by various literary magazines, therefore, the time that I devoted to *Stoma* was being drastically cut. I felt a natural affinity between all three mediums, that is, one began to complement the other. This stirring within various fields I believe is why I started the *Beige Copy* text, which I began to play around with late in 1985, but before I get into that I will round off a bit more from *Stoma.* In 1985 my "Theories of Poetics," section XVII of *Stoma,* came out via *Atticus* magazine, published by Harry Polkinhorn. The whole issue #10 contained twenty-nine pieces, from Stoma 601 to 639, which were written in the early eighties. There were also collages and a brief interview in the issue. This is the only time I've delved into my notions on poetry. I'll quote here briefly from a few passages: Stoma 605: "if the writer relies too heavily / on form / he will be misguided and lose the / spontaneity of nature / which is the flamed leaf of creativity. / form is spirit / a chance resolution / of the mind." Stoma 610: "w/ruler & equation / we stone / fix / the walls / of a new writing / on old turf." Stoma 633: "to overly stress coherence / in a creative work / is to throw out all mystery / for the reader to grab onto / and experiment with / so as to think obscurity can work / if it is a strong equation."

Prior to *Beige Copy* I wrote a series entitled "Collectables." This was in 1984 and about this time I was buying a lot of first edition books with the idea of becoming a bookseller, and in fact I came out with a catalogue of what I had for sale in 1985. So, between 1984 and 1986 more of my time was being taken away from writing. I was also holding onto a regular forty-hour-a-week job. A slim booklet of four of these "Collectables" came out via David UU and his Silver Birch Press. I'll quote here from the first poem in full: "Able to take pay dirt from pit of Century / able to murder veins of fountain in PLATZ / able to smell SOLAR polarus / in radius of bend / able to be in text of JAZZ / with lazy eye / & darting rhythm of applause / able to fit color in the MOUTH of surgeon / tasting liver." In the title "Collectables" I might have been sending myself little messages concerning the collecting of books. My lazy eye seemed to be swimming in the color of everything.

In the summer of 1981 Hugh Fox paid me a visit. He was going to do an overview of my work up to that time, and it was to be printed in *Stony Hill*, a review magazine put out by Diane Kruchkow who had published *The Ogden Diary* a few years before. Unfortunately the magazine folded and the overview was never published, but the words of Hugh Fox concerning my work would be heard further along the way. Also about this time I started to make connections with various editors in Toronto, Canada, which seemed to have more viable literary magazines than New York City. Such editors as John Curry, David UU, Daniel F. Bradley, and Marshall Hryciuk were beginning to take material of mine. During this period haiku was appearing within my *Stoma* text. John Curry and his CURVD H & Z Press printed Stoma 1322, which contained twelve haiku. Most of these appeared again in *One Hundred Haiku Selected from a Decade (1982-1991)* by way of O!!Zone Press, which is run by Harry Burrus. I remember making this selection in 1993 and had to choose from roughly one thousand haiku. Most of them were not connected to *Stoma*. From the book #12 goes: "In garden eclipse / a spotty leaf hangs / over deadly-night-shade." I recall

this poisonous plant growing outside our kitchen window in the second home that we had in Kent, Connecticut. Number 41 goes: "A heron begins / its dance / in hieroglyphics." I trace this to the sandbars, in Jupiter, Florida. Then there is #87: "the bare facts / of running away / with naked brides, unseen." This is a pun on a Duchanpian pun.

In early September 1984 I received a call from my father in Florida. His voice was flat and eerie. He said that he was told by his doctor that he had only six months to live. I walked out of my apartment in a trance, got off the subway at Fifty-ninth Street and Fifth Avenue, and without any interest at all began browsing thru the books displayed along the park. I suddenly closed an art book and heard a faint pop. I opened the book again to find a bug splattered between two pages. Nature had given me a sign to the explosion I felt within me.

I must have been working on Stoma 1676-1700 around this time, which was published in the middle of 1989 by Ghostdance. In Stoma 1679 I wrote: "art CRITICS / came / in beast head / their blind EYES / in net of Spring / they stared at a / RARE PIECE OF FIRE / in background image of duchamp / taking screen out of window / behind him a row of screen-doors / the mesh of fine wire to merge / into image of dust shaken."

In the fall of '85 I was working very carefully on Stoma 1701-1750, printed by Aegina Press in 1994, carefully, because I had thoughts of ending the series at that point. Aegina Press only published up to #1743, and did not include an important piece, #1732; in excluding it they listed 1731 as 1732, and so all the numbers after that are not correct. I start off in 1701 stating clearly, "this is an extremely / caustic & fabricated work / all hinges bare witness / in dark green rouge scent / of orange grove / a disabled handyman tinkers / with making a goddess / in naive nautical stance / forms a somewhat scarified / mermaid / launched from green pike / mood." In 1702: "a parody / in part sails / of her scars," and further along, "so be this disabled / swimmer now deified / by tradewinds." In this far from perfect world I begin with a disabled handyman, a somewhat humorous description and a disabled swimmer on the very next page. The words scarified and scars are mentioned in these pieces. What I am doing is putting a knife to this age and making a swollen mockery of it. Even gods and goddesses of the past can not play to the music of our time. I mention *Beige Copy* in 1711 and in 1714 and note, "thinking that the beige content / could be a dirty trap." I'm saying to myself, "am I going the wrong way in leaving stoma for *Beige Copy*?" But humor and cynicism are the lead steps in this work, for another example there are the last lines of Stoma 1717: "around curve a pale / car with windshield / reflecting the cosmos / chaos he says glued / to his seat & the evening / light." This is a dig on Creeley and his famous "drive, he said." The main thing you see here is that I'm having enormous fun with the universe as my poetry becomes more stinging while I probe my psyche.

In the fall of 1985 I felt that I needed a break from the epic. My painting and collage work were getting closer to center stage, so I was leaning more toward writing that would be more visual in texture. One day I began writing on beige paper, using different colored pens for certain words. I remember mentioning this to Harry Polkinhorn, that I would prefer not to type this text, but leave it in this more painterly fashion. Over the years I kept changing how it was to look on the page. Finally, the first twenty-four poems appeared via Nietzsche's Brolly in April 1991, and I titled it *Upper and Lower Translation of Text from Beige Copy*. I used a cross to divide up the text where I spread roots and origins of certain words that I had circled in the text, plus adding further poetic notes. Though my collage cover is in color it's a shame that the work wasn't kept in its original varicolored form. I would repeat the cross upon the page in future works. Marshall Hryciuk, the publisher of Nietzsche's Brolly, will also be coming out with Book II and III of *Beige Copy* later this year.

In 1986 Anna and I moved to Mill River, Massachusetts, a very remote town deep in the Berkshires. We lived there in a small house from mid-March until late August. If nothing else it was a great escape from city life. I concentrated mainly on painting and collage work. This period also brought back a lot of my memories of Kent in the forties. We returned to Queens and moved into an apartment just a few blocks from where we were living before. Due to money problems I got rid of my first edition collection, getting a meager amount for such a haul. I once again waded into *Stoma*

and *Beige Copy,* but my spare time was evenly divided between painting, poetry, and collage work.

I closed out the final years of the eighties working in these various mediums, but I also wrote haiku and created endless small collages, many of which became a series entitled *Piecemeal* that Bob Grumman published by way of his Runaway Spoon Press. Each of the eight chapbooks he did were thirty-six pages in length, thereby making it a rather expansive collection. Also, during this period Bomb Shelter Press and Photostatic Books came out with chapbooks of more of my collages.

In March 1990 Anna and I moved to the country once again. This time we tried coastal life and settled in Rockport, Massachusetts, a picturesque town on the last limb of Cape Ann and only thirty miles north of Boston. Over the months the enchantment of the place disappeared. I sympathetically recalled Charles Olson's scorn of the town, which had broken away from his beloved Gloucester, which didn't help in my assessments of the place.

While we were living there Black Tie Press published *Stoma: selected poems 1985-1989*. Peter Gravis, the editor, selected twenty poems from 1601-1700, seventeen from 1701-1800, six from the 1800s, 1901 and 1906 from the 1900s. I finished 1907-2000 while in Rockport. In 1901 I wrote, "treated to an / alliance / of fume & smoke / in this melting landscape / where carrots turn the / earth moving stones closer / to that smoky heap of gravel / placing chalk to skin / powder to cheek."

I worked on a three-act play while there and did several hundred collages and a number of paintings. I completed a new poetry series entitled "No Subject But a Matter." It consisted of thirty-two poems, the first half came out as a chapbook from Pangen Subway Ritual, another Canadian press. Daniel F. Bradley was the editor and publisher. It came out a year later. In number fourteen I wrote: "sticks of locust trees everywhere / there is no HILL TO FALL FROM / and gorky would make a point." I was referring to Gorky the artist who committed suicide not far from Kent in 1948.

In the fall we returned to Queens once again. From 1991 to the present it is much harder to pinpoint where I am going in my work. In '91 I began quite a different series called "Haiku-Vu." Over the next few years I did several hundred of them. Each piece consists of a concrete haiku and a collage, usually a bit below the words. Hugh Fox published Haiku-Vu 1-20 in 1993, under the title *wind owl, window howl.* He commented on this work and *Waiting for the Soothsayer* in his fine book the *Ghost Dance Anthology.* He did an extensive analysis of both works.

There is an enormous variety of works that I have been pushing out in the last few years, showing that my dance step is getting wider. For instance Runaway Spoon in 1991 published my chapbook *Vanishing Whores & the Insomniac* which is made up of thirty-three haiku along with sixteen collages and drawings. In 1993 I did *Damn the Evening Garden,* via The Berkeley Horse, 1994. Here I did ink drawings of the alphabet and wrote a short poem to complement each letter. Later in the same year I wrote *Too Far to Hear,* a series of twenty-six prose poems covering my days in Kent and Ashford. The first thirteen were put out as a chapbook by Leave Books and the latter thirteen came out in 1997 by way of Standing Stone Press. Again around '93 I created *Carved Erosion,* published two years later by Elbow Press. Steve Creson did an outstanding print job on the work which is a type of concrete haiku. Topography plays a big part in the text.

In 1994 I hooked up with Phil Smith again. This time in the field of art. He has a place called A Gallery, under the broader imprint Wares for Art. I've been a part of a number of his group shows at his space and in October '94 he gave me a solo show which I titled Spheres of Clouds and Skulls. In conjunction with this, Harry Burrus of O!!Zone Press came out with a book of forty-eight of my collages, using the same title. Almost instantly my thought process was translating my paintings into collage work.

In 1995 I wrote a sixty-page book of poetry called *Axiom of a Torn Pulley,* published that same year by Potes & Poets Press. In this text I finally utilize the cross symbol to the fullest extent. During that period I was doing a series of drawings and paintings much influenced by that text.

It is getting so that the writing is no longer isolated from my painting or collage work. It is beginning to mesh more and more, and experimentation within this process will become a continuous challenge. I regret that more of *Stoma* has not been published in book form, but it would take quite a large publishing house to undertake this task. It would probably require three volumes of 450 pages each to complete the endeavor. I have yet to package it in this way and might do so after reviewing the manuscript in its entirety. I could make this one of my goals in tying up my literary output. I could also develop a broader visual/verbal field, a kind of Post Beige Copy Text, using slaps of paint, pasted images, and blocks of words, passing passage of contents. My literary pulse is not an easy one to take, and it is getting more entangled as I go along.

XON: HEAD, THINLY FORMED IN SHADOWS: WINGS SMEARED; IT, I, ON, OR US GO ON BREEZE OF LIP, IN PECK OF WOODS.
XOR: DEATH CARRIED IN ITS POCKET A WIRE STUDY OF MAN.
XIT: YOU GO PAST YESTERDAY'S LEAVES INTO A VOCABULARY OF STARS TOO NUMB TO PRINT THEIR MEANING.
XUS: ON THE EDGE OF THE DREAM THE CIRCUMFERENCE IS SOWN CLOSER TO THE VEST OF NIGHT, SO CLOSE THAT THERE IS NO ROOM FOR MOVEMENT.

BIBLIOGRAPHY

Poetry:

Backroads and Artism, Moonlight, 1979.

The Raw-Robed Few, Applezaba, 1982.

Stoma: selected poems 1985-1989, Black Tie, 1990.

One Hundred Haiku Selected from a Decade, O!!Zone, 1993.

Stoma, Aegina, 1994.

Carved Erosion, Elbow, 1995.

Beige Copy II and III, Nietzsche's Brolly, 1997.

Contributor to anthologies:

Poems of Death and Suicide, Shelly's Press, 1978.

Contents Under Pressure, Moonlight , 1981.

The View from the Top of the Mountain, Barnwood, 1981.

American Poetry Confronts the 1990s, Black Tie, 1991.

The Ghost Dance Anthology, Whitston, 1994.

Author of numerous chapbooks, including *Razor with No Obligation, City Shingles, Wind Owl, Window Howl,* and *Book of Elevations.*

Bruce Boston

1943-

FIFTEEN EXPLANATIONS IN SEARCH OF A LIFE

Outsider

Nearly all of my life I have felt like an outsider, sometimes an outsider in the company of others, yet an outsider nonetheless. At one time I thought that as I grew older I would mellow and become assimilated, that I would feel at home in the everyday world that surrounds me, the people that inhabit it, and the attitudes that prevail. Instead, quite the reverse has happened. Approaching the age of fifty-five, I have never felt more alienated from American society and culture than I do today, never more at odds with its values and practices.

Some of these feelings are the result of intelligence. On most tests measuring aptitude I score in the ninety-ninth percentile. I find myself stranded with little company at the far right of the bell curve, looking over my shoulder at a mountain of relative mediocrity looming behind me. This is a mountain I have never been inclined to scale, though my life has been influenced by the shadow it has cast upon it. All through school and in any job I have ever held my native intelligence, which I have never learned to dissemble, has caused resentment from fellow students and workers, from teachers and bosses. Plenty of intelligent people are fully integrated into society, but I'm not one of them. Other factors set me apart.

I am an only child. My father was a Catholic of German and British descent. My mother was Jewish, of Russian and Polish descent. Neither practiced the religions of their parents and as a child I never attended church nor received religious instruction of any kind. My mother, believing with good reason that anti-Semitism was alive and well, concealed the fact that she was Jewish her entire adult life, even from me until I was twelve years old. I maintained this subterfuge myself until I was twenty-one. Her

Bruce Boston, El Cerrito, California, 1979

parents, both of whom died before I was born, never accepted her marriage to a Catholic. And my mother, for the most part, cut off ties to the rest of her family. Although I am half Jewish by blood, I received little or no cultural heritage on this count.

My father's parents accepted the marriage, but he also rejected his family, moving my mother and myself two thousand miles from Chicago to Southern California, ostensibly to escape the midwestern winters. This move occurred when I was five years old. Though I met most of my paternal relatives over the years, I never knew any of them well, actually never more than casually. It was a large immediate family—five sons and one daughter—and as much as I can judge from childhood memories and my father's stories, it was full of internecine conflicts and

Parents, John and Lillian, Chicago, 1938

long-held resentments.[1] These differences would inevitably simmer and boil over any time there was a family gathering, which generally involved drunkenness and at times physical violence. Though my father managed to leave all of this behind geographically, he never left it behind emotionally. Events from forty and fifty years in the past would continue to plague him into his senior years.

Thus, except for my parents, I have been familyless my entire life. I have never started a family of my own, and at the time of this writing my only contact with relatives is with one cousin on my mother's side, and again that is only casual. This familyless condition is not something I regret. Despite the current call for the strengthening of the American family and a return to family values, most of the families I've been exposed to seem to me much like my father's, that is, full of underlying differences and resentments, as much or more negative than positive in their overall influence on individual members. The only family I've ever known that I thought I might want to be a

part of was that of a friend in high school. It seemed like a loving family that was understanding and supportive of all its members. This turned out to be an illusion, at least over time. That particular family's history dissolved in infidelity, divorce, and ongoing hostility.

No Gold in California[2]

Psychologists claim that one's early years are the most formative, and if this is the case, I was fortunate. Up until about the age of ten my parents provided me with a secure and loving environment. I never lacked for food or shelter or parental attention. Despite the fact that my father and mother came respectively from lower- and lower-middle-class economic backgrounds, and my father worked as a manual laborer, I had more toys than most of my far-more-middle-class playmates. While I was still in grammar school my father set up a basketball hoop and a tetherball pole in the backyard of our apartment. As a result, these were sports at which I excelled, the only two at which I ever really excelled. I was tetherball champion of my grammar and junior high schools, and I could have played on my high school basketball team, only by that time my aspirations were more creative and intellectual than athletic.

My earliest childhood memories, of Chicago, are practically nonexistent, or at least impossible to sort out as real memories from stories my parents later told me. When we first came to California, in 1948, we lived in a trailer park in Pasadena. This I do remember, and the memories are mainly good ones of childhood play and laughter. A mental oddity I developed at the time, which has stayed with me to this day, was that whenever I heard someone's name I immediately associated it with a color, a color that seemed inextricably linked to that name. My own given name and surname were both blue. My mother's name, Lillian, was yellow-green. My father's name, John, was black. Judy was red. Frank was yellow. The only difference today is that the colors I associate with names are less primary, more full of shadings and variegations, resembling the canvases of abstract expressionism.

By the time I started first grade we had moved to an apartment in Monrovia, a small town about twenty miles northeast of Los Angeles. Why my parents picked Monrovia I can't imagine, unless because it was so different from their own backgrounds: a Catholic and a Jew, both liberal Democrats, both more lower class than middle, settling in a community that was conservative, practicing Protestant, and solidly middle class. They never really fit in, never established any roots in the community or any lasting circle of friends.

My mother did have middle-class aspirations. She wanted to buy a house. She wanted to start a business, a restaurant. She even went so far as to pick out the first and to select a site for the second. And for a time the money was there to realize both. But my father would have none of this. On the house he backed out at the last minute. The restaurant never got beyond the dream-planning stages. Part of the problem was his reluctance to take on any responsibility. He was a man inordinately proud of his working-class origins, always a strong union member. The bosses, from his vantage the middle class, were the enemy: duplicitous, pretentious, morally corrupt. Their world was one he had

At age five, trailer park, Pasedena, California

no desire to enter. The first time he was promoted and put in charge of other workers, on a bridge-construction job, he took to it like a flea to rice. After that he always turned down promotions.

I have no doubt that my parents loved each other. It was obvious in the camaraderie they shared and the ways they cared for one another. But love wasn't enough to sustain their marriage, not in light of my father's drinking. What caused his excessive drinking, what particular demons haunted him, I've never been able to determine in any definitive fashion. When he was sober he was a charming and generous man with a wonderful sense of humor. Give him a few drinks and he became even more charming and affable. Give him a few more and at some unpredictable moment he would suddenly Jekyll-Hyde to hostile and abusive, all the negativity he had suppressed in his everyday life surfacing with a vengeance. His own father had been an alcoholic, a binge drinker who would stay sober for months at a time and then disappear for weeks at a time. My father's drinking had been a problem as far back as I can remember, only during my early childhood it was a rare problem, occurring only a few times each year.

By the time I was in sixth grade, 1954, this frequency accelerated rapidly to at least once every week. The first sign of trouble would be when he'd fail to come home from work on time. My mother and I would spend the evening on tenterhooks, knowing he would turn up eventually, usually before midnight, and when he did he would be drunk and very hostile. He never physically abused my mother, but there was plenty of verbal abuse, tirades that would go on for hours, dredging up resentments accumulated over the years. By the next morning he would be hungover and sick and very contrite. "You know I didn't mean any of that, I was drunk," was the standard refrain, a refrain no doubt echoed in millions of households throughout the world to this day. And my mother would always forgive him . . . or at least she did up to a point. Meanwhile, the savings my parents had accumulated over the years—more than ten thousand dollars, a neat sum for the 1950s—was soon dissipated in drunk-driving fines, sky-high auto insurance so that my father could keep his license, and gambling losses, often incurred while drunk, at nearby Santa Anita Racetrack and in trips to Las Vegas.

Although my mother hadn't worked for more than twenty years, not since her early years of marriage and the Great Depression, she threw herself back into the labor force, at first as a keypunch operator, eventually as an instructor in data entry at a junior college. During my first year of high school, 1957, she made her first attempt to separate from my father. Unbeknownst to him, she rented another apartment in Monrovia. While he was at work, we moved out. The separation lasted only a few months. My father tracked us down, promised he would stop drinking, and my mother took him back. The promise didn't last for long. He never drank again with the intensity that had caused my mother and myself to flee, but by this time alcohol, smoking, and finally a serious auto accident had destroyed his health. In his early fifties, my father went on disability and never worked again except at occasional odd jobs.

My parents divorced in 1961, during my first year of college, but they never really separated. Although they lived apart they continued to see one another several times each week, spend evenings together just as if they were married, and even take vacations together. My mother lived eighteen years beyond my father's death in 1974, but she never remarried or became involved with anyone else. She never stopped loving my father, never stopped missing him.

Bad Old-Fashioned School Days

I was not one of the popular kids in school, but I never lacked for friends, usually one or two close friends and a handful of others. The close friends were always in some way outsiders like myself, at least within the narrow confines of Monrovia. In my early years of grammar school my first best friend was Leonard Romo: half Italian, half Mexican, practicing Catholic, whose background was also lower class and whose father was a laborer. At this point school was very easy for me; I always received good grades without trying. Also at this time, about fourth grade, I began to have a strange take on the adult world. First, most adults, even my teachers, didn't seem very bright to me. Second, and more significantly, the adult world seemed rife with hypocrisy: people saying things they didn't mean, acting in ways that in no way reflected their true feelings, habitually wearing false faces atop their own. This is a perception that has never left me and a mode of behavior I've never learned to imitate with any skill.

In my first year of high school, 1957, I fell in with a rough crowd. In the parlance of the times we were known as "hoods." We smoked cigarettes, turned up our collars, engaged in minor acts of vandalism—such as breaking all the sprinklers on the front lawn of the high school—and shared a common disregard for authority figures. That same year *Sputnik* went into orbit and saved me from a potential life of crime.

God-fearing America decided it was losing the space race to godless Communism, and a good part of the problem was education, or more specifically the lack thereof. All across the country public schools began singling out the brighter students and segregating them into special classes. At my high school these were called MCL (More Capable Learner) classes. For the first time in my life I was grouped with

As a senior in high school, Monrovia, California, 1961

others, who at least in terms of intelligence, were outsiders like myself.

Monrovia High was no different than most Southern California high schools in the fifties. Athletics, particularly football, had always been considered far more important than academics. The most popular kids in school, the social elite, were the star football players and the cheerleaders. All of this now changed, or at least was challenged by a new intellectual elite. At the core of this new elite, or at least among its most visible members, were myself and my closest friends, friends who were clearly outsiders in more ways than just intelligence: Judy Roberts, a Jewish girl with a uncommon talent for the dramatic attending a high school with no drama department and only a handful of Jews; Steven Kuromiya, a Japanese boy who had been born in a World War II internment camp attending a high school with virtually no Asian-Americans; and my best friend during both these years and my first years of college, Ed Paparteys, a lapsed Catholic of Polish descent whose sar-

donic sense of humor can still bring a smile to my memories today.

We were an arrogant bunch. We looked down our noses, not so much at other students in general, but at the social elite. We ridiculed many of our teachers, both behind their backs and at times in front of them. We compiled a list of quotes from teachers that demonstrated how narrow-minded and dimwitted they were. And, of course, like most teenagers, we spent hours talking, talking, talking, though our conversations just as often revolved around literature, philosophy, and politics as they did the usual teenage gossip. In a sense, our rebellion was no different from that of the "hoods" I had left behind. It just took a different expression.

There were a few adults who did gain our respect, teachers who knew their subject matter, could convey it lucidly and with a contagious enthusiasm, and who, most difficult of all, could relate to teenagers. Most notable among these were Lois Mayer, who taught all the MCL math classes, and Frank T. Jansson, who taught MCL senior English. They were both exceptional enough as teachers and as individuals that they inspired me to think that someday I might want to teach . . . provided all of my students could be MCLs.

One day in my senior year an event transpired, political in nature, that was to foreshadow the political upheavals of my senior year in college. Without warning, we were pulled out of our American government class, hustled to an auditorium and shown a movie. Said movie was produced by the HUAC (House Un-American Activities Committee), which was one of the last holdovers from the McCarthy era. It depicted demonstrations that had been staged against the HUAC earlier that year during hearings the Committee had held in San Francisco. Most of the demonstrators were students from the University of California at Berkeley; one we even recognized, a former MCL student from Monrovia High who had graduated the previous year. We saw the demonstrators fire-hosed and arrested, handcuffed and carted off in paddy wagons by the San Francisco Police. In the film, all of the demonstrators were portrayed as Communist agitators or Communist dupes. My friends and I were politically savvy enough to know what nonsense this was. The next day and throughout the following week we protested long and loud, drawing fire from

Boston (right) with high school and college friend, Ed Paparteys, Yosemite, California, 1963

teachers and other students who had seen the film and bought every word of it. Soon we were labeled as Communists and Communist dupes ourselves.

Although Judy Roberts was the central force in instigating and leading our protest, I was the most verbal and the most vocal. Consequently, I was singled out by the school authorities as the primary source of the trouble. I was called to the office of the boys' dean and told that unless my attitude and behavior changed it would be detrimental to my college recommendations. Naturally I balked at such blackmail. Being full of myself and my righteous outrage, believing that I did have free speech as the United States Constitution promised, my behavior didn't change.

I don't know whether or not I was black-listed on my college recommendations. I applied to the University of Chicago, Cal Tech, and as a fallback, the University of California, Berkeley. Although my grades and test scores were high, I was rejected by the first two schools. I was disappointed at the time, but it turned out to be a blessing in disguise.

Crack the Books, Start the Revolution

In the fall of 1961 Ed Paparteys and I took off for college together, and roomed together for the first year and a half. I intended to major in math, become a mathematician and a teacher, and to write novels on the side. Ed planned to become an engineer.

College was a revelatory experience both in terms of my perceptions of self and the world at large. First off, it knocked down my estimation of my own intelligence by more than a peg or two. I may have been a math whiz at Monrovia High, but U.C., Berkeley, was a different proposition. The competition was much stiffer, but that wasn't the only factor at work. Whereas Lois Mayer had brought my interest in mathematics alive, my college professors proceeded to kill it with rote lectures in class and assignments that consisted of one round after another of tedious problem sets. Rather than being a whiz, I was now just another one of the drudges—a capable drudge, I pulled Bs in my freshman calculus classes—but clearly I was not destined for a distinguished career with numbers. I was now thankful I hadn't been accepted to Cal Tech, which would have had little to offer me beyond mathematics.

Even in my liberal arts classes the competition was stiff enough so that I was no longer a whiz, at least not without trying. Given that I'd never done much studying in high school I don't know where I found the wherewithal to begin cracking the books now, but crack them I did. I began studying maniacally, often long into the night, particularly when finals rolled around.

Meanwhile, my friend Ed had taken a freshman schedule far more difficult than mine, nearly all science and engineering classes. He was also encountering stiff competition for the first time in his life, but he responded to the challenge differently, by not really responding much at all. Rather than cracking the books, he continued to crack smiles, spending most of his time socializing with the other students who lived in our rooming house. As a result, by the middle of his sophomore year his grades were so abysmal there was no point in continuing. He returned to Southern California and went to work for the Los Angeles County Road Department as a draftsman. Although we had been the best of friends, our lives were now to take such different courses that eventually we would have nothing left to say to one another. Ed stayed at the road department, advancing up the civil service ranks to a position of high authority and a hefty salary. To my knowledge, he remains there today.

As for myself. . . . By my sophomore year it was clear that I needed a new major. Given my interest in literature and writing, English seemed the likely choice. I had to see an advisor in the English Department to get my change of major approved. While waiting outside his office, I found myself sitting next to two graduate students in English who were discussing Shakespeare in great critical detail. Given that the conversation must have gone on no more than fifteen minutes, it seemed one of the longest and most boring conversations it has ever been my misfortune to overhear. By the time I entered the advisor's office I was beginning to have my doubts, and what he had to tell me confirmed them. Because I had taken Speech 1A-1B to fulfill my freshman requirements rather than English 1A-1B, he wanted me to start all

over. I couldn't take any other English courses until I had completed both of these, which would have left me a year behind in terms of my major.

Again this may have been a blessing in disguise. Almost everyone I knew with aspirations to be a creative writer who majored in English at U.C., Berkeley, became so critical in their orientation they could no longer write more than a few sentences without dissecting them endlessly. I finally settled on economics as a major. It seemed to be a subject where I could combine my mathematical and verbal skills. Also, I had scored higher on the tests in my basic economics class than any of the other students. I was following my abilities rather than my interests, which would ultimately lead nowhere.

In 1964, my senior year, the Free Speech Movement erupted on the Berkeley campus. In many ways it was the granddaddy of all the student demonstrations that were to follow, both at Berkeley and through the rest of the country over the next decade. Against the draft. Against the war in Vietnam. Against "How-many-kids-did-you-kill-today?" LBJ. For civil rights and free speech and People's Park. I took part in most of the San Francisco Bay Area demonstrations. Marching down city blocks for miles. Marching in circles with picket signs. Sitting in at sit-ins. Chanting the slogans. Halting traffic in San Francisco's financial district with human blockades that would quickly form, dissipate as soon as the blue-suits arrived with their tear gas and billies, and then reform on the next block.

We were a generation with high ideals. We had been raised to believe in America the Beautiful and all of its constitutional guarantees. We were now confronting the reality of America. Not only did its beauty seem terribly flawed, at times it was mud ugly. School soon became secondary to fostering political unrest. There were times when we thought a revolution was brewing, that we would set things right and create a country with liberty and justice for all.

By the time I graduated, whatever passion I had harbored for economics, hardly a passionate subject to begin with, was seriously spent. I had already begun publishing poems in literary magazines. I was more disenchanted with the establishment—business, government, academia[3]—than ever, and it seemed clearer to me than ever that the life of a writer was my

*Left to right: Boston, Rona Spalten, and Charles Entrekin of the Berkeley
Poets Workshop & Press, Oakland, California, 1972*

calling. I only went on to graduate school in economics to avoid being drafted and sent to fight in Vietnam.

Insider At Last?

If college was a revelation for me, the Sixties were a kind of transcendence. I am capitalizing the Sixties here to indicate an era, roughly 1964-72, rather than the chronological decade of 1960-69, an era demonized and ridiculed by the American media both while it was occurring and ever since. To my mind the Sixties is the most interesting and misunderstood era of my lifetime, and from a personal standpoint, the most worthwhile. It was the only period of my life when I did not feel like an outsider. Instead, I became a member of a whole subculture of outsiders, namely hippies, who were without doubt the leading force in American popular culture of the times. The ideas, the morality, the music, and the fashions that domi-

nated this era, all had their origins in the hippie movement. Even if much of it was chemically induced, the worldview promulgated by the hippie culture was more full of joy and a love of life, more humanist and tolerant and optimistic in its orientation, than anything we have known since. In comparison to the Sixties, the decades/eras that have followed seem to me to be lackluster and depressing, like new cars already in need of paint jobs.

Make no mistake, the Sixties scared the bejabbers out of the powers that be. It threatened to topple the existing structure, both political and social. It suggested that there were ways to be happy other than accumulating material wealth and exercising control over other people. It even had the unmitigated gall to imply that states of consciousness had more to do with America's well-being than gross national product.

No doubt inspired by Kerouac's *On the Road,* and by my own father's tales of riding the freights to California during the Great Depression,[4] I began hitchhiking in the Sixties: at first in California, eventually to New York and back. In the summer following my senior year I became a hippie and lived in a house with other hippies that could only be called a drug house.[5] Over the next several years I took LSD—Sandoz, windowpane, blotter, sunshine—on a regular basis. I smoked marijuana—Acapulco Gold, Panama Red, Thai Stick, San Diego Shake—on a daily basis. I also experimented with a suitcase or two full of other drugs: amphetamines, opium, cocaine, hashish.[6]

I am well aware that drugs, particularly addictive drugs, have destroyed their share of lives. I'm not only aware of it, I've seen it happen more than once. However, both at the time and viewing it in retrospect, the effect of drugs upon me always seemed to be positive. School and all of the reading I had done for years had left me locked within my own head, my existence far too intellectualized. Drugs woke me up to my body and my senses and the pleasures they could provide in a way that would have never happened until years later if at all. I enjoyed food more, sex more, music more, living and breathing more. Drugs, in particular psychedelic drugs, stimulated my imagination and creative energy, and as a result became a source of inspiration for my writing. They broadened my perceptions of reality and the world in ways that no amount of travel ever could. They gave me spiritual experiences that resulted in the only religious beliefs I've ever held, most succinctly described as pantheism. And ultimately, they even saved me from the draft and the war in Vietnam.

I had been on probation all through graduate school and finally managed to squirm through with a terminal master's degree. By the time my draft physical rolled around, I had already made plans to flee to Canada. I stayed up the entire day and night before the physical, smoking marijuana and popping amphetamines. This contradictory combination gave me enough wild-eyed bravado to convince an Army shrink that I was not only an addict but crazy as Christmas in June. I received a 1-Y deferment.

There are many reasons the Sixties failed to change American culture and society in any lasting fashion. One reason that is seldom mentioned has to do with human nature itself. As an outsider, my own nature was ready-made for the Sixties. I already embraced many of its values and ideas before they became popular, and

continue to do so to this day. Most people, I've since realized, are far less constant in their beliefs. Most take on the values of a time mainly because it is the stylish thing to do. Thus many of those I felt at home with in the Sixties were not outsiders like myself at all. They were merely playing at it until the next style came along.

The Greenback Blues

Living in a country where material wealth has become increasingly the be-all and end-all of existence, I've never cared much about money, an attitude that perhaps more than any other brands me as an outsider. All I've ever wanted was enough money to get by and enough time to write what I want to write. Since the writing has never supported me (see the section "Wordmonger . . . Not!" below), I've had to find other ways to make a living, ways that did not consume most of my time and energy. This has been and continues to be the central conflict and conundrum of my life.

When I was a senior in high school I was given a series of tests known collectively as the GATB. If memory serves, the acronym stood for General Aptitude Test Battery, and it was supposed to let you know what jobs you would be qualified for in adult life. The test consisted of both written sections and a physical section, including such dreary tasks as fitting pegs into holes. In retrospect, I can only see the results of this test as a supreme irony. My friend, Steven Kuromiya, who wanted to be an architect, qualified in every category of the test except the one that included architecture. Nevertheless, he did go on to take a degree in architecture and eventually worked with Buckminister Fuller. As for myself, I not only qualified in all of the tests' categories, I scored higher than anyone had at my high school in the previous ten years. In short, a successful career should not be a problem for me, no matter what kind of work I chose.

I suppose the GATB was accurate in that I can *do* any kind of job, yet totally useless in terms of predicting success. In the course of my life I have worked as a computer programmer, college professor, substitute teacher, gardener, movie projectionist, book buyer, editor, retail clerk, ghostwriter, copywriter, bibliographer, research assistant, technical writer, math tutor, furniture mover, free-lance book designer, assembly line worker, and warehouseman. It makes me tired just thinking about it. Nearly all of these jobs, particularly after I had them for a while, seemed to me to be mind-deadening and soul-deadening routines. Of course the worst were office jobs.[7] Whenever I've worked full-time in an office it has left me feeling physically sick—chest pains, stomach pains—and emotionally/mentally on the verge of a breakdown.[8]

I have never had a job I looked forward to going to, except for teaching. I've never found any single activity that I could tolerate for forty hours a week, fifty weeks per year, except for writing. Apart from teaching at the college level, the only jobs I've ever enjoyed to any extent were ones that did not claim my mind, such as moving furniture or working in retail stores. And even in teaching, where I did enjoy using my mind, my intelligence and ability eventually worked against me.

About three years into my part-time teaching career in creative writing, students were asked to evaluate their professors on a scale of one to ten in a number of categories: knowledge of subject matter, ability to communicate, fairness, and so forth. My evaluations averaged out as a nine. The evaluations of my immediate supervisor, head of the English Department, averaged out as a four. From that day on, my days as a teacher were numbered at that particular institution. Students attempting to sign up for my classes were informed that they were not being offered, even though they were. I'd show up for the first day of a new semester to discover that no classroom had been assigned for the class I was teaching. Students didn't know where to go, and I didn't know where to meet them. Eventually, creative writing was eliminated as a major altogether.

In many ways my own education ill-prepared me for the workaday world. First, because being a student is far more interesting than being an employee. There's no two ways about it. Studying the in and outs of the Russian Revolution or reading about American expatriates in Paris in the twenties is a more fascinating way to spend one's time than designing inventory maintenance programs for the phone company or writing technical manuals on electronic security systems. Second, the criteria for success in school and work are very different. Whenever I applied myself in school—researched my papers and turned them in on time, studied for tests, participated knowledgeably in classroom discussions, demonstrated that I had mastered the material the course was teaching—I received the appropriate reward, a good grade.

My experience in the working world, from clerking in a liquor store to programming computers to writing science fiction, indicates that beyond a certain minimum level of application and achievement, what is far more important in determining success is attitude. You have to act friendly—not just polite, but friendly—to people you don't like, take part in social activities that don't interest you, pretend to be effusively enthusiastic about projects you care about only because they are providing you with a paycheck. Hypocrisy in spades, rearing its ugly head once again.

In sum, the only work I've enjoyed on a long-term basis is writing. Although there are times when arranging words on a page seems to me to be the hardest work I've ever done, or at least the most challenging, more than a few friends who are not writers have told me that it isn't work at all. They claim that because I like to do it, it is really only play.[9]

Friends in Deed

If you are the only child of an alcoholic parent it's supposed to make you overly responsible in adult life. Perhaps that is the case with me. When I make commitments, particularly to friends, particularly if they are about something serious, I make every effort to keep those commitments. And I expect the same from others. To roughly paraphrase Camus, very roughly since I am recalling a passage I read thirty years ago: "When I was young I expected too much from my friends and I was always disappointed. Now that I'm older, I've learned to expect nothing. Thus all of their acts of kindness impress me to the fullest." I'm afraid I've never achieved Camus's state of grace.

As in school, I've never lacked for friends as an adult. Yet my post-college friendships, most of which have been with other writers or those involved in publishing, have never had much longevity. I don't expect my friends to shower me with spontaneous kindness, but I do expect them to be responsible and trustworthy. And I'm usually disappointed. Fewer than a handful of my adult friendships have survived

With wife, Maureen, El Cerrito, California, 1978

the years, and none have achieved the depth that I encountered in friendships earlier in life.

My closest friends to this day are friends I made in college: Dennis Healy, now a realtor, Jack Poley, a corporate vice-president and composer-musician,[10] and Gerry Chmielewski, who works with computer hardware and software. Whatever bonds I formed with these three during our coming-of-age years seem to have held. Despite geographic distance and different lifestyles, I can still share good times and good conversation with each of them. And we can still trust in and depend upon one another.

Love and Marriage . . . Love and Marriage . . . Love and Marriage

This is not a subject I'm inclined to explore in any depth short of oceanic, that is, two or three novels, which I don't have the time or space or bathysphere for here. Suffice to say that I've never been legally married, though I've actually been married and in love three times. First, for two years in the late sixties. Second, for four years in the early seventies. Third, to my current wife Maureen, since the late seventies. Both of the first two marriages were open relationships as the mores of the

era and subculture we inhabited dictated. This contributed significantly to their eventual demise. Both of the first two marriages were based primarily on physical attraction and a superficial compatibility. When the attraction began to pale, there wasn't enough common ground to sustain the relationships.

My marriage to Maureen has never been an open one, but more than that, beyond the initial physical attraction, we have discovered that we see the world in much the same way, our values and attitudes are simpatico. Maureen has always been emotionally supportive of my writing in a way that was lacking in my first two marriages. As a voluminous reader and *my* first reader, she has often provided valuable criticism that has helped to make the writing better.

If You Are What You Eat, Do You Write What You Read?

I have always read eclectically and my writing seems to reflect it. My poetry ranges from traditional rhyme[11] and meter to unpunctuated free verse,[12] from the deadly serious to the darkly humorous to surrealism, with numerous layovers and side trips in between. My fiction runs the gamut from what *The Encyclopedia of Science Fiction* calls "densely surreal"[13] to traditional mainstream,[14] with science fiction, fantasy, and horror sandwiched in between.

My earliest memories of the written word include Golden Books and the poems of Robert Louis Stevenson, read to me as bedtime stories by my parents. My mother at one time had writerly aspirations herself. She had worked on her high school newspaper and wanted to become a journalist. However, she was from an age and economic strata where women seldom went to college. She also met my father when she was eighteen and they were married by the time she was twenty. It was only natural that she transferred a share of her frustrated ambition to me. She taught me the alphabet and the rudiments of reading before I attended school. She took me to the local library, a blocky ivy-covered structure from the Carnegie era, and signed me up for my first library card at the age of seven. Most of all, she imbued me with a great respect for books and knowledge.

My library card at first led me to science books for children, usually about astronomy, and

*During his days as a furniture mover, Oakland,
California, 1980*

to the Walter Farley "Black Stallion" novels. About
the same time, I developed a mania for comic
books, mostly Classic Illustrated comics, and would
sometimes spend an entire day reading and
rereading them, either alone or with friends. I
must have been about nine when I discovered
science fiction and fantasy, and coincidentally
decided that I wanted to be a writer. I think
my initial attraction as a reader was similar to
why I remain attracted as a writer to sf/fantasy
today. In one sense this can be viewed as an
escape into worlds far more fascinating than
the everyday. In a more positive sense, speculative literature in contrast to mainstream is a
literature of possibility and hope, a form that
explores potentialities for both the individual
and the human species. It also gives imagination its freest rein, and for me imagination has
always been an essential part of the creative
process.[15]

The first science fiction novel I read was
Heinlein's *Red Planet*. I was hooked immediately, and within a few years had devoured all
of the science fiction and fantasy Monrovia Library had to offer, was buying paperbacks and
science fiction periodicals at the local newsstand,
and had joined the Science Fiction Book Club.
Some of my favorite writers from this period
were Asimov, Clarke, A. Merritt, Robert E.
Howard, Poe, A. E. van Vogt, Jack Vance, Edgar
Rice Burroughs, and Charles Eric Maine. But
the two books that impressed me the most,
continue to impress me to this day, and influenced me most in the direction of science fiction, were Alfred Bester's *The Stars My Destination* and *The Demolished Man*.

My MCL classes in high school led me away
from science fiction for a number of years to
literature, the kind with a capital "L." My most
significant influences in this area have been
Dostoyevsky, Hesse, Melville, Henry Miller,
Lawrence Durrell, Gunter Grass, Kerouac, and
Nabokov. In terms of poets: Poe, Ezra Pound,
T. S. Eliot, Dylan Thomas, and Allen Ginsberg
are the names that first come to mind. Apart
from college, I've never read a great deal of
nonfiction, at least not in comparison to fiction. The nonfiction writers and books that have
influenced both my view of the world and my
writing the most are Norman O. Brown's *Life
against Death* and *Love's Body,* and Colin Wilson's
The Outsider.

The kind of science fiction I like the most,
speculative, has to a large extent gone south
in recent years, in favor of space operas or
novels where the accuracy of science matters
more than the wealth of speculation. Now I
read mostly mysteries for entertainment, though
more often than not mysteries from decades
past, writers such as John Dickson Carr, John
D. MacDonald, Jim Thompson, Ross Macdonald,
and L. P. Davies. In terms of more literary
work, Mervyn Peake and Steve Erickson are the
last two writers I've encountered who have impressed and influenced me.

Another major influence on my writing was
the Berkeley Poets Workshop & Press, a group
founded by poet Charles Entrekin in 1969. In
the course of its existence (1969-87) it published thirty issues of its magazine, *Berkeley Poets Cooperative,* and more than twenty chapbooks
of fiction and poetry. It also held regular workshops in poetry and occasional workshops in
fiction. These workshops were different from
almost all nonacademic writing workshops I've
encountered, that is, they weren't just support
groups. Mainly due to Entrekin's influence, the

workshops provided an environment where one could get sound criticism that could make one a better writer. They helped me a great deal in polishing my craft as a poet.

I was a member of the Berkeley Poets Workshop & Press for most of its existence, led workshops in both fiction and poetry, and served as an editor for the magazine and the chapbook series. I learned the basics of book publishing during these years, knowledge that has served me well both in terms of employment and in overseeing production on some of my own books.

Word Play

I am known primarily as a poet of science fiction, fantasy, and horror (a.k.a. a speculative or genre poet) because this is the portion of my work that has received the widest recognition from readers and critics. To my knowledge, I've won more poetry awards than any other contemporary genre poet. I am one of a handful of poets listed in the *Encyclopedia of Science Fiction*,[16] and the other leading reference book in the field, *Anatomy of Wonder*, describes me as "probably the most fecund and critically acclaimed SF or speculative poet."[17] Reviewers often refer to me as the preeminent poet in science fiction, and *Fantasy Commentator* credits me with "almost single-handedly revolutionizing the form [of sf poetry]."[18]

In fact, I never set out to be a poet at all. I've published nearly as many books of fiction as poetry, and my fiction has also garnered a few awards. The poetry first evolved due to time constraints. I've never had much luck writing fiction, particularly longer works, unless I can devote large blocks of uninterrupted time to it. I've seldom resolved my economic situation for long enough to afford such blocks of time.

I would characterize myself as a writer of both traditional and speculative fiction and poetry. In a more general sense, I see myself not specifically as a writer but as an artist who uses words as a means of expression. Sometimes this takes the form of fiction, sometimes poetry, though even my poetry often leans in the narrative direction. If I couldn't write, I would undoubtedly find another means of artistic expression. When I was in my thirties, several ophthalmologists told me, incorrectly, that I was going blind. I believed this for more than a

year, during which time I taught myself to play guitar and wrote nearly a hundred songs. A few of these songs have been performed and one recorded. Many of the lyrics from these songs have since been published as poetry.[19] In short, the creative process is what I seem drawn to more than writing per se.

I often use images and themes from sf/fantasy/horror as the metaphorical framework for a poem or story that is actually about something contemporary. I think there's some truth in the cliché that fiction (particularly sf) tends to be more about ideas, and poetry (even sf) tends to be more about emotions. Add the compressed and imagistic language of poetry to this equation and you have an arena where even hackneyed science fiction themes, ideas, and images can be explored in different and imaginative ways, and if successful, can strike the reader with a fresh intensity. My collection *Accursed Wives* portrays the plights of the wives of various archetypes from science fiction and fantasy: werewolf, mad scientist, ghost, telepath, and so forth. At the same time, nearly all of these poems are metaphors for contemporary relationships and the different ways in which women are victimized.

Literary movements and styles interest me, but to embrace one method or philosophy of writing to the exclusion of others seems both pretentious and limiting. Surrealism in general and Dali in particular have influenced me, especially in my speculative poetry. Dali once said that his method of painting was to sit in front of a canvas with a coin held in one fist. When the coin hit the floor, that is, when he fell asleep and his hand relaxed, he would then paint the vision that was in his mind. This was his method of getting in direct touch with the unconscious. I've never used this method in writing poetry, but some of my best poems do seem to emerge in my mind full-blown from an unconscious source. Although many of my poems have a distinct surreal flavor, and others use surreal images, I've never considered myself a surrealist. If I had to try on a label as a poet, I'd call myself an imagist.

Those poems or passages of prose that seem to flow onto the page from an unconscious source are often complete as soon as I write them. I change a word here or there and I'm satisfied. Other works go through endless revision before I feel satisfied with them, and in some instances I never am. My poem "In the

Darkened Hours,"[20] which won the Rhysling Award for the best long poem of the year from the Science Fiction Poetry Association in 1989, is a work that has always seemed incomplete to me. Unlike some writers, once I am satisfied with a work that feeling doesn't change. When I look back at stories or poems I wrote and published more than twenty years ago, my opinion of their worth remains much the same as it was at the time.

I also regard humor as integral to my writing. You can find it salted liberally through my novel *Stained Glass Rain*. I've written any number of humorous stories,[21] and more than a few humorous poems.[22] Humor seems to me an essential part of the human experience, one of the emotions that keeps the darker sides of life at bay. It is also, like a toothbrush, a very personal thing. One of the reasons I like Henry Miller as a writer is because I find him uproariously funny. Some people read Miller and see only darkness and despair.

When I sit down to write I tend for the most part to follow my imagination and creative impulses rather than the dictates of the marketplace. I never have any trouble with inspiration or coming up with ideas. Like the old pop song says: "Walk right in. Sit right down. Baby, let your mind roll on." It's as simple as that. My notebooks are full of ideas, more than I could use up in a lifetime even if I were writing full-time. The problem is finding the time and wherewithal to transform them into complete stories or poems. Inspiration comes from anywhere and everywhere: books, movies, dreams, personal experience, items in the news, comments from friends.

My writing habits tend to be sporadic, again due in large part to economic necessity. I think this is a viable way for a poet to work, much less so for a fiction writer. During the periods of my life when I've been most successful at producing fiction, when I could write full-time, I've worked on a schedule: beginning in the morning, putting in four to six hours, and then perhaps another hour or two in the evening.

Of the assorted positive aspects of writing—seeing one's name in print, recognition, praise, remuneration—I'd have to go with the creative process itself as the main attraction, the high it engenders and the sense of accomplishment I feel when I finish a work. Writing as a catharsis or release makes sense to me, but the idea of writing as therapy has always seemed awry, a bit like pulling oneself up by one's bootstraps. I also believe it is a writer's responsibility to somehow connect with his/her own time and speak to its problems and conflicts (see the section "Political Expression" below).

I write both to entertain and illuminate. A few of the themes I've attempted to explore in my work include: the nature of identity and consciousness and the potential for changes in both, spiritual transcendence, the multilayered fabric of reality, and the future of the human species both immediate and distant. My favorite among my own work is the novel *Stained Glass Rain* (see the section "Tacit Censorship?" below). Other favorites include the fantasy novelette *After Magic*, the mainstream novelette *Houses*, and an early short story "Soldier, Sailor."[23] I have lots of favorites among my poems, most of which can be found in *Sensuous Debris: Selected Poems, 1970-1995*.

Tacit Censorship?

If I have a work that could be considered a *magnum opus*, it would be *Stained Glass Rain*: a coming-of-age novel set in the drug culture of the Sixties, 150,000 words, mainstream with speculative elements. Stylistically the book is diverse and ambitious. It is written mostly in third person, some in first person, and even a tad in second person. It includes diary sections, dream passages, letters, poetry, a play, and a short story written by one of the characters.

The first draft of *Stained Glass Rain* was completed in 1973. I had an agent at the time who tried to market it to New York publishers. Two junior editors at Simon and Schuster wanted to publish the book. It even reached the stage where my agent called from New York with a tentative contract to see if the terms were acceptable to me. They supposedly wanted to publish the book as a mass-market paperback in an edition of 100,000 copies and give me a $10,000 advance against royalties. This was fine by me, but their senior editor ultimately nixed the deal.

Stained Glass Rain languished for seventeen years, until Lee Ballentine of Ocean View Books, which had already published my poetry, asked me if I had ever written a novel. Since Ocean View had never published a novel, or any book approaching that in length, I thought he was

Boston (left) receiving Asimov Reader's Choice Award from Asimov SF Magazine *editor Gardner Dozois, Nebula Awards Conference, San Francisco, California, 1990*

merely expressing a reader's interest in my work. I eventually passed the novel along to him. Much to my surprise, after reading *Stained Glass Rain,* Lee decided he wanted to publish it. By this time I wasn't entirely satisfied with the novel the way it stood, and I spent six months, part-time, rewriting it. After additional delays from Ocean View, the book found its way into print in late 1993, more than twenty years after its first draft had been completed.

Stained Glass Rain was well received by both readers and critics. It posted more than twenty positive reviews, mostly raves, to one negative. It was likened to works such as Phillip K. Dick's *A Scanner Darkly,* Jim Carroll's *Basketball Diaries,* Truffaut's *Jules and Jim,* and even Mervyn Peake's *Gormenghast. Tangent* called it "the best novel yet written about the sixties and its drug culture."[24] Two readers—a twenty-year-old man I'd never met before and a fifty-year-old woman I knew casually—told me it was the best novel they had ever read. More than a dozen others told me it was the best novel they had read in a year or more. With reviews and kudos in

hand I once again approached major commercial publishers, only to confront a brick wall.

Part of the problem was that although *Stained Glass Rain* speaks mightily to certain readers, it is too literary and too outrageous for most contemporary readers. More than that, it is my firm belief that a tacit censorship exists among New York publishing houses regarding serious novels about drugs and the Sixties. There are plenty of novels about coming of age in the fifties, the seventies, and now even the eighties. There are novels about the Vietnam experience. But serious novels from commercial publishers about coming of age in the drug culture of the Sixties are rare birds indeed. The only one I know of is W. J. Craddock's *Be Not Content,* which appeared from Doubleday in 1970.

Wordmonger . . . Not!

In any age, in any country, it has always been difficult for artists to make a living, and writers are no exception to the rule. It's usually feast for a handful and famine for the rest. The feast in contemporary America generally goes to writers who are not artists at all.

Although I've been publishing stories and poems for thirty-five years, and appearing regularly in commercial publications for the last twenty-five, I've never earned even a subsistence income from writing for more than a few months at a time. Many of the commercial genre periodicals where I publish haven't raised their pay rates in almost twenty years. Major anthologies from major publishers, such as *Year's Best Fantasy and Horror* (St. Martin's), and the *Nebula Awards* (Harcourt Brace) currently pay lower rates than the genre pulp magazines were paying in the mid-1940s. Most writers are in the position blue-collar workers would be in if there had never been a union movement. Now, when I sell a poem or story to a major commercial market, I feel as if I'm being exploited.

I've abandoned any serious attempt to grapple with the market. I think if I were going to succeed as a commercial writer, it would have happened by now. Both in mainstream fiction and genre fiction, the lowest common denominator is far lower than when I started writing—dumb it down! dumb it down!—and the use of language, one of the strengths of my work, doesn't seem to matter much anymore. I don't feel that my failure to succeed commercially in any way reflects the worth of what I write. If anything, the opposite may be true. In my estimation, many of America's greatest writers—for example, Faulkner, Melville, Thomas Wolfe—would be commercial failures if they were trying to publish for the first time today.

Comparing the critical applause I've received to the money I've made from writing, the old adage rings true like a chorus of Sunday bells: "Praise is cheap . . . cheap . . . cheap!" Since fame and acclaim have never meant that much to me, I would readily trade all of my recognition and awards for total anonymity and a steady income from writing that would free me to pursue it full-time.

Political Expression

My politics have always been radical and individualistic. Early in life I thought of myself as a Democrat, a label I inherited from my parents. Since my college days I've had little use for either Democrats or Republicans. At one time I thought communism, the small "c" variety, would be a better system than capitalism. Now I think the system doesn't matter so much as the moral values of the people practicing it.

The contemporary economic and political realities of America appall me on a daily basis. The rich get richer while nearly everyone else gets poorer. Individuals who have worked hard their entire lives are abandoned jobless as corporations seek cheap labor abroad. Politicians play to the media and pander for their largest contributors. America's real ills—health care, education, the homeless, AIDS, the environment, et cetera, et cetera—are drowned out by saber-rattling on foreign shores and endless debates about taxation and the budget. I rarely vote because I've long since grown weary of choosing the lesser evil. I once found effective political expression in the demonstrations of the Sixties, and given the right circumstances, the right causes, I can see myself demonstrating again. For now, I find political/social expression through my writing.

If *Stained Glass Rain* doesn't have a political agenda, it certainly has a political stance, as does the novelette *Houses.* Many of my poems, in the guise of science fiction, are actually political poems.[25] My poetry collection *Nuclear Futures* portrays the dangers of nuclear proliferation. Part of the income from this book was donated to Greenpeace. The poems in *Chronicles of the Mutant Rain Forest,* co-authored with Robert Frazier, comprise a cautionary tale about our ongoing destruction of the Earth's environment. A portion of the income from the poetry collection *Accursed Wives* is being donated to a shelter for battered women.

Sustenance

Approaching the age of fifty-five I don't have much hope for the future, either my individual future or the future of planet Earth.

A few years ago Social Security sent me a notice regarding my retirement benefits that was based on the assumption I would continue earning income at the same rate I have in the past. It might be just enough to live on, provided I could transform myself to a domestic pet, a cat or a small dog. Clearly my contribu-

Bruce Boston, San Francisco, California, 1994

tions to American society would be viewed as more worthwhile if I'd devoted my life to a career as a fry cook or a claims adjuster, or in countless other ways, rather than writing award-winning poems and stories.

As for America and the planet as a whole, I anticipate more of the same. More wanton destruction of the environment. More greed and hypocrisy. More wars based on racial and religious bigotry. More mass culture at the expense of individual expression.

Even without hope, I have found other things to sustain me. First there is my rage, rage that still burns brightly. Its existence and some of its objects should be clear in the above. Second, there is my sense of humor, of which you may have noticed a few dollops in the above. In my better moments I can laugh at the absurdity of it all. Finally, and most significantly, I have my writing to sustain me, the creative process itself. When I pen a story or poem, when the words upon the page take on an existence and reality of their own that can ultimately live for others, I experience a high

and a sense of satisfaction that few are privileged to share.

Tomorrow and Tomorrow

I will no doubt continue to write poems and stories. I may even finish my novel-in-progress, science fiction, working title *In the Garden of the State*. If books and periodicals survive the Internet, much of this work will no doubt find its way into print, some will be praised, and some may even garner awards. Odds are I'll be underpaid for all of it. I'll probably add a few more temporary occupations to my already weary list. And for certain, as long as I'm still kicking, I will remain an outsider.

Endnotes

1. Most endnotes refer the reader to my own poems or works of fiction that relate to the text being referenced. Publication information on books cited can be found in the bibliography following this essay. Here, see the poem "When Your Uncle Knifes Your Father on a Sunday of the Saints" in my collection *Cold Tomorrows*.
2. See "Anesthesia Man" in *Dark Tales & Light*.
3. See "In the Groves of Acanemia" in *Houses & Other Stories*.
4. See "Anesthesia Man" in *Dark Tales & Light*.
5. See "Harvesting the Krill" in *Houses & Other Stories*.
6. See the novel *Stained Glass Rain*.
7. See the poems "In the Silent Kiss of Laser Ink" and "Abused Ignition" in *Specula*.
8. See "Broken Portraiture" in *She Comes When You're Leaving & Other Stories*.
9. See the poem "Curse of the Science Fiction Writer's Wife" in *Asimov's Science Fiction Magazine*, January, 1996.
10. Jack composed and performed the synthesizer music for my poetry audio tape *Other Voices, Other Worlds*.
11. See the sonnet "The Sins of the Fathers" in *Faces of the Beast*.
12. See "The Tiger Does Not Know" in *Sensuous Debris*.
13. *The Encyclopedia of Science Fiction*, edited by John Clute and Peter Nicholls (New York: St.

Martin's Press, 1993), p. 145. See "All the Clocks Are Melting" in *Hypertales & Metafictions*.

14. See the novelette "Houses" in *Houses & Other Stories*.

15. See "Jackbird" in *Jackbird, Tales of Illusion & Identity*.

16. Op. cit.

17. *Anatomy of Wonder 4, A Critical Guide to Science Fiction*, edited by Neil Barron (New Providence, N.J.: R.R. Bowker, 1995), p. 388.

18. "Songs of the Stars" by Gary William Crawford, *Fantasy Commentator*, no. 49 (1997), p. 49.

19. See, e.g., "Song of the Eternal Sailors" and "The Human Blues" in *Cybertexts*.

20. See *The Nightmare Collector* or *Sensuous Debris*.

21. See, e.g., "Interview with a Gentleman Farmer" in *She Comes When You're Leaving & Other Stories* and "Striker Out" in *Dark Tales & Light*.

22. See, e.g., "i hate aliens" in *Specula* and "Love Song of the Holo-Celebs" in *Conditions of Sentient Life*.

23. See *Jackbird, Tales of Illusion & Identity*.

24. "Hallucinogenic Realism" by Howard V. Hendrix, *Tangent 1*, no. 5 (March/April, 1994), p. 19.

25. See, e.g., "And Soon a Wolf for Every Door" and "Pandemic Cinema Horreur" in *Faces of the Beast*.

BIBLIOGRAPHY

Poetry:

All the Clocks Are Melting, collages by Andrew Joron, Velocities, 1984.

Alchemical Texts, collages by the author, Ocean View Books, 1985.

Nuclear Futures, collages by Robert Frazier, Velocities, 1987.

Time, collages by Robert Frazier, Titan Press, 1988.

The Nightmare Collector, illustrated by Gregorio Montejo, 2 AM Publications, 1988.

Faces of the Beast, illustrated by Allen Koszowski, Starmont House, 1990.

Cybertexts, illustrated by Alan Giana, Talisman, 1992.

(With Robert Frazier) *Chronicles of the Mutant Rain Forest*, illustrated by Robert Frazier, Horror's Head Press, 1992.

Accursed Wives, illustrated by Ree Young, Night Visions, 1993.

Specula: Selected Uncollected Poems, 1968-1993, Talisman, 1993.

Sensuous Debris: Selected Poems, 1970-1995, Dark Regions, 1995.

Conditions of Sentient Life, illustrated by Margaret Ballif Simon, Gothic Press, 1996.

Cold Tomorrows, Gothic Press, 1998.

Fiction; short stories, except as noted:

Jackbird, Tales of Illusion & Identity, Berkeley Poets Workshop & Press, 1976, reissued in hardcover, Borgo Press, 1991.

She Comes When You're Leaving & Other Stories, Berkeley Poets Workshop & Press, 1982, reissued in hardcover, Borgo Press, 1991.

A Bruce Boston Omnibus (boxed set contains *Jackbird, She Comes When You're Leaving, All the Clocks Are Melting, Alchemical Texts,* and *Nuclear Futures*), Ocean View Books, 1987.

Skin Trades, illustrated by Allen Koszowski, signed limited edition includes booklet of four poems and additional illustrations, Chris Drumm Books, 1988, reissued in hardcover, Borgo Press, 1990.

The New Bruce Boston Omnibus (boxed set includes *Jackbird, She Comes When You're Leaving, Nuclear Futures, Time,* and *The Nightmare Collector*), Ocean View Books, 1990.

After Magic (novelette), illustrated by Lari Davidson, The Eotu Group, 1990.

Hypertales & Metafictions, collages by t. winter-damon, Chris Drumm Books, 1990.

Short Circuits (prose poems and short-short stories), collages by t. winter-damon, Ocean View Books, 1991.

All the Clocks Are Melting (short-story booklet), Pulphouse, 1991.

Houses & Other Stories (and novelette), Talisman, 1991.

Night Eyes, Chris Drumm Books, 1993.

Stained Glass Rain (novel), Ocean View Books, 1993, reissued in hardcover, Borgo Press, 1994.

Dark Tales & Light, Dark Regions Press, 1998.

Has produced audio tapes, including *Reading at Sercon, Interview by Faustin Bray,* Sound Photosynthesis, 1987; and *Other Voices, Other Worlds,* music by Jack Poley, in *Hypertales & Metafictions* (see above). Author of broadsides, including *Musings* (four poems on writing), illustrated by Russ Miller, Eldritch Emu Press, 1988; and *The Last Existentialist,* Chris Drumm Books, in *Night Eyes* (see above).

Maria Espinosa

1939-

For Carmen Espinosa

I

I came into the world on a cold, snowy night on January 6, 1939. "You tried to come out the wrong way," said my mother. "The doctor had to turn you around. I was afraid you had been brain damaged, because for days your head had a strange pin shape from the forceps. When I looked into your eyes, they were black and hostile. In that first instant I knew you were a fighter."

During her pregnancy she had experienced dreams that reflected her fears. In one dream she found a china doll hidden in a cupboard. It was stuffed with straw, and it caught fire. In another, she encountered a group of small children on a beach. They were friendly, except for one dark-haired girl whom she particularly sought out. This child was downcast, and she shrank from my mother's touch.

A few weeks after my birth we moved from Manhattan to Buffalo, where my father, Robert Cronbach, a sculptor, worked on a WPA project for the next two years. They named me Paula, after Paul Block, a sculptor friend of my father's who had died fighting for the Loyalists in the Spanish Civil War.

I was their first child. My mother, Maxine, was nervous and inexperienced with babies. She herself had been raised by nurses and governesses. In early photos, she seems afraid of holding me too firmly. As for my father, a photo shows him squatting and holding just the tip of my finger as I stand next to him in a ruffled pinafore. I was six at the time.

After the WPA project ended, we moved back to Manhattan into an apartment on upper Central Park West. My father had a studio downtown in Chelsea. When I was five, he joined the merchant marine, and we moved in with his family in Saint Louis. Life there was a great contrast to what I would experience afterwards.

Maria Espinosa

We lived in a large, comfortable house with spacious rooms, a mahogany banister down which I could slide, a tall grandfather clock, and a huge second floor landing which gave a sense of grandeur. Every morning Nanny, my father's mother, would brush my hair and dress me with care. I attended an excellent private school, where I quickly learned to read. My brother Michael, who had been born in 1943, was a chubby baby. Lee, the youngest of us, was born in the spring of 1945. There were servants: a chauffeur-gardener, a live-in maid who had been with the household for many years, a laundress, a nurse for the babies. We went to the theater, the zoo, and we were well cared for.

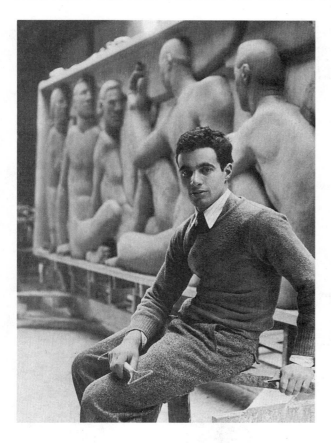

Father, Robert Cronbach, before his first sculptural commission, 1933

During those early years we used to spend the summers with my mother's parents in a rented house in the Ohio countryside. Granny and Grandpa Silver provided an extra measure of stability and caring. At the age of three and a half I had still not begun to talk. Mother feared I was autistic. But Grandfather Silver said, "Paula could understand when I asked her where the linen closet was. She showed me silently where things are." Shortly after that, I began to speak. Grandfather taught me simple arithmetic. Later he bought me a tennis racket and sent me to summer camp. They were gracious, kind people. Having inherited wealth, they felt a sense of social responsibility or *noblesse oblige.* Grandmother Silver's composure and her calm in times of crisis—which she passed on to my mother—would later serve as a source of strength. Perhaps it saved me, embedded as it was underneath the hysteria and panic I later felt.

Gertrude and Leo Stein had been among their inner circle of friends at Harvard and Radcliffe. Gertrude had invited my grandmother Ruth to live with her in Paris, but my great-grandmother, scandalized by Gertrude's Bohemian ways, had refused to let her. Gertrude's life was held up to me as a cautionary tale. According to Granny Silver, Gertrude had been infatuated with my great-uncle, also named Leo, but she had remained a spinster because she spilled food on her clothes and fastened her skirt with a safety pin! Not a word was ever breathed about Alice Toklas.

That fall the war ended, and we moved into an old house in Westbury, Long Island. Our house towered over the others on the block. But it felt shabby with its bare, black-painted floors and creaking stairs in comparison to the one in Saint Louis. We were surrounded by Italian and Irish-American working-class neighbors. Each night my father came home cheerfully from his Manhattan studio. From my bed I could hear his whistle and the sound of his steps on the sidewalk. However, my mother was lonely and out of her element. During those first years, she was ill and spent much time in bed with excruciating back pain. Finally, she found relief after surgery.

My brothers attended a cooperative nursery school and, among those parents, she began to make new friends in her suburban exile. As for my father, he obtained a part-time teaching position at Adelphi College, which he held for many years. With my grandparents' help, it was enough to get by. Later my mother began working as an administrator in the Drama Department at Hofstra College. However, there was always a sense of lack, of not having enough money for things we wanted.

We had a Swedish nurse named Anna, whom Granny Silver sent to help my mother out that first year in our new home. Anna was a strict Lutheran who filled me with her ideas on religion. I had nightmares of God, dressed in pajamas, leading me down cellar steps into hell. Troubled, I asked my father about God. "Let's look him up in the phone book," he said.

My mother did not share his pragmatic atheism. While he had long discussions about politics with his artist friends, she might fall asleep, thoroughly bored. She had a more mystical outlook. "The germs of Hitler are in each of us," she said one day in her soft voice as she pruned rosebushes in the garden. Often her sentences would trail off, implying a wealth of information that she either would not or could not formulate in words . . . or perhaps she had forgotten the listener.

When I think of her then, I see the sadness in her face, and I see those eyes gazing past me at some point in the distance. I felt responsible for her unhappiness. Somehow I failed to please her.

Mother gave me a thick green volume of *Grimm's Fairy Tales,* and I would read it, spellbound, for hours. I had to be physically torn away for dinner and bed. I began to read all the books I could lay my hands on, finding far more satisfaction in imaginary worlds than in everyday reality. With so many tales of witches and ghosts going through my mind, I began to imagine these beings around me. Words had magical properties. Songs cast spells in my mind. Rhythms and words haunted me. But so did numbers, shapes, and colors.

Many years later in Paris I took mescaline with an Australian artist named John. The street lamps cast a golden glow over the pavement. Things took on a new clarity as we walked very late that night. We are all psychic underneath, I thought. And we spend so much energy covering up our knowledge. Words seemed like heavy stones.

As we walked, visual reality took on a compelling quality, and I thought, this must be how a visual artist, a painter, designer, or sculptor perceives the world. I recalled how compelling the visual world had been when I was a small child. However, at a certain point I had stopped trying to express things through my drawings. They did not progress beyond stylized techniques I learned at the age of seven or eight. Certain barriers, directional signals, had propelled me into the path of words.

What were they? For one thing, my father's criticism of my early drawings. He seemed intent on having no rivals, and to ensure this, cut off any buds. Neither of my brothers has ever taken up drawing.

For another, my mother's compulsive cleanliness and order. There was no place in the house to risk making a mess with clay or paint. If I did, she would severely scold me.

I thought of my father's "tin" ear. As a child, his senses, too, had been wide open. But there was little music in his house. His mother sent him to art classes, where he shone. As a sculptor, he expressed her unfulfilled creativity.

Later that night as John, the Australian artist, and I lay in bed, not touching, I could feel a tube connecting us. It was not physical, although I visualized it as thick and white. Power flowed through the tube. He was drawing power from me. Then for a while the process reversed. I realized that people were constantly draining or receiving power from each other on an invisible level.

John and I journeyed to London a few days later. Within a week, he broke up with me. Feeling very lonely and rejected, in a freezing cold room in a London flat—we were staying with friends of his—I prayed. A maternal spirit comforted me. I felt it was the spirit of my father's mother. This gentle, lovely spirit nurtured me in the way I had always longed for. You are beautiful and you are good, and I am here to protect and guide you, whispered this immaterial mother. A desire to have a child welled up in me. As I lay in bed alone, I sensed that either I would give birth to a child within the next couple of years, or I never would at all. "Hear the cry of the unborn," I had written years ago. Now in that cold London flat, I believed that I could hear my own child waiting to be born.

Within a year, she was. But that comes later.

When I was seven, I broke my arm. It happened like this. Winnie and I were riding our bikes. She lived on the next block, and she was not of our "class." Therefore, my mother tacitly disapproved of her. We had been singing happily, and after Winnie went home, I came into the kitchen singing a popular song (of which my unhappy mother also disapproved). She scolded me for something, maybe for tracking dirt in the house. Those years her unhappiness simmered beneath the surface. She could not bear for me to be insouciant or happy. Those were moments to prick the bubble and remind me of some minor sin, such as forgetting to wash out the rim of the bathtub.

Her disapproval centered itself inside my head. But I was hungry for crumbs of her approval. I went outside again to bike some more, and I sang on happily, daydreaming about being a singer when I grew up.

Then I thought about how my father approved of tomboys. He didn't want me to act like a girl. I would win his love. I wouldn't be a coward. I would overcome my fear and do something I was afraid of doing. I would ride directly over the curb onto the grass. But at the last instant, I swerved. The bike fell. I stuck out my right arm to break the fall, and as I landed the bone cracked. In this split second my future changed. The bone healed crookedly. I was told the bone could not be set without destroying nerves. "The doctor said you might never regain the use of your arm," my mother later told me. "I prayed." This was something she did only in times of great crisis.

I am very much in my body, and I love to dance. Dancing can be a way of clarifying my thoughts. As I move, thoughts and emotions unwind. Many years too late I learned that my arm could have been set properly when I was a teenager. If it had, perhaps I would have become a dancer. But fate arranged things differently. There are coincidences, lapses, circumstances that seem to arrange themselves according to a hidden, magnetic design. I can only make sense of these phenomena in terms of fate or karma.

Its crookedness was not acknowledged at home, although I would entertain my playmates by extending the arm until it became grotesquely double-jointed. I learned to camouflage its angle by holding my arm somewhat stiffly and not ever straightening it all the way. I learned to avoid short sleeves that accented its crookedness. But I could never move freely, without holding back from movements that would reveal its deformity.

Some time after this, I began to fear that my mother could perceive my thoughts, as if my head were made of glass. This was projection, for I was constantly picking up the thoughts of others.

A substitute teacher in fourth grade decided to amuse us with guessing games. Whoever guessed the object she was thinking of would win a prize. Each day I won, and I could not understand why the others didn't. It seemed so easy.

After a while, the clairvoyance lessened, but it was still there.

When I was about ten, a hurricane hit the area. As we stood inside my parents' study, we saw trees swaying in the wind. "That one is going to fall," I said, pointing to an elm near the driveway. "Nonsense!" said my father. But soon cracks appeared in the earth. The elm swayed violently and crashed against the house.

I felt like Cassandra of myth. My perceptions were keener than those of my family, yet they were constantly discounted or mocked. My mother loved to entertain her friends with funny

Mother, Maxine Cronbach, as a young woman

stories about us, and she did so with no idea of their effect. For years I felt faintly ridiculous. Anything about me could be motive for amused laughter.

I was absent-minded and terribly naive. At first the other children considered me different, but after a while they grew to accept me as a leader, as I could always think of new, interesting things to do. I was a tomboy, partly because girls' activities like jumping rope and playing jacks seemed tame compared with boys' sports like baseball, football, wrestling, and boxing. Also, my father seemed to despise women's activities. Before the age of six and a half, I had been intensely feminine, with a love of flowered dress and brightly painted nails. But then I tried to bury this aspect of myself. Whenever possible, I dressed in boy's clothing. Once I startled Aunt Alice, my father's sister, at a birthday party for my cousin, Elizabeth, by coming dressed as Tom Sawyer with a can of live worms!

When I was eleven, I entered a period of painful sensitivity, upon entering adolescence. This was a point of no return. I lost the ability to chat amiably with other children and would become tongue-tied. At this time my parents decided to send me to a school on the North Shore of Long Island, after my fifth grade teacher told them I was "too bright" for public school.

In the new class there were thirteen boys and only six girls. The other girls were all friends.

They would walk arm in arm with each other, giggling and telling secrets. I became a pariah. I neither looked nor acted like them. I was darker in coloring, and I was more developed physically.

During recess and lunch period I would sit alone, trying to hide my tears. I was sure that something in me was irrevocably changing because of this rejection. To make things worse, for a long time I felt too ashamed of the situation to talk about it with my parents. I feared they, too, would reject me, because their acceptance seemed to depend on other people's. My parents appeared blind to the social differences—the others were richer, better dressed, belonged to country clubs. My mother was blind to the fact that we were Jewish, even if only by descent, while the others were mostly WASPs.

Furthermore, I lacked the clothes that other girls had. Grandparents paid tuition. But money was scarce, even though by this time my parents were both working. "We can't afford it," was my mother's constant refrain. I was furious, because they seemed to spend a great deal of money on luxuries.

By the time I entered seventh grade, I wanted to die. A sense of unworthiness preyed on me nearly every waking moment. Finally, unable to bear it any longer, after a miserable class party at the end of the year, I broke down and wept, begging my mother to let me return to my old school. She refused. Neither she nor my father took my laments seriously.

Looking back, I wonder why I didn't go on strike. They could not have physically dragged me to school, if I had simply refused to go. But something in me had been paralyzed. Although I had not ever been physically beaten, the invisible force-field that surrounded me inhibited overt rebellion.

Often I thought about running away. But where would I go? Manhattan seemed a dangerous place, and how would I survive?

My parents were absorbed in themselves. They seemed to move together in a dream world, barely conscious of their words and actions when they were alone with their children. My brothers, who were much younger, were close to each other and slept in the same room. I was the only one isolated, alone. There is strength in numbers. If there had been two of us—a twin sister or one close to me in age—how different it would have been.

At night sometimes my mother would come and sit by me in the darkness before I went to sleep. While I lay in bed she would listen, draw me out, and she seemed full of compassion. But in the morning it would be as if we had not spoken at all. She seemed to have no memory of the unhappiness I had expressed about school. No changes were ever made. Those nights took on a dreamlike quality.

As for my father, he was full of energy, boyish, buoyant, and left the household and care of children to Mother. Yet he was also very controlling. He wanted to—and did to a large extent—control my thoughts, my perceptions. All this of course was subliminal.

Memory is not rock solid. It shifts and changes. A miasma of conflicting energies and unspoken thoughts filled that house. I began writing a diary in order to keep a record of what was actually happening, as opposed to what I was told.

Here is a poem my mother wrote during these years:

Am I me?
Am I a mother?
The person in the office
Incidentally, your wife
                and lover
The fire that warms the hearth
The cold empty house that
                comes to life when I walk in.
Can you not do without?

Can you not walk in
And the house be warm without me?
Oh I am sick with the old sicknesses,
                torn and rocked
But you come, pulling at me
Little hands, big hearts

Flowers turned toward the sun.
I will not be your sun.
I would be no one's sun.

I, too, turn toward the sun
Kindled, blazing,
Consumed in its rays.

—Maxine S. Cronbach

Invisible energies form the medium in which we live, which we breathe in and out like air. This substance has always seemed very potent. In my writing, I try to deal with this substratum beneath our words and actions.

*"My parents, Robert and Maxine Cronbach,
at Coney Island,"* 1936

My mother's envy was almost palpable. At the same time, she deeply wished me well, and she longed for communication we were never able to attain.

Menstruation was not something to celebrate but of which to be ashamed. When I bled heavily during my first menses, mother treated this as something to be hidden from my father. Quickly we washed the sheets. I felt ill at ease in my changing body, and I feared my mother's jealousy. If I confided in her, this seemed to jinx things. Perhaps my fear of her jealousy was crazy, because she would tell me she loved me.

But I had strange dreams. In one dream, mother ordered me to pedal my red bicycle to the bottom of a lake. Obediently, I did so, although I knew I was going to die. But then

I found myself on gray rocks, surrounded by gray sea and sky, and although I had died, I still existed.

II

In high school I had few friends. I took refuge in long walks, rising early to do so before going to school. And I read almost everything that fell across my path—poetry, drama, psychology, philosophy, as well as fiction.

I struggled over term papers, unable to relinquish any that I had not honed to the best of my ability. Sometimes I read them to my mother as she lay in her bath—her favorite place for listening. She was an exacting critic, instilling in me her sense of esthetics and style. She introduced me to writers that she loved, such as Virginia Woolf, Jean Rhys, and Marie-Claire Blais.

In the attic I found old writings of hers, and I was deeply moved by her talent as poet and storyteller. Many years later, as she lay dying of cancer, the one thing she would regret most was not having written more. During those last months, she scribbled notes about her life, which she gave to me along with her other writings. I typed them and had them bound.

I felt impelled to express what was in her that yearned for expression.

When I was sixteen, I took up modern dance and drama. The dance studio was in midtown Manhattan. Twice a week I would take a train into the city. The last two summers of high school I attended drama workshops at Adelphi College. Acting opened up new dimensions. I loved it, and I wanted to become an actress.

My father had a puritanical streak, at variance with his own life and his social world. Although he had friends in theater, this was not acceptable for me. The conditioning in me ran so deep about conforming to his expectations, that actually preparing for a theatrical career seemed impossible. I prayed to become an actress, as if praying for a miracle. What I was really praying for was deliverance from the spell of his conditioning. The condition was so binding, so blinding.

Years later, my brother Lee, a musician, told me of a nightmare he once had. As adults, we have grown closer, and he shares many of my perceptions about our past. In his dream, we were all in the attic bathroom with its dark green walls, and we were mutilating each other with knives. Blood flowed all over. Then our father took out a hermaphroditic doll. "See how cleverly it moves," he said with pride. As he manipulated its puppet strings, a miniature penis emerged from the miniature vagina. In this dream, just as he manipulated the little doll, our father was controlling us all with puppet strings.

During these years I wrote and wrote and wrote in order to loosen the bindings. I wrote in a large, scribbling uneven hand, pages and pages of ramblings which have long since been lost or destroyed.

I needed my parents' approval and affection. Since they were rarely direct, a mere word or gesture, discounting through silence or changing the subject would profoundly affect me. Hooked on people's words, naively believing them, nevertheless I was aware that they were often false.

In high school I studied hard and was class valedictorian. One afternoon three letters came in the mail. They were scholarships to Wellesley, Vassar, and Radcliffe. There was no question as to where I would go. My mother and Grandmother Silver had gone to Radcliffe, although neither stayed for more than a year. I would follow in their footsteps and please my mother.

But that afternoon I felt an unexpected letdown. I had studied hard, and getting in was very competitive. But nothing I did could make me feel all right about myself.

The psychiatrist R. D. Laing writes that schizophrenia is caused in part by double binds. At home there were double and triple binds nearly choking me. My father never touched me casually or with tenderness. His embrace was furtive and passionate, so that I was a little afraid of his touch. He had a way of gazing intently at me, as if I were inanimate, which made me very self-conscious. I hated that stare. I wore shapeless sweaters to hide my breasts. Yet it never occurred to me to speak up about it! I had been too well-conditioned into silence.

Both my parents had lovers, although I learned about my father's affairs years later, while mother let hints of her life slip out. At this time she spent many afternoons in Manhattan. I was vaguely aware that she had erotic encounters with various men. It was her way of rebelling against the strictures around her and her way of creating a secret life and a secret source of vitality.

She was not a trustworthy guide.

"Having sex is like shaking hands!" she once remarked.

At college I emerged from being a wall-flower to being much in demand. It helped that the ratio of men to women was about four to one!

When I tried out for plays in the fall, I received principal roles in three pieces. The one I chose was that of an older woman in an Adams House production of *Our Town*. I covered my hair with white powder, and our photos were in the *Harvard Crimson*.

They put me into an advanced English class, and I was sure it was due to a clerical mistake. My self-esteem was so low that I couldn't deal with success.

During that first semester I had a kind, tender boyfriend, a Harvard sophomore named Howard. Our romance was self-lived. The *coup de grace* came with a Thanksgiving visit from my mother. Although her reasoning was a bit shaky, she covertly disapproved of Howard. Why?

Maria at three or four

She was vague. He wanted to marry me. He too was a scholarship student, and he came from a midwestern Jewish family—ah, in that lay the rub. He was Jewish, and he truly cared about me. At the time, I could not bear it. To stay with him, I feared, would diminish me in my mother's eyes and would incur her amused scorn, far more devastating than anger. Acting impulsively out of panic, I broke up with him as soon as she had left. And I still regret it.

Later I realized that any man who loved and valued me would arouse her disapproval and her fear.

"Don't you realize your mother is jealous?" asked a friend a few years later. "You are more intelligent, and you are beautiful." I was shocked. I didn't know that others saw us in this light. As for being more intelligent, I felt greatly inferior.

Without Howard, I was really alone. Because my mother's influence was so deeply ingrained, I didn't seek fellowship with other Jews. But I wasn't a WASP. Harvard was a snobbish place in the late fifties. One student confided in me that his grandmother was Jewish, but I must *never* tell anyone! Anesthetized, shell-shocked, I did not react.

After breaking up with Howard and getting terribly drunk at a cast party, I was put on probation. My father wrote stern letters to me. He considered acting and dance workshops as well as social life to be mere distractions. The only things that counted were grades.

At times during lectures I was afraid of my impulses. What if I were to touch the young man in front of me? Caress a woman? In my family no one touched each other in a casual, affectionate, or tender way. I was clumsy. I didn't know how to go about it, except through sex. Touching another woman filled me with dread and nervousness. Once I had reached up to embrace my mother who was standing behind me, and inadvertently I had grazed her breasts. My embarrassment was profound. Of course, neither of us mentioned it.

The summer after my freshman year at college I rented a tiny room in Manhattan. At night I took singing and dance classes, while I worked at an office job during the day. The City filled me with its frenetic energy. There was so much to explore. I wanted to get beneath the false surface of the world in which I had grown up.

When I emerged from my room, having spent the day reading or writing, sometimes words would stick in my throat as if they were rusty. There was no one to talk with except strangers.

The seeds of my novel *Dark Plums* lie in this summer. Many people, including my own father, thought the work was autobiographical. However, I have not lived Adrianne's life except through the imagination. It is the story of a young girl who prostitutes herself out of love for an artist.

Prostitution for me was a metaphor. I was deeply disturbed at how people sell their bodies and their spirits. The latter seemed far more pernicious to me, and I had observed it close up all my life. My mother suppressed her own considerable talent to nurture my father's sculpture. I observed how this affected her, for talent is a two-edged sword. Unused, it injures the possessor. At the brink of adulthood, was I going to prostitute myself under the guise of being a wife or working at a job that stifled the spirit? Many years later when I read George Sand's views on the subject—so like my own—I felt a great kinship with her.

Of Adrianne, I wrote,

> She wandered the streets each night, talking to strangers, absorbing something of them to nourish herself. . . . Everywhere now she looked for a man to break down her barriers so that she could love . . . he would accept her intense emotions. Yet since she was worthless, he would cast her down, dissolve her into molten liquid. Then she would be recreated whole.

Like Adrianne, I met a man in whom I sought a mentor, father-mother, guide. George was a jazz composer. He had just recorded his first album, and I fell in love with his music, playing it over and over again. It echoed so much inside me.

I have always found it difficult to write about him. A knot of frozen traumatic energy surrounds him. Of course, he was married. Otherwise I would have fled. I needed someone for whom I could yearn, who was remote, and who would not invade me with his needs.

He took me to jazz clubs where he knew many of the musicians, and he would talk to me about the music. We made love in hotel rooms and later on, with a great lack of discretion, we would make love in his apartment.

Afterwards we would talk about art, philosophy, religion, sex, our lives.

He absolutely overwhelmed me. He was older. He was so gifted. An aura of glamour surrounded him. It was the first time anyone had taken me seriously. After he read a short story I had written, he said, "Cut out this acting and singing and dancing shit. You're a genius. You're meant to be a great writer. Drop your job. Drop college. Just write."

His words threw me into turmoil. Maybe they were just a seductive ploy, although he didn't need one. I had no one else to turn to. I felt that my parents were trying to process me, as if I were a product in a factory assembly line.

In September when I returned to college I felt disoriented, torn apart. I didn't want to go back at all, but I distrusted my instincts, and my parents found it inconceivable that I drop out even for a while. Seeking to clarify my confusion and inspired by *The Outsider* by Colin Wilson, I read dust-covered books on Hindu meditation that were hidden away in the stacks of Widener Library. No one had checked them out in decades. Without a spiritual teacher, I was lost. I would focus on the tip of my nose or the inner eye, according to instructions. This all had an effect, but not a salubrious one. I felt even more spaced out and disconnected from my body and will. For hours I would stare into space in my bedroom. I could not bring myself to go to classes or write papers or study. I felt out of control, almost possessed. A few years later, meditation would become trendy with Leary, Alpert, et al., but I was ahead of my time.

That fall I studied creative writing with John Hawkes. He only accepted a few students of the many that applied. For his class I wrote frightening, sharp vignettes. This was the only course I managed to pass.

I dropped out of acting class after the student teacher told me that it was as if I were surrounded by glass, that I failed to connect with anyone onstage. I did not know how to say, "Please help me. I'm in pain. I want to connect, and I don't know how."

Although I went every day to a jazz singing lesson in Boston, I could never make it to my 9:00 A.M. Greek class, and could not bear the prospect of failing that course. It would be unthinkable, like falling off an invis-

ible cliff. Then I would lose the scholarship, and the consequences would be unimaginable.

Years later I wrote a scenario in which Old Women were knitting earmuffs for children who had no ears, mittens for children with no fingers. "It does not matter," they chanted. "It shows our love."

One cold winter day Peter and I were having coffee in Harvard Square. As Radcliffe freshmen, we had been warned about Peter. Avoid him, they told us. That was enough to lure me to his bed. Now he said, "Let's make a porno movie. We can raise some cash that way." I thought it was a great idea. It was a way to get back at the establishment and get the money I needed for singing lessons, for which I hated to ask my parents, as they would certainly disapprove.

He set it up. At the last moment, something warned me not to go. But another stronger voice said, "You promised." Yet without an instant's hesitation I had backed out of dates (the more attractive the man, the more likely I was to back out). I had backed out of going to Greek class.

Common sense had vanished. I had never learned gracious ways of saying no, and instead created bizarre stories. For instance, I would say I was a lesbian rather than frankly saying I wasn't attracted to a man. I was afraid of being harmed if I were frank.

It was as though someone had stuck a hypodermic needle into my brain, numbing and paralyzing the intelligence. It has taken many years to overcome the numbness. And some of it still remains.

So that day I took a taxi to Peter's apartment, and we made the film under bright lights. One of the student photographers betrayed us by giving shots from the footage to Harvard officials. As if we posed a threat to national security, they contacted the FBI. Late one afternoon during exam week, a Radcliffe dean called me into her office. My parents had been summoned from Long Island, and they were told to take me home by morning.

My mother was weeping. My father wouldn't speak to me. This went beyond any shame I could have inflicted in my wildest imaginings. They were like sheep before the college officials. Not a word did they say in my defense. Leaving half my possessions behind, I fled.

Humiliation overwhelmed me. I had failed my parents. I could not face the world. For

*Maria, née Paula Cronbach, on leaving
for Europe in 1962*

years I had wanted to see a shrink, but my parents had not listened to my pleas. Now my father sent me to three in one day. I came away from the interviews totally undone by those professionals, who seemed like voyeurs. Only the compassion of my parents' friend, Hans van Weeren-Griek, who invited me for a drink at the end of the day, helped me retain a shred of self-esteem.

But his tiny glimmer of acceptance was not enough to overcome the huge clouds of darkness. People seemed flat and two-dimensional. I had visions of jumping off a skyscraper, dying to escape the pain and humiliation. Words stuck in my throat. Sensory stimuli overwhelmed me. On a Manhattan bus, I felt undone by the angry remark of a driver. I was wandering around in a daze.

I received letters, some sympathetic, others jeering and satiric, from students. They had nearly run a feature article in the *Crimson,* but one girl had stopped them, saying, "No. Don't humiliate her more."

She is schizophrenic, said the psychiatrists. She does not have a sense of identity. Because she is a good actress, for years she has covered this up.

What is schizophrenia? It is a convenient catch-all term. I would study the root of "schizophrenia" in dictionaries, hoping to find a clue to what it meant.

The doctors did not have a clue. I was trying to liberate myself from something I could not name. I had been reflecting and expressing my mother's dreams, following her fantasy life of hidden afternoons where she bedded

strangers and which may have seemed dreamlike to her. Because she lived half in a dream.

III

Last night I found some old journals. My handwriting is scrawled, and I wrote as hastily as my hand would go. Ideas for stories came to me in the form of dancelike images. Slowing down enough to clarify scene, plot, story progression was beyond me.

Words could create windows of perception. Writing almost automatically, I would follow a thread that sometimes led me to a kernel of truth. *Becoming a Writer,* the classic by Dorothea Brande written in the 1930s, greatly helped me. I read it a few weeks after leaving Radcliffe, when I was still in shock. Following her advice, I would write at top speed, not giving myself time to judge or edit. In this way I could reach beneath the surface of my word-littered mind and, ironically, through these same words I could go deeper.

The hospital was in Queens. Its iron-grilled fence protected me from the chaotic outside world. The routine was comforting, something to grip onto. Bed at 10:00, after juice and cookies. Lights out. An attendant would walk by with a flashlight, checking to see that we were in bed. Wake up bell at 6:30. Breakfast, lunch, and dinner at set times in the cafeteria. There were scheduled activities. Individual and art therapy. The first picture I painted was of a nude girl falling through dark space and a witch's face in profile. With malign pleasure, she was watching the girl.

Years later I viewed some paintings that Carl Jung had collected with a shock of recognition. In one, the *anima,* great mother of the world, was tearing a male body in two. Blood streamed from his body, while a strange, sad smile lit her face.

In addition to scheduled activities, there were many free hours. At first, my mind was so scattered that it took a great deal of time to do simple things like wash my hair, iron clothes, wash out underwear, and file my nails. But when I had accomplished these mundane tasks, I felt a great sense of relief.

Daughters of two women my mother knew were in the same hospital. The girls' names were Cheli and Martha. On visiting days, all six of us would gather. My mother suffered enormously over my situation. She would be trembling and forgetful. Clearly it was anguish for her.

In the hospital for the first time I felt a sense of belonging with other young girls. We were there long enough to create deep, close friendships. This was in the days before massive use of drugs to supplant psychotherapy. Four or five of us would gather together at mealtimes or other free times and read our poems and writings to each other. Two of our group loved each other. Fern was chubby and boyish, while Linda was slender, pale, with floating dark hair. I could not understand why psychiatrists tried to separate them.

After a few months I was transferred from a locked ward to a "cottage," where there was greater freedom. Cheli and I used to wander out on the lawn, sit under a tree, and write poems. We made it a point to write at least one poem a day. I also wrote a long narrative, supposedly a novel but having little to do with that form. I just wrote, trusting that this plethora of words amounting to nearly a hundred pages in scrawled, uneven writing would eventually amount to something.

After we left the hospital, I saw Cheli again only once. It was in Manhattan five years later and she was on her lunch hour. We had each married foreign writers. She had gone from fat to thin, regaining her delicate beauty. She seemed happy.

Martha never did fully recover. She still lives with her parents, who are now very old. Occasionally I hear about her from my cousin, Elizabeth, who grew up with her. Martha had been popular, a cheerleader. In high school she had revealed no hint of emotional disturbance. I remember her as skeletally thin and pale, always dressed in black, with brown wavy hair. She had a quality of extraordinary purity and sensitivity. Her shrinks would become infatuated with her. What caused her to break down?

The culture of the '50s was a difficult one for young women. Pressures that caused me to crack were felt by many others.

Here is an excerpt from an unpublished manuscript of mine:

Meona watched the women at cards from a distance. This was the open ward. Although the doors were locked at each end,
she was allowed to move through the ward whenever she wanted. She was groggy from months of sedatives. Outside it was raining. The bare trees were blowing in the wind; leaves were blowing on the grass. What month is it? she asked. It is November, said the nurse, pinching her lips in that peculiar gesture of hers. November, said Meona. My favorite month. It is the month of death. Meona left with these words and walked to the window at the end of the corridor which looked out on the grounds. November . . . April is the cruelest month, bleeding dead shoots. November. In November I am inside myself, nearly ready to be born.

The walls protected her; the locked doors protected her; the institution protected her from the unknown in herself. The institution protected her from the world. She was relieved not to think, not to feel, to have no responsibility. The wild panic inside her which seemed a bottomless jungle of hysteria, which caused her outside the hospital to have nerves stretched so taut that she was continually in a state of fear and exhaustion, that former life no longer existed. She had metamorphosed into a plant. She had gone downwards to a lower state of incarnation. The old women at cards seemed shadows to her. This world which she saw through her eyes did not compel her attention; she observed it half-consciously, like shapes gliding across a mirror.

A group of men were walking across the grounds. They were wearing raincoats, and their heads were bent towards the ground. One attendant was in front of them and another walked beside the last one. They were walking fast. Probably they were coming from one of the other buildings for the first dinner shift at 4:30 in the afternoon. They all seemed to be like puppets with their central cords broken, held together with tape, their spines bent in a broken manner.

From above came a woman's scream. Her screaming continued for a long time. At first the women in the ward looked up towards the ceiling, towards the place from which the screaming came, and then they ignored it.

The day finished with a meal, with pills which made Meona heavy and dry and made her fall asleep. The next day would be like the one before. She dreamed of Thin Jane, the woman who walked through the corridors in a slip, leaning in languidly against the wall and lifting one leg to dangle a slipper . . .

octors at Hillside had considered me a curious specimen, an "interesting case." They held a special conference with twenty or thirty psychiatrists and psychologists gathered together to examine me. How many books did I read a week? Three or four? What did I write? Why had I left college? As I got up to leave I was highly mortified to discover that, under the stress of their questions, my menstrual blood had soaked through a double layer of Kotex as well as my dark dress and had left a huge stain on the chair.

Upon getting out of the hospital, for months I clung to a self-imposed regime of discipline which was a great contrast to the chaotic life I had led before. I was terrified of relapsing and wanted above everything else to get "well," although I wasn't sure what that meant. Every morning I rose early and practiced dance. Later in the day I would go to dance classes—modern, ballet, and African. Every night I was in bed by 10:00, following the former hospital routine, even though I longed to stay up and walk along the brightly lit streets which pulsed with life.

I saw a psychiatrist four times a week. He charged thirty-five dollars an hour, which was expensive in 1959. The money came from funds I had inherited from Grandfather Silver. The psychiatrist was a middle-aged Hungarian who considered himself worldly and who had fled with his family to America during the 1956 revolution. He was a Freudian, and he would keep silent in the classical Freudian tradition while I talked and talked . . . and I would leave the sessions often feeling a strange malaise.

Gradually I realized that he and I had very different values and that his advice—the rare times he did break silence—was untrustworthy. While I could go on for hours exploring my thoughts with him, it was expensive, and I seemed to be getting worse.

I enrolled at the Columbia School of General Studies and obtained a bachelor's degree, although it was difficult for me to concentrate on academic work. My mind raced along in *beta*. I wanted to write, but my mind would not slow down enough for me to visualize and create. Filled with tension and fear that erupted into panic states, I was only able to write short poems, jottings, and one-line "ideas" for stories, usually in the form of visual images.

George and I resumed our relationship. It became intensely sexual, obsessive, and disturbing.

I alternated between rigid abstinence, turning down a Broadway cast party, and desperately fucking anyone at all.

I believed that my father secretly either wanted me to be a virgin or promiscuous. Promiscuity without bonding would create the same effect as virginity. It would keep me belonging to him alone. How much of this was my projection? How much based on sensing the internal reality? It was probably a mixture.

Despite the fact that I spent hours each day practicing dance, despite my teachers' assurances that I was ready to try out for professional Broadway shows, I held back.

"It's a shame about her arm. What a terrific dancer she would be otherwise," whispered an African dance teacher during a student performance where I sang and danced in a red satin dress.

Those whispered words were enough to undo my confidence.

As if under a spell, I did not think of seeking another medical opinion about my arm. The words I had heard at age seven—"can never be set"—were etched indelibly. Once I went to some kind of physical therapist I'd found in the Yellow Pages, but I'd done it under cover, as if going to an illicit assignation.

My parents seemed to take it for granted that I must finish college. Only a college degree counted, and an academic one at that. Dance and theater didn't count at all.

One incident—a departure from this, a revelation of the secret manipulations at work—comes to mind. One summer evening, when I was home for the weekend, my mother burst into the attic bathroom, where I was combing my hair. I remember she knelt on the floor and almost wept. "It's all right with me if you want to be an actress," she said. "Although your father doesn't want it."

Those years at Columbia were bleak. For most of the time I lived in a one-room apartment on upper Broadway. What sustained me was visiting Hans and Jetje in Vermont, which was peaceful, especially in winter when the countryside was covered with a thick blanket of snow. Their warmth and good company nourished me. They were cosmopolitan, generous, good-hearted people. Although I did not know it at the time, Hans was also deeply involved with my mother.

Hans was tall and portly with white hair and ruddy skin. When he came to the City, he would be impeccably dressed. He had an air of authority, a largeness of spirit as well as body. Jetje was petite, graceful, with closely cropped white hair, and a cheerful personality. She was also very strong in spirit. During the war she, a Jew, had worked for the Resistance in Holland as a Red Cross driver. Her first husband had perished. Her parents had, remarkably, survived concentration camps, and they, too, remained unbroken.

At night Hans and I would go snowshoeing in the woods. It was so beautiful and still and calm and white beneath the stars.

Hans was a gifted artist. Also Dutch, he was more troubled and complex. He had worked as curator at a number of museums, but would end up picking fights with anyone in authority over him.

With Hans and Jetje I could pour my heart out.

They had built the house in Vermont themselves, with the help of neighbors. He had learned how to do construction, plumbing, carpentry out of books. And he was a meticulous craftsman. Jetje had sewed and upholstered furniture. The house had great charm. From the picture window by the dining table, one could see mountains and wilderness.

I discovered Anaïs Nin's collection of stories, *Under a Glass Bell.* Her work excited me because she was writing through a woman's consciousness as I had never seen done before. I loved the rhythm and beauty of her work, her ability to abstract the essential. Furthermore, in her stories I actually found a few phrases identical to ones I had written: *"hear the cry of the unborn . . . collision with reality blurs my vision . . . lies create solitude . . . I await the phantom lover—the one who haunts all women, the one I dream of who stands behind every man with a finger and head shaking 'Not him, he is not the one.' Forbidding me each time to love . . ."*

I wrote her a letter, which she answered in elegant handwriting on pale blue stationery. She praised the short poems I had sent her, and she encouraged me, as she did so many writers.

This may have been one of the poems I sent her:

A tongue in the mouth
Prevents the feeling of emptiness.
They love in the next room.
The memory of him is warm in my body.
I roll him over
as I would a morsel
with my tongue.

For many years my writing often almost felt automatic, as if channeled. There were words that I put down without knowing why, but sensing they were keys to something I did not yet understand, I would not erase them. When I began writing poems, the words took on luminous qualities when the poems "worked." I might rewrite a poem thirty or forty times, without knowing why I did so, ceasing only when it felt right.

In 1961 I traveled to Europe for the first time, carrying in my backpack a small black Bible, volumes of Yeats, Blake, ancient Greek poets in translation, Anaïs Nin, and Chekov. When I got to the village of Lindos on Rhodes, I settled down to write a story called "Adraia" that I felt absolutely compelled to write. Certain words I had to put down, certain rhythms I had to follow, without quite knowing why, but I was compelled.

This was the first time I was able to follow a disciplined writing schedule. It was so easy in that little whitewashed room. The room had two levels. It was cool, yet airy, and with enough light. Religious icons hung on the walls. The furniture was old, burnished wood and metal. The woman who owned the house would bring me plates of figs and fresh water while I typed on my Olivetti portable. It was astounding to me that the family respected the act of writing. This was certainly different from what I had experienced in America.

I would write all morning, break to eat lunch and swim, then write all afternoon. In this tiny village there were few distractions.

The story was about a girl who wanders aimlessly through Greece, obsessed with a lover who has rejected her. She goes mad and finally dies inside a church after making love with a shepherd whom she believes is Christ. He stabs her in the heart, then walks out into the fields.

I wrote the story in two weeks. But I could not let go of it. For many years it haunted me until, after countless drafts and transformations, more than thirty years later it was published as *Dark Plums.*

Back in Athens I met poets and artists at cafes on Kolonaki Square. They seemed to accept me as one of them. Here I felt far less isolated than I did in the United States, and I was reluctant to return to New York. All summer long I had been fearing the return trip by plane on a student charter from Paris. In fact, I had feared it so much that before I left for Europe I actually switched charter companies. But I journeyed back from Athens to Paris, and I took a taxi to the airport. As in my childhood dream, I was obediently performing the equivalent of bicycling to the bottom of a lake. The plane was delayed in its arrival. "Let's go out to dinner," someone suggested. "The Last Supper," I murmured. Around midnight we learned that the plane wasn't coming at all that night. The others were furious. But I *knew* that I had been delivered from death. The next morning I learned that the plane had crashed. There were no survivors.

Why had we been spared? This incident caused me to write with increased fervor, because I thought my life had been spared for a reason.

IV

After I graduated from Columbia, I left almost immediately for Europe, where for several months I traveled through Greece, Switzerland, Italy, London, and finally settled in Paris. The city led me to open up my senses, to explore the narrow streets with its ancient buildings, its rich odors and sights and sounds and people. Manhattan, in contrast, had seemed a place of sterile, gray concrete and rushing energy. There I had wanted to curl into myself to avoid overload.

It was on a cold November afternoon a month after I had left London that Mario and I met in a cafe on the Left Bank. A few days later I moved into his apartment on Rue Beautreillis. He was a journalist. Four years earlier he had come from Chile on a small grant from the French government. When I met him, he made a bare living doing odd jobs. He worked as a painter, handyman, freelance writer, and as superintendent of our eight-hundred-year-old building.

For me, he was like a crazy Zen master. It was as if he had no skin because he was so sensitive to people around him. He could be cruel, but he could also be extraordinarily generous in ways that most people did not understand. He felt driven to help people express what was latent in them, whether sexual or artistic. And he pushed me to write the hospital narrative after I told him how the entire experience still filled me with shame.

"You have too much talent," he would say. "You must write." And he demanded that I write two pages a day. "That's enough," he said. "That's all Thomas Mann wrote." But my two pages were often incoherent ramblings.

"Calm. Relaxed. Common sense." I kept scribbling these words in large, irregular handwriting in my diary, like flashing street signs, because I feared losing him. After one of our violent fights, I often feared he would go off and never return. But my need exerted a magnetic hold on him.

He believed we needed to live out our sexual drives in order not to pass them on to our daughter, Carmen. "You are *refoulée*," he would say. "Children pick up and live out what has been suppressed by their parents."

Here at last was the mentor, friend, soul mate for whom I had been searching. But how much was illusion on my part? What was real? Our relationship was intense, stormy, often telepathic. He was one man my family certainly could not ignore. In the past, my parents had treated various men I went out with, including George, the composer, simply as if they did not exist. They were polite, but their lack of concern or interest, their lack of response when the man had left their presence, had induced in me a strange sense of unreality. No way could they do this to Mario! He was in their faces, pulverizing lifelong facades, creating turmoil and anguish. He illuminated much that had been driving me crazy. In this way, he helped lead me out of mental illness. But it took its toll on him.

I clung to him with desperation. A passage from *Longing* describes this:

> She had always felt as if no harm could come to her when she was with him. No matter how cruel, how irrational his actions might appear, she always believed that some deeper, vaster intelligence of which he was barely conscious directed those actions (insane in the eyes of the world). His apparent craziness seemed akin to the acts of a Zen master, intended to awaken her. He was Protean. He took on many guises. His personality could change twenty times within one day. But she must stick with him, as in the Greek myth, stick with him through all his monstrous changes until he was forced to reveal himself in his true form. Then she would acquire a power which had been her birthright but had been stripped from her. He would empower her. But if she left him, she would be lost forever.

A few months after we met I became pregnant. Mario predicted Carmen's sex, coloring, premature birth, and even her eyeglasses. He foretold other qualities about her that unfolded many years later. For my part, Carmen was the child whom I had envisioned a year ago in London.

When she was four months old, I took her back with me to Westbury. Mario followed a few months later. While his sojourn with my family was traumatic for everyone, it opened my eyes to the underlying realities, to the conflicting desires and needs of my parents that had caused me to become so disturbed.

When she was with Mario, my mother sparkled with the vitality of a girl. So much in her had been suppressed and invalidated. I ached for her and wanted her to flourish. Yet I was terribly jealous. I did not feel adequate for Mario. She had qualities I lacked—wit, maturity, social composure. As I loved both of them, I wanted them to be able to give each other what I couldn't give them. They connected with each other on so many levels—perhaps the physical least of all.

In autumn, 1964, Mario and I moved to California. For the next few years we lived in Sausalito and Mill Valley. Although we divorced in 1965, we lived together off and on until Carmen was six. However, even when we were apart, he would sense if I were in crisis.

Carmen's eyesight had suffered as a result of her weeks in an incubator. These are inundated with oxygen, which in excess can cause blindness in infants. However, I did not learn this until many years later. By the time Carmen was four, she could barely see out of her left eye. In order to read the words in a children's picture book, she had to hold it just an inch or so from her face. Doctors prescribed thick glasses and a single contact lens, which we promptly lost at a Ravi Shankar concert. I took this as a sign to look for an alternate method. We were very fortunate in finding Anna Kaye, who taught eye exercises in San Francisco. She adored Carmen and thought of her as a spiritual daughter.

Every day Carmen and I did eye exercises outside our little house in Mill Valley. Her vision improved tremendously. She obtained almost normal vision in both eyes without glasses. These results were not permanent. She still has poor vision in one eye, and she wears strong glasses. But she can drive a car, and she can function normally. If she lived in a place with lots of light and she had time to do the exercises again, no doubt her vision would improve.

In 1966 I wrote in a journal, "Words create a prison out of which a narrow channel leads still further inward to a deeper reality." Writing had a paradoxical quality. It provided windows out of the prison of self, but it also created a prison composed of blocks of words.

"Ideas" for stories were vivid, dancelike images. One was "A flame encounters a girl encased in mirror in the Paris metro. Energy interchanges. The girl flies out of the mirror. The flame vanishes."

Mario was the flame who shattered the glass. See me, hear me, feel me, he would yell. If he did not get attention with words, then he used his fist.

And he was compelling enough that I wanted to sense his feelings. For the first time in my life I was forced into truly full awareness of another person.

"He was abusive. He battered you, Mom," says Carmen. She is now a psychologist who works with battered women.

She is also a dancer, a writer, and a fledgling filmmaker.

But she doesn't understand about the invisible glass.

The first time he hit me, he wept afterwards. Then he made me mop the floor, while

"With Mario and our daughter, Carmen"

we were both in tears. Something inside me that had been tortured into amnesia could only be brought back to life by violent impact.

"Who is the victim? Who is the victimizer?" wrote Penny Skillman in her review of *Longing.*

"Calm. Common sense. Faith," I kept writing over and over.

During these years in Sausalito and Mill Valley, he worked at various jobs, and he wrote. He held low-paying jobs as a cook or construction helper. Impeded by his poor English, he was impatient with language classes. We still communicated mainly in French, as we had in Paris. I worked at office jobs, for the Department of Employment and, ironically, as a teacher of English as a Second Language.

I owe much to Carmen's excellent caretakers during this period. Mary Lessig, who came from the Canary Islands, took care of Carmen until she began going to nursery school. Then Carmen Broomis took over. Each of these women had a son the same age as my daughter, and each took several children into their homes during the day.

Meanwhile, Mario had little luck getting his work in Spanish published abroad. Discouragement filled him. He felt alien in this North American culture. He hung out at bars in Sausalito. He became increasingly eccentric, discouraged, and angry. Mornings in Mill Valley during our last year together, he would rise late, smoke meditatively, and write. When he worked at a job, he tried to get a night shift. But he was constantly losing jobs.

At night after I came home from work and Carmen had gone to bed, I wrote poems and struggled to learn how to write stories.

In the summer of 1966 I had begun to study hatha yoga and meditation with Kri-yananda (J. Donald Walters), who was then teaching at the Cultural Integration Fellowship in San Francisco. Later he founded a spiritual community, Ananda World Brotherhood Village in Nevada City, California.

These physical and mental practices helped me to slow down into a calmer state, inspired my writing, and helped give me a sense of freedom. I realized that I had the power to release myself from the past. In a flush of euphoria, one day I decided to call myself Maria, which I had wanted to do ever since I was eighteen, as it felt like my true name. On June 6, 1966, I simply went down to the Motor Vehicle Bureau, filled out a form, then filled out another form for Social Security. Although aunts and uncles and cousins objected, as if I were casting off my birthright, my parents and brothers seemed relieved, as if by this change of name they too could throw off the past.

During this same summer I decided to go ahead and self-publish some poems in a chapbook, *Love Feelings.* Anaïs Nin wrote me a beautiful letter after I sent her the book. She called it some of the only "genuine" poetry she had read by North Americans in the last twenty years. However, the booklet had a strangely disconcerting cover. Only after it had been printed and stapled did I realize that the mischievous printer to whom I had entrusted the work had made an abstract design which resembled a woman's lower torso. I suffered months of agony over this cover. Many years later it was reproduced in a Chilean newspaper article about Mario, along with one of my poems which someone had translated into Spanish. I like the poem even better in that language.

With great tact and kindness, Mario insisted that the cover was fine. However, he arranged with Herb Beckman, who then owned The Tides Bookstore in Sausalito, to reprint these poems along with others in a larger edition. *Night Music* came out in 1969 under The Tides imprint with a beautiful black-and-white collage cover by Glory Rananda.

By then Mario and I had separated for the final time.

He moved to nearby San Rafael and worked at another job as a cook in a boys' institution. He no longer took pains to shave or groom carefully, and he whimsically wore cast-off clothing from friends or thrift stores. He had grown so thin that his pants looped around him, held up by a belt cinched as tightly as it could go. The sleeves of his short-sleeved shirts flapped around his thin arms. For him, life was a big bad cosmic joke.

Years after he died, I read about the effects of mercury poisoning. When Mario was about twenty-one he had been treated with mercury for syphilis, as they did not have penicillin yet. Mercury can cause nervous agitation, anxiety, and psychosis over time. No physician to whom Mario went for help ever mentioned this, and I don't think his family in Chile realized it either.

V

A postcard invitation from Anaïs Nin to her book signing at Cody's in Berkeley indirectly affected the direction of my life. There in June 1966, I met Judd Boynton. Four years later I moved in with him.

He lived in the Berkeley hills in a wonderful house he had built himself. It had many huge picture windows overlooking the Bay, and he knew fascinating people, such as Aldous Huxley. It was he who had introduced me to Anaïs Nin at that book signing years earlier, as I was so much in awe of her that I was afraid to approach. He looked a little like Ernest Hemingway, with his reddish brown beard and his tall, stocky build. Judd was the youngest of eight children and grew up in the north Berkeley hills. His mother had taught modern dance in her Maybeck house, which she called the Temple of the Wings. She and Isadora Duncan were close childhood friends. According to Judd, the two of them invented modern dance! He believed that Isadora had actually been his grandfather's love child and that the girls were half-sisters, although it was all kept under wraps.

Judd was a gifted dilettante: an architect and builder, an astronomer, a writer, a musician. He could be expansive, full of wit and apparent sympathy, and he could also be extremely destructive. In a mischievous way, he loved to "stir the shit pot," as he called it, and he could cause incredible complications in people's lives, pitting them against each other.

At the time, he attended a writing class taught by Leonard Bishop on Monday nights. I began attending the class, too. Leonard was crude, incisive, funny, vulgar, and cared passionately about writing. His white hair was as short as a GI's; he always wore navy pants and tee shirt. With even a short manuscript, he would type pages of single-spaced comments. It was impossible not to take one's writing seriously with such voluminous feedback. Leonard taught his students how to craft scenes, how to develop characters and stories, how to rewrite . . . and rewrite . . . and rewrite, adding details, perhaps changing point of view, cutting, enlarging, shaping. It was in his classes that I learned how to slow down and change my dancelike images into something fuller and richer. The class pulsated with vitality.

The story "Adraia," which I had written long ago in Lindos, still held me in its grip. In an

Maria and daughter Carmen in Sausalito, California

ill-advised moment, I had thrown out all my copies. But my mother had saved the original yellowing onionskin pages in the attic. She mailed me the manuscript, and I spent many months turning it into a long narrative about a Greek girl.

During this time I also participated at open readings which Herman Berlandt sponsored. For the first time, I tried accompanying my reading with my guitar. He published a few of my poems in his Underground Poets' Commune publications. I also worked with some dancers to combine words with music and dance. We performed at one of Herman's events at the Zellerbach Museum.

Carmen, meanwhile, was attending school at the bottom of the hill, and although she had a difficult relationship with Judd, she was thriving. She studied modern dance with Judd's sister at the Temple of the Wings. She took piano lessons. She planted carrots in the garden. She played with his dog, Shiloh. She had good friends. And she loved the house, with all its sunlight, which was helping her eyesight. However, I was growing increasingly fearful for her safety. Judd's only son had been injured at a young age in a firecracker explosion. I felt that Judd was in large part responsible. Carmen would come home from short drives with Judd and report that, although she habitually sat in back, she had knocked hard against the seat when they came to an abrupt halt.

In 1972 Carmen and I moved into the flatlands, into the thick smoggy air that we had floated above for the past few years.

I was consumed with the need to turn "Adraia" into a full-length novel. The long narrative about the Greek girl had been a technical exercise, which I quickly discarded. I went on Welfare, as this was the only way I could obtain the time I needed.

Only through writing would I find my identity, and this was a gamble. In my journal I wrote, "The only way out of my hole is writing and writing and more writing until the fear is gone . . . inside me are great lakes of panic, fear, worthlessness."

I thought it would take a year at the most, but it took five. Then it took another two years of rewriting before it finally was published, and even now I'd like to have another go at it. "A book is never finished, only abandoned . . . "

We lived frugally and simply. I supplemented our income by cleaning houses. We rode everywhere on bicycles after I sold my car. With a big basket strapped to the back of my bike, I could carry laundry and groceries. I sewed curtains, painted, laid linoleum tiles, learned to do simple carpentry.

Still I managed to pay for Carmen's piano, violin, and dance classes, get braces on her teeth, and raise her with things she needed. She says she didn't feel poor during those years. In contrast, I had always felt poor as a child.

Fairy tales come to mind in which a prisoner is held captive until the completion of a certain task. I recall one tale in which a princess had seven brothers who had been transformed into swans. She could only set them free by sewing each of them a special mantle, and she was given seven years. At the end of the allotted time, she had finished all but the final fringe of one garment. The swans were changed back into humans. But her youngest brother retained one webbed finger.

I could only set myself free by completing what I had to write.

Often I wrote as if guided. I felt somewhat afraid of the characters that came into my mind. I felt the presence of spirits, some of them malign. To write of certain things such as injury or death aroused my fear, as if writing about them could cause them to happen.

Max, who is one of the main characters in *Dark Plums,* appeared to me full-blown in a vision. I had not planned to put him in the story at all. But suddenly he was there, an old German Jew, plagued with guilt, who had escaped the concentration camps but whose family had perished. He had a generous, loving nature, and he flashed a jeweled ring.

In order to give him substance, I began to attend a local synagogue. Carmen decided to enroll in their Hebrew school. Max was leading us back to our roots! Strangely, he bore my mother's name. I think he embodied her frustrated, underground love. For underneath all our differences, my mother and I were connected by a powerful bond of sympathy and understanding. She was awkward in intimate encounters. So was I. We had deeply hurt each other, and neither of us had the skill or knowledge or insight of how to repair the rift.

As I wrote draft after draft, the jeweled ring vanished. It did not reappear until I was preparing the manuscript for publication many years later. Then the ring with its red and blue stones suddenly flashed into my mind, and I included it in the final scene.

In the course of this apparently endless writing task, I read a great deal. I would read Joan Didion's *Play It As It Lays* over and over again, trying to capture how she put things together. I copied an entire novella by Flannery O'Connor.

At some point I came across André Maurois's biography of George Sand. This led me into reading her work, both in French and English. Amazed that I could not find her most autobiographical novel, *Lélia,* which Maurois had actually used as a title for his biography (thereby causing some confusion), I began to translate it myself. Doing so was an enjoyable process, much less demanding than my own fiction. Written in an almost operatic nineteenth-century style, her heroine shared some of my own confusion. Like me, she was searching. Who was she? She fell in love, but could be faithful in her heart to no one. She tried to live as a nun, as a wife, as a courtesan. In the end, a fanatic priest kills her. In reading Sand's journals, letters, and accounts of her life, I felt strengthened on my own path.

The heroine says, " . . . to be lover, courtesan, and mother. These are three conditions of woman's fate that no woman escapes whether she sells herself in a market of prostitution or by a marriage contract." This echoes my theme in *Dark Plums*.

The early seventies was an era of encounter groups. I joined one, and it was very disturbing. For days after each meeting, I would mull over what had happened. However, I persisted in going because I believed I needed to learn.

But a few good things resulted. In a women's group I met Barbara Atchison, who became the sister I never had. Her warmth, charm, and intelligence have brought much into my life. For many years we have remained close, despite some really difficult times. As with Mario, she and I communicate uncannily without words. Helene Knox is another enduring friend from that time. It was she who helped me find a publisher for the *Lélia* translation by persuading me to attend an MLA conference in New York. Penny Michael, who died of cancer several years ago, was another person to whom I felt linked almost as if by blood. All three were discerning readers, to whom I could turn for valuable feedback. A large part of the difficulty of writing comes from knowing how readers will react. Penny, who was very much a Jungian, encouraged me to be daring and honest. She was never shocked—except by poor writing. "Write as if you were writing a book for yourself to read in three hundred years," she once said.

Around this time I learned that my arm, which I had always camouflaged, which I still held stiffly, which had so affected my life because of its crookedness, could easily have been rebroken and set properly when I reached the age of about fifteen.

I was furious. I confronted my parents by letter about this as well as about many other things from the past, which we had never discussed. They responded with denial and anger. To deal with all this, I sought the help of a woman therapist. A year later I had surgery on my arm. When it healed, it was less crooked than before. Something inside me, too, spiritually felt healed, although I was still murderously angry.

VI

A month later, as if a spell had been lifted, I met Walter Selig, whom I would later marry. It was at a Greek dancing taverna in Berkeley. On a whim, Carmen wore her Jewish star that night. Walter, who came from an Orthodox Jewish family, struck up a conversation with her. On our first date we went swimming with all four of our children.

Walt and I felt as if we had known each other for a long time. The kindness in his eyes was the first thing about him that struck me. If there are relationships that are arranged before birth, then ours certainly was. We've been together off and on now for twenty-three years. We have married, divorced, and come together again under the most difficult and unlikely circumstances. Although we are very different, we seem to fulfill deep needs in each other.

At the time we met, Walt was working as a research chemist for Lawrence Livermore National Laboratory. He had just gone through a turbulent divorce. His wife had custody of his children, Lisa, Naomi, and David, but they were with him on weekends. They ranged in age from nine to thirteen. Later on, they would live with us for periods of time.

Three years after we met, we got married at my insistence, which I would later regret. I rented a writing studio near our house in Lafayette. It provided a refuge in which I did some of my best writing. I worked part-time as a paralegal in Oakland.

During this time I was attending San Francisco State University where I obtained an M.A. in Creative Writing in 1981. I had some excellent teachers. One of them was Bill Wiegand. In his class students critiqued each other's writing as they had in Leonard's, but the tone, set by Bill, was entirely different. Some of the students who met in his class formed a group of their own, which lasted for many years and was very helpful.

Irving Halperin taught an inspiring course on Jewish literature. While doing research for his class, I came across a book called *The Expulsion of the Jews* by Valeriu Marcu, a German author of the 1930s. In describing the expulsion from Spain, Marcu wrote, "Then the Jews lay down by their ancestors' graves and wept. They left the keys to their houses with those who remained behind, hoping for better days."

Instinctively, I knew that some of my ancestors were those who stayed behind. In my parents' dining room hung a portrait of a somber lady dressed in brown velvet and pearls. Shortly before she died, my mother told me that this lady was related to my maternal great-grandmother, Rosa Judd, and that she had emigrated from Spain to Brussels in the late eighteenth century. The portrait in our possession was only a copy. The original hung in a Brussels museum. Recently an uncle confirmed my mother's story, adding airily, "Oh . . . they left Spain so that they could express their views more freely," which is somewhat of an understatement for the possibility of being burned at the stake.

When I read Marcu's passage, a missing piece of a puzzle snapped into place. Centuries of concealing their identities continued to affect my mother's family. It helped explain why they were perturbed by my Jewish looks, my dark hair and eyes. It helped explain their aping of WASP culture. Beneath the snobbery lay fears for their survival. It explained a curious photograph of Granny Silver among a group of smiling nuns. When her children were little, she had taken refuge each autumn at a convent. It explained hundreds of trifling details which cumulatively had a powerful effect.

I felt compelled to write a novel on the subject. At this point it is nearly complete.

During those years I wrote four drafts of *Longing,* but all of them seemed sterile. I could not crack the surface until one weekend in 1980 when I attended a Tibetan Buddhist seminar in Berkeley and was instructed in *shamatha* practice. Through this form of meditation, I was finally able to crack through the ice to the running water beneath.

In January 1981, Mario died alone in the southern California desert of cirrhosis of the liver and a heart attack. Many years later Carmen wrote the following poem:

For Mario

You were an unfortunate
    alienated
    alien-hated man

    a clown
    a beggar
    a storyteller

yet you were the only
one who knew the

"My good friend, Barbara Atchison"

truth about the ones
you loved.

was that your fault
you knew too much?

they wanted you
dead more than
alive

was that what
you wanted too?

Did I want him dead? I asked. "I'm referring to his family in Chile," she said. "The ones who gave him a one-way ticket to Paris long ago." He was the black sheep in his family, the one who perceived things they wanted hidden. But perhaps her poem applies to all of us! Truth is uncomfortable.

For a time I went away to the mountains of southern California. We were having a difficult time at home. There I stayed in an isolated place called the Galaxy Motel. I had lucid dreams where I would know that I was dreaming. To some extent I was able to tell myself what I wanted to dream about. And I felt the presence of Mario's spirit. He had died close by. His death deeply disturbed me. I needed to deal with it alone.

That month at the Galaxy Motel was a spiritual high which ended in physical suffering. A few months earlier I'd had a hysterectomy, which brought about emotional changes. It also evidently affected my back, causing me such severe pain that Walt flew down and drove me back.

Six months later I moved into an apartment alone in Berkeley, where I rewrote *Longing* quickly once again, and I was much more satisfied with this version, although not completely so. Like "Adraia," *Longing* was a story I had to write. And I had to write draft after draft. I wrote nine drafts in all. *Longing* deals with my family, and I felt I had to write about things so long suppressed in order to keep—or regain—my own sanity. It was a very difficult book to write. During the final draft, my back hurt so much that I had to get up from the typewriter every twenty minutes to crawl around and stretch. My back became such a problem that I took up the study of physical therapy and massage in order to get better. This worked, but it took years.

To my parents' credit, when I told about the novel and asked how they felt about its being published, they gave their consent. "You must do it," they said. By the time it appeared, my mother was no longer alive. The book still troubles my father.

My mother died two years after Mario on the day of his birthday and my brother Michael's, April 3, 1983. Here is a poem she wrote towards the end of her life:

Espinosa with her second husband,
Walter Selig, 1977

The Prisoner (June 5, 1982)

The person
has always been a prisoner
even when he burst
from his warm and watery confines
the person inside
was a prisoner.

When after long years
the mind wanders free
the person inside
will no longer be a prisoner.
No one can follow him
to his secret land.

(The thoughts have flown away
There is no prisoner.)
Death takes him by the hand,
He is free.

Sometimes I imagine that Mario and my mother have been reborn as brother and sister in a traveling circus. In this new life they swing from trapezes and ride bareback together.

I sent a draft of *Longing* to the editor of a university press. He returned the manuscript with a letter expressing regret that my heroine was not stronger, more heroic and assertive in the mold of Katherine Anne Porter's heroines.

Other editors and literary agents repeatedly rejected it because they found the book too depressing and the characters too negative. Like the university press editor, they wanted more assertive models of femininity. The ending wasn't upbeat enough for them. An editor for a large New York publishing house said she had argued in vain all morning with her associates, as she wanted to go ahead and publish the manuscript.

Through this period Nanos Valaoritis, whom I had met at San Francisco State, encouraged me when I was ready to give up hope. He believed in the book and laughed at the rejection letters.

Meanwhile, I had started to lead an informal writing group with four or five women. One of them, Maggie, had a yen to start a publishing cooperative and decided that *Longing* should be a priority. She gave me one excellent editorial suggestion: reversing the order of the first and second sections.

In September 1985, just as *Longing* was in the process of being prepared for publication, Walt and I separated bitterly, and I made the mistake of staying with Maggie. Intimacy did not breed love. She began acting strangely. As soon as I could, I moved out into a depressing apartment, went through a miserable year of financial panic, divorce papers, working part-time as a massage therapist, and looking for other work. I also oversaw the publication of *Longing,* in which by now I had invested thousands of dollars, as Cayuse Press, which is what we had named the cooperative, was not set up to pay our printing costs.

Under enormous stress, I commissioned a cover which must rank among one of the most hideous ever done. I was sick at heart over the cover, the publishing fiasco, and the divorce.

Nanos was a great support at this time. He held court in a coffeehouse near Telegraph Avenue where he met with students and friends. His literary knowledge, his cultural sophistication, his humor, and his acceptance of things—and of me, flawed as I was—were of great help.

He wrote on the back of that first cover, *"Longing* is a work of exceptional courage, honesty, and originality which one finds seldom in the Western world, more often in Russian dissident literature. This makes the work a rare document in human relations. In our society it also makes the work automatically a kind of experimental writing of the Western *samizdat* type, which official established literary bureaucracy will only recognize later after prolonged battle . . . "

In June 1986, there was a faint dawn. Penny Skillman gave the book a decent review in the *San Francisco Chronicle.* Several teachers used the book (hideous cover and all) in their college literature classes.

Eventually Cayuse Press dissolved.

I moved into a house in Oakland where I rented out rooms. I used to pray that none of my housemates would be home when I was there, and I pity anyone who had to share that space with me.

During this time I began to teach at New College in San Francisco. This is thanks to Carmen. At her graduation, where she performed a dance, one of her teachers expressed interest in having me work there. I taught Creative Writing from the winter of 1986 until the summer of 1990. That last year I was also co-coordinator of the Creative Writing Department, and I taught a contemporary literature course.

I enjoyed teaching, but began to feel that it was sapping my own work. I wanted to quit, and perhaps arranged things subconsciously so that I would have to do so. In the fall of 1989 friction arose between me and faculty administrators.

That summer I resigned from New College and moved to Tucson. The last few years had been extremely difficult, and the desert was a good place to lick my wounds. The beauty of vast open space was healing. I loved the sun and heat. The following summer I stayed in a tiny town named Patagonia near the Nogales border. I got a job as a dishwasher in the restaurant next to the house I had rented. In the fall, with regret I moved back to Tucson to teach English at a community college. But Tucson was close to the wilds. A short drive would bring me to Saguaro National Park with endless trails.

I worked on a novel about my mother, for which as usual I did many drafts.

Meanwhile, Walt and I had undergone joint therapy which helped resolve some of our anger and bitterness. Through circumstances I can only understand as karmic, we got back together with the help of his friend, Sally Headding. In February 1992, I came back to live with him.

Sally read the *Dark Plums* manuscript, then titled *Adrianne.* She became very enthusiastic about it and revived my flagging interest in finding a publisher.

Then in late August 1992, I went to a PEN West party hosted by Floyd Salas where I met Lucha Corpi. She made the surprising suggestion that I send *Adrianne* to her Hispanic-American publisher, Arte Público Press. Roberta Fernández became my editor there, and she painstakingly worked with the manuscript.

I owe much to Lucha. Had it not been for her suggestion, the book would probably still be unpublished. Over the past few years she has become a good friend and has helped guide me through the unfamiliar terrain of promotion.

That summer Sally suggested I paste a plain gray and black cover over *Longing.* I gave this camouflaged copy to Lucha, who passed it on

"My daughter, Carmen Espinosa"

to Roberta. It ended up in the hands of Nick Kanellos, director of Arte Público. This press is perhaps the most European of U.S.-based publishers. Nick Kanellos has published many writers whom others would consider too risky, too controversial, too blatant. He decided to issue a reprint. In November 1995, it appeared in its new incarnation with a wonderful collage on the cover by San Diego artist Leslie Nemour. The cover of *Dark Plums* is also a collage of Leslie's. I am very pleased with both. It is Roberta who chose Leslie's work, and who gave the original go-ahead on both *Dark Plums* and *Longing*.

In 1996 *Longing* won an American Book Award.

Anastasía Papas Konstantinou has translated *Longing* into Greek and has arranged with Delfini Press in Athens to publish it.

Longing has begun to find acceptance in the world.

However, it may take another decade for *Dark Plums* to come into its own. Recently an elderly man pursued me around a room, where I had given a talk, shouting angrily that the heroine, Adrianne, was stupid. He seemed absolutely outraged that she would go off to bed with strangers so easily. "My daughter is a feminist—a liberated woman—and she agrees—no woman of any intelligence would just go off like that with a stranger. She tells me Adrianne is stupid!" He was personally affronted, nearly ready to fight. I had hit a nerve.

Editors of a local paper, I am told, did not review *Dark Plums* because they considered it pornographic. However, my intent was not to arouse lust, but rather portray experiences with full intensity and clarity. In order to do this, I needed to be graphic. German Expressionist paintings have been a strong influence. When I read recent works by writers like Philip Roth, in comparison my work pales. The double standard still flourishes. Copies of *Dark Plums* keep disappearing from the shelves of local libraries. "It would be cheaper for people to buy them," said a librarian. To certain readers, the book speaks strongly.

For the last six and a half years Walt and I have been living together. I rent a writing studio, as I need this personal space. Six months ago we remarried. Once again I teach English as a Second Language, which is both exhilarating and demanding. It provides a way to give something immediately to people and provides a balance to the solitary work of writing.

As I look back over this account, I feel as if I am another person from the one who experienced the things I have described. One night long ago when I was riding back on a Greyhound bus from Vermont, I was struck by the fact that all of me that remains of the past is ghostly. A series of ghosts, of shed selves, like frames in film that run very fast. In another ten years, who will any of us be?

A few months ago I went on a firewalk. A New Age leader led us through visualization exercises and revved us up with singing, chanting, dancing. When we felt ready, we walked over a bed of burning coals without incurring any injury. The point of this was not the physical feat—which is rather an absurd one—but to demonstrate the power of spirit to transcend physical laws. Later that night, the leader gave healing instructions for those who had suffered any blisters. "The blisters will heal very fast," he said. I had felt a stinging sensation on my right arch the second time I walked over the coals. But when I looked for the blister, there was none. It had healed within minutes.

BIBLIOGRAPHY

Fiction:

Dark Plums, Arte Público, 1995.

Longing, Arte Público, 1995.

Poetry:

Love Feelings, Four Winds Press, San Francisco, 1967.

Night Music, The Tides, Sausalito, 1969.

Translator:

George Sand, *Lélia,* Indiana UP, 1978.

Jean Cocteau, *Plain-Chant [and] l'Ange Heurtebise* (bilingual), Sun & Moon, forthcoming.

Also translator of one chapter from George Sand's autobiography *Ma Vie,* edited by Thelma Jurgrau, SUNY, 1990. Contributor of poetry, articles, and short fiction to anthologies and periodicals including *Alameda Poets' Anthology, Anthologies of Underground Poetry* edited by Herman Berlandt, *Bay Area Poets Coalition, Cayati, Crab Creek Anthology, Golden Isis, In Other Words, Poetalk, Studies in Literary Imagination, Three Penny Review, Tidings, Voices of America,* and other publications. Translation of *Longing* into Greek by Anastasía Papa Konstantinou, Delfini Press (Athens), forthcoming.

Ronald Johnson

1935-1998

UP TILL NOW

Ronald Johnson

EDITOR'S NOTE: Ronald Johnson passed away on March 4, 1998, while this volume was in production. We thank the members of his family for agreeing to posthumous publication of his essay.

I

I was born bawling with red hair, November 25, 1935, smack dab in the dustbowl: Sun, Moon, and Jupiter in Sagittarius, and Aries rising. All direction and fire. Combined with the grit of settler grandparents in a covered wagon, come to live in a sod house to get land. However habited, my family never got "land." My mother's father became the editor of the *Clark County Clipper* in the days Ashland, Kansas, had an "opera house" for traveling culture. Hank Mayse had some education and a current, lively sense of vocation. His style was a sprightly vernacular, which he crafted, week after week, into what news there was to be lifted from the telegraph to be pithily fleshed out. Gossip was done apparently by a female, but we imagined it was by the telephone operator (who listened into every conversation), so right were the comments.

His wife, Hattie, was a typical resourceful settler's wife, who turned promptly out a family of eight roistering kids, mostly boys, my

109

mother Helen and my aunt Marjorie the only females. They made up games of their own, passed down as legend, on the three-sided verandah of a large Victorian house. Hank made a good living, as did his brother Bob, a bachelor who became the town lawyer in an apartment above the town center bank. Though, of course, they never made the big money like those who held on to the land, grew wheat, and raised cattle.

I remember being placed as a child in a blooming field and getting an allergic reaction, and I decided then and there "you will *not* have a negative reaction to the outside—this is enough." Some surrender, but that was not my way. I learned quickly I was "different" as well as how to assert my masculinity when necessary. I had an imaginary friend called Morris, and later, when I discovered the Oz books, believed until puberty there must be some way out of the prairie, some magical way I somehow associated with sitting in the middle of a huge lilac bush between my grandmother's house and ours. Robert Duncan was the only one I know who grew up with this expectation also. I had an uncle and aunt who both became blind in their teens, and I had always a dread of this inheritance. To this day I jubilate in seeing, as if a gift. This is certainly an element in my work, as were Baum's books. My most poignant moment of childhood was finding in a bookshop in Dodge City a long shelf of Oz books I'd never read and having my mother say (after I asked for some as a Christmas present), "No, you read them too much as it is!"

There was an old-fashioned high school where I learned perhaps more than kids do these days. There were no outlets artistically—though I remember a radio version of *Farewell to Arms* (with lots of rain) and discovering Ravel there, one late afternoon just before dinner.

My father hauled into town an almost derelict farmhouse which he placed on a basement and renovated into a fine commodious home next to my mother's mother, where she lived after Hank died. I reckoned later that Honey (my father's name for her, picked up by me as a tot and perpetuated in the family to her death) wanted to train a daughter on her own trellis. Other than that, we had a storybook existence of the American middle-class—my parents never divorced, as is so common and disturbing to kids these days.

My mother was a fine and inventive cook, if a sloppy housekeeper. My father was employed under his father at the local lumberyard. I once asked my mother how she had managed a household during the Depression, and she replied, "But we didn't know we were poor." She kept a chicken house and a large garden. We had a huge, still-bearing pear tree, mulberries, white and purple fruited, lining the front sidewalk, black walnuts cornering my father's lumberyard across the street, and gifts of apricots from great-aunts and cherries from an uncle. We churned vanilla ice cream on the back porch until the fireflies came. The family fished a lot and did some hunting. A quarter of beef was a pittance then, so we always had that in the local freezer; only the liver was eaten fresh.

I inherited from my mother fancy, and from my father resourcefulness. She took on many creative projects which finally went incomplete when enthusiasm waned, while my father doesn't rest until a project is finished. They were well suited and celebrated their fiftieth anniversary a few years before her death of cancer of the bladder.

My grandfather Johnson, called Jack, was, I understood even then, the last of a breed. He added up the day's total with an adding machine, but then added it up himself just to check the machine. He summed up an applicant for work by how they sharpened a pencil with a knife, and a plus was given for one with his own knife. (My father carries a small knife on his key chain to this day, and gave me one with the admonition that if I kept it sharp it was sure to come in useful.) His wife, Maggie, also raised up a large family, and became lame in one leg upon her last delivery. In her late years she became very religious and turned mostly to her bible.

I went to church, sang in the choir, and attended Presbyterian church camp where I played a Mickey Rooney role and started a show for the final bonfire. I found it fine to be somewhere I didn't have a sissy reputation, and made friends effortlessly. At home I was often pursued by yahoos in pickups and ran home to their taunts, sheltering behind the large elm trunks along the way, wondering if I could make it home before they rounded the block.

In high school I only did track, for I turned out to be a formidable runner. I played trombone in the band, and as first trombone was pivot for formations. I loved it. And my junior

Ronald (center) with neighbors, 1940

year I prepared a monologue of a crazed (or going crazy) inmate in a jail. This was called a "tour de force" (which took a long while for me to decipher) by the judge of the state contest. The next year I cut my own monologue from Shakespeare's *Richard II,* which led to my acceptance into the drama department at the University of Kansas (KU), where I was resourceful though not enough to be an asset. Besides I decided the theater was full of folks which I did not want to become. Then there was the audition for *Death of a Salesman,* with the discouraging comment, "don't ever wear bluejeans on stage again" (I wear blue jeans to this day.)

My only consolation was the piano, which I played for all the years growing up. The trouble was I did not have a very good teacher, and my hands were not really wide enough to become a professional. I also tried my hand at painting, but found I was not a draughtsman.

At graduation I held hands with Kay Randall as we went up the aisle to "Pomp and Circumstance," as a seal to the past perhaps. Now we were to become welcome to choose our destinies. I'd saved up from working after school and summers so elected to go to KU, for at least a year—though my monies barely lasted that long. I was duly installed in a house, where

instead of rent, I was to provide general housecleaning with extras like polishing the stairs and washing windows. I painted the studio, at basement level but with a whole wall of windows and a terrace, an apple-green, with accents of Wedgewood blue and white, a splash of red pillows. I thought it very stylish and gave small parties.

Being gay, for the first time I'd a "set" of compatriots. And I could seek kindred spirits in the arts. I made friends with Norman, a fine pianist from Canada whom I imported to Ashland for Christmas. This was the first time I had ever experienced conversation with someone who wanted to talk about the meaning of life and where were we going. I also made friends with A. and C., one from the library department and the other a teacher of vocal delivery. I sat at their lunch table in the cafeteria while they played an ongoing game. Each brought two lines of poetry and the other was to guess who wrote them. This was the crux, I now think, when I decided maybe I would become a poet. I did write rather flimsy poems, one which won third prize in a school contest, and was influenced by a two-volume set of Emily Dickinson's *Letters* I found on my room's shelves. Switching from Drama to Art to English Lit. I had at last found a home.

I also had an affair with one of the faculty, learning all kinds of friendly etiquette in bed and how to properly scramble eggs with grated cheese, and was introduced to the recordings of Mable Mercer—the ideal cafe singer. Frank Sinatra said he learned phrasing from her, and she was the fount of Bobby Short.

I didn't have enough money for a second year at KU, so I volunteered for the draft, at the hind-end of the Korean war. We were in a company apart, in order to be mobile for atom bomb tests, and I was head of Personnel for it, volunteering as a typist and making myself useful. My great regret was that I could send friends to coveted Europe, but could not send myself. This was Fort Huachuca, surrounded by the purest desert, fragrant with herbs after the infrequent thundershowers. Rains could be seen miles away, perfumes arose in swathes. I learned there to love the Southwest. My mother questioned me what I had learned in the army. I replied that I'd learned how to polish boots and drink Scotch. And thank God I didn't have to go on a bomb test.

I took a job in Topeka writing letters for Blue Cross/Blue Shield (BC/BS). The ones they thought unanswerable came to me, by some consensus, as the only male. You learned to pare down sentences, make no paragraph longer than four lines, and be very definite while being compassionate. That must have made some impact on my style.

I met airforceman John Sampas, later to be the Kerouac executor. He has been a friend these long years—and I occasionally help with the Kerouac estate business, which is considerable these days. Who would have thought we'd be connected a lifetime?

When John Sampas later became established in Washington, D.C., he urged me to get out and come east. So I did, and never regretted it. I lived in a house suited to the poet's imagination—a large brick house, its road leading to DuPont Circle. The King-Smiths collected what they called "artists" and themselves gave piano lessons, Mrs. K.S. having taught with Isadora Duncan. Mary, in the spacious second floor studio, was a mezzo and taught voice, at a second baby grand. Next door was an aspiring pianist whose grand took up most of his room. It sometimes was like living in an Ives sonata. I thrived, while answering phones at the BC/BS in Washington. I started "writing" poems from clipped-out words and phrases from the daily news. These were my first experience making visual poems.

At the pianist's I met Jonathan Williams, who was to change and give direction to my life. Jonathan was not only a Black Mountain poet, but published, with Jargon Press, most of the early poets who mattered, traveling endless miles selling his handsome editions out of the back of his old blue Pontiac to make the printer's bill. "With Black Mountain abandoned," he said, "New York is bristling with ex-teachers and students, so why not, since you have money from being a vet, go to Columbia? I know M., who can recommend you in the English department." That worked out, and we moved to M.'s upper floor on Staten Island.

M. drank about a gallon of Virginia Dare sherry a night. Slurring his fake F. R. Leavis accent as the evening progressed and the nine cats grew more unfed. We entertained Allen Ginsberg, the Zukofskys, had Fielding Dawson sequestered there one weekend to make collages for JW's *Empire Finals at Verona*. One disastrous evening I made a spinach soufflé for LeRoi Jones (then known under his given name) who simply didn't show up. His only excuse was that "something better showed up." On the plus side I discovered that soufflé was just *fine*, flattened and chilled.

One night, at about the height of tipsiness, the phone rang, Jonathan answered, and I caught it was undoubtedly M. I got the phone to hear him say, "You know, my dear, he's not quite a gentleman," something he kept saying to me about Jonathan! I dropped the phone, sprinted downstairs, opened the door to the cat stink of the "drawing room," found him giggling in an alcove, and socked him between the eyes, "sheddy" and all. The next day, of course, we were asked to leave.

After leaving home I've always seemed to live in picturesque surroundings. Moved to the Arvia Hotel I found that exotic, with its small room and reach-in kitchen, inevitably roach-infested, where I learned to make a quickly sautéed dish of thin veal with black grapes for the visitors who were intrepid enough to come dine. I was on the G.I. bill and JW wrapped packages at the Eighth Street Bookstore, so we had the only affordable thing. I was thrilled to be at Columbia and with New York, with contacts almost nightly at the Cedar Tavern, where your boothmate might be Franz Kline or de Kooning with a pronounced female, Fee Dawson, Charles Olson when in town, or Allen Ginsberg. It was all talk of what might art become, particularly at the Art Club meeting once a month, to which anyone in the creative world came. We were in the midst of a New York leading the world with abstract Expressionism to a new way of seeing. Surely this was as heady as expatriate Paris in the twenties. There was also the vibrancy of the Living Theater's productions of a new kind of theater, a new kind of world we lived in. I have a background shot at a booth selling Jonathan's books, all preppy from Columbia, in the lobby of the Living Theater. Cage gave concerts there to open our ears. There was also Charles Mingus in the downtown club, whacking the best bass in the business, whom Jonathan courted to write his memoirs. Along with Stefan Wolpe, Harry Partch, and Lou Harrison, this made for another education. Everything jumped and reverberated with the new. Never has been such a sounding board for a poet.

Jonathan and I took the Brooklyn ferry from Staten Island to meet Zukofsky and his wife Celia. We'd eat in a glorious Italian hole-in-the-wall where the order was passed up a dumbwaiter, which would descend with steaming and always succulent dishes from the kitchen above. We had ample red wine to prepare for the rigors of the Zukofsky household,

where everything was tiny. A cigarette had to be smoked down to the butt to put it out in one of their ashtrays. Miniscule drams of what they had laid in were served. They weren't stingy, it's just that they *lived* small. Louis was the exact opposite of Olson's sweep of generosity; even with little money, he once served us roast duckling from a stove which had to have the door tied with rope, and when he found I had never tasted lobster, took us to the best hotel in Glouscester and ordered four.

Louis became my mentor, after Olson, inspiring Jonathan to do a few Catullus translations when Zuk was translating them sound for sound: O that "blue-eyed lion"! I translated a few of Horace; the only line I remember: "O Chloe callow doxy / knock-kneed in the trees." The translations were published by the *Columbia Review,* which also printed a longish poem of mine that won the Boar's Head Prize in 1960. Louis became my last mentor, and the best for my purposes all in all. Except for the late Basil Bunting, I have learned most from Louis, with Pound always in their background of course. His close boxing with the language, its give-and-take, is what I modeled my poetry in *ARK* to emulate (but always to make sense, which late Zuk often doesn't). Jonathan always knew anybody who was anybody, of course, and I learned, and mostly listened.

The year I graduated, JW suggested we might get a lot of material by hiking the Appalachian Trail. So we set off at the Georgia end, Dorothy Neal driving us, from Demorest. Dorothy has been a lifetime friend. It was in her spacious, gracious house I later wrote *The Book of the Green Man,* ensconced above the studio for sculpting, with a huge loom in an alcove. Ms. D's late husband Charles was one of those men who could enchant one and all, and though he was not himself creative, he encouraged the young like Jonathan. He sent their adopted son Arnold to a renowned art school to learn to make pots, had the best sound system in the South, planted a garden half useful, half roses. And it all worked until his early death, when the household was hurled apart. There were some fine paintings from the thirties, as well as furniture from that period. It was for me a happy place to be, and to write in. Dorothy liked to cook and eat, and it was there I finally became a good cook. Dorothy taught me also about birds, and bought me binoculars one Christmas (which I still use, though the strap is broken).

Walking the trail *was* useful, for we carried a bird book, a book on wild flowers, and one on trees. And after about twenty miles, up and down, in fair or dripping skies, we made a small fire of wood left by others who'd used the shelter. And we wrote out what we'd encountered or seen. Nothing much came for either of us for poetry, but I developed a keen sense about when my body needed sugar, as well as an appreciation of the song of the winter wren.

The year was getting on, and with New York looming ahead, we agreed this was enough to say we walked the Trail. So we decamped and practically wore our backpacks to the Cedar—heroes of the hour, in the days before marathons. That was long ago, but still sometimes I dream I'm on the Appalachian Trail. . . .

Back in Highlands, with his parents, JW worked to get us to England, setting up itinerary, friends to stay with at first, people to go out of the way to meet. So in 1962 we were aboard *New Amsterdam,* on our way to visit the haunts of Dickens, James, and Oscar Wilde. And certainly a lot of other writers, such as Stevie Smith, Christopher Middleton, Ian Finlay, Hugh MacDiarmid, Nathaniel Tarn, Anselm Hollo.

We hiked the Lake Country where we stayed in hostels. One morning after returning from a visit with a poet and his wife, who cut swatches of chives for us to take, I put cut chives into scrambled eggs. The British, who never scramble eggs for breakfast, were aghast. (One was delegated to enquire of the American, "Why do you put grass in your eggs?") We quickly learned how to order in pubs, but restaurants were more difficult in those days. Once, in a lackluster Italian restaurant no Italian had ever entered, we asked if it were possible just to have sautéed garlic on spaghetti. The waitress almost dropped her order book, saying, "O Sir, we don't put garlic in anything!" There were then many leftovers from the war: canned baked beans on toast and denatured sausages. I asked Barbara Jones once about this, and she breezily explained, "They got used to them during the war."

It was in England I started collecting the objects—mostly rusted metal—that I was to turn into sculpture years later, as well as the sea-sculpted stone that I carried back from the beach at Clovelley, which I made my "cornerstone." In SoHo a couple of years later I was walking with Bill Benton and picked up a perfect Chamberlain "wave." Bill said, "I think it was Raushenberg who said: 'If you go around the block in New York without seeing something to put in a picture, then you've not been looking.'" I held on to this "wave" for years, saving up bits and pieces that would bring it out; until living in my Dad's basement in Topeka, where I had weathered wood and electric saw to construct objects I'd saved for years for want of a studio for my second wave of sculptures. Thus, when I found my métier was rust, not paint, I finally became a visual artist.

I lived again in "interesting" surroundings, on the top two floors of Barbara Jones's Hampstead house. Barbara, everyone said, was amusing, and she was indeed, with an eye for unusual things. On the walls of her bedroom there were fine watercolors of volcanoes (preferably erupting) from the nineteenth century, and a small sitting room featured a half-size camel made of curly maple, which folded out into a writing desk. I was once summoned to

help because Gypsy Rose Lee was coming to film in her kitchen and it was too dingy, so she sent me to Woolworths to find plastic flowers to cover up cracks while she painted the dishwasher as an owl—its handle the beak. Barbara had written two books about the follies and grottoes in Britain, and she once took us on a trip to visit different sites to see how these were being maintained. It was one of the most thrilling trips into the countryside imaginable, with me in the back seat of Barbara's convertible Morris, of course with the top down. I huddled with her "wartime wallaby," chilled and buffeted. She gave us a lesson in how to handle servants when she wormed her way into an estate: "A lady never looks a servant in the eye—then they let you get away with anything." So we had access to a particularly fine folly, which she breezed into, scarf blowing and gloved hand set to sunglasses. I was in a novel by Evelyn Waugh. For me she was a kind of Auntie Mame, and it was she who first made me notice the work of naive artists who built palaces out of found objects.

Her house was on Well Walk in Hampstead, a few blocks from Keats's house and the Hampstead heath. There I set out to explore the recently published Elizabeth David books, where I learned what cuts of meat were and how to shop for them. I learned how to make spare but tasty stews in the French manner; how to be elastic as to servings and able to turn out a lovely omelet for a famished poet or painter, wherever kitchened; how to end a meal with a sprightly cheese, and generally enjoy serving a good meal for company.

Jonathan sat in his studio writing a dozen or more letters a day to keep Jargon afloat. I flew to Paris to meet a friend who showed me the city, which was appropriately puddled to reflect the street lamps and chestnut trees on the way to the Arc de Triomphe. To fall out of love in Paris, in the spring, is not the ideal; nevertheless, to this day I can still smell it, savor it: Paris. We lived in two different worlds with their own responsibilities—but what a fling.

My first salvageable poems date from about this time—my translations into poems of Satie's notes to *Sports and Divertissments.* The first selections were printed in *Poor. Old. Tired. Horse,* and several years later Ian Finlay suggested I complete the series. Later the late William Masselos insisted these be printed in

The author in 1961

the program when he performed them. I also translated the notes Le Facteur Cheval and Raymond Isidore left into poems. These are kind of Urstones from the building of *ARK*. I take Pound's experiments in translation to be the ideal. All of mine were just notes which I shaped into a poem. The act of real translation has always escaped me. I attempted Jules Supervielle since his feel for words was similar to mine, but after trying for years I gave up, especially on lines such as "Le Soleil sur Venus se lève." It was he who taught me not to fear being "too much" in such lines as "Cellophane in cellophane of salamander slid within the flame," as well as the cocky banter of Wallace Stevens's "chief Iffucan of caftan in tan, in henna hackles, halt!" Or Edith Sitwell reading "Facade," as well as her explanation of poetics in the introduction to her collected poems: *Canticle of the Rose.*

Through Thoreau I was seduced into cosmology as reflected in nature, on all levels. From Ives I learned how collage could be used to effect. From Stan Brackhage I learned the virtues of cutting for speed, and from the painter Jess how to reconstruct a puzzle so the seams became the seen (and vice-versa). From R. B. Kitaj, that anything might happen in the way of connections. From Duncan I learned to see

the angels in Rilke, and to *trust* them. For years I was highly influenced by Guy Davenport's sprightly prose, and through decades of correspondence in which his lively wit sparkled unendingly.

When we came back to the States I settled into a studio at Dorothy Neal's in Georgia, and wrote *The Book of the Green Man* from my copious reading of the British naturalists, as well as my notes from our far-ranging hikes. I wrote "Autumn" first influenced by Samuel Palmer's visionary landscapes. The late Sir Herbert Reed particularly admired this. *The Green Man* was published both by Longman's Green in London and W. W. Norton. Denise Levertov was Norton's advisor on poetry at the time, and got them to publish me and Zukofsky— bless her! So I was well reviewed from the beginning. *The Green Man* was my attempt, as a brash American, to make new the traditional British long seasonal poem, and is a preview of what I was to do for American poetry in *ARK*.

I remember a night on stage in London with Robert Lowell, Jonathan Williams, Stevie Smith, and (I think) Christopher Middleton. I read my most buffaloed poem. Jonathan charmed. Stevie alarmed. At the party after, Stevie and I tangoed and drank Black Velvets (half Guiness, half champagne), which she remembered from the twenties. She taught me that readings should never be

boring and later I learned by watching James Broughton's "Two Men and a Harp" how to use just a chair as a stage prop. Once I even shamelessly used a fedora, in a classroom of all things, just that way. So my little experience in the theater came to be useful at last.

Jonathan said Barbara's house was free the summer of '63, so why not go again? It turned out that, with my *Green Man* a success, we had an act on our hands and greener fields ahead. Crossing again on the *New Amsterdam* (JW had a friend who got us best accommodations in second class at bottom prices), we took up again the Hampstead residence. We entertained artists of all kinds, both British and American. I remember one visit of the Creeleys which was particularly fine. I took Bobbie to the then fashionable Carnaby Street, where she picked up a slinky, rather flimsy frock trimmed with feathers. And Jonathan took them to a Mahler concert, which they had never experienced. (It is hard to think now that then Mahler was a relative rarity.) We also, with Barbara on vacation, gave a whole house party. The only thing I remember vividly of this was a Hampstead matron enquiring of William Burroughs about what drugs he was on. "Oh, just a little Psylocybin and a rye on the rocks," tossing the ice with his right thumb. It was a rather difficult party to give, having to trot the lower jammed floor up two flights, placing a celebrity or two on each floor. So I took on the distribution, leaving mostly the elderly the first floor. Finally, they started to circulate and I could relax. It ended on the third floor with people decorating the carpet in a room where the lights from Keats's house twinkled and the blackbird sang at night almost within reach.

Later we set out for Europe, subleasing to Muriel Rukeyser. It was a super tour. Through Germany with surfeit of rococo, bier, and wurst. Trips to some of the Concrete poets there. We were driving a VW bug Jonathan had bought, and picked up Dorothy Neal in Paris to tour France and later Italy. In those days it was not always necessary to make reservations, as there seemed always a pension available at reasonable prices. I swear the room JW and I shared on a canal in Venice is the one in which Merton Denscher stayed in *Wings of the Dove* (or perhaps my memory fleshed out the book).

Though we crossed the Atlantic only the four times, I feel grateful to have lived in a time this was possible. Somehow to go by ship was as interesting as Europe itself, and much more civilized than an airplane. I've known people who swear by lovely Florence, but in those days Venice was my choice. Saint Mark's Square, which Henry James called "the great drawing room of Europe," city of waters for a visitor from much-parched Kansas, with great paintings like confetti in the churches, reached by arched bridges (we could not afford a gondola). And one most memorable day when Jonathan and I entered into the presence of Ezra Pound. We knew he'd not really talked to anyone for several years, but Jonathan had him talking after a chance remark that he published Mina Loy. Pound's ears pricked up at that and we chatted comfortably for an hour or more. Then, with Miss Rudge, he took us to the canal where *A Lume Spento* was written. We discussed Olson and Dahlberg, William Carlos Williams, and Creeley, I seem to remember. They invited us to join them for dinner at Ez's favorite tratorria. Alas! We had dinner reserva-

tions with Dorothy at the Gritti and had to go change. That was a loss, but the mashed potatoes JW ordered, after too many days of pasta, were the best I've ever tasted—just right in texture and tasting of the essence of potato. I should have ordered a side dish.

At my urging, we stopped in Hauterives where the Le Facteur Cheval had erected his Ideal Palace out of found objects and honest cement. This is the first of my inspirations for *ARK.* Later Jargon Press would issue *The Spirit Walks, the Rocks Will Talk,* which made poems from Cheval and Raymond Isidore, who built a mosaic house and garden in the shadow of Chartres. Unlike Simon Rodia who left no writings about his Watts Towers, they both left notes. After a tour of this most amazing structure, I insisted we go to La Pyramide for lunch, M. Point's restaurant given four stars in the *Michelin,* and one of the best in France at the time. There we lunched on the terrace under mild sun, and I ordered for them the famed *pate-en-croute,* asking the sommelier about the best wine to accompany it. He presented a Moulin-a-Vent of the best vintage. I understood then which wines were merely drinkable, and which divine. I've seldom had more than a sip or two of the divine (and never enough caviar.) It was a memorable day. From there I only remember Carcasson on the way, through Paris for too few days, hence to the Holland America line, for home. I'd had the Grand Tour.

Again at Dorothy Neal's, I wrote *The Different Musics* in which I first invented the centered line which was to be used in *ARK,* long down the road. "The Letters To Walt Whitman" are probably my most republished poems, and were to show me just how comfortable the centered line could be. In *Assorted Jungles* I attempted poems as if an equivalent of Rousseau. In the "Unfoldings" I met a stumbling block: how to resolve this book. It ended with rather too many pyrotechnics and applause of real galaxies colliding. I pruned my first book to add to this, and it was published as *Valley of the Many-Colored Grasses* by Norton in 1969. Critically, it was a success—my last appearance from a New York publisher.

Next summer Jonathan was at the Institute in Aspen, and I worked as a bus boy at the Copper Kettle Restaurant. Gus Blaiddell, who was then working for the University of New Mexico Press, visited for a week, and I cooked Southwestern dishes for him. He said, "We could really use a good cookbook at the University of New Mexico Press, why don't you write us one? So I did research in Aspen and wrote my first cookbook—which was a top seller for them for quite a few years. I also cut and pasted the mock-ups for *Balloons for Moonless Nights*. Doyle Moore got his class in Indiana to make silk screens of these, to my color specifications, size, etc. And he produced a very handsome boxed set of them. This was my almost final foray into Concrete poetry: three assemblies of one-foot squares, my favorite being a three-by-three foot maze of moonlight—gloss and matte black, silver, dim platinum, pure moonlight and shadow. I don't know now who bought complete sets, but I made rather a lot of money on them. That year I visited Glen Todd and Dave Haselwood in San Francisco, and I fell in love with the city. It wasn't just that this was only a year down the road from "the Summer of Love," though that spiked the brew. The city was full of energies—like New York earlier—creative artists of all kinds at work to make it new. I felt I'd finally made it to the Emerald City, and indeed I wrote all of *ARK* there.

II

Yes, I fell in love with San Francisco, the climate, the varied neighborhoods, the newly painted Victorians flaunting subtle colors, the ease of getting around, the different kinds of people all living in harmony. All in all S.F. is the most civilized city in America. I was privileged to live there a quarter of a century, from the golden years where all was possible, all permitted, to the grim AIDS years which tested moral stamina. The ten or so years I visited friends wasting away is indelible in memory as those wastrel muscled nights we spent in bars (smoky) and beds (mostly lucky).

Since the goldrush the city has always been easy on deviant lifestyles. Famous for its drag shows, mostly seen by tourists; for San Franciscans there was the glorious Charles Pierce. His routines still go through my mind: "Dial A Deviant" and his triumphant Bette Davis shooting her fur stole, then (pause) "Get up!," but his signature was appearing on a swing while singing to Jeanette MacDonald's "San Francisco," all in a glitter of sequined tulle. That always brought down the house. There was a fine bal-

let, opera, symphony, theater. There were interesting friends to meet again, Rexroth and Duncan, and new ones to make, Thom Gunn, for instance. Thom and I could talk (but not in bars), and I drove Robert Duncan once a month over the bridge to Berkeley to shop and have lunch. I've heard the cowed say that Dunc was only a monologist, but we talked endlessly, brilliantly. This was the first poet who treated me as a peer. Smoking was banned in his and Jess's home, except in the garden, but Robert didn't blink at my smoking in the car with the window down a slash. We shared many a new recognition, past and present, in my vintage VW bug.

During my first years in San Francisco, I wrote my translation of the notes left by Le Facteur Cheval and Ramond Isidore, making their notes into poems in English as I had done earlier with Satie. Next, after Jonathan had written short poems for every movement of Mahler's symphonies (perhaps his best work), I decided to do his "Songs of the Earth." This finally turned out to be a series of Concrete poems—not translations but small squares in the spirit of the work—surely the most lyric work in all of Concrete poetry. Glen Todd set this at Dave Haselwood's Auerhahn Press, now taken over by Andrew Hoyem as Arion Press. It was one of the most perfect collaborative experiences I've ever had with a printer. Handset type, which can achieve effects now unknown with computer-generated stuff, is mostly a lost art. *Songs of the Earth* was to be published by Hoyem, without consulting me, in a tight, hard binding with a cover, like wallpaper, of pastel balloons reminiscent of the nursery and completely opposed to the openings of my text. We quarreled over this unfortunately, as we had been friends from my first days visiting San Francisco.

Songs of the Earth was my requiem for a now lost movement of my youth. Ian Finlay and I were the only two to come through into a wider realm using the essential visual tools of Concrete poetry. I admire him immensely and feel there is a connection of sorts with his gardens and park works and the architecture of *ARK*. We don't correspond much anymore, but my heart is with him always.

The next work I completed was *Eyes and Objects* in which I tried to make short lyrics with the immediate *effect* of a concretion. This was published by Jonathan Williams in a lovely edition, marred perhaps only by Doyle Moore's use of blue for italics, since the type he chose did not have an italic. It was published in 1975, and is one of my favorite works.

The next book was begun while I was teaching at the University of Washington. A student brought a recording of Lucas Foss, with a piece using Handel in which Foss strips away a lot of the notes and comes up with something he could not have composed any other way: "I composed the holes," he says. I immediately went out and bought an old edition of *Paradise Lost* and began to omit words so I had a text emerging that was completely other than Milton telling the old, old story. I remembered Blake rewriting him, and his etchings. And on each page I attempted a kind of etching away of text to make a visual effect. This is perhaps my most loved work, for people open it expecting a deconstruction and find an arching continuity, which finds the story of Orpheus and Euridice unexpected in the biblical story. I titled it *RADI OS* to show from the first the method of construction by extracting letters from Milton's title. Strangely, it also reads aloud very well, though it becomes too long to read to an audience.

I found DDD, the apotheosis of the South of Market biker crowd, single, just moved to the city from Seattle. I learned everything about this niche of gay life, and was to several years later open a notorious leather bar called The No Name. To be specific, I inherited it from KD, who had a motorcycle accident, and I turned it into a bar infamous enough to attract tourists from Europe and New York. Within a year I had to maintain a line at the door. I believe—and Thom Gunn would concur—The No Name, encouraging fantasy, was the farthest-out bar ever. We were the last to have a jukebox, which made music more democratic than the tapes of today, as favorites were truly popular for a time, until the focus shifted. I established a billboard where like-minded could meet, and the intervals between 45's were fine for people to move about in search for a partner. Earlier, a group of us had started a bike club called the Rainbow Motorcycle Club, and I used these members as a family for staffing. We gave notorious parties. I remember we gave a Bacchanalia, à la Petronius. I had posters made so there was always something louche to talk about. I fostered the idea that every night we give a party, and encouraged a sense of humor

not ordinarily associated in South of Market bars.

At the apex of our success, the owner sold the bar, and for several years it coasted on The No Name's reputation, then grimly drifted into just another dark hole. I then unwisely went to work for this same owner, creating a restaurant, a classy Brasserie before South of Market got jammed with upscale restaurants. I opened it wearing a tux, with a cabaret act, and it was a sudden success. However he (the owner) turned into a painwracked she before my very eyes. She got to hanging around, with two Cuban transsexuals we called "the Cuban Heels," and the atmosphere kind of curdled as they brought in coke-sniffers, etc. So I got out, along with half the staff, and started to write *The American Table*—a "diet of the tribe," to paraphrase Pound. It won a "tastemaker award" and was reviewed in glowing terms, and I was invited to a cookbook conference in Philadelphia, with luminaries like Craig Claiborne. I thought I was on the way to being the next James Beard. And it was a fine way to make a living: creative, without getting in the way of poetry.

Unfortunately Simon and Schuster took me on. First, they disapproved of my title "When the Cupboard Is Bare," so it came out as *Simple Fare,* with no suggestion it was for the cook on a thin budget. It got fine reviews from M. F. K. Fisher, Marian Cunningham, and Leo Lehrman, but of course didn't reach its audience. Then they didn't care much about my *Company Fare* on how to entertain without a lot of fuss, and they didn't send it out for reviews or get it in chain bookshops, so I got a "box office poison" reputation unfairly, as it is a wonderful and useful book. I wrote then a book of American desserts, titled "Floating Island and Hummingbird Cake," which no publisher would touch, and finally my best cookbook, for single cooks, which has the potential of interest for the unmarried, the divorced, and the widowed, and is certainly a most useful book. But New York disagreed; they said though it was beautifully written "Singles don't cook, they eat out," ignoring, as usual, that there is a whole country of singles out there who don't have a cheap little Chinese restaurant around the corner and are tired of awful little microwave offerings. So I have two fine but unpublished cookbooks on hand. If I had lived in New York "net-working," as they say, it probably would have been different. But even that might not have helped in a New York that becomes, in the cookbook world, sillier and more expensive every year.

During the years I made a living writing cookbooks, I didn't actively pursue a full-time teaching job for I found my creativity went into that, rather than into my own poetry though I was asked to hold a semester's residency at both Stanford and U.C. Berkeley.

To begin writing *ARK,* I started with Pound's gleaning from the Greeks that poetry was composed of Logopoeia, Phanopoeia, and Melopoeia, which gave me a trinity of The Eye, The Ear, and The Mind, and determined the ultimate form of three books of thirty-three sections each. So these three form cornerstones for a threefold structure. I then wrote the whole thing in sequence, except for the Windmill, which I pushed ahead to become, fittingly, the end of The Spires. I didn't know until much later that *ARK* was to become a spaceship and its end line would be "count down for liftoff," though there were hints along the way.

The first section, The Foundations, begins at sunrise, and ends at noon, which suggests the whole would be a single day. The next, with lightning at its core, is epiphany. I used the titles of these as "Beam," which includes the double meaning of the beam of light and the beam as a structural element. Beam 3 begins what will eventually become a mandala. Beam 5, The Voices, is about perception, and ends with Euridice dancing like Pavlova. Beams 6 and 32 were written after the first capsule we sent into space, with Bach and the Beatles given equal meaning. They are modeled, obviously, after Christopher Smart. Beam 8 was written with Charles Ives in mind. It seems to come at the world from every angle, almost at once. Though it resembles in technique *The Different Musics,* it goes suddenly faster. Looking back, it seems to me almost too fast, though we have all become accustomed to flash cutting with MTV, etc. The dancing of Fred Astaire has been an influence here, and later on I will do a tap-dance of birdsongs. Beam 9 is a descent of our Mars landing; Beam 10, the core.

Beam 11 is an experimental flight in a spaceship. Beam 13 is probably the structure of the universe. In the middle of The Foundations, I plunked down a quote from Thoreau's notebooks as a middle cornerstone. From him I learned how, from stating some observations, it

is possible to have the unconscious click in. Beam 16 is about the most swift of them all, and is, I suppose, about becoming a poet. Beam 17 is dedicated to Robert Duncan as mentor. It takes ordinary short paragraphs to tell the story: Euridice as slip-knot muse. Smart, Blake, and Duncan himself were influences here. A Memorable Fancy continues the idea that Angels are made of light and we do not see them because they go at the speed of light. My palm print in Beam 18 is an echo of Cocteau's *Orphée,* in which Orpheus enters the underworld by way of dipping his hand into a door or mirror of mercury. In 19, I plant a refracting mirrored ball, reflecting the rainbow cosmos. Beam 20 announces itself a labyrinth: the path to Euridice.

Beam 21 begins with the beginning of *RADI OS,* and continues with his descent into the underworld, thence to the use of the Psalms as a text. Palms announces the method, as well as using the entry by palm once more. My rules were that I had to take the psalms sequentially, with at least a word from each. It is one of my poems readers invariably like, though it is too long for a poetry reading. I didn't of course know where this would take me, but I trusted my intellect, eye, and ear to lead, and indeed it took the form of my myth. Toward the end, it compacts into six-line stanzas, like snowflakes, and ends finally with an open ten-line stanza to imitate the ten strings of Orpheus's lyre.

Beam 24 is a bouquet to the earth, and 25 my response to Charles Ives. Beam 26, continuing with 27, begins with the cell dividing (Prosper O cell!) and it continues to an imagined space-landing from, I believe, Burroughs (Edgar Rice, not William!). Beam 28 goes into the letters of the alphabet to see if they themselves can yield meaning—even an oracular one. It ends with the description of James Hampton's *Throne of the Third Heaven of the Nations,* from a newspaper article. Hampton was another naive builder whom I had not known about before I began *ARK,* but fit snugly in here. He was a black anitor who collected foil and anything that glittered to construct his vision in an empty garage in Washington, D.C. Apparently entry into this, after his death, was almost like discovering King Tut's tomb. Beam 29 is a kind of whirling pivot, rather like the DNA double helix.

Beam 30 plants a garden in the center of the work, and is dedicated to Patricia Anderson dying, it turned out, from cancer. This determined the end which radiates light down into the cells to heal. The end takes a passage from Newton's investigation into the nature of light. It probably is as close as I can get to creating an Arden. The Mind is 31, and 32 is another Musics. Still radioing out to space what we are, and were, and might be. The end turns the actual more slowly, a kind phoenix nesting prairie. These are The Foundations.

The Spires, dedicated to Jonathan Williams, begins with Emily aspiring, and Melville stating the structure. I had a vision of a tall, tall spine to start off, and had collected a harvest of words and phrases to build with, and it started to just tumble out of me. After the first page I learned that Zukofsky had died, and it turned into an elegy, a proper pyre on the prairie of existence. It is also a poem that suits my voice and gesture, so I always read it in public. 35 is a tour of construction so far, and 36 tells how angels may become human, as well as how it feels "ascending." ARK 37 is a quilt made from both dark and bright bird songs culled from Roger Tory Peterson's *Birds of the Eastern United States*. 38, to answer Prospero, is Ariel's songs. I had a commission to record something, so I took recordings of western birds and with the help of a technician recorded snippets I thought I might use and over six weeks or so, we completed six songs. The afternoon we finished The Emptying of Hell, I emerged to hear of the Jonestown massacre—synchronicity indeed. ARK 39 was dedicated to my patron during the difficult years when six hundred dollars a month really meant something. It was inspired by an equestrian statue on San Francisco's Market Street—Don Anderson, flag in hand, horse arear in greeny bronze. He lives in Roswell, New Mexico, where he has constructed an amazing house with built up hills, a pool with a fountain, strutting peacocks, a sculpted folly with a furnished banqueting hall inside, and a spiral stair to the turret. It has the most ample stanzas in all of *ARK*. 40 is a herm. In Lot's pillars I do not always know I got there from here, but they are all modeled by the three note melody of "Taps." Inching by spare threes, you rise, to find the prospect "a statable estate."

The Rod of Aaron, blooming at the top, is one of my favorites for reading out loud. The Spire of Limbs is the return from a space probe; it ends with a sparrow I buried as a child, growth from a matchbox.

All the fountains are a jeu d'esprit in full plash of ideas. Next, from my hometown, I turn it into a wasteland, haunted by a volcano quoted from Doughty, spraying its ash (Ashland). It ends, however, with an eruption created by reading Henry James's piece on Niagara Falls back to front, so it goes up in the air to cool off the desolation (the Majesnehry being an anagram of Henry James). Masthead was written with an eye to the prairie as a Sea of Grass, with the covered wagons called prairie schooners. ARK 50 gives, I suppose, Adam another chance. The Pencil Spire was inspired by Jess's huge pencil drawing of Narkissos, incredibly detailed—a labor of years. If he ever decides to paint it, it could take to the end of his life. Those who have been permitted to view it have been astonished at its intricacy. Starspire, dedicated to Bucky Fuller, begins with a quote from Henry James and proceeds to lay rungs up. Like with Fuller, everything seems to *fit*. The Jugular Spire is also Juggler. ARK 55 ia a building block Spire. My Balachine Spire is my tribute, after years of seeing his illuminating ballets. I took notes from several books, including his, to get the lingo right. It could, perhaps, actually be danced by a ballerina, to Scarlatti.

The Gaia Spire is a hymn to the earth and all its diversity, wrapped its mantle of animals and light. ARK 58 is what it says it is, and is kind of a joke, and 59 is also self-evident. The Fireworks came after watching with friends from the top of a Market Street apartment building—and for once they were not fogged in. I attempted this by scintillant words and quick cutting. I thought of the speed and flickering lights of Stan Brackhage's films, and it is dedicated to the composer Bill Hibbard who was so impressed by my line "in ecstasy of palimpsest" that he began writing a piano piece with that title—left unfinished at his death from AIDS. ARK 63 is an attempt at another space launch. 64 is, of course the rainbow bare. The Windmill on the horizon, a proper Kansas icon. 66, dedicated to Pound, is meant to be, since it is just dusk, the still-illumined mountain tops. It is the highest Spire.

The Ramparts are arches illuminating, through the changes of the night, all that went before. I found my inspiration upon finally visiting Simon Rodia's Watts Towers. I spent quite a few visits in L.A. trying to convince someone to take me there, but every one put their hands up in horror of visiting Watts—the scene of

At Men-an-tol Stone, Cornwall, England, 1965

the famous riots. But I finally found a couple of friends who didn't mind. I knew from photographs the major towers and some of the mosaic work, but I was not prepared for the majesty of the actual. I had several hours to simply look, look, look. The walls surrounding the spires were a bricolage of broken tiles, colored glass and mirror, broken crockery set in a mosaic arch after arch, an intricate trash in patterns like a Persian carpet. L.A. once tried to demolish it, and left not a dent. A committee mostly of artists requested they give it landmark status. It will probably be among the rubble at the last trump.

My arches were formed the same way: bits and pieces of life, words and phrases picked up along the way. They are printed as they came, night after night. The first lines present a theme and I try to keep up the tempi and meaning. Some of these take a text for inspiration, like Van Gogh's letters, or Thoreau's notebooks, for the possibility of finding another range of vocabulary and experience. One begins with a waking dream: "Riddle iota sublime," which later swept up most of America the Beautiful: I am patriotic, unlike some poets, for the democracy has awarded me sharpshooter's medal, an education at Columbia, and veteran's complete health coverage for life.

There are also a series of three Arches, collaged from the Protestant hymnals into a kind of Paradisio. People have often imagined paradise boring, but I believe it fascinating as earth itself. ARK 83 gets the animals on board (as 86 and 89 the vegetation and minerals). It is dedicated to Glen Todd after his sending me a list of collective nouns from the eighteenth century. So they go not two by two, but tribe with tribe. There are arches for the painter and collagist Jess. There are also arches for Stan Brackhage who had, he claims, completed a movie about *ARK* which predated much of the imagery I put in the poem! Another instance of synchronicity.

By 99 I had everything on board, and take off—it should have been foreshadowed—on a spaceship. Off to explore the universe with enough of the old blooming buzzy earth to get on with under alien skies.

Now I am in full stride, but New York will not publish either my poetry or cookbooks. Gus Blaisdell had to create a new press just to publish *ARK,* and next year he'll be putting out my *Collected Early and Shorter Poems.* There were a few fine reviews of the book by those who had kept up with the work over the years, but it is only fair to say it is a huge chunk to digest for a reviewer new come to it. The only attention in the East came from Boston University which awarded *ARK* best book of poetry of 1997 (chosen by Robert Creeley, from formidable competition).

Even with my fine record of teaching, I cannot find a job as poet-in-residence. So I've come back to Kansas to live with my father, where I cook for my supper and work on a government program, half time at minimum wage, in a beautiful park, where I bake loaves of bread and cookies. Rather a comedown, but satisfactory all the same. As Pound remarked, "Ovid had it a lot worse." If I've outstripped my early appreciative audience, they'll catch up some fine day, I trust. My cup has always brimmed.

BIBLIOGRAPHY

Poetry:

A Line of Poetry, A Row of Trees, Jargon Press, 1964.

Sports and Divertissements, (contains poems written by Johnson from Eric Satie's notes, in French, to the piano pieces "Sports" and "Divertissements"), Wild Hawthorn Press, 1965.

Assorted Jungles: Rousseau, Auerhahn Press, 1966.

GORSE/GOOSE/ROSE, and Other Poems, Indiana University Fine Arts Department, 1966.

The Book of the Green Man, Norton, 1967.

Valley of the Many-Colored Grasses, Norton, 1969.

Balloons for Moonless Nights (limited edition), Finial Press, 1969.

The Spirit Walks, the Rocks Will Talk, Jargon Press, 1969.

Songs of the Earth, Grabhorn-Hoyem Press, 1970.

Maze/Mane/Wane, Pomegranate Press, 1973.

Eyes and Objects, Jargon Press, 1976.

RADI OS I-IV, Sand Dollar Press, 1977.

ARK: The Foundations, Northpoint Press, 1980.

The American Table, Morrow, 1983.

ARK 50, Dutton, 1984.

Cookbooks:

The Aficionado's Southwestern Cooking, University of New Mexico Press, 1968.

Southwestern Cooking: New and Old, University of New Mexico Press, 1985.

Simple Fare, Simon & Schuster, 1989.

Company Fare, Simon & Schuster, 1991.

Contributor to anthologies:

An Anthology of Concrete Poetry, Something Else Press, 1967.

Young American Poets, Follett, 1968.

Holding Your Eight Hands, Doubleday, 1969.

Under 30, Indiana University Press, 1969.

Inside Outer Space, Doubleday Anchor, 1970.

The Voice That Is Great Within Us: American Poetry of the Twentieth Century, Bantam, 1970.

This Book Is a Movie, Delta, 1971.

Shake the Kaleidoscope, Pocket Books, 1973.

John Martone

1952-

MINOR YEARS: MEDITATIONS AD MATREM

John Martone's father's family's passport photo, with his father on the far left

I

A falling black globe, turning more massive as it falls, but shrinking; shrinking but more massively small, until it is everything, and at that moment everything's gone. Everything. Nothing earlier than this feverish delirium at eighteen months in the downstairs bedroom of the post-war-gray Cape Cod, 67 Cross Street, Williston Park, New York. It was the last house on the dead-end street, and honeysuckle pressed through the neighbor's chain-link fence. Across the way was a red house with salamanders and bull-frogs in galvanized pails and, further on, St. Aidan's.

II

Certainly I did once see the immense Christus on the crucifix over the altar turn his head from right to left. Certainly once weep on my knees at St. Mary's altar, wondering innocent at Lent why she was shrouded in purple head to foot, where the movers would carry her off to? Certainly help the dolphin-voiced blind boy to the communion rail, his mother giving me a Braille embossed thank-you card. The blind boy my first saint. Certainly genuflected outside the church, just passing it, if a door happened to be open. Certainly gave Monsignor a statue of the Sacred Heart and was called to the rectory with a friend to be asked why.

III

The Chasuble

Make-Up and Present Use. *The outer vestment covering nearly all the other vestments from the priest's shoulders to his knees, back and front; hence, with large cross on its back, it becomes the most familiar of all vestments.*
History of Former Use. *Used as a circular cape without sleeves; with a hole in the middle for the head to pass through; this garment completely enveloped the body; a practical outdoor garment of protection against the weather. Called "chasuble" from Latin word "casula" meaning a little house.*

Ah, why wouldn't you get me child-sized vestments, chasuble, maniple, stole, alb and cincture? I celebrated Mass with a sherry glass and Wonder bread in the dormer, dreaming of missionary Maryknollers in Uganda, houses on stilts as in the geography book, everyone in the world speaking Latin. And there were miracles everywhere.

Libera Nos, quaesumus, Domine, ab omnibus malis, praeteritis, praesentibus et futuris: et intercedente beata et gloriosa semper Virgine Dei Genitrice Maria . . .

IV

But my first words Italian, surely. First six months upstairs in grandpa's house, surrounded by uncles. Grandma in red floral-print dress, reading *Il Progresso Italo-Americano,* talking steady as the music of the spheres, not a word of English. And my raven-haired mother never confessing to know a word of Italian, nodding, myself between the two of them. We all understood one another perfectly!

The house smelled of immigrant cooking gas, onions, and garlic. Tomato plants grew to my shoulders with caterpillars I was never afraid of, thicker than fingers. Towering basil, peppers, rows of cabbage, endless rows in the tiny yard like a maze to get lost in. And each fall we pulled the fig tree over to overwinter and buried it under dirt and burlap.

In the cellar a wine rack of 7-UP and White Rock bottles filled with tomato sauce.

And a pocket-sized Berlitz book carried around and studied like a missal.

V

Locus Amoenus: Eisenhower Park

Running. A picnic tablecloth blanket spread on the ground, Mother sitting on this. Dogwood close to the ground, forming a dome, a cave, so like the letter M to crawl into, hide within, spend all of life there since all of life is there. Rolling hills beyond, the endlessness of M and perhaps other picnickers. Raven-haired mother.

VI

Kitchen of the Cross Street house, listening to Phil-Rizzuto-Yankees-Ballantine-Knickerbocker-Rheingold radio on the counter. The window open, letting the song lyrics drift out. Hands and elbows newsprint smudged from *New York Daily News* centerfold bathing beauties lying in Jones Beach sand, soprano harps of rib cages and O's of navels. In the back of the paper, strange entertainments, female impersonators, and *Mondo Cane* scandal, *I Am Curious Yellow,* and coaxing piano music.

We were beginning to experiment: stuffing cardboard toilet paper tubes with Calgon Bouquet talcum powder, detergent, whatever household chemicals we could find to build rockets with on the back porch. Mother, oddly tolerant, watching from the distance of the back door, knowing what we were up to, where we were going.

And making metal radios—#8 copper housewire wound around a cast-off flashlight battery and a jewel-bright glass diode with a red end? a colorful banded resistor? Walking down Cross Street persuading friends, who persuaded friends, we could communicate great distances at night.

And one night I saw the Sacred Heart, a hovering red votive light, in the bedroom's darkness. And a friend did too. The same time. In his room.

Eternal Father, I offer thee the Sacred Heart of Jesus, with all Its love, all Its sufferings, and all Its merits: to expiate all the sins I have committed this day, and during my life. Glory be to the Father, etc.

How often my birthday fell on Easter!

VII

Once at breakfast, a kitchen cabinet fell from the ceiling and my father, propping it up, told mother to get a TWOBYFOUR from the basement. She, not knowing what he meant, came back with something else. He yelled. She stood across the kitchen from us, eating alone, and he sat at the table with two eggs sunny-side up, strips of bacon, toast.

The consequence of their origins—trying to keep all worries and quarrels from us, who therefore never heard of tax time and bill man, surely in the background, and the hulking dark Depression lurking over their memory-shoulders.

VIII

Driving to the mystery of a house going up, harpwork of studs at sixteen inches, and walking through invisible walls room to room in the new development where peach trees grew in rows, pine trees further back: we would live in the secret, eating peaches, climbing oozing pine limbs, adhering to trees. And Grandpa fashioning a nimbus of earth at the foot of a dogwood to keep the water in, and having me hold the hose to it.

The ancient stone house to the south, with its bottomless pond, and further still the sound of trains. Arrowheads in the dirt. Whose rooms? Whose?

IX

Mortified *ad mortem,* wearing a tie to public school and standing up to answer a question! Making up for it wearing an oral-report-suit of Reynold's Wrap armor (studying the Middle Ages) that fell apart before I reached

the front of the room. Good Mr. Guder remembering one-room schooldays with Dad: "The Russians can have the U.N.! You should worry about the water!" He came to school in the summer to help us build a wind tunnel for balsa-wood wings. But best of all we wrote a novel about Colonial Long Island, Nathan Hale's light and improbable witch trials, and he took us outside to meet his writer friend from the east end of the island, who came to see us in his pickup truck camper and with his poodle Charlie. And me innocent for years, lost later in *Cannery Row, Of Mice and Men, The Red Pony,* and *Grapes of Wrath,* writing long summer-vacation novels.

I won a little gold statue of a fireman on a marble base for an essay I wrote about a house burning down.

X

Anatta, Anicca

There's no story any more than there's a self, just a *pater*-patter of images, a spring shower. Don't make any more of it than that. The problem is we put on too many clothes in the rain. Do you remember the first time you were aware *it's spring*? In fifth grade, standing alone at recess, looking up the hill at maples completely out!

All appeared New and Strange at the first, inexpressibly rare, and Delightfull and Beautifull. I was a little Stranger which at my Enterance into the World was Saluted and Surrounded with innumberable Joys. My Knowledg was Divine. I knew by Intuition I saw all in the Peace of Eden; Heaven and Earth did sing my Creators Praises and could not make more Melody to Adam than to me. All time was Eternity, and a Perpetual Sabbath.

—*Thomas Traherne,* Centuries of Meditation

XI

Cold Spring Harbor. The secret place. *Microbe Hunters* and a plastic Gilbert microscope from 60 to 400 power. Life begins as a single cell by the sea. So *Four Years before the Mast* and science and widened worship. After all, in

"My mother is second from the right with all her siblings"

the seventeenth century Cold Spring Harbor was a whaling town. What difference in the imagination climbing a ship's rigging or a ladder of DNA? And they had found the secret of life right there, across the bay in that monastic cluster of brick buildings. But how close would I ever get?

My eyes always a problem, being nearsighted enough to see muscae volitantes any time I looked at the light, much less in a microscope. And how much the dust looked like life! Blue-green algae? Volvox? They'd turn and dart so that I couldn't tell the difference. Did I ever see a real amoeba? I carry the paramecium's body plan from *Adventures with the Microscope* in my head to this day. "Infusoria may be found in every body of stagnant or fresh water. Indeed, you need only take a drop of such water and you will be pretty sure to have captured some form or other." A timeless creature—I'd put it on my coat of arms!

Single-celled. Island. The bedroom with my brother (half my age, a shadow, but he'd become the biologist!) and life alone. Such a strange house—all of us monks—Jeanette off by herself drawing, Diane playing with pink plastic model Showboat, playing the flute, or cheerleading. And what did my father do, engineering Northport power plant turbines and Shore-

ham nuclear pools that glowed blue with light-speed neutrons? What did my mother? The intimacy of six silent people.

Years later I would understand Sinclair Lewis's mental radio at once. Weren't we able to read one another's minds? Wasn't speech in such a setting something like a wedge?

XII

Mildred Caecilia, my mother. Hers the smallest bedroom closet in the house, the most crammed, and through it the crawlway to the attic with its antiquities and Christmas lights. Closet crammed with baby clothes, old fur coat, the wood box of oil paints, drawings from long ago . . .

Long ago when she lived in Elmwood: almost an afterthought beside the greenhouse, the two-room house ten children grew up in, less room for people than plants! Sleeping crosswise to fit four to a bed and going behind the drapery to dress. Happy at Christmas with an orange for a present; sad when brother John died of his heart murmur while skating. And then she was given to the Sisters of Charity convent (which took in children of the poor during the Depression). Dressing the convent statue of the Infant of Prague (closest thing to a doll) in nicer clothes than she ever had. Tremendous thunderstorms in the Pennsylvania mountain forest.

As if this were the family of Therese of Lisieux, one sister, Ellenita, stayed for a life of laundry work and mystic happiness and silence in medieval habit with a great starched bow and collar (handing out holy pictures, scapulars of the Sacred Heart, tiny gold statues of the Blessed Virgin Mary and St. Joseph, phials of holy water when we were allowed to visit, and a rosary with transparent beads that I have today) which turned into old age depression. And one brother took a ten-year vow after his time in the navy, a cop after that, and then despair. Whose was that tiny crucifix locket that opened revealing a single red hair of St. Agnes? And where is it now?

But Mildred left and took up commercial drawing, to leave that in turn behind because the family needed income. She kept it all in the closet: her box of oil paints (palette stained from its last use) and newsprint sketches of late '30's models. She herself, who later turned so reclusive, became a salesgirl at Macy's in the city, then rivetted Grumman Avengers at Bethpage during the war, turning down at least one young blade's offer of wild flight in a fighter!

Years later memories slipped out of friends from then, someone on crutches, a black girl, and Ruby, who surely had red hair and stood six feet tall, broad-shouldered without '40's shoulder pads, and who kept a menagerie of raccoons, snakes, rabbits, squirrels, and was my mother's truest friend, the only one from that time lasting into my childhood—her huge old house somewhere near Huntington Station.

All Mother made—airplanes and art, not to mention us—but years later would never pick up a pencil, leaving it to her daughter Jeanette (four years my junior). Some nights she lay in the dark listening to news radio 88, 9:30 on a Friday night, when there was nothing to hear, or looked out the small octagonal window at the front of the house on Thursday afternoons. Her eyes were not good enough for close work like drawing or painting and her confidence had been shaken by moonwalks and new women. After all, to her sisterly ways, service was all and ambition an ill, poverty a virtue, the mustard seed of respect, and the zero a nimbus. So much to teach my own children:

(like
mother)

study
clouds—

show re
be
kah
how to

look—
pass it

on
(passing
by

—from *Astilbe*

XIII

The Genesis of Radioland

Hallicrafters
Hammarlund
Vibroplex
Instructograph
Collins
Allied
National

I began to inhabit the basement, Radioland, after kitchen nights with my father assembling a Heathkit GR64 shortwave receiver, intoxicated with lead-solder fumes and singed circuit. Of course it didn't work at first—an important lesson there—but Dad had the touch and a suitcase-sized vacuum tube tester and VOM with red and black probes, alligator clips, and army surplus (U.S. Army Signal Corps!) headphones. The 80-meter dipole reached from a pine tree at the back of the lot to one in front, and half-inch thick 75 ohm coax cable, ending in a shiny PL259, ran from the chimney in through the cellar window. This was travelling: alone in the damp dark basement taking in VOA and BBC and Radio Moscow propaganda, Cuba, WWV pulsebeat at 5 megacycles, 10, 15 and so on. Writing off for QSL cards that came in the mail saying "yes, you heard us!" and taping them to the pegboard wall. Coming of age at last: an Official Shortwave Listener!

XIV

And David Weintraub, ah, meeting you in junior high, a year older, with your house in Huntington Station full of Russian airplane transceivers, Hammarlund and Hallicrafters, Lafayette, Blitz bugs, telegraph keys, and 1-kilowatt tubes (not to mention 007-novels and Get Smart impossible anticommunist plottings)—

16. What are the recognized abbreviations for: kilocycles, megacycles, Eastern Standard Time, Greenwich Mean Time, continuous wave, frequence modulation, amplitude modulation?

I learned the code. The jolly old high school physics teacher gave me the test and I was WN2TOM, who sent his signal out nightly and connected with no one but the neighbor's TV. And once, for an instant, G——, someone in England, but just for a second, and what could you say to a stranger but 5-7-7: an intimate "you are here."

But still it was only a lonely boy in the cellar against ABC, NBC, CBS, WOR, WPIX million-dollar movie, and the entire metropolitan area's TV time, and mail poured in from the FCC threatening axes crashing through doors, pirate equipment confiscated, fines and jail for me and guardians if the buzz of my telegraph key didn't stop.

XV

And then came my one failure. Rode to Manhattan (such dirty streets, I thought, they were supposed to be gold) to take the general-class exam in a dingy building, but I choked and couldn't get the 13 wpm at all well enough. So I resigned myself to Technician class WB2TOM, ARRL Official VHF Experimental Station.

21. Draw diagrams of, and identify by name, variable-frequency and crystal-controlled oscillator circuits such as the Hartley, Colpitts, Pierce, etc.

89. What is the formula for finding the resonant frequency of a tuned circuit?

The formula for resonant frequency is $f = 1/2$, square root of LC, where f is the frequency in cycles per second, L is the inductance in henrys, and C is the capacitance in farads.

And I concocted alchemical capacitors with shifting fluid dielectrics (Dear OM: Many thanks for sending your contribution to "Hints & Kinks." We are always glad to receive material for use in this section of the magazine and appreciate your taking the time to write. Your Hint & Kink will be held for possible use in *QST*. We hope to hear from you again. 73, Walter F. Lange, W1YDS), delicate antennas Calder would have loved, but spoke to no one, heard no one except in my mind on my two-meter transceiver with a single ammeter, bouncing imaginary signals off the moon and neighbors' houses, and not even the FCC complained anymore. It was all magic and miracle as vital as Lourdes. I was in my own world, taken with the beauty of diodes and grids and plates of vacuum tubes, the basement's damp with its furnace and water heater and dehumidifier and the small iron door behind which the cinders fell from the fireplace upstairs.

XVI

Even then it was all art, resonance deeper and more thorough than any radio oscillator's. It was all spirit and consort with angels, the glow of vacuum tubes replacing sanctuary lamp and votive candle, the glass diodes instead of holy water phials, the braided wire instead of Franciscan ropes, QSL cards instead of holy pictures, the code instead of Latin, the tapping telegraph key instead of a rosary. And the solitude of prayer.

My Vocation in Life

Pray fervently to make the right choice of the married, single or "religious" life. On it depends the happiness of your own soul and other souls in this life and for all eternity.

Twenty years later, I made my *Ocean Vows:*

the silences in me

To find
the silences in me

adolescent   the boy has strung a wire
between the pine trees
at night he leans to a radio
to cross the ocean

in bed the woman
almost appears beside him
he can almost feel her hand
at the base of his spine

he dreams of drifting in darkness
to the end   he knows
no words can cross this
emptiness   can reach him
he listens

if he ever speaks
he will confess until
we see the earth
blue with its oceans
spinning
like an empty spool

he will have made something beautiful

XVII

Two weeks of summer spent far away—an Adirondack cabin, lake dense with water lilies and islands, near Lake George. Rowing myself out of parental sight and floating tangled in green and overhanging branches. Solo time to fantasy other lives. Girls in the cabin next to ours. Ticonderoga crowds, cannons, and lead musket balls. And what must winter be like up here.

The company ski lodge in Vermont another summer had vast dormitory rooms and stacks of Sears Roebuck mail order catalogues with lingerie sections lingered over in the recesses of that house (where are those ladies now?). Mountainsides to climb in back.

XVIII

But I can hardly tell anymore what I remember from what I imagine. There was a movie, for instance, about a boy who falls asleep in what must have been the American Museum of Natural History in New York and wakes to find himself in primordial time on a boat, of course, ferns and dinosaurs around him, all the dioramas come to life, all the Cambrian, Devonian, Ordovician and Paleolithic ages jumbled

together. Of course, what could be learned from such a jumble had nothing to do with paleontology: this was the landscape of the soul, the black and white TV by which I watched *The Boy with Green Hair.*

XIX

Not that we went places but that the places came inside. I made a world at home.

XX

At the time, amusement parks designed like Buck Rogers Spacelands were all the rage: Spaceships of imponderable concrete painted pastel blue (already flaking away) nestled in sand with stairs to climb inside, portholes to look out of, still to be seen in the silence of Super-8 mm projector gears (I recently did). And even at that time the parts and cameras seemed dated and archaic, not convincing as fantasy at all, already memory.

XXI

Robert K. Toaz Junior High, just this side of the other side of the tracks, on a triangular lot (near the *L-Shaped Room* bar and brothel glimpsed from school bus window) where it all fell apart in accelerated math. Didn't belong there, much as I admired the calculus book in the glass-front bookcase. Word problems which I got lost in like stories, solved but never correctly, a racing train or a ship sinking at so many miles per hour, hardly able to raise my head or look at other problems slick as glass, nowhere to get hold. Pleading for better than a D and told the D was a step up because of all the homework I'd done (if not correctly).

And shameful Spanish in the same room the next period, showing no respect for the awkward first-year black woman who taught and cringing when the blonde-haired girl behind me said "I can't sit here behind him with his DANDRUFF."

Mr. Nickerson, dark-mustachioed choir director, "it's harder now your voice has changed." Everyone's did, but where the Irish tenor went to a rich bass, I went nowhere good and couldn't hear the notes on the page and left my sheet music behind.

One moment of joy on Halloween off Oakwood Avenue, groping in the bushes with a flat-chested red-haired girl whom I've tried to remember the rest of my life.

Cleveland Institute of Electronics (CIES) advertisements in the back of ARRL (American Radio Relay League) magazine: Be a TV repairman, be a refrigeration technician. Study at home (the best of all places I thought) at night (best of all times). Some hope for me yet, though my father was taken aback at these possibilities. What, no college?

XXII

There was a beatnik woman (bobbed black hair) English teacher (everyone said she spent her free time in the chemistry closet with the science teacher). She surely lived in the other-worldly Village, a long commute, and she liked what I wrote about Walter Mitty. That he wasn't just another character, for all his characters, he was real. Did she know I was Walter Mitty lost over there on the right-hand side of the room?

XXIII

There was torque inside, need to turn around before too late (it was almost too late), and I actually asked for parochial school next year, feeling catechism, rules, and uniform could piece me together. The radios started gathering dust, the dipole rusted.

XXIV

Among other things, there befel me a most infinit Desire of a Book from Heaven.

—*Thomas Traherne*, Centuries of Meditation

I looked at the moss under a pine tree, green as the sacred heart had ever been red, but with no thought of the sacred heart. This was life.

The books were best if they were small. Pocket books, no larger than the *St. Joseph's Missal,* or the Anchor *Life of St. Dominic* or St.

Francis. Washington Square Press. O. Henry was best because he was short. It could all be done in a few words. And Tennyson:

Flower in the crannied wall
I pluck you out of crannies.
I hold you here, root and all and all in all
Flower in the crannied wall.
If I could understand you
Root and all and all in all
I would know what God and Man is.

There didn't have to be another word, and such words were as close as you could get to silence.

XXV

No upstate that summer. My father decided to build an addition onto the back of the house, a room to see the woods from, and we spent the summer mixing and pouring concrete first (sixteen shovels of sand, a bucket of cement, and a hoseful of water in the red mixer). Then driving in masonry nails. Then raising the frame of two-by-fours, craftily shimming windows all around and hanging two doors, banging tongues into grooves of siding, carrying rolls of tar paper barebacked onto the roof. A beautiful structure. A beautiful structure to sit in at last and look back to the pine trees out back. To imagine in.

XXVI

Mother would ask what the two of us talked about on our long rides to the lumberyard. The truth, nothing. It was enough to be and be with, lugging eight-foot boards and ninety-pound bags of cement. These were the only times together, silently building radios, plastic B-52s, and now a house.

Only learned years later from his older brother Nick, family historian, that he spent the first eight years of his life with Grandmother in Neapolitan Frigentum while Grandfather carpentered here, sending money back. Came to him on the Count Biancamano, to Ellis Island, dragging the big suitcase, Nick laughed remembering it, trying to be helpful in any way. In the old country once he spilled a big pot of spaghetti, ruined the family's dinner. Always trying

Maternal grandfather in front of the two-room house where ten children grew up

to take on something maybe too big. Himself saying nothing of this time except, "We were *very* poor."

What upheaval, suddenly to be a "guinea," a "wop" in New York learning English, encountering a stern father for the first time, caddying for the well-to-do, grateful for running water. Lonely in Mineola High School Yearbook with the blackest hair of all and wire-rimmed eyeglasses. (Chemistry Club, Prom Committee.) And hardly at home when the war took him off to nightmare Pacific islands, kamikazed troop ship, and best friend dying beside him. What's to be trusted? Who knows what's to come? How could one not be strong? And not say what can't be said . . .

XXVII

Walking to the high school bus stop took me through Steve Engel's yard, site of endless pubertal madness and admiration and love, let's say, for he was all anyone dreamed to be. Wiry enough to be a pole-vaulter and tennis-player, and smooth with girls who fell over each other,

and an easy talker inheriting his father's vaudeville musician hands that could play anything that came their way, and everything did—six-string acoustic and twelve-string and bass, mandolin, violin, banjo, ukelele, and yes even Ravi Shankar sitar, not hard at all for him to tune with its sixteen strings. In my clumsy chubby way I bought a sixteen-dollar Kent guitar (bad as that brand of cigarettes, we joked), which I couldn't even tune, or manage more than barchords on of "Louie Louie" (E-A-B-A-E).

But the chemistry between us had mostly to do with explosives at first. The Engels had a four-foot backyard pool they'd assemble every summer and otherwise store in a small wooden shed. Summers that shed became our lab. Steve's first discovery: pool chlorine mixed with sulfur (of which he'd bought a huge five-pound jar) made a powerful (if unstable) kind of dynamite. So he collected empty CO_2 cartridges from neighborhood air-rides and seltzer makers and filled them with the powder. These could be used almost interchangeably as hand grenades, rocket engines, or bazooka shells. We escaped with limbs intact, though we blew ourselves over once or twice and luckily missed a neighbor mowing his yard when our copper pipe bazooka rocket missed its target. Once, though, Steve burned his hands on an engine that hadn't finished burning and ended up in an emergency room where the resident took advantage of the situation, threatening to call police and innoculate us both against tetanus with a needle two-feet long, it seemed, and a syringe that might've come from a large animal clinic.

This by no means put an end to the experiments. We discovered that styrofoam turned to jelly when mixed with gasoline. One morning we smeared and ignited a goodly bit of this on the wall of a bank as we waited for the bus. Just an experiment, and we rode off to school none the richer through a dissipating cloud of black smoke. We planned to mortar Huntington Harbor. We built multistage rockets and planned to put frogs in orbit.

XXVIII

Of course we knew, somehow, biology was behind such antics. We stood aghast at explicit pictures complete with plastic transparencies in our life science textbook. Ah, poor notorious strict Sister Grace Angela, assigned to teach us human sexuality, saying if we were shy we might write out our questions and leave them anonymously on her desk. How the pile of notes grew, whatever they asked, till her desktop spilled over and crates had to be brought in, but none was ever answered. And poor me, who didn't know the class conspiracy to flunk the unit exam, compelling the good Sister to repeat her lessons. In a class of such exquisite F's I had an A, the only one, but Sister said we had to get on to amphibians.

What an abysm of ignorance that A belied and suspicions that shaking hands could make girls pregnant and that every girl on the bus could read my mind and knew my wet dreams and frantic solo misbehavior, and that was why they wouldn't talk to me.

XXIX

I learned the ritual of confession in second grade but only needed it now: to put it all in a word or two and say it to another and

Mother in New York

be forgiven. To recite Hail Mary ten times in penance (and lose track at eight or nine and scrupulously wind up saying the prayer a hundred times) and leave the church buoyant as never otherwise in life, joyful, eager to be struck down by a speeding truck on 25A.

How beautiful the confessional itself, a redolent pine chest environment dark as the grave and self, the grate between oneself and the priest, between sacred and profane, upon which the martyrs were grilled. So much statuary, stained glass, painted stations of the cross, and a few words repeated until they were real beyond any art.

XXX

At the same time in the cellar playing the same records over and over, self-pitiful Herman's Hermits and Association playing over and over, till even I began to sense something not quite right, since hours passed with no human contact and all this repetition.

And imperceptibly at first the need to follow the right path through the house, counting floor tiles, hands held close to body, not brushing against the wall, yet keeping close to it, and certainly never touching the doorknob or an article of clothing worn the wrong time and not washed since, hair not brushed since I couldn't touch a hairbrush, and sitting just on the corner of the bed, and not pulling my chair in too far at the kitchen table. Mother in tears, and Dad turning off the water after my shower'd run an hour (still soapy, but the pattern ruined, so having to start over). Dishpan hands and soap-discolored forearms smelling of perfume that won't wash away since it's in the soap. And permanent despair, devising suicides, swallowing boxes of No Doze to wake myself out of the nightmare of once more and the right way . . .

XXXI

A textbook case, but all the textbooks wrong, teaching horrid lessons. Freud and Menninger secreted into the house and the illusion of unspeakable repressed Oedipal trauma, ulterior perversions, and torture on the rock of the return of the repressed. Trying to stop until I believed in nothing. Hope dried up with my serotonin.

XXXII

Did the best I could to keep up appearances: took up acting. Always the heavy in the school play—psychopathic Judd Fry in *Oklahoma!* and convincing, I thought—and despair became entertaining, even funny, as I slouched across the stage, 170 pounds in thirty-eight-inch huskies in the dream ballet, "dancing." Later as William Jennings Bryant eating a bologna sandwich and raging in *Inherit the Wind,* choking to death on the names of the Bible's books, and a Southern racist senator in *In White America* foaming at the mouth about Southern womanhood as he tears the white suit jacket from his body. (And secretly in love with Ceci, to whom Cicely Tyson does not compare.) Even in *My Fair Lady,* the villainous Zoltan Kaparthy.

XXXIII

And wrote apocalyptic plays about nuclear war inspired by memories of Bay of Pigs—a more optimistic side of me! During those days (I knew it was serious when Dad left for work telling Mom that if anything happened there were twenty gallons of water in the water heater) our house filled up with pamphlets from Civil Defense:

Facts
About Fallout

Radioactivity is nothing new . . .
The whole world is radioactive.
But normal amounts are not dangerous. It is only when radioactivity is present in highly concentrated amounts, such as those created by atomic and hydrogen bomb explosions that it becomes dangerous.
Don't get discouraged.
Don't get panicky.
Prepare a shelter area in your home.
Stock your shelter with a 7-day supply of food and water.
Americans are hard to scare.
This problem can be solved—as others have been—by American ingenuity and careful preparations.

Editorial

The plot of On the Beach *is based on two assumptions about the nature of radioactive fallout. Both assumptions are false. And they lead directly to the false assumption implicit in the blond girl's question—that anything, including surrender to Communism, is better than nuclear war.*

I put together what we would need in the basement. Lots of insulation, buckets for human waste, a shovel, and just enough room for the four of us to spend two weeks under the ping-pong table.

It was an image of eternal life, the family in a kind of womb of itself, out of time, a *Buried World.*

XXXIV

What an irony that the high school was Holy Family, brand new and immaculate cinder-block institution with a convent on the fourth floor. Since 1970 was to be the first graduating class, the six hundred of us had the building to ourselves at first, spoiled oldest children in tumultuous times. For although the school was secluded under huge oaks on Wolf Hill Road, books and words from the outer world got in. *Go Tell It on the Mountain* and *The Fire Next Time* and *Soul on Ice* and Jonathan Kozol's holy *Death at an Early Age.* What the hell were those nuns teaching us, my father steamed, but let me stay. And principal Father Rowan quietly prompted and let things stir, himself active for Catholic conscientious objectors (Oh oxymoron!) to Vietnam. In eighth grade I'd wanted Goldwater! And I'd grown up knowing Communism was evil and persecuted the church, but how could you love your neighbor (much less enemy) and bomb cities, burn children, and watch monks of all people burn? There were "debates":

First Affirmative Constructive

Because John and I believe that American foreign policy should keep pace with the times, we hold it "Resolved: that Congress should prohibit unilateral U.S. military intervention in foreign countries." In order to make for a clear understanding of the proposition in the context of the affirmative case, the affirmative team defines "Congress" as the legislative body of the United States, "prohibit" as to prevent by constitutional means, and "unilateral military intervention in foreign countries" as the active involvement of preponderant . . .

I was always surprised that no one agreed, that Frank Antonucci with his loudly boasted vocation to the priesthood didn't want to hear of "faggots" and cowards. How strange it was to see lines drawn between the majority supporting the war and ostracising those who didn't, nuns and five or so foolish utopians.

With one of whom I fell in love for good reason, for Sister Regina, though older and taller, was full of poetry and encouragement as no one else had been and had me reading Merton's *Original Child Bomb* and Dag Hammarskjöld's *Markings* and e. e. cummings and even Kahlil Gibran and Ferlinghetti's *Coney Island of the Mind.* She had the most magnificent bold handwriting and ignited everyone, it seems, especially the sad and sleepy souls overlooked or down on themselves or possessed of hidden talents. Quite literally charismatic, God-intoxicated, and mystic. Too much for the convent, anyway— her energy drawing scornful when not jealous looks and some ill will—and so she left at the end of the year.

She gave me *A Child's Christmas in Wales,* and Fern Hill committed to memory "young and easy under the apple boughs." I checked out his notebooks from the Huntington Public Library and pored over them, crossing out words

on my own pages (backs of forgotten telegraph notepads).

And David Ignatow's "You who are living / rescue the dead." And Allen Kaprow's happenings, autistic performers and sanctums of private religion. Paul Carroll's *Young American Poets,* a book to dream by with scriptures of Jon Anderson, Vito Acconci, Kostelanetz's "Tribute to Henry Ford," and Wakoski's gun pointed at you. And even then Ian's sundials were a compass to me.

I was also in love with a red-haired actress who played in *Our Town,* encountering her as she made her way down a slushy Main Street in the company of two men—she was wearing Frye boots—and I said I liked her . . . in the play. And she smiled thank you, and the men laughed it over, as the three went their way, and where is she now?

XXXV

The Chicago convention on our big TV, the whole world watching, and Daley's cops'

The greenhouse

clubs coming down on skinny backs and legs. Too much even for my father (who wanted to scatter thumbtacks in the street for barefoot hippies in Cambridge, Massachusetts). Both of us sitting in our room, silent with history.

A long bureaucratic counter. A line of us with right hands raised. Nixon on the far wall, glass visibly covering his face. I would be shame-faced 2-S (burning it at Father Charlie Gonzales's Mass, but never arrested), then 1-H, then I-A with number 159, and so through it, my one sin to have slipped by, luckier than Chesty Puller's son who legless and armless wrote his truth of the time slowly coming to light and took his own life. Luckier than Bao Ninh, too. All my studies thereafter of Japanese poetry and Mustard Garden Tao and Buddha, of Thich Nhat Hanh and Suzuki, Nyanaponika and Takuboku root in this shame at taking life. Two million plus fifty-seven thousand. Such numbers never go away: when faced with such shame, my generation turned from fantasies of gentle community to cynical credit card glut in the free marketed world.

XXXVI

And what of my other teacher-friend Charlie, new drama director with more panache than Regina or any diva, glad to do a dance step and confess what he really wanted was to do costumes for the opera! Ah the football and lacrosse coaches (ex-marines both) didn't know what to make of him (though it was nothing nice), convinced he was leading us off like the Pied Piper to homosexual perdition. But I never took this seriously or saw that it mattered. Yes, he fraternized, thank God: I drove his MG and had nightlong conversations, but he opened secret doors to Shakespeare and Whitman—

On Montauk Point

I stand as on some mighty eagle's beak,
Eastward the sea absorbing, nothing but
sea and sky . . .

And one day on the steep road home from school he asked where my melancholy came from (for everyone saw the doom of my obsessions and compulsions, but how could I confess, knowing at that point only my sickness).

XXXVII

J.S., we were so much alike, but I never knew half your despair. That huge old house that burned to the ground, the humiliating school PA announcement asking for clothes. You had such a voice, singing with Steve "A Bridge over Troubled Waters," but the comparisons to Mama Cass nothing you liked, nor just being everyone's friend and chauffeur, sad in the black 1950 Chevy with three on the column which everyone learned to drive, and marijuana in the back seat. Your blue prom gown and sad expression, and when I put my arm around you as we sat on the beach at midnight, you said, "You don't have to do that, I don't want your pity." And you disappeared into the void of Chicago drive-through banks.

O innocence, innocence, innocence.

XXXVIII

The nameless history teacher: maybe the most honest, hiding his draft-dodging brother in the closet when the FBI stopped by with questions, and all of us in terror—no honest living left in our "history," which he didn't dare teach, but digging clams in Northport bay with long wooden rakes, dreaming of anonymity in lonely rooms and greeting burned-out speed freak Ginger Baker on Kerouac's street.

XXXIX

One night I sat in our white '66 Corvair outside a music-blaring tavern thinking "This is the end of an empire," reflecting on presumptious Caracalla, his Roman baths and murder of an entire generation of Alexandrians, and I wonder now, was I about to *enter* or *leave* the tavern and career my teenaged way home? The empire careened, too, then as now, drugged with privileged evasion, and the whole earth felt the "control" room's rock-and-roll.

XL

That summer I lasted two weeks working with migrants on, what else in the suburbs, a sod farm. Rising at 4:45 and then in the fields, vast lawns-to-be, folding sheets of sod and stacking them on pallets. The Mexican beside me my age, never been to school, riding busses up and down both coasts, another sort of education. (And with all my high school "Spanish," I was the one who couldn't talk.) The foreman boasting of his dozen wives and twenty children—did I want to see? And because I couldn't keep up (though the only one making two dollars an hour "because you're white"), the bosses sent me to Wading River to move sprinkler pipes up and down a field all day. By noon collapsing under a water hose. And that afternoon knowing I didn't have the wrists or arms, despite bench-pressing two hundred in the high school gym, to do a day's work. And couldn't go back, not even for back pay.

XLI

But I went on to the power plant, LILCO's Northport generating station with its two units on line and a third going up. The personnel manager's one demand: "Cut your hair, college boy." And that's what we were—college boys (or soon to be) among those who worked for a living and had no escape. The first day encircled in the welding shop, "Do they like pussy? Boy, do you like pussy? Maybe the boy likes boys?" And the circle getting smaller, but in the end sent off to scrub urinals and mop floors and stand over cesspools reaming out clogged lines till day's end, spattered with shit.

The best job was digging. When the boilers went down, mountains of rock hard ash had to be shoveled into fifty-five-gallon drums. A front-loader could do this in an hour, but we were make-work cases and unreal. And once Ed Abey, foreman who went back forty years with my father, saw me covered with the stuff and said, "Afraid to get your hands dirty?" just New York working-class put-down, but it went right through me—did he know?

And wearing asbestos suits inside the boilers to scrape them down, balancing on sixteen-inch-wide planks, air hoses leading outside. Or in rubber suits in eight-inch crawlspace under the condensers, scraping mussels, blue crabs, horseshoe crabs and whatever else gathered in the cold salt-wet darkness.

I never questioned the scorn we were held in, the brick dropped on "Red's" hard hat with its peace sign on top, or how another John

was taken to the fan room which pumped millions of cubic feet of air per minute into the boilers, and stripped, and had his hands and feet bound, and was slathered with paint and left for a workday in the screaming blast of air. He had tried to buddy up, get along with full-timers. . . .

But the place had everything to do with American power and politics, a living allegory, with its offices we never got to see and immense 350-pound chief engineer and his secretary, the much lauded only pussy in the plant. There was the space age turbine floor and control room with "operators" who could read and write and never got dirty. And there was the rest of the plant, like Ellison's *Invisible Man's* paint factory with two-hundred-feet high boilers and pump rooms, tank farms, and antipollution scrubbers. My first experience with real drugs on a catwalk at 160 feet, spraying trichlorotrifluoromethane cleaning fluid onto dirty boilerplate and reeling happy. "Permanent HIGH school," Red said, given the antics of those forty-year-olds their total timecard.

XLII

Tragic times with Chris. Most talented of all, able to simulate Dickens's Pip or Stoppard's Rosenkrantz or recite from memory reams of Shakespeare. We decided Friday afternoon to go camping that night at Montauk, a three-hour drive almost, and though we had no equipment, off we went, turned away at the gates at 9:30 because we had no tent. Finally we stopped at a town park somewhere east, exhausted, and unrolled our sleeping bags. Chris, foolishly I thought, insisted on his joint as I slipped off, awakening at dawn's early light to a policeman walking our way, frisking us, then going through the Corvair, miraculously finding nothing, telling us to leave and never come back.

And that night a second miracle, lost as ever, finding a room in a rambling old house/hippy-bordello (we didn't know), though the manager said he wouldn't put on new sheets for our five dollars. Girls in long nightgowns asked if we had stuff; and though I was naively eager in so many ways, Chris was suddenly stingy with dope. So I drifted off again, only to be awakened an hour later by the "Whack, whack" of Chris swinging his bloody shirt, killing mosquitoes that filled the room.

And then awake an hour later to desperate cries of "We're busted!" as motorcycles blasted into the driveway, headlights flooding the room. But this was but a local biker gang, not the police, and we cowered the rest of the night and made our escape.

XLIII

Twenty-five years later, I run down 25A through Cold Spring Harbor, passing signs that plead for endangered sea turtles sometimes washed up. My senses abide on a long lost island. The tiny brick library's gone, and Oscar's bookstore is gone, and the air is thick with car fumes.

EPILOGUE

I

First Street

Six years married to you, Marjorie, in our mid-thirties, *nell mezzo del cammin* in our first house in Thornton Wilder's *Our Town.* An 1890's bungalow with white paint peeling and a gravel drive.

And first thing after hanging a mezzuzah was to plant a Japanese maple in the ten-foot-square front yard to look at while working, a memory of New York. And how much work any house needs, the back door rotted from winter storms torn out and the floor rebuilt, and a brand new peachtree door (ah, like Huntington peaches!) and the toilet floor too, a bumper jack underneath holding up the whole works, and a few months later the attic catching fire, old knob-and-tube wires no good. And we settled there, a block from the park, two-year-old messiah Rebekah showing us how.

So much time with her in our laps, reading and rocking, twenty-thirty books an afternoon, simple books naming things—circle, square, *some things go together.*

And Vivaldi, Telemann, Hayden, Mozart, when not the sons of Cage, and whale song always over our shoulders.

And Rebekah's delight in Fisher-Price Little People, lining up crowds in the plastic city, blonde-haired mother in blue, and green daddy.

And such angelic Henry Miller watercolors we made, spattering paint, or our hands in it, crumpling pages and flattening them out. And how much swinging, delightful corkscrew twisting-up the chains and flying how many ways at once, over the top of the swingset, above the houses like *The Red Balloon.*

How mystic you were, Rebekah, aloof from others your age, not killing insects! And persevering so, hours with your little people, or on the footbridge in Morton Park all day, happy with odd things, spinning, in your own world even though we were beside you, autonomous. So different from born-in-the-blizzard Eva yelling "Here I am" at birth and crawling at four months, high-jumping out of the crib.

But, ah, both of you together:

washing rebekah and eva's hair

```
        more
        than
        one       streams
        to
        any
        one       strands
                              how
                  spines      close
                              a
  late                        part
  May
  white
  tub

  they
  close
  their
  eyes
  &
  laugh

                          —from primer
```

II

I found Larry Eigner's *Selected Poems* by chance in a city I visited only once, and I wrote him and he wrote back some months later. I wanted to frame the page, cry it from the rooftops so in love was I with the current of his words, clear as the four streams of Eden. Life pure and simple: what unfolds before the eyes, music George Herbert would've loved, not to mention Spinoza with his GOD IS ALL AROUND, GOD IS EVERYTHING. Larry lived this every second of his trembling life. And finding my way in Berkeley, world of flowers, up from BART, then right, past the Y, to 2338 McGee Avenue with its ramp and poems everywhere, outside (exposed to the weather—thank God for so little rain!) and in, the house overflowing! Poems instead of furniture! And in the kitchen, alone with him, how long it would take to eat a meal! Eggs, maybe, or oatmeal . . .

III

And Cid Corman's faith:

> In the hills
> for a few days—
> couldn't write
>
>
> Gone further found
> less—maybe
> you know the place

And ten plus years of weekly letters back and forth. A whole LIFE in those letters, insistent utter clarity—*POETRY IS LIFE,* he wrote, and—*My poems ARE my life and my life is, if anything, poetry. So—my commitment is, of necessity, beyond like/dislike, to life.*

And—

The first thing of the Noh I was shown after seeing an empty stage/theatre—which in itself knocked me out (for it was precisely the theatre I had proposed to myself)—was a Noh mask, the classic female mask, the most common of them all. And the old man (dead now), beard-sensei they called him, with a long white flowing Chinese-style beard, quietly showed me how the seemingly flat face altered incredibly from the light-angles as it was tilted slightly this way and that. So that in performance the same mask, transfigured by words, voicing, tilt, can seem to be laughing at one moment and weeping the next, etc. They often said the mask was the play. So, it isn't a matter of robbery, usurption, maya, etc., but of good use, as Charles Olson also knew (though knowing isn't doing).

And—

Family, wherever it is (feels), warrants the deepest respect—And when I complained about faulty plumbing at our First Street house, he wrote

The family: John Martone and Marjorie with their daughters (from left) Eva and Rebekah

back: . . . *without flush toiletry for nearly 25 years here. We have 2nd hand hot water heater for the sink . . .* My closest neighbor.

And in these letters and the friends that sprang from them the *Origin* of *t-l.*

And what joy to meet Cid in the mountains one summer, at home, so far away from home for both of us.

IV

Rebekah had no friends and could not play with Eva and more and more had to have things just so and no loud noises, no eye contact, no spontaneous greetings, no eye-hand coordination either, or drawings that looked like people or the world, for all her joy or ability to bounce a ball one hundred times. A nightmare day of kindergarten.

V

Followed by a nightmare round of refrigerator doctors alleging in 1990 we did not discipline this child enough and needed "to put the screws to her" (no wonder they worked in a child *dis*ability clinic in THE NATION'S SEVENTH LARGEST GROUP PRACTICE. But by chance a speech-language pathologist saw her and knew at once.

VI

Reading Lao Tzu's *Tao Te Ching* again and again—it was my Bible on First Street, especially "know the male but keep to the role of the female / and be a ravine to the empire," and "Thirty spokes / share one hub / Adapt the nothing therein to the purpose at hand and you will have use of the cart. Knead clay in order to make a vessel. Adapt the nothing therein to the purpose at hand and you will have use of the vessel. Cut out doors and windows in order to make a room. Adapt the nothing therein to the purpose at hand, and you will have use of the room." And so, in *primer:*

> *home, life, the tao*
>
> long
> weed
> yard
> creeper'd
> steps
> hinge
> rusts
> shade
> soon
> in
> as
> out

Hand in hand with this came Simon Cutts, his coracle. Little poems of his found in a Washington bookshop that seemed written in eternity.

Later I would hear in Robert Lax the yin-yang of silence and syllable of the shingyo.

> ma
> ka
> na
> ha
> ra
> mit
> ta
>
> and the ocean's rhythms of pulse and
> breath at last inevitable in my own.

VII

The epilogue makes the beginning possible—the children's childhood recovers another.

SELECTED BIBLIOGRAPHY

Poetry:

The Transparent Dancer, The Blue Guitar, 1979.

Ocean Vows, Copper Beech, 1983.

The Buried World, archived at Shadows Project Museum, Milan, 1983.

consequences, Northern Lights, 1990.

trousseau, Runaway Spoon Press, 1991.

far human character, Runaway Spoon Press, 1991.

primer, Runaway Spoon Press, 1994.

dwelling, Irving St., 1996.

wild flower book, Longhouse, 1997.

birthplace, Bull Thistle Press, 1997.

an array, Pentagram, 1997.

Astilbe, Backwoods Broadsides Chaplet Series, 1998.

no roof, Longhouse, 1998.

heartwood, Bull Thistle Press, 1998.

Editor:

tel-let, numbers 1-65, 1988— (ongoing).

Shadow Play 5 (Larry Eigner Issue), (Grande Isle, Vermont), 1997.

Contributor to Anthologies:

The Last Decade: III International Biennial of Visual/ Alternative Poetry, Mexico, San Diego State University (Calexico), 1989.

Bob Arnold, editor, *50 Numbers That Just Happen,* Longhouse (Brattleboro), 1994.

Rupert Loydell & David Miller, edtors, *A Curious Architecture,* Stride (Devon), 1996.

David Miller

1950-

David Miller at the Grand Canyon, 1993

Prologue

It has never seemed to me a fruitful or suitable pursuit for a writer to wonder about his or her own position within contemporary literature. But if I had to turn my thoughts in this direction, I would have to see myself as in some sense out of place and out of time. Dislocated—quite literally, dis-located—from where I am. For a British writer whose formative years were spent in Australia, and who has related himself mostly to American writing from an early age, the idea of "belonging" to any national tradition is peculiarly vexing. As to my writing being "out of time," suffice to say that I do not mean this in the sense of some non- or anti-contemporary literary practice, but rather that what I write rarely coincides with currently fashionable theories, movements, or "styles," and even then only as a coincidence.

The author's mother, Florence Miller, 1991

I was born in Melbourne on October 2, 1950, a third-generation Australian of mixed Portuguese, German, and British descent. My mother, Florence (Severino), was from the Victorian country town of Maryborough; my father, Archibald, or Arch, was from a small mining town in Tasmania called Zeehan. Their first child, my sister Beverly, was born four and a half years before me; I was their second and last.

A small foundry occupied the lower part of our two-storey house in South Melbourne, and it was here that my father worked; indeed, he ran the business single-handedly. My mother was a milliner, working from home when I was a little boy and in a factory when I was older.

My father was a good-natured, kindly man, yet very reserved. He had kept me amused with wonderful fictitious stories about himself when I was small; later on he became increasingly a listener rather than a talker. Of my mother, I will only say that she has been a great source of encouragement to me throughout my life, and that she is a woman of independence, spirit, and perseverance, as well as sympathy.

Childhood was largely spent in solitary ways, due to my shy temperament and lack of interest in sports or even in many games. My school days, at Dorcas Street Primary School and more especially at South Melbourne Technical School, are in most respects an unpleasant memory. I was sent to a technical school at the age of twelve, partly because my father wanted me to be an engineer, and partly because I had the idea I'd like to be a draftsman—without any real idea of what this would mean in relation to architecture or engineering. As it turned out,

I had no aptitude or liking for mechanical drawing. The staff at SMTS were by-and-large strongly disciplinarian—in a few cases, cruel—while the boys had a deserved reputation for rowdiness, bullying, and violence. I did, however, find a few companions over the four years I was there, and was befriended by the school librarian, Margit Funk, and the English teacher in my final year, Kay Butterfield. But this didn't stop me from loathing the time I spent at SMTS. When I was sixteen I dropped out of school. My father had died of a heart attack the previous year; I was going through a distinctly unhappy time, and it didn't seem possible to continue my studies. (As it happened, I wouldn't return to formal education for another twelve years.) Concentrating on writing, music, and painting, while working intermittently at unskilled jobs, was from now on my chosen way of life. It would remain so for well over a decade.

I had been studying the clarinet from my twelfth year, while also developing a serious interest in drawing and painting. Two or three years later I became interested in writing, having discovered modern poetry and fiction—as well as various writers from earlier periods—simply through browsing in the local library.

> I don't think it's possible to say *why* I started [writing]; except that I'd discovered certain authors who excited me—writers as various as Arp and Dante and Henry Miller. (I should add that it was Dante's *La Vita Nuova* which I read and reread, rather than the *Commedia*.) Reading these people seemed to involve an *invitation*, to participate in this extraordinary activity of writing. I was influenced by a large number of writers—I think it would be pointless to try to name them. But in the years immediately after my first attempts as a writer, Nerval and Malcolm Lowry were probably most influential.
>
> (From "An Interview with David Miller, 1983," conducted by James Crouch)

As well as those mentioned above, the authors I was drawn to at this time included the English Metaphysicals (Donne, Herbert, and Vaughan, in particular), Blake, Hopkins, Whitman, T. S. Eliot, Sandburg, Jeffers, H. D., Joyce, and Kerouac—an eclectic selection. Through an interest in Thoreau's writings in this same period, I was led to embrace a form of pacifistic anarchism. (My thinking is still influenced by anarchist ideas, inasmuch as I remain opposed to social hierarchies and deeply distrustful of all varieties of power.) Reading around in comparative religion was also part of my private curriculum. As I said in the interview with James Crouch:

> My parents held vestigial Christian beliefs, but they made very little effort to bring me up as a practising Christian. I felt free, when I was growing up, to investigate various religious traditions, without having to feel that this went against inherited beliefs.

I should also mention here my early exposure to the details of Simone Weil's life and thought, initially through Jacques Cabaud's beautiful biographical study, *Simone Weil: A Fellowship in Love.* Weil had been both a political radical *and* a religious mystic—this was an important reason for my fascination with her, since I, too, was interested in mysticism and political radicalism, and desired some sort of confluence between these concerns. But confess it: she also exerted an ambivalent fascination through her extremism and her strange combination of generosity and intransigence.

Margit Funk and Kay Butterfield had encouraged my earliest attempts at writing, during my final year at SMTS. But it was after I'd dropped out of SMTS that I came into contact with someone who would be vastly more important to my creative development—Ken White, the elder brother of one of my acquaintances at school. Ken was seven years my senior and was involved in what seemed a heady world of jazz performance, painting, and animated filmmaking. His considerable talents as musician and artist were already evident and would continue to grow over the years. (Recent meetings in Melbourne and also in Edinburgh—where Ken was showing his paintings at the Leith Gallery and playing guitar at the private view—have confirmed that this is still the case.) Ken astonished me by immediately suggesting we collaborate—despite never having read a line of my writing. His openness and generosity were exemplary. Apart from writing a song or two together, we never did collaborate; however, I found myself for the first time in a friendship that encouraged and extended my sense of what was possible for me as a writer.

Ken introduced me to his friend James Crouch. James was deeply concerned with comparative religion, mysticism, and spirituality; he also had a lively, eclectic, informed interest in the arts. It's hard to imagine how I would have fared without my talks and correspondence with James, both then and since, for he has remained a close friend for the past thirty years. I would certainly have been the poorer, as a writer and as a person.

Another significant friend from these years was a young painter named Norm Roberts. Norm and I met when we were working together in a bookshop in one of the Melbourne suburbs. I found I could talk with Norm about art and writing and music; moreover, I was able to witness, and hence to some extent share in, his attempts at articulating and developing a very real creative vision—a process that seemed difficult in the extreme, and not for any lack of skill. (There is probably no one else I've ever met for whom art is quite such a tortuous and problematic activity.) Norm and I have continued our talks intermittently over the years—in London, when he stayed here in the late '70s, and in Melbourne, during my visits in 1980 and 1996.

During this period of my life I was equally involved with writing, visual art, and music, and I was influenced in the one art-form by what I read or saw or heard—or did—in the others. For instance, it is utterly inconceivable that I would have ended up writing the sort of poetry I've written without having listened intently over the years to improvisational musicians like John Coltrane, Jimmy Giuffre, Roscoe Mitchell, Dave Burrell, and Joseph Jarman—alongside a wide range of other music. In particular, I've always been interested in the notion of exploring similar paradigms in different art-forms, a notion that I investigate in an essay entitled "Interrelation, Symbiosis, Overlap."

At one point I branched out into the theater with a play, since destroyed, of highly heterogeneous elements juxtaposed in a collage form. The owner of a small theater in Melbourne wanted to put the play on, but insisted I direct it myself—and also find a cast for it! My play went through a number of rehearsals with an ever-changing ensemble of friends and acquaintances, as well as friends of friends and acquaintances. The rehearsals never improved from one week to the next, and I finally cancelled the play a fortnight before it was due to open. (So much for my experience with the theater!) Film was something else I wanted to try my hand at, and I got as far as writing a script for a short "experimental" film and sending it to the American filmmaker Bruce Baillie for his advice. Baillie was kind in his comments, and I valued the contact, however brief, with the maker of such extraordinary films as *Mass (for the Dakota Sioux), Castro Street, Quick Billy,* and *Roslyn Romance.* The truth, however, was that my filmscript was a non-starter.

My interest in cinema *did* have an effect on the way I developed as a writer—partly through what I gained from the work of "experimental" filmmakers such as Baillie. But I'd also want to mention the influence of Robert Bresson's filmmaking, especially with regard to his nonpsychological approach to the films' thematic concerns and his powerful use of ellipsis. But this is to skip ahead about a decade.

The contemporary American poets I'd discovered, initially in the pages of Donald Allen's great anthology, *The New American Poetry,* were the major influences on the poetry I was writing at this time. Robert Duncan, Robert Creeley, and Charles Olson, in particular. (I sent a letter to Duncan at one point, and received an extremely gracious, encouraging reply.) As I later wrote in "Interrelation, Symbiosis, Overlap":

> The aim of these poets was to disclose or make manifest in the words of the poem an apprehension of things which was not part of a familiar knowledge. The emphasis on disclosure rather than on imposition of meaning and order, entailed the poet being taken up, in his or her composing, into an intuitive awareness which was not restricted by rational control; and it was coextensive with the idea of an "open form" which expands or frees the process of composition rather than inhibiting it.

This notion of an "open form" poetry was deeply congenial to me and has remained central, however much it may have been combined, dialogically, with other approaches. I was also reading Pound, Williams, Stevens, Hart Crane, David Jones, Basil Bunting, Gael Turnbull, and the (then) younger generation of British poets, like Lee Harwood and Tom Raworth, alongside the German poets Celan, Bobrowski, and Piontek in translation. I discovered Concrete poetry through the Emmett Williams, Stephen Bann, and Mary Ellen Solt anthologies, which led me to the work of Robert Lax, an Ameri-

can poet who has sometimes been grouped with the Concrete poets. Lax's writing has been extremely important to me, as I will relate in due course. The philosopher Ludwig Wittgenstein was someone else I became passionately interested in—after hearing a musical setting by Elisabeth Lutyens of propositions from his *Tractatus Logico-Philosophicus*!

Although it was mainly American and, to a lesser extent, British poets whose work "awakened" me to contemporary possibilities, I read a great deal of Australian poetry during my formative years. I still feel a real nostalgia when I hear the names of certain Australian poets. It was Francis Webb, a legendary and tragic figure in Australian letters, who came to mean the most to me of all Australian writers, but that was years after I'd left Australia. I have a recording of Webb reading from his poem "A Drum for Ben Boyd," which I find extraordinarily moving—there is such evident humanity, grace, and subtle emotion in Webb's voice. (The only living poet I've heard who reads in any way like this is the American Fanny Howe.) I should say, however, that I was more drawn to Australian artists than writers. In *South London Mix* I wrote:

> I am haunted by the absence of meetings. —Meetings made impossible by deaths—such as those of Godfrey Miller and Roy de Maistre. Or the cessation of meetings, either by ruptured friendship, by the intervention of distance, or again by death. There are interiors I will never sit in, and interiors I will never know again.

The painter Roy de Maistre certainly interested me; however, Godfrey Miller and Ian Fairweather were the two Australian artists whose work I most cared about, and I eventually published essays about both of them (in the *London Magazine,* in the early '80s). Roger Kemp, Fred Williams, and Len Crawford were others I admired, and I *could* have met all three during return visits to Melbourne—through my friend William Gleeson, a fine painter and stained-glass artist. I put off doing so, and then it was too late. More recently I've become fascinated by Syd Clayton, Australian composer, jazz musician, and writer; in his case, I was only made aware of his work after his death, when friends in Melbourne began telling me about this extraordinary person. (Ironically, I'd worked alongside one of Clayton's main collaborators, Robert Rooney, in the same bookshop where I met Norm Roberts.) Clayton's composition *Archaeopteryx (The First True Bird)*, which the composer Warren Burt sent me on a privately recorded tape a couple of years ago, is a work of unadorned beauty and rare distillation.

I have been emphasizing my involvement in the arts—in writing, especially—during those years in Melbourne. Something of a very different nature occurred when I was eighteen: I was conscripted into the Australian army. Like many of my generation, I had specific objections to Australia's involvement in the Vietnam War—indeed, to foreign intervention in Vietnam as a whole. But I was also a strict pacifist at the time, and it was my pacifism—more than anything else—that made me register as a conscientious objector. However, I was not a member of any recognised pacifist organisation, nor would I have been willing to do non-combatant service—so it was very unlikely I would have won a verdict in court. Spending two years in prison did *not* appeal to me. As it happened, the courts had too many conscientious objectors to deal with, and I was offered the chance of taking a medical examination and being released from any obligations to the army if I

was found unfit. I took the medical—and flunked it.

At the very end of the 1960s I began to publish in Australian little magazines and to meet a handful of poets—notably Charles Buckmaster and John Jenkins. Charles was possibly the most gifted poet of my generation in Australia. Sadly, he was subject to mental problems and committed suicide when he was still only twenty-one years old. John is still writing—both poetry and music criticism. (I've recently read an essay that he wrote about Syd Clayton.) Unfortunately, John and I lost touch many years ago.

In my late teens I converted to Shin Buddhism, a form of Mahayana Buddhism that developed in Japan. (Many years later I wrote an essay on Shin, "The Self and Language in Buddhism," published in two issues of the Kyoto journal *The Pure Land* in 1980-81.) I was eventually put in touch with the Australian poet Harold Stewart, a Shin devotee who had been living in Japan for many years. Together with his friend James McAuley, Harold had been responsible for the infamous Ern Malley hoax—a much-publicised incident which probably set the cause of Australian literary modernism back

David, immediate left of the teacher, Dorcas Street Primary School, Melbourne, Australia, 1956

David, seated at the extreme left, South Melbourne Technical School, 1965

two decades or more. (Michael Heyward's book *The Ern Malley Affair* recounts the story of this hoax.) For obvious reasons, Harold and I didn't see eye-to-eye about poetry, and I don't think I ever sent him anything of mine to read. Our correspondence was almost entirely about Buddhism. Harold kindly offered to help me if I visited Japan to further my knowledge of Shin. I fully intended to do so, but decided to go to England first and meet a few of the writers and artists whose work interested me. I would then go on to Japan before returning to Australia—that was the plan, at any rate.

In June 1972 I travelled to Singapore by ship, and a few days later caught a plane to England. The brief time I spent in Singapore constituted a shock: I had never seen such poverty before, so many people either without homes or living in makeshift housing. (The sight of large numbers of people living on the streets is of course utterly—and appallingly—commonplace in cities like London nowadays.) I had never been publicly importuned to such an extent, either, or approached by pimps at every turning. As much as I was unpleasantly taken aback by aspects of Singapore, I was fascinated to find myself in a place geographically unlike anything I was used to, and delighted by the temples, and intrigued by the little I was able

to see of Singapore's contemporary art. England was nowhere near as strange. Yet I confess that London, where I came to live, was at first overwhelming and disorienting to a shy young man from a small city like Melbourne.

I introduced myself to a number of people during my first months in England, including older artists like William Scott and Ivon Hitchens—it seemed important to learn what I could during what little time I imagined I had at my disposal. Most significantly, perhaps, I made two visits to the poet and painter David Jones, who was living in a Catholic nursing home in Harrow-on-the-Hill, Middlesex. In many ways, David Jones seemed exemplary to me: in the way he involved himself in two different art-forms; in the relationship between art and spirituality in his work; in his essential modesty, integrity, and lack of "careerism"; and in the high achievement of his poems, essays, paintings, and painted inscriptions. Jones received me in a very kindly, gracious way, and talked with me for several hours on each visit—in fact, he seemed reluctant for me to go, and I suspected he was somewhat lonely.

At the time, [Jones] was receiving attention from academics who wanted to quiz him about the sources for his writings, in a way that annoyed him; so much so that he wanted to talk about art rather than about writing. (I remember him exclaiming, "If I'd known this would happen, I'd never have written the bloody things!" But the remark, out of context, suggests a thorniness or asperity which I suspect was alien to him—he struck me as altogether a gentle and good-natured person.) I found that, for example, we agreed about Ben Nicholson's importance as an artist (although I already had an idea of this from reading *Epoch and Artist*), and that we both greatly admired Georges Braque. But he talked about quite a number of things, and I made no notes after my visits. . . .

(From "An Interview with David Miller, 1983," conducted by James Crouch.)

One of the first people I looked up in London was the songwriter and poet Sydney Carter. (Sydney is probably best known for his song "Lord of the Dance.") I'd briefly met Sydney during a visit he made to Australia, when I gatecrashed a reading for the students at Melbourne University and stayed to talk with him afterwards. (I was in the habit of working in the library at the university, eating lunch in the college refectory, and even participating in two student discussion groups, one on contemporary poetry and the other on comparative religion. I told anyone who asked me that I was a postgraduate student, but of course I was never registered with the university and had never taken a degree anywhere.) Sydney let me stay at his house for a couple of nights while I was sorting out accommodation, and quickly became one of my first English friends. I was impressed by his individual, often unconventional, approach to things, whether it was song-writing or making a living. Also, his emphasis on the spiritual and creative value of uncertainty was extremely interesting. In Sydney's case, this was largely a matter of uneasiness about final or rigidly held interpretations or ideas—one of his collections of poems is in fact entitled *Nothing Fixed or Final*. In my own case, it led, eventually, to an engagement with negative or apophatic theology,

with notions of unknowing, of a process in which one suspends any sort of rational certainty, so that in Nicholas [of Cusa]'s terms one is entering into what, with regard to reason, can only be regarded as a darkness—

where one doesn't *know*, in that sense, at all. That interests me because, let's say, I find it's the most congenial way in which I can think about and deal with questions of the invisible, the immaterial, and so forth. And that concern is basic, I think, to what I am doing as a writer.

(From "An Interview with David Miller, 1992," conducted by Andrew Bick)

I've gone into this question of "unknowing" in an essay entitled "The Dark Path," where I note that:

Keats' negative capability and the mystical tradition of apophatic theology parallel one another in their emphasis on uncertainty (understood in terms of a negation of *rational certitude*). In both cases, one proceeds by way of a dark path towards some illuminative discovery or revelation or ecstasy which cannot be willed or obtained through rational knowing.

When the artist Andrew Bick asked me if I could see "the possibility of any form of faith . . . , or would [I] say that the idea of faith is important because of its very impossibility?," I answered: "I think the notion of faith is important to me as a poet inasmuch as it relates to doubt and uncertainty" ("An Interview with David Miller, 1992"). Sydney Carter and I are vastly different as writers, but I think he would have approved of this reply. During the time I knew him, Sydney was working on a book project that would be published, years later, as *The Rock of Doubt* (and then revised as *Dance in the Dark*). He was having a great deal of trouble with writer's block. I would later find myself periodically afflicted with the same problem. In those years, by contrast, I was writing a considerable amount and almost effortlessly.

It soon became apparent that Harold Stewart was too difficult a person for me to rely upon as my one-and-only contact in Japan. Harold had promised to help me find work, as well as to introduce me to various people, but in subsequent communications he made it apparent that I would only be welcome at a certain time of the year, that he expected me to learn far more Japanese than I had any hope of doing in the time at my disposal, and so on. I gradually abandoned the idea of going to Japan. Rather than returning to Australia, however, I stayed on in London—and gradually abandoned the idea of going back to Australia to live.

I have already mentioned my interest in the novelist Malcolm Lowry. While still in Melbourne, I started a correspondence with Lowry's widow, Margerie Bonner Lowry. I also wrote a short book, *Malcolm Lowry and the Voyage that Never Ends,* which I took to London and submitted, in revised form, to Alan Clodd of the Enitharmon Press. Alan was interested in encouraging young writers, and I benefitted from his encouragement in having both the Lowry book and my first collection of poems, *The Caryatids,* published by Enitharmon. However, the publication of *Malcolm Lowry* was delayed for three years, so that when it finally appeared in 1976, it seemed like a minor addition to the growing corpus of Lowry studies. Margerie Lowry genuinely liked it, as far as I could tell, but for the most part it went unnoticed.

The Lowry book *did* receive one lengthy and enthusiastic review, however—in a Mexico City newspaper, *Excelsior,* the year after the book's publication. This came about through the good offices of Mathias Goeritz, a wonderful sculptor, experimental architect, and Concrete poet, who had long resided in Mexico. I'd begun exchanging letters with Goeritz in 1973 after having been impressed by reproductions of his work. Mathias and I never met, but in the course of a lengthy correspondence he gave me a great deal of encouragement, and his *Messages*—a powerfully evocative series of abstract images developed in response to Biblical passages—influenced my work at a much later stage, when I began writing *Spiritual Letters.*

An even more important contact was made around this same time, when I wrote to Robert Lax. I made my way to the Greek island of Patmos to meet Lax in October 1973. (More accurately, I encountered him by chance on Kalymnos, while we were both *en route* to Patmos for the proposed meeting. We went on to Patmos together.) Bob quickly became my mentor as a writer. Various people have called Bob "saintly," which must embarrass him, as he is a modest person. He is certainly a most kindly, generous man; unworldly, too, and lacking in ambition, as far as any sort of fame is concerned. At the same time, he is *totally* dedicated to his chosen art of writing. I consider him an exemplary figure, both for his personal qualities and attitudes, and for the individuality and artistic achievement of his work. I've written about Bob

on a number of occasions, but perhaps this brief quotation will suffice to show how I feel about his writing:

> Robert Lax has sometimes been grouped with the Concrete poets, and indeed in his avoidance of rhetoric, his cultivation of an economical, "stripped-down" language, and his concern with such structural devices as permutation, repetition and variation, his poetry would seem to be related to that of Finlay, Gomringer and the "Noigandres" poets. But it is important to note that these poems of Lax's comprise only part of his literary output, which includes journals, fables, prose poems/narratives, etc.; more to the point, there is a strongly contemplative quality to all of Lax's work, which tends to set it apart. His development as a writer has been a very individual one; and his clearest affinities are probably with the abstract painter Ad Reinhardt, who was a close friend of his. Like Reinhardt, Lax uses structure to get beyond structure; uses form to let the "formless" manifest itself. With Lax, this "formlessness", this "nothing", is at the same time the world of earthly (including personal) existence. As Nicholas Zurbrugg observes, "the content, the structure, and the sound of his poems are all primarily related to his explorations of natural transitions, and of the more personal, introspective rhythms of "'a person talking to himself.'"

(From "Interrelation, Symbiosis, Overlap")

I was also making contacts with writers and artists in England, mostly expatriates like myself—Denis Mizzi, George Alexander, and Kerry Leves from Australia; Bill Manhire from New Zealand; Carlyle Reedy from the United States. Someone else I came to know was the English poet Allen Fisher, who subsequently introduced me to other writers, such as the poet and translator Pierre Joris and, at a somewhat later date, the design theorist J. Christopher Jones. I always found visiting Allen a delightful experience; he had a remarkable intellectual curiosity and a respect for many different kinds of artistic endeavour, and although we seldom see each other these days, I'm sure he's still the same. An amiable, generous person, Allen was more than willing to share his discoveries and enthusiasms. During the next few years I established friendships with a number of other British poets, including John Riley, Ken Edwards,

Robert Hampson, and Philip Jenkins, as well as the expatriate American poet Asa Benveniste, with whom I shared an interest in Jewish mysticism.

I'd written both poetry and prose in Melbourne—by prose, I mean prose poetry and fiction as well as critical prose. In my earlier years in England I concentrated on poetry, while also writing essays and reviews. It was with a book of prose poetry, however, that I found my own way of writing, or at least, a book of prose poetry that also included poems as "inserts." But the line between poetry, prose poetry, and fiction has often been an arbitrary one in my work, making nonsense of genre classifications. (I've written about this subject in my essay "Interrelation, Symbiosis, Overlap," pointing out the irrelevance of rigidly defined classifications for such works as George Borrow's *Lavengro* or John Ruskin's *Fors Clavigera*.) The book of mine in question, *South London Mix*, was written in 1973 and published two years later by Gaberbocchus Press, the publishing enterprise of novelist and poet Stefan Themerson and his artist-wife, Franciszka. *South London Mix* was assembled from textual fragments, as this excerpt will show:

> String unwound from her mouth. Or clouds.
>   Floating out.
>
> Drinking. Cups. Blue smoke.
>
> And earth; and light:
>
> *
>
> Brief flash of sunlight across the eyes, bringing one into a different (almost non-visual) space for a second or two, before seeing oneself reflected in the glass of the door.
>
> *

Publishers like Alan Clodd and the Themersons were extremely conscientious about every aspect of what they did in bringing an author's work into print; I was fortunate in being involved with such serious and caring individuals at this stage of my writing life. However, I was also to experience the exact opposite of this approach when two of my texts were included in an Australian anthology, *The Outback Reader* (Outback Press), in 1975. The published ver-

Miller in Melbourne, 1972

sions of my texts were a travesty, pure and simple. I wish I could say this has been an exception in my experience of publishers; it hasn't, by any means. I hate to think about how many of my publications have been compromised by the carelessness of editors, publishers, and printers, the worst example being *Background Music* (Tangent Books, 1980), which I was forced to disown.

Strangely, I didn't write anything else quite like *South London Mix*, nor did I write any more prose (apart from critical pieces) for several years. I was writing free verse, but as a writer of free verse it took me until 1975, when I wrote *The Story* (Arc Publications, 1976), to catch up with what I'd accomplished in *South London Mix*. My writing became denser and more allusive in some subsequent texts, yet always with a strong tendency towards compression; there has also been a complementary or contrasting pull towards limpidity in various of my later work. If I had to pick out some of my own favourites from the books of poems I published in the 1970s and '80s, I'd name *Appearance & Event* (Hawk Press, 1977), *Primavera* (Burning Deck Press, 1979), *Unity* (Singing Horse Press,

1981), and *Losing to Compassion* (Origin Press, 1985).

Mention of Origin Press brings me to Cid Corman, the American poet, translator, and editor of *Origin* magazine and its associated book-publishing ventures. My contact with Cid dates back to 1977. I'd written to another American poet, Frank Samperi, after seeing a ridiculously condescending review of Samperi's great poetic trilogy, *The Prefiguration, Quadrifariam* and *Lumen Gloriae,* in order to let him know how highly I, for one, thought of his poetry. After Frank had read some of my own work, he kindly recommended that I get in touch with Cid, who was just starting up the fourth series of *Origin.* Cid not only included me in the magazine, but also asked me, a few years later, to be an associate editor of the fifth series. It was through Cid that I came to know many of the writers I've felt close to over the years, including John Levy, George Evans, Clive Faust, Will Petersen, Michael Heller, John Martone, and Billy Mills. Cid has also been a loyal friend for the past two decades.

I was playing improvised music a great deal in these years, mostly privately, in workshop situations. It was my good fortune to know and play with a number of talented musicians, including Mark Pickworth, Roy Ashbury, Julian Wales, Ye Min, and Robert Smith. I also took part in informal sessions with Lou Gare, ex-AMM saxophonist, and the flautist and electric guitarist David Toop, who has since become very well known as a writer on music. The person with whom I developed the closest musical bond, however, was a clarinettist named Jessica Mills. I have lost touch with all of these people, but it's Jess Mills I miss the most. Not only was she a gifted musician, she was also as charming, sympathetic, and sweet-natured a person as I've ever known. Much of my interest in playing music had faded by the beginning of the '80s, and when my clarinet was stolen in 1982, I simply gave up music. It's only in the last year or so that I've begun playing again.

I had been working at short-term jobs, mostly in bookshops and public libraries, since coming to England. However, I was forced out of work for several months when the Home Office decided I was too close to gaining residential status under the then-current immigration laws and requested my departure from England. This left me with the option of filing

The American poet, translator, and editor of Origin *magazine, Cid Corman, in Boston, 1982*

an appeal but not the option of earning a living while waiting for my appeal to be heard. I was eventually granted residency (and several years later took out British citizenship). Unfortunately, this period of enforced unemployment had made my already patchy work-record look even worse.

J. Christopher Jones was in touch with some of the English contingent of Joseph Beuys' Free International University and managed to get me invited to teach under their auspices. This proved to be an impractical arrangement, as there didn't seem to be any funding available. I found I required an alternative. Chris Jones had been deeply involved with university teaching at one time, and I believe it was my association with him that was partly responsible for the decision I now made—along with my need for some sort of further educational qualification to improve my job prospects.

What I did was to enroll for a degree at Middlesex Polytechnic (now Middlesex University). Originally, I set out to do a combined Art History and English Literature degree, later changing to History of Ideas with Philosophy as my secondary subject. This was a far cry from teaching for the FIU; yet given my circumstances, it seemed a more appropriate course of action.

I was at Middlesex from 1978 until my graduation in 1982. The lecturers were an odd assortment, or so it seemed to me. But I certainly found a handful of good, sympathetic teachers and formed a particularly friendly and stimulating relationship with the philosopher Doreen Maitre. Even more importantly, I met David Menzies, a fellow student who quickly became one of my closest friends. A gifted writer, David has so far published extremely little, partly due to temperament, partly because of the unusual and at times unclassifiable nature of his work.

My time at Middlesex helped me to clarify my thinking and develop my essay-writing. I found myself moving from Heidegger's philosophy, which I'd been reading for some while, to a closer identification with Levinas, Ricoeur, and, most especially, Gadamer.

Somehow I managed to save up the money to make a trip back to Australia in 1980. As well as seeing my mother and sister, I had the opportunity to spend time with old friends, such as Ken White, James Crouch, Norm Roberts, and Bill Gleeson, and to engage in lively talks with a more recent friend, Australian poet Clive Faust. My links with Australia are in some respects attenuated, and become more so as time goes by; yet in other ways they remain a very real and important part of my life, due to family ties and continuing friendships.

After a period when I had ceased to practise Buddhism, I became involved with Shin again, and wrote my only essay on the subject, "The Self and Language in Buddhism." It was my intention to study for a doctorate in Buddhist philosophical studies under Hisao Inagaki, who was teaching at the School of Oriental and African Studies (London University). Unfortunately, Hisao suddenly decided to return to Japan. After having made some enquiries into the possibility of studying the subject with someone else, I decided to change to English literature and write a thesis on the novelist and naturalist, W. H. Hudson. Robert Hampson, who was lecturing at Royal Holloway, another of London University's colleges, agreed to be my academic supervisor. I had thought about writing on Hudson for years—in fact, ever since I'd read *Green Mansions*, with admiration, sometime in the mid-'70s. Pound's high praise for Hudson was another reason for my inter-

est. In the Preface to *W. H. Hudson and the Elusive Paradise* (Macmillan & St. Martin's Press, 1990), which developed out of my thesis, I set out the main symbolic concerns of Hudson's work:

> Hudson's fiction and non-fiction share the same fundamental symbolism: that of the elusive Paradise. Through attention to the concrete details of the world, in certain moments at least, Hudson apprehends an invisible or supernatural dimension. These moments might appropriately be termed epiphanic. What I shall call "affirmative" epiphany affirms the earthly by revealing the divine through or within it; it is either directly paradisiac, or assimilable to a vision of the earthly Paradise. In contrast to the "affirmative" epiphany, there is also "negative" epiphany which opens up a chasm of terror and dread. Violence, affliction, and human submersion in evil are amongst the things that play into the notion of "negative" epiphany. In Hudson's fiction there are also indications that evil is written into the network of chance and natural law; so that the "darkness" or evil disclosed by "negative" epiphany can be seen as ontologically prior to the actions of the human will. The paradisial endures as a fractured and elusive aspect of experience, constantly threatened by contingency, violence, or evil.

The thesis took up four years of my life, from 1981 to 1985. For some months in 1983 I resided in what had been Hudson's own house in St. Luke's Road, Westbourne Park (West London)—in fact, the very part of the house that he had lived and worked in, the other floors having been let out to lodgers. Extraordinarily enough, I was offered the rental of the top floor flat purely by chance.

I began some important friendships with other writers during this time. Guy Birchard, for one. I met Guy and his wife Anne during one of their sojourns in London, after George Evans had suggested that Guy should look me up. As a poet, Guy has an extremely fine ear and a marvellous feeling for detail; more importantly, his best work has that combination of strangeness and inevitability that one finds so rarely these days. Guy is based in Canada, yet more often publishes in the United Kingdom (and sometimes in the United States); consequently, his work has suffered neglect from those eager to "place" a writer, quite literally.

"With my good friend Petros Bourgos," Meligalas Messenias in the Peloponnese, 1984

Gad Hollander, poet, prose-writer, filmmaker, artist, is another friend I want to mention here. Gadi and his family have been so much a part of my life for the past fourteen years. I've written about Gadi's work in "Interrelation, Symbiosis, Overlap," mentioning "his exploration and mastery of a number of different art-forms," and commenting that he "has extended his concerns as a poet to the making of films more successfully than anyone else I know. " I would add that he is, in my belief, one of the finest writers of his (and my) generation. I was delighted to take part in Gadi's film *Euripides' Movies* (1987), where he cast me as a "blue cap poet" because of the cap I often wore in those days. Edouard Roditi was yet another writer who befriended me. Roditi was more important to me as a literary exemplar than anyone else, apart from Bob Lax. I began corresponding with Edouard in 1982, after reading his book of poems *Thrice Chosen*. I'd been struck by the way that he dealt with aspects of Jewish spirituality in those poems, and in fact it was always that strand of his writing—rather than the Surrealist texts, say, or the short stories—that drew me to him. At the same time, I was aware of his wide-ranging knowledge—amazed by it, too; it was both exhilarating and dismaying to begin a conversation with Edouard on a contemporary artist or writer and find him moving into a recondite area of philosophic thought, or else

some aspect of Kabbalistic literature. I was Edouard's guest at his house in Dieppe on three occasions, besides meeting him when he was in London and keeping up a correspondence with him. Edouard was a wonderful host, and he was unfailingly generous in his attempts to help me publish my writing. As well as the preface to my novella *Tesserae*, he provided one of the two blurbs for my Hudson book (Guy Davenport having written the other one). I owe my friendships with the prose-writer and poet Lawrence Fixel, the critic Gregory Stephenson and the poet David C. D. Gansz to Edouard. (Leonard Schwartz was another poet Roditi wanted me to be in touch with, but it was only after Edouard's death that I contacted Leonard, having been impressed by his translations of Benjamin Fondane.) During the last visit to Dieppe, in 1990, my friend Petros Bourgos videotaped an interview I conducted with Edouard for a film project, together with an interview between Edouard and David Menzies. Sadly, the film was never completed. Edouard's death in 1992 was a terrible shock. I continue to miss him.

It was Roditi who, noting my interest in Buddhism, attempted to make me focus more on Western religious traditions, in the belief that one should explore one's own historical, cultural, and spiritual heritage—including both good and bad aspects—before attempting to engage with other traditions. (Another influence towards Western spirituality came from Rev. Elizabeth Welch of the United Reformed Church and her husband Peter Skerratt. Elizabeth and Peter had been friends of mine since the mid-'70s.) If many of my earlier writings were informed by my Buddhist leanings, the later ones often derive themes and imagery from Christian and Jewish sources. When I occasionally returned to Eastern traditions in later texts, it was with a deeper sense of my own Western perspective—and a greater sense of the levels and degrees of understanding and misunderstanding that may inhere in any particular perspective. "In the Field" is the text that most specifically derives from these concerns:

1.

'don't turn away where are you gazing
and whatever are you gazing at?'
'there was a huge golden man'
the girl said 'lying down on a couch
and the couch was in a field'

2.

details reproduced through layers levels
the dream coming home in day's hours

3.

a line in vermilion
brushed onto paper
gold body-color
anticipations of black
on white revealing birds
and immortal beings

4.

'throughout that field there were outbursts
of crying' but the children take on the
   aspect
of celestial nymphs and a love
from before birth's remembered
unearthly life stirring in faces

5.

and the tribute which he offered
was a picture of the Lord of Heaven
and of the Mother of the Lord
altogether improper things he brought
   bones
of supernatural beings they are superfluous
   things
which ought not to enter the palace

6.

disseisin *where were we now*
where else could we be
than in that same field

Those writings of mine that focus on Western traditions of spirituality often do so "in the spirit of someone attempting to retrieve or recover what has become obscured," as I say in a text entitled "Thesis," noting that this involves a process of disrupting or rupturing "the flow, the continuity, of time, narrative, history. " Yet as I also say, "one places oneself in the present (there is nowhere else to be)." My interest in heterodox spiritual perspectives has always been investigative, exploratory, never deriving from any sort of dogmatic position. Something of this interest can be indicated by the following brief quotations:

The other people there wanted to talk about art; he didn't.
There was a glint of hysteria in his eyes. He said: It was a vast secret society, calling itself the Agapé. Its leaders authored the Christian Gospels, and circulated them for their own worldly ends. They assassinated those whose power they coveted. Montanus wanted to reform the Agapé; he was condemned at Rome, and committed suicide. . . .

*

On the notebook's cover a girl stands in a ballet-costume, her face covered in white make-up. Her hands gesture to the sky, an arc indicating lost and soteriological spaces. A secret society calling itself by love's name? I keep thinking of the woman whose ecstatic utterances were nothing the churchman could challenge with argument, leading him to resort to a third type of utterance: exorcism. The woman's followers stopped him from completing the act; yet he had won, just the same. A ring was unknowingly dropped in the dark. Beneath the night, the ground's caked and bleached.

(From "Dark Ground")

She appeared to him in a dream, and said:—*I am pursued like a wolf from the sheep. I am not a wolf. I am word, and spirit, and power.*

*

Blue crystal. At the centre of the thicket.

*

A house that you reach by a series of narrow lanes past the sea-front. Inside, a door opens upon weeping, bleeding, speaking, in their variety of colors.

(From "At the Heart of the Thicket")

My friend John Levy was living in Greece in 1984, and I decided to go out and visit him, giving me the opportunity also to see Bob Lax again and to spend time with my good friend Petros Bourgos. I met up with Petros in Athens and we drove to Meligalas Messenias in the Peloponese, where John and his girlfriend (later wife), Leslie Buchanan, were staying. John and I had friends in common, including Corman and Will Petersen, quite apart from the poets and artists John had put me in touch with, such as John Perlman and Linda Bryant. The highlight of the trip, however, was my reunion with Bob Lax, with whom I spent several highly enjoyable days on the island of Patmos.

In 1986 I was approached by a young poet, painter, and publisher, Rupert M. Loydell, who wanted me to contribute to an anthology of prose, subsequently entitled *The Serendipity Caper* after one of my texts. (The greater part of my creative output since 1977 had been—and continues to be—in prose, so I welcomed the invitation, especially when it became evident that Rupert was including fiction, prose poetry, and less classifiable forms of imaginative prose.) This was the beginning of a long-standing association with Rupert and his imprint, Stride. Besides a collection of stories, *Darkness Enfolding* (1989) and my novella, *Tesserae* (1993), Rupert has published my selected poems, *Pictures of Mercy* (1991), a selection of my essays, *Art and Disclosure* (1998), and two books about my work, *At the Heart of Things: The Poetry and Prose of David Miller* (1994) and Michael Thorp's essay, *Breaking at the Fountain: A Meditation on the Work of David Miller* (1998). Rupert and I have also co-edited two anthologies, *How the Net Is Gripped: A Selection of Contemporary American Poetry* (1992) and *A Curious Architecture: A Selection of Contemporary Prose Poems* (1996), both published by Stride.

Following the completion of my doctoral studies, I did some casual work in museums for a couple of years. I'd been suffering from arthritis since 1983, and it was especially severe in its effects in the first few years, prior to a fairly successful treatment being found. Consequently, holding down a full-time job wasn't easy at this time. In 1987 I began working in university libraries, specializing after a while in the field of small presses and little magazines— that is, noncommercial, nonmainstream publications involving literature and the other arts. In this capacity I've organised exhibitions of small press publications at London's Royal Festival Hall, Durham University Library, Staffordshire Polytechnic, University College London, and workfortheeyetodo, a notable London gallery and bookshop. My co-organiser, in each case, has been Geoffrey Soar, a former librarian and an authority on this subject. (Someone else I should mention in this context is R. J. Ellis. Dick Ellis was the person behind the exhibition at Staffordshire Polytechnic. He is someone with a keen, scholarly interest in

little magazines and small presses, which he has pursued in various writings, and I hope to be able to work with him on a project about little magazines in the near future. Dick also published *Cards* (Sow's Ear Press, 1991), a book I co-authored with John Levy.)

I was writing art criticism during the 1980s and early '90s, both as a reviewer for *Artscribe International* (1985-88) and as a contributing essayist to a handful of exhibition catalogues, beginning with Jennifer Durrant's show at the Serpentine Gallery (London) in 1987. As already mentioned, I also wrote essays on the Australian painters Ian Fairweather and Godfrey Miller, which were published in the *London Magazine* (1983 and '84). My involvement with visual art has extended to my own books; in the case of my earlier publications, I let the publisher decide about the artwork, occasionally with sorry results, but since 1984 I have taken care to work with artists whose activities have complemented my own, in one way or another. The artists in question have included Jennifer Durrant, Denis Mizzi, Graham Gussin, Emily Hoffnung, Ian McKeever, and Andrew Bick. Andrew Bick deserves special mention here. When Andrew and I first met in 1990, at Rupert Loydell's instigation, I immediately recognised him as a fellow spirit. Besides his admiration for Bob Lax's poetry, Andrew was deeply interested in the Christian tradition of negative theology, ranging from Dionysius the Areopagite to Meister Eckhart and Nicholas of Cusa. (Someone else we both greatly esteemed: Ad Reinhardt. And we both knew and respected the poet Thomas A. Clark.) Andrew's work as an artist is highly significant, I believe, in its strongly realized response to spiritual perspectives. I was delighted to have the chance to write about his art for the catalogue of an exhibition at the Todd Gallery (London) in 1990. Since then, Andrew has been involved in several projects with me, including the publications *A path a lake the very breath* (RMG Publications, 1994), *Stromata* (Burning Deck Press, 1995), and *Spiritual Letters (1-10)* (EMH Arts/Eagle Graphics, 1997).

A significant event that needs to be mentioned here is the publication of the anthology that Gillian Allnutt, Fred D'Aguiar, Ken Edwards, and Eric Mottram put together, *The New British Poetry, 1968-1988* (Paladin, 1988). This was an especially important sampling of British poetry from the period in question, even if it didn't include a number of poets I, for one, admire—Gad Hollander, Philip Jenkins, Peter Dent, Tony Lopez, for example. I was pleased to have been represented in it, thanks to Ken Edwards's interest in my work.

With the novella *Tesserae*, I ended my fiction-writing—for the time being, at least. My fiction had become more complex in these years, especially with the long short story "True Points" (incorporated in a collection of the same title from Spectacular Diseases Press, 1992) and *Tesserae* itself. In Robert Hampson's highly perceptive essay, "'Beyond Allegory, Beyond Dream': David Miller's Prose Texts," he refers to the "polyphonic, discontinuous narratives" of some of my stories, and to the "loose but carefully articulated, meditative narratives [produced] through a montage of epiphanic moments." I couldn't do better than direct an interested reader to Hampson's essay for an insightful reading of my fiction.

I began a number of significant friendships with fellow poets during the 1990s, including Stephen C. Middleton, Rosmarie and Keith Waldrop, and Fanny Howe. Stephen Middleton is a poet whose knowledge of the history of post-World War II jazz and jazz-related forms of improvised music is staggering. It would be hard to imagine having the exchanges I've had with Stephen on this subject with many other writers. (Norman Weinstein is one of the few I can think of.) Keith and Rosmarie Waldrop had published my booklet *Primavera* from Burning Deck Press in 1979, but I didn't really get to know them until 1992, when they were staying in London. While I'd been an admirer of Rosmarie's poems and translations for some time, it was only after meeting Keith at this point that I began to read his poems in earnest, and to discover the strikingly independent qualities of his work. Indeed, I consider Keith Waldrop one of the finest poets living. I later stayed with Rosmarie and Keith when they were in Berlin on a fellowship. Later still, they were to publish one of my best books, *Stromata*. I've written about Fanny Howe in my essay "The Dark Path"; I'll quote just a short passage, from the Postscript:

> Fanny Howe's writings are occasions or loci for a "leap" of insight; sources or supports for spiritual illumination. Like the poems of otherwise dissimilar writers like Frank Samperi, John Riley or Robert Lax, they are

exemplary in the way they demand that poetry be seen as spiritual art.

I would only want to add that Fanny and I sensed an affinity between each other's writings from early contact.

My first trip to the States was in 1993, with three subsequent visits over the next few years. I've come to feel a special affection for San Francisco, which I consider one of the most beautiful and pleasant cities I've ever spent time in. Difficult, of course, to divorce my feelings about the city itself from the people who have made my visits so enjoyable. The poet Benjamin Hollander, Gadi's brother, comes first to mind. Ben means a great deal to me as a friend, through his many kindnesses, his lively mind, his warm and relaxed companionship. Lawrence Fixel also comes to mind here. Larry has let me stay in his and his wife Justine's house on two occasions, and has been a generous and caring host. As well as a unique writer of prose poems, fables, poems, and stories, Larry is a person for whom ideas are, indeed, his daily bread, and he is a stimulating partner in intellectual conversation. (My first reading in San Francisco was given with Larry Fixel; the occasion was made especially memorable by the presence of my late friend Frank Samperi's daughter, Claudia.) Other writers I've enjoyed contact with during these visits to San Francisco would include Carl Rakosi, Edward Mycue, Jack Marshall, Aaron Shurin, Peter Money,

American writers John Levy (right) and Robert Lax, Athens, 1984

Morton Marcus, and my old friend George Evans. (I would also like to mention the jazz vocalist Patty Waters, even if Patty and I have failed to meet on each of the occasions when I've been in California. I got into contact with Patty in 1993, after many years of listening to her music. She was a legendary and mysterious figure, who at that time had only recorded two albums under her own name, both in the mid-'60s. But more than that, she was an inspiring example to me in the way that she explored the emotional, imaginative, formal, and technical possibilities of her art. To receive mail from Patty and talk with her on the telephone just seemed like a dream.)

Tucson and Phoenix are other cities for which I feel an affection; again, my feeling for these places is hard to separate from the feeling I have for certain people. John Levy and his wife Leslie Buchanan have made me feel at home in Tucson, just as the painter and poet Linda Bryant has in Phoenix. On my first visit to Arizona, John and Leslie drove me to the Grand Canyon, and then to Flagstaff, where we met up with Linda. John had put me in touch with Linda many years before, and I had enjoyed a lengthy and warm correspondence with her. Linda and I spent the next few days driving through desert landscapes in her jeep, visiting Hopi and Navajo sites, before going on to her home in Phoenix. I later wrote "Landscape" to commemorate the time we spent driving through the desert together:

> a black so chill
> it numbs the eye
>
> you favored rocks
> I spoke up
> for the comfort of trees
>
>   *
>
> in a desert landscape
> these Polish lamentations
> are lifted breaking
> through a wash of static
>
> cholla and prickly-pear
> seen from a moving car
> the soprano's voice
> that sings of grief entire
>
> a confluence unstable
> that ear shapes with eye

With Edouard Roditi, 1986

A more recent trip, to Los Angeles this time, enabled me to meet Douglas Messerli, whose Sun & Moon Press will be publishing my collection of prose texts, *The Water of Marah*. I was also able to see some extraordinary work by Wallace Berman, an artist whose example has been very important to me. But the main reason for the trip was so that I could spend time with Guy Birchard and his wife Anne, who have moved to Los Angeles for the time being.

One day the publisher Alec Finlay phoned me to suggest that I do a collaboration with Ian McKeever, a painter we both knew personally, for Alec's Morning Star Folio series. I was delighted by the idea, especially as I was convinced that Ian was one of the most significant—if not *the* most significant—painter in the United Kingdom. I'd also found him to be a friendly, engaging, highly intelligent, and articulate individual. Working with Ian McKeever proved to be one of the most enjoyable creative experiences of my life. We spent several months during 1995 exchanging drawings and poetic prose texts, using a notebook which was sent back and forth through the post. The drawings and prose poems "commented" on each other, but only in an indirect way. The collaborative development of visual images and text was, for me at least, an exciting, intensely involving, and often very surprising process. The unexpected nature of Ian's contributions led me to write in a way that I'm sure wouldn't have happened otherwise. A small section of the notebook is to be the basis of *(For Simone Weil)*, which Alec Finlay will publish. There are no definite plans as yet to publish the entire work, which is entitled *The London/Hartgrove Notebook*.

Beginning in October 1995, my life was over-taken by a series of personal events, deeply distressing in nature, which involved the sever-ance of relations with a friend I'd cared about deeply. For professional reasons, my former friend and I could not avoid contact, and this led to an intensely troubled situation which was as painful as it was long drawn-out. I still bitterly regret the severance, which was my friend's idea, not mine—as well as regretting everything which followed from it. As Gérard de Nerval wrote in *Aurélia*: "Each one of us can search his memory for the most heart-rending emotion he has known, the most terrible blow that fate has inflicted on his soul." The reason for mention-ing this matter within the present context is that it had a profound effect on my writing. *Spiritual Letters* and *Suite* were written out of personal crisis, and are undeniably informed by this fact. However, *Spiritual Letters*, in particu-lar, also bears witness to my interest in the *Zohar*'s mystical commentaries and elaborations upon Scripture, and is indebted to the collages and assemblages of Wallace Berman, with their very individual engagement with Kabbalism, and to Mathias Goeritz's *Messages*. In common with other texts of mine, *Spiritual Letters* is informed by a "dialogic approach to structure and im-mediacy, plan and impulse," to re-employ a description from "Interrelation, Symbiosis, Over-lap." Here is a section from *Spiritual Letters*:

> . . . *letter by letter*. Having no wish to be detained by clever fabrications, stories that might distract. A dark courtyard, a lecture on aesthetics.—And if art is only lies, for the sake of rapture and power? Facing the wall, away from the wind, she struck a match for her cigarette—the flame drawing my look. Feckless, volatile girl; in the dream she be-gan shouting at me as I turned away from her.—Flung across the hospital room by the Holy Ghost, the musician said. A phone-call: the driver survived; he died—the friend I'd stopped seeing. I thought of how he'd in-sisted on reading poem after poem to me at dinner; I'd looked (but not wanting to) at the spittle ejected upon his lip as he spoke the words. Faces of friends by my bed. Memory's unquenched: her long hair that

she tossed around her neck; her hand that reached for mine. *Eye toward eye*. . . . Slow phleboclysis (drop by drop; into the vein).

To quote from Benjamin Hollander's com-pressed and insightful essay, "On David Miller's *Spiritual Letters*":

> What the text of these *Letters* suggests, in part, is a meditation on the (im)possibility of a rationally conceived aesthetics of writ-ing which would represent us in our mo-ments of transcendence, in our acts of re-membrance, in our experiences of poverty and isolation. . . .

Partly in order to take my mind off the situation with my estranged friend, I began to put together the manuscript of my *Collected Po-ems*. This had little effect on my state of mind, let alone the situation itself; but it did result in a book that I felt was worthwhile. The *Col-lected*, which was published by the University of Salzburg Press in 1997, enables the reader to obtain a coherent and comprehensive view of my free verse writing. *The Water of Marah* will provide an overview of my imaginative prose, from 1973 through to the early '90s. Other collections might do the same for my short stories, which are not included in *The Water of Marah*, and for more recent prose texts.

In a highly perceptive essay on my poetry, "'Thought, itself, ruptured': The Spiritual Mate-rialist Poetics of David Miller," Tim Woods writes:

> Miller appears to have always engaged with disjunctive form and fragmented structures as a principled method of overcoming the easily commodified messages of contempo-rary popular culture.
>
> Yet these experimental initiatives appear to add up to a different concept which domi-nates Miller's poetry: namely, *ethics*.

As Tim Woods also says: "This space carved out for and by the face and love, the ethical sphere, has always interested Miller."

> How the ethical gazes out
> irrevocable, from iris and pupil
>
>   (From "Fire Water")

With particular reference to a text of mine called *The Book of the Spoonmaker* (Cloud, 1995), Dr. Woods writes that:

The ethical "I" results from casting off the hegemony of the ego, moving away from oneself, and is consonant with Miller's poetics and its desire to resist the imperialism of the subject's impositions on the world.

I should also like to quote the conclusion of Dr. Woods' essay, which manages in a few lines to go quite some way towards revealing what my work is about:

> Like his literary mentor W. H. Hudson, David Miller is equally in search of an "elusive reality," to which he hopes to gesture in his poetry through diligent and careful negotiation with the phenomenal world. His poems eschew the form of the "well-wrought urn"; but the "Thought, itself, ruptured" . . . , the shards of language which make up Miller's oeuvre, are far more likely to pierce the fabric of perception, than the smooth, classical surfaces of an Attic grace.

Some other writings about my work deserve mentioning here. Robert Hampson's essay "Producing the unknown: language and ideology in contemporary poetry," included in *New British Poetries: The Scope of the Possible* (ed. Hampson and Peter Barry, Manchester University Press, 1993), involved a notable attempt at an overview of my poetry, but as such it was overshadowed by Hampson's excellent Introduction to my *Collected Poems.* Robert Sheppard's "A Gap at the Heart of Things: The Poetics of David Miller" (in *At the Heart of Things*) constitutes another fine piece of critical writing, as does Michael Thorp's essay, *Breaking at the Fountain.* It might be worth noting Michael Thorp's point, that I've suggested "an alternative to style and an affirmation *through* negation" in my writings—referring to my engagement with negative theology, on the one hand, and my concern with disclosure, on the other. In my own words, from an essay entitled "'The End of the Kingdom of Necessity, Servitude and Inertia'":

> Style rests upon a schizomorphic separation of form and meaning. In certain types of art and literature, the pre-existing "matter" becomes less and less important, and the mouldings and pressures of the formal conventions—"style" *per se*—become predominant. The history of this process is a history of impoverishment.

My interest here lies solely in pointing to an alternative to style. This alternative is what I believe to be found in the most significant art and writing of the present (and, indeed, of earlier historical periods). If style consists in the writer or artist manipulating elements of what he or she already knows, re-presenting them in a new manner or form so that the artwork is persuasive and gratifying, disclosure has to do with modes of being that are unknown, i.e. not part of the familiar sphere of "knowledge." "To produce is to draw forth, to invent is to find, to shape is to discover. In bodying forth I disclose." (Martin Buber.) Or as I have written elsewhere: "Art makes manifest unfamiliar modes of experience, existence, being, in such a way that this making-manifest is thoroughly embodied in a concrete or sensuous form, and can only be approached through the form, more, the physical being, of the work."

Whose work has been important to me in recent years? Apart from that of Wallace Berman, I'd especially mention George Tooker, Paul Thek, Christian Boltanski, Gerhard Richter, Jaime de Angulo, S. Y. Agnon, William Goyen, David Rattray. (Musicians and composers? Too many to list—and my interests are *highly* eclectic.) I'm no longer at an age when I feel I am *influenced* by others in my writing, but I do feel that I am stimulated, encouraged, by the example of such creative artists as Thek or de Angulo; just as I am by conversations with longtime friends like Gadi Hollander, Guy Birchard, or the poet Wendy Saloman, as well as more recent friends such as Sharon Morris or Jeff Hilson.

I realize that there are various aspects of my life that I have not even attempted to deal with in this essay. Fair enough, I think; the emphasis has been on my life as a writer. Those friendships that have been significant to me as a person *and* as a writer are what I have chosen to emphasize, and if I've mentioned a large number of people it's for the sole reason that these people—and others that I have not managed to name—have all been important to me, in one way or another. On the other hand, there are others I don't see the relevance of mentioning in this specific context, however dear the people concerned. Other things I simply prefer to leave to silence. Discretion and reticence are traits that I value.

What plans do I have at this point in my life? I intend spending a good deal of time playing music, making up for all those years when music was no longer an active part of my life. I still hope to publish my collaboration with Ian McKeever, *The London/Hartgrove Notebook.* A book about Robert Lax, co-edited with Nicholas Zurbrugg, has been in progress for a long time, and I very much want to see it through its final stages. (It will be good to know that the finished book is in Bob Lax's hands, as well as those of its many contributors, and those of Bob's admirers and admirers-to-be.) —I will, I trust, continue to write.

January, 1998

Sources

All poems and excerpts from David Miller's prose writings are copyrighted by the author. "Interrelations, Symbiosis, Overlap" was included in *Interaction and Overlap: from the Little Magazines and Small Press Collection at University College London* (with Geoffrey Soar), workfortheeyetodo, London, 1994, and reprinted in *Art and Disclosure: Seven Essays,* Stride Publications, Exeter, 1998. *South London Mix* was published by Gaberbocchus Press, London, 1975; it was also included in *Pictures of Mercy: Selected Poems,* Stride Publications, 1991. The two interviews, with James Crouch (1983) and Andrew Bick (1992), were both included in *At the Heart of Things: The Poetry and Prose of David Miller,* Stride Publications, 1994. "The Dark Path: Notes for/ from/ about Fanny Howe," appeared in *Five Fingers Review,* 17, San Francisco, 1998. *W. H. Hudson and the Elusive Paradise* was published by Macmillan, London and St. Martin's Press, N.Y., 1990. "In the Field" was originally published by tel-let, Charleston, Illinois, 1992, and republished in *Collected Poems,* University of Salzburg Press, Salzburg, 1997. "Dark Ground" was included in a festschrift entitled *Emotional Geology: The Writings of Brian Louis Pearce,* ed. Rupert M. Loydell, Stride Publications, 1993. "At the Heart of the Thicket" was published in *At the Heart of Things.* "Thesis" appeared in *First Intensity,* No. 6, Staten Island, N.Y., 1996, and was also in a festschrift for James Hogg entitled *Summoning the Sea: An Anthology of Contemporary Poetry and Prose,* ed. Wolfgang

Görtschacher and Glyn Pursglove, University of Salzburg Press, 1996. "Landscape" was published in *Elegy,* Oasis Books, London, 1996, and in the *Collected Poems.* The excerpt from *Spiritual Letters* appeared in *Spiritual Letters (1-7),* tel-let, 1996, and *Spiritual Letters (1-10),* with artwork by Andrew Bick, EMH Arts/Eagle Graphics, London, 1997. "Fire Water" was included in *Stromata,* Burning Deck Press, Providence, R.I., 1995, and in the *Collected Poems.* "'The End of the Kingdom of Necessity, Servitude and Inertia'" was published in *Morning Star Folio*s, 2nd series no. 3, Edinburgh, 1991, to accompany poems by Robert Lax and artwork by Andrew Bick, and reprinted in *Art and Disclosure: Seven Essays.*

The excerpt from Gérard de Nerval's *Aurélia* is taken from the *Selected Writings* translated by Geoffrey Wagner, Peter Owen Ltd., London, 1958 (reprinted by Panther Books, London, 1968). Benjamin Hollander's essay "On David Miller's *Spiritual Letters*" is unpublished to date. The excerpt included here is by courtesy of the author. Tim Woods' "'Thought, itself, ruptured': The Spiritual Materialist Poetics of David Miller", is to be included in *The Poet's Voice,* New Series, Vol. 4 no. 2, Salzburg, 1998. Michael Thorp's *Breaking at the Fountain: A Meditation on the Work of David Miller,* was published by Stride, 1998.

BIBLIOGRAPHY

Poetry:

The Caryatids: Poems 1971/3, Enitharmon Press (London), 1975.

All My Life: Poems 1973/4, Joe di Maggio Press (London), 1975.

The Story, Arc Publications, 1976.

Appearance & Event: 16 Poems, Hawk Press (Paraparaumu, N.Z.), 1977.

Primavera, Burning Deck Press (Providence, R.I.), 1979.

Unity, Singing Horse Press (Blue Bell, Pennsylvania), 1981.

Losing to Compassion, Origin Press (Sedro-Woolley, Washington), 1985.

Messages, Torque Press (Southampton), 1989.

Pictures of Mercy: Selected Poems, Stride Publications (Exeter), 1991.

A path a lake the very breath, with artist Andrew Bick, RMG Publications, 1994.

(With John Levy) *Cards,* Sow's Ear Press, 1991.

Stromata, Burning Deck Press, 1995.

The Book of the Spoonmaker, Cloud (Newcastle upon Tyne), 1995.

Elegy, Oasis Books (London), 1996.

Spiritual Letters (1-7), tel-let (Charleston, Illinois), 1996.

Suite, Longhouse (Brattleboro, Vermont), 1997.

Collected Poems, University of Salzburg Press (Salzburg), 1997.

Spiritual Letters (1-10), artwork by Andrew Bick, EMH Arts/Eagle Graphics (London), 1997.

Fiction and other prose:

South London Mix, Gaberbocchus Press (London), 1975.

Darkness Enfolding: Eight Stories, Stride Publications, 1989.

True Points: Eight Prose Texts 1981-1987, Spectacular Diseases Press (Peterborough, Cambs.), 1992.

Tesserae, Stride Publications, 1993.

The Water of Marah, Sun and Moon, forthcoming.

Criticism:

Malcolm Lowry and the Voyage that Never Ends, Enitharmon Press, 1976.

W. H. Hudson and the Elusive Paradise, Macmillan (London); St. Martin's Press (New York), 1990.

Notes Written at a Night Window: On Ad Reinhardt, Form Books (London), 1994.

Art and Disclosure: Seven Essays, Stride Publications, 1998.

Editor of:

Robert Lax, *Journal C,* Pendo Verlag (Zurich), 1990.

(With Rupert Loydell) *How the Net Is Gripped: A Selection of Contemporary American Poetry,* Stride Publications, 1992.

(With Rupert Loydell) *A Curious Architecture: A Selection of Contemporary Prose Poems,* Stride Publications, 1996.

Contributor to anthologies:

The Serendipity Caper, edited by Rupert M. Loydell, Stride, 1986.

The New British Poetry, 1968-88, edited by Gillian Allnutt, Fred D'Aguiar, Ken Edwards, and Eriac Mottram, Paladin, 1988.

Mark J. Mirsky

1939-

As I approach sixty, the curve in a bow of the years bent from birth begins to make itself felt. Last night I dreamt again of a dark corridor in an apartment my grandfather rented, or a corridor I imagined at three years old at our house at 46 Warner Street where my memories begin. Both long hallways lead back to Boston's Jewish Dorchester. It seems as if my grandfather, who died when I was four and a half, his friends, the old totems of the house, are still alive, and their world is the one with weight, importance, where decisions are made. The shadows of Europe fill that corridor; the syllables and stories of a town surrounded by impenetrable forests and swamps, Pinsk, my father's and grandfather's city. In the dark, magical objects are held, give off light; and the languages, Yiddish, Hebrew, mingled with English, promise at every moment to disclose secrets.

Between Grandpa's house and ours lay a frozen bay of ice through the winter, an ocean of lawn in spring and fall. Franklin Field, its grass short at the edge, rose taller, burying its golden dandelions, until the stalks reached like the ferns of a jungle over my head. At five, six, I began to wander down the crossword puzzle of streets from my front porch across the trolley tracks of a busy avenue to the rustling mattress of the grass.

So much of my fiction tries to reach back to the riddle of those moments, the first dim ones in which one was conscious of the old ones to whom I, the child, mattered so much, and to whom my father and mother were only children themselves. If I could decipher those memories, I would have that insight into myself, the past, that would make the future a matter of calm anticipation.

The book I have written about my father, his sisters and mother, and my grandfather coming from Pinsk to America, *The Broken Voyage;* my novels about the world of the Jews abandoned in the streets of Dorchester and Mattapan, published and unpublished; *Dante's*

Mark Jay Mirsky

Kabbalah, a manuscript that maps my country of neo-Platonic dream; or the dusty chambers of hallucinations through Manhattan—novellas like *Knock* or *The College Magician;* even my foray into another borough, "The Brooklyn Golem" (to be found in an issue of the magazine *Fiction*); and the castles back in time that I am working on now have their origin in that corridor. There I set my steps every few years in a dream that promises to return me to that moment before one has forgotten the world one was sent from.

I can recall a half a minute, by a little bridge over the water—my aunt Sonya told me that they had taken me to Springfield, Massachusetts (or was it the Public Gardens in Boston?) and the excitement, in part the creation of the adults, of seeing the swan boats. Sunshine flickers over these images. My aunt Rochelle, my father's half sister, said to me a few years ago, "Mark, you were such a happy child!," her breathless exuberance masking a caustic wit, and the implication that at five or six, I lost that. She and I laugh over the yellow yoke and congealed whites she stuffed up my nose and ears in Montreal, when I refused to eat the unfamiliar scrambled eggs she had prepared for breakfast. I had been dumped on my aunt and her husband, the rabbi, for a night and day by my parents. Many years after, the smell of scrambled eggs was still poison to my stomach.

Scent is the Messianic trait, and my novella *The Messiah's Nose,* in the novel *Franklin Park Puddingstone,* speaks of it. In that lost corridor, I smell old pipe tobacco, my grandfather's. I put it into my nose—cherry mixed with the snuff of the American Indians, the cinnamon and cloves of the silver towers that are shaken between the Sabbath and the weekday. Decaying leather straps from the mysterious boxes of phylacteries spice the air, and then the sharp tang on the rocky cobbles of the street just beyond our porch at 46 Warner—horse shit.

I was born just as the horse and wagons were leaving the city streets. Daily a few feet from the curb, a fresh heaping mound of manure, twice as big as my foot, buzzed with blue and green flies. Milk wagons, junk wagons, grocery wagons, ice wagons, drawn by horses, they clattered down our quiet street. Their passage, even when silent, sealed in the stamp of manure, sprinkled with hay shavings.

There is a bitter, brutal stanza of Jonathan Swift's, a writer who has always exercised a peculiar hypnotism for me, mocking the romantic in his poem "The Lady's Dressing Room," as the lover catches sight of the toilet basin— "... finishing his grand survey, / The swain disgusted slinks away, / Repeating in his amorous fits, / Oh! Celia, Celia, Celia shits!" As Swift concludes, however, "He soon would learn to think like me, / And bless his ravished eyes to see / Such order from confusion sprung, / Such gaudy *tulips* sprung from *dung.*"

Other writers in this series have spoken of a childhood discovery: the power of attraction to the body of another. I might soften Swift, so to speak, by thinking about those games, played with twigs for thermometers on the scuffed, unpainted steps in front of my house at 46 Warner Street in Dorchester. A neighborhood girl—or two—and I explored each other, front, rear, in games of doctor and nurse. How or why did this curiosity about the smell of the opposite sex suddenly stop? My mother may have caught us and shaken over me the finger of taboo? I still see the bench in Franklin Park where it was first disclosed. Did I ask in our living room again to see it? My baby-sitter, pale, Irish, who seemed so grown up, though probably no more than fourteen, soft creases in her cheeks mottled with pink, lifted her skirt and drew the band of her panties down to show an appendix scar. By five, off to kindergarten, the neighborhood girls were lifted by our maiden teachers into another sphere, even the tomboys. We approached the thrones of these Jewish princesses with chaste reverence, cherishing unrequited courtly hopes. A lifetime later, at ten, the world of the erotic again loomed in the Dorchester streets, a whisper between the desks, down the schoolroom aisles.

The pavement beyond the front steps became a dangerous highway through which one ran, or retreated, before the cruelties of juvenile criminals who had discovered in me the child who cries easily, a classical victim. On the way to public school, on the way home, playing on the front porch, one had to have eyes in the back of one's head. Nothing could draw them off, not even my father in his three-piece attorney's suit, shouting red-faced, flailing a broom seized from our entryway, chasing them down one street, then another, finally into their own house. My father's temper, murderous, matched their own. He had been kicked to the side by the Polish soldiers in Pinsk when they grabbed his uncle and pushed him against a wall with thirty-six other Jews—a massacre that briefly touched the world in 1919. The kids, the Burkes, who regularly beat me up were not kidding. (In the U.S. Air Force, serving my six months of active duty, I would get a news clipping from my mother, telling me that the Burke brothers had been arrested for robbing a bank in Uphams Corner with machine guns.) Our street was only one over from the railroad tracks, where the New York-New Ha-

"My father, Wilfred (Velvel) Mirsky, just before his immigration to America," Pinsk, Poland, 1919

The Boston Flower Market was pure aphrodisiac. My grandfather had been a wholesaler for the growers and under the great glass roof of the old Cyclorama building on Dover Street, his cronies still remembered Israel. Joe Price, the florist, who sold orchids, would always give my father a free box and tell, after some coaxing, a tale of the Jewish Legion in which he had fought during the First World War, facing the Turks in Palestine.

I am muddling my entry to that childhood Eden, the Flower Market.

My father from his very first days in America had worked beside my grandfather, Israel, in the latter's stall during the 1920s. Dad was used to getting up at 4:30, 5:00 in the morning. By 5:30 A.M., he was impatient for company and would begin to whistle, put on the radio—Strauss marches blared out at that hour of the morning. If all else failed, he came into my bedroom and gave me a shake. My reward was a corned beef sandwich at six in the morning at the G&G delicatessen, where Dad met one set of his clients, salesmen who had to be out on the road early, and then we hurried to Dover Street and the market. At six thirty, quarter of seven in the morning air, the intoxicating breeze of carnations, gardenias, roses, filling the glass dome of the market, sent one round and round in circles of joy. Echoes of Grandpa, who had come to America nine years before his children arrived, still seemed to go up and down the aisles as men spoke of Israel Mirsky with affectionate familiarity. Most of the stalls were closed by eight thirty, the day's business transacted.

This was the poetry of childhood. Its prose was the bitter understanding that I had failed my father, Grandpa, and so disappointed Mother as well. I was not a genius—in fact, a bit of a dummy.

I came from a place situated between Russia and America—one of those immigrant communities that throw up a circle of covered wagons to defend what they have brought from their old civilizations. I belonged as much to the *blottes*, the swamps of Pinsk, as to the Algonquin woods of the Blue Hills, or the Yankee and Irish tribal lands staked out in the Commonwealth and city.

ven roared up and down to Boston. It was the haunt of poor families. "You killed Jesus," the brothers shouted, jumping me with a boy named Plunkett, who had one eye of glass. These names, famous in Irish history, would haunt me as would the malice that seemed to bubble in their eyes.

Smells held one in thrall—the "schoodies," or non-Jewish thugs, smelled of beer, piss, not the cabbage and lemon of Jewish hallways, stuffed meatballs, *kishke,* or the sweet liver-stuffed *knishes.* Even the lace-curtain Irish, along the better streets off Codman Square, had their particular perfume, something we smelled in the grand ladies who were our elementary school teachers. This was part of my childhood paradise, the smell of foreign hallways in Boston. For I often trailed after my father, a political figure in the city as well as a lawyer, who took me along to keep him company as he climbed the stairs to many strange entryways.

The unhappy experience of school—this now intersects with the autobiography of the spirit. "When I think about it, I must say that my education has done me great harm," Kafka repeats in his diary, as if that strain of his harp gives redeeming pleasure. This "reproach" in my case is tempered by the bifurcation of Hebrew and public school education. In the Boston public schools through the eighth grade, I was a good but not spectacular student. This was "a thwart, disnatured torment" to my father. He had come to America from Byeloruss without English at thirteen and within a few years torpedoed through all the elementary grades into the city's most demanding, classical high school. I was an average student in public school—and that was painful in the fiercely competitive streets of Jewish poverty where the son of the "fruit man" was held up, his superior points suspended over my head—an example of true genetic growth. In Hebrew school the extent to which I was stunted became apparent. I went from the room of my first grade teacher, a handsome tall Miss, who reflected from her olive complexion and sturdy breasts the sun of Palestine, to a short, gray-haired Mrs. in the second, pale with the sunless whitefish cheeks of Eastern Europe, angry beyond words. My father was a director of the synagogue that oversaw the school. Escape was impossible. "Mirsky, you idiot!" Mrs. B would scream, hurling one of the prayer books which served as our textbooks down the aisle at my head, breaking countless pointers on the blackboard. She was the first to whisper the horror of the Holocaust in our ears and to cry the tears of Isaiah over Roosevelt's betrayal—a shock to our liberal ears raised on the psalmody of the Democratic party. Evidently the talented Hebrew students in the class had a different experience of her teaching. The film director Alfred Maysles, and Arnold Band, the Biblical scholar, everyone it seems who lived in this corner of Boston has a story about her. She appears in two of mine, "The Last Boat to America" and "Lessons," presiding at Beth El, the gloomy altar where we sacrificed the after-school hours, when the rest of the world was free to run around the streets and back lots. She was one of those characters who loomed large in small geographies like the Dorchester streets.

I tried to sketch this world directly in a piece called "The Deep Blue Hill" that I wrote originally for the *Dutton Review.* The pages landed in *The Boston University Journal,* bound together with photographs that Elsa Dorfman took of Blue Hill Avenue, accompanying me on a trip

with my father in and out of its failing butcher shops and delicatessens.

My wife, a Norwegian, complains about the insular, almost rude behavior of the Chinese shopkeepers who have slowly crept up the Bowery, Elizabeth, Mott, Mulberry, since we took up residence on that old Dutch farm lane of Peter Stuyvesant, displacing the Italian and Jewish stores. I recall that the wrinkled faces of the generation who tended similar bungholes of commerce, more comfortable with Yiddish than English, left behind in the mad American immigrant scramble for success, were equally suspicious, if not hostile, toward strangers who came in from the "other worlds" to look over their merchandise.

My father's career, first as a lawyer who had graduated from both Harvard College and Harvard Law School, then as a State Representative in the Massachusetts legislature, his first two terms between 1948 and 1952, meant that the "other worlds" of Massachusetts were part of my childhood. I was, in fact, half out of the Jewish streets, almost from the outset. Of course the teachers in public school were almost all Irish-Catholic spinsters, forced by a nasty quirk of the Boston School Committee to remain unmarried if they wanted a job. Eccentric, they played the roles of secular nuns without the consolation of a religious vocation. My elementary school was almost entirely Jewish. There were a sprinkling of Protestants—I remember my father and mother's friendship with a Christian Science family just around the block—but most of the children on the fringe were Irish Catholics, poor families who had to live in the marginal housing on the edges of the Jewish blocks. The teachers spoke the language of another world—"novenas, Catholic retreats, saints," their small talk of a forbidden reality—through those sick years of religious reaction. The textbooks we were handed belonged to yet another America, not just Dick and Jane, those happy tintypes out of *Reader's Digest,* but the American Revolution, old Boston, its heroes Samuel and John Adams, Israel Putnam, Puritans like the Winthrops, Bradfords, Endicotts—our schools and streets bore their insignia. They were the real Americans, not we, the Jewish kids, or our Irish teachers. Our history and English classes right through high school suggested that Jews, Irish, Italians, Polish, our classmates, and, more painfully, our teachers, did not really exist in the United States. I have always felt that Joseph McCarthy's hypnotism was part of that parody that the Irish have such a genius for—the parody of American patriotism—hinting that the *echt* (genuine) America could never be acted out by Yankees, but only by their successors in rock-ribbed conservatism, the Irish Catholics.

Public school was rational compared to Hebrew school. Here the process was crueler. The teachers identified a few geniuses on which they doted. The rest of us were "idiots." Why? "Hebrew School" education began as a Zionist ex-

The author's Aunt Hilda (from left), Grandfather Israel, Aunt Sonya, and father in Boston after a nine-year separation, 1920

periment. Its founders enlisted dedicated and intelligent members of a Jewish community locked into the shtetls and small cities of Poland and Russia, recruiting teachers to create Hebrew as a living language and with it the ideology of return to the Land of Israel. My work on the town books, *Yizkor* volumes, of my father's city, Pinsk, to be published by Stanford University Press, brought me into contact with students of this generation. I met them as old men, bright-eyed, laughing, often heroes of the War of Independence in Israel. Their stories, love for the teachers of those "new" or "reformed" Hebrew schools of Eastern Europe, have given me the measure of the distance between their Hebrew education and mine. In the United States, the experiment degenerated into a foredoomed attempt on a part-time basis to teach both Hebrew and the fundamentals of the Jewish religion to restless children. American culture beckoned. Oh, to be Dick and Jane in our few free hours of play, though instinctively we understood them as ideals far removed from our fun. Over the orange ash of the coal barrels that were spilled out on the icy sidewalks of Warner Street by the wooden tenement at the corner, I galloped, Red Rider across the barrens of the far West. In the spring, the neighborhood broke off branches from the privet hedges for bows and arrows, fixed chips of slate in the split green wood as hatchets, wild Sioux, lurking Pequot, and longed to go naked but for breechcloths.

One sat in Hebrew School forever—hours that would not pass. I counted them off in the small thick wafers of a candy known as Canada Mints, moving them on my tongue until they dissolved and seemed to take the bitter taint of failure off with the five minutes of sucking they tolled against the clock. Four or five mints brought me to my daily request for the bathroom; a stronghold of fifteen minutes against the boredom and misery of being called on. My teachers could not reach me, did not try.

My father had been a Hebrew teacher in an earlier generation when to study Hebrew was a radical idea. He studiously ignored my disaster, apart from his scowl when the report card arrived. Each year I grew more depressed, less attentive, as the Hebrew words flew out of my head, and I measured time in that metronome of sugar licked into motes until the bathroom could be requested. The moment of my bar mitzvah arrived. This rite, which my father

took pleasure in reminding me was not celebrated in any unusual fashion in the Pinsk of his childhood, has been transformed in the United States. It is a pre-adolescent male "coming out," a debutante party. My father made mine into a political rally for his third term candidacy in the legislature. Besides our large family, spread from California to Canada, he invited as many people as he could afford in the district he represented. He could not countenance a disgrace by me on the high altar before a thousand people.

And so began a very different back and forth.

My father, Wilfred (his Hebrew name, *Zaav* or "Wolf"), when he had a mind to do it, was a talented instructor. He had earned his way through Harvard Law School as a Hebrew teacher, and former students ran his first political campaigns. A complex man who defined himself as an "agnostic," taking equal pleasure in the Talmud and Spinoza, he drilled me to recite the passage from Isaiah, talking about the prophet's anguish and encouraging me to make my performance echo it. To look for the drama in the Hebrew words and "act" as if I was Isaiah in my recitation was an entirely new idea of what you might do with a Biblical text.

My relatives were stunned, my father happy with me. The bar mitzvah after the religious ceremony was a mass rally—my father's most detested political opponents pumping hands in the crowd. Our family was engulfed in a crush of *shleppers* from the surrounding streets, pushing in for a free lunch. One of the waitresses behind the buffet, not recognizing me when I reached for an extra piece of *lukshin koogle* (noodle pudding), slapped my hand away.

We moved. In a larger space I could reserve many pages for what it meant to move from Warner Street in Dorchester to Hazelton Street in Mattapan. Both addresses were within my father's district—Ward Fourteen—which he represented in the legislature. In Mattapan we were surrounded on three sides by greensward of peculiar countryside: a Catholic cemetery, a broad pasture behind iron pikes, the very bottom of the state insane asylum's meadows, and an empty lot where tombstones were displayed for sale. Still, Mattapan, which is Algonquin for "landing place" (a ford of the Neponset River), was a step up in the sociology of Boston's Jewish streets. There was a library, an elegant one with Georgian details, at the very top of the street where it met Blue Hill Avenue, that central artery of kosher existence. And I was freed from Beth El, a gloomy Orthodox academy, and sent to Beth Hillel, a Hebrew School whose synagogue had become "Conservative." In my grade, the fifth at Beth Hillel, they recruited for the Purim play. Here I got my first chance to act. My teachers and parents hardly recognized the gloomy boy at the back of the class who bounded out. I played a crazy Persian king, swinging a baseball bat as a scepter under a jester's cut-out cardboard crown, riddling the air with Yiddish swear words, *a klog oif ihr!* (a curse on her)."

Yiddish! This was the first time I was encouraged to speak this language, my father's first tongue. It was the secret palaver of the house, and its rhythms ran like Alph in the sunless sea of our basement lives. I still don't speak but a few broken words and phrases; however, it is as precious to me as the testimony of descent from King David.

August 11, 1997—it is my birthday. A fearful moment for me. I have been working this summer on an introduction to Robert Musil's *Diaries,* large excerpts of which we printed in the magazine *Fiction* in the past year. Bringing out the magazine in the wake of Donald Barthelme's death, Max Frisch's, and Harold Brodkey's, all those adopted fathers and elder brothers, is in part thankless. Associating oneself with this great European novelist who died in poverty and neglect, an exile in Switzerland from the Nazis, gives some piety to the task. A passage from late in the *Diaries* recalls one of those strands that runs through my own history, easily forgotten and yet a cable to this moment.

"Nietzsche. Did I absorb in my youth, even as much as a third of him? Despite this, a decisive influence." I am in my late fifties today, about as old as Musil was when he wrote that line. I read Nietzsche in high school—not of course in class—there was only one teacher one might suspect of appreciating him (characteristically, a Jew, Sidney Rosenthal). The curse of Hitler's distortion of Nietzsche still lay over his works. We read Nietzsche by way of Colin Wilson's *The Outsider,* which introduced me and a few other schoolmates to the spectrum of Existentialism—Sartre, Camus, Hesse, Kierkegaard, and their promise of sexual and intellectual freedom. Giurdieff and Ouspensky, deep forag-

ers into the supernatural, were beyond me. Musil makes so clear the promise of that "other reality," the mystical, but I think, in retrospect, its waters have been muddied by most of the Existentialists we read. If not outright anti-Semitism, there was suspicion of Jews among many of the boys at the Boston Public Latin School, and enthusiasm for Nietzsche was sometimes part of this. Our city's angry ethnic politics in the 1950s encouraged it. A boy I considered a close friend suddenly sneered at me as a "Jew." It meant not only stingy, but tied to the material, particularly in erotic matters. My frankness in speaking of women, of Jewish young women, whose tight skirts and translucent blouses flaunted their adolescent attractions—though they kept one at a distance (certainly from the "final consolation" of the Medieval handbook)—must have irritated this "friend." I was wary of Nietzsche, but his doctrine of man going beyond man, always trying to surpass, was a hypnotic idea, leaping beyond the boundary. How strange it was to hear these sentiments on the lips of Rabbi Soloveitchik, that overarching authority of Orthodox Judaism, whom my grandfather Israel had helped bring to Boston. Some fifteen years later, deep in the Brookline night, the "Rav" or "Teacher" as he was known, rose on his tiptoes, a frail man in his seventies, before an audience of gray-bearded men, boys with pious curls around their ears, a scattering of college professors like myself, to evoke the footsteps of man and woman in the Garden of Eden and the necessity of risk. "It's man's nature to be always reaching out. Man's task is to go beyond boundaries." This circle of friends, reading forbidden books, trying to live the ideas of Dostoyevsky, Nietzsche, Sartre, to make ourselves "aware" of each other, of ourselves, these companions were the round bobbing ring that bore me through waves of despair, four dreadful years of being condescended to in the Boston Public Latin School.

One of my non-Jewish classmates, who was part of the circle that met occasionally at my house in Mattapan to discuss books, saw one of the first paperbacks on my shelf—I believe it was *The Anchor Reader.* Among its contents was "Yalta" by Alger Hiss, and "The Sexual Failure of the Beautiful Woman." This boy borrowed the book and brought it into school. Caught with it, he defended himself by saying, "It's not mine—Mirsky gave it to me." The Headmaster called me in. I'm not sure which of the two articles angered him more. He was a gravel-voiced Irishman who read the Psalms at school assemblies as if they were threats not songs. Since I had not brought the book into school, there was nothing he could do officially. He shepherded me into his office though, snarling, "If I were your father, I would take you behind the woodshed and give you a whipping." In my house an unabridged copy of Rabelais with illustrations had been on the shelves free for my perusal. From childhood no book was forbidden.

In my senior year, I mentioned James Joyce's *Portrait of the Artist* to my English teacher, thinking because of his Irish ancestry he might be touched by my curiosity about the world of Dublin. His red cheeks flamed as he cursed Joyce. "Where's your ashes?" he cried down the aisle one Wednesday. The Irish boy who toyed with agnosticism was not a student to these masters, but an errant sheep.

Mark Jay Mirsky at age three, Boston, 1942

One came close to the Irish though, in their anger, their sense of religion as embattled, precious, a mystery to be guarded. At fifteen in school I felt oppressed by the Irish Catholic masters' fears, the anxiety that the self-appointed seer of American patriotism, Joseph McCarthy, this community's hero before the Kennedys, was spreading through the United States. I did not appreciate the pain that lay concealed in McCarthy's mockery of the American Puritan.

Nietzsche preached the ideal of the lonely hero, Zarathustra, the man who through will overcomes the boundaries set to normal human life. That was a necessary idea to keep one's head above the waters of the shabby Jewish streets, the rote memory exercises of the Boston Public Latin School, the dreary conversation of girls I met, moving toward the impossible, far-off goal of a college of stimulating thought, of a woman who could be a partner in thought, of a task one could master and in doing so go beyond one's own capabilities. I had known that in one place—the stage.

I was a high C and low B student at the Boston Public Latin School. My father went there only two years after getting off the boat from Pinsk. "I won the Classical Prize my freshman year with an English dictionary in my back pocket," he said, staring at my abysmal grades. (Years later I was to discover on his shelves the book he received as a sophomore for the Modern Prize as well.) By dint of effort, hitherto unknown to me, and the skill of a teacher known as "weepy Murphy," I did get an A that year in Latin. This white-haired gentleman with the lilt of Dublin in his voice would catch a cheater and lean over whispering, "I'm sorry, Mr. ..., but you're out." Little tears would appear in the blue, guileless eyes of the Master. It meant expulsion from the school. Latin as taught by Mr. Murphy was not only clear, but echoed of ancient history, a subject that fascinated me, which I learned reading the college textbooks on my father's shelf. And I was determined not to repeat the disaster of Hebrew School. I was credible in English and history but my sophomore year the English teacher was bored and I caught his disease. History was taught only in the freshman and senior year. In my second language, Greek, only the dismal performance of the football team which had enrolled alongside me saved me. My father had easily mastered German, since the Yiddish spoken during the occupation of Pinsk in the First

World War by the Kaiser's armies was colored by them. I determined to at least perish in a language in which I could not be taunted with comparisons. There was a certain nobility in baring one's breast to the inevitable in Greek. The class average sunk so low, however, that I was saved by the curve. I had little talent for languages. (I learned, however, to read the Greek alphabet, to sound out Greek, and this, like my flirtation with Latin, would profit me many years later, for I would finally read Homer haltingly in Greek.) In French I diddled, uninspired.

More or less 800 students entered the Boston Public Latin School in each class, some in the seventh grade, others like myself in the ninth. Of these only about 180 survived to graduate in my class, 1957. "Look to the right of you, look to the left of you," was the Master's sardonic boast. "Only one of you will survive." Boston was a stew of angry children who flunked out and skulked off, feeling they had been flushed into the gutters. (My sense of Louis Farrakhan was turned upside down upon learning that he had dropped out of the school. He must have known what I knew, suffering beyond words the crucifixion of rote memory in Western Civilization.) There were those who were just geniuses. The rest of us didn't sleep at night for four or six years without nightmares in which we had failed and been expelled.

And from this torment one talent released me—declamation. It was a trial for most students to get up and recite several stanzas of poetry aloud in class. My memory, untrustworthy in Latin, French, Greek, Hebrew, held words in declamation. I remembered sentences, paragraphs, passages with slight effort. The silver and gold medals I won at the schoolwide competitions glittered in the midst of my mediocre grades. I copied Gielgud's deep-throated sighs as Hamlet, and the next year writhed on the stage as the hunchback, Richard the Third, in a voice which mimicked Lawrence Olivier's. On the headmaster sitting stonily in his chair by the curtains of the proscenium, I cast an eye of insanity borrowed of Richard Burton's wicked King played on a mining camp's makeshift stage in the movie *Prince of Players*.

This one gift of dramatic mimicry would eventually speak in my writing. Luck brought me an English teacher in my junior year, Sidney Rosenthal, who was filled with enthusiasm for the Russian classics, Dostoyevsky, Tolstoy; an instructor who wanted to know what we thought, instead of vocabulary words we could reproduce with correct spellings and identify in context. Again in my senior year, Paul Pearson, with real enthusiasm for history, gave me the kind of encouragement that brought me to the top of his class. And I recall for a moment in an hour with our Latin Master, Mr. Dolan, hearing the sudden flash of Virgil's voice in *The Aeneid*.

The rest is silence—for I was twisted, like poor Richard, out of shape. There were no girls at the Boston Public Latin School and very little time to pursue those who lived in our quickly crumbling Jewish neighborhood or the wealthy suburbs whither everyone with daughter to be married was fleeing. I came home from Boston Public Latin by trolley, stopped at the corner drugstore where I ordered some kind of cheese doodles that I chewed on with a raspberry coke, and rifled the soft covers whose pages were often just stapled, behind the regular wire rack where the stiffer paperbacks with the conventional stuff, Mickey Spillane, etc., spun. I had about an hour to find enough passages about unwary young women trapped into "intercourse," a word that trembled like the body one dreamed beside one in the afternoon nap before the long night of study that extended into the morning hours. I got up at seven or eight, choked down a meal, then sat until one or two in the morning, trying to get tenses straight in Latin, French, Greek, and sandwich my reading and mathematics in between. In the early morning I often woke in the grip of a nightmare that must have repeated itself four or five times a month. I had failed the test the day before and had been expelled. Only slowly, as the gray, cold light of the long Boston winter entered my window did I recall that I had managed to scrape through yesterday's examination.

This is too dreary to be an entire representation of my years at Boston Latin, but there were many hours spent trudging up and down Blue Hill Avenue in the yellow light of a district where failure meant being consigned to a self-imposed ghetto. One would take a job as a shoe salesman, a short order cook, a delicatessen slicer in a restaurant. I lived outside of books, and acting, in a fantasy world, part of it concocted from the scraps of history, part from my other reading in which I doodled maps and drew figures of young men who were leading troops on an island in a perpetual war for its liberation from an invasion of Turks. *"Enteuthen exelaune,* from thence they marched" was Xenophon's cry in the *Anabasis,* and in this kingdom drawn in my lined notebooks, I was constantly retreating before a superior force into mountains where I would hide, to strike back when least expected.

The thick green paint of the doors and window frames, the massive red brick of its walls, the sun filling the windows in the morning on the side that faced the Boston Lying In Hospital, the white marble of classical statuary in the entryway, these still float before me as if I could put my teeth against them and taste the school.

My father, despite a political defeat in the middle of his legislative career right after my bar mitzvah, was a major figure in Massachusetts politics throughout this period in my life. The house resonated with issues that were reflected in the Boston papers, and the glamour of his exploits and speeches cast a glow over our family, though often emphasizing how far I fell short of him. In the morning he would often drive me to school, asking me to read to him from journals like Winston Churchill's during the Boer campaign, or telling stories about Alfred North Whitehead to whose teas he had gone at Harvard. At sixteen, I took the wheel, and he read, an extension of the companionship that had begun with the bar mitzvah lessons.

At the end of my junior year, the horizon widened further for me. My mother, looking for free vacations to send me on, had dispatched me to Boys' State on the campus of the University of Massachusetts in Amherst. I had some experience of the red-faced, burly men who ran it, walking behind my father at the State House and at the Democratic State Convention in Worcester. I was only fifteen but had my father's delegate pin on my lapel to get in and out of the auditorium. Knocko McCormack, the rotund brother of the Speaker of the U.S. Congress, and his cronies pushed us up against the back wall, beery-eyed, swearing that if we didn't support their choice for the governor's nomination, "You and the f...n' Jews are gonna be out of Massachusetts politics for fifty years." The convention of boys in Amherst were to choose a governor, lieutenant governor, and attorney general. The supervising Legionnaires covered themselves with more medals than Soviet generals. They jingled, walking in beribboned uniforms.

It was obvious that the Irish boys had been organizing for elections far in advance of the convention in Amherst. The nominating process was a foregone conclusion, stacked against Jews, just like the Democratic party in Massachusetts. I volunteered for the newspaper and published my first poems in it. I had watched my father cast the single dissenting vote in the legislature. At the nominating convention, I jumped up on a table and declared in a voice loud enough to carry across the hall without a microphone, "I'm going to run for governor as an independent. In the proud tradition of Aaron Burr and Henry Wallace!" The last name struck dynamite. A crowd of boys actually chased me across the campus screaming "Communist!" I had to lock myself into the newspaper's room in a dormitory basement and promise to withdraw from the race.

Still, I had a newspaper column, and the journalist who supervised us was a wily old veteran who had that touch of outlaw wit that gives the Irish such spunk. He allowed me to snipe at the convention in the paper. I ridiculed the speeches, mentioning that the candidate for attorney general, a handsome six-footer, thought his medals as an Eagle Scout were a qualification for office.

Ted Kelley came by to ask what I meant by making fun of him. We immediately became friends. The prospective attorney general had a real curiosity for books, ideas, as well as manners far more polished than mine. He invited me out to Wellesley High School where he was the class president. Here for the first time, with the exception of my father's twenty-fifth reunion at Harvard when I was fourteen, I met the middle-class Protestant world of America. Ted was not a Catholic. His girlfriend, Pam, had the beauty of magazine centerfolds. I was introduced to a circle of young women my own age who were not desperate to date marriage prospects three or four years older than they were—some lived in books as I did. The realtors of the 1950s had barred Jews from owning property in Wellesley. I was strange and curious to these girls of seventeen—a visiting celebrity from Siberia.

At the end of my senior year, Ted asked me to join him with a group of boys from Wellesley who were going hiking on Mount Katahdin in Baxter State Park. This was my first experience of the American wilderness. Here I

Mark with his mother, father, and sister, Deanne, 1945

took communion, though I did not know it, with the deities of Concord.

The Wellesley parents were often suspicious, but with a new circle of friends, I slowly walked out of four years of shadow. To everyone's surprise, most of all the masters at the Boston Public Latin School where my average never rose above the mediocrity of a low B, I did so well in my Scholastic Aptitude and Achievement Tests, I found myself admitted to Harvard.

The college I went to is gone. It is a mark of how rapid change has been in this twentieth century that not just buildings, but the flow of time in the streets, and what those streets clung to, has long gone down the river. It need not have been so. My father's Harvard was still there when I entered it—despite many alterations. The college has such a poor ear for its

own echo. The somber resonance of religion that the New England universities and their cousins, Princeton, Columbia, represented for the classes that passed through them, whether Catholic, Jew, the hundredfold denominations of the Protestants, that unique aura has been lost. The slightly musty Harvard of the 1950s was provincial, and it sold that shadowy birthright for the pottage of success like so many other American institutions. To have stood against the flood tide was perhaps impossible, but why did no one even imagine doing so? As I read Thoreau over, I sympathize with his suspicions that as a writer one can never be sentimental about education, or the places in which it was housed. The lasting value of Harvard for Henry David Thoreau was its library, the instruction he received in the classics, perhaps the bond it implied with his neighbor, Ralph Waldo Emerson.

I was so eager to escape Blue Hill Avenue—perceived as a curse, the image reflected in its storefronts in the glass of countless promenades through adolescence, the Hebrew school failure, potential public school dropout—that I drove to Harvard Square to live there. Seeing my chagrin at being accepted at his alma mater but asked to live at home, my father bought me an old Buick convertible. I slept in its leather cushions through the Cambridge night. A second-class pass to Paradise had arrived in Mattapan. Harvard denied me a place in its dormitories. I was so upset when it came, my admission on a yellow slip of paper rather than a crisp certificate, that I threatened to go to Dartmouth or Bowdoin where I had been accepted without conditions. My father thundered into the room where I was sniffling in bed and cried, "You want to be a big fish in a little pool?"

In June, before Latin School's classes were officially over, I began spending every day and evening in the cafeterias of Cambridge. They were the indoor stoas of the harsh New England climate. The Waldorf, Hazen's, but, in particular, the "Bick," where Harvard undergraduates, professors, graduate students sat arguing. Here, and at Cronin's, a beer hall down the street, no one asked how old one was, but behaved as equals. If one listened, as I did, afraid to reveal how little I knew, brave new worlds came flooding into view. For four years at Harvard, I found my true New Lecture Hall at these cafeteria tables. (I would never be an adequate beer drinker.) There were tales by one wild abstract painter about being thrown through the plate glass window and finding himself unharmed on the sidewalk outside. In the same breath he enthused about Henry James and poured scorn on everything as being "so *existential.*" It was the voice of Bruno Latini, "*Qual maraviglia!* "

I went off for the summer to an apprenticeship at the Theater on the Green on the Wellesley College campus. Jerome Kilty, who had been one of the original Brattle Theater Company, was directing some of the best young actors, American and Canadian, in the English-speaking theater: Nancy Wickwire, Barry Morse in Shaw and Shakespeare. I would come back a second summer when they worked together with that genius of the British Music Hall, Max Adrian, who was so funny in Molière and the Restoration Comedy that night after night apprentices and actors alike tried to contain their laughter in the wings, as they watched his mischief bring the madness of an almost lost stage art into these texts. Among these all too brief productions was a *Merchant of Venice* in which Adrian loomed as a savage clown. Kilty and Adrian had to suppress the vivid colors of their cartoon after the opening night, which brought screams of laughter from some but silence from others down the descending seat banks under the open sky of Wellesley. The *Merchant* was being played in a town where Jews were still locked out of purchasing homes. The staging was too resonant for the audience, which included a number of middle-class Jews from the nearby towns of Brookline and Newton. I saw that night, however, what I believe was Shakespeare's Shylock, a Jew with the criminal instincts of Fagin, immensely funny, penny pinching, a caricature whose pungent antics make one uneasy as it hints at an evil as amusing as it is unsettling. When I read Christopher Marlowe's *The Jew of Malta* at Harvard, I immediately felt the kinship to the Richard I had played and to Adrian's Shylock. I dreamed of performing it at Harvard and almost got to direct it on the Loeb stage, but at the last moment, Harry Levin, a professor whose Jewish background had so far disappeared from view that all and sundry pronounced his last name Le Vin, would thwart me of that ambition, perhaps wisely.

In my first month at Harvard, I was swept up into a dizzy whirlwind that would never quite stop spinning me for four years. I went for auditions and was cast in DeGhelderode's *Escurial* as the mad king. John Van Italie was the director and Roger Klein, who in his tragically short career would become one of the most important fiction editors in New York City, played opposite me as the jester. At the same time, I was cast in a production of *The Master Builder* as the old father, Bravik. My son was played by Daniel Selznick, and Richard Jordan played the lead. Danny's mother was the theatrical producer, Louise Selznick, his father the well-known Hollywood director, and his grandfather, Louis Meyer. My father, whose maternal grandfather had owned the circus grounds in Pinsk, talked familiarly of the Selznick grandfather and some of the other Hollywood moguls whose background sprung from those back lots in Eastern Europe where turn of the century entertainment bridged every sort of travelling wonder and side show. Performing was a heady introduction to a wider world after the pavements of Blue Hill Avenue. Most of the young men and women I was acting with in the Harvard Dramatic Society were seniors and some came from sophisticated backgrounds. Daniel Selznick's mother, Irene, after seeing a Harvard Dramatic Society production, had helped introduce Arthur Kopit's play *Oh Dad, Poor Dad, Mother's Hung You in the Closet and I'm Feeling So Sad* to Roger Stevens. The undergraduate's play was produced on the New York stage. Success in the theater meant one became a local celebrity. I would walk through Harvard Square wondering who I was. Where had the sad boy, never to escape the pickle barrels of Dorchester groceries, gone?

In my first year at the college, I tried to write as well as act and direct plays. I didn't know, however, what to write about. The gifted English teacher of my junior year, in my senior year had become faculty advisor of the Latin School *Register*. I had published a story steeped in self-pity, trying to evoke the redbrick walls of the school, the flaking green door of its back door, colors baked under the sun of hopeless afternoons. My freshman writing instructor at Harvard was more than kind, but I knew that the stories I wrote were sentimental. In the spring of 1959 I was acting in downtown Boston, a bit player in a lavish production of *The Power and the Glory*, on the stage of the Wilbur Theater. How I got there would involve more pages on the succession of roles I played as a freshman and sophomore, including Gloucester in *King Lear* at the Peabody Playhouse where I was opposite an uncanny fiery King Lear, danced by the Black actor Harold Scott as if the British monarch was a tiny dervish. Trying to be a professional actor and maintain my studies at Harvard was too much. (I had also kissed a young lady with mononucleosis a few weeks earlier.) Collapsing with a high fever in the middle of the production, I was carried off to Stillman Infirmary on a stretcher. Through my first two years at Harvard I was so eager to be away from Blue Hill Avenue, its Jewish streets, and angry that Hillel House had turned away Ted Kelley who accompanied me there for a freshman mixer, that I filled in "agnostic" on all the forms that asked me to declare a religion. Going through the doors at Stillman, I must have been truly frightened. "Jewish," I whispered on the admission card. Like Jiminy Cricket beside my bed, the new Hillel rabbi showed up, Ben Zion Gold. I

was suspicious and obnoxious, as my temperature had begun to fall rapidly, teasing him about Alfred North Whitehead, many of whose remarks I knew by heart. "You're misquoting Whitehead," I crowed to Ben Zion, who took my cocky attitude in stride. He kept coming back for more abuse, and slowly I understood what a remarkable man he was—unlike any American rabbi I had met. Ben had survived Auschwitz, was deeply knowledgeable about rabbinics, Polish culture, the world of Heschel, Rosenzweig, Nachum Glatzer, Buber, figures from the German Jewish renaissance that had taken place at the beginning of the century, prematurely cut off by Hitler. Ben was eager to meet students at Harvard who were not traditionally Jewish. We often disagreed, but he listened carefully, and I found myself being drawn to the worlds he spoke about.

I often recall the first line I was not entirely ashamed of having written, and I refer to it in the pages of that premature book of mine on American Judaism, *My Search for the Messiah*. I had just come from a long talk with Ben Zion Gold in the Hillel House. Its 1950s home was a ramshackle mansion (was it stucco or brown shingle?) on Bryant Street, a quiet lane of middle-class houses. The path to the door was some twenty feet or so from the sidewalk, and turning to the right at the fence for the long trek back to Harvard Square, a line jumped into my head as if I was a ventriloquist's dummy. "So, it was Epstein the Butcher's boy who had painted the swastika on the wall of the Beth El Hebrew School. Oy." I, of course, was Epstein.

I had made my way, as you may have guessed, into the Harvard dormitories. My mother artfully declared that the stress of living at home was harmful to me—judiciously omitting her own share of my abuse—and in the middle of my freshman year I found myself a resident of Harvard's Matthew Hall, a roommate of John Nathan, the prodigious scholar of Japanese. His room, the larger of the two in the suite we shared, had as its principal decoration an oversized bottle of sake on the mantelpiece. The sheets on a bed that was never made trailed half their length on the dusty floor, until my mother, who came banging on my door demanding my dirty linen, saw his gray windings and gave them the benefits of laundering. The next year in my sophomore year, Tom Glick, now a professor of history at Boston University, and I inherited the room that John Van Italie and Roger Klein had just left.

It was William Alfred who now put the harp in my hand. Bill used to come for lunch to Kirkland House.

The first glimpse of William Alfred was arresting. He wore a hat with a crown that was unusually flat and low, with a small brim that looked suspiciously like clerical headware. It was set at a rakish angle, jutting forward. On his back he bore a green book bag of the kind I had abandoned in high school. Bulging, looking heavy enough to bring a husky schoolboy to his knees, the load bowed the professor's tall back slightly. Like Gershom Scholem, the great sage of Jewish mysticism (who comments revealingly on Martin Buber), William Alfred's ears were large, intimidating. What stopped me, though, in the foot traffic of the Square's sidewalks to stare after his retreating back was the smile that flashed across his face. It was at once mischievous and private, with a touch of the beautific. I would go seeking that quixotic halo in Bill's living room for many years after I had graduated Harvard.

William Alfred had written a verse drama, *Agamemnon,* some poetry, and was teaching Anglo Saxon at Harvard. I never took a class with him. The course he taught in Chaucer belonged, during the year when it was required of me, to another professor. I may have been afraid to turn the friendship that he offered every day at lunch into the more formal relationship of teacher and student. (I did gather the courage to write my undergraduate thesis under his direction.) At the table where Bill sat, however, he taught like Socrates, by sheer wit and insight. I would try again and again to memorize his remarks about Shakespeare, Aristotle, the Broadway theater. Conversations ranged from ghost stories, our own ghosts, to the plays of Eugene O'Neill and our childhood. As all of us—sophomores, juniors, seniors, and the tutors and the younger professors who sought out Bill's table—talked, it was natural to take a turn. Trying to come up to the standard, to find what was interesting in my own life, for I was only a callow nineteen, William Alfred's tales of his own infancy in Brooklyn among the fierce clans of Irish awoke in me the courage to speak of Dorchester, Mattapan, Roxbury. The counterparts of Bill's churches were the synagogues where the wail of Eastern European mountains went up on the High Holy Days. In the sacred

hours, men ran up and down the aisles raising money with the furious palaver of tobacco auctioneers. Bill encouraged me to take this childhood seriously. He listened to a multitude of questions and complaints and, in moments of the distress when my girlfriend had run off with someone else, it was to Bill's living room I trailed, to tell my tale of woe. His associate in wit was Robert O'Clair, the senior tutor at Kirkland House, as red-faced, raunchy, bulky, and Falstaffian as Bill was slender and religious. To hear them read in the Kirkland House Junior Common room—Bill, Chaucer; Bob, Dickens—was to be carried back into literature bodily, to be in the presence of the writers, and to understand what teaching is—to carry a student out of time.

Bill Alfred's table made me look back at Blue Hill Avenue, and the shock of meeting Ben Zion Gold gave me the voice to speak of the streets of childhood. I would never, however, have thought that I could be a writer, if I had not met in my senior year Albert J. Guerard, Jr.

When I was a junior, Ben Gold had asked me to be the literary editor of a magazine he wanted to start at Harvard Hillel, *Mosaic.* Though I had taken a class in creative writing that year, the instructor who belonged to the polite Yankee hierarchy (his wife was Robert Frost's secretary) was not enamored of what I was doing. As a senior I applied to Archibald MacLeish's writing seminar, which was considered the charmed circle for aspiring prose writers. I applied as well to Guerard's. I got a summons a few days later from Albert Guerard, and when I sat down in his office, he began by saying, "Well, I see that you applied to MacLeish. You probably are going to take his seminar...."

I cut him off. "No, MacLeish didn't accept me."

"What!" Albert looked surprised. And that was the beginning of my life-long devotion to this uncanny teacher, who convinced me that I belonged to a tradition, that I was an "anti-realist." I have taken many of Albert's habits of teaching into my own classes. He would simply mark a story with x's next to bad sentences, and check marks next to ones he thought were good. I was so in terror of his approval and disapproval that it would take me months before I could look at the manuscripts, but they pointed the way to a prose voice worth speaking.

Like Bill, Albert engaged his students in a way that implied an equality of endeavor, if not yet understanding, or depth of perception. "Why are you staring at me?" he asked at the beginning of one class, as if it mattered. I had to explain that I was only looking, perhaps too fiercely, for his approval. He brought his own fiction into class, read it, and took what was often stinging criticism. He wasn't afraid to talk about the weaknesses in his work and quoted other writers like Herb Gold on that subject. Albert constantly made himself vulnerable in the class, but woe to one's own work when it fell below the standards he had set. Glowing with the praise he had shown the first work I submitted, I dashed off a hasty, overambitious story, sloppily typed with corrections penciled in. By chance I met him at the sock counter in the Harvard Coop. "Have you...?"

He interrupted me. "I'm not going to let you read it. The class would lose all their respect for you." (Since one of the class, Annie-May de Bresson, had looked my way with favor, this warning had more than literary consequences.) Fishing in his bag, Albert left me with the manuscript in hand. That was one I went through right away, for it was covered with comments, not just checks and crosses. It was my discovery of "voice," and how far I had strayed from my own, or rather how immature and cliché-ridden my voice became when I tried to talk about events that were contemporary to me. I had tried to unriddle my romance with the Canadian girl I had been in love with as a junior and who continued in my senior year to unsettle me. There was no story articulated in those pages, only my distress, confusion. I saw clearly in Albert's handwriting how many dead tags of language I had brought from my house in Mattapan, the detritus of television, *Time* magazine, my father's and mother's careless American conversation. It was a speech of a kind that Harold Brodkey's later books parody so mercilessly in the persona of the mother who adopted him. (Harold, who also studied with Albert Guerard, did not, however, take to him.) It was the shock of Albert's rejection that sent me back to write the first story where my voice was consistent, "Noodle Pudding." For two heady years now, Ben Gold had been plying me with books like Bernard Malamud's *Magic Barrel*, collections of Yiddish stories, Isaac Bashevitz Singer, and I had discovered Philip Roth's *Good-*

by Columbus. Suddenly, there were signposts and directions up in American Jewish fiction. Another influence on me was Riesman's course, where I wrote about Jewish identity, and the shock of Erik Erikson's lectures, and personal charisma in the same fall semester I began studying with Albert.

The summer before my senior year, acting at Provincetown, I had met Norman Mailer. His wife, Adele, was one of the extras in a musical comedy there, wanting to act. Among other roles, I was playing Major Melody in Eugene O'Neill's *Touch of the Poet*. Once introduced to Mailer, I found myself deserting the playhouse whenever I could to sit at his habitual table by the front window in the Old Colony. Dwight MacDonald appeared there after Mailer got into a fight with one of the police commanders, calling out "Taxi!" after a patrol car. The conversation of actors was trite in comparison to the talk that buzzed around Mailer, though one couldn't engage him on the subject of Malamud, Roth, or Bellow. He wasn't interested, and I recall one moment when I turned to the writer sitting next to him, a slim African American, who sympathetically discussed with me this circle of Jewish writers in whose footsteps I would try to follow. He was James Baldwin.

Mailer's *Advertisements for Myself* had just come out. I immediately understood that Mailer was a writer I wanted to know as I groped for my own voice. Irving Howe would remark to me that Mailer's best fiction, *The Time of Her Time* and *The Man Who Studied Yoga*, were in this collection. Equally important to me was the essay "The White Negro," in which the texts of existentialism, my underground reading in high school, were given fresh relevance. "I was so aware of him, he was so aware of me," its refrain, was given vivid meaning to me one afternoon. Cocky with the success of my acting as the rubicund Major Melody (a role which a mature Eric Portmann played in the Broadway production), and encountering Mailer at a street crossing in Provincetown by the playhouse, I fell into step beside him. We were both headed to the town's West End. It was a walk of fifteen or twenty minutes. I began to talk about acting, delivering what became a long monologue, until we came to a fork in the road where our common route parted.

He broke his silence. "I haven't heard a word you said." He turned to the right and didn't look back.

Several weeks later at a party, I stood a few feet away, staring at Mailer's back or profile for ten minutes, wondering how he could be so cruel. He turned to me abruptly, "Now, that's acting!"

The theater was my preoccupation. I spent two seasons at the Provincetown Playhouse. At Kirkland House I staged a *Waiting for Lefty* that starred the Black writer William Melvin Kelly and Betsy Bartholet, now a professor at the Harvard Law School. A demure Miss Porter's School graduate, Betsy played a proletarian housewife, standing in a slip above an ironing board, so sweet and vulnerable in her slip she broke the audience's heart. My senior year I directed Ben Jonson's *The Alchemist* on the main stage of the Loeb Theater, then rushed from the graduation ceremony to a stage in Branford, Connecticut, where my former roommate, Steve Randall, was doing a season of summer stock. Here I would appear opposite a young Sally Kirkland in another O'Neill play, *Anna Christie*. Sally hauled me off to the New Haven docks so we could do a "sensual." Alas, "sensual" did not include any hugs or kisses, just deep breaths of the foggy Connecticut night, despite my pleas that we dispense with our roles of father and daughter.

The following summer I acted at Woodstock. In a production of *Three Penny Opera* I played its police chief, Tiger Brown, next to Estelle Parsons' Mrs. Peachum. She would send us all rushing to the back of the auditorium to watch not "acting" but a "performance," that eerie reaching toward the unknown where an actor fills a theater's space with such presence that one's own identity seems to slip away. One is swept into the frightening hypnosis of the audience, the "crowd," and briefly taken out of the body.

It was not yet clear to me that I wanted to write. Mystical power could be distilled in giving oneself up to roles on the stage, more in directing from the back of a dim theater, moving actors and actresses in play that brought the audience into strange worlds. The experience of a book conceived in dreams, passing into strange hands, its events taking place again, would seem, as voices crowded my head, the most mysterious projection of all.

I pause and wonder about my last sentence. Was it instead a freak of politics that sent me in one direction, not another? I thought I

had a Fulbright to study with Joan Littlewood in London. Littlewood's *Oh What a Lovely War* seemed to me the most exciting direction in the theater since the productions mounted by the Russian stage director Vselvolod Meyerhold, murdered by Stalin. I was introduced to Meyerhold in a class Robert Chapman taught in stage managing, one that forced one to really grip the theater. (Professor Chapman was kind enough to put up with my challenges, my ill-considered bravura. I was not a well-behaved class member.) The approval of the New York Theater Committee was tantamount to the Fulbright Award, and I was already receiving congratulations when it was overruled in Washington. The State Department evidently had the last say. (Later my father would be scolded by a relative who worked as the administrative aide to a Long Island congressman—evidently a word from a congressional office would have removed the objection.)

Instead I went on a Woodrow Wilson Fellowship to Stanford—a university that had refused to admit me as an undergraduate. I was following Albert Guerard who had taken a chair there, named for his father. Albert, however, was not allowed to teach in the graduate M.A. program in creative writing at Stanford. Wallace Stegner, who ran the program, regarded not just Albert as suspect but the "anti-realism" that Albert championed as the most important direction in fiction. "I don't know where you could take this," Stegner said to me the first time I met him, in regard to the pages of my first novel, *Thou Worm Jacob*. I had begun this in my last semester at Harvard, desperate to fulfill Albert's requirement of sixty pages. Stegner confided in me that he had always been very friendly to the "Jewish boys" when he taught at Harvard. This set the tone of our conversations that year. My sister would later marry the son of Stegner's close friend, Bernard De Voto, and he would genuinely embrace me when I returned to Stanford to teach. During two quarters of graduate study, however, I wrote clumsy stories, trying to imitate the world of Mark Twain, hoping to come closer to the Western realism that was the mark of Stegner's work. I got a B in his seminar, and in Richard Scowcroft's, his associate. They didn't know what to make of me, though Stegner got along fine with Philip Roth and Ken Kesey. George Higgins, the detective-novelist-to-be, was lurking about the Stanford campus in some capacity. George had been a successful candidate at that American Legion Boy's State. George, a friend named Frank, and I went to see Stegner, somewhere in my third and last quarter at Stanford, driving up to his ranch in the hills. I remember getting a headache, trying to concentrate on his remarks, which were intelligent but deliberately low-key and frustrating to me in their litany of common sense. Bent in close as Stegner spoke, trying to make more of the conversation, one sentence of his from that afternoon stuck in my head. I had read Wallace Stegner's *Big Rock Candy Mountain,* one of my mother's books, when I was in high school. Asking him about it, Stegner drawled, "I wrote that book too early. I wasn't good enough as a writer to tackle the mate-

rial. Now I've spoiled it. I can't go back to that world again."

In *My Search for the Messiah,* there are a few portraits of me as a Stanford graduate student, switching between engineer boots, leather jacket, and motorcycle to a three-piece suit with a Phi Beta Kappa key dangling from the vest pocket. It includes my trip to Tijuana with Albert in search of the neo-Platonic form of beauty through the downtown strip joints. Here I have to speak of women. Sharon Cobb, now Olds, was a close friend—we had a brief romantic interlude—though I was in love with a Radcliffe sophomore, and trying hard through a regular correspondence in the mail to hold on to her. Sharon was one of a circle of Stanford seniors

"My mother being sworn in as a member of the Massachusetts Immigration Board by Governor Paul Dever (1948-49), with her sister-in-law Ruth, her brother Simon, and my father, State Representative from the Dorchester, Mattapan, and Roxbury Districts"

grouped around *Sequoia,* the Stanford Literary Magazine, and their nest in the Stanford Union became a second home to me. Another close friend was a freshman named Charlotte Low, now Charlotte Low Allen, with whom I remain in correspondence on politics and religion. Charlotte likes to recall herself as a gawky adolescent; however, I remember her as a statuesque young woman already girdled into her Roman Catholic principles, but with a blush that always awoke me to fresh admiration. And there was a princess of the far West, Cindy Harwood, a campus rebel, who regarded me with curiosity. I was terribly lonely at Stanford. The friendship of these women, as I sat in my little shack off the El Camino Reale, trying to cook for myself and ward off the depression that came with the steady winter rains, meant everything to me. In the spring, a friend in Cambridge called to tell me that the Radcliffe girl was seeing someone else. After a series of frantic and expensive telephone calls to her, I fell apart.

I was walking along the Stanford campus, mumbling to myself, wondering how I could hold together through my examinations, when I stumbled into Irving Howe. He had been a very important teacher the previous semester when we went back and forth in a class he taught in American literature, a very different influence from Albert, but with a sharp and open mind. There was something funny about Howe. He talked about Huck and Nigger Jim in *Huckleberry Finn,* the "ecstasy on the raft," delivering a glowing peroration about friendship, then fled the class to avoid the eager group of graduate and undergraduate students rushing up to his desk. I teased him about that. Howe had bought a bicycle from me, and Albert and he were good friends, so our paths crossed out of class. He was recently divorced and had bought a shiny red convertible. Riding in it with him one night, we began to talk about one of my fellow graduate students, a young woman with a warm Southern accent, a beaming smile, and an attractive figure. I had taken her out for a date once, but she kept me at a distance. "There's something about her," I said, "that just isn't sensual."

Howe was furious. "Don't ever talk about women that way!" he snapped, with that slight lisp that always made him seem vulnerable. Later I found he was dating the young lady.

Now, however, seeing me in tears, he asked, "Mirsky, what's the matter?" I began to pour out my distress. "Come on, have a cup of coffee," he said, taking me by the arm and steering me to the Stanford Union where he proceeded to make much fun of my romantic agonies, in the spirit of a kinder, gentler Howard Stern. The real Bronx "geshmack" was in his raillery.

I was forced to laugh at myself and give up the bravura of thinking to throw myself off a bridge. "Well," I sighed, at the end of the half hour he spent skillfully making me see the folly of self-pity, "I guess when I am your age, it will be easier."

"No," he replied. "The older you are, the harder you fall."

That was my closest moment with Irving Howe. The next time I saw him, years later at Harvard Hillel, I was with Susan Wick, a girl I had fallen in love with, a spirit of the pure Appalachia. "Who's the *shicksa?*" Irving Howe asked me. I was very hurt. Howe should have been so important to me as a young Jewish writer, and yet like Kazin he seemed to dislike not just me, but the generation of writers who were succeeding Roth, Malamud, Bellow, the companions of his youth. "I didn't know you were a 'mystic,' Mirsky," he called out, at a public assembly at YIVO, when Cynthia Ozick awarded me that title. When I tried to discuss the problems overwhelming us at City College in Open Admissions, Howe waved me away from him in the corridor with a grandiose gesture.

The chairman of the English department offered to give me a full scholarship and a free year traveling in Europe, but Albert Guerard had told me not to stay in graduate school. Did he fear I would fall into his own dilemma, spending more time as an academic than a novelist? Without Albert's support there seemed no point in continuing at Stanford. I had never really considered an academic career. The Ph.D. in English required, I thought, a real facility with foreign languages, one that still eludes me.

I returned to Cambridge and began looking for a reserve unit. It was the age of the draft and there were no deferrals once out of school. "You're not going to make a fool of me in front of all those Irishman," my father barked. In Harvard Square at the Hayes Bickford there was a perpetual seminar on this subject. Taking Epsom salts to speed up your heart rate, feigning craziness, homosexuality, screaming when they told you to take your clothes off. The tables debated a dozen ways of evading responsibility. Dad was the appeal agent for the local draft board. He was sympathetic to all the rest of the Jewish boys trying to slip out of military service in the district, but he had wanted to serve during World War Two and regarded me as his proxy. Later, taking down his memories of childhood—the helplessness of the Jews before the armies that rampaged through his birthplace, Pinsk—I would understand why it was important to him that I learn to "bear arms." I hung around Cambridge after a summer of acting at the Woodstock Theater, where my roommate Steve Randall directed a season of stock. I had met David Packard, Jr., son of the founder of Hewlett Packard, at Stanford. David, embarking on graduate study in Classics, offered to sublet a room in the apartment he was renting on Hingham Street. My father, growing anxious at seeing me neither in school nor working while I waited for a place in the Reserves, secured a substitute teaching position for me in the Boston Public Schools.

Girls' High was in one of the toughest parts of Boston, just above Dudley Street Station. Its population of young women reflected that even though the students were drawn from all over the city. I had no idea what I was doing but was thrust as a substitute into several classes to teach American history. "Don't push the girls too hard," one of the older teachers told me, "They're not that smart." The class I remember best had a substantial number of Black students. Most of them were polite and curious— after all I wasn't much older than they were, though from fourteen, fifteen, sixteen, to twenty-three is an awesome leap. One of these adolescents flashed at me during a lesson when I was trying to make the dry facts of our textbook real to them, "Why the hell should I care about Marbury versus Madison?"

Attractive, impatient, rebellious, she voiced what most of the room, bored by my recitation, felt. I threw the book down on the desk. "If you have a hope of getting out of a segregated society in the next few years," I said, with a rising voice, "it's because of Marbury versus Madison." And I began to talk about the Supreme Court, the principle of judicial review, the separation of powers, the constitution, in terms of what was happening and could happen in their lives. The anger in the class was like a fuse that lit up the pages, and I was

excited, coming back to that class, day after day, to try to recover the real attention of every young woman in it. A majority of the class was white, poor Irish kids, but they were as alive to the inequities of American society as the young Black who had challenged me. It was a privilege to teach in this atmosphere. One very shy but deeply intelligent student, a Miss McCarthy, came up after a class and asked me for a book list. I began to bring my own books into the class, and after I left for the military asked my parents to let her borrow from the shelves in my room. My mother was suspicious and did not encourage her one or two visits in my absence. Sitting in the Hayes Bickford, staring through the windows at the Cambridge High School girls, the wanderers from prep school, the Radcliffe freshmen, with Jonathan Kozol, who had been a student of Albert Guerard and was now, after publishing *The Fume of Poppies,* at loose ends, I mentioned how sad I was going to be to leave my teaching post. He was suddenly interested, twenty-two dollars a day—? My rent was only thirty-five dollars a month on Hingham Street. A week's work was enough to pay for the next thirty days' living expenses. "Your father has the same contacts with the School Committee as mine," I laughed. And Jonathan went into the public school system as I left it. As a prep school graduate he had a slightly different perspective on the system. In his book he gives a vivid description of its corporal punishment. I had been rattanned—it wasn't the physical pain that stung, it was the shame. Discipline in most of the classes was built on that.

One of my friends from Harvard, in the same fix as I was, had found a medical reserve unit that would take us. I volunteered to be a psychiatric ward assistant. In my senior year the course with Erik Erikson had led to several stormy sessions between us. He first asked me to lecture, as a director on *Wild Strawberries* by Ingmar Bergman, then got up and physically pushed me off the lectern because he didn't like my conclusions. I have a raft of Erikson stories, but again have to hurry on. Erikson's course had piqued my interest in mental institutions. Romantic fascination with madness was a very strong part of my character. Talking about blood, however, even subjects like the circulation of the heart, makes me so queasy I get faint to this day. This dates from the age of

Mirsky as Major Melody in Eugene O'Neill's Touch of the Poet, *Provincetown Playhouse, 1960*

five. Tripping with two milk bottles, I fell down the front stairs of my house on Warner Street, cutting my palms in the shattered glass. Bleeding profusely over the sidewalk, I was lifted up and rushed to Children's Hospital in the milkman's wagon—one of the first engine-driven ones. When I came home, the flies were still buzzing over the fresh blood.

We flew to Houston, Texas, and Lackland Air Force Base. I can't write easily about the next two months. It recalled the worst moments of the Boston Public Latin School. I thought Harvard and Stanford had set me beyond bullying and sadism. My head was shaved. College was a liability. The sergeants deprived us of sleep, pushed us into a punishing set of physical exercises, created a surreal set of standards for the toilet kits we crammed into our drawers, set upon us in a deliberate hazing. For the first two weeks I cried in outrage against my pillow in the few hours between midnight and three in the morning, when one was hustled out into the cold Texas morning, the wind whipping from Canada. One came nose up against the mean and tight assed in America. "White Christmas" and "Rudolph the Red-nosed Reindeer" blared from the loudspeakers. A Baptist minister at a religious assembly, meant to instill morals in us, snapped in the midst of his sermon, "Sit up on your butts!"

I was in the active military from December of 1962 to June of 1963. There was a certain comedy to it since the Vietnam War was only a very distant static, not even a rumble, which I would encounter in the mental wards where its first victims were showing up.

Our flight was called Sixty-Nine, an immediate challenge to the imagination of the sergeants. A strange lot, these boot camp instructors, most of them "hyper." For the first three weeks our hours were spent in a prolonged nightmare. The sergeants assigned to us were incompetent and so all the other sergeants at Lackland descended on our formations to harass us. It was a form of prison camp and not funny. A closet homosexuality in some of these instructors visited upon us a dangerous sadomasochism. Our terror excited them. They were watching for a victim to run to the ground. I saw one tall boy, a gawky adolescent from a rural backwater, who seemed to be suffering from malnutrition, pushed to the point where he collapsed. He wasn't able to run the laps or do the push-ups required of him, but the sergeants just doubled the load. We watched the abuse, helpless. He died of a heart attack beside the track.

One of our sergeants was from an Irish family that had known the McCormacks, that pre-eminent clan of Massachusetts politicians (a bad sign to me, since I remembered Knocko McCormack at the State Convention). The sergeant took an immediate and visceral dislike to me. He used to pause in front of my place in the line, sniffing, as if he could smell the "Jew" in my undershirt. "Did you wash, Mirsky?" he asked one day. The corporal under him bore me no particular malice, but he kept making mistakes. Our flight would show up late, go out in the wrong gear, not be coached about proper procedure in arranging our bunks or bureau drawers. The officers who came in to inspect the barracks shook their heads, and the sergeants accompanying them were screaming at us. Our marching was a disgrace. The rumor was that we might be kept back for another round of basic. A groan went through the flight. With the exception of a single Black recruit, we were all college graduates.

One day we were set to clean the ovens in the mess hall. There was a malicious wink in the eyes of the sergeants from the kitchen, set to supervise us, as they herded us into the cooking area. They put steel wool and scouring powder in our hands, told us to take off our shoes and jump into the maw of these coffins, about four feet high, eight feet wide. The metal was still hot. I hopped from foot to foot in my stockings, and they barked at us to scrub until the steel gleamed. My friend from Harvard, a Protestant, thought I was being picked on as a Jew. At the time I laughed it off, since I assumed everyone else was forced to do it— but I can recall the fear of having the steel oven door swung closed on me, skipping on the burning surface. After five minutes or so

they let us jump out, but it was a sobering reminder of just how helpless you were as a draftee in 1963. The military imagination wished to reduce each man to a common denominator who could be manipulated or "counted on" to fulfill an order without thinking.

The regimentation ran against the grain of the American myth I had grown up with. The young rabbi who met with us the second week— Chanukah coinciding with Christmas—closed the door behind him and whispered, "I know it's terrible, but you'll get through it." Those of us who had been segregated for this short service from the mass of Christian airmen sighed in relief. There was one sane person among the officers. He went on to assure us that we could request to see him, if we couldn't take the pressure or were being abused. One of the men in another flight, a classical musician, took this escape route as his salvation from a sergeant known as "the gray fox," an older man who seemed to delight in driving recruits into the ground. I recall him in the distance, standing over the dying boy. I wondered if I would have to dash to the rabbi's back door. The whole flight was beginning to smell ominously as our sergeants cursed us, and we saw them losing stature in the eyes of everyone around them. One day in the midst of our hopeless drilling, stumbling from left to right, a high nasal Appalachian whine cut through the cold Texas afternoon. The lackadaisical voice of the corporal counting cadence had drifted off a few moments previous.

"One, two, three, four...."

"Never seen a sadder bunch before!"

The voice broke out with a panoply of swearing, mocking, cursing, all on the edge of obscenity but avoiding the obvious four-letter shortcuts, rather indulging rhymes, epithets, of fresh and often stunning improvisational skill. He came right up to our ears, not barking but insinuating, cajoling, teasing, correcting, then backing off, his voice cracking over our heads, "left, right, left, right," wheeling us back and forth, back and forth. It went on and on past what we knew was the time assigned for drill.

"One, two, what a sight."

"Don't get fed, till you get it right."

That voice was a teamster's whip. For the first twenty, thirty minutes we thought we had been put under a madman, as our confused legs tried to make sense of what he was doing to us. After an hour or so, our aching calves and bruised heels began to feel the difference. The lash of the voice knew just when to flick, and our muscles found their stride, our aching lungs their second wind. We began to march, coming down on a single foot. Even the least competent marchers, two short, stocky Jewish pharmacists from Philadelphia, caught the cadence. Sergeant Rip, I will call him, whose voice was snapping in the crisp air, would have to hide them in the center of the formation when he put us on parade, but they learned how to disappear in these inner rows. As the sweat trickled down our necks, the first moments of understanding came; the flight moved for a moment or two as a body unified. At the Neighborhood Playhouse where I had spent a stint one summer learning acting, elocution, and dance, they had tried in vain to instill through the elementary steps of ballet a sense of company movement in me. Now in this unlikely venue I felt the thrill of being under a master. There was more to Sergeant Rip than just a genius for drilling raw recruits.

The night following our day of exhausting footwork, we met with him in the barracks for an orientation session. He began to go through some of the rules again, ones that had been tripping us up.

"What's the reason for that?" someone asked, encouraged by his ironic recitation of the regulations.

"There's no damned reason for it," Rip drawled. "Doesn't make a bit of sense. Just a page out of Mother Fletcher's manual. Don't look for any meaning in it. Just *do* it." He threw up his hands in the air as if struck by holy insanity, a hillbilly Kierkegaard explaining absurdity in the military universe.

That was as much comfort to the flight as the Rabbi's assurances had been to his misplaced tribe. We sucked in a breath of enlightenment. If it was understood that what we were asked to do was idiotic, it was easy. The demand that we as college graduates take the rules seriously had been demeaning. Sleep deprived, and constantly the targets of insults, we lost our sense of humor almost from the outset. Rip's confidence in himself was such that there was nothing personal in his bark as a sergeant, and he seemed to lean back and look at us with curiosity, even affection. A few days after Rip took over, he was sitting in the barracks office, trying to solve a crossword puzzle. Someone walked down to my room and asked me

to walk up to his desk in the middle of the bunk house. "What was the name of a magician in the Bible?" Rip asked. I guessed Solomon, since the king was reputed to speak to the birds and consorted with a half-demonic Queen of Sheba in the Midrash, mythology that the rabbis had spun. It fit the spaces in the newspaper. I became a confidante of Rip's collection of erotic dreams and tales of the other sergeants. He told me of a field of waving private parts, the tender grass of women; of a Korean prostitute who had tied a red ribbon around the most prized possession of hers, a single stalk, and who kept a sharp knife in readiness beside the bed for the man who would dare to pluck it. What struck one in a world where four-letter words were common was how inventive Rip was, rarely if ever resorting to them. A formation of WAFS marched by, shouting, "One, two, three, four, we are the fighting Forty-Four...." The sergeant rapped out our cadence in the brisk Texas morning, dropping his hands in cups to mid-chest, "Forty-four, forty-four, wish I had 'em, wish I had 'em!" Our flight roared it back, to the smiles of the passing WAF recruits, "Forty-four, forty-four, wish I had 'em, wish I had 'em." Rip was what William Carlos Williams called "one of the pure products of America." He told us how he had come down from the Appalachians, hardly knowing how to tie shoelaces and never having seen a toothbrush. The air force had given him an education. He wanted to become a fireman in the military, a form of hazardous duty, but one where there was scope for heroism. Strangely, he admired the "gray fox" and other sergeants who seemed dangerous to us because he recognized in them a streak of the unconventional and prized it. Under Rip's guidance we began to parody the spit and polish requirements, taking hold of saluting, looking "smart," and returning the "yes, sir," and "all present and accounted for," with the enthusiasm of Mother Fletcher's children. The harassment abruptly stopped, and the other noncommissioned officers gave us a wide berth. As an actor I happily took on several Prussian characteristics that seemed to stand me in good stead, barking out my responses during the quickly diminishing inspections.

The last weekend, when over a thousand of us were suddenly let loose for four hours in the downtown of San Antonio, wandering back and forth over the sidewalks, hoping to find a young woman outside the bars, still has the sharp outlines of a daguerreotype. With one or two friends, I followed six or seven young women who were laughing in Spanish over a bridge, the arroyo below empty of water. We were afraid to speak to them but simply followed, dumb. The presence in this barren world of schoolgirls caught up in their own lives was an assurance of an existence we might resume.

After basic training in Texas, we went north to Alabama for medical training at Gunter Air Force Base, just outside the capital, Montgomery. Here we regained some freedom. General Walker, who had led the protest against desegregation in nearby Arkansas, came to speak in Montgomery. I watched white racists who were also making anti-Semitic remarks on the local television. In our Air Force uniforms, heads shaved, we were anonymous, and so my Harvard classmate, who had relatives in the city, and I were admitted without question to the balcony of the hall where we heard the General rant. The South was still a place of surreal prejudice. Our captain down in Texas had been African-American and the sergeants' surly nickname for him was "Captain Midnight." After our first weekend liberty in Montgomery, I heard the story of how our one Black flight member had been refused entry into the White downtown bars where he had gone with several friends from our unit. They went with him to a Black bar, but there, his White compatriots were told they could not be admitted.

The formation was filled with professionals: lawyers, architects, psychologists, even a German scientist whose residence in this country had made him liable to be drafted. One of the architects, Caldwell, came from Franklin County in Louisiana. In his spare time, he would drive out into the country and sketch the shacks and barns in whose shapes he claimed to recognize African influences. It got him into some trouble despite his deep Southern accent and Caucasian complexion, because any stranger was suspicious, especially someone taking pictures or drawing. Later, he invited several of us to spend a long weekend at a girlfriend's mansion in Franklin, and it was my first insight into the still-living romantic South of literature. It was a weekend of heavy drinking, waking to be served in the morning by Black servants of such politeness that one felt ashamed to be cooked for by them until they set you at ease. An oil rig pumped in the midst of the fields,

and we were taken for a trip deep into the bayous. One saw some of the stereotypes of Tennessee Williams very much alive, the exaggerated politeness, the flirtatious curiosity of the women, the amused detachment of the domestic staff. In particular the accent of Franklin County, "The toity-toid," for the "thirty-third," which sounded so close to a quickly fading Brooklyn pronunciation, fascinated me. One afternoon we went deep into a terrain of alligators and cottonmouths, where the host's family owned land. In the bayous, among the French-speaking Cajuns, I saw "heart of pine" floors polished to a gloss in one shack that looked from the outside as if they were the haunts of rickety poverty. The simplicity of the interiors, the natural elegance of their furnishings, contrasted with the glittering pyramid of discarded beer cans rising out of the canal just outside.

Earlier I had visited New Orleans, going down in an automobile for the Mardi Gras. The holiday rippled with danger through the French Quarter. People were out in the street, holding bottles and glasses of alcohol in hand, couples in tuxedos and ball gowns, already half-cocked. In the midst of the merriment, faces would loom dazed, slashed in the cheek, forehead, pouring blood. There were knots of young and older men, brawling, screaming, shouting. It was drowned out in turn by loud singing. Black teenagers slithered angrily through the predominately White crowd, and animosity between the races was implicit. As if out of the pages of the *Reader's Digest,* through the chaos of drunken men, women, pimps, and prostitutes, walked a smiling family of six: father and mother in their Sunday best, four children, ages seven to eleven in pastel coats, with the curiosity of tourists treading through a movie set's backstage.

It was impossible to find a room to rent. The landmark which had been recommended as a place for us to assemble was called La Casa de Los Marinos, a big, rough bar, catering to dock workers and the rivermen. Through the night its crowd surged out into the street, and there was no elbow room at the bar. I slumped against the moist shell of an enormous porcelain urinal in the lavatory, trying to catch a few winks of sleep. Earlier I had accompanied a young woman with whom I'd struck up a conversation, a college student from Tulane, out to her campus on a trolley, talking, hoping for an invitation to spend the night on her floor. She politely turned me away. Returning to the center of the city by dawn, I was hardly able to stand. In the first streaks of light, I went to a doughnut and coffee shop on the waterfront where they made the chicory coffee that was a New Orleans specialty. By the Jax Beer place, Black stevedores were singing as they swung the sacks up on the boats. I had listened to work chants in the folk-song collections of Harvard's Woodberry poetry room and on a recording of John Jacob Niles, but I thought they had passed from the world of the United States. All the fatigue of the hours searching for a place to lay my head whistled away down the Mississippi. I lingered by the riverfront, kept coming back until our hour of departure, hoping to hear more of a precious litany I knew was fading from the century.

The last two months of active duty were spent in Florida at Eglin Air Force Base just outside Fort Walton Beach. For the first time we were on a work schedule. My intuition when I signed up was that duty in a psychiatric ward would be a window into another reality. One had the privilege of wandering through wards where the diagnosis of mental illness has made rank of only relative consequence. There was a general who claimed he had sexual problems, but whom the doctors regarded as simply lonely in retirement for the ear of subordinates. More interesting were those whom the fundamental insanity of the Cold War had driven off the edge, a colonel who told us the tale of pretending he had operational missiles under his command on a Pacific island to his far-off superiors in the Pentagon, while his immediate superiors had stripped off all but one in some strange "scam" that seemed endemic to this terrain of Mother Fletcher. On the first day, I saw a dumpy looking young man in the corner, obviously depressed. Since our assignment was basically to sit and talk to the patients, I squatted beside him on the couch and began to draw him into conversation. Over the course of a week, we talked frequently during the ward hours, and when we made out our reports, the doctors called me in. The patient had been scheduled to go off to a state mental institution as a hopeless case of depression. Was he really as willing to communicate as I had remarked in my notes? In the six weeks I spent on the wards, I was able to witness his turnaround. Like many of the patients in the wards, his situation in the military was the cause of

his withdrawal. I recall another case, an airman who had left college, recruited for training as an interpreter in an intensive course of French. The training took place under the aegis of the Military Police. When the course he was supposed to be enrolled in collapsed, the foreign language student found himself on patrol duty, walking in circles around planes on windswept airstrips eight hours on end. None of the regular air force ward attendants had much sympathy for these cases. One learned that your ability to draw a patient out of distress had to do with a strange and unpredictable chemistry. Other members of my unit, for whom I didn't have much respect, were successful in getting patients to talk who turned away from me.

It was at Eglin that I, and others, first heard the stories of what was really happening in Vietnam. A crusty, tough first sergeant had been locked up for fighting with his superiors, trying to report what he had seen on the ground there, a criminal corruption among the Vietnamese he was supposed to help train. He had been sent out without any preparation and began to lose patience with the lying, the futility, the human cruelty of what Americans were being drawn into. There was nothing demented in this man's anger, or about the colonel who had finally flipped, trying to pretend that he was commanding missile batteries when there were no missiles. As reservists, we listened with respect and fear, understanding that something awful was in the wings for the country. Later in the mental wards during the Johnson administration, the soldiers taken off the planes, mud still sticking to the bottom of their boots, would be giggling, talking about pushing Vietcong alive out of helicopters.

In lighter moments, I organized an impromptu afternoon of Gilbert and Sullivan with the patients. I watched my dumpy patient of the first week come out of his depression on the stage with several other inmates of the mental wards to the astonishment of the nurses and the women who volunteered—one of the latter pumping on the piano as the patients sang and did a sort of dance, assembling in a kickline at the edge of the game room stage.

I was thrown into such shock during basic training that I lost what had been a constant of my life since adolescence, that is a dizzying joy in the dream of sex. I must have

In Norway, 1976

experienced what animals and civilizations do when they are paralyzed with terror. Only slowly in Alabama and Florida did I recover my fantasies and my desire.

On the base or in the bars, degrees from Harvard or Stanford were meaningless and conversation about books or culture impossible. The beach along the Gulf of Mexico was beautiful and still unexploited, with long stretches of sand and grass, but however attractive the women were in their bikinis, there seemed nothing to talk about with them. I asked my parents to ship my motorcycle down to me. It had been crated to Boston from California. I had started a novel about Blue Hill Avenue at Harvard in Albert's class, but put the pages aside while at Stanford. The rabbi at Eglin, another sympathetic figure, loaned me the use of his office when I got off the wards at eleven o'clock in the evening. I worked at his typewriter and,

when I had a few hours free in the morning, wrote in a notebook on a deserted spit of sand. It was at the end of a trail which I had discovered on my bike.

Eglin Air Force Base, beyond its landing strips and military barracks, was a lost stretch of Eden. The tropical Florida through which the Indians had wandered was still intact through many of its acres. Creeping in my lowest gear, cursing the sound of the muffler, I rode down a hardly discernible track to the inlet at the bottom of what must have been a game trail. A hog that looked to be the size of a horse was crashing through the underbrush one morning. On another, I saw a banded rattlesnake as thick as a fire hose slither across the sandy path in front of me. Too late to avoid it, my wheels rolled over the creature, which wriggled without harm under the tires and into the brush. Except for the occasional scream of the jets above, I was as entirely alone on the Gulf of Mexico as Robinson Crusoe.

On the wards I met women, but dating patients was forbidden to us. I was detailed to watch an old man who had pneumonia and was apt to thrash around. He was tied down, and they asked for a psychiatric ward attendant to sit by the bed so he wouldn't break the IV bottles attached to him or get up and start wandering. Since the patient slept most of the time, and there was little activity in the wards after 3:00 P.M., when my duty started, I got to re-read Milton, *Paradise Lost* and *Paradise Regained*, books that I had crammed down at Harvard. I wanted to absorb Milton as a writer, gain some of his brooding puritanical voice, not just swallow the poetry but add its chords to my own voice. In the midst of the solemn movement of dark angels, I was summoned across the ward to the bed of a German girl to help with an injection. She was the wife of an American sergeant, her fragile white complexion framed by jet black hair on the pillows. She had attempted suicide and, staring into her frightened, intelligent face, I knew the reason. During our two weeks on the women's wards, again and again, the wives of enlisted men would come in, some of them rigid, their bodies frozen in postures of horror. It was our duty to talk to them, try to draw them out of their hysteria. It was dangerous, though, because as they talked, it became obvious that the problem often lay in a marriage that was a disaster. Were you responsible for a conversation which brought them to recognize this? What was I to say—run away?

One of the WAFS who had worked as an orderly wound up on the psychiatric ward. "Babs" was her nickname. I asked why she had tried to kill herself. She answered in the flat nasal dialect of the mountains, "It was like I cut off my nose to spite my face. And my face...didn't care."

A member of our flight did date a patient despite regulations. She was an officer's daughter with red, red hair that streamed like a fiery bunch of cherries down to her waist. The first sight of this extraordinary woman, eighteen or nineteen, lolling like a Hollywood star in a bed was electric. Between laughing and flirting with all of the medical reservists, she talked incessantly about her religion, Baptist. The way she walked across the ward in her pajamas, top open to show her full breasts, and rolled her hips, the invitation in her eyes, spoke to different pieties. The aftermath of the date, on a weekend when the hospital allowed her a one-day pass, was another suicide attempt. It was a grim reminder to most of us that the taboos were rational.

The most powerful bond I formed in my weeks on the mental wards was with an Ojibway. I knew him for only two or three days. We were sent to sit together in a cramped small office on the mental wards. He was a big man, with a figure imposing rather than heavy: thick in the chest, shoulders, legs. His voice mesmerized me—its strange melody of the western tribes in English as if sentences were not statements but questions, half rising in the air. My ear would catch a similar music, years later, listening to Hopi and Laguna Indians.

I was to take down his autobiography. Was this just luck, or did my stories of knowing Erik Erikson at Harvard touch one of the psychiatrists (I had let it slip in conversation) and influence their choice of me as the American Indian's interlocutor?

The Ojibway was there for threatening his superior officer, perhaps even hitting him. An aura of hero clung to those broad shoulders. Such deeds were the folklore of the mental wards. American Indians, Mexican-Americans, men from a background where mockery rang out as a challenge to honor and required a response in proportion to its nastiness often ran afoul of the United States military. The insults meant to shape up a soldier, put him in his place, had the opposite effect on them. The noncommissioned officers all secretly admired these objectors of conscience.

From the first moment, what struck me was the Ojibway's sweetness, the poetry in his way of thinking. I ought not to have left those notes behind, though it was forbidden to copy them. He began to tell me the story of a bus ride a few months before. The Ojibway was in love with a girl on one of the neighboring reservations. It was a thirty-six-hour trip by Greyhound and local bus from where he was stationed. He had to travel from the bottom of Texas to a small town close to the Canadian border. Getting off the final bus in this anabasis, he saw the girl walking on the opposite side of the street. He waved at her, then turned around. If he was going to avoid being AWOL, he had only a few minutes to mount a bus leaving in the opposite direction and return to Texas. He told this saga with gentle self-mockery: the moment in which he raised his hand to the girl, having shown her what he felt. The difficulty of accomplishing the trip was its romance. I left the room in a state of disbelief. The Ojibway's story of his bus ride, like the description of the Sioux who rode out in battle to just touch their enemies with a stick, to "count coup," not to kill or wound them, was a moral tale. The rhetoric of the Hebrew Bible lingered in the simplicity of his expression, laughing, direct, striving to make clear an experience that could not be put in words.

In my year of graduate study earlier at Stanford, I had met a mechanic named Mike, who worked in the motorcycle shop down the street where I had bought my Zundapp, a balky 250 CC running on a mixture of gas and oil, capable of some seventy-five miles an hour but best kept between fifty and sixty. Its mufflers covered me in a veil of smoky fuel that soaked into my pants and shirts, left my fingers gritty. Mike had moved in with some Mexican workers who rented rooms in an alley behind the motorcycle shop. Lean, shy young men, they lived from one week to the other on a foot-deep pot of chili: beans and a bit of meat over a bed of rice. Mike proudly showed me the pot he had cooked for himself in the first week of his attempt to join them. He got sick on this regimen. A stocky French-Canadian, he wasn't made for their diet. Trying to reduce his life to basics, he didn't think much of motorcycles. They were high-strung machines, constantly in need of attention, tuning, alignment, though he had magical hands as a mechanic. When I stopped by his room after hours, he would lean over my gasping, sputtering two cycle, restoring it to a smoothly running machine with a few flicks of his wrenches. He preferred the utility of motorscooters and drove a banged-up Vespa. Mike listened without enthusiasm to paragraphs I recited from my work— too literary and special for his taste. He had read Henry Miller. Touched by his essay on baking loaves, Mike drove down with a loaf of homemade bread to give to Miller. Mike was full of tales about Topanga Canyon from which he seemed to be in exile. One of his friends there, Mike said, had driven up to Marilyn Monroe's front door to make love to her, arriving with the same good faith as Mike had knocking on Henry Miller's with the bread. The Ojibway whose face glistened, describing the wave of his girlfriend's hand, like Mike was searching for a secret way.

I have spoken only briefly about the young women I sought to find my own polar star in. The lines of the present autobiography do not report what occupied many of my waking thoughts. The pages of a fuller chronicle would represent me to the cautious auditor as a fool. Blushing, I quote to myself the lines of Miguel de Unamuno: "There are people, my Don Quixote, blind to these adventures of sighing and leaping into the air without more ado. Only a man who has slapped his shoe in the air or is capable of doing so is fit to round out great ventures. Wretched is the man who is sane in private and who takes care to see that others may see him so." And a few lines on, "The mad antics kindled his love for Dulcinea, and that love was his compass and the lodestar of his actions." Looking back forty years, I see the child of Dorchester's and Mattapan's streets maddened by too much Dostoyevsky as an adolescent, throwing himself into the gutter of Massachusetts Avenue, across the street from Harvard's gates, in front of a girl from Radcliffe crying, "Natasha Pavlovna, I love you." The young woman was from Cincinnati, not Moscow, not, of course, "Natasha" but a more prosaic, American name. She had, however, a thrilling figure and a statuesque beauty that mingled with sadness in cheeks touched with faint roses that made my own flush with the fires of literature. (Shall I admit that I walked around in boots and a fur coat that freshman year?) I saw myself as

Prince Myshkin in *The Idiot*. She tolerated my foolishness though nothing more. Her anguish flashed across her face. She left college that first year, drifted to New York City where she worked as a model in the Sixth Avenue garment industry. Her father would arrange for her to be locked away in a mental institution, and it would be several years before she was released. I wrote to her occasionally, and her letters spoke with a sparse immediacy that left me feeling ashamed of myself—pretentious when not just loquacious. Still numb from the breakup with the young woman whom I had been in love with my senior year at Harvard, in the solitude of the air force, I wrote more frequently to this American Natasha. Her letters back quickened my hopes. On the day of my release from the air force, I buckled on my leather jacket, packed some clothes in the leather bags that hung from the blue Zundapp, and began a pilgrimage from Montgomery, Alabama, through its hill country into Tennessee and Kentucky toward Cincinnati, where she lived. I would ask Natasha to marry me.

America in the 1960s was still lit by the glow of redbrick store fronts trimmed in white Victorian gingerbread. From its machinery one heard the squeals and pipes of the late nineteenth century. Caldwell, the architect, had found the shapes of African villages in the circular roofs of the field shacks. The hoot of train whistles and flash of the steam engines' pistons ran alongside me through the night as I raced on the motorcycle down the long valleys of Tennessee and Kentucky; wound up the mountain tops on narrow roads that followed the instincts of game trails and river beds. Old granaries of finely grouted brick and granite, wooden clapboard half encased in asphalt tile, the coal mining shanties of tin roofs, broken-down porches, sad Mother Goose boxes on the wrong side of the tracks—the Appalachians' lost worlds dotted their worn-down mountains. Even horse farms in the Blue Grass country were set out in a landscape still unspoiled by the glitter to come. Along this vertical line of twisting road on the map, there was no interstate, no notion of fast food, supermarket, very little concrete, and that in imitation of limestone block. Everything slumped, handed down, half-broken, inherited from discarded decades. The gas stations' signs, survivals from the 1930s, were museum pieces. The dew collected on my helmet, visor, and leather jacket as I dismounted for one more doughnut and coffee at a truck stop nestling in a diner that was indeed an abandoned railroad tender. I had ridden without sleep through Tennessee until the dawn streaked the horizon in Kentucky.

It was midmorning when I swung the motorcycle over a rattling wooden bridge that spanned the Ohio River and descended into the North—Cincinnati, Ohio. The riverfront and downtown were a collection of motley redbrick of the nineteenth century, broken window struts, decaying decoration in that greening copper sung as "wintry bronze." Blond-haired little boys and girls in ragged pants and skirts, living figures of delft china, played in the mud under the sober gaze of better dressed Black shopkeepers and passing workmen. Here, across the river, the horn of Appalachia and the Old South poured out their different worlds into the border city. When I rode up the hill to her house, my idyll was over. The "Natasha" of my dreams gently told me that she was in love with a young Englishman, her future husband, who had come to Cincinnati to study American business techniques. She nevertheless put me up at her handsome mansion. I spent a few days there before riding on through Pennsylvania to my aunt's home in Teaneck, New Jersey, where my parents were scheduled to meet me.

It had begun to rain as I left Ohio and turned onto the Pennsylvania turnpike. I kept riding. The Zundapp had an annoying habit of quickly stretching its rear chain. One had to keep checking, and I never mastered the art of tightening links while keeping the wheels in alignment. In rain it was a very messy procedure. After plunging hands into the oil and grit of the chain adjustment, you lay down on the ground beside the bike to eyeball the front and back tires. Somewhere west of Harrisburg on the turnpike, in a tunnel, the loose chain fell off its sprocket. The grade was downhill, so throwing in the clutch I leapt off the motorcycle, grasping the handlebars, and ran, though it was top-heavy with saddlebags and gear strapped on the seat. A big truck behind me saw what was happening and braked, then very slowly followed me rather than trying to pass, protecting my rear. After six or seven minutes of running, praying, with the motorcycle beside me, the end of the tunnel loomed and I gratefully pulled over just beyond it. One of the workers from the station at the end came over to my bike, helped to tighten my chain, and then

Mirsky and wife-to-be Inger Grytting, Norway, 1976

motioned me to get going quickly. A series of cars with smashed hoods and staved-in trunks slowly emerged and filed by as we bent over the motorcycle. The truck slowing down to save my life had caused a ripple of violent braking behind it.

The rain kept up all the way to Teaneck, New Jersey. My aunt in whose garage I left my leather jacket (it was too soaked even in the morning to put back on) complained that puddles kept collecting under it for a week. I left the motorcycle behind with the jacket and let my parents drive me up to Boston.

My father had decided to run for the city council. Election was a forlorn hope. Councilors no longer ran in districts which had guaranteed several Italian and one Jewish city councilor, but for the past few years had been elected on a citywide basis. This eliminated the Jewish seat, though the population of Jews in the city was, in any event, on the wane. What was always painful, often humiliating—going up and down strange stairs, standing on street corners asking people to vote for my father—this time was useless. People both in and outside the Jewish streets looked at us as if we were crazy. When I tried to dissuade my father, he lost his temper and raged. He had to run. His law business was going downhill. Everyone had forgotten him. My mother's appointment as a commissioner on the Industrial Accident Board was over. So we went clambering all over Boston. Instead of sending me off on my own, however, it seemed as if he needed me next to him. We climbed the steps of loft buildings in downtown Boston through the wholesale garment district, trying to collect signatures on his nomination papers from the women at the sewing machines.

When my father had been in the legislature, the Jewish factory owners had greeted him with open arms. Now at most doors they could smell defeat. I could feel the sting of that slap in his face, being turned away in front of his son. It was a large part of what soured him on the Massachusetts legislature.

In his first terms, my father had enjoyed the confidence of Governor Paul Dever and the Speaker of the Massachusetts House of Representatives, Tip O'Neill. The Democratic governor, however, had been defeated when he sought a third term; and O'Neill had departed for Congress. The honor and dignity that my father had felt in the House began to fade. One of the succeeding speakers, who liked to brawl, barked obscenities at my father, meeting unexpectedly at the elevator of the ornate marble lobby. I stood there, angry and embarrassed. When I asked Dad years later, "Why did you give up your seat?" he answered tersely, "I couldn't stand another term under that drunk."

My father was limping as we reached the top of the third or fourth building whose stairs we had climbed in the absence of elevators. His legs knotted with varicose veins were beginning to give. I begged him to stop, but he kept knocking on the glass doors, introducing himself to the owners, asking if he could go down the long tables of the factory and solicit signatures. The bosses were usually behind a set of glass doors within the lofts. I was about to turn away again, accustomed to the refusal, when a white-haired man stuck his head in the hallway. "Mirsky?" he asked.

We were invited into the factory. "Your name is Mirsky?" the owner repeated, motioning us to chairs—someone had gone to summon him to the door when my father first knocked.

"Yes, I'm Representative Mirsky..." Dad replied, using his former title as a state legislator, and about to begin his monologue of past achievements.

The man shook his head. "Are you the son of Israel Mirsky?" he interrupted.

"Yes," Dad answered, taken aback.

"Israel Mirsky who was the shammes at the Fowler Street Shul?"

My father nodded.

The man took a deep breath and leaned forward. "Your father, Israel Mirsky, spoke to me when I came to the shul to recite Kaddish for my wife. I didn't know how I was going to get through the next few weeks. What your father said to me saved my life. I'll never forget him. He wasn't just a kind man. You should know, he was a person of tact and nobility. If you are the son of Israel Mirsky, I am happy to do what I can for you." The owner took my father down the long loft, from table to table, with the nomination papers in his hand, asking the women to sign for Representative Mirsky and to remember him on Primary and Election Day.

Coming down the stairs of the loft building, my father buoyed by our success, I felt the shame of balking, not wanting to go another step.

At home my mother was on the telephone from morning to early evening, calling her share of the thousands of registered voters in Boston, urging them to come out on Primary Day and give her husband, Wilfred, a vote. She was also supervising the mass mailings, letters that had to be folded by hand in three, stamps and flaps licked, sealed, the boxes trekked to the post office. The friends who usually helped at these moments and with the task of hanging up posters, running sound trucks, ringing their neighbors and relatives, were conspicuously absent. I suspected that Mother, like me, was depressed by the pathos of my father's campaign. She was too loyal a partner, however, to complain in front of us. In the midst of this, my sister decided to get married to my classmate at Harvard, Mark De Voto. My mother had always been upset when I brought home non-Jewish girlfriends. Although it was my father who had the background in the Judaism of Eastern European piety, the Talmudic learning, the fluency in Hebrew, and the skill at leading prayers, it was Mother in whom the loyalty ran to unfathomable depths. Two thousand years of clan were suddenly at an end. Though a reform rabbi performed the ceremony under the traditional Jewish wedding canopy, the chuppah, at the Signet Club, a society of arts and literature to which Mark and I both belonged, Mother, a meticulous driver, crashed our car on the day of my sister's wedding. Departing for New York City to try my luck in the theater, it felt like I was fleeing Boston.

That summer, while I was still in Boston, I was surprised by a call from Albert Guerard. He was on the campus at Tufts University, attending a conference on the reform of education for the humanities. He couldn't officially invite me to the proceedings, but did I want to come out and say hello? I drove to Tufts and took a seat in the hall where the discussion was still going on. As usual it was hard to keep quiet and I put my two cents in. The organizers invited me to the next conference. It was being run by John Hawkes and Walter Ong, a Jesuit priest, while Professor Zacharias, a mathematician at MIT who had been instrumental in the reform of teaching in mathematics, hovered at the edge of the proceedings. The U.S. Department of Education was funding this, and it soon evolved into a series of meetings.

In Manhattan, I had found a tiny two-room apartment on Thirteenth Street, kitchen and narrow bedroom with a third space hardly larger than a closet, the bathtub in the kitchen. Nick Smith, whom I acted opposite at the Provincetown Playhouse, met me on the street and asked where I was living. When I told him I was looking for a place, he brought me to his landlady, a genial, big-boned Italian. An agent had seen me work at Provincetown and asked if I would let her represent me when I came to New York. She sent me for one Broadway audition where Boston's pronunciation was my undoing. "The accent goes away in the paaht," I insisted, but the director shook his head and didn't give me a second chance. In "paaht" it was also the fault of the Neighborhood Playhouse and the Method which had instilled in me a sense that I had to be natural in auditions and not assume an accent that was not my own before I had assimilated the character as well. For a few weeks I scanned *Backstage* and *Variety* for casting calls, but quickly realized it was a humiliation I could not survive. (Little did I know what publishing had in store.) I began to look for work as director. Nancy Cooperstein had been one of the most talented actresses in my class at the Neighborhood Playhouse, and she was now working at the New Playwrights. She arranged a nonpaying assignment to direct a stage reading for one of their authors. A young Tony Lo Bianco was in the cast, but neither

he nor the playwright listened to my suggestions, since I was by far their junior. I was living on the Unemployment Insurance that my father had explained I was entitled to as a result of my six months of military service. The Equity card allowed me to search for employment in the theater, but as the fall wore on, I began to get apprehensive about my benefits running out. I was living on water and biscuits for a day or two by the end of the week, the eighty-five-cent meals at the local Polish restaurants out of budget. I ran into Chuck Mee, several classes ahead of me at college, and he asked if I wanted a job at American Heritage where he had been taken up as a "wonder kid," working as a staff writer. I felt a bit strange. I had walked out of a production that Chuck had directed at Harvard of *The Good Woman of Setzuan*, put up to it by Steve Randall who had directed when I played Gloucester as a freshman in *King Lear*. Steve was a brilliant director and it was inevitable, when he decided to act in Chuck's production, that they would clash over Chuck's decisions. Caught in the middle, I let loyalty to Steve prevail over sense. Now, five years later, Chuck shrugged off my apologies and arranged for an interview. I got the job. My boss, Alvin Josephy, remarked to me after a few days, "You're a square peg in a round hole," or perhaps it was the other way around. On the project to which we were engaged, writing an "Encyclopedic" Guide to the United States, I was able to choose the folklore of the States and hide therein. Alvin Josephy was passionate on the subject of American Indians, and the small library at American Heritage had a good selection of books on them. Alvin was tolerant of my disappearance from the building on what became almost daily trips to the New York Public Library, a few blocks away. The journals of the American Folklore Society became my Bible, their numbers running far back into the nineteenth century when the collectors, in order to preserve the obscenity of their American Indian sources, transcribed them in the vernacular of Cicero and Ovid. I began to revive my limited skills from Boston Public Latin.

The first weeks at American Heritage, I began to sweat uncontrollably at the desk I was assigned to. The idea of actually sitting in a chair from nine to five, with an hour's break for lunch for the rest of my life, threw me into shock. After two hours I had soaked through my pants and had to run into the men's room to pat myself dry between the legs. This was to be the genesis of a play, "The Leak," still unproduced, inspired as well by Le Roi Jones' *The Toilet*. Jones, I felt, had not plumbed the depths of his metaphor, the public stall used merely as a backdrop.

That fall in New York City, I had finished my first novel and sent it to another Harvard friend, Allan Rinzler, Claude Brown's editor at Simon & Schuster. Allan boasted that he had extracted *Manchild in the Promised Land* from Brown with a tape recorder and helped to pull its pages together. My novel, Allan declaimed, was unpublishable, but as a sop, he asked if I wanted him to put my name in for a fellowship at the Breadloaf Writers' Conference. "Sure," I said.

To my surprise the Air Force Reserve was understanding about the fellowship and released me from part of my summer training duty. The personnel office at American Heritage was upset, though, about me exchanging two weeks of military obligations for time spent at Breadloaf. Their pique destroyed any illusions I harbored about being able to fit in there.

Breadloaf gave me a sense of horizons I have never quite reached. John Ciardi, who was running the conference, had read my novel and would later repeat the extravagant praise he greeted me with, in sentences he furnished for the book jacket. I briefly wondered who I was. Ciardi gave me an enthusiastic recommendation to his publisher, Houghton Mifflin—though of course they were hostile to most work that smacked of the other side of Boston. Howard Nemerov, who was also in residence, consented to look at the manuscript and wrote me an appreciation of the book that still makes me tremble, words that every prose writer dreams of receiving from a poet. Among the other fellows was Jerome Charyn, who became a close friend, and Russell Mead, soon to be elevated to headmaster at Concord Academy. Stanley Elkin and Muriel Rukheyser would come down to see us at the Fellows' cottage and share our circle of conversation. And there were a host of handsome women and pretty waitresses, students who were serving the more affluent participants at table, in order to offset their conference fees. Among the latter, Jerome Charyn found his wife, Marlene, though Stanley cast a melancholy and covetous eye. Stanley, though happily married, was particularly lonely and in need of the at-

tention of young women. Grumbling, he would come regularly to sit with us, the Fellows, declaring that our society was preferable to the other faculty. He complained bitterly through the first few days that no one liked him and that he was unappreciated. His academic lecture was difficult to follow, and the lack of overwhelming response threw him into a dudgeon. Late in the conference, however, Stanley read his fiction out loud. He was a superb actor of his own characters. When he read several years later at the City College, the students and I had to slam our fists on the floor and walls, trying to stop laughing. That night the Breadloaf audience burst into loud applause. I saw Stanley run off the stage and throw open the glass doors at the side of the lecture hall. As they banged shut behind him, he cried to the moon and stars, "Now can I get f...?"

In the fall of 1964 I left American Heritage, despite an offer from them to relocate to another project. I was still feeling very much a square peg. This time I had a small reserve of cash to see me through and decided to take another fling at the theater. Anne Oehlschlaeger had been a loyal assistant director at Harvard, and she managed my foibles with tact. She had found a spiritual home at Saint Mark's Church in the Bowery. The pastor there, Michael Allen, was interested in the arts, and Anne suggested that I go and have a talk with him. Since my childhood beatings at the hands of the Irish lads on their way home from Saint Leo's in Dorchester, churches made me nervous, but Michael Allen quickly set me at ease. "The whole of the East Side is my parish regardless of the faith of the inhabitants," he remarked. I wanted to use the church for a project that had been bubbling in me ever since my courses in the pre-Shakespearean theater and the world of early Tudor drama. Why not form a group of actors who would be proficient in classical and modern drama, starting at the very beginning of it in English, the mystery plays, and slowly proceeding in a progression of plays into the twentieth century? Michael misunderstood me when I asked for the parish hall and offered the main sanctuary. I was stunned for a moment, then realized that the high-ceilinged space where the congregation worshipped was appropriate for plays that had been engendered in religious festivals. However bawdy, they were part of the whole cloth of religion that covered both street and cathedral. "Why not do them in the service?" Michael suggested, leaning back in his chair by the coal fire that burned on the hearth of the stone rectory. We were a few yards from the final "resting place" of that notorious anti-Semite, the last Dutch governor of New Amsterdam, Peter Stuyvesant.

The most exciting theater I knew was that which established a direct link between audience and the play in front, overhead and around them. I decided to take Michael Allen up on his offer.

One of the best actors at Theater Genesis—a place where a number of Sam Shepard's plays were first put on—Kevin O'Connor was among the four carpenters fastening Jesus to his cross in the *Crucifixion* of the York pinners' guild. Warren Finnerty, the star of the Living Theater's *The Connection* and Anne Oehlschlaeger's boyfriend, played another. Kevin had a boisterous energy and a cunning actor's intelligence, but he was dangerous on a set. More than once, the mallet in his hand went flying. Warren by contrast projected a hypnotic malevolence, though off stage he was remarkably modest for an actor whose reputation was already large in the city. Matthew Lewis, who had played Albany opposite my Gloucester at Harvard in the production of *King Lear* in 1957 at the Peabody Playhouse, was a compelling Jesus. He suffered on a cross made of castaway timbers we found outside the restaurant supply places on the Bowery. The joke or "play" of the short drama is that the pinners of the guild at work on the son of Joseph are incompetent. They mismatch the holes they make in his body to those they drill through the limbs of the wood. The arms and legs of the crucified man are broken and stretched to fasten them. Jesus becomes a disposable piece of botched furniture. The action made the church audience wince and wriggle in their seats. We toured the production to several churches and, in one of the poorer parishes in Brooklyn, the children seated in front began to laugh at the pranks of the workmen while Jesus swayed unhappily above the mockery. The adults were horrified but I was carried bodily into the world of the Middle Ages.

The success of this Crucifixion led to an offer by CBS-TV to televise nationally the Easter production we had planned. Stunned by this opportunity, I decided to cast actors who had hitherto been unavailable. Nancy Cooperstein took the role of Mary Magdalen, and Frank Langella, whose performance in *The White Devil* had brought him to prominence, was cast as Jesus. Judd Hirsch, at that time relatively unknown, but a close friend of Nancy's, agreed to play Pontius Pilate. Rehearsals went wonderfully, but when Easter morning came, Nancy and Frank, who were supposed to do a sly ballet of flirtation, froze into a conventional exchange of amenities. My chance to shock a national audience when it was still relatively naive—1964—was lost. Only Judd rose to the occasion as a towering, storming Pilate. I still have the outsized robe that was made for him in my closet.

Albert Guerard and Jack Hawkes, meanwhile, had begun an experiment at Stanford University called the "Voice Project." My book was bouncing between editors. Albert needed a young writer who had already published a novel. I recommended Jerome Charyn. Jerry told me to go and apply at City College for the job he was leaving. The day of my interview, a speck of dust caught in my eye. It was watering fiercely and during the interview, which I thought went badly, I kept rubbing the socket. Ed Volpe, the chairman of the City College English Department, asked me how I wrote when I told him I had finished a novel. On a typewriter, I replied, since my handwriting was so messy it depressed me to look at it.

"I always write with a pen. It seems more...." I forget Ed's exact words, but the sense of the stylus digging out syllables on the page was implicit, and ever after I wrote my lines of fiction first in longhand. Offered the job of teaching Freshman English, which I have now taught for over thirty years, I came there on the strength of my work as a director.

My first novel?

It's the kind of story my wife hates me to tell, for it casts me again as a fool. I repeat it because it speaks to the pain of thinking oneself a writer. I had gone up to see William Alfred and in a childish fit, stung by yet another publisher's rejection, I threw my manuscript on the floor of his living room at 31 Athens Street. "I've just been fooling myself," I cried.

"No, no," he exclaimed, bending to pick up the pages. "Let me show it to one of my students."

It was James Wade, who was just starting as an editor at Macmillan. He liked the manuscript, but felt he was too young to take it on and handed the book to Richard Marek.

Thou Worm Jacob was the title we settled on—to my mother's discomfort.

"You'll never sell a book with a worm in the title," she said harshly. In a sense she was right. One of my friends-to-be, the historian Francis Russell who would write a rave review in the *Christian Science Monitor,* calling me the successor to Isaac Bashevis Singer and "The Magician of Mattapan," once asked Roger Donald, who had toyed with the idea of publishing me, why I wasn't more successful with the large Jewish book-buying audience.

"Mirsky doesn't tell them what they want to hear."

Thou Worm Jacob got wonderful reviews when it appeared in the newspapers of Boston, Houston, San Francisco, and journals like *Partisan Review*—everywhere but the place that was most important. It was assigned to Martin Levin who did a dozen or so capsules at the back of the *New York Sunday Times Book Review,* and he savaged it. Still, the novel was on the best-seller list in Boston, and Macmillan went into a second printing, aggressively advertising it. Suddenly this stopped. I asked Dick Marek what was happening. The Six-Day War had just finished in Israel. "Books about Jews in America aren't selling," he explained. "We don't want you to be typed as a 'Jewish writer,'" Marek told me, though Macmillan had signed a two-book contract. I had written my second novel, *Blue Hill Avenue,* in a wild rush. It would be "New and Recommended" next to Donald Barthelme's collection of stories, *Sadness,* in the *Sunday Times Book Review* after a long enthusiastic review there. But Marek didn't want to publish it at Macmillan, rejecting as well *Proceedings of the Rabble,* which I offered as my non-Jewish book. One of the characters named through an oversight in *Thou Worm Jacob* had threatened to sue me and Macmillan. The suit, fortunately, was dropped, but perhaps that had something to do with these editors' loss of enthusiasm. That is my most charitable thought.

I was at Stanford when the novel was published. Albert had hired me for the Voice Project on the strength of the contract Macmillan offered.

Again I have to take a step back.

The Tufts conference on curricular reform in the teaching of English had been succeeded by several others. For someone who was living on twenty-eight-odd dollars a week, the per diem check of one hundred dollars a day, plus hotel and restaurant fees, was a form of manna from the federal government. In New Orleans I listened in awe to scientists cut through the linguistic nonsense of professional educators and lay out strategies of teaching that would involve students who didn't conceptualize in conventional ways. Ben De Mott rose up on the podium to eloquently declaim, "The greatest disaster in American education has been this country's failure to imagine the life of the Black person." In the early 1960s, this cry rang out with urgency. It was at a subsequent conference at Sarah Lawrence, however, more narrowly focused on writers as teachers, that I found my church and synagogue. Jack Hawkes and Albert Guerard assembled Grace Paley, Donald Barthelme, Susan Sontag, and John Barth among others. Not rhetoric but wit ruled as Susan rose to describe her favorite high school teacher covering papers with the red ink of endless corrections, a suggestion for curricular reform that sounded vaguely of De Sade. Like her espousal of the *Book of O,* it made one sit up and think twice. Barth, eerie, staring off into space, the very image of his mesmerizing hero, Jack Horner, in *End of the Road,* towered a good six inches over every other head at the conference. It was noticeable, therefore, when he got up and just walked out at lunch time, departing for the train station as if oblivious to the debates of the conference or its social amenities. I blathered of Girls' High to the amusement of Jacques Barzun and others. A few months later Grace Paley was playing the mayor of New York in the churchyard of Saint Mark's Church in the Bowery. After the troupe's performance, I came up and reintroduced myself. She had used a paper megaphone, and I leaned back to show her how to bounce a voice off a wall and double its volume. Laughing, Grace took me under her wing as we walked to her home on West Eleventh Street. I had a permanent invitation often exercised to share the bowl of spaghetti on her table. A young Radcliffe student had given me Grace's *Little Disturbances of Men* with the awe of a disciple handing me holy gospel my first year in Manhattan. At Sarah Lawrence, the most interesting face belonged to a handsome man, some ten years older than me, who sat silent with an enigmatic smile. This was Donald Barthelme. He exercised on me a hypnotism that I still feel. At that time, Donald did not know Grace, though they lived almost exactly across the street from each other on West Eleventh Street and were in the course of time to become the closest of friends. From the few words that Donald did speak at the table, I felt what Kent speaks to King Lear when he comes back in the guise of servant, "You have that in your countenance which I would fain call master."

"What's that?"

"Authority."

Donald was exceptionally shy at first. When he did speak about books and writers though, one felt the gavel of an impersonal judgment that was absolute. He was, of all the writers I have met, the best read, and his interests ranged from the Frankfurt School to Thomas Burton's *Anatomy of Melancholy,* which he gave to me as a Christmas present. Donald's apartment was decorated with the austerity of a postmodernist museum. He had been a curator at the art museum in Houston. (One of his wives, Birget, told me that he had come to New York in pursuit of Elaine de Kooning, who was a frequent visitor in their house.) I often camped at the tables of Blimpie's on the corner of West Eleventh Street and Sixth Avenue, staring out of its wide glass windows, hoping that Donald would wander out in the late afternoon. Seeing him about to pick up a magazine at the little store across the street, I would fly across the sidewalks to say hello. More often than not, Donald invited me back to his house for a drink. From these hours I would take home a reading list, Gabriel Garcia Marquez's *One Hundred Years of Solitude,* S. J. Perelman, *The Road to Milltown,* William Gass's *In the Heart of the Heart of the Country,* everything of Flann O'Brien's. It was Donald who wouldn't let me drop the idea of starting a magazine in newspaper format; an idea that the novelist Rudy Wurlitzer and I had discussed as we sat kibbutzing in an Avenue B luncheonette. Anne Waldman, who had become the center of a group of poets at Saint Mark's Church, told me about the new printing process on web press with cold type that had cut the cost of putting out a magazine to below a thousand dollars. When Donald offered to do the layout, I knew whatever it cost and however I collected the money to do it, I was going to.

At the least, it was an excuse to go over and listen to him talk. Donald could be extremely abrupt, even cruel, but once he extended friendship, his loyalty was absolute, though tinged with irony and danger. Again, though, memories are outracing the slender thread of chronology in these pages.

It is the fall of 1966. The year at Stanford stands out as a turning point, though at the time it did not seem so. I was still involved in the theater, with a book scheduled to be published. When I was invited to join the Voice Project, Albert asked what course I wanted to teach in addition. Stanford through those years offered "freshman seminars." Senior faculty were recruited to teach a course in a field of research they were presently involved in, but the students were incoming freshmen. I asked to run a seminar on directing. My idea was that if I trained directors, I would spawn not one production but many. The freshmen in my seminar put on stagings of T. S. Eliot's "The Love Song of J. Alfred Prufrock" and Lewis Carroll's "The Jabberwocky." Their work was done in tandem with Larry Friedlander, who had come out to Stanford to teach Shakespeare. Together we assembled a freshman drama group. They performed in the freshman halls. The staging of *The Knight of the Burning Pestle* had all the madness and panache of the Christmas productions I had witnessed at Harvard in the dining halls. I told the actors playing apprentices, who had been seated among the audience, to bring garbage to pelt the stage. Mayhem ensued as several members of the faculty, whom we had induced to sit as the honored upper crust of the Greengrocer Guild, tried to defend themselves against the assaults upon the stage—flying banana peels, rotten grapefruit. Four years later at their graduation, this group would send me an airplane ticket to come back to see the production of *King Lear* they staged. As for my own work as a director, I talked the Stanford Chapel into loaning me the church for a *Magnus Herod.* A full cast on donkeys and horses processed through the Stanford quadrangle, evoking the Corpus Christi processions of London in the sixteenth century. Among the three kings was the Stanford chaplain, the student body president, David Harris, who was Joan Baez's boyfriend, and the freshman dean as they wended their way to Bethlehem, in medieval robes under paper crowns—three backs bent in real and earnest conversation on some political issue of the community.

What was most important, however, was the Voice Project. John Hawkes had the intuition that if you set good writers in the classroom, they could discover the principles of what made each student's voice unique and, by freeing that "voice," give the student a sense of how exciting writing could be. Of course since this experiment was being urged by those who wished to emulate what had been done in the teaching of science, there was a desperate attempt to find equipment, identify formulas, that would justify the expense of sending writers into high schools and sections of Freshman English. None of this mechanical part of the experiment came to anything, but as Leo Litwak remarked to me some years later, what seemed foolish at the time, as one looked back on it, was serious and important. Searching for the "voice" of each student awoke my ear to some of the lessons I had learned collecting folktales and boiling them down to the few paragraphs that *American Heritage* required. What most troubled me about my work at that magazine was that in the process of condensing you lost what was unique, the voice of the speaker. The cardinal rule of collecting in folklore, as I learned it from books like Richard Dorson's, was that you had to record exactly what the speaker said, albeit clumsy, redundant, or obscene, for the way of saying something was what was magical.

Since I had taught in a tough high school in Boston, the Black public school in East Palo Alto, Ravenswood High, fell to my lot. The students there were even more exciting than the ones in my freshman section at Stanford, who somewhat overawed me. One of them had been Miss Hawaii the previous year. Their level of sophistication was certainly above mine. I recommended another articulate, attractive student to Norman Mailer as a secretary for the summer. (According to Norman's wife, Beverly, the student caused a fair amount of problems in her interpretation of a secretary's duties. "Beverly is upset with you," Norman teased me, on the steps of the Department of Justice that fabled day before he set out for the steps of the Pentagon and *The Armies of the Night*. I was on reserve duty for two weeks at a nearby air base and had tiptoed in for the beginning of the peace demonstration.) Even in the conventional precincts of Stanford Freshman English, where one was battling the "country club" culture of

the wealthier students, it was possible to break through to a voice. "Write a story you're afraid to tell! Write two essays, one praising, the other insulting me—you have the rest of the period to ask damaging personal questions." I cribbed my best exercise from Philip Roth through Seymour Simckes (another of Albert's disciples, Seymour's father was the local rabbi through two generations in Dorchester-Mattapan and a friend of our family). It was based on Kafka's *Letter to His Father*—"Write a letter to your father that you are afraid to send!" I peppered this class of mostly White, middle-class freshmen and women with tall tales collected by Zora Neale Hurston. This was at a moment when she was forgotten. I had discovered Hurston by accident in Botkin's *Southern Folklore*. "Write about the hottest day, the ugliest man," etc., though this exercise would strike far deeper roots at City College in the dialects of New York's streets.

At the grave of Reuben Mirsky, the author's great-great-grandfather, on the Mount of Olives, 1986

The company of writers Jack assembled for this project, Mitch Goodman, Jerome Charyn, Denise Levertov, John Barth, Leo Litwak, Clive Miller, and William Alfred (who had been lured for a semester from Harvard) were fun to work with. We were often irascible. Jerry got up at one meeting to announce loudly, "Jack, sit down. You don't know what you're talking about." Stanford offered me an assistant professorship if I would stay on, but I was in love with Manhattan, and the students at City College I felt needed me in a far more personal way.

During my year in California, however, I discovered a new world. I had arrived early from New York City for my year of teaching at Stanford. Leo Litwak loaned me his apartment in San Francisco for a week. Clive Miller, who was a class ahead of me at Harvard, another one of Albert Guerard's disciples, let me stay at his place just off the Stanford campus for a few days while I found rooms to rent. The Stanford library had open stacks that I was familiar with from my days as a graduate student and on the half-deserted campus I wandered into them since classes had not yet begun. Here for the first time I discovered Talmud in the Soncino translation.

Perplexed by the long row of volumes, not knowing where to start exploring, I went to the Talmud's index and looked up the entry on death. Taking out a notebook, I copied out the columns of references that stretched over several pages and began systematically to work my way through them. It was the entrance to a garden of storytelling. I was wound up in the world of my father, grandfather, great-grandfather, and the fantasy of the rabbis became my preoccupation. A few months later, I would write my first story in that voice, "Mourner's Kaddish," and the writer who lived opposite me on the landing of East Thirteenth Street, Marvin Cohen, would carry it to *New Directions,* where it became my sole contribution to their *Annuals.*

As I look forward, I see that I will not be able to draw the bow past my twenty-ninth or thirtieth year, though I am approaching fifty-nine. Still the arrow, never at rest, in flying has to pass through some of the years beyond that.

I came back from Stanford. My mother and father had visited me there and were not enthusiastic about my return. They were thinking of pulling up stakes in Boston and spending a few months in my Palo Alto orbit every year. California was an old dream of my father's. His career in Massachusetts was over. I, however, felt the pull of the Lower East Side; the kosher restaurants of Avenue D, its pushcarts; the crazy shoe-box synagogues, dairy eating places between Houston, Delancey, Grand, and East Broadway. My mother was angry at me because I would not make up my mind about Sue Wick, a young woman I had been dating almost from the beginning of living in Manhattan. "I don't know whether to love her or not," burst out of Mother one day. I couldn't talk to her about what was or was not happening between Susan and myself.

The dial flicking past those pretenses at popular sociology that call themselves "Talk Shows," I heard a host ask the actress Goldie Hawn what she wanted most in the world. The answer froze my fingers on the button. "To please my mother."

A few years before her death, Aunt Sonya, my father's younger sister, said to me, "You know when you first came to New York, Mark, your mother told us not to be too nice to you."

I looked at her, bewildered.

"She wanted you to come back to Boston."

I laughed. "She told me from childhood, when I was twenty-one she wanted me out of the house." If she had asked, I would probably have stayed. It's difficult to speak directly of what I felt for my mother. Those readers who seek out my short stories will perhaps find a more articulate description of my feelings.

My mother knew far too many of my secrets. She had a habit of pursuing me with questions that unlocked my tongue, but left her shocked, unable to make sense of what I was doing. Still, during this year in California, I had received letters from her that were not the correspondence of a mother but of a young girl, shy, even romantic. Behind the hostile stare of disapproval, an electric and unexpected curiosity flashed. I went up, without Susan, to spend a week with my mother and father at the end of the summer at our beach cottage in Hull. My sister had come with her two little girls for the entire summer and my mother happily fussed over them. When we came back from Logan Airport, my mother stopped me on the upstairs landing. In an uncharacteristic gesture, she opened up her bathrobe and asked me to look at her stomach. I was horrified. Her belly was bloated, and when I reached out to touch it—hard. In the alcoholics' ward at Martland Medical Center in Newark, during my monthly reserve duty, I had seen bellies like this. They were liver damaged, the stomachs of men in an advanced state of cirrhosis.

"How long has this been going on!" I shouted, and then cried for my father. "Why haven't you taken her to the doctor?" I was scheduled to ride back by bus to New York City later in the day. After a rancorous hour in which I threatened to fly up from New York to take her to the hospital myself, they agreed to go and seek medical advice. In six months she was dead. Everything changed.

Nine years before, Ben Zion Gold had put Gershom Scholem's *Major Trends in Jewish Mysticism* in my hands, but I found the book esoteric and unreadable. Now I picked it up as a guide to the other world, one that I needed. Dante, whose *Commedia* I had read, joined it on the shelf that kept me from tripping into the abyss.

Fragments of those months of nightmare exist in a number of stories published in the pages of *Fiction, Kerem, Another Chicago.* Her death, and that of my father twelve years later, form the principal axis of an unpublished novel, *The Boston Ghost.* In a year when everything was in upheaval, my father took me to the synagogue. He had been hostile to religion for a long time. Mother's death made him more so, but now he completed my bar mitzvah instructions of sixteen years ago, teaching me how to put on *tefillin,* the black boxes strapped during morning prayer to the head and right arm of an observant Orthodox Jew. He stood beside me in the pews of one of the almost empty halls of prayer on Blue Hill Avenue, prompting me in the Mourner's Kaddish. "Recite it for your mother," he mumbled in an undertone, but the grief in his quiet voice had the authority of Law. "It's an honor for her."

I began going regularly to the synagogue in the morning and late afternoon, both in Boston and when I returned to New York City. In turn I had a request. "Take me to listen to Rabbi Soloveitchik." This was the one rabbi of whom my father had never spoken ill. Another world floated into view as Dad talked with a light in his eyes that he reserved for the professors at Harvard who had left their mark on him: Alfred North Whitehead, Harry Wolfson.

He would boast of the radical decisions Soloveitchik had made as a young man, challenging Orthodoxy's conventions. The details of my first visits to the rabbi's lectures in Brookline are in a chapter of *My Search for the Messiah.* Through Rabbi Soloveitchik's hypnotic discourse, I seemed to recover my grandfather Israel, lost to me at four and a half. I began a journey back to Pinsk, his city in Eastern Europe, and my father's. I took copious notes during the Saturday night lectures at the Maimonides school, where Rabbi Soloveitchik spoke to crowds of two hundred people. The "Rav's" thoughts spoke to me again and again in the essays I wrote after I heard him speak, and still do, years after I published some of these in *My Search.*

For eleven months, from 1968 to 1969, I recited the Kaddish for my mother. In the summer of the latter, the young woman from Cincinnati, who had gone to live in London with her husband, asked if I would like a free trip to England. There were extra seats on some of the flights her husband's business had chartered. I jumped at the chance to travel and, again, the commanding officer, Colonel Frimpter, of my Air Force Reserve unit was understanding. Marvin Cohen, the writer on my East Thirteenth Street landing who had brought my book into *New Directions,* gave me several lists of people to see. Some, he told me, were good for free meals, others were important as literary beacons. I skipped the meals, but I was eager to meet other poets, novelists, essayists. Among the names I was given was that of Alastair Reid.

Alastair, one of the translators of Borges, was living on a houseboat moored to the bank of the Thames in Chelsea. When he heard that I planned to visit Dublin, he pressed on me the name of Anthony Kerrigan, another of Borges' translators, mentioning that Edward Dahlberg was in the precincts of the River Liffy. The sentence "I had heard of Edward Dahlberg from Fanny Howe" does not do justice to what came before. Landing in Dublin, taking a hotel room quite by accident a few doors down from where Bloom had lived, I walked through Tony Kerrigan's doorway a few hours later and fell in love with him, his wife, his daughter, Antonia, and the ferocious character of Edward Dahlberg, who bundled us into a car and drove around the city looking for a female graduate student of his. Dahlberg had castigated Tony as an inadequate host for not immediately attending to my needs as a writer. Dahlberg with

Oriental largesse had proposed this young woman as someone who might give me *sensual* comfort during my lonely stay.

It was from Tony that I first heard of the *Tain Bó Cuailnge* and Flann O'Brien's *At Swim Two Birds.* It was through Tony that I would be introduced to Jorge Luis Borges, Unamuno, and meet Camilo Cela. Edward Dahlberg, his essays, his book *Because I Was Flesh,* turned my prose style upside down. I went back to Manhattan with new riches in my head.

As the numbness of my mother's death wore off, it became apparent that Susan Wick and I were not going to be able to live together any more. I won't speak of those events, though at the time they overshadowed everything else. We parted just before the summer of 1971. The next year, I corresponded with a Norwegian student I had met in Cambridge, Massachusetts, Inger Grytting, who would become my wife. In the spring of 1972, I began, together with Donald Barthelme, the magazine *Fiction,* now in its twenty-sixth year of publication. As in balance to the *Rav,* or the "Teacher," as Soloveitchik was known in the Orthodox world, Donald became the other major influence on my intellectual life. His death in 1989 tore something out of my life that can never be replaced, although friendship with him was often very difficult for me.

Here I break off. As literary biography, the best remains ahead: my trips to Switzerland to see Max and Marianne Frisch, the stormy friendships with Arthur Cohen and Harold Brodkey. I loved writers and sought them out—Cynthia Ozick, Cabrera Infante, Bernard Malamud, William Phillips.

There are so many tales to tell. How Jorge Luis Borges begged me to visit him in Buenos Aires, then pushed me out the door. How I rescued Manuel Puig's *Curse of the Spider Woman* from obscurity. My dance with the PEN club, founding the Teacher's Writer's Collaborative with Herb Kohl. The times I spent with Lawrence Stern of the *Washington Post,* one of the few men I have met who was absolutely a "mensch" and Ben Bradlee's "rabbi." I was drawn into the circle of *Partisan Review* by Caroline Herron. How I worked as a speech writer with Liz Holtzman. How I helped to convict Richard Nixon! How I played "rabbi" where angels feared to tread in Southeast Washington, D.C.—on a platform with the Black Muslims. Those who go riding high and erect through the stars will

no doubt be greedy for such details, but I am running out of space. Rather than taking an abrupt departure, though, I thought I would tarry a bit, what Jewish tradition describes as a Day of Lingering at the end of the long holiday of harvest.

I am never consciously difficult or even experimental. And I revise again and again, believing that I can be more lucid. I've done purely journalistic pieces, but I have absolutely no interest in them. They are sawdust. I don't exist in them. I don't think one can "conform" and write anything that someone else is going to take to heart. I do think about my audience—but only in terms of making them think of me. I was ready to read a piece about a teacher falling in love with a student at a recent reading of students and faculty. It was dangerous, but danger is "the secret in yourself." Acting taught me something about that—you go out on that stage to become aware and to draw the audience into that "act." If you can't surrender the self-consciousness, or rather let the audience share in your self-consciousness, you don't belong on the stage. What you are doing is going through a role by rote memory.

In creative writing classes, I insist that students go to the root of their feelings and speak honestly about them. I was asked recently if I was "obsessed" by sex. And, higgledy piggledy, whether I thought the Messiah would bring "peace." Finally, my interlocutor wanted to know if my mother, who at one point as she was dying whispered to me, "Use it. It's material," was giving me her weakness to turn into strength.

My thoughts on the Messiah exist most directly in the novel *Puddingstone,* which Sun & Moon has listed as coming for five years now. The Messiah in the Jewish world is part of this search for love—and to speak of the Messiah bringing "peace" is curious. The Messiah is feared in the Jewish sources because of the cataclysms that are prophesied to accompany his advent. The Messianic, however, is something each of us can look to in our own life, and this is bound up with the joy of mystical union. That union, not sex, is what I am obsessed by. The Jewish rabbis, whom I read with increasing curiosity, make it clear that the attraction to one loved is the closest experience we have of that union with the Unknown.

My mother did not give me her suffering out of weakness, or tell me to make of her "weakness" a strength. This is a reading which betrays a religious bias foreign to me. My mother gave me in her last months what she had always hidden from me, her nakedness. Only at the last moment, when her dignity was compromised by her suffering, did she wave me away. She gave me mystical union and that is love. She overcame many middle-class taboos to let me know just how fiercely she loved me. Some rabbis spoke of Messiah as a woman, or the Messianic experience as a union with the Female Presence of the Divine, so as to try to experience it with the strongest force of love they could imagine. I am afraid of death—and love seems to me the only power with the hope of overcoming its crushing threat of meaninglessness.

When Dante tried to imagine what love was in the highest circles of Paradise, he surrendered to geometry, or abstraction. Love, however, is never abstract, except when the sentimental is posing as love. (Not to suggest that Dante was sentimental in these final cantos, rather that grappling with a close approach to the Unknown, he recognized that the human image was inappropriate to the vision.) Love is a walking out of yourself toward others.

The Messiah in Christianity, at least in Catholicism, is reserved for those who believe in Him. There is no salvation or Messiah without belief. In Judaism a Messiah is not dependent or even interested in belief. A Messiah only requires acts of loving kindness between men and, of course, women. To speak of this as the "law" is to misunderstand the term in Hebrew, which is not "law" but rather "ha-lakah," the way to walk. I received from my father and mother so many deeds of loving kindness that I was carried far beyond the law, and far beyond the normal paths of human beings. That's what I seek in this life, that mystical love. Thoreau, questioned whether he was prepared for the world-to-come by a religious busybody hanging about the Concord writer's deathbed in the last days, answered, "One life at a time." The insistence that life here can be suffused with this intense, overwhelming emotion is what draws me to Robert Musil's work, his *Diaries,* the short stories, and *The Man without Qualities.*

Although I have always felt that Freud's use of myth was often purely speculative, i.e., the Oedipus Complex, or the story of Moses as an Egyptian prince, nevertheless, as a Jewish thinker, it seems to me he grasped the root of the Rabbinic understanding of the way man walks in the world. He saw that the powerful impulse of Eros underlies human action in many subtle and not so subtle ways. Scholars like Harry Wolfson have showed that condescension towards the sexual gained an irresistible grip on the early Church's thinking through Saint Augustine. There is a similar condescension in some passages of the Talmud, but it never gained the status of doctrine. But this is an open debate I have with Catholic friends, Charlotte Low Allen, and Fanny Howe, thinking about the boundaries of religion in this century and past ones.

One of the problems that I set myself in my novel *The Red Adam* was the danger that Judaism has always seen the image as a prime source of evil. I have so much respect for Rabbinic sources because of their laughing respect for the "worm" of sexual desire, the "shaper to evil," as they call it, seeing this drive as the prime mover of life. They have no wish to exclude it, cut it off. The idol rather is anathema to them. Not to fall victim to the image of a person, the illusion, but in sexual experience and in love, to find something that can be gripped as real—that is the most difficult task. It is twinned with birth, procreation. My fiction is an attempt to understand these riddles. I discovered that the rabbis were trying to do the same, and that they pursued the questions beyond this life. I feel that they are often "radical," just as I feel that Dante and Musil are "radical." The uncanny power of images to evoke reality and to draw one away into dreams, to seduce, and to suggest what one would normally regard as forbidden, fascinates me. As an actor I learned to "embody" an image, to project it so that others believe in it. I have always feared this off the stage, to become an idea of yourself. And yet ideas do form one. To become a forbidden idea, to summon a real person as an idea, or to treat a person as an idea—these were some of the riddles of *The Red Adam.*

In walking with a friend, just a few days ago, discussing his separation from a woman he had fallen in love with, I praised the distance, because it gave one a chance to idealize the person, so that one's ideals preceded reality which was often destructive of romantic illusion.

"Don't you believe in reality?" he asked.

"All love, I think, is based on an idea of the other, a genius for letting the ideal form dance ahead of the flesh. Ideas of beauty stir us to reach beyond ourselves, and beyond the other as well."

It was just this year that I met this neo-Platonic wisdom in Saul Bellow's small novel *The Actual.* Since I was one of the judges, I was happy to help give the Award in Fiction of the Jewish Book Council to a writer whom I had regarded with respect but distance. I write and I read fiction in hopes of entering, if only briefly, what Robert Musil, to whose *Diaries* I am currently writing a preface, calls, "The Millennium."

To write serious fiction is to search for the boundary between dreams and what we consider real, asking how dreams create the latter. In essays on architecture, particularly landscape architecture; in my single academic book about stage games in the Shakespeare text, *The Absent Shakespeare;* even in the political articles I have written for *Partisan Review* or *The Progressive,* my question is the same. Reading Schliermacher's essay "On Translation" and some of Novalis' aphorisms in the past month, trying to grip Musil's thought more intimately, I was made aware again of how important it is to understand all thought as a form of translation, from one world to another. My interest in family history and all the work I put into the unpublished manuscript about my father and grandfather coming from Pinsk to America, *The Broken Voyage,* is part of this curiosity about worlds that preceded my own. The book I just referred to is a manuscript of voices, and I wanted as much as possible to keep those voices intact, so that the story could be understood in their context. Charles Olson does this in his *The Maximus Poems* where New England, old and new, echoes in its language. Again my devotion to publishing the histories of Pinsk, the *Yizkor* books, or "books of remembrance" of my father's city in the swamps of Byeloruss, which seems to have finally borne fruit in the form of a contract from Stanford University Press, reflects, I suppose, a desire to "translate" not just my father's but my grandfather's voice into my own. The whole history of their city, Pinsk, which formed them, is an obsession for me. When I hear my voice, I recognize with surprise my father's inflections. Often, walking in the street, I sense that I am striding in his gait, my shoulders hunched like his. And some-times, listening to folly attempting to abuse me to my face, I catch my mother's side of the mouth pucker, her ironic silent dismissal moving down the line of my nose.

In a book I would publish far too early, *My Search for the Messiah,* I made fun of myself and my search for voices that would speak through me from worlds that had passed, or to use the Biblical metaphor, worlds that had gone before me. The laughter, however, was a "stimulant" to think further. In sexual experience one has a taste of Messiah's promise. The presence of the Unknown is overwhelming, and Maimonides, the super-rationalist among the rabbinical commentators, uses the image, obviously personal, of man's love for woman to describe the overwhelming of all rational boundaries in the approach to the Unknown.

Amen to Novalis, "Mankind, metaphor."

BIBLIOGRAPHY

Fiction:

Thou Worm Jacob, Macmillan, 1967.

Proceedings of the Rabble, Bobbs-Merrill, 1971.

Blue Hill Avenue, Bobbs-Merrill, 1972.

The Secret Table (novellas), Braziller, 1975.

My Search for the Messiah, Macmillan, 1977.

The Red Adam, Sun & Moon Press, 1990.

(Editor with David Stern) *Rabbinic Fantasies: Imaginative Narratives from Classical Hebrew Literature,* Jewish Publication Society, 1990, reissued by Yale University Press, 1998.

The Absent Shakespeare, Fairleigh Dickinson and Associate University Presses, 1994.

Contributor of articles and short stories to *Ararat, Boston Globe, Identity, Massachusetts Review, Mosaic, New York Times Book Review, Partisan Review, Progressive, Tri-Quarterly, Village Voice,* and *Washington Post Book World.* Editor, *Fiction* magazine.

James Scully

1937-

MAN RAY'S FLATIRON: TOWARD A LITERARY AUTOBIOGRAPHY

James Scully (pencil drawing by Mondo Jud Hart), 1997

I was born 23 February 1937 in New Haven, Connecticut. My mother, Hazel Donovan, did housecleaning. With the Second World War she got her first factory job and that became her work. She went from major corporations such as A. C. Gilbert, Talon Zipper, and Whitney Blake to family-owned sweatshops—for example, baking enamel coating on lipstick tubes—until she retired at sixty-five with arthritic hands. My father, James, had immigrated from Clydebank, Scotland, which he referred to as "the old country." He worked as a plumber's apprentice, but by 1937 he was a glassgrinder and shipping clerk for MacAlester Bicknell, a laboratory apparatus and chemical supply house. He had this

*job for the rest of his working life, until he was
fired for alcoholism a few months shy of retirement.*

*My writing and politic are conditioned by this
family history, which starts from systemic exploitation
rather than psyches or sensibilities. It takes reams
of mental and emotional contortion to rationalize
such a system. Cultural institutions are part of the
rationalization, a circumstance that has made me
ambivalent toward poetry—poetry not as language,
but as culture. Poetry as a cultural institution is
necessarily system-blind. What it does observe is a
decorum of social silence.*

*

Nearly everyone lives a mess of lives—from
one time to another, and at the same time.
Yet living is one thing, narrating another. The
story as told leaves much of the story out. To
put a skin on an autobiography is less a documentary
than a political act. Which is what this
is. My assumption is that the auto in autobiography
is overrated. Life stories make more sense,
are less mystifying, when we understand that
they are unique instances of a social history.

*

I'm on the floor, playing. The radio is on.
My grandmother is sitting at the kitchen table,
tears running down her face. I'm eight years
old, and I have never seen her cry. It is the
only time I will see her cry, ever. Her one strong
opinion, as far as I know, is that Bing Crosby
is wonderful and Frank Sinatra is "a bag of
bones." It is April 1945. She's crying because
the radio is playing the death of President
Roosevelt.

*

In time the house would be racked with
throwings and hollerings, but my early childhood
was a happy one. Between the early caring
and the later eruptions of inexplicable adult
rage, I grew up painfully shy. While my mother
worked, my grandmother took care of me. I'd
go to her house, a three-room railroad flat,
and listen to Morton Downey's Coca-Cola Hour
on a wooden cathedral-shaped radio, which was
in the front room with the windup phonograph.

The bedroom was in the middle and the kitchen
to the rear. My grandfather always seemed to
be working, so my grandmother and I would
walk in the park or take the open-air trolley
to Morris Cove, off New Haven Harbor. I don't
recall if she swam or not, but she would stand
in the water and bounce up and down, wallowing
in it. She was a bosomy lady. Afterward
I rode the merry-go-round, wanting to catch
the brass ring and terrified I would. What if it
jammed and pulled me off the horse?

*

She was dark, my grandmother. Deep dark
in summer. Her husband, Clarence, was white
white. Partly that was him, partly his job, which
had him indoors ten hours a day tooling rifle
barrels at Winchester's. The war—World War
II—meant constant overtime. Poppy, as I called
him, would come home late from the factory,
all oily and worn and wanting quiet. He would
sit there and eat, reading the newspaper. On
Sundays he became a dandy: clean, white-shirted
with arm garters and, in summer, a white panama
hat. He had a black 1929 Chevy he kept spotless,
reserving it for weekends, which he could
do because Winchester's was close enough to
walk to. In 1946 when he gave the Chevy up
it was still running and shining like new, except
the black had patches of green patina.
Ten years later it was a battered old machine.
One of my uncles had it churning over the
field on his farm. The last I saw of it was in
the early '60s. It lay moldering in the woods
in Bantam, Connecticut, near another uncle's
tar-paper shack. The road to it was gone, grown
over. The old Chevy had become exotic, vinecloyed
. . . just *there*. Later I would see it again,
at MOMA, in Dali's dank, vegetated rain taxi.

*

*Freud said the Irish were "one race of people
for whom psychoanalysis is of no use whatsoever."
He might have said the same of Chinese farmers or
multinational sweatshop workers (of whatever 'race').
And Fanon noted that Freud, Adler, "and even the
cosmic Jung did not think of the Negro in all their
investigations." But, he says, "they were right not to
have. It is too often forgotten that neurosis is not a
basic element of human reality." Not all repression*

is psychological. When push comes to shove, the psyche and its analysts are exposed as a culturally specific, class-bound construct.

*

There is a point to this. It bears on what I would and would not write. I grew up in a world that in life rhythms and technologies was very different from this one. There was more social time, less *stuff*. Yet life was no less class-specific than it is now. There are those who own and accumulate, and those who must work for them and be written off. We no longer talk about class. It's an embarrassment all the way around, to be acknowledged only by socio-logical euphemism—the mystifying notion that class is a matter of income or occupation or something called life-style. But class is more richly systemic than that. What evolves through rela-tions of production radiates though all the di-mensions, including what is called the spiritual. Every system has its narrative. It shapes psy-chology, aesthetics, the contours of knowledge. Not truth, but knowledge. The fact is that class also expresses itself as the power, or the pow-erlessness, to define and accredit social reality. And because in some sense all writers set out to be writers of reality, class becomes a defini-tive writing issue. That is why I can't be dis-creet about it.

This writing life has everything to do with class—and with the peculiar, melancholic rage that piles up behind the silences imposed by class boundaries and markers. Not just the si-lences, but the distortions and misunderstand-ings. And as it has to do with that, it has sec-ondarily to do with race, which has the mini-mal advantage and the considerable disadvan-tage of being more graphic.

Race was *always* out there, the opaque "given" of social limits. In 1940s New Haven, race meant black. The ghetto was rigidly defined—it could have been laid out by a surveyor, like a planned community—bounded by the Dixwell/Shelton junction on the north and by Lake Place, just short of Broadway and Yale University, on the south. Dixwell Avenue was the main street of the ghetto. My grandparents lived in a Shelton Avenue tenement two doors from the border. One day, as we were driving through, some black people double-parked or got in the way. Poppy started muttering about "jigaboos" and

With grandfather, Clarence, New Haven, Connecticut, 1940

"jungle bunnies." The language was so startling, so vehement and unexpected, it was scary. Or-dinarily he was a mild man who said little. But I also remember this same man taking me down Dixwell once to get a haircut in a black bar-ber shop—something as unheard-of then as it is now—and a number of times to be treated by a black dentist, Dr. Fleming, a courtly gentle-man with a feathery touch, though what im-pressed me more were the two panels of stained glass flanking his front window.

I was nearly five when the War began, eight when it ended. However horrible for oth-ers, for me it was a grand time, a time of living in one big community bound by a com-mon purpose, arcane codes and fetishes shared by young and old alike. The mood was up-beat, can-do. For "the war effort" we collected aluminum foil and lard, selling it to the A&P.

There were blackouts, black shades on the windows, and shields like eyelids blacking the upper hemispheres of auto lights. My father was an air-raid warden, and we made raw, icy ice cream in a galvanized churn bucket. Somehow, in my mind, the two are related. Then and later we listened to the radio—Edward R. Murrow, Sam Spade, The Shadow, Abbott and Costello, Jack Benny, and the Friday night fights sponsored by Gillette. When margarine came in, owing to the butter shortage, the dairy lobby insisted it be sold uncolored, in pallid lardlike blocks. The kids got to knead the dense plastic sacks, bursting the bubble of red dye which spread through the margarine, then, diluting to a yellowish color.

Most of the servicemen we knew were in the Pacific, so our war was more against Japan than Germany. One cousin was killed when his ship went down, but I did not feel what that meant. The living and their souvenirs were more real. My uncle Patrick, who was in the Seabees, brought back a long, heavy sniper's rifle, the papers and ID photograph of a smiling Japanese sailor, and a pair of Japanese sneakers with the big toe separated from the others. The sneakers looked like awkward foot mittens. Once I glimpsed a picture of Patrick with two bare-breasted women in grass skirts. His only wound was a deep, jagged forehead scar where (he said) he was "kicked by a horse." Home on leave, he came in drunk with his girlfriend, Nelly, singing "Cuddle up a little closer" while my mother hushed my sister and me in the darkened bedroom, keeping us out of the way.

On V-J Day there was a great street celebration. People built a bonfire and hanged a life-sized effigy of Tojo or Hirohito, I forget which. When the war ended and Patrick got his discharge, he came to live with us. He and I shared the three-room flat on the top floor of the house we had moved to, thanks to the wages my parents earned working overtime during the war. The front room was mine, the middle was Patrick's. They were garret rooms with slanting walls. The rear room was screened ceiling to floor along two facing walls. These built-in wall cages were filled with my father's canaries. So many I never bothered to count them, though for all those growing-up years my room thrummed with muffled canary warbles and the cooing of wild pigeons under the eaves.

*

My father came to this country with his father and mother, two brothers, and three sisters. Two older sisters came earlier, working as maids and saving enough to bring the others. Their father had worked at a Singer sewing machine factory in Glasgow, but from the day he arrived in the United States he refused to work. The daughters would find him jobs and he would quit or be fired, usually the same day. I met him just once. He sat in a rocker—distant, with a severe aspect—looking like a Smith Brother on the cough drop package. The rocker was the only furniture in the room. By the time I was born his wife had already died. My father said she would put a pillow at the windowsill and lean on it, watching people pass in the street. In Scotland she liked to visit castles. The few details suggest she was a romantic, though maybe she just wanted a break. She'd had thirteen children in all, five of whom died in childhood. All my father remembered about the castles was his playing with frogs in the moats. Which makes sense. He was a good father, but a man more at home with animals than with people. I think he respected animals because, unlike people, they are what they are. He was swarthy, with bright blue eyes, though his intense look was more generalized than piercing. He was as *un*topical as anyone I have ever known. When he spoke it seemed to be from some indefinable space rather than from a particular place and time, an effect heightened by his caustic pithiness. Though he hadn't finished high school he had a remarkable vocabulary—superior to, and used more freely than, that of most U.S. college students. I used to think it was a generational thing, but now believe it was owing to the Scottish educational system, which unlike the English system is not only prized but is genuinely public. Or was. I don't know what goes on now, but in his day it did not systemically discriminate on a class or economic basis.

*

While I was growing up my father did not go to bars and, except on extended family occasions, was not a drinker. The alcohol ravaging came later. But early and late the one constant in his life was animals. Beside the canaries he raised homing pigeons, show pigeons such as pouters and ruffish-collared jacobins, chickens, bantams (colorful and vicious), guinea pigs, tropical fish, a dog—he always had a dog. A springer spaniel called Midnight had a mouth so soft it would carry a hen's egg, intact, from the coop to the porch. Which was just one of the lesser wonders. When a crow turned up with a broken leg, my father fixed it. One day it followed his car as he drove to work, and when he went out back for lunch the damn thing, as he called it, was waiting on a fence by the railroad tracks. So he shared his lunch with it. This went on the next day, and the next—he began packing extra food for the crow—till one day a kid stoned it and the damn thing, as he never failed to call it, flew off down the tracks.

Though he had a few buddies, mostly Poles, his human relations were with animals. There's no other way to describe how he was socialized. Because there is only rudimentary psychology in human/animal arrangements—which are based rather on behaviors and discretions—they are spared some of the more refined meannesses that creep into psychological negotiations. My relationship with my father, like his with animals, was also based on behaviors and discretions. We did not talk intimate personal feelings. He would have felt awkward about that, as I still do. At the same time there was no bullying, just different decorums for different occasions . . . some of which could be raucous. When the Scots got together for weddings or anniversaries there'd be heavy drinking, with bawdy dances and songs—the kids joined in as well, it was more fun than anything—but none of it was personal. Your personal life was yours . . . if that makes sense. That aside, what my father and I actually *did* together was hunt, once in awhile, and fish. When we fished freshwater, brooks or lakes it made no difference, nothing but trout would do—which meant hanging out in silence, watching dragonflies or "sewing needles" balance on the tip of the rod. Other fish we threw back: sunfish, perch, pickerel, bullheads, suckers, and eels. There was more action in salt water. We rented a rowboat, went out into the Sound, threw droplines, and pulled up a bushel of flatfish which we shared with neighbors. A few times we caught very small sharks, called dogfish. Skates and eels we cut loose before they snarled the

line. The skates—also called devil fish or stingrays—were especially fearsome. I learned that you respect animals by recognizing them and by not reading yourself into them.

When you can't see how one thing relates to another, when you live the ignorance of a child, confusion creeps in. You do not see it coming. As little time as I spend with my father, I spend less with my mother, who is working and has another child. My sister, Carol, is four years younger. There's pressure to stay out of the way and not track dirt through the house. My mother is irritable. As we have no family routines, I'm on my own. Then school comes to the rescue. For the first time, though not the last, I am unofficially adopted.

*

Our family was not religious. We said no prayers, had no icons on the walls, held no religious beliefs. But as parochial schools were considered better than public schools, I attended St. John the Baptist grammar school, which was run by the Sisters of Mercy. The first-grade nun was a dwarf who beat us with a pointer when we made mistakes and beat us again if we tried to erase them. It was Dickensian, without the redeeming prose, and the more terrifying because she came at us on *our* level, her face inches away. The genius of this arrangement was that by second grade the worst had passed. We'd still be hit or have our ears pulled, but for reasons we could understand. Punishment was predictable and linked to rules.

The nuns teach writing by the Palmer Method, which we practice by making big spiraling loops, like Slinkies. Anyone who writes with the left hand is beaten. Which I do, and am, and so never learn to write script. At least, not without deliberation. All I can *write* spontaneously is my signature. . . . I taught myself to print by copying typeface. And because I could never print fast enough to keep running lecture notes, I trained myself to note key phrases and later to remember or deduce from that—which would become a helpful disability, as it forced me to analyze while listening.

At St. John's I became an altar boy, had straight A's after the first grade, eventually played on the baseball and basketball teams, had the lead in the school play, and was in general looked-out-for by the priests and nuns. The church and school were more a social institution than a religious one. When I didn't have sneakers, they bought me a pair. And when I couldn't pay tuition to the Catholic high school—I didn't even know there was tuition—a priest surreptitiously took care of it, for me and others, though I did not learn this till years later. His name was Father Carukin and he was a mild man, unusually educated for a parish priest. Above all he was a Boston Celtics fan, a student of proper spacing, and a believer in the bounce pass, which is near impossible to intercept.

*

Things had gotten worse after the War. My mother would fly into screaming rages. She'd throw anything, even an iron, in any direction. Or put her hand through glass. It was horrific because she knew no bounds. Anything might set her off. To meet her now, long past the throwing and the screaming, no one would guess what that was like. But back then I stayed out of the way, as did my father. We lived more or less outside, coming in only to eat or sleep.

In one of Randall Jarrell's poems, a woman, a "soul in space," blurts out: "Shall I make sense or shall I tell the truth?" Along with the rages—or maybe it was only a finer form of raging, a vapor off the same boiling—my mother had dreams for my sister and me. The dreaming was of singing and dancing. I'd have to take my sister downtown to Madame Annette's dance studio for toe and tap lessons. On my mother's bureau there's a picture of Carol, dead many years now, posing in the bellhop hat and short, satin skirt that was her tap dance costume. Later, I think later, my mother had me take singing lessons, of which I recall nothing except having to escalate scales. I sang Saturday mornings on WELI radio, a boy tenor trying to knock out show tunes such as "Somewhere over the Rainbow" or plodding along with "Peg O' My Heart." I also recall singing "The Surrey with the Fringe on Top," though I had no idea what a surrey was. The pianist was a large, gravelly voiced lady named Frieda. Frieda had dyed red hair, lots of eye makeup, a huge emerald ring, and the air of someone who was way ahead of wherever we could hope to get to. It was incredibly reassuring to be around

her. With such a person backing you, you could not miss. But how my mother managed all this is a mystery to me. There'd been no 'culture' in her background, and for all her ferocity at home she was timid about going places she had not been before. To this day she has never lived further than two miles from the house she was born in. Before getting married she'd gone a few years to Commercial High, then left to do housecleaning. She got pregnant, married, had one kid, went into the factories, had another kid, and . . . ? I used to assume, without thinking, that her dreams swirled over from '40s and '50s dance musicals, where romance and sexuality were played out for the general public. But those films were the popular culture of *my* early youth. Hers had to have come from the 1920s, and from the Depression that ended her school days.

*

Horrendous moments sink in in a heartbeat yet may not resurface for years. I was about fourteen, walking with friends down Dixwell Avenue. An old woman came shuffling up from the other direction. She drew even, then passed. I drifted to the far side, mingling with the others, relieved she hadn't recognized me. The old woman was my grandmother. Three or four years earlier my grandfather had had a stroke. One side was paralyzed. He made awful yawning sounds, unable to speak. For awhile I wouldn't see him in the convalescent home because I was afraid to. When I did go he broke down and cried, which is my last image of him. I don't think he was crying about me only, but what I reminded him of. After the stroke my grandmother had taken the insurance money and run off with a nursing home attendant. When the money ran out, the man left her. My mother never spoke to her again. My grandmother would come up on the porch and ring the doorbell, but my sister and I were forbidden to answer. It was like with Patrick and Nelly, when they were courting in the kitchen and Carol and I were hushed. But then, this was not at all *like*. Years later, after my grandfather Clarence died, we'd be dunned by the welfare department demanding reimbursement for my grandmother. They threatened my mother with jail. She said she would go before she would pay, and she would have. So the day I passed by my grandmother on Dixwell Avenue was not only the first time I had seen her in some years, it was the last. That moment, so small and natural then, a trifle awkward, has become astounding to me. Here and now I can't begin to say what my feelings are, they're so near to nonfeelings. It's like having a crumb of dry ice inside my chest.

I don't know what became of my grandmother, nor where she is buried. I don't know where she or my grandfather were born. Her name was Gertrude Signor, and from her looks and jet black hair and dark burnished color, and from something dismissive my father said in passing—intimating French Indian—I assume there was some indigenous history behind her. She herself never referred to a past. My maternal grandparents seemed to have no relatives, never said where they came from, left no documents.

Now it's called Newhallville. Then it was "around Bassett Street," an Italian-Irish working-class neighborhood. It was so thoroughly what it was, without any 'other' to compare it with, we had no notion of class. Nor, really, of white poverty. The closest I came to that was a Cub Scout den on Division Street. The den mother was one of the Salvation Army poor who were sprinkled discreetly around working-class neighborhoods. I was struck by the squalor—our own house was clean to a fault—but she was a warm woman and the warmth took over. I should also note that though we lived among immigrants and accents—nationality was not an abstraction but a concrete reality—as kids we were indifferent to ethnicity. Everyone was pretty much the same . . . until high school.

St. Mary's drew Catholics from different backgrounds. One girl would arrive in a chauffeur-driven limo! We were all Catholics, yes, but with differing expectations. No one had to track us, we tracked ourselves. I started out as an honor student and quickly became a hood: severely pegged trousers, DA, suede shoes instead of bucks, the works. I got into petty criminal activity—occasional burglaries, numbers running, and gang fights—but nothing out of line with the standards of the time and place. Hoodishness had more to do with attitude. As part of the tuition payoff I was supposed to play basketball for the school, but didn't. One night, as one of two white players on an otherwise black team from the Y, I found myself playing against

my own high school. No one dared say anything, and anyway I was hardly the only one at odds with the school. There was ongoing antagonism between the nuns and the working-class male students—which was resolved, a few years after I left, when the school stopped admitting male students.

In high school I learned two things. One was how to type. The other was a political lesson. In a prom referendum the students voted for the wrong band—one led by a Jew, not that run by "a good Catholic"—and the nuns overruled us. Everyone walked out, even the respectable students. Our indignation was not over the chauvinism or the *de facto* anti-Semitism—had the bandleader been Protestant the nuns would have reacted in the same way, obsessed as they were with Protestant evangelism—but at the injustice of the overturned vote. And at getting an unhip band.

*

Sex and sports were generic, but gangs and jazz meant growth and survival. Gangs socialized me, teaching solidarity and organization. By learning to resist the daily challenges and threats—there was no way to avoid them without losing face—we developed so much confidence in ourselves that I have never had to envy or be in awe of anyone else, no matter what their status or wealth. As for jazz . . . rather than functioning primarily as a social revelation, as seems the case for many middle-class whites, for me it opened the prospect of real live *intellectual* activity.

I belonged to two gangs in two different areas of the city. One was local. Despite tension with a neighboring gang and occasional skirmishes, the Aristocrats, as we called ourselves, was more social club than anything else. We had our own jackets with emblems we ourselves designed. We put together trips, even rented a summer cottage—though none of us came from a professional family, nor from a family that ever had a cottage, and none was older than seventeen. With informal leadership from one especially intrepid Italian kid, the gang was a training ground in self-organization. Most of the Aristocrats became successful later on: in business primarily, but also in the military and the police. They still work with and keep in touch with one another. The other gang was more volatile: loosely knit, unnamed, a wider and older range of ages, and capable of serious violence. *Unlike gangs now, with their lethal mix of automatic weapons and big money drugs, our confrontations were hand to hand with chains and clubs. Only once was I in a fight where shots were fired, and then the shooting was defensive, aimed over heads.* This gang was based on State Street, and I had come to it through other hoods from the high school. I had the impervious attitude, but could also dance. At block dances they would clear a space for me in the street. This was in pre-rock, R & B days. At parties we bopped to *doo-wop*—The Scarlets, The Orioles, groups like that—but in halls or at block dances we did a kind of swing, which was wider ranging and quicker footed, less up-and-down, than rock and roll. Lacking the backbeat and the syncopation, rock has always seemed more like exercise than dance. With rock you started from the arms and legs, making it somewhat mechanical, whereas the other stuff had to be tuned in the gut. Not metaphorically, but physically in the gut. *I've seen huge Finnish ladies whirling around a lodge floor doing polkas and stepped-up waltzes, so light on their feet they could have danced on eggs. They weren't dancing with arms and legs but inside out, letting it flow from there.*

Along with the dancing I did a lot of listening, either at a local jazz club called MacTriff's or in New York. I started going to clubs at fifteen, with a false ID, and though challenged once or twice was never thrown out. Some of the attraction was the romance of it, the sense of being *where it's happening*. Here's Basie and Joe Williams at Carnegie Hall. Or a seedy midtown Manhattan hotel bar, where local guys are honking and banging it out among the pimps and prostitutes. The musicians are cynical, but sometimes they become interested in what they're playing if *you* become interested. Or you're in Birdland, at the bar, and thirty feet away there's Dinah Washington poured into a glittering, shoulderless, white-sequined gown, singing "Willow Weep for Me." I mean, what can surpass that? Or Zoot Sims comes to the bar between sets, weaving through the smalltalk. Or you're at the Metropole and the band perched over the bar is in a sweat of *wailing*, percussing like mad. But more than that, after years of dead schooling I had my first exposure to unabashed intellectual activity—which I identify, most dramatically, with a 1954 or 1955 appearance of Bud Powell at Randall's Island. It was shock-

ing. Powell seemed kind of crazy—not with 'stylin' but with thinking through. You had to listen, and listen hard, or the stuff would scatter into little notey pieces. But then all the great improvisers—not the musical quoters, being cute and lazy, but the improvisers—were engaged in a superior form of thinking. Years later when I came across Yeats's saying, of a dancer, that you could almost say her body thought, I'd associate that with jazz, which is so thought-saturated it can *only* communicate as inside-out body English. In time this became a writing ideal—not the scenes or subjects of jazz, which are limited, but its kinesthetic intelligence.

This was between 1952 and 1955—I also followed, religiously, the cool of Progressive or West Coast Jazz—when the nuns passed me out of high school though I did not have the grades to graduate. My entire senior year my homeroom teacher refused to speak even one word to me because, as she said, I was hopeless. By then school had no reality for me. Nor did literature. My father's vocabulary notwithstanding, we had fewer than a dozen books in the house, all but two of them Wednesday matinee prizes from the Dixwell Avenue movie theater, which ordinarily gave away Melmac dishes. *When I was younger, going to Saturday matinee, my mother would hang a little cheesecloth bag of camphor around my neck to ward off polio.* The books were novels by Mark Twain and Sinclair Lewis, and the sea stories of James Fenimore Cooper. I'd read them when I was home, sick, with nothing to do. The other two books belonged to Uncle Patrick: Ovid's *Amores*, which he kept among the stacks of bodice-busting true detective magazines, and the poetry of Robert Burns. Our Irish surname notwithstanding, my father and uncle and their parents had all been born in Scotland. They were culturally Scottish and thought of themselves as such. The exception was my father. Though everyone called him Scotty because of his burr, he did not habitually socialize with other Scots, as his brothers and sisters did, and would insist he was "an American." Ironically, almost a year after I'd gotten out of high school, it would be Burns's poetry that mediated my way into *writing*.

*

How could a teenager afford the music, the clubs, the trips to New York? Well, being a hood is a posture, not an occupation. The fact is, I worked: part-time in winter, full-time in summer—sometimes at two jobs—and during Christmas break. The jobs: in the repair department of a jewelry store, coding prices and ferrying items between the retailer and the manufacturing jeweler down the street; setting up duckpins at the Union League; dealing at a cigarette gambling booth in an amusement park; chloroforming and skinning rats in a state agricultural lab conducting routine dairy testing; and doing rough carpentry and roofing in tract house construction. One summer I worked as a church janitor, and for a few seasons as a parking attendant for stock car races. For awhile I did stoop labor, mostly picking green beans (the farmer would come to the city and collect us in his truck), but we were paid piecework and it was not worth the trouble. I also did house painting (external) and in a church/city political patronage job worked one summer on an overmanned crew, painting white divider lines down city streets. My last job was as a night gas station attendant. I know it was the last because I was fired for reading on the job—a sign that my life had begun to change. *Evidently my Scottish grandfather, who'd refused to work, had become a perennial extension student. Well into his sixties he was taking courses at New Haven College. The* New Haven Register *had an article on him, the oldest student in the city, noting he liked to talk "philosophy."*

With father and mother, about 1941

I was the first and only person in my family to finish high school. Which left me at an impasse. At seventeen I had joined the Naval Reserve for eight years, three regular and five reserve. I'd gone to boot camp in Bainbridge, Maryland, and worked in the neurosurgery ward at St. Alban's Hospital on Long Island. Now I had a troubled relationship with a girlfriend and didn't want to do full-time service, not yet, though nearly all my friends had headed into the marines or the army. I was at a loss. This became an acute crisis—which, out of guilt at having thrown over so much of church and Catholic school, and having ended the relationship with the girl, I interpreted as religious. So I went back to the parish church, where I hadn't been in years, went to confession, and said I wanted to become a priest. That was how I got the job, with seven other potential seminarians, painting white lines down the middle of New Haven's streets. Toward the end of the summer the parish priest—a rough-hewn American Irish man, very straightforward, with no irony—took me to the seminary for a look around. The immaculate, polished floors made me uneasy. The looks and smells were too reminiscent of grammar school corridors, giving me a nervous stomach. So when the priest introduced me to the purple-satined monsignor with the damp, soft handshake, that did it. An unctuous fraud is an unctuous fraud, no matter what the outfit. We left there, I left the patronage job, and aside from weddings and funerals and one baptism, I did not participate in a Catholic church again.

Anyone could get into New Haven State Teachers College. Also it was only a mile and a half away, within walking distance of my home. This was in 1955, when the college was not only free but had open admissions. Public higher education *was* public. I had only to pass a general test. When they called me in to discuss the test results, the first thing the interviewer said was "You scored so high, why are your grades so low?" I said, "Because I didn't like the nuns." Give or take a word or two, that was the interview. They admitted me. Looking back, I don't like to think what my life would be if they hadn't. It's not just a question of job opportunities. I had been living with the unrelieved expectation of violence. Though violence was always awful—there was nothing appealing about it—that did not keep me from being short-tempered, dangerous to others as well as to myself. Of course there was music, which I respected and learned from. But music was not enough. What college provided, in time, was access to understandings that could inform and articulate my rage. The understandings were not psychological but social and political. A dozen years later I would recognize a motivation similar to my own in *Letter to a Teacher*, which was written by peasant schoolboys who'd been flunked out of the Italian school system. The boys had gone to a dropout school run by a village priest, had mastered the skills they'd failed, and then used those skills to critique the class-based educational system that is conceived to fail them.

*

With the square-backed DA, the pegs, the Mister B collars, the slouch, and the rest of the hood/hip paraphernalia and attitude, I resembled no one else in the teachers' college. Two of the professors, independently, had me to their apartments for dinner. One was a genteel, elderly woman who taught theater. (Once, when I'd done a monologue for her class—Hamlet's "O what a rogue and peasant slave am I"—she said she wished she was directing again, and I felt very proud. She was a reserved woman, someone who in those days would have been called a Brahmin, and in no way given to casual praise.) The other was an art teacher who was showing me to her husband, a Yale professor, who made me uncomfortable with questions about my life. Yet they had good intentions and were respectful, which took the edge off. With my look and bad language, my ignorance of rudimentary manners—never mind social protocol—I probably came across as a "wild child" who, incredibly, had thoughts and perceptions. Whether from arrogance or inno-

cence, I never hesitated to say what I thought. I was no wild child, though. Just someone who'd gone feral for awhile and didn't know their rules. Before high school I'd had a fiercely disciplined, if unintellectual, education and a tremendous out-of-school *verbal* education from attending to my father, who used words as though they meant something. He did not blather. Very early on, also, my grandmother had coached me through children's books. To this day I remember the five-or six-year-old triumph, it felt prodigious, of learning to read the word *steamshovel*.

At the teachers college I found a home among the bohemian set: students, and a few teachers, who were queer, foreign, or independent women, plus freethinking Korean War vets, working-class intellectuals, painters, and other 'others' who didn't fit anywhere else. The queers were not closet but undercover. That is important. Closet implies fear, yet it took courage for them to live as they did. I should also clarify that "bohemian," in a mid-'50s commuter college, did not mean avant-garde. Avant-gardes are driven by middle-class kids from elite colleges, the rejectionists who make up countercultural or elite movements. This was not that, nor a brand name bohemia, but an unpublicized generic one. We had no quarrel with established culture—some of us because we loved it, others because we'd never encountered it. For me it was a novelty. I had nothing to base a prejudice on. In twelve years of Catholic school curriculum we had read not one novel, seen not one work of art, other than religious icons, and heard not one piece of classical music. All I knew was what I'd heard on the Texaco-sponsored opera hour which aired on the radio every Saturday afternoon. I didn't think of it as classical music—classical was not a meaningful category in my life—but listened because I enjoyed it, hood or no. And when a professor from the teachers college took me to a Jascha Heifetz recital at Woolsey Hall, I was as thrilled as I'd been a few years earlier hearing Brubeck and Paul Desmond in that same concert hall.

A group of professors encouraged me to take the courses I wished to take, regardless of requirements. There was a spring blizzard, and classes were called off. As it was March 17, I got the notion of writing a dialect poem: a Scot complaining of a Saint Patrick's Day parade. I knew what Scots sounded like, having grown up with it, but didn't know how to write it. So I dug out Uncle Patrick's copy of Burns's poetry and used that as a glossary and spelling guide. The poem, written in rhymed quatrains, won the school's literary prize. At the presentation an older, Irish student gave it a dramatic reading. I was nineteen, and that was my first poem. It's sobering to realize that by then, before I had written a thing, I was already *stamped*—socially and mentally no longer in formation but 'given.' My understandings, analyses, and elaborations would become subtler and more strategic, less purely reactive, but the social outlook was what it would be.

Flush with achievement I wrote a one-act play—*The Flower Box,* very trash can, with domestic violence—then more poems, one Eliotic but most Mallarmé-ish, being cribbed from Roger Fry translations. Pastiche and outright mimicry aside, I trained myself to write prescribed forms. Without pretending to do more than exercises, I went through Babette Deutsch's dictionary of poetic forms making verses in nearly every formula in the book. Went through literally, beginning at the beginning and ending at the end, which took months. I suppose this is how novice artists teach themselves to draw—though not, I hope, with such doggedness. And as it's possible to tell, with painters, those who can draw from those who can't, so too with poets. In so-called free verse the difference between those who can manage prescribed ("formal") verse, and those who cannot, usually shows in the syncopation and in the line breaks. The syntactic energy levels are different. With the discipline of prescribed verse, free verse line breaks may still have the charge of bona fide punctuation (even in unsayable, "visual field" poetry), but without that discipline the breaks tend to give way to syntactic or rhythmic exhaustion, as though their spring were sprung. Of course someone may come along and put the lie to this, leaving another generalization with one leg less to stand on, but that remains to be seen.

After the professors taught me how to eat, to speak, to dress, and how to have my hair cut—all of which they did—and after I'd taken the courses I wanted to take, they arranged my transfer to the state university, figuring it would be more challenging. I thought little of it then, having no basis for comparison, but in retrospect what they did is amazing. An academic world with self-acting people in it, and those people not stars, is hardly imaginable now.

In 1957 I left New Haven. My sister dropped out of high school and went to live on her own. As little contact as we'd had before, there was less now. My parents stayed where they were, working separate lives from the same address, though everything around them was changing. The ghetto border had lost its mysterious power. Italians were moving en masse to the suburbs—it was like a migration—as black people moved up into Winchester Avenue, to the east of us. Meanwhile redevelopment (urban renewal, aka "negro removal") was destroying the un-Yaled side of downtown, cutting it off from the actual city. The one constant was Yale itself, whose power and wealth prevailed.

Frequently I run into people whose only association with New Haven is Yale, as though Yale were New Haven. In fact there wasn't even a cultural reverberation. As far as I knew, the good of it had been a few concerts at Woolsey Hall and Tony Lavelli's hook shot. The rest was iron-gated gray stone, fronted by waterless moats, forming a *cordon sanitaire* along two sides of the New Haven green. This was a university that produced no bohemia, not even the *buzz* of one. It could not support Whitlock's, the lone independent bookstore sitting in its shadow. If New Haven were X-rayed from outer space, say by alien anthropologists, Yale would have appeared as a massive implosion in the heart of it. Possibly the institution has reformed since then, though recurring labor put-downs suggest not. What's certain is that in the 1950s the relationship of the university to the city, to the people of the city, was appalling.

*

I arrived at the University of Connecticut in the fall of 1957. Making up for the required courses I had not taken at the teachers college, I took science classes. For the next two years I had six courses a semester, getting waivers to exceed the allowed credit load. With the staggered timing of labs and lectures, I'd wake in the morning panicked, thinking there was a course I'd forgotten. But years of parochial school discipline had left me with at least one useful compulsion, and I never missed a class. I'd rush from one end of campus, having studied empiricist philosophers, to a gimmicky psychology lab in the remote area of campus called "Rostov," after the town in Siberia, and there was nothing except a schedule to connect the two. I did not dance, listened to little music, did not play sports, did not attend a single sporting event, and did not notice I didn't. There was no time to.

I lived in an agricultural dorm, though it was not so much Ag as it was an encampment of students outside the fraternity system. Some were foreign, mostly Latin American and Caribbean. And there were Korean War vets like those at the teachers college. It's remarkable how many had problems that later would be associated with Vietnam vets. Some could not have attended without the GI Bill, and these added to the class mix. There was something reassuring about their political skepticism and savvy. But most of the time my speeded-up schedule and bare-bones regimen kept me in an institutional tunnel. Though I was not poor, and the university did not charge tuition, still it was a financial struggle. The room cost three hundred dollars per year, which I paid for with summer work. I could earn no more, so my father sent ten dollars a week, a considerable sacrifice on his part. The ten dollars went for books, cigarettes, and food, in that order. I ate one meal a day. At graduation I weighed 135 pounds, 35-40 pounds below normal weight, but was too single-minded or preoccupied to notice.

My entertainment was films, student plays, free chamber music concerts, and hootenannies. Bergman, Pirandello, Beckett, Genet, Sartre, Camus, and Hesse were cultural icons. The hoots were held in a cellar-level greasy spoon, a converted bowling alley, run with limitless tolerance by a Chinese man, his German wife, and her sister. The hoots had their too-sweetish side, the curiously cleansed traditional lyrics, but there was social commentary too. Despite stereotypes of the '50s, signs of unrest did break through the backwardness. I recall two major demonstrations. One was brought on by the expulsion of the student newspaper editor, who had published a cartoon satirizing the university's president. *Yes, a student could be expelled for satirizing the president. And women, who were not allowed to wear slacks or shorts to class, were locked in their dorms at 9 P.M.* There was a series of protest actions, even as the student editor took refuge in the house of a sociology professor. The other demonstration was over Arthur Miller. The students had invited him to speak on campus, but an administrator disinvited him be-

cause he'd refused to testify before the House Un-American Activities Committee. Oblivious of political history, I knew little about HUAC. Five years earlier I was not particularly aware of the Rosenbergs being executed. They meant no more to me than murdered Iranians or Guatemalans did, and do, to most Americans. My single impression of the McCarthy hearings was of Secretary Welch rising in indignation, saying, "Have you no decency, have you at last no decency, sir?" and that only because it was replayed over and over on television. This level of politics hadn't registered in my hood world—nor, as far as I know, with my parents. Neither Communism nor anti-Communism was of concern to us. I joined the Arthur Miller demonstration for the same reason I protested when the high school nuns overturned the prom band vote. It was unfair, and it was an affront. In a way, that motivation was not unlike what had given Secretary Welch the spine to rise off the craven floor of the McCarthy hearings. But for me it was a reflex, not a burst of moral or political clarity. It has been a long struggle to turn, or try to turn, that streak of combativeness into healthy social rage—in particular, at the brutalizing exploitiveness that forges such anger in the first place.

*

Sandy Taylor, who was a local high school teacher, and another student and I started a literary magazine. We hand printed the *Wormwood Review*, without electricity, on an old flywheel letterpress in a barn. When we misprinted a poem by e. e. cummings—a slug of linotype had drifted in its tray—he wrote us scathing hell. Which was strangely gratifying, and left us feeling we had scored a coup. Other contributors, James Wright comes to mind, were plain generous and decent. For some reason—maybe because writers in residence were a rarity, there being fewer opportunities to make a career of poetry writing—there was less careerist egoism than now. The egoism was temperamental, amateur, not driven by substantial reading fees, salaries, and titles. A range of poets felt free to take interest in other poets' work. And the homosexual omnipresence—adaptable and tolerant, not yet a politicized identity—contributed to a cosmopolitan ambiance. That was the upside. The downside was that few women were admitted to this poetry world, and fewer blacks or other people of color. Working class or populist or politically-tinged whites were extraliterary novelties surviving in stray anthology pieces . . . something by Kenneth Fearing, say, or Muriel Rukeyser's quiet, stunning "Boy with His Hair Cut Short." Or a few of Karl Shapiro's "Wurlitzer Wit" poems—though not populist, at least quotidian, the poetry of soda fountains, flies, Dynaflow Buicks, and Sunday nuclear desolation—also might turn up. British poets were another matter. They could be 'political' and they could write about machinery or docks or workers, and still be poets. As long as they were British.

With 1997 hindsight it's obvious that as the literary world has opened up in some ways, it has shut down in others. Balkanization of identities has been no more liberating than in the actual Balkans, the former Yugoslavia. New gender and ethnic recognitions were supposed to expand cultural horizons—and might have, if informed by a universalizing vision. But with the commodification of identities, and the proprietary attitude taken toward them, the whole business has shrunk to a zero sum game of competing properties. The provisional gains of the civil rights movement of the '60s and early '70s, the openings for other-than-white and other-than-male, were broken down into identity movements and tossed back into the national spoils system. The rules of capital, which presume a war of all against all, have become the mentality of culture itself—with the further ignominy that this latter-day culture war is fought by toy soldiers. Nothing dies but the spirit. It's not too much exaggeration to say that earlier there had been the illusion of universality without the reality. Now the illusion has been trashed, and rightly so, but also trashed is the ideal the illusion spoke to.

In 1959 I graduated from college. The Soviets had challenged U.S. technological superiority by launching Sputnik, the first manned space vehicle. To restore U.S. preeminence the DAR lobbied for National Defense fellowships. I was offered one to Washington University, another to the University of Connecticut. For personal reasons I stayed in Connecticut, but my situation had changed in one significant way. Not only was I self-supporting, but my work life had become categorically professional. My values and reflexes were still working-class con-

ditioned, yet objectively I was moving 'up' into a stratum of the middle class. Without plans or goals, however. I just kept going where the openings were.

But then what? I was *in* a middle-class professional world, not *of* it. I didn't respect it enough, or feel its reality powerfully enough, to accept the fundamental articles of its faith. Later on this would come as a shock to some colleagues, a betrayal even, because I would use their language to speak a world that middle-class culture—whether 'high' or *avant* or countercultural, it makes no difference—knows only through stereotype and caricature. And yet working-class life—which, stripped of resistances, is nothing more than categorically exploited life with its demon ignorances and rages—is still the most powerfully instructive reality I know. Not that such life is intrinsically virtuous or healthy, it's not, but from within it you can feel the point of the pecking order. You're in a position to know *concretely* how the world is structured and how we are disposed by it. On the other hand, it is almost impossible for the relatively privileged to appreciate the depths and sublimities of their own privileging. *Uneasiness may creep in, however, and did—heralded by the Beats, who broke not from outside but from within the same elite universities that underwrite cultural privilege in the first place. Poets who earlier would have 'been' the world, mentally and in their writing, were now simply in it. Historically scaled vulnerability, and a sense of being besieged, came through then in Snodgrass's 1959* Heart's Needle, *in Lowell's* Life Studies, *in the earliest of Berryman's* Dream Songs, *and most vividly in Plath's* Ariel. *These were highly individualistic and self-mythifying recognitions, however. Their strictly limited social and historical dimensions were de-realized, becoming reflections of the poet's own subjectivity. In the end, despite their battered state, these poets continued to speak from a culturally privileged space.*

*

I don't know when my father started drinking. He and my mother were living in the same house but now totally estranged. With the fellowship money, and the possibility of renting half a cottage, I had less contact with them than before. We never wrote. Also we were of a generation, this I shared with them, that did not feel comfortable with phones. We had not grown up with them—nor with a refrigerator or washing machine or shower or oil furnace, much less a TV. We shovelled coal, hauled kerosene from the gas station, and got ice from an iceman who, like the ragman, came in a horse-drawn cart. Every Saturday I bathed (we'd have said *washed*) in a tub of too-hot water that turned gray and scummy even before I got to rinse my hair in it. This was not an inconvenience or a deprivation but simply the way folks lived there and then, at that stratum of life. My garret bedroom had North and South American wallpaper, a rudimentary map repeated over and over as though the western hemisphere were all the world—but there was no heat up there, and on winter mornings I woke with the room temperature below freezing. My breath hung on the air as I ran downstairs, clothes in hand, to get dressed somewhere warm. In that version of the world—where strenuous physical activity coexists with an almost gelatinous passivity toward the social and technical conditioners of life—the lack of communication felt natural. As though by some great gravitation, we seemed ever on the verge of slumping back into the landscape.

*

I'm sharing a forty-dollar-a-month cottage with Ira, a graduate student in psychology. He has composed a cantata to be performed at Hillel, the campus temple, and he has asked me to sing in it. But when we arrive for rehearsal an argument breaks out. The cantata has a Zionist text. Some others there don't want me singing it. I don't take this personally—sitting to the side, I sense that one woman is intent only on shielding me from involvement in the text—but Ira is adamant, and I sing the cantata. I don't know what Zionism is. A burning issue, clearly, yet this is the first I have heard of it. When we get down to it, it is difficult to square the passion of the discussion with the poetical blandness of the lyrics.

A condition of belated education—acquired like a "five-year plan" rather than grown up with—is that you're always something of an autodidact. I think of autodidacts as solitary souls who bore aching tunnels of light through the densest of darkness, so dense they can only chip away at it. There is no flooding illumina-

tion, no sudden access of panoramic vision. If the self-taught are not looking directly at something, they don't see it. Well, that was me. The advantage was that the darkness, or ignorance, helped ward off the ideological conditioning of sanctioned educational systems. By the time you got into that, you were not so easily polished off by it.

*

The head of the English department couldn't compete with elite private universities for the top academic students, so he looked for *interesting* ones. And it paid off. In grad school we educated ourselves, in class and out, talking literature, politics, political history, films, and European theater. The key was Grandin Conover, a playwright from DC via Swarthmore. Grandin was a great appreciator, a person of the world, with a more complex life than the rest of us. He wrote a play, which was stolen

Sister, Carol, with Mother and Grandmother Gertrude, about 1942

from the trunk of his car, so he left school to rewrite it. *As the Hawk Sees It*, set in late 1930s Berlin, was produced in Chicago in 1962. Later Grandin was literary editor at *The Nation*, and in 1967 another play, *The Party on Greenwich Avenue*, was produced by Barr and Albee at the Cherry Lane Theatre in New York. I don't like writing about Grandin. But he's crucial to this story, and I will have to say more about him later.

My first and only creative writing course was a tutorial with John Malcolm Brinnin—a wry, humorous man, too sophisticated to be prescriptive. He'd written a book on Gertrude Stein, though her work did not figure in the academic world of that time. He'd also published an account of Dylan Thomas, whose beleaguered tour agent he had been. John's own poetry, up to that point in 1959 or '60, was richly allusive—somewhat in the vein of English "apocalypse" poets, immersed in language *qua* language—but he drew me to clarity. I tended to be cryptic, overconcentrated. Writing myself into a world that felt more provisional than 'real,' I wielded English with the hyperconsciousness of a foreigner: literalizing idiom and weighing individual words as though they *were* their etymologies. It was much too much of a good thing. John coaxed me out of that. Even so the strain of balancing one consciousness over against another, the split between class consciousness and class reality, kept pushing me into an ironic posture. The irony was not literary, though irony was a New Critical fashion of the time, but a consequence of the bind I was in. Lacking the real-life means to resolve the impasse, I tried to beguile it with sheer writing. Literarily, the ploy worked. One day John sent five poems to Howard Moss at *The New Yorker*, who took them all. It was so casual, I had no notion how rare this was.

That entire period seemed both magical and commonplace. Anything might happen, anyone turn up, and I neither knew nor wondered why. It was like getting a series of small hits on the lottery. My wife, Arlene, and I were invited to dinner at James Merrill's, whom I knew of only as "an Amherst poet." Some time after that it was suggested I apply for a grant from the Merrill Foundation, which I did, getting the three thousand dollars that Arlene and I used to spend the better part of a year in Rome, going later to Yugoslavia. Still I had no map of the literary world. At Merrill's

I'd been in a long conversation with a Mrs. West. Not about literature, but one of her kids. As I was near her son's age, she thought I might help her understand him. A few days later someone who'd been there said that "Mrs. West" was Mary McCarthy. I knew the name, of course, but as I hadn't read her it didn't mean much. What did matter was that she'd been a straightforward, unaffected person. And in an incredibly overlaid way so was Merrill when we got to know him, though we never knew him well.

One spring morning in 1962 I received an honorable discharge from the U.S. Navy, which I'd forgotten I was in. After entering the teachers college I'd stopped attending Reserve meetings. The Third Naval District lost track of me. Now the eight years were up, and I was discharged according to schedule—with the same archaic, procedural illogic as Sleeping Beauty being bussed by the prince. *"The World was all before them,"* says Milton. *Whatever, he did get that right.*

Arlene and I had begun dating in May or June of 1960. We didn't really know one another, it's unlikely we knew ourselves, yet by September we were married. The wedding took place in a Congregational church, officiated by a Harvard-educated minister with theories about the virtue of clear-glass Protestant windows as over against the world-denying properties of Catholic stained glass—a man with whom I'd also had a long prenuptial discussion about William James's *The Varieties of Religious Experience*. Before the wedding, while the minister, the best man, and I waited in the sacristy, a fly circled and landed on the floor just inches from the minister's patent leather pump. He edged the gleaming shoe slowly toward the fly, which buzzed off. What was he going to do? Even if, miracle of miracles, he caught up with it? Protestant or no, he reminded me of the purpled monsignor in the seminary five years back. But then Arlene came down the aisle, crying. . . . This was thirty-seven years ago. I thought then that she and I could have been anybody marrying anybody, and it may be so. But we've gone through many different lives since then, remaking ourselves for better and for worse—*as Pasternak says, living a life is not like crossing a field*—and are more married than ever. But that is another story, not to be tossed in with this ideo-literary ransack.

*

In the fall of 1962 we boarded the *Baska*—a Liberty ship converted into a Yugoslav freighter—stopping over in Casablanca, tied up there by a dock strike, and later passing through Tangiers before we disembarked in Genoa. The fare was $110. At sea an argument broke out among the Yugolavs. It had been triggered by Tito's arrest of Milovan Djilas, who advocated political democratization. On one side were the captain and a doctor, a woman, who were against the jailing. Their opponents were the ship's steward and another doctor, also a woman. The argument advanced by the steward, interestingly, was not ideological. "For us there must be one way, and one way only, otherwise we will be killing one another." He was referring to the vicious civil war that had been fought inside the Second World War. Tony, the steward, invited us to his home, though by the time we got there the following spring he was at sea again, heading for New York. We stayed with his family, who were peasants living in Brela, a tiny Dalmatian hamlet on the Adriatic coast. These hospitable people were our first experience of a traditional patriarchal household. Excepting one of the younger women, who translated—we had some Italian, she had some English—dinner was eaten at table by the men and Arlene, included because she was a guest. The women served. After dinner the patriarch, Stipin, a very old and very nice man, a tall proud man with broken glasses sliding down his nose, permitted the women to come sit along the walls and listen while we talked. Doubtless every culture has a version of this protocol, which makes it all the more puzzling why anyone supposes it progressive to base a politic on ethnicity or culture.

But Yugoslavia came later. In 1962–63 we lived in Rome, reading the remote alarms of the Cuban missile crisis in the *Herald Trib.* I wrote little, being too taken with everything. Except for boot camp in Maryland I hadn't been further from Connecticut than Manhattan, and I'd never gone to a museum there. We had a one-room cold-water flat in an old Roman neighborhood equidistant from the Piazza Navona and the Campo dei Fiori, a twenty-minute walk across the Tiber from the Vatican. The entrance to our building was an ancient sagging door, ajar against the door hole, with a fifteen-watt bulb over the stairway. The people upstairs had loud, glass-smashing arguments which we did not know how to respond to. I don't think we ever saw what they looked like. That year was the coldest winter on record—the fountains froze—and some mornings we'd be the only ones in the Sistine Chapel, as even the guards had gone off to warm themselves. We walked all over Rome and took trains to Florence and Siena, spending time in the Pitti and the Bargello, finding Martini and Cimabue and other revelations, from Giotto in Padua to Signorelli in Orvieto. Sometimes Bob and Sally Bagg, who were also there from Connecticut, took us touring in their blue VW bug.

Arlene did secretarial work for an Australian yellow journalist who made up human interest stories, putting a fantastic spin on kernels of truth—such as the story of a "mountain town without men," all very lurid and tongue-in-cheek, neglecting the fact that the young men had gone to Australia as guest workers and that the real story was not some sexual mother lode but sex and humanity cut off, hung out to dry, by the migrant labor system. In the realms of capital there is no "village life," though I realized this only in retrospect. At the time, the "town without men" seemed merely exotic. And, finally, anticlimactic.

*

In the fall of 1963 Arlene and I went from Europe to New Jersey, where I had a job at Rutgers. I had never taught before and so was overwhelmed by the four introductory courses with their onslaught of required papers. We lived in a rickety flat over a butcher shop on Raritan Avenue, our little Fiat 500 did not start in the cold, etc. It was a rat race. President Kennedy was assassinated that November. A month later we had our first son, John, who was born the old-fashioned efficient way, with forceps and knock-out pills, which was hard on Arlene.

New Jersey jump-started our political education. Ron Grele, a graduate student in history, organized a self-styled Randolph Bourne Society. Arlene had known Ron from the University of Connecticut, where as a Korean War vet he'd organized a political party of independent students. (Till then, student government and activities fees had been controlled by fraternities and sororities.) Randolph Bourne, a New Jerseyan, was a short-lived World War I pacifist intellectual who opposed nativist chauvinism by arguing against the notion of America as a "melting pot," which he considered a subterfuge for getting new immigrants to submit to an Anglo-Saxon cultural norm. Instead he proposed a "Transnational America," a new culture that would be a cosmopolitan "weaving back and forth of many threads of all stripes and colors." This meant conceiving American culture not as something given from the past, but as a project to be realized into the future. American cultural tradition "will be what we all together make out of this incomparable opportunity of attacking the future with a new key."

Though more activist than scholastic, the Bourne Society did have cultural interests. One member, a university archivist, was assembling materials on Paul Robeson, who'd gone to Rutgers, been all-American everything, and had then been airbrushed out of the all-American picture because his internationalism and his Communism had made him too big for it. For all the talk about multiculturalism now, Robeson was one of the few who have ever demonstrated it. He was truly a citizen of the world.

Downtown New Brunswick, the corporate home of Johnson & Johnson, was a ghetto devastated by redevelopment. There was block after block of vacant lots, some of which had been razed ten years earlier. The Bourne group founded a Community Action Project which set up a storefront day-care center and began a modest campaign to have a public swimming pool built on one of the desolated lots. Meanwhile Arlene was also active with Women Strike For Peace. Pushing John in his baby carriage, she picketed the IRS . . . and was attacked most vehemently by other women, who understandably felt more challenged by this than the IRS did. Women Strike, though, was a tough-minded group. Some were old CPers (former and possibly ongoing members of the Communist Party). They didn't rise and sink on waves of sentiment but had fairly tempered analyses and did not fear street action. I recall them leafletting the first showing of *Doctor Strangelove,* redirecting its out-there mythification back down into our lived reality. One of the women, a blue-eyed blond who looked the very stereotype of a cheerleader, rented a small plane from which she dropped leaflets on Camp Kilmer, an army base.

Toward the end of the school year we heard about two women from Nagasaki who were "missioning" the United States with their wounds, their story, and an Airstream trailer carrying A-bomb memorabilia. Another guy and I volunteered to host them, but no one wanted anything to do with us. Finally a man at the YMCA permitted us to park in front and to use their sidewalk plug-in—provided we did it extralegally, with no agreement. So we did, and for three or four nights passers-by came pounding on the trailer, rocking it, and shouting anti-Japanese slogans. My cosponsor and I looked for corporate and private groups to host the women. No one wanted anything to do with them, except, and this is the incalculable part, the Boy Scouts of America—who had their national headquarters in New Brunswick, and who greeted the women with huge Japanese and U.S. flags atop their building—and a ladies canasta club, whose members were probably also old CPers. To get a hall for a public talk we petitioned the town's Protestant ministers at their

With wife, Arlene, April 1969

association brunch. We sat through it, without being offered so much as a cup of coffee, only to be told no one could rent to us. Next day, however, the Dutch Reformed Church called and rented us their hall. *It was only years later that I learned the Dutch Reformed Church had been the chief moral support for apartheid in South Africa.* The meeting was well attended. Also, affecting. The women from Nagasaki were unusually modest and dignified. The neck of the older and taller woman, the shy one, looked as though it had been melted and had run and then cooled. The tendons stood out like tree roots.

That academic year, my first as a teacher, President Kennedy had been assassinated. The other signal event, Martin Luther King's rally in Washington, had been preceded by intense speculation as to whether or not "they" would riot . . . before King rose above the fear and the crap with his "I have a dream" speech. Meanwhile I'd finished my thesis, gotten a doctorate, and accepted an offer to return to the University of Connecticut. When I told the department head at Rutgers that I was going back to Connecticut, he was concerned: "But what about your career?" I had no idea what he was talking about.

I would teach at the University of Connecticut, off and on, for twenty-eight years. As an institution it was like most: life stirred in the cracks, and there might be challenging or original work carried on in the corners of it, but the basic structure was meant to domesticate faculty and students. Excepting certain individuals, the university was not categorically different from the high school I'd passed through. There was an anxious, overarching tedium to it, as though its mission were to make sure nothing happened.

My father's drinking had gotten worse. For three years he was confined to Laurel Heights, the state's TB sanatorium. When I visited he would talk about the rules, the nurses, and how patients tried to outmaneuver them. He was taken with the workmanship of the sanatorium, a 1930s structure the WPA had built with fieldstone and a lavish use of copper flashing. He could not believe all the copper. He also described fights between the black and Puerto Rican patients. Because TB is largely a poverty disease, it affects minorities disproportionately. For that reason, and because this was a public institution, my father was one of the few whites

there. He passed the time crocheting wool caps. Released, he was no less caustic than before, only now there was an air of desperation. I did not like it.

What had been oracular in his heyday degenerated into DT hallucinations. His pronouncements could be horrifying, they were so unaffected in their ruthlessness. He was drying out in the hospital, tied hand and foot to the bed with strips of linen, when he noticed my mother in the doorway. He looked startled. "What is she doing with all that raw meat on her?" Genuinely puzzled. And once, he was sitting at the kitchen table describing how two attendants could not hold him down in some hospital bed and how "a big black nurse" came and threw herself across his body and stilled him so that he could not move—when he finished telling the story he said, quietly, "I should have married a nurse." This with my mother in the room. Even the expression of his humanity, then, was brutal. *He* wasn't brutal, but in those miserable circumstances human truth-telling had to come out that way, to that devastating effect. Everyone around had to be strong. It was no place for weak people.

When the visioning talk passed, he was broken and aged.

*

The years 1964–67 are jumbled. I was teaching, not knowing how to. A typical semester would include two sections of freshman composition, plus one modern poetry course and one Shakespeare. In December 1965 we had a second son, Aaron. We were renting a farmhouse, and about three months later two friends from New York delivered Grandin at our doorstep. They said he needed "fresh air." For days he roamed the house and the fields, raving. He came in bloodied from the barbed wire. I'd race off to school—teaching *Hamlet*, of all things—and race back, fearful of leaving him alone with Arlene and John and the baby. He didn't sleep. One night we smelled smoke. We got up to find Grandin pacing the kitchen, and I called the volunteer fire department. It turned out to be a furnace fire, an ignition had burned out. But that was it for us. A few days later I drove Grandin to Yale–New Haven Hospital and committed him. All during the drive he dangled a whisky bottle behind my head, his arm slung over the seat, and I really didn't know if he was going to smash me with it. I thought, if he knows what I'm doing, he will hit me. But he didn't. Before his "interview"—they knocked him out with a shot, as though he was being shanghaied—he kissed me on the forehead and walked in with the orderly. He *knew* I had betrayed him. After that I visited Grandin weekly, and for a long time he would not talk to me. Then it didn't matter. The basis of our understandings changed, or maybe just got overwhelmed. It was June. I was sitting in a supermarket parking lot, reading a newspaper, with son John in the front seat and Aaron sleeping in the rear. When I looked around, Aaron was still. Like stillness itself, not the smallest hint of breath. I looked and I could not find it. I could not admit I could not find it, him ceasing like that. It was so awful.

*

My father and Grandin, who never met, had this in common: when they spoke from where they were they spoke totally, gnomically, without euphemism or tailoring. It's been years since I've heard anyone talk that way—which is not verbal manipulation, but a conceiving that speaks to the jugular. Above all it was unconscionable honesty, as though a person could speak from where a person is, without self-interest and without regard for the self-interest of others. Which is rare and cannot be willed. Most speech is thrown off by the storm of junk feelings and junk voices, the impressive buying and selling of hysterias and half-truths, that takes the heart out of the world.

*

The Marches, my first book, was discreet enough to win an award. The discretion was not calculated but followed from literary inertia and formal preoccupations, something I have written about elsewhere. It's interesting, in retrospect, how many of the poems touch on social and sociopolitical realities, as well as intensely personal ones. At the time, that did not register. The meditative voice and the parabled speech did not force such recognition. Now, some are obvious ("Chicken Coun-

try," "An American Airman," "The Old Order"), but who could know that "Midsummer" was a Cold War (i.e., nuclear) poem written at the moment of the Berlin crisis? Or that "The Glassblower" was a near-literal detailing of the fauna of my father's drunken stupor? Or that "Facing Up" was a rendering of Grandin's turning up, for help, the time I committed him? The personal references in particular were *very* guarded.

Through David McKain I met Arthur Cohen, my editor for *The Marches,* and Arthur's wife, the designer Elaine Lustig Cohen. They and their collections brought me, visually, into the twentieth century. It's one thing to visit a museum, quite another to have hands-on access to works over a period of years. What got my attention was not New York contemporary, however, but Constructivist graphics, Dada, and the Bauhaus project. I would sit on the sofa next to Man Ray's flatiron, which was perched on an end table, running my fingers over the needle-sharp points as we sat with brandies late into the evening, talking. The iron had, for me, an iconic power condensing tremendous domestic misery and rage. But beyond that, and more relevant to my writing, Constructivism and Dada and the Bauhaus were all movements whose works had an exceptional clarity to their social aspect. Had I been an artist I would have known then what to do. But I wasn't and didn't. I had to work this out through what Platonists have called "the tangled and inept medium to which we are condemned." That is, not through 'pure' images but through discursive speech—historically implicated, hopelessly compromised language.

*

In those days social upheaval began before breakfast. It was as though there was no sleep. I cannot believe the energy we burned. Technically I was the faculty advisor to SDS (Students for a Democratic Society), but really it ran on its own. I was involved in a general range of ad hoc and reactive actions against the Vietnam War. The race struggle, never central on campus—there were so few students of color—took the form of antagonism between the Black Students Union, which had a radical anti-imperialist analysis, and the African American Students Association, which was culturally nationalist, politically conservative, and cool to the antiwar movement.

Some demonstrations ended in pro forma civil disobedience arrests: prospective arrestees would queue up as though for a movie, a ritual that made dissent sacrificial without actually disturbing anyone or anything. Other demonstrations broke bloody and chaotic. Classes were disrupted—a chemistry professor threw acid at protesting students—the faculty club was fire-bombed, and there were uniformed and undercover cops all over campus, including six from Army Intelligence alone. The state police had a secret command post in the basement of one of the buildings, which I discovered only because I was escorted there for an interview one afternoon.

We took over the ROTC building and repainted it, declaring it a day-care center, though the army was undoubtedly more concerned about the demonstrations against recruiters from Dow, Olin, and Honeywell. There was occasional guerrilla theater, but constant picketing. I made it a point to smile for the undercover cops who stood filming us at the picket turnaround. It was not enough simply to demonstrate. They had to understand you were not intimidated by their surveillance. Some colleagues would cite "the sanctity of the classroom," becoming indignant when an undercover cop enrolled in their class. But when was any classroom sacrosanct? What the cops were doing was not a matter of individual morality, nor a personal affront. It was one thing to oppose them, but it made no sense getting righteous about it. They were agents of a social system, a function of its logic. The classes themselves, with their framed and posed subjects, were a function of the same logic. The system was the problem, not its agents—who anyway didn't give a damn what was taught, wanting only to keep tabs on student and faculty bodies prior to moving on them. Besides, there were no secrets. We were all open books. Yet the distinction between the system and its agents, and the priorities implied by that distinction, got lost in the rush of actions and reactions. It was hard to stay focussed.

I was writing *Avenue of the Americas*, an omnivorous collection of poems. And our daughter, Deirdre, was born in January 1968.

Late '60s, early '70s. Arlene and other women organize a socialist-feminist discussion group. Later they include men, because if anything is to change then *everyone* has to change. Even men. But the group cannot get past the re-

sentment that fuels it. This emergent feminism carries a powerful strain of misanthropy, literal man-hating, driven by the anger of middle-class, university-associated women who have sacrificed their own careers and ambitions for their husbands and families. A stubbornly class-bound gendering takes over, leaving the socialist project behind. The priorities of women who are secretaries or janitors do not come up. Which is a fact, but not the whole truth. There is an exemplary selflessness to some of the women's motivation. When the university purges dissident faculty—which I escape, having early tenure—some of the same women picket the administration. A TV reporter asks Arlene if her husband knows she's out here. She asks him if his mother knows he's out here. It's exasperating, but that is the level of sexist presumption. It could not be admitted that women might engage in a principled action. Whatever women did had to be personalized, which is to say trivialized. Usually when protest is not criminalized it is trivialized. Here the trivializing was a gender smear.

*

In 1968 I took leave from the university to teach at the newly created Hartford Street Academy, a high school for dropouts in the north end of Hartford. Everyone was black except me and a math teacher. When a Puerto Rican showed up, he was warned not to come back. That's how it was. Just by being around day after day I became invisible enough to see, to appreciate, how bottomless the racist pit is. This was laid out casually, without threat, via regular deliveries of *Muhammed Speaks*—in the soft rounded features of the cartoon blacks and in the pointy chins and noses, and the black hair stubble on the cheeks, of the cartoon whites. This was also the era of afros, and of the slogan Black is Beautiful. Once, in front of me and everyone else, a dark-skinned Jamaican—a straight-up type with no tolerance for junkies, who'd brought a keyboard one holiday so he could play "I Heard It through the Grapevine" over and over, like a raga—dissed a light-skinned guy: *What you saying, black is beautiful? I'm black, man. Look at you, you're yellow.* Excruciating. And there was sexist racist ugliness I will not repeat. But none of that was the last word on race at the Street Academy.

The last word was the Black Panther Party. Our building was their unofficial headquarters. Effectively they ran the place—an old, two-storey, brick grammar school—keeping it clean and functioning, holding off the heroin junkies. I admired their selflessness, their organization, and their freedom from the cultural nationalism that was so widespread at the time (via the Muslims or Ron Karenga, later the founder of Kwanzaa, whose "U.S." had Nixon administration backing to promote Black Capitalism as a string of black-owned gas stations). One day we're sitting in the lounge, watching TV, as San Francisco State students battle Hayakawa and the San Francisco police. What has everyone engaged is not the melee, but that black and white students are shoulder to shoulder. *Now we'd call the protesters multiracial, but then everything was viewed through the lens of black and white.* Guys are using "brother" indiscriminately, including whites. They are so relieved—I am so relieved—to get the dead weight of *race* off our backs.

Preconceptions keep breaking down. Someone donates cameras, and the Street Academy students go off to take pictures. Cameras are a college fad. It's not uncommon for college students to photograph 'gritty urban scenes' of trash cans and dozing alkies and old, abandoned shoes and the like. We expect our students to do the same, but no. George comes back—he's a charming con, and a junkie—with what will turn out to be a gorgeous close-up of an ice-cream cone. That is one lesson. We have another lesson when George steals the cameras to supply his habit. . . . Years later he would die in the exhaust vent of a restaurant. He'd climbed in to rob the place, gotten stuck, and wasn't found in time. I tell this not to wrap George up—there is no wrapping him up— but because the line between his life and mine was as arbitrary as a shade of translucent yellow . . . and I knew it. Only a fool would have illusions about that.

We were studying *The Autobiography of Malcolm X*, the very model of a "growing up" book, when the Street Academy came to an abrupt end. Alex Rackley, an accused police informer, had been murdered by Black Panther Party members in New Haven. They'd dumped the body in Middlefield, midway between New Haven and Hartford. The FBI raided us and brought down not only the Hartford Black Panther Party but the Street Academy as well. Of course we'd been under surveillance anyway. An acquaintance in the state education commissioner's office saw photos of me—taken from inside the academy, well before the murder—that FBI agents had circulated while soliciting information about people connected with the academy.

Connecticut is a small state. I'm never far from where I grew up. My parents continue to live in the same house in the same neighborhood—which, however, is not the same. As used to be said of such neighborhoods, in the poetic quaintness of race language, "it got dark." The ghetto border I'd crossed with my grandfather, getting treatment from the gentle Dr. Fleming, is gone. Not that segregation has ended, but at least the black population can spread out. By simple inertia, just staying where they are, my parents become the last whites in their neighborhood. And then, when no one remembers it had once been white, they become the only ones. My father is a face-battered alkie, still casually racist: *Why don't they bring home books instead of basketballs?* Yet by living in a black neighborhood he himself has become *de facto* black. That's why, when the cops caught him out, they didn't just arrest him. They put the claw on his bicep—the claw looks like a single handcuff except it has a ratchet handle, for tightening—and squeezed till the arm went black. It was so bad the desk sergeant refused to book him. They took him back out and dumped him. The arm had been crippled. Anyone could see it was weaker and thinner than the other, without full movement, and so it stayed. He could just about pick up a coffee cup with that arm. I suppose he'd said something. When he got his back up he could be *really* insolent. But if they'd caught him in a whiter part of town they wouldn't have gone as far as they did go. So racism got my father, too, no matter what color he thought he was. Though he never talked about the arm. Maybe he was embarrassed. Then again, he could have taken it as the banging-up you get naturally, as you go along. In his world, unlike the one I'm writing in, you *expect* scarring and disabling.

*

I'm thirty-one years old, a teacher at the university, and I'm supposed to be writing poetry. But the reality I want poetry to speak to, "poetry" has no language for—not counter-cultural poetry, which rides on the broad back of cultural privilege, nor protest poetry. I'm more sympathetic toward protest but am put off by the moral overdrive. Besides, neither "countercultural" nor "protest" has enough specific gravity to do justice to the reality of the life I am describing . . . life which is virtually beneath cultural notice. It *is* beneath poetic notice.

As I recall, the first contemporary writing I came across that did have that power was not a poem but a story in *Off Our Backs*, a then-new radical feminist tabloid. The piece was "I Stand Here Ironing," by Tillie Olsen, whom I had not heard of. For me it was not only the first contemporary literature that did not cartoon working people, but the first to realize the powerful emotional nuance within the circumstance of a working person's life. And the life of a working woman at that, which was yet more unimaginable. Having grown up fending off my own mother's rages, I had not had the luxury of understanding where the fury was coming from.

*

Grandin was institutionalized again in the spring of 1967. *The Party on Greenwich Avenue* had been edited into incoherence, slammed in the *Times*, and shut down in less than a week. At some point he was arrested on morals charges.

Grandin Conover, April 1969

Then the following year, I think it was then, he was brought bloodied to Bellevue and subjected to shock treatment. Worse than the pain was the humiliation. He'd been writing amazing poems: visionary pronouncements from the heart of where he lived. Rather, from where *we* were living, as Americans. At that time "American" was still felt to be a viable category. Institutions wanted him to behave, but to him behaving meant "taking the crooked way." *"Animals behave,"* he said, *"people conduct themselves."* I took issue with some of what he said, bothered by the aestheticism. I could appreciate it as an occasion for grand gesture, but despised the politic. In those days I wrote lots of letters, but this time—I'd been reading Chinese and other letter poems—I wrote one in verse. Grandin responded in kind. We exchanged verse letters a few more times, until June 1969, when he was to join Arlene, the kids, and me at a farmhouse we'd rented on the Maine coast. When he didn't show up, I called. Who answered was not Grandin but the cop left to watch the body. Grandin was barely thirty-three when he killed himself. Now he will always be thirty-three. It seems strange and awkward to be growing old over his memory. The way, I imagine, a field of autumn stubble must feel. How did it come to this?

In 1970 our verse correspondence was published as *Communications*. Bob Bagg, who proposed the chapbook, wrote a brief introduction. Then the University of Massachusetts Press published *Ten Years*, the poetry manuscript Grandin had left with me.

Avenue of the Americas was accumulated from the rush of Grandin's apocalyptic end throes, the comings and goings of the Street Academy, the specific political crises and intellectual turmoil of the time. I had given many political speeches, much out of character, and it was the only time in my life I would do so. With rare exceptions, on that or any other stage, I have much preferred to be a spear carrier than a principal. But *Avenue* was also shadowed by my own physiological breakdown. After a year and a half of chronic pleurisy and periodic drainings, complicated by state-administered TB medication—twenty-eight pills a day, though I did not have TB—I went down with an enlarged heart, a collapsed lung, and a malfunctioning liver. It took a year to recover. In *Avenue* the poetry that came of this concatenation was literal. Not, as in the first book, parable-like. The voice was as true as I could get it—but still ironic, as I was furious to unload some of the cultural baggage I'd accumulated. *Some of, not all.*

We were so absorbed in those electrifying times, *and this too is the story of a generation that knew it could always get a job, coming of age before the creation of mass homelessness, before casual panhandlers had given way to more or less professional beggars,* hardly anyone I knew gave thought to literary or professional status. We didn't care about success because we knew we could always make a living. We were free to follow our noses, and many did. But when you follow your own nose instead of constantly checking to see where you're supposed to be, you end up in unforeseen places. Locally, based on earlier work and awards, I had some respectability. From that perspective *Avenue* seemed a betrayal, an anticultural fit, though it was only an attempt to speak unfictioned, in a more directly connected way. Political engagement or no, the middle-class-bound world of poetry had never seemed real to me. Poetry as language did—writing was intensely engaging—but not poetry as a cultural institution. Worse, the well-being of that class-bound poetry world could seem almost an affront. I'd wonder who are these rosy glowing people with their cleanliness and their teeth, and what are the teeth smiling about? The presumptions of privilege were not visible to the privileged—who *are* privileged to see a great deal, but *not* where they are, nor what life-support system sustains them. I could not credit the simulated reality of the world their class-specific privileging had constructed. This wasn't a moral or a political position. Not at that time. It was a failure of faith, simply: my failure at maintaining their faith. I could share in the material perks, but emotionally and spiritually it was like living in a stranger's arbitrary dreamworld. In time that sense of unreality extended to much 'political' poetry, whose professed politic clearly began and ended *with* the poetry. But then it had been written from the same class-bound platform as the other stuff was. Because the political and moral sentiment of that poetry had little basis in political practice, it came out as void and inconsequential as untheorized activism is. Dehistoricized sentiments, like unstrategized political activities, degenerate into a treadmill of postures: the illusion of motion.

*

My father had been found lying across the railroad tracks. A black man, a stranger, pulled him off the rails and brought him home. He knew where my father lived because my father and mother were unique. They were the only whites. I think about this, and about racism—including the casual, indifferent racism of these last and only whites, my parents—and I think that though racism is a vicious symptom, it is not the problem. What is is the mythical category of race. Race is a crime against humanity. *As a category it is a virtual nuthouse. My Scottish grandfather's 1934 U.S. naturalization papers list his nationality as British, his 'race' as Irish!*

Our free radicalism ended in Chile—an end that began with a letter from the Guggenheim Foundation. Donald Hall, a poet I'd never met, whose writing and politics had no discernible relationship to mine, had suggested that the foundation invite me to apply for a fellowship. Which I did. The whole thing seemed magical then. A "break." Now I'm more impressed by the magnanimity of the gesture.

It was 1973. Allende's Popular Unity government was experimenting with a bourgeois electoral "socialism with a human face." With the fellowship we decided to emigrate to Chile. We were en route, studying Spanish in Mexico, when the CIA-backed military bombed the presidential palace, killed Allende, and rounded up so many people they had to put them in the national soccer stadium. We went on to Chile anyway, figuring the military would assume I was a U.S. agent. Which they did. Access to the Pudahuel airport outside Santiago was restricted to soldiers and DINA—the intelligence police, mostly guys in business suits carrying automatic weapons—yet they didn't even check our bags. We were North Americans, our kids were blond, we were arriving on the heels of the *golpe*—who else could we be but who we had to be?

An Argentinean acquaintance has recommended a school for John and Deirdre. The moment we step inside, we feel the tension. The director is flushed. Her speech turns vatic, oblique. "This is the rain that kills the little birds." A Chilean proverb about the heavy rains of spring is her barely coded way of describing the effects of the *golpe*. She is torn between

The author's children, Deirdre and John, Machu Picchu, 1973

wanting to speak truth and wanting to get rid of us. For the same reasons we passed through the airport so easily, she is profoundly terrified of us. Our kids should go to the American school, they will be happier there. The American school is called *Nido de Aguilas*, Nest of Eagles. The interview is starting to sound like *Strangelove*. But we persist and the kids stay, becoming the only foreigners in the school . . . *Without Spanish it must have been hell on them— John was nine, Deirdre five—but they did it, even taking the bus on their own. We became friends with the director, and some years later Curbstone Press would publish her poems,* De Repente/All of a Sudden, *under the pseudonym Teresa de Jesús.*

We lived on the ninth floor of a downtown highrise. Isabel Letelier was under house arrest in the building nextdoor. Her husband, Orlando, had held a number of government positions— he'd also worked for the Inter-American Development Bank—but at the time of the *golpe* he was Allende's defense minister. He'd held that position for all of one week before being arrested and imprisoned on Isla Dawson in the Strait of Magellan. We kept Isabel company, and she would tell us stories—a few of which turn up in "Isa Mar," a poem I wrote to commemorate verses Neruda had scribbled to her on a napkin, and which the military had confiscated, along with all other papers in the apartment, the day they arrested Orlando. For awhile Isabel had contract work translating business proposals into English. Sometimes we helped her with English idiom. One proposal was for *Cocina Dos*, or Second Kitchen, a fast-food business that would go *to* Chilean workers so they wouldn't waste time by leaving the job to eat. Already the neoliberal economic scheme was busy commodifying the as-yet-uncommodified little 'rest areas' of life.

Isabel knew nothing of our other activities. We were working with the MIR (Movement of the Revolutionary Left), the most active resistance group. One afternoon we'd gotten into a shocking riff of political allusions with a middle-aged store clerk, who revealed more about her politics than she should have. Later, not trusting who we were, trying to cover her tracks, she came to visit with a young guy who was presumably her lover. She called herself Quena, after the Chilean flute, and he was Pancho. They were dressed as hippies. That way, if Arlene and I were associated with the U.S. government, we wouldn't take Quena's political indiscretion too seriously. Or so their reasoning went. *We'd had an amusing, vivid encounter with two Gypsy women in a government office. Arlene and the younger one ended up behind a giant door spitting in one another's palms, exchanging bracelets—Arlene somehow getting the better of it—while I read a government form for the older woman, who was illiterate, and who kept asking me about American hippies. She'd seen pictures and she was convinced that they were, as she put it, "como me." "Like me." No, I had to tell her, they dress like you, but they're not really like you. I felt chagrined, as though I was letting her down.*

Pancho and Quena dropped the hippie charade. After further visits and discussion they allowed as how they "knew some people, if we wanted to help out." I had a copy of *Avenue of the Americas*. Pancho took it to "some people I know," returning a few days later. Their review? "A little bit hippie, a little bit Left, a little bit Trotskyist." And then, smiling, "but very definitely Left." That was how it began. Our apartment became a safe house. MIRistas met in the bedroom, always in groups of three. Sometimes we'd be there, but mostly not. We also recruited people to MIR—"Guerrilla" was occasioned by one such failed attempt—did money laundering, mailing, and propaganda leafletting. Sometimes the leaflets were tiny stickers. Or we'd leave Post-it sized papers on kiosks and storefront ledges, to be scattered by the wind.

There was little to do during curfew except read and write. I finished a cotranslation of *Prometheus Bound* and reworked some of Jesús Lara's Spanish versions of Quechua peoples poetry. It was too dangerous to write our MIR activities, but I could write about what happened to others. One such was Fernando, a member of MAPU, who was held by the air force and made to witness both real and mock executions—though I did not write about him

till after he was exiled, and I took care to write *my* experience of his experience, not pretending, as in fiction, to have suffered his. *Undoubtedly I muddied the line at times, but it seemed especially important, especially there, to honor the distinction between life lived and life heard about. In a poem about Victor Jara I did not say he was singing "Venceremos" when they shot him, but that "his legend is" that he was. Beyond that, it was unthinkable to write of surmised lives.* And some things I did not write about but should have, if only to save the memory. For instance, Fernando was made to watch as one cadet in a firing squad refused to shoot. The cadet was himself put against the wall. But others I did not write about because they seemed less spectacular or compelling at the time. M was a very nice guy, easy to be with, not in the least 'foreign.' All he wanted was to translate Frost, smoke pot, and listen to Brazilian music. (For all the good his harmlessness did him, he too would be arrested.) More interesting, he was the spiritual image of any number of North Americans we'd known: apolitical, benignly cynical, liberal, cultured, harmless as a grass haze. I hadn't considered how such a profile might measure up under a military junta but saw now it didn't. The overwhelming instinct was for accommodation. We began to appreciate how easy it would be to run a coup by liberal North American academics—run it by them not just physically, which is one thing, but ideologically. M could not even *think* resistance.

By early summer, which is the Chilean winter, we were no longer untracked foreigners. When I walked out of the American Institute, where I taught English to secretaries and business people, I'd be followed. Downtown Santiago is designed so that the ground floors of office buildings are tunneled with glass-fronted galleries. Walking through the galleries is like moving through a maze of semitransparent mirrors. When you look into them, you can't help but see the ghosts of those who are passing or standing behind you. The tail was easy to spot. Even without a uniform standing over them, military shoes have an obsessive glow. Civilians do not wear such dandified things. One afternoon the tail and his shoes came up to Arlene and me in the Parque Forestal, making smalltalk. He'd seen us talking with another North American, a guy from Amnesty who'd come out of Isabel Letelier's building. The tail was trying to find out who that was. Someone from the

U.S. Consulate, we told him, which seemed to be the right answer. We danced around one another. He'd been in the air force (Chilean) and had trained in Dayton, etc. We talked about that, how we'd never been to Dayton, and about the kids on the swings across the way—maybe we even talked about the weather—all the while Arlene and I recalculating, feeling our world grow smaller and more fragile. We prepared to leave Chile.

There was a snag at the airport. Because we'd registered late for identity cards, our papers were incomplete. The plane was on the tarmac, revving, loaded, ready to go—except for us, being held back in the terminal. The DINA agent ordered the plane to wait while he called the Investigaciones office. After confirming we'd begun the paper process and had provided the required information, he let us and the plane go. Next we knew, having rushed out onto the runway and up the boarding stairs, we were cruising the snow wall of the Andes, toward Lima, so relieved we burst into tears. The Chilean political warp was so pervasive we had warped ourselves with it. Everyone had. It was grotesque. Now the sudden rush of freedom felt more harsh than sweet.

Later we heard about further arrests of friends: Pancho, Quena, another MIRista, and others who were not. No one was killed as far as we know. Three were exiled. One we never did find out about—just that he'd been arrested. Him we knew least of all, having spent only a day in his company. He and his girlfriend drove us to Pomaire, a little town known for its clay pigs. Clay pigs are *muy Chileno.* Soldiers stopped us once along the way—we were driving the wrong way down a one-way street, near a police station—but after giving him a summons, checking out the girl and looking us over, somewhat disdainfully they let us go. Except that they were soldiers and not police, it almost felt normal.

*S*antiago Poems was Sandy Taylor's concept. I thought of poems as engagements, adventures into problematic junctures, by-products of a life—not as elements in a narrative. Not thinking of my life as a narrative or a career, why should I think of poems in that way? At the time, Sandy had a cottage press that printed translations from Danish. He wanted the Santiago poems to inaugurate a press that would be wider-ranging than *Threepenny* or *Trekroner,* as his Danish

chapbook series was called. And that's how Curbstone Press started. *Santiago* came out early in 1975. It was not a distributed book—I recall being in San Francisco, trying to get City Lights to carry it on consignment, failing even that—but I loved the integrity of the work: literary, visual, moral. (I do mean moral, not political. It is not what I consider a political book.) And the 'idea' of it—I felt together with it, if that makes sense. It gave me a feel for what a living, acting gesture a book of poems can be. Nothing was decontextualized. All was part of the same reality, even the great clay head filling the cover—not a convenient image picked up from anywhere, but a photo of one head, from an entire wall of heads, both small and monumental, that Jeff Schlanger had sculpted and fired in response to poems and letters I was sending him out of Chile. Sent, of course, without return addresses. The wall, called *Estadio Chile,* still exists at Jeff's Studio Spirale in New Rochelle, New York.

One night we got a call from Venezuela. Orlando Letelier, whom the Venezuelan government had gotten out of prison, was thanking me for "Isa Mar," the poem I'd written for his wife, Isabel. Later the Leteliers moved to Washington, DC, where Orlando organized international opposition to the Pinochet regime. We joined him and Isabel once in New York, at a Chile benefit on the Lower East Side. Arlene, John, Deirdre, and I also visited them one weekend at their home in Maryland. This was in the spring of 1976. As we had never visited Washington, except for demonstrations, Orlando took us sightseeing in his oldish Chevy. We drove down Embassy Row, where he'd once served as the Chilean ambassador, and past Dupont Circle, which was more his world than ours. It is *still* more his than ours. Three months later, in September, driving down the same street in the same car, Orlando was blown up by a remote-detonated car bomb. An American co-worker, Ronni Moffitt, was murdered with him. A few years later Michael Townley, a Chile-based American, and two anti-Castro Cubans were tried and found guilty of the murders. Three DINA officials were indicted but never extradited. Of course this had nothing to do with poetry as we are supposed to understand it, yet it had everything to do with the specific gravity of poetry. This order of reality—which is not bizarre or mysterious, but fundamental to the way we live—is a kind of test case. No poetry has to deal with this reality, not even indirectly, but it must be able to *stand in* with it. What is the good of poetry that cannot hold up in the actual range of the world, or that only gets along in some fantastically convenient version of it?

I began looking toward work from South and Central America, Eastern Europe (mostly there), and on occasion the Middle East. Most contemporary U.S. poetry seemed remote, as though it couldn't touch reality but had to keep veering off like some poor exhausted thing in a circle of Dante's hell, never getting where it needs to be going. The exceptions were sporadic, isolate bands of wanderers increasingly difficult to trace. A little Baraka here, a one-&-out magazine there. For all the restiveness and impatience, none of it seemed able to turn the corner on itself. Nor muster the selflessness that might raise our level of understanding, including our understanding of 'integrity.' *As late as 1986 some friends and I started a magazine called CCC, for Communist Committed Culture. It lasted one issue.* Of course the culture apparat kept turning dissidents of whatever stripe into cultural nonentities. But that was not the only problem. Much dissident work was writ shorthand, having lost touch with the full range of reality. Or perhaps I was seeing it differently after the experience of Chile. And there were other, objective factors. When it came to *consequential* work, foreign poetry was actually more available than domestic was. University and small presses would publish and distribute entire books of it. Being foreign, it was not considered a cultural threat. But then poetry was not all the writing I looked to. Before Chile I'd read some Marx and Marxist literature, though without bearing down or following through. Now my readings of those works became systematic.

*

Eight or nine months after returning to the United States we moved to Willimantic, a mill town whose population reflected the history of the American Thread Company. There were only fourteen thousand people: a distinct mix of Yankees, Poles, Russians, and Hungarians from early in the century, French Canadians brought in as strikebreakers in the mid-1920s, Nazi-sympathizing Ukrainians and Latvians from after World War II,

and, more recently, the Puerto Ricans who made up nearly a quarter of the population. The mills went back to the Civil War, but after World War II this labor-intensive industry began losing out to Asian textiles. One of the last things made before the final shutdown was thread for auto seat belts. Now the town was in chronic economic depression. Our mortgage was so low— $89 a month—I could afford to take leave from the university every other semester, which I did for seven years. Arlene worked at the town's Learning Center, first as a secretary, then as director of Adult Basic and Community Education. It was such a small, untransient town that if we didn't know a person, the odds were we recognized him or her, and they recognized us.

We were doing everything at once. Along with writing, teaching for part of the year, and volunteering weekly at Curbstone Press, I and Arlene (always Arlene) engaged in organized political activity, which ranged from the theoretical to street level—study groups, campaigns,

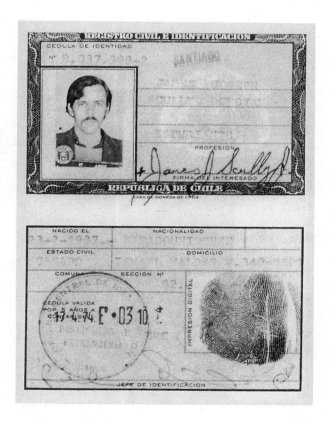

Chilean ID card, 1974

demonstrations, hostings, scuffles, and eventually an arrest.

My association with Curbstone, which was within walking distance of our house, began in 1975 and ended ten years later. I edited books of poetry, collated pages, bound books (we used an old hunk of railroad track to hold the glued pages down), typeset books, and designed pages as well as occasional covers. Sandy Taylor and I did the printing on an old offset machine in the basement. When Judy Doyle joined the press she took on the printing and the design work, being more skillful at it than we were. Toward the late '70s I started "Art on the Line," a series of six-by-four-inch booklets with a cover featuring a 1920s male cheerleader logo (which I'd found in an odds-and-ends shop in New York, in a pile of old lead slugs). The mission statement on the rear cover read: "A series of essays, interviews, manifestoes &c. by 20th century artists: socially conscious &/or politically engaged artists speaking to, or from, the point where their commitment and their art interact." My intent was to challenge the aestheticism and reflex anti-Communism that had become the ideological accreditation agency of U.S. poetry. (One working hand in glove with the other: anti-Communism the hand, aestheticism the glove.) The first booklet was Roque Dalton's *Poetry and Militancy in Latin America*. The next two were by César Vallejo (including an attack on Mayakovsky *from the left*), the fourth reprinted Mayakovsky's "How to Make Verses," and the fifth, the last I did, was an original collection of pieces by George Grosz, John Heartfield, and Wieland Herzfelde. This was called, after one of the contemptuous pieces in it, "Art Is in Danger!" I planned other booklets, by Erich Fried, Paul Robeson, Tadeusz Rózewicz, and David Siqueiros among others, but had neither the resources nor the support to do them.

Each cover flap in the "Art on the Line" series had the same slogan: "To the song of resistance / only revolution does justice." Which meant—reapplying Marx's XIth thesis on Feuerbach—it's not enough to complain of or to deny an oppressive reality. It is necessary to *negate* that reality. That is, to change it.

Chile exposed the fatuousness of independent radicalism, which like counterculturalism depends on social, economic, and political privileging. On returning to the United States I joined the Committee Against Racism—and, later,

the Marxist-Leninist Progressive Labor Party (PL). I would remain in PL for nearly five years. Some of the people we organized and befriended show up in poems ("Angel in Flames," "Esperanza," "Frankie Reyes' Poem," "Down Home Prison Poem"). I learned something from every one of them. But the party machinery, unlike those people and their world, had a flattening determination to it. I still had a writing life, a university job, a Curbstone commitment, and traces of an earlier, more conventional literary life that was all but running out: for example, serving as juror for the 1976 National Book Awards or on the editorial board of Wesleyan University Press. Literary service activity acquainted me with literary fashion, but mostly I looked forward to it because it put me together with people who could understand and discuss *writing* issues. The political understandings of fellow editors and jurors were different from mine, but invariably they acted in good faith, which meant I could argue for work that ordinarily would not have gotten consideration. I did manage to get National Book Award nominations for P. J. Laska and for Carolyn M. Rodgers's *How I Got Ovah*, which was as well written as much prizewinning work and more intense than most—but which had the wrong issues expressed in the wrong terms, having been written from the wrong-class, wrong-color neighborhood in Chicago. But literary justice was not a primary concern for me. By then I was preoccupied with political struggle and with the tensions running through PL itself.

At the university we dealt with racist incidents involving faculty and students. But in Willimantic, where the majority of politically active people were working-class and welfare Puerto Ricans—young people, thirty- to forty-year-old adults, and a few truly unfazed grandmothers, *one of whom would slap and scold her religious statuettes when she didn't win the lottery*—we conducted protracted campaigns and demonstrations around the police station, protesting police abuse, and around city hall, protesting the vicious and humiliating impositions of the town welfare officer. Not only would she go through people's purses and pockets, but she forced mothers and children to wait up to six hours in an unheated hall, threatening them with loss of their place in line if they left even for a moment. We also took part in out-of-town actions: "Workers United" records a demonstration at the Brooklyn Navy Yard. And once a week I'd drive to

Spanish Harlem for international committee meetings. But usually we organized and spoke up where we lived and where we were known. Unlike activists in major cities, we could not demonstrate and walk away afterward. We lived with what we did—even if it meant, as it did mean, getting a few small-calibre holes in our windows or being denounced by name on the local radio station. I think about this, sometimes, listening to the righteous speeches of agitators who will later vanish under the cover of crowds. If you can walk away from your saying, in poetry no less than in politics, what can the saying be worth?

The KKK began a national campaign in northeastern Connecticut. They were brought in by a local landowner whose family had been Klan since the 1920s, when nightriders attacked Catholic French Canadians. We went right at them—a tactically correct move, but a strategic error, as it distracted us from the larger systemic struggle. The skirmishes went on for years. Two samples:

Scotland, Connecticut. A national Klan rally in rural Connecticut, the first of many such rallies in a years-long campaign. This one is met by a massive counterdemonstration of townspeople and others brought in by PL—men and women of all ages, the majority Puerto Rican and Dominican, all marching two miles up a lonely country road which the state police have cleared of vehicular traffic. What's striking about our march—to me, accustomed to the antiwar and civil rights demonstrations of the '60s and early '70s—is the near absence of students. Also, not that those earlier demonstrations didn't on occasion turn violent, they did, but this one feels dicier, less ritualized. We notice the police have disappeared. They allow Klan members and their allied bikers to come up the same road, among us, figuring that *they* will take care of business. Instead, the bikers who try to push through are themselves stoned, clubbed, driven running through the fields. Chains, sticks, and golf clubs have materialized among the marchers. Though cars are not permitted, one comes racing at us from the opposite direction—a pistol is being fired out the window, but into the air. The car flies by. Another comes, but is stared down by a marcher who steps in front of it with a boulder in his two hands. We watch the car back all the way down the road and out of sight. We go on. In front of a farmhouse, not thirty yards off, some-

one rises from a lawn chair and fires a shotgun directly at us. We hit the ground but nothing happens. He has fired a blank. Now a phalanx of state police comes at us from over a hump in the road. Chaos. Meanwhile the newspapers feature liberal academics and ministers who denounce us for attacking the Klan. Other townspeople are simply intimidated. One man's business is torched. And before town meetings that have been called to deal with the situation, Klan members loiter by the roadside displaying shotguns. This is how the years of renewed Klan activity began. Incidents were not rare but almost weekly.

Meriden, Connecticut. Maybe three years later. The Klan rally on the steps of the city hall, which is on a grass-aproned knoll. The Meriden cops form a protective cordon, riot batons held out at waist level, as they march in a line down toward the surrounding anti-Klan demonstrators. As they near us I put my hand out, palm down, thinking to grab the baton if the cop in front of me tries to raise it. All I want to do is stop him from hitting me with it. To my surprise, he stops. The whole line of them pulls up. They look sideways at one another—and stay that way, in a stand-off with the demonstrators. Then I realize what has happened. I'm wearing my old navy pea jacket and a watch cap, which makes me a little 'straighter looking' than the other demonstrators. The Meriden cop has probably assumed I'm an undercover state cop and that my extended hand is a signal that the city police should stop advancing. . . . After we'd left, believing the Klan had left too, the situation deteriorated. Having hidden the Klan inside the city hall, the police tried to escort them to their cars. Together they were stoned by residents of a nearby housing project.

A lawyer, an acquaintance, says the state police think I was involved in the stonings. Strange things happen. Odd phone stuff, unlikely volunteers, one an out-of-work trucker trying to clear himself of incest charges, another a personable young black guy come up from somewhere downstate. *Sometimes I think we all come from central casting.* Once, when Arlene and I are away for a few days, Deirdre comes home from school to find an undercover cop coming out of our house. He has an orange in his hand, but other than that he has taken nothing, not even a ten dollar bill that is sitting on a table. *I have wondered about that. Was taking the orange like 'counting coup?' Was it a state-*

ment? Some of these guys have odd humors, like Mafia hit men. I suppose the sensible, nonconspiratorial view would be that he simply felt like eating an orange.

Littérateurs deride party slogans: the supposed simplemindedness, the vehemence, the metaphorical violence. But as I have written elsewhere, slogans are just a language that conflates knowing with doing. They are *our* classical rhetoric, and are already everywhere. Civic space is unthinkable without them. *To recapitulate.* "Within the party my problem was not with slogans, nor with the violence of party language. Why take offense at violent language when the language of non-violence, of peacemaker missiles and democratic imperialisms, of the purity of arms and of pacification programs—*pacification programs*—is a rancid anthem of exploitations, oppressions, state terrors and other atrocities? Rather, the problem was that this particular party's slogans pressed on like stripped gears. Actual practice could not keep up. Having projected themselves into a ritualized, symbolic language—a language posted like commandments at the end of time, where none of us lives at the moment—these particular Marxist-Leninists did not mean what they said. They were more considered in their practice than in their speech, which was grindingly heroic." Verbal inflation, intended to project strength, did just the opposite. I left the party in December 1979.

With Arlene in Willimantic, Connecticut, 1975

*

In 1977 *Scrap Book* was published by Ziesing Brothers, the lone Willimantic bookstore. The brothers had begun as comic book retailers, later branching out into science fiction and anarchist/libertarian tracts. In a small town no activist can afford a righteous politic—principled yes, righteous no—so there was give and take all around, and everyone was the better for it. Of course Ziesing's was not just the publisher of the book, but the only store ever to carry it.

Three years later Roger Mitchell, editor of the *Minnesota Review*, offered to publish *May Day*. He gave me a free editorial hand, and I designed the cover, the pages, and did the typesetting. As with Curbstone and the Chile poems, Mitchell wanted *May Day* as an inaugural *Minnesota Review* book, using it to launch a book-publishing press from the magazine. I don't know what came of the project. *May Day* itself was sent to *Minnesota Review* subscribers but did not get general book distribution. So the poetry written and printed during that period was not generally available. "Cold Rags," from the *Minnesota Review* book, marks the end of my association with PL.

Where did everyone go?

Enemies depress the air.
Friends have gone home.
What's left
is comrades.

If only *these* were not so
remote, righteous, intimate
as gossip in snow.

If they would stop
lying to themselves.
Or if the lies
warmed, were not
wrinkled
and stiff
flapping at the skin.

In such comrades
a comrade could freeze to death,
to death
pushing this brilliant future,
this communism, this human
truth
like a needle that has lost its thread.

Yet party organizing had gotten me to 'write people' in a historically concrete way. Twenty years earlier I'd written my father into his own social muteness, not challenging it. In "The Glassblower" he was stranded inside the dehistoricized silence of a snow globe. Now, in "Enough!" I could not only write him *and* my mother, I could connect them with their place in the world, touching on what they may and may not envision from there. The aesthetic mystification was dispelled. Which from here seems a modest achievement, though it did not come easily.

*

My sister, Carol, was killed in the spring of 1980. She and a coworker, whose car had stalled in the rain, were victims of a hit-and-run driver as they walked along the highway. Carol was thirty-nine, had a lovely daughter from a bad marriage to a heavy drinker, and worked as a barmaid. She'd lived for years as a lesbian. Heavy smoking had given her emphysema, though her job couldn't have helped. After the funeral, at our mother's house, one of her friends looked at me and said: "Carol never mentioned she had a brother." I didn't know what to say. The woman was suspicious, perhaps assuming Carol's lesbianism had estranged us. In fact Carol and I had had little communication in twenty years, including during her marriage. We hadn't been family at home, and there was nothing to build on. But what compounded the estrangement was not sex or gender but class. Even as I'd struggled to articulate and fight for working-class interests, interests as much spiritual as material, my education and job and ability to write had taken me out of that class. Not that this was news. I just hadn't felt the recognition so viscerally before. I'd gotten away from where we'd started in life, while Carol had stayed. Rather, she'd drifted from our parents' world into something Marx might call *lumpen.* Of course our father was headed in the same direction, with very nearly the same battered aspect. But he went in solitude. Carol did not. She had a community. Despite remarkable nastinesses in the world she lived in, some of which came out after the wake, in a larger, supra-individual sense that world had to have been nonjudgmental enough, unexpecting even, to make her feel at home in it.

A couple of months later, about to visit a friend in Puerto Rico, I stopped to see my father. For some years he'd been living in my old bedroom, and now he was lying ill in it—*in the same hammock-like mattress I'd tried to sleep in thirty-five years before, and it was old even then!* The minute I stepped inside the door, he said: "Don't get too close. I wouldn't want you to get what I got." A week later I caught an emergency flight back from the island. He had died of lung cancer, though no one knew he had it till the autopsy. *I wouldn't want you to get what I got.* But it was too late. I had already gotten what he had. It was the very condition of my existence.

People from the Communist Workers Party had been shot to death by the Klan in Greensboro, North Carolina. The same could happen in Connecticut, where the Klan was catalyzing a mix of Eastern European emigres, Birchers, and leftover Minute Men who years before had shot it out with police at the pacifist farm in Voluntown. Amazingly, they were still around. With the next Klan rally, then, a friend and I determined that if anyone was going to shoot at anti-Klan marchers they were not going to do it with impunity, as in Greensboro. So there we were, driving around, when three guys in an old Ford pulled in front of us. The driver looked in his rearview mirror and gave us the finger. My friend grabbed a camera, snapped . . . and lights started flashing. We were pulled over. The driver grabbed me—it was a hot day, eighty degrees or so, and he had leather gloves with lead or something stuffed over the knuckles—and he said to me: "Scully, you've been doing this for years." I'd never seen the man before. He was with the Criminal Intelligence Division (CID) of the state police, which is also the Red Squad. We had a shotgun and a rifle in the car and were arrested on weapons charges. After uniformed state police booked us in a commandeered school gym—and before we were taken to the venerable Brooklyn jail, which is so old that the abolitionist William Lloyd Garrison did time there—we were transferred temporarily to the local police. The cop who cuffed me was a guy I played pick-up basketball with at the local Y. Neither acknowledged this, and a week later we were playing as usual. Actually, that game went on for years, every weekday at noon. It was the most racially and economically inte-grated event in town. Not even the town meetings could compare.

The case hit all the state's newspapers. Connecticut's attorney general was desperate to get us, and especially me, as I had a file going back fifteen years or so. Fortunately a bail bondsman put us on to a tough-minded lawyer, a former prosecutor, who took the case for next to nothing. Some years back he'd defended a man who had been charged with trying to blow up Spiro Agnew at the Coast Guard Academy! (Is anyone *really* capable of imagining reality?) In the end, after three years of passing through various courts and judges, the charges were dismissed "with prejudice." *Historical reality check. . . . After the Clinton administration's "anti-terrorism" measures eliminating traditional protections against unwarranted search and seizure, if the same thing happened today I would go to prison. This is not to say whether I should or should not have gone, but to note how significantly the legal rules of engagement have been changed.*

While I was growing up, home violence kept me on the street. Yet having such a background, I never looked for violence. Even in gang days I did not go beyond the necessary minimum. Like others I had a switchblade—but did not pull it, because then it would have to be used. Later, an attraction of college had been the promise of a way away from street violence. Or, what was more nerve-racking, the unrelieved *threat* of violence. But in Chile, with the viciousness of the repression and my inability to imagine a political response, old junkyard reflexes surged back. I was writing *Raging Beauty* when suddenly . . . there was frustration, reaching for its rusty knife. It was disconcerting that I hadn't shaken the pall of violence. And now, beyond gangs, well after Chile, I was not only arrested on weapons charges, but if someone *had* started shooting at the marchers, I would without question have shot back. Because not to defend those people—who were not supposed to stand for themselves, but who did—would have been shameful.

*

Nineteen eighty-four or eighty-five, visiting my mother. Upstairs in my old bedroom, where my father once lay dying—*I wouldn't want you to get what I got*—a little machine spews out a ribbon of paper. All over the place. What's going on? The son of the man who fired my father— a police groupie who used to ride around with a scanner in his car, chasing the calls—has put some of his FBI agent friends onto my mother. She's the one white person for blocks around, and they want a secure, local station for their machine, which must be recording something. My mother, not knowing better, has allowed the agents to use the room. Every four to six weeks they collect the spewed-out ribbon of paper. She's bemused, sort of. I say nothing, having failed once again to imagine reality.

*

The poems of *Apollo Helmet*, so-called after the ingenious U.S./Iranian torture instrument with the inspired name, were written in the early 1980s. By then it was obvious there was no cultural place for what I was writing, not the way I was writing it. Because the particular way of writing was a particular way of living, and neither was on the U.S. poetry map. "Political poetry," marginalized even as a concept, had come to mean poetry-as-politic: the politics *were* the poetry, having little existence outside it. There were still some old-style social lyrics capable of lighting themselves up, but what made them good-feeling also left them inert. I admired the idea of a Thomas McGrath, yet if the actual work did not seem *necessary* how could it mentor a future? And workerist poetry kept pointing to and ending in itself, like a thematic version of local color. Without a transformative politic, it lacked transformative power. Ditto the identity poetries, which mimic the old cultural nationalisms but without their exuberant hubris. Finally, nearly all the so-called political poetries were about the right kind of sentiment. What is the politic of striving to achieve *the right kind of sentiment*? And what do you have when you have it? Not that I was immune. The best of it I could get a general feeling from—like from a not-bad movie—but politically, as a working writer, I could not communicate with it. Besides, talking back and forth was not a concern of that poetry, which was basically chanted out, one-way, like ripples from an already sunken stone.

My interest was in strategic working papers: drafts toward a future. Which may be why, to put the distinction in terms of two canonical

figures, Neruda seems a wonderful but done-with poet, whereas Vallejo is still being written and is still writing us . . . beyond ourselves. I certainly didn't aspire to that—but to the extent I knew what I was doing, I tried to write into the impasse of social contradictions and to do so in a transparent, idiomatic language. There was a reason for this. The interplay of reality with ideology is so complex, in writing *through* it it is crucial to keep the language lucid, not giving in to opportunistic complication or specious concreteness. (Concreteness is not in things-in-themselves but in the social relations that produce them. Only in the elaboration of those relations do things assume *vital* density and dimension.) Finally I came to feel this couldn't be done through poetry, or it could but not by me, and not under present cultural conditions. Anything written as poetry would be read, if read at all, as "poetry." The irony is that the class-bound cultural institution has so discredited poetry as a full-blown mode of human speech—of people speaking with all they have, from the reality of the world we live in— that poetry can no longer be read with the seriousness that prose is sometimes read. In part, that is how I came to write essays. I still wrote poetry, working on a manuscript called *Words without Music*, but with the recognition that *socially* the poetry had become what the IRS always knew it to be: a hobby.

For twenty-nine years I taught for a living. Throughout I was assigned to teach creative writing and canonical English poetry (from Chaucer on). It is only one of many ironies that I taught the full range of canonical texts more frequently, and over a greater number of years, than anyone else in the department. Early on I also taught composition and Shakespeare. My preference was a "variable topics" course, an elective for faculty, which I did as often as the department allowed. Some of those courses, evolving from the '60s into the '90s, were a team-taught Versions of Paradise (Milton, The Living Theater, Marquis de Sade, a book on bonsai trees, Wallace Stevens, etc.), Marxist Approaches to Non-Marxist Literature, Comparative Translation (multiple historical versions of selected poems by Sappho, Catullus, Horace, Dante, Villon, etc.), Modern Poetry in Translation (Hikmet, Brecht, Cavafy, Rózewicz, Attila József, Vallejo, and others), The Social Production of Literature, Critical Theory (taught from

With Arlene in San Francisco,
New Year's Eve 1996

a materialist position), and other one-time courses I no longer remember. In the Third World Literature course, whose title I did a critical history and analysis of, I began with *The Tempest* and went on to texts from current hot spots, mostly from Central America (Menchú, Payeras, Cardenal, Dalton, and others), Southern Africa (Head, Mphahlele, La Guma, Themba), and occasionally the Middle East (Kanafani, Sahar Khalifeh, Adonis, Darwish, Mahfouz). The "hot spots" were supposed to ground the literature, bringing it to life by connecting it with current geopolitical and human interest concerns, but in fact the majority of students did not read the international news. Occasionally I'd try to engage their personal concerns directly, say through the generational conflict that is one aspect of Ngugi's *I Will Marry When I Want*, or I would wrench course categories by teaching, say, Agnes Smedley's *Daughter of Earth* as a Third World text, a tactic that did get results. The essays in *Line Break* emerged from some of these courses, notably Third World Literature, The Social Production of Literature, and Critical Theory. Only in later years did I find a way really to teach. A student would question a comment, on Auden, or on an issue, or something as simple as a verbal distinction, and I would organize the following class around the student's question, and so on. At times a single class would accordion out into three or four succeeding ones. The procedure was not efficient, but it had more sheer *educational* value

than any other I'd followed or been exposed to in the past.

Much of *Line Break* emerged from this process. Though the essays are occasional, the overall project was not. I was trying to provide tools for substantive, genuinely critical literary analysis. Without that, as I came to realize over the years, our writing would have no way to develop. As writers we'd be predetermined, which is to say dehistoricized: signed and sealed inside lines and lines of unselfcritical reflex, blind sentiment, and yet blinder impressions. *Line Break* was an accumulated, organic response to this situation. The form of the project was dictated by circumstance. I couldn't take time out to structure a book. Not only was my teaching load heavy, but as a matter of policy I would not do two sections of the same course. If I was teaching three courses they would be three different ones, and no one course was ever the same from semester to semester. If I couldn't learn while I was teaching, I couldn't teach. Given those self-imposed handicaps, I built the *Line Break* analyses from examples that came up in classes, whatever they might be, and from extra-academic happenstance. In one case the occasion was an abortive panel. In another, a commission. In yet another it was a planned Tendency Poetry anthology the prospective publisher lost interest in. But whatever the particular occasions, the book was meant as a (necessarily sketchy) analytical primer, the beginnings of a critical toolbox that could be augmented and applied by others who had the time or the interest for that. I included back-fill footnotes, assuming most readers would have no knowledge of the primary literatures and concepts that the analyses were based on. Nothing came of this, of course, but then why should it? Such projects cannot be realized by individuals. Critical development has to be grounded in social movement. That is the first step, not two or three 'bright ideas.'

*

In 1992 Arlene and I moved to the Mission District of San Francisco, where we live the life we've always lived—though, owing to circumstance, in a more diffused form. Among other activities I began teaching myself to write plays. In 1994 Azul Editions published *Raging Beauty*, a selection of poems that includes work from the unpublished *Words without Music.* Because the editor, an old friend and "Art on the Line" associate Richard Schaaf, felt that few readers would recognize the historical and social contexts, I wrote an afterword called "Culture War." Which is what this is about, anyway, and why a poem or a book *would be* "raging" beauty rather than be sent raving *by* it. Beauty, like poetry or religion or anything human, is historical and socially specific. It's nothing more nor less than what we make of it. But who does the making? And what is the making for?

BIBLIOGRAPHY

Poetry:

The Marches, Holt, 1967.

(With Grandin Conover) *Communications,* Massachusetts Review Press, 1970.

Avenue of the Americas, University of Massachusetts Press, 1971.

Santiago Poems, Curbstone, 1975.

Scrap Book, Ziesing Brothers, 1977.

May Day, Minnesota Review Press, 1980.

Apollo Helmet, Curbstone, 1983.

Raging Beauty: Selected Poems, Azul Editions, 1994.

Translator:

(With C. J. Herington) Aeschylus, *Prometheus Bound,* Oxford University Press, 1975.

(With Maria A. Proser) *Quechua Peoples Poetry,* Curbstone, 1976.

(With Maria A. Proser and Arlene Scully) Teresa de Jesús, *De Repente/All of a Sudden,* Curbstone, 1979.

(With Arlene Scully) Roque Dalton, *Poetry and Militancy in Latin America,* Curbstone, 1981.

Editor:

Modern Poetics, McGraw, 1965; revised edition, *Modern Poets on Modern Poetry,* Collins, 1966.

Essays:

Line Break: Poetry as Social Practice, Bay Press, 1988.

Contributor to periodicals including *Critical Quarterly, Harvard Magazine, Left Curve, Massachusetts Review, Minnesota Review, New Yorker,* and *Poetry.* Editor of "Art on the Line" series for Curbstone Press.

Lewis Shiner

1950-

WHAT AM I DOING HERE?

According to my mother, I stood completely upright the entire time she was pregnant, arms crossed, kicking her now and then in the stomach. On December 30, 1950, I grudgingly emerged feet first and two weeks late into a frozen morning in Eugene, Oregon. From the start my parents and I were destined to disappoint each other.

*

My mother suffered from asthma and left me increasingly with a neighbor to raise—culminating, when I was less than a year old, in a stretch where I lived at the neighbor's full-time while my mother was in a hospital in another town. I have to take her word for all this, which is of course one of the major ironies of autobiography: the most profound and inescapable influences of your life hit you when you're too young to remember them.

My first actual memories are from Tucson, Arizona, where my father had gone, in his thirties, to get his Ph.D. in anthropology. By this time we'd already lived in five or six different houses, not even counting my stint with the neighbors back in Oregon. I remember a house behind a drive-in theater where I would get up in the night and stand at the window to watch *Disney's Living Desert*. I remember another house with a low, white picket fence and a porch where I would sit with a boy doll I called Boy Baby and eat homemade grape popsicles.

Much later a therapist told me I was using Boy Baby to try to demonstrate proper parenting to my own mother and father. It didn't work—my father was disgusted to see his male child play with dolls. When we moved away from Tucson I threw Boy Baby out the window of the car and began to cry hysterically. My father went back for the doll once, but warned

Shiner as the full-time fiction writer at home with his cat Liz, late eighties, Austin, Texas

me he wouldn't do it again, and when I tested him he was as good as his word.

I was apparently tired of moving and was fighting with the only weapon I had. My father could simply have taken that weapon away from me and put it in the trunk, but it seemed

237

important to him that I take complete responsibility for my actions, even at age three. My mother went along, just as she did for the rest of his life, whether he was right, wrong, or even clearly insane. All of which leaves me with the thought of that doll lying in a ditch on the side of the highway, with gum wrappers and paper bags full of half-eaten hamburgers, as the cars roar by.

*

One side effect of my enforced early adulthood was that my parents had already taught me to read. This spared them having to read aloud the tiresomely juvenile books I liked at the time—*The Pokey Little Puppy* and *The House at Pooh Corner* come to mind. When I finally started kindergarten, though, I was deeply bored, and it gave me a distaste for school that I never lost.

We'd left Tucson because my father had joined the National Park Service as an archeologist. After stints in Seaford, Virginia, and in Macon and St. Simon's Island, Georgia, we moved back to Arizona, this time to a small copper-mining town called Globe, in time for me to start third grade. We stayed in Globe

Lewis Shiner: *"My earliest memories are of this yard, this fence, in Tucson, Arizona. I was two and a half."*

for three entire years, two of them, incredibly, in the same house. That two-year period stretches like an eternity in my memory, even though I spent the summers in New Mexico, where my father was rebuilding the ruined pueblos at Chaco Canyon and Aztec National Monuments.

By age eight, when I arrived in Globe, I was in many ways a fully formed miniature adult. My parents had taken me to grown-up parties as far back as I can remember, where I would converse brightly with the other adults (whose approval, of course, I was desperate for) about the stock market or politics or literature, and then I would quietly go into a corner and read. My parents got lots of compliments on how grown-up and well-behaved I was, and that seemed to not only make them happy but to justify all the punishment, both mental and physical, that had shaped me to that end.

Jules Verne was my major literary hero at the time, though I was also deeply into various Grosset and Dunlap adventure series: the Hardy Boys, Rick Bryant, and my favorite, Tom Corbett, Space Cadet. I'd started my first (unfinished) novel the year before, at age seven. It was called *The Deep Blue Sea* (as in, between the devil and). It chronicled the adventures of Tim Richards, scuba diver, and my memory of it is that it was a bit episodic to have amounted to much commercially.

Shortly after that I started a novel about a descent into a volcano, also unfinished, and then I wrote a series of short novels (very, very short novels) about a group of nonsuperpowered heroes called The Planets. Other than the fact that they wore blue sweatshirts just like my best friend Dicky Benny and me, they were pretty much indistinguishable from the Challengers of the Unknown of DC Comics fame.

My favorite memory of Globe—which fueled a later short story called "Twilight Time"—is of the National News Stand on the three-block-long main street of downtown Globe. Well into my thirties I still had dreams of walking to the plywood rack against the far wall and finding one of my favorite comics there: *Sea Devils,* or the *Atom,* or *Rip Hunter, Time Master.*

I was also writing and drawing my own comics, which I would sell to kids at school for fifteen cents (a nickel more than DC was getting at the time). I drew them on newsprint, with slick shelf paper for covers, and finished them with colored pencils. One of my characters was named the Brain; he lived in a cave, wore a skin-tight purple suit, and outsmarted his enemies.

While still in Georgia I'd heard Elvis and the Everly Brothers and had only been able to think how much my parents would hate them. In Globe, however, it was the end of the fifties and all the grade-school kids were listening to Buddy Holly and Ray Peterson and Johnny Horton. I also especially loved Ray Charles, who I remember hearing on the jukebox at Upton's soda fountain.

I don't know why my memories of Globe are so vivid and emotionally charged. Maybe I had some mistaken conviction that we were actually going to stay there. Maybe there was just something about Arizona, about the deserts and the clear air and clean water. Maybe it was the fact that my father was in the field eight months a year (though we did join him for the summers) and being away from his moodiness and heavy-handed discipline for weeks at a time gave me some much needed breathing room.

In any event, it didn't last. In the summer after my sixth-grade year my father quit the Park Service because my mother had been diagnosed with breast cancer and they wouldn't let him stay in Globe with her. Though my mother was very sick, and in Phoenix for radiation therapy much of the summer, I don't remember this as a particularly bad time. The one credit I will give my parents is that they were good in a crisis. They'd always taught me that when there was real trouble you got through it first and worried about the repercussions later. There was a sense during the summer of my mother's cancer that we were all pulling together, and it may be as close as we ever were as a family.

My mother made a full recovery; my father took a job with the Museum of New Mexico that took us first to Santa Fe—where I had a hellish seventh grade among Chicano gangs—and then to Africa, where the Aswan Dam was about to flood a wealth of early human sites.

We spent a month in Europe on the way over, six months in the Sudan, and another month in Europe on the way back. In many ways we were the boorish American tourists that make Europeans cringe—my father with his mangled attempts at French and hatred of non-

Lewis, age seven, at his paternal grandmother's house in Laredo, Texas

representational art; me wanting only to find a passable American-style hamburger, or more importantly an English language bookstore so I could get more science fiction.

We arrived in the small, doomed village of Wadi Halfa in October. We were on the East Bank of the Nile, a flat, rocky landscape with occasional towering *jebels* that looked, as much as anything, like the mesas of northern New Mexico. The only vegetation was a band of grass and gnarled trees along the Nile. The village itself consisted of low, one-story shops open to the street, a block-long market, with sides of fly-blown beef and lamb, and block after block of nearly identical houses, all made of thick adobe blocks. Everything came in shades of off-white: the dry dirt streets, the plaster on the houses, the parched blue-white sky.

I spent most of my time there wandering the streets, or reading whatever I could scrounge in English. This ranged from James Bond novels to *Catch-22* to the international edition of *Time* printed on flimsy air-mail stock. The novel I remember working on from this period was called *Dog Star*, concerning the sole survivor of a mission to a deserted planet in the Sirius system; this was still not quite isolated enough for me, so I topped it off by blowing up the Earth he'd left behind in a nuclear war.

*

Shortly after we got back from Africa we moved to Dallas, where Southern Methodist University had hired my father as part of a new graduate program in anthropology. I'd been supposed to read all my eighth-grade text books while in Africa, but of course I'd hardly bothered. The principal of the war zone that passed for my junior high had given me full credit for the year anyway, saying that what I'd learned on the trip was much more valuable than what I would have learned there.

These pretty sentiments weren't much help when my parents put me in a private high school in Dallas with what amounted to a substandard seventh-grade education. By working insanely hard I managed to make Cs and a few Bs my freshman year; my report cards said I had a lot of potential but didn't seem to be applying myself.

Up to this point I had been in many ways my father's son—smug, arrogant, racist, misogynist, walled off from the world by my intellect and a dozen kinds of fear. I liked the same easy-listening music my parents did, and hated queers and communists, like my parents. But all of that began to change.

I saw that my teachers had no idea of who I was or what I was going through. I was stuck at an all boys' school when the only thing I wanted in the world—other than to write alienated novels—was to meet girls. I knew how to make friends quickly, but only because my entire experience was geared to losing them quickly too.

September 24, 1965, is as good a date to mark the change as any. My sophomore year had barely started, and my best friend, Jim Savage, had talked me into going to see Bob Dylan. Jim was a military brat and as bitter, introverted, and intellectual as me. Unlike me, he was smoking, drinking, and listening to rock and roll even as a freshman. He'd played me some of Dylan's stuff, which I liked, but seeing Dylan in concert literally changed my life.

It was only the second stop on Dylan's first electric tour. Later Dylan would be booed all over the world for betraying folk music, but not in Texas, and certainly not by me. Staring at the huge blue shadow of the bass guitar on the white backdrop, hearing the drums echo across Moody Coliseum's basketball court, listening to the high wail of Dylan's voice and

Robbie Robertson's guitar, I got the message loud and clear.

The music literally set me free. I became the poster child for the evils of rock and roll: by the end of my sophomore year I too was smoking and drinking, and had gotten my first guitar, a cheap Sears Silvertone with nylon strings. My parents, not surprisingly, insisted I had no musical talent, but I was just starting to believe they might be wrong.

That summer, like the one before, I was part of a high-school summer-stock theater group called Harlequin Players. Women, again, were the big draw, especially a sexy blonde named Adrian that I'd met the summer before and would pursue unsuccessfully through my junior year. ("You're different," she would say when I complained about the other boys she slept with. "I *love* you.") The season had barely started when I ran a Skilsaw brand circular saw that was missing its guard into the flexor tendon of my left index finger. I spent the rest of the summer in the hospital, and when I got out my hand was in a useless and painful traction device; I was never able to bend the finger again. Worse yet, they'd given me Demerol all summer long, leaving me a teenage drug addict.

If I'd known where to get heroin in Dallas in 1966 I would have done it. After I got out of the hospital I went for a couple of weeks literally without sleeping at all. I couldn't get my driver's license because of my hand, couldn't play guitar, and it was weeks before I stopped being in constant pain.

I was not willing to give up on music, though, and by the winter of my junior year I'd made the decision to switch to drums. Another close friend, Mike Minzer, was a good bass player and a great natural singer. We teamed up with a classmate named Eric Vogel on lead guitar and, with occasional rhythm guitarists, started playing parties and coffeehouses.

Eric, like Mike and Jim and myself, was on the fencing team. The choice had been inevitable for me because of all the Edgar Rice Burroughs novels I'd read, all of whose heroes were swordsmen. Fencing seemed to attract all the weirdos and outcasts in the entire school—certainly all of my friends were there.

Another fencer was John Alberts, who was famous for drawing Bruegelesque cartoons in class and for falling helplessly in love with women who humiliated him. John had a big family—

"Summer vacation in a Martian landscape," Chaco Canyon, New Mexico, about 1960

an older sister and two younger brothers—and his parents encouraged him to bring his friends home. (As opposed to my father, who tried to start an argument with any of my friends he got in a room with.) I formed an attachment freshman year with John's father, who not only listened to me as if I were an adult, but was the first father I'd ever seen who was physically affectionate to his children. I knew instantly that I'd been missing it. And while I liked my mother's cooking well enough, the food at the Alberts' was gourmet quality. I spent as much time there as I could, listening to Bill Cosby and Lenny Bruce records, playing pool or ping pong, or touch football.

Then there was John's aforementioned older sister, Mary. She was not only drop-dead gorgeous, she was the very picture of the high-school socialite—cheerleader, beauty queen, prom date of football players—the exact opposite, in short, of the kind of girl who would ever have anything to do with me. Despite my being her little brother's friend, despite my being weird and undesirable, she was kind to me and, in

time, would talk pleasantly to me even when other people were around.

I know a lot of people—my friend John Kessel, for one—who might not have made it through high school if it hadn't been for science fiction. SF didn't mean much to me then; the thing that saved my life was rock and roll, either listening late into the night to the transistor radio next to my bed, or putting one of the few albums I owned on my parents' ancient monaural hi-fi, or playing with the band. I was still reading, but I was into Len Deighton, Irwin Shaw, and James Jones. When I wrote it was usually another attempt at a novel, like *Yellow Valley,* a novel about an eponymous prep school in Texas. The narrator was a depressed, overly creative teenage misfit, and the plot revolved around his out-of-control best friend, who bore a strong resemblance to Jim Savage. By senior year this had mutated into a long story called "In the Car at Crabtree's," taking its name from Crabtree's Electronics, where the band bought a lot of musical supplies. I also published stories in the student literary magazine, the *Marque*—morbid and obvious pieces full of masochistic nobility and stifled longings.

*

I finished my junior year in May of 1967. On the rest of the planet it was the Summer of Love, but in my house it was the summer of my father's near-fatal heart attack. He was forty-nine, just three years older than I am as I write this, and he'd been playing tennis in one hundred-degree heat with one of his graduate students. When he got off the court he sucked the smoke from one of his Roi-Tan cigarillos deep into his lungs. Then he drove home and told my mother his stomach hurt. He ate a banana and lay down and after a few minutes finally let my mother call the doctor, who listened to his symptoms and immediately phoned for an ambulance.

The things that culminated in his heart attack—his bitterness, his rages, his paranoia—had led me to finally admit to myself that I hated him. At that time, and in the context of my friends and the society around me, it was a chilling, completely forbidden thought. And yet he'd left me no alternative. I was finally making good grades at school—good enough to make the Cum Laude Society senior year and to be a National Merit finalist—but nothing pleased him. There was always more work to do around the house or in the yard and nothing but criticism for the way I did it. He had finally stopped hitting me, but he insulted me constantly—for my appearance, for my taste in music, for my opinions—until in the weeks before his heart attack I began to have dreams about him dying. I'm sure they were more wish-fulfillment than prophecy, since they usually involved a car wreck rather than a heart attack, and because I was so disappointed when I woke up.

It was late summer when he came home from the hospital. I remember standing in the driveway, watching him slowly shuffle toward the front door in his pajamas and robe, barely able to walk unassisted, his face as gray as the cement under my feet. He turned and looked at me with contempt and said, "I can still kick your ass, you know."

Twenty years later I wrote a story called "Match" in which a midthirties version of my-self takes his aging father onto the tennis court. The father says, "I can still kick your ass," and the son says the words I should have said as I stood on that driveway back in 1967, words that I was able to think but not to say out loud: "Prove it, old man."

In the story the father has a second heart attack on the tennis court and then, like some creature from a fifties horror movie, shakes it off, refuses to acknowledge defeat, keeps shambling on. It's still difficult for me to read that story because of the utter lack of compassion it brought out in me, and for the truth it tells about my father. He continued to find ways to hurt me and defeat me until almost the very end.

*

Senior year, especially the spring, was an eye in the storm of my adolescence. Other than two rather feeble attempts to run away from home—one ending in my own lack of resolve, the other in betrayal by my mother, who promised to get us counseling and didn't—I had a pretty good time of it. I'd been in one school for over three years now, a new record, and I was even getting along with most of the football players. I'd quit the fencing team for tennis, which enhanced my reputation, as did my writing on the Senior Follies and my band's performance at the party afterwards. And I was having a very grown-up relationship with a beautiful girl named Tricia Alexander, whom I'd known as part of the extended drama club family since sophomore year. We saw an incredible succession of concerts that year, from Jimi Hendrix in February (our first official date) through the Jefferson Airplane in late summer, with Cream, Vanilla Fudge, the Doors, Country Joe and the Fish, and the Mothers in between, not to mention great local bands like the Chessmen and the Novas.

I'd made some progress as a writer as well. I won the Creative Writing Cup at final assembly and a short-story contest in *Our Generation,* a local teen magazine, that earned me twenty-five dollars and, at age seventeen, my first professional publication.

If you looked hard enough, though—which no one bothered to do, despite my running away from home twice, publishing a story about suicide in the school literary magazine, and the almost-unheard-of act of going to school drunk on several occasions—you could see that everything was not quite right. I did all my homework in study hall during the day, and at night I sat alone in my room listening to the radio. I had a blue gel over the desk lamp that was the only light in the room. I didn't read. I didn't write. I didn't practice my drums. I just sat there, night after night.

Given my father's social status as a professor, college was not optional for me. Between my parents and the guidance counselors at St. Mark's I was maneuvered into choosing Vanderbilt, a nice conservative Southern school, where Mike Minzer also decided to go. What I wanted was to go to a technical school and get an apartment with Tricia and live in the real world, doing real things. I never stood a chance.

I was supposed to be an English major, but rebellion was getting to be a habit with me. I found the English department stuffy and repressive, and committed to a Russian major instead—despite no aptitude whatsoever for the language. It seemed practical, since I could earn money as a translator, and in the back of my mind I still thought I might have a career in espionage.

And so, after an uneventful freshman year and a summer of construction work in Dallas, I started my second year at Vanderbilt. Early that fall, Tricia sent me a dear-John letter that ended an increasingly awkward long-distance relationship. I had Russian language at eight in the morning, taught by a Vietnamese émigré with an unintelligible accent. I was in a band, the Nashville Blues Group, that was getting work and even had a tape that the student radio station was playing, but practice often didn't start until eleven or twelve at night.

I grew my hair and spent a lot of time in my dorm room, brooding. The previous year I'd rewritten "In the Car at Crabtree's," adding fantasy sequences that featured midget alter egos of the main characters. With the new title "Adam Rhodes at the North Pole," it had won the Henrietta Hickman-Morgan Award for Freshman English, which consisted of thirty dollars' credit at the student bookstore. Alone in my room sophomore year I put that story together with some other related stories, added a final section called "Adam Rhodes at the Circus," which incorporated badly drawn cartoons

with the prose, and ended up with a book I called *Volume One.* I sent it out a couple of times and got a couple of rejections, and by that time my life had changed again.

*

It was spring of 1970, and students were getting killed at Jackson State and Kent State. Despite having drawn a disastrously low number (three) in the nation's first draft lottery, it was becoming increasingly clear to me that I couldn't stay on at college. I didn't care about anything they had to teach me; all I wanted to do was play rock and roll.

I had plans to hit the road with my band at the end of the school year. Instead it turned out that the band's new promoter had his own drummer (a situation I went into in some detail in my novel *Glimpses),* and I ended up in Austin, in a one-room apartment with giant roaches, unable to find work, trying to put together a band with a guitarist who'd only been playing six months, an organist who'd only ever played classical, and a bass player who disappeared in his ice-cream truck somewhere between Austin and Houston.

To pass the time, and to keep myself from thinking about how poor and how desperate I was feeling, I wrote a novel, in longhand, called *And Then Palestrina* (from a line in Dylan Thomas's *Under Milkwood,* a Harlequin Players staple). The main character was a depressed, overly creative nineteen-year-old misfit whose girlfriend dumps him. He takes up with a depraved older guy named Reese with whom he commits random murders and then, in the novel's climax, attaches a fifty-caliber water-cooled machine gun (which he nicknames "Roger Iron") to the back of a convertible and machine-guns an entire town to death. (David Lynch, if you're out there, the film rights are still available.)

*

When my money finally ran out I went back to Dallas and worked construction again for my old boss. I started looking for a band again and eventually hooked up with an awesome and strange guitarist named Phil Graef (rhymes with "waif"). Phil, in turn, introduced me to a bass player named Arthur Hoffman, with whom I became friends so immediately, with such complete lack of reservation, question, or even perceptible ramp-up time, that only some theory of reincarnation can explain it. Within weeks we were tied inextricably in a web of standing jokes and unspoken communication, and Arthur remains one of my best friends in the world at this very moment.

Arthur and I made a great rhythm section, and Southern Cross (a name we stole from Mike Minzer) was a great band. But Phil was determined to do only original material, so we had a tough time getting jobs. Our big moment came when we played for about fifteen hundred people at a pop festival in Grapevine, Texas, an event we referred to sarcastically as "Grapestock."

The end of the summer of 1971 found me retired from the band and house-sitting at the Alberts'. John's parents were on vacation; John himself was in Pennsylvania rehearsing a play; Mary was married and living in Oklahoma, and everything I owned was in my car. Once John's parents got home I was either going to move to Hawaii (I don't know why, it just seemed like a good idea at the time) or go back to school. In the end I decided maybe I did want an English degree after all. I could get free tuition at SMU because of my father, and it sure beat working for a living.

*

Besides Arthur, my other best friend at the time—and for decades to come—was a guy named Julian Gamble, who I met at the Alberts' that summer. He was an aspiring actor, a superb poker player, a serious drinker, and an incurable romantic. As Arthur and I were two halves of rhythm section, Julian and I were two halves of a comedy team. When the director of a local girls' school kicked us out of his production of *The Little Foxes*, he gave us the nickname that we adopted with pride: The Trained Dog Act.

About the only things I did for the next two years were drink with Julian, and drink and study. I found that if I kept drinking I was perfectly content to sit home reading all night—every night—and so alcohol led me to straight A's at SMU.

My favorite professor was unquestionably Ted Tucker, an Englishman who taught Chaucer and

Old English and loved American baseball. He showed me how profoundly important mythology was to all of literature and took me to a couple of Rangers games, where he knew the batting average of every player on both teams.

A close second would have to be Marshall Terry, who taught the senior fiction writing class. I gave him a short-story version of *And Then Palestrina* as an audition piece for his class, and he let me in anyway. He called me Shoeless Lew because I came to class barefoot in warm weather, and gave advice and encouragement as I took the two main characters from *Palestrina* and put them in a science-fictional retelling of Jason and the Argonauts that I called *Soldier, Sailor*. (The title is from the song "Tinker, Tailor, Soldier, Sailor," which the Yardbirds covered on their final album—the same album that contains the song "Glimpses.")

I'd found my way back to SF because of my astronomy class junior year, where we'd been required to read Clarke's *Childhood's End*. I modestly thought that if somebody could combine the mythic potential of SF with a real literary sensibility they might really have something. A couple of years later I discovered that Roger Zelazny and Ursula LeGuin and J. G. Ballard, among many others, had beaten me to the punch.

Getting my undergraduate degree was all the college I could stand, and I resisted the faculty's attempts to lure me into graduate school. Instead I joined Arthur's new band, a country-rock outfit that we jokingly called T. T. Taylor and the Rice Paddy Raiders. Unfortunately we never sobered up enough to come up with a real name.

We played three nights a week at a club called Booger's off Lemon Avenue, making twenty dollars each per night. By eating lots of chicken pies and confining my really serious drinking to the free beer at the club, I was able to live off the band for quite a few months. Eventually, though, the liquor control board made Booger's start carding their patrons; the under-eighteen set stopped coming; the band broke up; and Arthur got me a job at the record store where he was assistant manager.

Arthur eventually became manager; I eventually became assistant manager, but that only meant longer hours, driving my actual dollar-per-hour figure below the minimum wage I'd been making before the promotion. The Sound

Town philosophy was "We can replace you with a sixteen-year-old" and eventually I let them.

It was now the summer of 1974. I had some savings, a little money my grandmother had given me, a girlfriend with a job, and a conviction that it was now or never. Like so many others before and after me, I decided I would try the Harlan Ellison write-a-story-a-week-until-you're-famous plan.

I was living at the time in an efficiency apartment near SMU at 3420 Rankin, #1. I would get up around ten in the morning, shower and eat breakfast, watch a Perry Mason rerun at eleven, and at noon I'd hoist my massive, ancient electric typewriter onto my lap and go to work. The first week I wrote an SF story called "Tinker's Damn" about an artificial intelligence who falls in love. I wrote three drafts, working late into the night, and when it was finished I put it into the mail and went on to the next one, an adventure story about underwater treasure hunting and sharks.

I believed that plotting was my biggest weakness, so I read Raymond Chandler and Ross Macdonald in the evenings and tried my hand at some mystery short stories. One of the first was called "Buyin' My Heartaches a Beer," about a construction worker who gets framed for his wife's murder. I got a nice long rejection letter from *Alfred Hitchcock's Mystery Magazine* for that one, and though I never did sell them anything, it was the first personal response I ever got on a story. It made me think I was on the right track. I followed it up with "Deep without Pity," featuring an Austin private eye named Dan Sloane. At the time nobody had done a private eye who was a Vietnam vet, and I had dreams that he would catch on and I could do a series of novels about him.

Along with the mysteries, I was reading J. G. Ballard, and I loved his idea of the "condensed novel." Of course I just happened to have a novel lying around that was in desperate need of condensation—*Soldier, Sailor*—and when I changed the protagonist's name to the sinister-sounding Kane and worked up a highly stylized prose that featured ampersands instead of the word "and" (an homage to Blake as well as a blatant attempt to seem literary) I felt I was really on to something.

Nobody else did, and the rejections continued to pile up. There were times when the frustrations were overwhelming—insulting rejection letters, manuscripts lost, manuscripts left at the bottom of a slush pile and sent back unread when the market closed, manuscripts mutilated by the post office or stained with spilled coffee. Once a magazine returned a story—after it had been completely copy-edited for publication in green felt tip pen—with a form rejection slip saying it "duplicates material already in our files" and no other explanation.

Yet at the same time I was slowly dragging myself up by my bootstraps, first wearing my influences like coats of bright red paint, then gradually internalizing them, then finally making my first tentative steps toward originality. I remember getting a tax refund and shelling out two hundred dollars for a reconditioned IBM Selectric. It was a profound and nearly religious experience for me to suddenly be able to produce such physically beautiful manuscripts. I loved the sound of the print ball, the smell of the ribbons, the wide "o" of the Courier font. I was determined to write something worthy of the typewriter and began a story called "Kings of the Afternoon."

The title popped into my head one day while doing dishes, and I still don't know where it came from. The story took me deeper into personal obsessions than anything I'd written before, blending UFOs, early Eagles songs (a band that to my mind has been unjustly persecuted for the crime of being popular), the myth of James Dean, John Ford westerns, and a hatred of capitalism into a finished product that had less calculation and more emotion in it than anything I'd written before. Using Dean let me put a character on stage who could actually lose control, and at the same time that I was uncomfortable with it, it was also immensely liberating.

I'd first wanted to write a post-apocalyptic western because of a writer's group I was in at the time. It was a Dallas offshoot of the well-known Turkey City workshop in Austin, which featured such local luminaries as Steve Utley, Lisa Tuttle, Howard Waldrop, Bruce Sterling, and old pro Chad Oliver. A guy in our local group had written a story where the protagonists tied their horses up to the parking meters in ruined cities, and I thought that was the wrong way around: they should have been riding motorcycles and big-finned convertibles through the desert, guns blazing.

Fortunately the guy didn't hold my criticism against me. Instead, when my money finally and completely ran out in the fall of 1976, after two long years of hunger and odd jobs, he offered me work as his assistant, doing technical writing for a local computer company. My personal pendulum, which seemed to swing back and forth between the need for freedom and the need for security every two to three years, had brought me back to the fear of starvation again, and I took him up on it.

*

I'd always wanted to learn more about computers, and I made the most of the opportunity. I volunteered to write the manual for the proprietary language the company used, and learned to program in the process. I then turned that into a programming job with a VP who left to start his own company.

Meanwhile the years of work had finally, grudgingly, begun to pay off. A couple of weeks after I took my first computer job I sold "Tinker's Damn" to *Galileo,* a small SF magazine out of Boston that later gained a certain cachet from having published the first stories of John Kessel and Connie Willis, both of whom went on to major awards and important work in SF. When the acceptance letter came I didn't jump up and down with excitement, but instead felt quietly satisfied, as if some great injustice had finally begun to be set right.

Less than a month later my first Dan Sloane story, "Deep without Pity," sold to the new *Mystery Monthly,* and for the first time I dared to think of myself as a real, honest-to-God writer. Unfortunately, I was premature again. The editor at *Galileo* was "dismayed" with the rewrite I did for him, and I went a year and a half without knowing (or really much caring) if the story was going to be published at all. *Mystery Monthly* folded the month before my story was scheduled to come out. It was another three years before my next sale, when *Shayol,* a semi-professional magazine out of Kansas City, finally bought "Kings of the Afternoon."

By this point I was a full-blown alcoholic. I drank at least a six-pack a night, and maybe a couple of them at the regular Friday night poker game (which I described in my novel *Slam).* My joke at the time was that I drank to forget. If anybody asked me what I was trying to forget I would say, "I don't remember, so it must be working." Funny, maybe, but also the truth. I truly didn't know why I drank so much,

only that I was happy if I kept it up and that I didn't dare stop.

The reasons would not have been hard to find. I was twenty-seven years old, and I had none of the things I'd expected to have at that point in my life: no writing career, no music career, no girlfriend. I didn't even have my Rankin apartment anymore: it had literally started to fall down around my head, and the landlord was uninterested in fixing it. I'd set a new record there, five years in one place, and it killed something in me when I moved out. For years I dreamed about going back and discovering that my key would still let me in. Either the place was empty and I would begin a second, secret life there, or I would start a relationship with some woman who was living there. In either case, my former mailbox would be stuffed with mail for me—an indication of how much of my life there had centered on that mailbox.

In the summer of 1978, after a long vacation where I drove out to California and came back through Globe, I went back into discipline mode. I'd been taking notes as I drove for a suspense novel called *Red Weather* (from a Wallace Stevens poem), set in a computer company with clients in the oil business, just like the one I worked for. I used my coworkers as models for the characters, and my protagonist was a late-twenties, depressed, overly creative misfit named Jack Marshall who stumbles on a dark secret in the company's past. I made myself write two pages a night, every night after work, and after nearly a year I had the first draft of a decent, salable novel.

In whatever time I had left after writing the novel I wrote letters to my new friend Joe Lansdale. I'd met him at the 1978 World Fantasy Convention in Fort Worth, where we started talking about detective fiction and didn't stop for almost ten years. The letters led to a collaboration on a story about a Houston ex-cop with a bad knee named John Talbot, "Black as the Night," the first, we hoped, of a series. Joe had already sold to *Mike Shayne Mystery Magazine* and figured maybe we could sell there together.

Joe had an agent who he was willing to mention my name to, so in May of 1979 I sent her the first hundred pages of my second draft of *Red Weather.* I gave the final manuscript of "Black as the Night" to Joe to market, quit my job, sold my car (which had been breaking down with infuriating regularity), put everything I had in storage, and went to Mexico.

It had been a bad year. Bad luck with romance, bad weather, the aforementioned car trouble, long days working for somebody else. A badly butchered version of "Tinker's Damn" had come out in *Galileo* and the first I'd heard of it was when one of my poker buddies mentioned having seen it. I remember my lack of enthusiasm when he told me. I guess my disappointment that I hadn't sold again, and that my one sale wasn't even on local newsstands, kept me from feeling much of anything. As I got on the Greyhound for Laredo I was thinking that I would come back when my money ran out, or my career got going again. I didn't much care at that point if I came back at all.

*

I spent a month in Mexico City, and the change of scene got my creative juices going again. I found a wonderfully shabby hotel room near the Alameda Central and spent my days reading, exploring the Anthropology Museum, eating fabulous meals for next to nothing, and writing a new novel in longhand while sitting in Chapultapec Park.

The novel was called *In Transit* and was high adventure in the *King Solomon's Mines* tradition: hard-boiled hero, ruthless villains, Mayan and Incan ruins, and treasure. Once I knew I was going to write about the jungle it became inevitable that I go see it, so eventually I made my way to the Yucatan and the ruins at Palenque.

The rain forest had a completely unexpected emotional impact on me. I'd expected it to be alien and frightening and instead it felt peaceful, welcoming, and (relatively) cool. As for the ruins, they were not just breathtakingly beautiful but also spiritual. I spent three days there but could easily have stayed for years.

Finally, just over two months into my trip, I arrived in Cozumel, where I called my parents and got the news: Joe had sold "Black as the Night" to *Mike Shayne* and his agent wanted to take me on. I was back in Dallas within a week, where I washed all my clothes, got my typewriter out of storage, and moved to Austin.

*

After a few weeks at the Lexington Suites ("A Day or a Lifetime") Bill Alberts found me an efficiency behind his apartment on Duval, near campus. His sister Mary was in town as well, with her then husband, and she saw to it I had a good home-cooked meal from time to time. I finished the rewrite of *Red Weather,* put it in the mail to my new agent, and immediately started a Dan Sloane detective novel called *The Slow Surrender.* The theory was that since my agent liked *Red Weather,* I wanted to have another mystery ready to go when the first one sold. Besides, *In Transit* still needed some fairly expensive research—a trip to Machu Picchu in Peru—that wasn't likely to get done anytime soon.

Even though I basically thought of myself as a mystery writer, I was still doing the occasional SF short story, one of which I was particularly happy with. Bill's roommate was a pharmacology student, another ex-St. Mark's kid, and he helped me with the research on a story called "Stuff of Dreams," about traveling to dream worlds by means of an addictive drug called Adonine.

When I showed it to Lisa Tuttle, one of the Turkey City writers, she said, "Ed Ferman will buy this." I didn't believe her; Ferman was the editor of *Fantasy and Science Fiction,* a.k.a. *F&SF,* considered the most literary of all the SF magazines. I desperately wanted to sell there, and had a couple of nice rejection notes from him, but I'd also been burned too many times.

One of the great things about *F&SF* is that you find out you've sold there when you see your name on the check through the window of their envelope—a clear and unconditional response. Three months after I submitted "Stuff of Dreams," I got my check, and it felt like a major watershed.

It was. Everything in my career before it had been touched by heartbreak and frustration, and from that point on the momentum, at long last, began to build.

There were still setbacks. *Red Weather* never sold. *The Slow Surrender* never sold. I fired my first agent and a half dozen more over the next four years. My mystery short stories continued to kill the magazines that bought them. I wrote a couple of adult western novels, one with Joe Lansdale and one on my own, that never sold.

But my SF stories were starting to sell, and in 1982 I was the most prolific SF writer in Texas, selling almost a story a month to major markets like *F&SF,* the *Twilight Zone* magazine (under the enlightened editorship of T.E.D. Klein), and the revamped *Asimov's* under Shawna McCarthy.

My personal life had stabilized as well. I began dating Edith Beumer, a film student who lived in the apartment under Bill's. Though she was nine years younger than I was, she'd sustained her own damage in relationships; she was smart and pretty and funny and I very much wanted to feel settled. We got married in July of 1981.

Shiner signing his first novel at Bob Wayne's bookstore in Fort Worth, Texas, 1984

I quit the sixties revival band I'd been playing in right around the same time. And, somewhat to my surprise, I quit drinking. Part of it was physical—the mornings after were getting more and more difficult. The rest had to do with the reasons I'd been drinking in the first place. I had a writing career now, and a relationship, and I didn't need it as badly.

In 1982 I started going to major SF conventions on a regular basis. Some aspects were appalling to me after years of highly civilized Texas conventions: the fans with no social skills, the drunken and obnoxious professionals, the overloaded elevators, the bizarre costumes. On the other hand I got to know the editors I was writing for, and they got a face and a personal style (I always dressed well) to put with my name. I got to meet other writers my age who were just starting out, many of whom became friends for life, including John Kessel, Karen Joy Fowler, and Jim Blaylock.

I came home from my first WorldCon in September of 1982 to an unfinished horror novel called *The Darkling.* I'd shown part of it to an agent who didn't want to market it unless I finished it; I didn't want to finish yet another novel without some better reason to believe I could sell it.

I was sure, though, that I could sell an SF novel. More importantly, I knew that was what I wanted to write. I'd just had my interest in the field revived by Bruce Sterling, who gave me a manuscript of "Burning Chrome" by his friend William Gibson. The story stunned me. It was the first SF I'd read that was truly contemporary, not a relic of the fifties or sixties. It was SF that watched MTV, rode the subway, and read fashion magazines.

When I thought about writing an SF novel, two pieces of unfinished business came to mind. One was *In Transit,* now mutated into a time travel idea involving both ancient Mayans and the end of the world; the other was my condensed novel, "Soldier, Sailor." I took some notes, drafted a few pages, and finally decided to make *In Transit* into a short story called "Deserted Cities of the Heart" (from the song by Cream). With luck I could use it to break into the very high-paying and prestigious *Omni* (which I did) and maybe turn it into a novel later (ditto).

With "Deserted Cities" in the mail, I started to turn "Soldier, Sailor" back into a novel again. I decided to call it *Frontera,* after a song by

Roxy Music guitarist Phil Manzanera that had a minor, yearning quality that sounded like Mars to me. I also liked the denotation of "border" and the fact that there was a Frontera Truck Parts just outside Dallas on the road to Austin.

The first draft was a shambles. It started out in first person and ended in third; characters changed name, race, and/or gender in mid-paragraph; sub-plots appeared and disappeared without notice. I somehow knew that momentum was important and I didn't let myself go back to the beginning to rewrite. I just kept pushing on.

In the midst of all this I still had to make a living. At the time that meant going to Dallas every five or six weeks for a week to ten days of contract programming, ten to twelve hours a day. I hated the time in Dallas, not just because it was hard, lonely work, but because it meant staying with my parents. My father was as bitter as ever, my mother as critical and undermining.

I finished the first draft of *Frontera* and almost immediately started the second. I was still working on my IBM Selectric, and I retyped constantly as I went, getting a fairly smooth and consistent feel. When I had about seventy-five pages done, I sent photocopies to Shawna McCarthy at *Asimov's* and Ellen Datlow at *Omni*, hoping to get some word of mouth started.

The strategy worked. Betsy Mitchell, who'd been managing editor at *Analog* when I sold a story there, had just gotten a job at a new line of paperback originals named for editor Jim Baen. She mentioned to Shawna over lunch that she was looking for manuscripts, and Shawna remembered me.

I had two-thirds of the book finished when Betsy called me, and within a few weeks she made me an offer. I agonized a little before I signed the contract: her boss, Jim Baen, was a nuts-and-bolts, hard-SF fan, and I saw *Frontera* as an ambitious book that could get lost in his list. But in the end I'd been waiting too long to finally sell a novel, and I opted for the nearly instant gratification of going with the start-up company. I finished the manuscript around Christmas of 1983 and the book was in stores (including my local grocery) the following summer.

Sales were modest; reviews were sparse (as they always are with paperback originals) but very gratifying. I was a finalist for the Nebula and Philip K. Dick awards, and lost both (deservedly) to Gibson's now-classic first novel, *Neuromancer*.

*

Edie and I bought a house in the summer of 1984 and spent two months remodeling it. In fact I stopped putting up Sheetrock one afternoon in July to go to the local SF specialty shop where I saw my first finished copy of *Frontera*. It was strange to finally hold it in my hand. After seeing the page proofs and the cover proofs it was too familiar to seem entirely new, and yet I didn't want to let it out of my sight.

I was already at work on the novel version of *Deserted Cities of the Heart*. I'd gotten tired of SF and was reading mainstream fiction again—Robert Stone, Don DeLillo, Denis Johnson. I wanted *Deserted Cities* to talk about the end of the world (which the Mayans are expecting early in the twenty-first century) but still be set in the present day. I spent a lot of time weeding the backyard and trying to think my way through the contradictions, eventually deciding that it was enough to see the beginning of the end. There were plenty of omens in Latin America, from earthquakes to cults to political upheaval.

I assigned myself a daunting amount of research: classical Mayans and present-day Lacondones, revolutionaries and U.S. Army weaponry, socialist theory and New Age philosophy. My friend the pharmacology student took me on a psilocybin trip; a local helicopter instructor gave me a flying lesson and a look at a real military Huey. I even put together a plastic model of the helicopter to plot out the action scenes that took place inside it. It had only taken me a year to write *Frontera* (unless, of course, you counted the previous incarnations all the way back to *And Then Palestrina*), but *Deserted Cities* took more like three.

By the time I finished the first draft I knew where I wanted to sell it. Bantam Books had started a trade paperback line, Bantam New Fiction, meant to compete with the Vintage Contemporaries that I loved. Shawna McCarthy was an editor at Bantam now, and through her boss, Lou Aronica, she could get me into the New Fiction program. It was the mainstream credibility that I'd always dreamed of, and so when the auction for the rights came down to traditional SF publisher Ace Books and Bantam, I chose Bantam.

*

At this point my career had pretty much peaked. My work was starting to appear in both the *Year's Best SF* and *Year's Best Fantasy* collections. I had been labeled—along with Sterling, Gibson, and others—a "cyberpunk" and gotten a disproportionate amount of publicity as a result. I'd been able to buy a computer and do my contract programming from home, part-time, leaving the majority of my days free for writing fiction. I was on the phone every day with editors and other writers all over the country.

At the same time the life had completely gone out of my marriage. I found Edie cold and she told me I was unromantic. Though we were both unhappy, neither of us was strong enough to end it. The more I pulled away from her, the more involved I got with my career and my friends, the more distant I must have seemed to her.

I finished *Deserted Cities* in the spring of 1987 and ran immediately into trouble. I went back and forth for months with the editor of the New Fiction line, who refused to speak to me directly. I even line-edited the entire manuscript at her behest, though no one would give me a clue as to what she thought was wrong with it. The real problem, I think, was that Shawna and Lou had tried to foist one too many SF writers on the program. In the end Lou actually marked up a chapter for me, and when I saw what he'd done I literally took to bed sick for four days. I thought every change he'd suggested was for the worse, and with great sadness I declined to make them.

Needless to say I was washed up at Bantam New Fiction (though apparently I wasn't the only one who disagreed with their ideas of good writing, since the line didn't last very long). Lou gave me the choice of buying the book back (which meant going back to Ace, if they'd have me) or letting Doubleday publish it as part of a new hardcover SF line. Ace would have published it as SF too, and Doubleday would let me keep the gorgeous cover that was already finished, so I reluctantly let them keep it.

I hadn't been able to write since I finished *Deserted Cities,* despite the fact that I'd been taking notes on a new novel, *Slam,* since the previous winter. It sprang from a throwaway idea: what happened to the money that you always heard about little old ladies leaving to their cats? It seemed like the basis of a Harry Crews-type comedy, and maybe for that reason I had an unshakable image of a beach house and the sun rising out of the ocean—which I thought at first meant Florida. Then one day I realized that Galveston Island had an east coast too, and I was off and running.

The other half of the plot grew out of watching skateboarders from the window of my favorite Mexican restaurant near campus. I loved the circle-A T-shirts and the haircuts and the disavowal of sixties culture—*my* culture. I got deeply into *Thrasher* magazine with its deranged graphics and evocative language and developed a genuine love for the skate-punk band Suicidal Tendencies.

It was October of 1987 before I finally made my peace with Bantam/Doubleday, and once I did, the dam broke.

My marriage had degenerated into long silences and there were many nights when I slept in my study. Still I remember the time I was actually working on *Slam* as very happy. I wrote the entire first draft in ten weeks, knowing at the end of each day what I wanted to do the next, but sure that I was going to run out of ideas any minute. I never did, and most days I was smiling or even laughing out loud as I wrote.

When I had about fifty pages I showed them to Edie, to my mother, and to my agent. All three hated it, my agent even calling the protagonist a "layabout loser." My feelings were hurt, but I was otherwise undeterred—except that I did wait until I had a finished second draft before I showed it again. At that point everybody liked it, including Pat LoBrutto, who had taken over for Shawna when she left Bantam.

Pat was a bit disorganized from a business perspective, but he and I were kindred spirits, and he was the perfect editor for *Slam.* He completely understood what I wanted to do, was full of great ideas and encouragement, and had exquisite judgment. As a Bantam genre editor, however, he needed a mainstream Doubleday editor to sponsor the book. Unfortunately, between my second and third drafts, that editor bought a book called *The Firm* by John Grisham and lost all interest in me. Whether

"With my parents in Laredo, Texas, probably 1954. I describe this photo in my novel
Glimpses *where the protagonist imagines himself as the father."*

for that reason or another, *Slam* suffered the same fate as *Deserted Cities* before it—fabulous reviews, poor sales.

*

On November 16, 1988, about a month after I sold *Slam,* I got a phone call at four in the morning. It was my mother calling from Australia to tell me my father was dead.

At the time I hadn't spoken to my father for a couple of months. Our last phone conversation had been about *Deserted Cities.* "I read your book," he said, "and I've got a list here of your mistakes, both factual and grammatical."

At the time it was important to me to be able to take criticism of my work—a point of honor at Turkey City—so I cheerfully told him to go ahead. After a couple of quibbles he told me that no camera made had the F-stop setting I'd used at one point in the novel. I actually got my camera and told him the setting was right there on the lens.

"It must be some kind of Russian camera, then."

"Dad, it's a fucking Nikon."

"Well, it's the only one like it ever made."

In a moment of absolute clarity I saw I would never win an argument with my father as long as I lived, that he would never be able to praise me or show that he was proud of me. And I saw that it was his fault, not mine.

"Okay, Dad," I said. "Fine, Dad. Goodbye, Dad." I hung up the phone and never spoke to him again.

As in my novel *Glimpses,* where I (barely) fictionalized the incident, I continued to have some contact with my mother. According to her, my father's response to my continued silence was, "He'll get over it."

His death—also very much as described in *Glimpses,* though it happened in Australia rather than Cozumel—was mysterious. He was scuba diving on the Great Barrier Reef and, at the end of the dive when he should have been swimming up to the boat, he turned and swam downward instead. The dive master chased him and got him turned around at about ninety feet, but both were then out of air. By the time my father got to the surface he was dead.

Did he kill himself? He'd always said he wanted to die underwater. More importantly from my perspective, what was he thinking of when he started swimming down? Was he thinking of me?

After I finished *Slam* I started a novel about a late-thirties, depressed, overly creative misfit who goes to Cozumel (I'd never been to Australia and couldn't afford to go), both to see the place where his father died and to escape his crumbling marriage. I called it *In Transit* because I still thought it was a great title.

I worked on *In Transit* for close to a year, and despite all my insistence about being a mainstream writer, I knew something was missing: a spark, an energy, to carry me through the vast work of writing a novel. At this point I was living off the *Slam* advance and the money I was making writing comics—a sideline that I really enjoyed. I was not under any financial pressure, and I was able to set the novel aside for a while and work on something else.

That something else was a short story, an SF short story, which meant I might actually be able to sell it. (I'd never been able to crack an important market with any of my mainstream short fiction.) The idea concerned a man who could imagine a legendary lost album from the rock era and actually have it show up on tape. He'd get more and more into it and eventually have to choose between fantasy and reality. The fictional characters would interact with real people like Jimi Hendrix and Brian Wilson of the Beach Boys.

I started writing and couldn't seem to write it fast enough. For every page I wrote I had to backtrack and add two more. Before long I saw I was going to have to answer the central question of the story: who was this guy, and why did he need these albums so badly? I held out for days before I finally gave in to the obvious answer. He was probably a guy with a lousy marriage whose father had died under mysterious circumstances in Cozumel. In one bite the short story—which I'd been calling "Glimpses"—reached out and swallowed *In Transit* whole.

*

Edie had read the first chapter of *Glimpses,* the novel, and there was no question where I'd gotten the details of the protagonist's bad marriage. "Is Ray going to leave Elizabeth," she asked me, "or is Elizabeth going to leave Ray?"

"I don't know yet," I said.

The summer of 1990 was heavily booked. First I had a research trip to L.A. for *Glimpses,* combined with signings for *Slam,* which had just come out. Then I had an academic conference in Long Beach, followed by a week in Seattle teaching Clarion West, a prestigious SF writing workshop. Edie came with me for the first leg of the trip, and on the last day, before she flew back to Austin, we had one of the worst fights of our marriage.

I would teach every day in Seattle, then go into my room at night and continue my increasingly grim discussions with Edie via long distance. When I got back to Austin we agreed to separate. I left the next day for Dallas, where I was supposed to help my mother move out of her house and into a retirement apartment. Two days later I drove back to Austin and took the last of Edie's furniture to her new place.

Edie met someone very quickly, eventually married him and moved to Dallas. For me it was more difficult. I didn't want the marriage back, and I was happy enough to be living alone. I went out on a few dates, spent a lot of time on the phone or writing to friends. But I wasn't okay. I was angry a lot, out of proportion, it seemed to me, to the things that set me off. Other times I was consumed with self-pity. Much of what I did seemed pointless.

What was happening, in fact, was that my entire life had come to a head. Everything I had put my energy into since I was in high school—sex, alcohol, performing in front of an audience—had been an attempt to keep functioning despite severe emotional damage. By the fall of 1990 nothing worked.

I started seeing a therapist, a woman Edie and I had gone to briefly years before. My parents were a major topic, obviously, but the therapist also felt that I was trying too hard to define myself in terms of romantic relationships. She wanted me to pull back and be independent for a while. I might actually have done it if a chance encounter—or the hand of fate—hadn't sent me off in a completely unexpected direction.

I was still seeing a lot of the Alberts family. Bill had provided legal advice and lawyer jokes for *Slam,* and was my divorce attorney. On December 16, 1990, he and his wife had their annual Christmas party, which I'd been looking forward to for weeks. When I got there I asked about Mary, who I knew had been in St. Louis getting her master's degree in social work. She'd finished school, it turned out, and was staying with her father in San Antonio. The two of them drove up for the party that night.

She seemed as delighted to see me as I was to see her, and gave me a big hug. We hadn't seen each other in about eight years, since Bill's wedding, and I know I had changed—sobered up, published some books, and gotten a lot more self-confidence. Still it was unthinkable that she could actually be attracted to me. She was even more beautiful than she had been as a teenager, well-read, well-traveled, highly sophisticated, used to men with luxury cars and fat bank accounts.

Still we seemed to have so much to say to each other. I had always sensed a loneliness in her, and that night, when we ended up on Bill's back porch, talking intently, Bill's son Christopher ran into the house yelling, "Aunt Mary's got a boyfriend!"

She did indeed. I went to San Antonio the next weekend to see her and we stayed up all night talking. The next weekend she came to Austin to stay with me and both of us realized that, without warning, we were both in way over our heads.

She started a job at M. D. Anderson in Houston in February, and the next thing I knew I was giving up the house where I'd lived for six years, longer than anywhere else in my life, and moving to Houston to be with her. We each had our share of misgivings: I was just

out of a bad marriage; she'd had a succession of bad relationships. But for me this was a once-in-a-lifetime chance, a storybook romance, and I knew from the very beginning that I would gamble everything I had on it, without question.

I had written the first nine-tenths of *Glimpses* without really knowing how it was going to end, and the shape of my life after separating from Edie shaped the last chapter of the book. I figured out the ending on I-10 headed for Houston one Thursday afternoon, taking notes with one hand and driving with the other. Mary believed utterly in the book and gave me parts of her own life to add to it. I finished the second draft in late 1991 and sent it to my agent. She agreed with me that this could be my breakout novel and went looking for a big

"Happy at last," Lew Shiner with wife Mary Alberts at a serendipitous street sign in Dallas, 1998

offer. When it didn't come she started looking for any offer at all. In the end we sold it to an editor named Dan Levy at Delacorte for less money than I'd gotten for *Slam.* When your advances start to go down it's never a good sign, and I was afraid that the streak of luck that had let me, first of all, sell wildly diverse novels, and secondly, support myself with my writing, might be coming to an end.

I was right. Dan was a huge music fan, the perfect editor for the book, and he was fired before I turned in my third draft. His boss, Brian DiFiore, took over the book and then moved to Morrow. I'd always wanted to be a Delacorte/Dell author, but there was no one left to support the book there, so I did what I had to do and pulled the book. When we couldn't sell it anywhere else we took it back to Brian at Morrow, who bought it a second time, and then moved again before it was published.

The book got some great reviews but also took some hits. The *Village Voice* and the *New York Times* seemed disappointed that I was no longer hip, ironic, and distant, like I'd been in *Slam.* The hardback sold about the same as both my previous hardbacks, and despite my winning the World Fantasy Award, the paperback was a financial disaster.

But the story of *Glimpses,* in the end, was not about money. It was about Brian Wilson showing up at a signing for the book in L.A., and about my getting to know David Leaf, his friend and biographer. It was about meeting people, and getting letters and e-mail from people that had been genuinely touched by the book—people who would not have reacted in the same way if it had been hip, ironic, and distant.

*

Mary and I moved to San Antonio in February of 1993, shortly before *Glimpses* came out. My comics work dried up at about that time and my brief career as a full-time writer was over. In September I took a full-time job with a computer company.

I was heartbroken. I went two years after finishing *Glimpses* without really writing any fiction at all, and once I started working I quit writing altogether. It shouldn't have been a big deal; I'd gone long periods without writing before. Only this time I wasn't drinking, and I wasn't playing in a band. And this time I'd

been really close to making it, close enough to taste it.

I began to fall apart.

I couldn't sleep; I couldn't control my emotions; I could barely drag myself out of bed in the morning. Eventually it became clear, even to me, that I had to start writing again. I had to write not to become famous, not to become rich, and not to make up for a loveless childhood. I had to write for its own sake, for whatever satisfaction I could get from the act itself.

It was a new attitude for me, and it didn't come easily. But, with Mary's help, it has started to come. I wrote the first draft of a stage play, *Neverland,* which I will come back to someday. I wrote a complete draft of a novel, *Say Goodbye,* which I'm still working on.

Mary and I live in North Carolina now. It's been almost seven years since her brother Bill's Christmas party, and I am still learning what it means to truly love another person and be loved in turn. But that love continues to grow stronger and stronger.

Writing is still something between a pleasure and a need for me. There is so little time for the work I care about, so much time lost to the work that doesn't matter. I'm learning to make the most of the time I have.

I hate it that there's still so much to learn.

BIBLIOGRAPHY

Fiction:

Frontera, Baen, 1984.

Deserted Cities of the Heart, Doubleday, 1988.

Slam, Doubleday, 1990.

Nine Hard Questions about the Nature of the Universe, Pulphouse, 1990.

The Edges of Things, illustrated by Alicia Austin, Washington Science Fiction Association, 1991.

Glimpses, Morrow, 1993.

Other:

(Contributor) *Mirrorshades,* edited by Bruce Sterling, Arbor House, 1986.

(Contributor) *All about Strange Monsters of the Recent Past: Neat Stories* (science fiction), edited by Howard Waldrop, Ursus Imprints, 1987.

(Contributor) *In the Field of Fire,* edited by Jack and Jeanne Dann, Tor, 1987.

(Contributor) *By Bizarre Hands: Stories* (horror/fantastic fiction), by Joe R. Lansdale, M. V. Ziesing, 1989.

(With others) *Wild Cards* (comic book), illustrated by Barry Kitson and others, Epic Comics, 1991.

(Editor) *When the Music's Over: A Benefit Anthology,* Bantam, 1991.

(With Walter Jon Williams) *Epic: An Anthology* (comic strip), edited by Dave Elliott, Epic Comics, 1992.

(Contributor) *In Dreams* (horror/science fiction), edited by Paul J. McAuley and Kim Newman, Gollancz, 1992.

(Contributor) *Norton Anthology of Science Fiction,* edited by Ursula LeGuin, et al., Norton, 1994.

Jennifer Stone

1933-

Jennifer Stone, 1991

I was born on December 5, 1933, the day Prohibition was repealed. Mother told me this meant the rules did not apply to me. She was wrong about that.

My first published poem appeared in a student journal in La Jolla, California, in 1945. Something about a snake's eye view of a storm at sea.

Mother called herself Gretchen. My father called her Kiki. Her birth name was Gertrude Kiekentveld. At the time of my birth, my parents lived at 1930 East Sixth Street in Tucson, Arizona. They were both born in Michigan in 1902. My father's name was Robert Alan Hicks; he is described on my birth certificate as an M.D. and pathologist. I was born alive in Pima County at 4:47 A.M.; I am described as legitimate.

My parents were more or less on their own by their teens. Mother grew up in Holland, Michigan, and Bob grew up in Benton Harbor. I never called him anything but Bob which may lend some truth to the rumor that my biological father was a family friend and patient who came to Tucson with tuberculosis; this man's name was Walter Stockley, a writer for *Time-Life* whose Saxon style was said to be antithetical to Bob's bog-Irish aggressivity and flamboyance. I do not remember Walt Stockley very well, if at all. I seem to know him only from a few photographs and from the reports given me by my mother's close friend, Elsa Howe Richards. I do remember my confusion when Bob got drunk and wept over my mother's unfaithfulness. I tried to look up Walter Stockley many years later, in 1957, when I was a young actress making the rounds in New York City. I called the offices at *Time-Life* and they told me he was long deceased.

My parents were together for ten years before they had their first child. Mother got a degree in architecture and my father started a general practice. After they moved to Tucson, he concentrated on patients with arthritis and with the illnesses brought to the desert in the 1930s.

My mother had three children. I was the middle child. My older sister, Rolland Jeanette, was born in 1927. She was named after a male cousin of my mother's who died young. Apparently mother thought the extra "l" in Rolland would feminize the name. We called my sister Rolly, pronouncing it like Sir Walter Raleigh. I, too, was expected to be a boy, and as there was no feminine name ready, I was registered at birth as Mary Jane, after my paternal grandmother, who happened to be visiting at the time. Within a week, mother had decided to call me Jennifer; she noticed that the name was decidedly out of fashion in 1933. By the

Father, Bob Hicks, 1932

tution was much stronger than Rolly's and when they retired to Malaga, Spain, my sister sank into alcoholism and died in 1972. At the time of her death she was forty-four years old, just as my mother had been. For both of them, denial was the practice common to their milieu. Alcoholism was considered bad form and a lapse of good taste.

My grief for my family is heightened by the memory of how happy we seemed in the beginning. My early years in Tucson were a dreamscape. In the summer months, from the time I was three, my mother took us to La Jolla on the coast of Southern California. The drive over the desert during the cool hours of the night and our arrival at the cove, the beatific beach that smelled of salt and iodine and beckoned me with its tide pools and sensuous waves—this was enough to make me ecstatic for days on end.

The beach houses and the seascapes and the sensations of those days were the source of poems and fiction for years to come. Oceanic images gushed from my pen until I had to discipline myself to cool it. Like my contemporary, Sylvia Plath, my favorite girlhood poem was Matthew Arnold's "The Forsaken Merman." I didn't learn about Plath's love for this poem until many years after her death, when I read a biographical account of her early years which included her letters and journals. At the time, I put together one of those units (teaching is not my favorite task) about women writers and the sea: it began with Edna St. Vincent Millay's girlhood in Maine. It ended with scraps of Sigmund Freud and his rejection of oceanic feelings as infantile and narcissistic. I wanted my students to understand why Freud felt women were disloyal to civilization; to *his* civilization, that is. The students were thoroughly confused and serves me right. I digress.

time I could hear, I was Jenny. My father named his boats after me; he liked to chant, "paint it blue and call it Jenny."

When I was four, my parents finally had the son my father wanted so much. Michael was a blond angel, much adored by us all. He met tragedy following his years in Vietnam where he was stationed for many years during that war. He was a Navy Seal, or Frogman. Today he is a quadriplegic and an alcoholic. His wife was forced to leave him in the best interests of their three sons. Mike's story is still too painful for me to write about in detail.

My sister married an Englishman named Martin Vaughn Williams. He was old enough to be her father and had several children from two earlier marriages, so my sister's desire for children was not shared. Martin was a construction engineer who had lived in South Africa, Central America, and Mexico. Old school British; reminded me of the actor, Trevor Howard. Rolly was too romantic (or neurotic) to set limits. She drank with her husband and repeated many of the patterns of our parents. Martin's consti-

During World War II, my father was based at the San Diego Naval Hospital. The five of us settled into a beach house in La Jolla for the duration. There was much partying and wartime melodrama among the doctors and nurses and navy corpsmen. Beach fires and outrigger canoes and lobster pots fill my memory of that time. During one of the last invasions in the South Pacific, Bob was a commander on a hospital ship. When he returned, his blue black hair was iron gray. Whether it was the war, or too much drinking, or my parents' tormented personal relationship, their marriage fell apart and they divorced in 1945. Two years later my mother was dead.

During those years, my sister Rolly went to the Bishops School, then an exclusive girls' school complete with uniforms and Episcopal nuns as teachers. She turned into an Anglophile in short order, just as she had embraced Catholicism during a short stay in a parochial grammar school. She taught me the Keltic myths and legends, introduced me to English literature, and especially to the plays of Shakespeare. I was already addicted to the theatre, my first role being Mustard Seed in *A Midsummer Night's Dream*. My first stage appearance was with Mary McMurtry's Children's Theatre in Tucson. I still recall with much excitement my best moment with that group. I played the Scarecrow in *The Wizard of Oz* when I was thirteen. By that time I was living with a family friend, Ellen Slyter, one of the many mother figures who came into my life after Gretchen died.

During Gretchen's last year, I was sent away to live at Emily Johnson Duffy's Ranch School for Girls. Apparently the rough and tumble life of horses and the great outdoors was intended to distract me. This woodsy retreat in central California near the town of Fallbrook was not entirely wasted on me. I still remember the wild women who swam their horses in the rivers, stole out alone at night to meet boys, and got into all kinds of teenaged trouble. I was only in the eighth grade and already an adult-oriented, nearsighted bookworm. I looked with awe on the flaming red hair of the school's most reckless outrider; but I knew I could never compete with the athletic set, the fire-eaters. I began to live in my imagination. That was the place where I could be myself.

After mother died, I withdrew into poetry and silence. I read about the death of Virginia Woolf's mother when Virginia, too, was thirteen. Virginia tried to kill herself. I mythologized my memories then as well as later. There was denial and dissociation of course. I even repressed the memory of my own hysterics at the funeral, displacing this behavior onto my nine-year-old brother. The truth is, so far as I can remember now, Mikey was mute throughout the entire day. I was in my late thirties before I allowed myself to admit I lost it when I saw Gretchen bathed in blue light in an open coffin surrounded with gardenias. Someone asked me just the other day if I had worn a garde-

nia corsage to my high school graduation. I have never worn a gardenia anywhere. I was three months away from my first menses when mother died. I screamed my head off. Who wrote: "After the first death, there is no other."

When we arrived at my mother's gravesite in the desert, my father waved his German pistol in the air and threatened to shoot himself. It occurred to me then that he had upstaged my mother as long as I could remember. He was a scene stealer. He liked to recite poetry and if I complained he would say, "you'll be sorry when I'm dead and gone."

Over the years, he would arrive at my graduation ceremonies (sixth grade, eighth grade, ninth grade, twelfth grade, and college) with several large dogs, always drunk as a lord, and invariably all hell would break loose. After all these years, I still dream I see him in some new context, wandering the city alone. I watch and wait for him to see me, to cry out the way he did when I walked into the kitchen and saw him for the first time after Gretchen died. Ever after that, I felt I was his mother. In dreams I feel the anguish, realize he's drunk, that he's out of control again.

Selective memory is a survival skill. As the recovery movement has taught us, we remember only what we can handle (if we're lucky). My earliest efforts at writing were excavations into the psychic jungle of my childhood. Through a glass darkly and then face to face?

In my thirties, I discovered Virginia Woolf had had psychosexual trauma very much like my own. In my case, it was an older male cousin who "seduced" me, in a context which it took me years to understand was abusive, not consensual. I am still afraid to name the perpetrator. Worst of all, he was my mother's sister's son. I loved his mother deeply. Jeanette lived in Manhattan and was a career woman. It was she who told me that if I wished to succeed, I'd better get into advertising! Because my parents were alcoholic and quite unreachable when I was ten, it seemed natural to trust my cousin, to believe his affection for me was genuine. The horror of it is, on some level, I imagine he believed it was. And he knew I was too ashamed ever to expose him.

My first attempt to write about this trauma was a short story called "Blood Rust." It appears in the collection *Over by the Caves*, first published in 1977. Despite the current controversy over repressed memory syndrome, I have no doubt whatsoever about my own case. I never forgot the abuse, always knew I had to pretend everything was my own choice. I was startled to discover that I *had* suppressed some details. I was in my late thirties when my psyche felt safe enough to fill in the blanks. By that time, I was glad to know that my psychological health was better than I thought. How sensible to forget the blood on the bathroom floor. "Blood Rust" deals with the persona of a woman who is in denial, who is overly objective and dismissive of her own pain. This story was the first work of mine read on KPFA Pacifica Public Radio. One of my colleagues there, the black poet Adam David Miller, read it with the kind comment that it was ahead of its time.

Well, like so many traumatized teenagers, I developed my defenses big time in the years between dolls and despair. Virginia Woolf wrote: "I shall go on doing this dance on hot bricks till I die." Denial can become an art form. I got tough. People would ask me how or why my mother had died. I would quote Dorothy Parker: "She put all her eggs in one bastard!" Mother loved Dorothy Parker: "But I shall stay the way I am, because I do not give a damn." Drama was my defense. Theatre became my full-time passion. On stage, I could feel all the emotions, all the rage, fury, anger, and joy. I could do this without shame because it wasn't me, it was the character speaking. My first review in the *Hollywood Reporter* called my scene in a summer stock play (as a wispy spinster on her last legs) "a touching cameo." Offstage, I wore heavy make-up and made wisecracks.

Bob's take on all this was, "If you would just be *natural,* everyone would love you." In hindsight, it's not too difficult to see what was going on. My life was tied to Bob's as he went through four marriages, getting his wives' names mixed, searching everywhere for my mother, and in the end calling each new mate Gretchen.

Bob set up a practice in Wilcox, Arizona. He built a large hacienda and there was a new baby, Barbara Jean. Her mother was arthritic, a patient of my father's. Barby was my first charge, my first child perhaps. Things went terribly wrong for Bob after a few years, and he fled to Eniwetok, the Bikini Atoll where the hydrogen bomb was being tested. He had gone back in the navy to save his reputation. He'd had a manic depressive period in Wilcox and

gotten into a deadly fight with another doctor. He was also arrested for driving his ambulance to Tucson with the siren going; the police stopped him and found only a dead deer in the back.

He seemed to think he was Hemingway one day and F. Scott Fitzgerald the next. There were too many scrapes and scandals to record, but I was lucky enough to land in Laguna Beach with my stepmother and the baby. We were joined by Josephine, a dear Mexican mother/mentor who had lived with us when I was very young. She had come back from time to time, and worked for Bob as a nurse's aide. Now she came to help with my invalid stepmother and with Barby Jean.

Looking back now, it seems to me that while Bob was often in trouble with alcohol, he went long months between binges, worked long hours under great stress, cared deeply about his patients, and tried to give his children the kind of life he had always dreamed of. In fact, as Josephine herself told me at the time, he spoiled his children rotten.

I am grateful for those years in Laguna Beach. We lived in Three Arch Bay, and I acted in summer stock at the local playhouse. I graduated from high school as valedictorian in 1951. I was in love with the captain of the football team, and we had a glorious encounter at a party one night at Bette Davis's beach house. It was the kind of moment that stays in the memory into old age. The next day he was back with his cheerleader sophomore girlfriend and I was back at The Round Table, a gay bar which was my steady hangout.

There are endless stories to write about those days, about all the Hollywood actors who came to practice their craft in the stock company. I remember playing one of the parts in *Chicken Every Sunday* which had Bette Davis's sister, Barbara Barrie, in the lead. She was one of the softest women I have ever met. So shy, she did two plays and then retreated to the prop room to help out there. In hindsight, I see that in spite of their unconventional ways, they were an altogether gracious group. Over time, I have come to feel that theatre folk are more tender than the literary men and women I have known. But that's a glittering generality and probably has more to do with the impressionable age at which I was totally immersed in theatre. I did not come to the writing life until most of my vulnerabilities were exhausted.

My only published story about this period in my life is "The Walrus Bird," a take on my experience as a nude model for the then famous art photographer Paul Outerbridge. The story deals with the existential question of adolescent development: am I my body? It ends with my efforts to bury a dead mammal which has washed up on the beach. In 1967, a professor of medieval French literature, who lived upstairs from me (we baby-sat each other's kids), called this story post-symbolism. Indeed.

I might have done something in the theatre. I had a friend at (Hollywood's) central casting, Barbara Morrison, a British actress who worked in Laguna during the summers. I was all set to start at the Pasadena Playhouse after high school but Bob came to see me and decided I was on a slippery slope to decadence. He arrived at the Playhouse and saw me rehearsing for Anita Loos's *Happy Birthday* in which I played a bargirl on the arm of a sailor. In the second act, we became Lord Nelson and Lady Hamilton.

Bob was set up in the San Francisco Bay Area by this time. He was living with the woman who would become his last wife. He was lean and tan and working at the Oak Knoll Naval Hospital in Oakland because the Korean War was at full heat. He was happy and on the beam and wanted me to go to Mills College. I had tried to run away a few times, but at seventeen it seemed a bit redundant. I agreed to give it a try.

I arrived at Ethel Moore Hall, Mills College, Oakland, in September of 1951. I cried for a bit, then sought out two rebels who, like me, felt they had been coerced into attending a woman's college. Sally was the most beautiful and Saran was the cleverest. We hit the bars whenever we could. Sally had been sent to Mills to get her away from a young man her family disapproved of; the irony was that he joined the army and was stationed at Fort Ord on the Monterey Peninsula and Sally ran away to meet him there on weekends, finally marrying him and living there by the beach. I fell in love with him in 1956 in New York, where I had gone to make it in Manhattan. By that time he was a father and he and Sally lived in Chicago. There was a sorry scene between us following my marriage in 1957.

I had married Alan Axelson at City Hall on Christmas Eve. Alan had to fly back to his teaching job in California after New Year's. It was then I had to face Sally's husband Mike, had to admit I had done something on impulse, something I might regret. I said I'd done it because the landlord threatened to throw us out of the apartment for immoral behavior. Mike said it wouldn't have happened if I'd had a part in a play. Who knows?

But I'm getting ahead of my story. I stayed at Mills for four years and got a B.A. in speech and drama. The stage at Lisser Hall is still more alive in my memory than what I did last week. I played Andromache in *Trojan Women,* Desdemona in *Othello,* Madame Zinida in *He Who Gets Slapped,* Clytemnestra in *Electra,* Mistress Lovitt in *Sir Fopling Flutter or the Man of Mode,* Gwendolyn Fairfax in *The Importance of Being Earnest,* Mary in *Juno and the Paycock* and so many more it all flows into a long dream of days and nights spent inside the thoughts and words of playwrights. Classes with Elizabeth Pope in the English Department, with Dr. Walker, who selected my short story for the freshman prize, with Miriam Goldeen, who taught me more about the Greeks than even she knew, with Dr.

Jennifer at age seventeen

Headley, who went to the central valley in the summers to work alongside the migrant laborers in the fields, and with Evaline Wright, my advisor and acting teacher, who found me the money to continue at Mills after my father had thrown me out of his house after my sophomore year because he read my diaries.

I had to work seventeen hours a week in the library during my junior year and I was carrying a heavy academic load as well as acting in plays every night. One evening I was sleep starved and so terribly tired I had what seemed to be an out-of-body experience. I was walking under the trees after a long stretch in study hall. I had not spoken to anyone for perhaps thirty-six hours. I got lost in time/space and stood looking at an ancient street lamp. I seemed to be in another dimension, in another time and place. Later I felt quite rested, but had the lingering feeling that I was trying to find something I had lost, some other existence or even another person I might have been.

During the year following my father's rejection, I lived with my sister Rolly in her apartment close to Mills. She was by this time a medical records librarian. We did not get along very well because my friends filled her apartment and she had to clean up after our late night parties. In hindsight I can see how she was trying to help me, even though she had only a studio apartment and a modest job at that point. I was able to move back on campus with a full scholarship my senior year. My father came to see me finally, after I was back in Ethel Moore. In my diaries I had said some rather unkind things about him, called him a big ape, a veritable Neanderthal in fact. In the '50s, we didn't know that Neanderthals were relatively benign. It seems so absurd, looking back now. Dysfunctional family behavior is so comic, unless it's your own family.

I have gone back to Mills from time to time. The eucalyptus trees are still there. Of course, what I am really searching for is the feelings I had when I was so young. I fell in love a lot. The first one was Bud Moss, an actor I found at Parks Air Force Base. Bud did a number of plays with us before departing for Hollywood, marrying Ruth Roman and becoming an agent for Carolyn Jones. Buddy didn't love me for long. He loved Laura, the most beautiful woman I have ever seen in my life. Laura played the ingenue in the Russian play *He Who Gets Slapped*

(I played the Lion Tamer). She is a ballerina in the play, and she rides bareback with an acrobat, the man she loves. He turned out to be my children's father, my husband, Alan Axelson. Alan came to Mills through the good efforts of my dear friend, the late Lisa Lauterer, an actress who was married to Arch Lauterer, then head of the Mills Drama Department. Lisa persuaded Alan to play the role of a Scandinavian road builder in Ibsen's play *Little Eyolf*. I figure she set me up because before I ever saw him she said, this guy is going to look terrific in mountain boots! Alan and I became lovers when I was twenty. We married three years later.

Alan was nearly thirty when I met him. His marriage was coming apart. I have to say that I have probably done him no justice through the years. He gave me two sons, each of whom is infinitely subtle, eternally interesting to know, watch, love, and enjoy. My complaints about my husband were enough to separate us in 1966. I am not being self-effacing or noble when I say that the fault probably lay more with my

As Desdemona in Othello, *Mills College, 1954*

own character, my own restlessness and search for the ineffable. I had run off the rails in the last year of the marriage and found that having an affair while married felt wretched. It came about because I was susceptible, because I was lonely and housebound with small children. Or perhaps it was just a chapter in a life that has always spun me out of control.

The summer before my senior year at Mills, before Alan and I became lovers, I had flirted with the Beat culture in North Beach. I had the leading role (Dorine) in Molière's *Tartuffe*, which was staged at the old Bella Union Theatre by a group called the Interplayers. The *San Francisco Chronicle* called me "a natural actress," whatever that is, and I hung out at the Black Cat and made the scene. I had an affair with the play's director, Jules Rothman. Opening night we found ourselves together in a beatific house in West Marin. Jules was forty and I learned quickly that he was not marriage material. In the 1950s, most women's lives were still muffled with fears of pregnancy, with need for financial security, with existential dread of falling through the cracks in a social order that was cruel to women who broke the rules. (Not that much has changed.) I looked around at the women who were the support systems for Beat poets, women who had to do it all. I balked.

It's curious that many years later, after my divorce, I renewed my affair with Jules and found the shoe was on the other foot, so to speak. He found me more attractive and more skilled, sexually speaking. Funny, because I no longer felt real love for him. Dorothy Parker's quips come to mind. "I love them, till they love me."

Well, there's more to life than love. Someone told me that. Maxim Gorky writes: "Love is the failure of the mind to understand nature." Perhaps. Love can be a disease. The last time I felt the pain of betrayal, the bitterness that goes so deep there is no being in the same room with him ever again, I was fifty-seven. If I'm cured, if I'm free to look *with* love from now on, instead of looking *for* love, then I have truly made it as a woman of the wise blood.

Bad faith between man and woman has been a theme in my poetry and fiction. With time, I have tried to move away from the world of men and women and into the world of reality which is a little more complex. Susan B. Anthony wrote: "When love is tyranny, revolution is order." Women must first be free. Gender justice cuts both ways. Sexual politics is a paradigm for all political struggle. Gaia belief systems reject the dominator model which still oppresses both women and men. Fascism begins and ends at home, in the heart of the family. The personal is political and the task of the poet is to transmute the truth into something that can be solace to the soul. Thought breaks the heart, but passion can keep it beating.

The longing is all that lasts. That's why poetry is the only way out for those of us who insist on losing what we love. Whether this is neurosis or nonsense is not for me to say. For some of us, love is passion, and passion is suffering. Perhaps that's why we come to solitude as the cure for loneliness. Solitude is a kind of religion. I have always practiced it. Sometimes it was hard won, sometimes brief. When I was a college student, I never had a roommate. As a single mom, I stopped the car on my way home from teaching to sit by the ocean for an hour before picking up my children. Whether it is the stolen hour, or the surfeit of days I have now, it is precious beyond all else.

The payoff for the writer, for this writer anyway, is in the memory bank. Among my souvenirs, I find moments that rerun and fast forward so brightly I hesitate to seek any new experience for fear I will dim the glow of so much in the past. Most of my memories are ecstatic. Even more are just colorful, just human comedy. The fatuous '50s were more fun than you might think. I see myself playing the muse of history in a dreadful production celebrating the centennial of Mills College. I see the early morning fog when we had been up all night in San Francisco dressed in our Beatnik black with kohl around the eyes, and jazz jams till dawn and angst for the memory of the Jackpot, that gay bar down the alley from the India House, and for drives down the coast with ghosts in every cypress tree and cedar trees as sacred as stone. Big Sur and Carmel where my children's father went to high school and got out just in time to go to Japan for the end of World War II. And treks to Bolinas and to Mendocino, to the Pygmy Forest there and the Keltic twilight even here in California where you can hear the voices of ancient peoples around the redwoods where the tree stumps are burnt blue black and like hearths. And today, in the 1990s, I have friends up and down the coast, crash pads and even comfort zones like the hideouts in Half Moon Bay.

Cease, we said. Whenever we got to slicing the old philosophical salami a bit too thin, we said CEASE! and went back to the facts. Let us seek truth from facts: North Beach was our bohemian beat. The men at the Black Cat who held hands and sang, "God Bless Us Nelly Queens!" The jazz, the glass windows painted over in the restaurant called The Iron Pot, and the low-rent ease with which we moved from place to place. The eccentrics, the eclectics, the elitists, the collage of characters who cared, who gave a damn.

Sitting at the bar, top of the Mark Hopkins hotel, Korean war veterans thick in all the mirrors; mostly escorted by men old enough to be my father. Little black velvet hat with veil. Black sheath dress. Black underwear. Years later, in 1957, I got married in black. Whiskey sours and sharkskin dresses.

Why is it hard to remember the marriage? A decade of denial? The long red nails that

In 1957, the year of her marriage to Alan Axelson

vanished forever during the birth of my first child in 1960. Medical problems: cervical cancer, surgery, all of it too traumatic to write about. Just get it over with. Second child because they told me I couldn't, or shouldn't. No one writes about births and blood and all the stress of babies. Not in 1960. I've tried. The results were such a bore, no one wanted to listen anymore. And publication is still a problem.

In 1961, Bob died. It was a few months after both of us had spent the night at Brookside Hospital, me with a miscarriage and Bob with a trauma from a fight. The night before he died, it seems he got into another brawl at a bar down on San Pablo Avenue in Richmond. In the morning he drove to the Yolo County prison hospital where he was treating the inmates; apparently a brain hemorrhage killed him while he was at work.

At this time I had one baby and was trying for another. Medical complications kept me in a fugue state about this time, and I hardly remember what I felt. I do remember Bob's silence at his own funeral. And his voice that is now in my mouth. I went to my sister's house in Hayward for the night. She lived in a cul de sac in the woods with many sheep and other creatures. Her husband built the place and called it Cum Dingle. My children spent their weekends there for many years. It is now a public park and a refuge for threatened wildlife, especially wounded wolves and owls kept in tall cages; it's called Sulphur Creek Nature Center. I was alone there after the funeral and with no one to stop me, I drank too much whiskey and danced to the soundtrack from *Zorba the Greek*. Must have looked odd in my black maternity smock.

Divorce. Some things from this time I will take to my grave. Moral black matches, and a stygian black lotus. Truth may not be stranger than fiction, but it's often more lurid. My rhinestone era; all those alcoholic spasms we called love affairs. So many of us were illusion factories in 1966. The flower children of the pan sexual revolution. Followed our bliss, right to the bottom of the bottle, some of us. Read our Wilhelm Reich: my own quip was, an orgasm a day keeps the psychiatrist at bay. Sexual freedom is a contradiction in terms. As the poet Edna St. Vincent Millay put it: "Whether or not we find what we are seeking is idle, biologically speaking." Brightness falls from the air;

*Husband, Alan, shown in a 1945
photo taken in Japan*

Lesbians have died young and fair. We sure gave it a shot.

The picture in my mind is of the Caffe Mediterraneum on Telegraph Avenue in Berkeley. Male chauvinist prigs who cruise the scene for vulnerable young women. Ah, I tell the students that education is the willful acquisition of vulnerability. That's why it's so dangerous. We thought we were going to be free, free at last! Hippie heaven and beatnik bliss in a world where we could make money funny, dump the depressions of the age of anxiety, live in the moment, make love instead of war, never quite understanding that we were riding for a fall.

For the better part of a year, I slipped into Berkeley whenever I could. The end of my marriage meant moving back to the place where I could imagine myself as a real person.

Lafayette, California, was my last suburban home. I lived on Janet Lane. It was a very pretty house. I did a few plays in the local theatre. The world was waking up. I was reading James Baldwin. My husband wasn't. I saw a

French/BBC TV production, *The Mills of the Gods,* about what American military forces were doing in Vietnam. I didn't want to go on living where I was, doing what I was doing. I had picked up a teaching credential at U.C. Berkeley in the late '50s and had done some substitute teaching. I made the leap back into the world. I put the children in the car and drove to Berkeley. I found an apartment on the border between Oakland and Berkeley. My side of the street was mostly white residents. The other side of the street was mostly black folks. My next-door neighbor had five sons. She did child care. I got jobs in the Oakland public schools. I still remember the first time I stepped off the curb to join a political demonstration.

Bob Dylan and Joan Baez are my emotional food. I take the name Stone. "And I shall find a white stone and in that stone shall be a new name." It's the only word in the English language that says what it means, means what it says? Or it's my birthplace at Stonehenge? I begin to push my mystique. Freud brought Virginia Woolf a narcissus the only time they met. Like Narcissus, I fall in love with my own reflective soul.

Poets enter my life. One day I am outside the U.C. Art Museum where I have taken my children to play in a metal sculpture: "the world split open" it's called, and it spoke to me then as now. Sitting on the grass I see Bruce Hawkins selling copies of anthologies written by members of the Berkeley Poets Workshop. He stands by the Durant Street gate and I ask him where the poets meet and I go to hear them and I offer my ravings and I am hooked for life.

Teaching modern dance at Castlemont High School in 1967 after the so-called race riots. The days of the Black Panthers and the assassinations. The death of little Bobby Hutton (his sister Judy at my school when it happened and the unkind words in the teacher's room) and the fear and paranoia everywhere as people struggled to be wise and lost it when the pressure was on. Sahara Baldwin, the kid whose rock group was called The Mighty Aggressions. And the rise of paramilitary police forces in response to breakfast programs in the black community. Huey Newton's book, *Revolutionary Suicide,* explaining that a revolutionary is wide awake, knows the score, but goes for social justice anyway. A reactionary suicide, on the other hand, internalizes what society says about him, dies a victim of the system that created him. Sadly, Newton himself failed to achieve his romantic goal of revolutionary suicide. But his book still sits on my shelf. So many lives wasted because of fear. My best mentor was Roosevelt Brown, aged fifteen. He educated me. I thought I could teach him something that might save his ass. But in the end we were both laughing. BBC English wasn't his thing. Ebonics then was not even something we could argue about, to say nothing of study. Brown gave me the Gullah proverb: "Done been in sorrow's kitchen, and licked all the pots clean."

After a few years, I was purged from the Oakland Public Schools. It was simple hubris. I didn't really want to be there. I went to Herb Kohl's workshops at his alternative school and hung out with Collingwood August, an African scholar who called himself Herb's Man Friday. We worked out a unit on the distinctions between Christian fairy tales (good and evil as pretty and ugly, etc.) and African or Eastern tales in which the truth is never black or white and in which blame for human ills is shared by the whole community.

When my principal saw what I was doing in the classroom, I knew my time was up. He was an ex-football player, played for the Rams. Had a heart attack a few years after I left. Died young. He told me not to use the word "black" in the classroom. The students asked me why I taught Du Bois when their black teachers didn't. I bought a class set of paperbacks (Richard Wright's *Black Boy*) and got called on the carpet for dictating curriculum. I did honestly try to talk to students, talk about their real problems. But when the lid has been on so tight for so long, things just explode in your face. I wish it were better today. There is more free expression, but I am not sure there is any more depth of understanding, any deep desire to love one another and to acknowledge our shared fate.

The years following my divorce were romantic and revolutionary. They were also reckless and rough on my children as well as on my own expectations that life would become comfortable when I found my true context, my life as a Berkeley radical with money enough to help all my friends. When this scenario failed to materialize, I retreated to Albany, essentially a suburb of Berkeley, where life was easier for single mothers with pubescent sons.

The scores of people who passed through my life during those turbulent times are the subjects of stories, poems, and even of a novel. Astonishing women and men who became friends and lovers for a few days, a few years, or even for life. I met Jean Shelton, a lifetime friend, and we worked together at The Berkeley Repertory Theatre when it was in its nascent stage. She is now one of San Francisco's favorite acting teachers, and her school is at the heart of the Bay Area's theatre community. She and I managed a trip to Europe in 1989 and spent a year in Bolinas in the mid-'80s. Bolinas is the sort of seaside village that city folk like me imagine to be the ultimate escape, the refuge from stress and the tensions of urban living. My younger son, Peter, lives in Bolinas these days. His thirty-fifth birthday is August 21, 1997. I am planning for this event, even as I write.

After I was fired from my job as an English teacher in the Oakland public schools, I substituted in the Berkeley schools for two years and finally took a job typing and answering phones for a group of psychiatric physicians connected with Herrick Hospital in Berkeley. I stayed on for six years, watching the workings of psychiatry backstage. The work was strangely quiet after the riot of the schools. All messages were passed on in writing. I had an office upstairs where I was alone most of the day, and the window gave me a view of the trees. I talked with patients on the phone. I was so good at this, I decided to try radio.

In 1981, I began doing programs for Pacifica Public Radio. The first one dealt with female genital mutilation as it was perceived and resisted by Dr. Nawal el Saadawi, the Egyptian physician and activist who wrote *The Hidden Face of Eve* and numerous other books.

I discovered I was a closet introvert. I turned to poetry, feminism, film, and became a culture vulture as well as a critic. Over the years, my voice has become part of my community. Even the late Herb Caen quoted me in his column in the *San Francisco Chronicle*. My favorite quip appeared when I published a novel, *Telegraph Avenue Then*, just when the Los Angeles insurrection was sending waves of street disturbances through Berkeley. I had planned a book party in a downtown art gallery, and the shops and cinema next door had shut down and boarded up by 7 P.M. I simply put a sign in the window and went home. The sign read:

Book Party Cancelled Due to the Fall of Western Civilization. Someone sent the quote to Caen who seemed to think I was joking.

Chronology is helpful when we look back over our experience. The truth is, lives are like plays. Our acts being seven stages? I wrote a long poem in the '80s, using the years 1933 (birth), 1944 (end of the war and then mother's death), 1955 (graduation from college), 1966 (divorce), 1977 (first publication in national magazine, *Mother Jones*), 1988 (last love and final decision to convert to Zen minimalism and even get rid of the cat), 1999 (the seventh and final stage?). But life is never labels; the form is fun to draw on white pages, name and color and frame on the wall, in books, even pictures. What actually happened is an altogether different reality.

In 1978, I moved into a brown shingle mansion on Florence Street in Berkeley. Although I was distracted by the ambulances shrieking into the emergency room at Alta Bates Hospital, the location was serene and even elegant. This period allowed me to get in touch with my dark side. My notebooks were full of sketches and poems about Lilith. I had come to the realization that I was not going to find real companionship with any of the lovers who came my way. I remember a metal sculptor who felt quite domestic, with all his ex-wives and daughters. He gave me a collection of rare photos of Franz Kafka, so he must have understood my emotional state at the time. He was comfortable in the sense that his misogyny was the ordinary old-fashioned kind. He loved women. As many as possible. But these echoes of others seemed unreal. The real people seem to be my parents, my siblings, and my children. This has not been wise, necessarily, but it's late in the day to change my script. I ask myself if I could have loved women? But that is another book. Sensual life is the best life. Ecstasy, and the music and magic that go with the passionate devotion to another human being. But after a while, the Cupid and Psyche story kicks in for me and I find that I turn on the light at night, take a good hard look at my lover, and he splits. Remember, in that story it is Psyche's sisters who give her the lamp, candle, light that reveals Eros (Cupid) in his full dimensions.

One of the icons that still remains on my desk is a photograph taken on the Emeryville mudflats in the 1960s. The photographer is Bill Jackson, a black poet with a paranoid pose, one of those who wore himself out with resistance to ghosts. In the photograph there is a collage sculpture of wood with the evening light striking through the center; an image that feels crucifixion, a kind of epiphany. I keep it because it speaks to me. I sometimes wish that Bill and I hadn't been pickled in the crimes of our generation. Years of one-night stands because we never trusted each other, not really. Nothing is black and white.

It is a comfort to study the myths that explain our lives. Even when they are lies. I ask my friends to tell me their three favorite fairy tales, legends, even films they relate to with deep emotion. It's a shorthand to the soul. Carl Jung took it too seriously but it's an aid to literature. When writers get psychiatric, it's not so damaging as when doctors and therapists do what they do with drugs and shock treatment.

I asked my close friend (since 1976), the poet Alta, about her favorite stories. She chose Nancy Drew, Superwoman, and Cinderella. My own three favorites would be Hans Christian Andersen's *The Little Mermaid* (masochism and transcendence), the Greek myth of Psyche and Eros, especially as illustrated by the nineteenth century's Arthur Rackham, and the movie, *The Red Shoes* by Powell and Pressburger, made in Britain in 1948. This film continues to fascinate me because of the many interpretations which can be made: adolescent take was that love is worth any sacrifice; then the male oppression of the female object (dancer) is seen

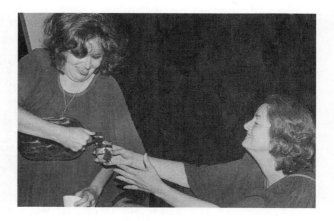

The author (left) pouring wine for Marion Scott during the production of Stone's play Three Hands Clapping, *Berkeley Stage Company, 1976*

in the behavior of the impresario (Anton Walbrook). Finally, the shoemaker himself, the one who created the shoes, the creative drive which took the woman on her path to destruction. Endless prism of possibilities.

In the late '70s, I am the poetry editor at Alta's Shameless Hussy Press. I do lots of one-woman plays and poetry readings at which my favorite persona is Lilith. My pal Sally Sleepwell writes short sketches for the two of us. Sally is so wise, so funny, everything special that came out of the '60s. Another woman from this period is my beloved Teresa Reitinger. She is still my touchstone for all that is authentic, even holy. She is an ex-nun who came to Berkeley, met a madman, had two children and became the kind of saint we saw in the '60s—someone for whom love was a verb.

Most of what I wrote in those days was inspired by these Lilith women. I saw them as prophets. They fled into the desert, into the wilderness, and were nourished from the face of the serpent. I have found only one reference to Lilith in the Bible. It's Isaiah 34:14:

> The wild-cat shall meet with the jackals
> And the satyr shall cry to his fellow,
> Yea, Lilith shall repose there
> And find her a place of rest

In 1977

In 1975, I got an M.A. in creative writing from San Francisco State. Fun to be in school twenty years after Mills. My years at U.C. Berkeley getting the teaching credential were very grim. That was 1959 and I had no heart for the work. At S.F. State I did an independent study with Kay Boyle. Grandiose woman, but deeply committed. I remember she disapproved of Gertrude Stein. (Said Stein paid the Nazis in France to leave her alone.) I did my orals in Stein. She wrote, "Patriarchal poetry makes no mistake." I discovered she was my favorite language poet: "What is poetry and if you know what poetry is what is prose." As Walt Whitman destroyed thirteenth-century verse forms, so Gertrude Stein, in the twentieth century, took an axe to syntax. She wrote, "If you are a thinker, you will change the language. You will not use the words the way the others do."

We fought to change the status of women at S.F. State in those years. We wanted an undergraduate major in women's studies. Kay Boyle told me the women were "combative" and I agreed. I wish I had been able to persuade her to be their mentor. When I suggested it, she said, "They haven't read Marianne Moore."

Before leaving Berkeley for Albany in the mid '70s, I lived at the corner of Oregon and Old Grove Streets. One of the reasons I moved was an assault, a rape which I suffered when a stranger broke into my ground-floor apartment through a window at three o'clock in the morning. I didn't report the rape, either because I was too traumatized or because I was afraid the police might target my lover, who was also black. My state of mind at the time was defensive. Siege mentality.

A few months later the rapist returned. This time I called the cops. The police broke the window used to enter the apartment. They also took me to Herrick Hospital Emergency to see a doctor, and I was terrified my sister would see the report because she worked in the medical records library at that hospital. My lover insisted I keep in touch with the police because they could watch the house, could "protect" me in some way. He was wrong about that. He also asked me if I hadn't met this man, the rapist, at the Steppenwolf, a popular bar on San Pablo. My usual hangouts were the Blind Lemon Bar and the Albatross, both on San Pablo where the action was.

The police took away my best bedclothes and my favorite dressing gown, a special garment I had bought at the Persian Caravan. They said anything the criminal touched was evidence. Indeed. I never got my things back, although I went to the police station several times.

I had a mild crackup about this time. It tied in with being purged from the Oakland schools and with some depression and burnout due in no small part to the roughing up my children were getting in the neighborhood. There was even a dog attack on my younger son which required stitches. It was obviously time to retreat and retrench. Some of the experiences from this time found their way into a collection called *Loose Leaves from a Little Black Book*. A later version was published in 1992 as *Telegraph Avenue Then*.

When I stopped teaching full-time, I began writing columns for the progressive papers and alternative magazines. I wrote television criticism for the women's paper *Plexus* for four years as well as contributing poems and profiles of literary women. I wrote a column called Bread and Roses for the Berkeley paper *Grassroots* for three years. Film criticism appeared in the *Berkeley Monthly* for three years in the early '80s and my last film commentary was published for eight months in 1995 in the *Berkeley Insider*. Film and TV criticism was synthesized in the collection *Mind over Media* from Cayuse Press. The collection which won the Before Columbus American Book Award in 1989 was *Stone's Throw:* an eclectic selection of literary and political essays covering ten years of my work.

Writing goes well when I have a reading scheduled. The pleasures of expression are needed to lift me out of the melancholy that comes when I write. It's lonely, talking to yourself.

Male children are a curious responsibility for a single mom. Mine are fire signs, like me. I'm a Sagittarius, Paul's an Aries, and Peter's a Leo. I think that means we understand each other rather well, but that doesn't mean we're at all alike. My sons provide me with some source material for stories, but in general I don't like to intrude upon their privacy. Once I published an essay on the mother/son issue. I thought it was rather clever. I described Paul's love of football (short-lived) and said that he worried about the mobility of the quarterback and I worried about the integrity of the image cluster; what we had in common was worry. The editor who used the piece called on the phone to ask for a group picture of the three of us. I was horrified. Paul asked if it needed to be done for the money, and so forth. He is sensible and would have done it if I asked. I told the editor we were three loners. As it turns out, we are still single, the three of us. Born in 1960 and 1962, these men are my touchstones for just about everything.

After I got my M.A. I did a number of writers' workshops and discovered that teaching drove me to despair. I spent my time at poetry readings and getting my own work published in all those journals and little magazines which nourish those of us who long to see our words typeset. Then I retreated to Zen minimalism, muttering about the arrogance of expression. Ultimate ambiguity of all human endeavor in an age of annihilation.

Berkeley's street poet, the Bubble Lady, Julia Vinograd, tried to cheer me up sometimes. She said we could stop saying poetry, start saying *spoken word*! In the late '70s, we read the poems at La Salamandra on Telegraph Avenue. One night, after an absence of several months during which I had tried to resurrect an old love affair, I came back to La Salamandra in my feathers and black cape. Julia wrote me a poem on her napkin:

> The power behind an intentionally broken
>   face
> The blue lips tearing control like a piece of
>   meat,
> with out thrown wrist turning an abstract
>   objection
> into a personal bite and the sort of affair
>
> nobody has these days,
>
> anymore than New Yorkers buy the Brooklyn
>   Bridge
> and jump off it
> in that order
> respectively
>
> What the hell
> Jenny you been gone too long

Julia knows my deepest need is for betrayal. How else can I escape, year after year. I can't do time in someone else's life, anymore than he can.

The work that synthesized during this period began in journals. The truth will tell, if you let it soak long enough. The past decomposes, the flesh falls from the bones, and you get to the marrow of things. Symbols surface and memory becomes mythos.

Journal writing is elliptical—my thoughts skip like stones across the surface of life. Like a seascape seen from a moving train, the beauty is glimpsed, not grasped. The trivial and the profound get equal time.

Synthesis, like style, has something to do with sedimentation; the settling of the sand of thought and the leaves of emotion into a compost heap of prose from which a poem may sprout, or a story ferment. As Gertrude Stein wrote: "mud settles."

In a journal it is possible to gnaw on the existential bone all day, and then use that bone to make stone soup for supper. Poems are found there and they die there. Trauma reflected upon in tranquility can produce stunning insights—literary light! It can also produce maudlin rubbish.

When I began to excavate my journals, it was all I could do to separate the garbage from the trash. But I always return to the notebooks because they contain the authentic feelings, the heart's blood. I am fascinated with the notebooks of other writers, always more so than with their finished works. I am a pathologist, like my father? And the formal depresses me: "The way to recognize a dead word is that it exudes boredom," wrote Anaïs Nin in *The Novel of the Future.*

Today's experimental poetry is exclusionary. In the '70s, there was hope that women might change the language. Gertude Stein led the way. Virginia Woolf wrote that all the older forms had become hardened by the time the woman writer took up the pen, but the novel might still be soft in her hands. Woolf suggests that the novel might be an outlet for the poetry in woman: "if a writer were a free man and not a slave, if he could base his work upon his own feeling and not upon convention, there would be no plot, no comedy, no tragedy, no love interest or catastrophe in the accepted style."

In 1982, I am at Briarcombe, a writer's retreat near Bolinas, just over the hills beyond San Francisco. I have with me my notebooks, and bits of the pithy play I am sure will write itself once I can be alone. I am on deadline to write a book review for the *San Francisco Chronicle;* a biography of Alfred Hitchcock which stresses his sadistic streak. By the time I finish, I realize how much I don't want to write criticism, how much I want to write my own stories.

I find a tiny room overlooking the sea, just a room and bath big enough to exist in for a year and a half. I write a novel: *Sophia, Last of the Wise.* It seems a bit like Sartre's *Nausea.* Perhaps I will go back to Bolinas again some day and write another novel. Bits of *Sophia* have been published here and there, but no one seems to want the whole package.

Journal passages from the Bolinas days find their way into the *Wormwood Review.* One piece was called "Notes from the Back of Beyond." I wrote a column for the *Bolinas Hearsay News* and it was personal and idiosyncratic; the style I use now for my column in the local women's paper, "Mama Bears News and Notes," which I have written for three years.

The village of Bolinas is still very special for me. It is more like my childhood than my childhood was; there I can sit on the sand and watch the evening light, the seals in the lagoon, and if I wait till the sun sets I can imagine the ancient peoples who lived there before the Europeans came. The native people didn't live there year 'round, I'm told. Only came there for their health at certain times of the year. I like it best in the fall, in the Indian summer when it's warm.

It is November, 1985, and I am a writer-in-residence at Steepletop, home of the poet Edna St. Vincent Millay. After Vincent's death in 1950, the house and 650 acres of these Berkshire hills in upstate New York became a retreat for writers and painters.

The thorn apple, or jimsonweed, a member of the deadly nightshade family, is a recurring image in the poetry of Millay. The thorn in my apple this month is other writers at the colony, one who can't empty a mousetrap and another who refuses to make her bed. Our housekeeper is a young mother whose husband is sick and whose children are hard to handle. She is also in charge of the ninety-two-year-old sister of Vincent, Norma Millay, who is ill and has to be taken to and from the hospital on cold mornings. Finally, I tell the writer who is cross because the bedsheets haven't been changed that writers should make their own beds; it's *experiential.*

I take off with a cheerful woman painter and we drive to Stockbridge, Massachusetts, where she visits Norman Rockwell's paintings at the Old Corner House. She tells me how Norman started out animated and ended up atrophied; that is, he was an enthusiast who stiffened up with time, with the arthritis of illustration.

Next morning I walk into the woods. Time to dust the graves. Here is Cora, Vincent's mother, born 1864, died 1931. Vincent lies beneath a great stone next to her husband, Eugen Boissevain 1880-1949. Vincent was born on February 22, 1892. She's a water sign, a nymph—Ondine? She used to read her poetry dressed in green scarves, a red-haired leprechaun of love. I put leaves on a milk-white stone near the graves: "in the grave, no flower."

Her spirit hovers by the deserted swimming pool. The place is overgrown, covered with detritus. There is a little bar in a lean-to, a drink in the afternoon in this grove with a statue of Eros. Nearby there is a tiny writing room, a house from a fairy tale with her sofa, chair, table, lamp, ashtray, and *clock* all enshrined for visitors to sigh over. The wood is still stacked outside for her stove.

I feel the cold, here in the snow, with deerhunters stalking the backroads, looking for something to kill. Vincent's voice from the grave: "Give me *thy* coat, get into mine."

In 1988, David Volpendesta writes the most flattering, well, supportive, review of my work that I have ever received. This profile appears in *In These Times.* I make a file of all the swell reviews and kind words I have received from critics and writers, as well as packets of letters received at KPFA Pacifica Radio. This is what I have to show for myself, as we said in school. Best of all is to walk the streets of Berkeley and know so many of the inhabitants of my village.

It is June 4, 1989. I am in Washington, D.C. With me is my dear friend, Maggie Switzer. (Maggie founded Cayuse Press in the 1980s. She died at the age of forty-seven in 1995.) We fly through the streets of this city neither

Sons Paul (left) and Peter Axelson, 1996

*Jennifer Stone (second from right) with four other playwrights
at the Rasputin Theatre in San Francisco, 1991*

of us has ever seen before. Then we collapse from the heat and allow ourselves to drink from the little stash in our hotel room. We have come to collect my Before Columbus American Book Award for an essay collection published in 1988 by North Atlantic Books.

On the plane, I tried to write an acceptance speech to deliver at the National Press Club. Leafing through my book *Stone's Throw*, I underlined some of my hopeful phrases sprinkled among the perjury, some fragment that speaks to the future.

By the time I spoke to the audience, the television sets in the hall just outside the conference room were shrieking the news of Chinese students dying in Tiananmen Square. I tried to address this tragedy even as it was happening. None of the other writers had done so. Later, over drinks, a Chinese American poet tells me that it is an old custom, this mass murder of dissidents in China; ten thousand scholars are as nothing if the emperor is displeased, and so forth.

This sort of talk reminds me of how conventional some radical writers can be. We have come together from all over the United States, and here we are in the capital, all seated at separate tables. The parable of the tribes? I find myself with a group of expatriate Irish writers, mostly male academics. Awkward and invisible in this context, I am rescued by Barbara Smith (founder and editor of Kitchen Table: Women of Color Press in New York); Barbara is a radical lesbian feminist who has connected with me through my programs for Pacifica Radio. She integrates me for the evening, and what's more I am introduced from the podium as a generalist! How hard it is to remain an outlaw, not to submit to a hardening of the categories.

It is October, 1989. It is a week before the Loma Prieta earthquake and I am in love again. Is it possible? Probably not. Who was it said the Irish use words for everything except expressing feelings? I suppose it is my father, his wounded past or even his race memory going back to the potato famine, to the time when he or his ancestors were inconsolable, when his longings were denied or traduced, and he became a fatalist. The Irish seek refuge in facade. My first acting teacher in college said I had a veneer an inch thick. It's my art form, I told her. A means of expression is all the heart needs. Sam Beckett: "I am sorrow's bone." Catastrophe is cyclical and eternal. In the land of Ire, the wrath of poets never ends. It isn't that the Irish are unwilling to say what they feel, it is only that they know such a task is beyond them. They know the stones may weep, but when they do, the soul in the stone is laughing. Only sounds make sense, and song makes sense without lies. Words cannot be what silence can do. The secret is in the stone.

It is 1991 and I am in the Manhattan apartment of my friend, Edith Konecky. She has gone to the MacDowell Colony for two months, so I have her lovely space to write my play, the one about women's inner lives and outer anguish. The play I've been writing for twenty years is all spread out on the coffee table and my solitude is complete. I have time to write several pages of tentative dialogue before I turn on CNN and discover that George Bush has started a war in the Persian Gulf. Ancient Mesopotamia was the place where blood feuds began. Well, one of the places. I telephone Prairie Miller at the *People's Weekly World.* I find myself with protectors over at St. John the Divine. My time to go within, to dredge up a drama from my deepest being, all wasted as I join the chorus of those who act out their parts (as in a Greek tragedy) by taking to the streets, by saying to the rulers, *hubris!* blind arrogance! Always the energy spent in wailing, in hand wringing. Is it possible to hold opposing ideas in the mind at the same time and continue to function? Can we be on the barricades one day and back in the books the next?

I am struggling with chaos theory and stone soup. My last poem dealt with the years of Persephone's *hegira.* The Greek word *hegira* defines a journey, a flight, or a trip, especially when undertaken as a means of escaping from an undesirable or dangerous environment (earth); or as a means of arriving at a highly desirable destination (hell).

Impossible to write poetry in a late age. The market economy is the latest great poem, a metaphor to puzzle on. Free market feminism is the subject of my last essay in 1997. Oh, and a few thoughts on Ebonics. In 1871, George Eliot wrote: "Correct English is the slang of prigs." Primate grandiosity is still with us in 1997. We still use language as a class marker. I believe my species is getting a little wiser with time, but I doubt if this will save us. Too much millennium in my diet?

This last decade of the twentieth century, this *fin de siecle,* seems to me a rerun of the past, or perhaps of my past? The mauve decade, the gay decade, the synthesis that comes before the new age begins. Jean Houston in *The Mythic Life* writes that this is not a new age yet. She says we are the people of the parenthesis. I call it the hinge of history. She has a chapter called "Buddy, Can You Paradigm?" Nice phrase for the '90s.

A letter from a friend in Maine. She is afraid critics will find her work (fiction) sentimental. I write her a note saying perhaps there are worse things.

Then I throw away some of my own worst work because I know just how she feels. What a horror, to think someone might discover that, in a moment of weakness, I wrote a love letter.

Let's hope that critics still know the difference between false sentiment and Eros; as Diane di Prima wrote: "The flesh knows better than the spirit, what the soul has eyes for."

In these sad times, the pathology of the spirit demands an autopsy, a psychic surgery. What are we becoming? Some men mistake cruelty for character, and some women find celebrity is sexier than sex.

A bonfire is a fire for burning bones. I use the last hours of the last day of every year to set out the bones, the things I want to burn. Pages, of course, and the letters, the dead letters and yellow tickets. I try to light the fire at midnight. Often I do this on the Day of Dead, All Souls Day, the Keltic Samhain. What hippie doesn't love Halloween?

Mostly I save things from the fire at the last moment. Like Pablo Neruda, I am a collector of shells, stones, amulets, beads, pictures, costumes, feathers, toys, leaves, snakeskins, rocks, sand, any- and everything that reminds me of earth spirits, of chthonic gods and elemental forces. (Will there still be vital reality as well as virtual reality in this postindustrial future that's coming?)

My last libation is drunk to Emily Brontë, who has been my psychiatrist and muse. For the poet, the lament and the praise song are one and the same. The beach fires that lit my childhood during dark nights by sacred grottos, these are the same fires I see on the moors, on the black sea that is women's history.

BIBLIOGRAPHY

Over by the Caves, Berkeley Poets Workshop, 1977, New World Press, 1995.

Mind over Media: Essays on Film and Television, Cayuse Press, 1988.

Stone's Throw: Selected Essays, North Atlantic Books, 1988.

Telegraph Avenue Then: Loose Leaves from a Little Black Book: 1966-1977 (a memoir), Regent Press, 1992.

Contributor of short stories, book and film reviews, poems, and essays to numerous periodicals, including *Appeal to Reason, Before Columbus Review, Berkeley Insider, Berkeley Monthly, Grassroots, Hard Love, Mother Jones, Plexus, Rosebud,* and *San Francisco Chronicle.* Has also had poems and prose published in Canada and the United Kingdom in such journals as *Herizons, Irish Quarterly,* and *Tears in the Fence.* A play, *Three Hands Clapping,* was produced by the Berkeley Stage Company in 1976 and was staged again in San Francisco in 1990. Two weekly programs on literature and media, written and produced by Ms. Stone, have aired on Pacifica Public Radio (KPFA) since 1982.

Keith Waldrop

1932-

Keith and Rosmarie Waldrop, Paris, 1994

"We lov we know not what: and therfore evry Thing allures us."

—Thomas Traherne

I know, in songs, how important the words are, how the melody is—in some sense—dependent on the words. And yet I almost always listen to, for instance, Schubert (or whomever) without taking the text into account, without in some cases any idea of what the song is *about*.

It seems, generally—this partial experience of the total song—adequate.

I have taught my last class of the semester, the end of a course on versification.

I was born on Sunday.

The sound of talk in another language can be quite distinctive without one's knowing the language, without even knowing precisely what language is being spoken. I sometimes hear, on a train, or in a dream, what seems a new tongue, enunciating what are probably common-places in an incomprehensible—and, thereby, magical—message.

Keith, age two

As a child, I was moved by the sound of certain words—or, rather, combinations of words—and memorized, among others, "Thanatopsis," an adolescent work:

> To him who in the love of nature holds
> Communion with her visible forms . . .

and have carried with me for years (by now I could, I suppose, say *forever*) the resonant declaration—where the meaning seems part of the sound:

> All that tread
> The globe are but a handful to the tribes
> That slumber in its bosom.

which, as a statement, is—someone now assures me—untrue. The defunct, it seems, are a minority, present treaders outnumbering the dead and gone.[1]

My first love was theatre. In kindergarten I played Peter Rabbit—chosen for the part, I should add, because I was the smallest child in the class, the one who could most easily get under a screen representing the fence around Farmer Smith's garden.

I have always despised the pompous sound of

> And death shall have no dominion

---

[1]Is this possible? My math is not good enough to verify or disprove it.

along with its silly message.

(I can remember other pompous, and even sillier, lines: e.g., "I think continually of those who were truly great.")

As a child, I was considered sickly, though I myself never took it seriously. Whenever my mother was not hauling me off to the doctor, it was my father. He was sure I had TB—or undulant fever—or *something*.

I looked up at the doctor's shingle, open-mouthed:

THOMAS P. BUTCHER GENERAL SURGERY

And in the Emporia cemetery, I found a tombstone with the single word inscribed:

LOVELESS

I think continually of the perdurance of particles.

My father was a railroad worker—and inventor.

He claimed to have invented the refrigerator. Only, Lord Kelvin was quicker with the patent. If he—my father—had just had the money . . .

Before the war, he kept trying to produce a synthetic rubber. A certain kind of fruit fell in Emporia streets: green, apple shaped, but sort of warty, rather smelly—inedible, I always assumed. We called them Osage apples. It struck him that this wasted organism was not only plentiful but *sticky* and therefore, to his inventor's mind, suggested rubber.

He gathered and brought home, at the season they fell, loads of Osage apples and heated them on the kitchen stove, with or without other substances, for hours on end. Their stink increased. When he forgot them, as he often did, they scorched and sent up acrid smoke. The kitchen reeked.

Nothing came of it but smoke and stink and ruined pots.[2]

---

[2]He did in fact get one invention through the patent office. He patented a self-wringing mop, with a mechanism so complicated as to preclude production.

"Before the war" means, in this case, before the Second World War (I was eight-going-on-nine at the time of Pearl Harbor), but I might note that my father had already been too old to fight in the First World War.[3]

My mother and I, along with my sister Elaine and my brother Julian, went to camp meetings. One camp, I remember, had a ramshackle dormitory where Mother and Elaine had a room on the first floor, and Julian and I shared a room just above them on the second.

Julian one night brought in a bucket of water (the dormitory had no plumbing) to wash his feet and, after accomplishing this, asked me to get rid of the water.

I prepared to throw it out the window, but Julian warned me to save the soap. Not about to reach into dirty water to find a bar of soap, I gently tilted the bucket, letting the water spill to the ground in a tiny stream.

Elaine, in the room below—and, no doubt, the righteous in adjacent rooms—immediately assumed that one of us was peeing from the upper chamber.

Ah, but I was not careful enough. The soap slid from the bucket after all and landed in the newly made puddle with a *plop*.

Jehovah's Witnesses, in my childhood, used to come by the house, hoping for converts and a little cash. They carried with them, in that era, a portable phonograph from which a ten-inch 78 rpm record gave out the essentials of salvation.

"Those old Fullerites!" my mother would say. Or, sometimes, "Those old Rutherfords!"

But she did not keep them out. On the contrary, she invited them in, got between them and the door, and preached another gospel to them, out-talking the recorded Watchtower message.

They were never converted, but after a few times—going down the block—they began to circumambulate our house, like a house of sin.

My father had catchphrases he produced whenever remotely appropriate. "It won't be long now" was invariably followed by "as the butcher said when he dropped the cleaver in his lap."

Crazy was always "crazy as a peach orchard boar."

"This world—and then the fireworks."

But what did it mean, that "peach orchard boar"?

Or was it "bore"?

My father always chuckled as he said it and my mother seemed scandalized, so I assumed—as a child—it must be some sort of obscenity.

I have, to this day, no clue.

In high school,[4] I combed my hair, religiously, once a day—just before going to bed.

Professor Baker, at Kansas State Teachers College (where I was a pre-med), said I was the worst chemistry student he ever tried to teach. His being so near retirement gave the claim a certain pathos.

I was drafted (the Korean War almost over) lacking six hours of my B.A. When I was about to leave for the army, a friend composed—and performed for me—a *Pièce héroique* for organ.

It is, in my career—military and civilian—the sole note of heroism.

I try to stay out of the sun. Shade is my element.

I am given to scratching around in second-hand book stores.

There was a secondhand bookstore in Danville, Illinois, run by a crony of my brother Charles.

I scratched around in it.

An odd-shaped book—wider than tall—caught my eye. I could make nothing of the contents,

---

[3]He was born in 1881, my mother in 1898.

[4]At a fundamentalist school outside Central, South Carolina—a school I renamed Sharon for my fictionalized account in *Light While There Is Light*.

so—even though it was only fifty cents . . .

. . . I put it back.

I went away.

But it stuck in my mind, the book with the odd shape, and I went back to the dismal little store, asked the owner if he knew anything about it. He had, he said, only recently bought the store, along with its stock. Clearly, he knew little about *any* book.

I went back a third time . . .

. . . and I bought the book.

Blue cloth binding: four and three-quarter inches tall by seven and three-quarter inches wide.

Fifty cents.

"IN SARA, MENCKEN, CHRIST AND BEETHOVEN THERE / WERE MEN AND WOMEN // John Barton Wolgamot //JOHN BARTON WOLGAMOT / 1944."

No further indications.

The right margin is unjustified in a way that suggests verse—but it is clearly prose, one sentence to a page, from which names project in clusters.[5]

My first year at the University of Michigan (on the GI Bill) I entered the Hopwood contest with three manuscripts: one poetry, one fiction and, for the essay contest, an old seminar paper.

My poetry got nothing. My fiction got nothing.

The seminar paper won me six hundred dollars. I kept two hundred to live on over

(From top) Keith, his brother Julian, his brother Charles, South Carolina, 1948

the summer and sent the rest to Rosmarie for her passage to the States.

She came over in December, 1958.

To marry Rosmarie, I was first required to send her astrologer father exact coordinates of my birth: day, hour, latitude, longitude.

For something so momentous, and so personal, he did not trust himself to cast the horoscope, but sent the appropriate details—of my birth and of hers—to a master astrologer whom he revered.

We never learned what revelations he received.

Except the lucky conclusion. It is all right, said Herr Sebald, after consulting the documents. We might marry.

Rosmarie's ship was a day late because of storms on the Atlantic. When she did arrive, it

---

[5]The first page:
In its very truly great manners of Ludwig van Beethoven very heroically the very cruelly ancestral death of Sara Powell Haardt had very ironically come amongst his very really grand men and women to Rafael Sabatini, George Ade, Margaret Storm Jameson, Ford Madox Hueffer, Jean-Jacques Bernard, Louis Bromfield, Friedrich Wilhelm Nietzsche and Helen Brown Norden very titanically.

was with three large wooden crates. The customs officials glanced at her, at the crates, began to stamp them without ceremony.

Then I became visible.

They reconsidered, made her open everything, went over it all with a Geiger counter.

That evening, we went to the City Center, where Balanchine was giving his new Stravinsky ballet *Agon*, along with the Brecht-Weill *Seven Deadly Sins*.

Allegra Kent. Lotte Lenya. For a long time after—in the wilderness of Michigan—Rosmarie would point out that she was given a misleading idea of what, in the way of culture, would be available to her in America.

We lived in the last house on a dead-end street called Turner Park Court, the street named, not for a person, but from a long-disbanded *Turnverein* (Ann Arbor having a large German population). It was an extremely small house.

The walls of every room we lined with books, all but kitchen and bathroom—for fear of grease and steam.

Between grease and steam, steam seemed the less dangerous and, when the volumes reached too great an overflow, we decided to put shelves in the bathroom.

So what books should go there?

Books, we decided, with something in title or author to suggest that locus.

We began. *Ubu Roi*, of course.

The Golden Pot.

Anything by Adelaide Crapsey.

The search gained momentum. The Sitwells. The Brownings. *The Golden Ass. Privy Seal. Free Fall.*

Let It Come Down.

Finally it was hopeless, any word at all doubling its meaning with an excremental shadow.

Howards's End.

Gone with the Wind.

John Crowe Ransom was scheduled to give a lecture on "Poetry and Religion" in the Rackham auditorium, which was packed for the occasion. Most of the audience was still there when he arrived, an hour late.

"Now Poetry and Religion," Ransom began in his soft drawl, "they're these two sistahs. And they don't awl-ways git along . . . "

And then an odd thing happened. He continued to talk, and the words seemed standard English, but I could make no sense of them. I did catch once that he was quoting Valéry (or someone he called *Val*erie) and the quote, strangely, seemed nonsense also. Eventually, when I had given up, there was a sentence I thought I understood:

"Well," he said, "I've talked about poetry, now I'm going to talk about religion."

And the blur recommenced.

By this time, a surprising number of those in attendance had fallen asleep. Snores resonated from different parts of the hall. Hardly anyone had physically left, but many heads had sunk—or fallen backwards, so that they seemed to be contemplating the stars painted on the auditorium ceiling (if only their eyes had not been closed). Those still awake were shuffling in their seats. It was excruciating.

But finally it was over, to perplexed applause. I was groggy and found others also rising slowly, as if stiff from a long journey. I saw Glauco Cambon leaving and I whispered,

"Did you understand that?"

"Not a word," he bellowed. Nor, it turns out, did anyone else, although one faculty wife— one who, as Don Hope always claimed, decided on her comments ahead of time, while thinking about what dress to wear—came out with,

"Why, that makes him a Platonist, if not a downright Aristotelian!" Those around her moved away quickly, pretending not to hear.

Amid the relief of exit, the most relieved was Rosmarie. Only just arrived, listening to the great critic, she was horrified to think how she must have overestimated her command of English, thinking that indeed she must know no English at all.

After the *Evergreen Review*'s issue on the San Francisco Renaissance, and other—vaguer—reports, there was much curiosity in Michigan about the Beat Generation, its poetry, its life-style. Under the aegis of a non-existent student organization, the John Barton Wolgamot Society, we—a group of teaching fellows, including X. J. Kennedy and I[6]—decided to exploit this interest.

Posters went up (this was May 1959) announcing a reading by three poets of the said renaissance, with excerpts from a new play "with jazz accompaniment." The poets were named Ronald Whalen, Felicia Borden, and Kenneth Kant.

We thought of it as a joke, but also an experiment. We would arrange the evening to become more and more ridiculous as it went along, to see just how far we could go before the hoax became apparent and our bluff was called.

We spent hours writing biographical notes for our poets, and minutes preparing words for them to read. We imported an actress from Detroit (Don Hope must have been our contact) to play Felicia Borden. Bob Dunn, who played Whalen, was a fellow student and therefore had to be disguised, so—reverting to my theatre-ridden days in Emporia—I made him up as a black.

I played Kenneth Kant. Unlikely as it may sound, I shaved to assume my beatnik role. Bob Dunn and X. J. put my hair into pin curls and used up an entire box of Toni—enough, by the instructions, for four home permanents. Just before the performance, the pins came out and I shook my hair loose (but did not comb it), and sprayed it more or less brown. I wore a pink shirt and a white jacket with, as lapel ornament, a syringe.

This transformation accomplished, I was doubtful, thinking that few people would show up, that those who did would already be in the know, or immediately recognize either Bob Dunn or me. But entering the formal ballroom on the top floor of the Rackham building, seeing the enormous, expectant crowd, my doubts dissolved.

It was a crowd unlike any I (or the Rackham building) had seen: jeans, motorcycle jackets, bare feet, green hair—a veritable prophecy of the coming decade. They had filled the chairs, they were sitting on the floor, the windowsills.

We persuaded Norman Nelson, then in his sixties, to introduce us. He looked appalled at the audience he was facing, but bravely read the biographies we had provided. Miss Borden, he read out, had been awarded a fellowship by the American Academy of Arts and Sciences—and had turned it down. *The audience applauded.* Kenneth Kant had been arrested in San Francisco for petty larceny and narcotics violation. *Grand applause.* After nine months in federal prison, he went to Japan and entered a Zen monastery, in Yoshiwara.

Professor Nelson (who was in on the hoax), having gotten through the notes at a great clip, made a rapid exit—indeed, a sort of dash for

Waldrop as Sir Andrew Aguecheek, Kansas State Teachers College, 1951

---

[6]Along with—among others—James Camp, Dallas Wiebe, Virgil Hutton, George Kennedy, Bill Kenney.

the door—and was not seen again that evening. ("I just knew," he explained to me later, "that they were going to lynch you, and I didn't want to be there to see it.")

X. J. Kennedy, as MC, took over then, maintaining a patronizing tone, as if dissociating himself (and, by inference, the English department and the university as a whole) from these uncouth intruders. One could feel how the audience resented his tone, already siding with the poets.

Felicia Borden, whom Henry Miller, according to our poster, called "the most authentic woman voice of the late school," read poems we had thrown together one evening. Felicia was the favorite of the evening, she was so obviously sincere. By comparison, Kenneth Kant came across as a bit crass, calling upon John Crowe Ransom to ram his textures up his structures, chanting

> Yap! Yap!
> Crap in your lap!

The audience ate it up. They wanted that one over. But the more sober among them did not entirely trust Kant, fearing he might be someone merely "exploiting the movement."

The climax of the evening was Ronald Whalen's play, *The Quivering Aardvark and the Jelly of Love*. Three casts (I say to their credit) agreed to do the play, then looked at the script and backed out.[7]

At the end of the play, Lance—I, that is to say Kenneth Kant, played Lance—shot everyone on stage, then fired into the audience crying, "One for that goddam aardvark!" There was a blackout to let the corpses get offstage, and everyone connected with the performance went home, leaving the audience in the dark.

---

[7]*The Quivering Aardvark . . .* was actually based on the final scene of *Francesca da Rimini* by George Henry Boker, a nineteenth-century American Shakespeare-imitator and one of America's worst playwrights. The plot was a little changed: Boker's Francesca has, as usual, been unfaithful with her ugly husband's handsome brother Paolo—originally played by Otis Skinner; the husband, Lanciotto, kills the happy pair in blank verse. In the Whalen version, a lovely dope fiend named Prudence falls for a square called T.S. and both are murdered by the hero-hipster Lance.

The play was, if anything, more appreciated than the poems. And especially the obscurity of its ending.

"It's wonderful," one spectator was reported saying. "They give you the perfect work of art, and then—*nothing*, the *void*."

Comparative literature, at Michigan, was a program, not a department. It was, in fact, staffed by appropriate members from several departments and chaired by Otto Graf (Autograph, as we of course called him).

It took some patience to get in to see Graf—there was always a crowd of students outside his office—but once one got in he was cordial. After he had signed something or other for me, I got up to leave.

"I've been thinking," I said, on my way to the door, "about a dissertation topic."

"Oh," he said, waving me off, "there's plenty of time for that."

"I was thinking," I said, my hand on the door, "of something to do with the aesthetics of obscenity."

"Sit down," he said.

My dissertation proposal went—by Graf's suggestion—to Austin Warren.

Coming out of a long vastation, Austin Warren had married his doctor. Their courtship was a series of theological discussions between Austin, who had been (at least) Methodist, Swedenborgian, and Orthodox, and Toni, whose Swiss Protestant background had given way to an unemphatic skepticism.

(Eventually, Toni's persuasion prevailed. In his later days in Providence, Austin's faith was gone, though he seemed to have kept hope, a more fragile virtue.)

To me, he often seemed—like an earlier sage—a bit scandalized at the idea of being in a body.)

X. J. Kennedy ran into Austin, just outside the office of the head of the English depart-

Waldrop acting in George Manupelli's film Histoire du Soldat, 1964

ment. Austin asked him to deliver something to me.

"In the *English* department," Austin said loudly, projecting his words towards the office door, "there are certain *gods* who would not approve of this," and handed X. J. my proposal, carrying now a boldly scrawled "NIHIL OBSTAT" and Austin's signature.

After which, laughing, he fell down the stairs. X. J. rushed to him, helped him up, and re-

ported that he went off uninjured, still chuckling.

We sometimes caught sight of John Heath-Stubbs, not yet completely blind, standing on the sidewalk, his cigarette as always between his fingers or at his lips. He seemed to be in meditation.

Then, suddenly, he would take off at a run—frightening for those of us who realized how little he could see—and after half a block, would stop, just as suddenly, stock still, as if in meditation.

He rarely seemed to collide with anyone or anything, although once in the lobby of Haven Hall—what the students referred to as the Fish Bowl—he tripped over a Saint Bernard.

Even as he fell, he was apologizing abjectly—until, close up, he found himself saying "Sorry" to a dog. Then he was terrified.

"I was frightened," he told me later, "that it would bite me. I know if I had been the dog, I would have bitten me."[8]

X. J. Kennedy and I found we shared a love for *Ubu roi* and decided to perform it. We talked the University of Michigan theatre department into letting us use, not their main stage, but a small studio theatre underneath it.

But what to call the play? I went to all my friends who had children and asked them what their children said when they needed to go to the toilet. I wish I still had the list I came up with.

"My daughter," Carrol Cox said, "yells 'Gopotty! Gopotty!'" I stopped there.

And so our posters announced that the John Barton Wolgamot Players would present:

GOPOTTY REX.

X. J. played Papa Gopotty. I played Mama Gopotty. Our costumes were made from old army blankets, which seemed the right color.[9]

It was rather a filthy production.[10]

I was supposed to be working on my dissertation.

I kept getting a yen for novels by Henry James, Jane Austen . . .

Rosmarie would check my reading. *The Spoils of Poynton,* perhaps.

"That's not dirty," she would say, and take it away.

I sat in on a semester of Japanese.

It did not take.

The only thing I remember how to say in Japanese is *good morning* which, considering my schedule, is not a useful expression.[11]

When I needed to see Austin, I went to his house and, without ringing, went in, and up the stairs to his library. Sometimes he was there, but often I sat a while, leafing through his books or checking over what I had brought—a few pages, perhaps, for my languishing dissertation. He slept, as he said, "like a pussy cat," i.e., whenever he felt the need, and when he woke—well then, if I was there, he found me in the library.

He had an altar there, with icons—not statues, nothing three-dimensional, since his current affiliation was Greek Orthodox.[12] They included, I remember, an etching of King Charles the First of England, whom Austin revered as the Martyr King. Austin had often insisted, I knew, that students and colleagues bringing him

---

[8] I produced Heath-Stubbs's play *The Talking Ass,* with Roger Staples as Balaam and X.J. playing "first half ass."

[9] For Gopotty's disposal of the Polish nobles, Chris Longyear (who had constructed the ass's head for *The Talking Ass*) taped a toilet. One at a time, nobles were shoved forward from a knot of terrified and scroungy aristocracy, to be sentenced, each in turn, "Down the trap!" At which, the noble was thrown out, Gopotty pulled the chain on his throne, and the loudest of flushes ensued. The next noble, ejected from the same knot, was always the same actor—only his hat changed. For *Gopotty,* Dallas Wiebe conducted what we called an orchestra—four ill-sorted instruments—in works by, naturally, Scheidt (and also "Good King Wenceslas"). His baton: a long green candle.

[10] Norman Nelson—having attended Harvard in the dim past—striding from the theatre, was heard to murmur, "Babbit, forgive me."

[11] John Cage once tried to convince me that Japanese has no syntax. Having failed to master that syntax, I was quite sure it was there, but I said, merely, that in that case they could hardly know what they are saying. Such is, said Cage, the fact of the matter. He claimed that the Japanese often talk for hours before discovering what they are talking about. At that point, some fool, who happened to know the language in question, interrupted our benign conversation.

[12] He claimed to be attending the Greek Orthodox church in Ann Arbor for the simple reason that there was available no Russian Orthodox.

manuscripts first lay them on the altar. He never suggested that my work be so consecrated. Perhaps its subject disqualified it.

"With a dissertation on obscenity," my friends kept asking me, "where do you think you'll ever find a job?"

It was a perfectly serious question, but I decided to treat it as a joke.

"Obviously," I said, "*Brown* University."

I seemed always out of phase. While artists and poets were busy cataloging their memories, I was circling around something I couldn't remember.

Now, however, anything I can recall . . .

There's less every time I turn around.

I asked Mary Ashley to design a cover for the third issue of *Burning Deck.*[13] She thought it over.

"All right," she said, "here it is. Just put *cover* on the front and on the back put *back.*"

Did she mean the title of the magazine should not be there?

That's exactly what she meant. Just *cover* and *back.*

"But," I stammered, "what if someone was looking for *Burning Deck*, how would they know this is what they're after?"

"No one," she pointed out, "was looking for *Burning Deck.*"

I had to admit, she had a point.

But the next time I saw her, she had reconsidered.

"Put *Burning Deck* on the front also," she now said, "along with *cover*. Because," she went on, "we shouldn't die for art."

Don Hope gave a lecture at Wayne State (W. D. Snodgrass providing a facetious introduction) in which he maintained that the spirit of Doctor Johnson was alive in the work of John Barton Wolgamot.

At the end of the lecture, Sam Astrachan asked Don why he had not talked about Thoreau. When Don admitted not seeing quite why he should have done so, Astrachan walked out . . .

. . . and wrote *The Game of Dostoevsky*, a novel in which a character named Hope heads a group of pretentious intellectuals who call themselves the "Wolgamuts" [sic]. Hope (the character in the novel, that is) speaks in a ridiculous, stilted manner which is, no doubt, supposed to be a parody of Don's elegant Augustan sentences.[14]

Don's dog was called Luke, short for Lucretius. Don had chosen that name because, he said, the dog derived all his knowledge from sensation and did not believe in the immortality of the soul.

I don't think I was ever a believer, even far far back, when I believed I was.

There is something particularly eerie in hearing the Credo—I believe—*sung*. Music, one might hope, should be a refuge from belief—indeed from ideas in general, whatever *could* be believed. (Which does not stop one, even an unbeliever reared in the lunatic fringe of American Protestantism, from a little regret for the Latin Mass.)

Songs—music with a text—do give in often to a didactic bent. In my own I find messages:

The core of the problem is . . .

or

---

[13]The magazine *Burning Deck* was edited by James Camp, Don Hope, and myself. It was printed by Rosmarie and me on a Chandler and Price job press we bought in Detroit and installed in the basement of our house in Turner Park Court. It was supposed to be a "quinterly," but there were in all four issues, the first in 1962 and the last—after we had moved to Connecticut—in 1965. After the demise of the magazine, Rosmarie and I continued under the same imprint to put out chapbooks and, eventually, books.

[14]Don Hope reported being accosted, in classes and in bars, with the question—the aggressively urgent question—whether he was or was not serious. He could not, he was told in no uncertain terms, be both *serious* and *not.* Don Hope edited the only publication of Burning Deck preceding the magazine, *The Wolgamot Interstice* (1961). He died in the seventies.

"With my wife, Rosmarie," Durham, Connecticut, 1966

. . . nothing's promised

that I would hesitate to put, undisguised at least, into a poem or a story.

The last page of Wolgamot's book refers to the Second Coming.[15]

I had found what I took to be another copy of Wolgamot's book, with a different title but the same text. I now maintained (was I serious, I wonder?) that these were the first two volumes of a trilogy, which would be completed with one more—with, again, the same text, from the same plates. A trilogy, *of great formal unity.*

---

[15]The last page: "In its very truly great manners of Ludwig van Beethoven very heroically the very distinguishably Second Coming of Jesus Christ had very ironically come amongst his very really grand men and women to Gregorio Martínez Sierra, Franz Liszt, Oliver Hazard Perry La Farge II, Jean Baptiste Siméon Chardin, Madison Julius Cawein, Vicente Blasco Ibáñez, Edgar Evertson Saltus, André Paul Guillaume Gide, John Van Alstyn Weaver, Richard Henry Stoddard, Walter Dumaux Edmonds, Katherine Anne Porter, Ernest Augustus Boyd, Emile Gaboriau, Felix Salten, Marcel Proust, Diego María Rivera and Gertrude Allain Mary McBrady very titanically."

The defence of my dissertation took place in Austin's downstairs living room. Besides Austin, there was Robert Niess, who had recently published a book on Benda, plus Ingo Seidler and Norman Nelson. A professor from the French Department also showed up, who was not on my committee. His field was seventeenth century, but a recent novel, which he found disgusting, had puzzled him and he was looking for an explanation or excuse for "explicit" scenes of—if I remember correctly—masturbation.

Austin had a way of delaying the first words of any comment. One would see a communication forming at the base of his throat and generally a slight grin—prophetic of irony—developed as the message became vocal. (It was this that made telephone conversations with him so difficult: without the visual clue, it was impossible to distinguish such preparations for speech from simple silences.)

When everyone was seated, awaiting Austin's first words to attain the level of sound, a chair—one of those sealed with the Harvard arms, VERITAS—went to pieces, and the French professor found himself on the floor amid a débris of sticks and splinters.

He was helped up. Another chair was brought in. The remnants of his earlier seat (the chair had not simply broken, it had shattered) were swept to one side. He sat down again, carefully, as though on eggshells, or something more dangerous.

This prompted an extended discussion of how much each person weighed. (Of those present, only Nelson might have been called heavy.)

Eventually, talk did come around to my dissertation.

There was a good question: when obscenities become current, Ingo asked, and dirty words are therefore no longer shocking, how then can you shock your public? I had an answer for this, but before I could get out with it, Norman Nelson offered,

Waldrop conducting Tardieu's Conversation-Sinfonietta, Providence, 1974

"Easy! You get on the stage and you take your pecker out." The specialist of *le siècle des lumières* almost went through another chair.

On the occasion of our leaving Ann Arbor, the Wolgamot Society planned a gift to the University: an allegorical statue.

Our Volkswagen had gone its last mile and the plan was to push it onto the green—some conspicuous spot—anchor it to the ground, open both doors wide, and spray it with concrete. The resulting figure, with its winglike doors, would be christened

THE VICTORY OF MICHIGAN

The gift was not accepted.

In my life so far, there are two compliments I remember with particular pride. An old history professor in Emporia,[16] after seeing me in the role of Pooh Bah, paid me the one I have found useful in after years.

"You have," he said, "not too little, not too much—just the right amount—of contempt for your audience."

Carl Viggiani came to me (this was in 1966 and he was head of the French Department at Wesleyan—it was my first semester teaching in the English Department) and pointed out that it was the fiftieth anniversary of Dada. He wanted me, it came out, somehow to help "mark the occasion."

Like how?

Well, he said, he'd get the Honors College for me some evening and I could do what I liked. I agreed, not really thinking much about it, and was startled a few weeks later when posters went up, confusing posters: some announced a lecture, some a reading; others promised a "happening." Some were vague. All agreed on time and place. All contained my name and, prominently, the word DADA.

There was not much time to think about it. I decided it would be easiest simply to read

---

[16]I have not set foot in Kansas since 1955, when I attended my father's funeral.

Dada texts: I translated a number from French, short snippets, and got Rosmarie to do some from German. The closer it came to the event, the sillier it seemed.

Perhaps no one would come anyway.

With a few days remaining, I ran into the head of the English Department. He apologized for having inadvertently scheduled a department party on the day of (as he called it) my "thing." I told him not to worry, that my thing would be short and that, when it was over, I would come to the party—to be at his place.

The more I thought about it, the more I dreaded, not performing badly, but reducing Dada to the dreariness of subject matter. It seemed to me that I must do something to lighten things and—almost at the last minute— I planned in two jokes, one for the middle and one for the end.

Frank Reeve said he would be there, so I implored his help. When, at the end, I ask if there are any questions, would he please rise *immediately*, say, So-and-So has written . . . and read a paragraph of something, anything—and follow it with, "Do you have anything to say to that?"

The hour arrived. The swank lounge of the Honors College, it turned out, was packed with students—I saw no faculty except Frank, Carl, and Ned Williamson, though Heinrich Schwarz and his wife were there on the front row.

Carl had arranged a suitable introduction: to read from his dissertation (on, as I remember, Sainte-Beuve) while a student drowned him out with a drum. Carl started reading before he noticed the student was not there, grew embarrassed, sat down.

I was in black suit and bow tie and had my texts in a footlocker next to the podium. I fished out a text, read it, rummaged for another. The students found them funny, applauded, laughed wildly—as was appropriate— though I proceeded to read completely poker-faced.

There was really no need for my last-minute jokes but, come to about midpoint of the

evening, I decided to go ahead with them.

Digging again into the footlocker, a little longer than before, I came up with something that apparently surprised even me.

I laughed.

I controlled myself.

I started to open the new item, broke into more laughter, snapped it shut, explained to my audience, between guffaws,

"Well. . . there was one time when. . . I have to admit, the Dadaists went, well, *too far.*" But trying to read it, I again burst out laughing.

With great effort, I controlled myself.

Tried again.

Burst out laughing again . . .

This went on . . . until, when I thought them about ready to come up and take it away from me, I showed what it was.

It was my Ph.D. diploma.

I threw it back into the footlocker and continued with other texts, poker-faced as before.

I read the last text, threw it into the foot-locker, said,

"Are there any questions?" And Frank Reeve leapt to his feet, brandished a book, from which he read, at top speed, in French, what seemed to me pages. I had not caught a word. He snapped the book shut.

"Have you anything to say about that?" And I replied,

"No."

So it turned out a jolly occasion, a celebration no doubt inadequate but in the proper spirit—well-worn gags and all. I put my foot-locker in the car and drove to the department party.

The party was in full swing, the house full of people, full of noise and smoke. I thought some were looking at me just a bit strangely, but perhaps—it was my first semester on the faculty—they did not recall who I was. Or maybe it was the bow tie. The level of tipsiness was up there.

Then the department head, a tall man, wormed his way to me through the crowd, his drink held high. Reaching me, he leaned down to my height and said (I thought for a moment he was speaking verse),

"I hear you MOCKED an academic deGREE."

"Well," I said, somewhat taken aback, "it's MINE."

And it passed like a joke—which I assumed it was.

This was in October. In November, I asked if I would be reappointed for next year. If not, I needed to start applying elsewhere. I was told,

"Oh yes . . . you're doing fine . . . Well . . . but I guess I have to ask the department. We're having a meeting next week." I felt reassured.

The next week, I was informed that I would *not* be teaching at Wesleyan next year.

I made no connection, until various gossips told me what happened. One member of the department was in fact at my celebration of Dada—I had not noticed—and, as one put it, "never forgave you for that *academic-degree* bit." He had convinced the assembled department that I was not fit to teach at Wesleyan.

From the library of Wesleyan University, I checked out a volume by the elder Henry James, *Substance and Shadow.* The last signature on the card, before mine, was from fifty years earlier. It was that of Austin Warren.

Edwin Honig—director of the Brown English Department for a single year—hired me. The same year, my first book of poems came out.

In that book I tried, by including a translation, to indicate (not pay) my debt to Raymond Queneau, whose poems I discovered while an undergraduate (from songs recorded by Juliette Greco). A list of the others who have taught me something—assuming I could make such a list—would not be very interesting, but there have been moments when a particular book seemed an essential pointer: Robert Creeley's *The Whip,* for instance, or *The World, the Worldless* of William Bronk.

My "desert island" book—assuming that even on an atoll the Gideons will have left a King James Bible under the palm—would be *The Golden Bowl,* or perhaps *The Wings of the Dove.* (Late James is something I get cravings for.) And if the island is equipped with a CD player, my one disc might be the *Winterreise* (or, well, perhaps the *Goldberg Variations*).

I have learned more from my students than I ever did from my teachers.

In 1971, we were in Paris on an Amy Lowell fellowship, in an apartment on the rue des Saints-Pères, which had been the office of the magazine *L'Oeil.* My old student George Tysh, having married his cousin Chris, was then living in Paris, and they often hosted readings by American poets passing through. But they lost their apartment and had no longer an appropriate space. We had only two rooms but one of them was rather large and for a while George scheduled readings there.

At one of these (the Québecois poet Robert Hébert was reading), two strangers, Claude Royet-Journoud and Anne-Marie Albiach, appeared. After the reading, Claude looked at the French poetry on our bookshelves and approved of the selection.

He noted in particular the three volumes of *Le Livre des Questions.* Those, I explained, we brought because Rosmarie had begun translating the first volume.

Claude, hearing that, flew across the room, kissed Rosmarie,[17] and tried immediately (unsuccessfully) to get Jabès on the phone.

---

[17]I trust this will not conflict with the account in Rosmarie's autobiography.

"With Rosmarie and George and Mary Oppen,"
San Francisco, 1979

Anne-Marie's first book, we learned, had come out from Mercure de France just the day before. As soon as they left, I went around the corner to Le Drugstore, bought *Etat*, and read it that night.[18]

The next day, Claude turned up again, with Edmond Jabès.

Back in the States, "sit-ins" were common and there had been a "be-in." I suggested to Bart St.-Armand that, on the anniversary of H.P. Lovecraft's death, we have a Providence *lurk-in.*

It was a passing fancy, but Bart and Harry Beckwith decided to carry it out. We would meet under the Faunce House arch at half past eleven the night of March 14, so that at midnight—Lovecraft having died on the Ides of March—we could begin a tour of selected sites.

It turned bitter cold. I was not sure I wanted to venture out, but felt I shouldn't disappoint Bart and Harry. (It had not been advertised, so no one was liable to show up.)

I arrived at the arch to find fifty or a hundred people there, a motley bunch with banners and torches.

We made our way, slowly, blocking traffic, to various places sacred to the Lovecraft legend. To the List Art Building, which had replaced his last dwelling. To the corner of Prospect and Meeting, where that dwelling now stands, across from the Daughter Church of Christian Science. To the Shunned House on Benefit Street. At each stop, a text of Lovecraft, appropriate to the spot, was read out.

Lovecraft himself, as we knew, showed visiting friends the city by night ("I am Providence," he declared), pointing out the beauty of widow's walks and fanlights.

We did not go as far as his birthplace at Angell and Elmgrove, let alone to Swan Point, where he is buried.[19]

We did visit the old churchyard that goes down the hill from Benefit Street and were challenged by the watchman from an institution next door, who demanded to know what we were doing there. Bart replied, matter-of-factly,

"I'm going to read a poem." The watchman, nonplussed, disappeared, and Bart read a sonnet out of *Fungi from Yuggoth.*

Edwin Honig and James Schevill decided to start a poets' theatre in Providence, and both Rosmarie and I were in on its founding. For a performance of the Wastepaper Theatre, the four of us—and selected accomplices—would present new work, limited (theoretically) to fifteen minutes each. My plays were often shorter than that and usually performed without a script. Recently I have written some of them down, from memory, in what I think of as "postscripts."[20]

---

[18]In 1971 I started translating *Etat,* and completed it twelve years later. I have done all of Claude Royet-Journoud's books into English, as well as books by Paol Keineg, Dominique Fourcade, Jean Grosjean. I also translated a selection of early poems by Jabès, to put beside his more important books which Rosmarie has done.

[19]Reports circulate to the effect that grass from the grave of H. P. Lovecraft is available for a price—and is much sought after for use in diabolic rites. This year (1997), someone seems to have tried to dig him up.

[20]Wastepaper Theatre performed, on the average, once a year for twenty years—1972 to 1992—mostly in the museum of the Rhode Island School of Design. Since then, Gale Nelson and I have founded a new group, Shandy Hall.

With Edmond and Claude, Rosmarie and I visited Arlette Jabès in the hospital, where she had gone for minor surgery. The other patient in her room objected to the enormous bouquets people had brought for Arlette, so Edmond had to take them home with him.

Afterwards, Claude, Edmond, and we decided to eat together. Edmond, without Arlette to check his intake of salt, opted for Italian.

Halfway through the meal, I began to feel ill. I tried not to succumb, but when it seemed serious, I announced that I had to leave and managed to get as far as the sidewalk, where I passed out. Claude, having followed me out, caught me and told Rosmarie to quick call *Police-Secour.*

I dreamt that I was throwing up and, like Adam's dream, awoke and found it truth. Rosmarie, meanwhile, about to call for help, realized the first question would be, Where are you? and realized also that she did not know. She came out to ask where we were and saw that I had recovered enough that a taxi home would be the best program.

Arlette called from the hospital to see how I was. (I was desperately afflicted with the epizooties, an unimportant twenty-four-hour horror.)

Recovering, I gave it to Rosmarie, who had a much worse case, but who—falling ill at home, not on the street—got less attention.

Edmond, from all the flowers he was saddled with, had an attack of asthma.

Looking up "Rhode Island" in the 1910 *Britannica,* I found on the map of the state a "Mt. Misery."

Recent maps list no such place.

I began asking around, among natives and longtime residents, and found no one (not even Bart St.-Armand) had ever heard of such a hill. Some, indeed, questioned the likelihood of the name.

I wrote a text, "The Quest for Mount Misery," and later used it as the title for a collection.[21]

Steve Palumbo (who with Ann Huntington directs the Po Gallery, which has several times exhibited my collages—each time at a different address) noticed the title.

Because, it turns out, he once owned a piece of land on this very Mt. Misery—near the Scituate Reservoir, which was not there in 1910—but sold it, to finance the starting of the Po Gallery.

The premiere of Robert Ashley's[22] *In Sara, Mencken, Christ and Beethoven There Were Men and Women* was in Bremen. He later performed it on the west coast. When it was scheduled for New York, it occurred to him that he had never asked Wolgamot—or anybody (except me!)—for permission to use the text.

The composition includes, in fact, the entire text of Wolgamot's book. Bob found that he could speak any one page without taking a breath. He recorded a page, took a breath, recorded another . . . When the whole book was on tape, he went back and cut out all the breath between pages.

Before a performance in southern California, a woman came to see him, to ask if that title—which she had seen on a poster—might possibly refer to a book by John Barton Wolgamot.

Bob was startled but stammered an affirmative.

The woman was delighted. She revealed that, at the very time the book was being written, she was an intimate of the author—in fact his "only confidante." When she learned that the piece was going to New York, Bob must, she insisted, make contact with Wolgamot. She was sure he would be pleased.

Now that she thinks of it, he must already be aware, subliminally, of the piece's existence.

---

[21]Turkey Press, 1983. The text is collected in *Hegel's Family* (Station Hill, 1989).

[22]My acquaintance with Ashley goes back to our Ann Arbor days. My first friend there was Gordon Mumma. The two composers, along with Roger Reynolds, George Cacciopo, and Don Scavada, founded the Once Music Festival. Ashley and Mumma did the music for my production of Paul Goodman's *Jonah* in 1962.

(This does not make Bob less nervous.)

Yes—the remembrance animates her—when, a few weeks ago, she had lunch with Wolgamot in New York, he said (these, absolutely, his exact words) he did believe something was "in the air."

And she, for her part, figures that he—Wolgamot—may now, "after years of self-imposed obscurity," be "ready for a little fame."

Bob, relieved, saw that she was going. But, the door open, her hand on the knob, she turned again, to say how happy she was to know that Ashley was going to contact Wolgamot. And, just before disappearing, closing the door behind her,

"Oh, and, by the way,

"You'd better bone up on the *Eroica*."

So Ashley and I went to see Wolgamot. We talked to him in the lobby of the Little Carnegie Cinema, where he was the manager. He said it was hard to imagine reading his book aloud.

"I suppose," he said, "it would have to be a sort of"—he hesitated, considered—"breathless reading."[23]

Wolgamot had written two books, he told us, and was working on a third.

"My first book was a complete failure." He had the copies destroyed. "The second began to gallop." And, in a murmur,

"But wait till you see the next."

He has been working for thirty-odd years on his third book.

The first was called *In Sara Haardt Were Men and Women.* The second, published a year later, is the one I found in Danville, Illinois. The two books were in fact printed from the same plates, with no change whatever, except for the title page and reduced margins.

I asked if the third will have . . . the same text?

---

[23]He did not want to hear Ashley's composition.

Oh, yes.

But a brand new title page.

In 1929, Wolgamot says, he heard for the first time the Eroica Symphony.

"I was bowled over." And as he listened, rapt, he heard, somehow, within the rhythms themselves, *names*—names that meant nothing to him, foreign names. It was these names, he realized, that created the rhythm, bearing the melody into existence.

He checked out from the library a large biography of Beethoven. And in that volume, he found, one after another, all the names he had heard ringing through the symphony.

And it dawned on him that, as rhythm is the basis of all things, names are the basis of rhythm.

"That's why," he said, "when a woman marries and gives up her name, she gives up her personality."

Names determine character, settle destiny. "You can see that in the great novels," he says. "Take Tolstoy. What does this remind you of: *Annaka rennina annaka rennina?*—it's a train, of course. She's killed by a train."

Wolgamot decided—about 1930—to write a book.

He wrote one name on each page.

But he knew it could be richer. Names react to one another.

He made long lists of names and held the list next to the pages of his projected book. When certain names came near each other, there was, he found, a spark, and thus he knew they belonged together. In this way, three names gathered on each page, and around them clustered multitudes.

And still something was lacking. Each page rhythmically complete, there was no impulse from one page to the next. There had to be a matrix, a sentence, to envelop the names. So far, he had spent a year or two composing his book.

The sentence, a sentence to be repeated, more or less identically, on each page—this sentence took him ten years to write.

"It's harder than you think," as he put it, "to write a sentence that doesn't say anything."

Our attic, where Tom Ahern was living, caught fire. We called the fire department and immediately went out of the house, into the front yard. Looking up, I saw smoke curling, not out of the chimney, but from around it, outside it, an envelope of smoke, rising about the brick column.

I watched that rising curtain of smoke.

The firemen—stationed, fortunately, just around the corner—came quickly, ran, and ran their hoses up the steep staircase. We heard them smash out windows and skylight. The roof was saved.

Before the firemen got there, while I saw that smoke rising quietly from the roof, everything, somehow, suffered combustion, became smoke—buildings along the street, any street, all streets, the city, the seven hills of the city and its harbor, tall buildings and long red factories and, of course, our wooden houses.

Circulation failed in one of Austin Warren's legs and the limb had to be amputated.

He described himself thereafter as having one foot in the grave.[24]

What is in my mind—or I should simply say, *what my mind is* (which is to say, my environment)—well, in a sense, that is precisely what I'm not.

In another sense, it is all in the world I am.

The scars of the saints, I read, *rise with them into Paradise and remain on their glorified bodies through all eternity, badges of martyrdom, stripes signifying heavenly rank.*

---

[24]Austin—who had moved to Providence—preferred funerals to weddings. A marriage, he said, you never know how that will turn out. He died at the age of eighty-seven in 1986.

The other compliment that I remember with much pleasure came long after the first. One of my students (one of my best students), meaning it—I think—as a compliment, one day after class said,

"You are a master of the antidote."

I thanked her.

I did not ask for an explanation, uncertain to this day if she intended to say something else—or if, in fact, she did say something else and I misheard.

The distinction between form and content is convenient, but it might be more helpful to distinguish, in a text, rhythm / melody / harmony.

Edmond Jabès was engaged to speak at the opening ceremony of a new program of Jewish Studies in Paris.

It was a particularly tense moment in Israeli–Palestinian relations, but we were taken aback at being frisked at the entrance to the auditorium. This special attention was explained when we learned that Edmond was not the only speaker. There was a long table of participants, and his talk was to follow one by the Israeli ambassador to France.

The ambassador—whose presence was as much a surprise to Jabès as it was to us—began by references to Palestinian "assassins" and his remarks became more hawkish as they proceeded. People in the audience started walking out. (I noticed Claude Royet-Journoud going out the door—and then, also, Arlette.)

We were not sure it was appropriate for us (foreigners) to join the protest. Besides, we did want to hear Edmond. Then, however, Jabès rose, gathered his papers, left the table, came off the platform, crossed in front of the ambassador, and went out.

After this, there was no point in staying. We went also, to find the corridor full. One of the ambassador's body guards was trying to get everyone either into the lecture hall or out of the building, but nobody would budge.

*Waldrop lying across (from left) Paul Auster, Dominique Fourcade, and
Claude Royet-Journoud, New York, 1984*

Soon the ambassador, his speech over, was hurried through. We returned to the auditorium, and Jabès delivered his talk.

Edmond told us later that when he started to get up from the table, the director of the school—sitting next to him—got a grip on his pants-leg in an effort to hold him. And claimed his greatest fear was that in his exit he would lose his trousers.

Edmond died in 1991, apparently while looking into a book which had just arrived, a French translation of my collection of poems *A Ceremony Somewhere Else*.[25] Arlette died a year and a half later.

I once claimed that the "ideal poem" should be a sort of *last words*, making impossible any sequel, and elsewhere suggested a project "to redesignate the world—mark it as a gravestone."[26]

In the first half of the seventeenth century—the age of melancholy—men walked the

streets, we are told, *as if mad and spellbound, looking at each other.*

And Saint Augustine: "What if, in this life, it became quite certain that you could never learn anything beyond what you now, already, know?

"Would you not weep?"

As a child, I disliked (stupidly) most of the music I heard, particularly popular music. In high school, I had no contact with pop bands or singers, though I had begun to listen to Mozart and Beethoven—and knew, of course, a large assortment of hymns.

The peculiar thing is that now, though I thought I had always avoided them, when I hear a popular song from that time, I often find I already know the song, words and music—not all, of course, but many.

An unmerited grace.

Blossom Kirschenbaum named her son Abram. I asked her why not Abraham? She gave me her practiced look-of-rebuke.

"He has to make his own covenant!"

---

[25]Translated by Françoise de Laroque (Fourbi, 1986).

[26]*Who, living, builds himself no monument, once dead will have no monument—disremembered even as the sound of the bell decays.* Somebody said that—I think a Holy Roman Emperor. I can't, actually, claim any great confidence in my own pile.

John Heath-Stubbs once told me that, as a young man, he opened—I suspect in the original Greek—Herodotus' *Persian Wars.*

The first sentence, he insisted, converted him to classicism:

These are the researches of Herodotus of Halicarnassus, which he publishes, in the hope of thereby preserving from decay the remembrance of what men have done . . .

With neither great and wonderful actions nor any sense of glory to report, I write *this—* or maybe it's *these—*against the decay of remembrance.

In *Light While There Is Light* I tried to give a sense, not of my early life, but of the world I passed through in that life, that previous life. I can say of this work, as of that one: nothing here is absolutely true, and none of it entirely false.

BIBLIOGRAPHY

Poetry:

A Windmill Near Calvary, University of Michigan Press, 1968.

Songs from the Decline of the West (Song-texts), Perishable Press, 1970.

The Garden of Effort, Burning Deck, 1975.

Poem from Memory, illustrated by Linda Lutes, Treacle Press, 1975.

Windfall Losses, Pourboire Press, 1977.

The Space of Half an Hour, Burning Deck, 1983.

The Ruins of Providence: Local Pieces (poems and a story), Copper Beech, 1983.

A Ceremony Somewhere Else, Awede, 1984.

The Opposite of Letting the Mind Wander: Selected Poems and a Few Songs, 1990.

Shipwreck in Haven: Transcendental Studies, Awede, 1991.

The Locality Principle, Avec Books, 1995.

The Silhouette of the Bridge, Avec Books, 1997.

Analogies of Escape, Burning Deck, 1997.

(With Rosmarie Waldrop) *Well Well Reality,* Post Apollo Press, 1997.

Fiction:

Wind Scales, illustrated by Linda Lutes, Treacle Press, 1976.

The Quest for Mount Misery and Other Studies, Turkey Press, 1983.

Hegel's Family: Serious Variations, Station Hill, 1989.

Light While There Is Light, Sun and Moon, 1993.

Translator from the French:

Claude Royet-Journoud, *Reversal,* Hellcoal, 1973.

Claude Royet-Journoud, *The Notion of Obstacle,* Awede, 1985.

Edmond Jabès, *If There Were Anywhere by Desert: The Selected Poems of Edmond Jabès,* Station Hill, 1988.

Anne-Marie Albiach, *Etat,* Awede, 1989.

André Breton, Paul Eluard, and René Char, *Ralentir Travaux,* Exact Change, 1990.

Paol Keineg, *Boudica,* Burning Deck, 1994.

Claude Royet-Journoud, *Objects Contain the Infinite,* Awede, 1995.

Claude Royet-Journoud, *A Descriptive Method,* Post Apollo Press, 1995.

Dominique Fourcade, *Click-Rose,* Sun and Moon, 1996.

Jean Grosjean, *Elegies,* Paradigm Press, 1996.

Translator from the Chinese:

(With Wang Ping, et al) Xue Di, *Heart into Soil,* Burning Deck and Lost Roads, 1998.

Other:

(Editor with wife, Rosmarie Waldrop) *A Century in Two Decades: A Burning Deck Anthology: 1961-1981,* Burning Deck, 1982.

(Editor with James Camp, X. J. Kennedy) *Pegasus Descending: A Book of the Best Bad Verse,* Macmillan, 1971.

(With James Camp, X. J. Kennedy) *Three Tenors, One Vehicle: A Book of Songs,* Open Places, 1975.

Contributor to magazines, including *Poetry, New Yorker, Open Places, Sulfur,* and *Conjunctions.* Cofounder and co-editor of *Burning Deck* (magazine), 1962-65.

Rosmarie Waldrop

1935-

Rosmarie Waldrop, 1995

Poetry is having nothing to say and saying it: we possess nothing

—John Cage

THE PAST, UPON SCRUTINY

Not green mountains embedded in strong feeling. More an exaggeration of fog than German poetry. Interval eclipsed.

I had no grandparents, my mother told me a few months before she died. Then burst into tears.

LOOKING AT A PICTURE OF THE LANDSCAPE IS EASIER THAN LOOKING AT THE LANDSCAPE

Sepia as an aid to memory. On a lap, chair, tricycle, sled, slope, skis. Next to a Christmas tree, bicycle, pool, bridge, potted cactus, father's motorbike, a wheelbarrow, my sisters. I wash (drown?) dolls in the tub, pet a black-and-white cat, throw snowballs. I hold up my *kulleraugen-*

puppe, a Raggedy-Ann doll, but male, with big, rolling eyes. The photo does not show the doll was named Ulli (my name had I been a boy).

I WAS AN ONLY CHILD

even though I wore hand-me-downs from my sisters. Most were *Hängerchen,* without waist. A source of mortification. I envied boys because they had pockets in their pants.

Snow drifted onto the balcony. The iron
    stove glowed red.
Father said, I raise daughters and cactuses.
Coupling curiosity with upright for speed.
I learned to tie my shoes, to swim, to ride
    a bike.
Wildflowers up to my waist. A whir of
    cicadas. Swallows perched on telephone
    lines. Adding up cobble stones against
    more unguessable events.
Father told stories of poisoned apples
    while mother's shadow grew longer.
Years after waking, words from the dream
    invade my long childhood.
Could a child be born from something
    not a mother?
Each slap revealed a face I had not
    suspected.

FOR REFERENCE

I was born on August 24, 1935, in Kitzingen am Main, Germany, the daughter of Josef Sebald, a high school teacher, and Friederike, née Wohlgemuth. My twin sisters, Annelie and Dorle, were born nine years earlier, in 1926.

HITLER ON THE RADIO, FOLLOWED BY LEHAR

I remember the voice. I heard it again years later, heard its hysterical pitch in the voice of an American evangelist. This was in 1959, at a camp meeting in Illinois that my new mother-in-law had taken me to. To disinfect me of Catholicism. The voice freaked me out. I began to see the tent as a Nazi rally, the people ready to do the evangelist's bidding no matter what. Keith brought me out of my panic: the collection basket held nothing higher than a one-dollar bill!

WAR CAME OUT OF THE RADIO BEFORE I HAD TIME TO SCRATCH ON A SLATE

I see us sitting around the wicker table with the radio on it, Father, Mother with me on her lap. She says, "This war is going to be over in four weeks. Our leader will take care of it." But maybe that was said back to her later, as a taunt. The phrase *die kochende Volksseele,* "the soul of the people boiling over," I read later. It was 1939. I was four and looking forward to going to school. Playing at it with my sisters' satchels and discarded books. Another photo.

MY FIRST SCHOOL DAY, SEPTEMBER 1941, A COOL DAY

I was taught. The Nazi salute, the flute. How firmly entrenched, the old theories. Already using paper, pen and ink. Yes, I said, I'm here. Even though the principal was a *brüllendes Ungeheuer* who struck children across the palms with a cane, wheezing, his face redder and redder with almost an asthma attack. Even so, anxious suspense was converted into the tongue as home. The calendar changed from moon to sun.

WAR, A SURFACE TO LIVE ON

All men were old. Shoes always too small. Cold oozed up through the holes. Uniforms moved with great speed. Mother thrust her chin forward with a new violence. Examined ration cards and missed coffee. At night the town gave in to the dark as if electricity had never been invented. So many things I did not understand. War as sufficient explanation. Balked in my simulation of childhood. Mother, I cried, extremely. At home in winter, wool pulled over my eyes.

At the sound of the siren everybody ran into the cellar.

IN FEBRUARY, 1943,

I burrowed into a heap of potatoes as the ground shook. People prayed. When we climbed out of the cellar there were no streets, no rows of houses. Instead: craters, heaps of rubble, mortar, stones, walls broken off, a craggy desert, air thick with dust. A few houses were left standing. They seemed out of place, incongruous with their insistence on boundaries, definite lines. Mother hurried me up to our apartment and tried to patch the shattered windows. Father came back late from digging up bodies.

It was the first drastic change of my world. A second followed in 1945, a not exactly Nietzschean "revaluation of all values." "Our leader" turned into "the criminal," "the enemy" into "Amis," "surrender" into "liberation." This went deeper. And took years to understand.

I have always thought of poetry as a way of building a world. *The* world is certainly not a given, even if it occupies more and more of the sky. Building a counter-world, not better, but other.

After this bombing, nobody would consider taking shelter in a cellar. Rather catch it in the open and a quick death. Rather jump on bicycles at the first alert and make for the woods. Or flat in the ditches as the planes came roaring.

School stopped. We kids ran wild. The ruins became our castles, with an undercurrent of terror that we might find real bodies in our imagined dungeons.

ALL HANDS IN THE FIELDS WOMEN OR PRISONERS

After a second bombing, we wandered from village to village, my parents and I. My sisters were drafted, one to a munitions factory, the other to an anti-aircraft unit. A few months with acquaintances here, a few months there. Then my parents found a way to ship me to my uncle's farm, an isolated place in the mountains north of Nürnberg, four miles of dirt road from the next village. I tended the cows and developed a crush on Felix, one of the two Polish POWs. Uncle Georg ("Schorsch") emerged from the mill white with flour. Aunt Margaret called me "thing" because "Rosmarie" required too much lipwork. Cousin Sybilla took out her accordion and sang "La Paloma."

One day, the Poles vanished; another day, my sister Dorle came walking toward the farm. Her anti-aircraft unit had disbanded and Uncle's farm was more possible to reach on foot than our hometown. Cousin Arno walked in next, in tattered Hitler-Jugend uniform, outraged at having been called "pig-dog" by an American soldier. I did not doubt his blatant translation of *Schweinehund*, as I had not doubted Old Shatterhand's swearing, "O thunderweather!" in Karl May's Westerns.

Then jeeps with Americans. One stopped. Soldiers ran into the house, empty except for Arno (15) and me (10). One soldier put a pistol to Arno's head, "SS?" I remember feeling cold, unable to move. Not how Arno convinced them there were no SS.

MY CAREER IN THE THEATER

was brief. In summer 1945, Father came on his motorbike and was pleased to find two daughters, but puzzled how to get us both home. Riding on the pillow strapped to the gas tank was bumpy, but the view superior to the back.

Jeeps became part of the everyday street image. So did Americans in pressed uniforms, sometimes handing kids that exotic delicacy, chewing gum. Pairs of motorcycles with goggled Military Police roared through town, a bit frightening, as if a vestige of past terror.

School did not reopen in Kitzingen until January 1946 (though the Berlin Opera started up as early as September '45!). I was hired by a theater troupe that toured towns and villages in an American army truck. Afternoons I was a dwarf in *Snow White;* evenings, in Wedekind's *Love Potion,* I played Enyusha (or was it Alyosha?), a Russian nobleman's son. I was proud to be paid like the rest of the cast, but soon got bored playing the same parts every day. I couldn't wait for school to start again.

NOT JUST POSTWAR FOCUS, BUT DEEP AND FETID

I dreamed I was human, but not sure it was possible. The naked part of morning had disappeared. Natural space lost to mirrors on the wall.

Things settled down to "normal." The quarrels, the silences. My sister Dorle married, and her apartment became my refuge. Mother cleared my throat. Every few weeks she moved all the furniture. Father retreated into his astral body, quoting Goethe and working the Rühmkorff pendulum. I barricaded myself behind books.

WHAT BOOKS?

There was no public library in my hometown. The high school had a few measly cupboards full. So had the Catholic church, where I avoided the devotional shelves and went for *Ben Hur, Fabiola, The Last Days of Pompeii.* Father's bookcase held the German classics, opera librettos, and books on flying (airplanes and more fantastic attempts). During one convalescence I read Schiller's *Complete Plays* and was amused to find, marked in his hand, the lines that made up half of my father's conversation. But there was a decent bookstore. I made friends with the manager, spent what pocket money I had, and managed exchange privileges.

A LONG LIFE OF LEARNING THE PRECEDING CHAPTER

History classes did not go up to the Nazi period, though some teachers talked about it. Few parents seemed willing to. Relation of did not perceive to did not happen. We, my friends and I, talked, shared the books we found. Reports from the camps, war memoirs, new novels. The first book about concentration camps I tried to read was Ernst Wiechert's *Totenwald.* Tried, because my mother took it away: I was too young. I found ways to circumvent her belated efforts at sheltering.

We tried to hold on to the idea that the Holocaust had been so horrible that nothing like it could ever happen again—that anti-Semitism, any form of racism, was now impossible. And we knew we could not distance ourselves and say "they." *We* had done this, *our* country. It was by a hair, by a few months, that I had escaped the Hitler-Jugend. In fall 1945 I was ten and would have been drafted. And brainwashed. How would I have acted? Brecht's *Galileo* was helpful. Heroism is the exception; most human beings are not cut out for it. It helped us accept our parents who, even if they had not been active in the horror, had made it possible by going along, conforming, *Mitläufer,* fellow travelers.

WE SWAPPED KNIVES TO PEEL OFF CHILDHOOD LIKE SO MANY SKINS

The last three years of high school were co-educational. With the change of school, I noticed a change in myself. I had been a tomboy, a rabble-rouser. Now I became quiet. I thought it was because my father taught physical education in the same school. More likely the presence of boys combined with the hormonal state of my sixteen-year-old body. Hot weather firmly implanted in the pelvis. Between flesh and mirror. Unsure how to behave. I already knew I had no talent for "charm" from

a disastrous experience. During my last year in the girls' school, we had been given a lecture on charm—a concession to femininity, along with dancing lessons. The lecture stressed we should practice smiling at people till it became "natural." Next thing I knew, a classmate scoffed: "What a crush you have on Kurti Höhn. I couldn't help laughing when I saw you pass him." I was humiliated. Kurti was a neighbor, an old playmate. I had been *practicing.*

At least I had sense enough not to follow the advice of the priest (firmly lodged in my mind as an outrage): "You are very bright," he said, "but if you were *really* bright you would not show it."

Other injunctions to silence were harder to shrug off. My German teacher's dismissal of a poem: "Try to learn something first." Or Adorno's: Poetry is not possible after Auschwitz.

BUT MUSIC

was everywhere. Piano lessons. Flute lessons. Mother singing. She wanted to be accompanied on the piano, but I preferred playing in the

Rosmarie with her parents Josef and Friederike Sebald, and older sister Annelie, about 1940

"With my twin sisters, Dorle and Annelie," 1939

"youth orchestra" my classmate Hermann Rupperti conducted. I was in love with Hermann. Later he became a dentist.

MUSIC ENTERS THE BODY AS MUSIC

but hollows it for emotion. Christmas 1954 we gave a concert for the American soldiers. (Kitzingen was flanked by two army bases from Nazi times, which the Americans had taken over.) Our orchestra numbered many more heads than the audience, but afterwards, over coffee and doughnuts, dozens of soldiers wanted to chat. Keith Waldrop had been at the concert. He invited a bunch of us to listen to his records. We were ecstatic. None of us owned records. For the next four months, until he was discharged, he once a week lugged records and player to one of our homes. He and I also met to translate poems. Reflexes reach marvelous complexity in damp climates: the first poem I chose was not some Rilke, but Nietzsche's "Tanzlied," with the line, *Doch alle Lust will Ewigkeit*, "all pleasure wants eternity." Was I *already* thinking marriage?

THE SYSTEM WAS NERVOUS

In the fall of 1954 I had started commuting (a half-hour train ride) to the University of Würzburg. I voraciously gobbled as many lectures in literature, art history, and musicology as I could fit into the week and promptly got indigestion. Apple wrapped in snake. I took matters in my own hands and checked out both *The Faerie Queene* and *Paradise Lost* over Easter vacation. It would have been a steep project even if my English had been perfect.

Of course my discontent had variable wave lengths and more than one cause. Cold skin more abrupt than abandonment. Fingers closing on desire. By the next fall I was a ghost. Torpid, fainthearted, in despair. Without knowing what was lost. Not paradise. Getting up became difficult. Speaking, impossible.

The one thing I could hold on to was Bach fugues.

I stopped going to class, which went unnoticed, and played the piano all day, which did not.

Herr Jaeger, on the floor beneath us, complained. He had already offered to buy felt slippers for the whole family if we promised to wear them the moment we entered the apartment. Mother, no matter how dissatisfied with her children, rose like the proverbial lioness the moment she perceived an "attack" from the outside. She on the spot invented a future musical career for me. My practicing was professional necessity. Herr Jaeger sued. A team of experts arrived with a "noise-meter" and measured the decibels I produced. I got an injunction not to play between 12 and 2 P.M. or after 10 P.M. Which I had never done.

HOW DARK

was the night of my soul? And how was it joined to my whole body? I had been brought up a lukewarm Catholic. Father went to Mass on Sundays, but his real church was the forest, his religion a mix of pantheism and astrology. My mother's only involvement with her Protestant church: singing in the choir. By age thirteen I had lost all faith and considered myself a rationalist—only to rejoin the church at eighteen, copying my deeply religious sisters. Firmly focused on infinity, without an inch to spare. I watched them praying, tried to participate in their stillness and fervor by sheer force of concentration. Courted their passion in the belief that I was courting God. The towers of the church rose into red shifts. The snowflakes drifted slowly in the opposite direction. I stuck out my tongue for Communion, but the Holy Ghost did not come to roost.

Once my imitation fervor lost speed, I did not act on my feeling, but hung on. Trapped in notions of consistency. You walk into abandoned reasons: directly, driftwood, some trick of the current. It took several years before I gave up the struggle to deceive myself, stopped pulling the strings of my own puppet. My sister Annelie was preparing to enter the Carmel. I came to my senses before she was returned to hers, declared too neurotic for convent life by the nuns.

HOW TO STRETCH MUSCLES AS FAR AS THE MEDITERRANEAN

Keith found he could use his GI Bill abroad, and we conspired to spend the school year 1956–57 at the University of Aix-Marseille. The foreign students were segregated in their own institute across town from the main university so that it was hard to meet French students. But like all lovers we knew the time that was given and the time we must take. My landlady put her finger on it: "Your French is still poor, but I understand your English has improved greatly." Lack of money, however, sent us back, separately, to the United States and Germany.

LONGING IS INCONTESTABLE. YOU FEEL A SPLINTER AND KNOW WHERE IT CAME FROM

Before going to Aix-Marseille, I had transferred to the University of Freiburg to avoid living at home. It must have been in my first year there (1955–56) that Germany got an army again. The students were set against it. But all that meant was we talked, debated, like the anarchists in Conrad's *Secret Agent*. It didn't occur to us to act, to demonstrate. It was probably the year after Aix that Heidegger came down from his mountain to give a lecture: *"Das dichtende Denken ist ein denkendes Dichten."* The announcement caused both indignation and curiosity. Suddenly everybody had stories: how, during the Nazi time, Heidegger had eagerly replaced Husserl as *Rektor* of the university. And kicked out other Jews. How Professor Rehm, on the contrary, had turned pale but continued lecturing on Kafka when a gang of Brownshirts came and sat in the front row. In the end, we did not obstruct the lecture, but sat with backs turned.

My great Freiburg discovery was Musil. Professor Rupprecht frequently referred to *The Man Without Qualities,* but admitted not to have a grip on it. This made me curious. The "grip" no doubt eluded me also, but the delight, pleasure, richness of both language and thought did not. Musil's concept of identity rang true to me: consisting of multiple selves, with "character" and "qualities" being our most impersonal traits because they are what is reinforced from the outside. And I was fascinated by the way the narrative calls itself into question, both thematically and by always pitting a two-dimensional grid of details against the famous "narrative thread." This became important for my own method of composition: the tension between clusters (lines or single words) scattered on a page and a temporal sequence.

I WENT WEST, INTENDING THE MILKY WAY

In 1958, Keith won the Hopwood Prize at the University of Michigan and sent me a check: Come.

In December of that year I set sail for my third change of world, for a wholly new identity, I thought, for the steep program of the pleasure principle. It was a rough crossing. The boat took eleven days instead of the scheduled ten. I was seasick during five of them and swore never to set foot on a ship again.

In New York my crates were being cleared by customs. I was practically waved through—until Keith walked up to help. The customs officials took one look at his beard and long hair—this was before it became a familiar look—and went over all my belongings with a Geiger counter.

That evening, we saw Balanchine/Stravinsky's *Agon* and Brecht/Weill's *Seven Deadly Sins* at the City Center. With Allegra Kent and Lotte Lenya as the two Annies. It was not exactly representative of life in the United States. Neither was the night at Daniel Robins' apartment. Daniel, though several years younger, had declared himself Keith's grandmother (a metaphysical relationship, granted). One room of his cold-water flat was completely filled by a baby grand—it touched three walls, barely allowing room to squeeze by without scraping the fourth. Daniel put on his ballet slippers and did pirouettes. He had been discharged from the air force because he fell out for reveille in a costume for *Firebird.* The next morning, as we were leaving for the bus to Michigan, Daniel, itching for mischief, took me aside: "I'm so glad Keith is getting married. I didn't know he liked girls."

I CARRY YOUR NAME AWAY FROM OUR INTERSECTION

Married we got. Though with obstacles. I still wanted a Catholic wedding. Keith patiently submitted to "instruction," but was baffled when the priest demanded an affidavit that he was baptized and unmarried. Keith's mother could write it. But it had to be notarized by a priest. To Keith's mother, the Catholic church was the Great Whore of Babylon. She would never go near a priest. Who would? Daniel Robins, who had wanted to become a Trappist monk, but been rejected because he was Presbyterian.

Daniel sent back a statement that he had *witnessed* Keith's baptism and a note that it had taken him a week to find a defrocked priest to sign it.

After this, Ann Arbor did not seem strange at all.

I WAS SHOCKED AT MY LACK OF CULTURE SHOCK

Of course, Michigan had a large German population. We lived on Turner Park Court, named after a German exercise club, a *Turnverein!* Fittingly, it was a dead-end street.

Graduate school was a pleasure. Small seminars instead of the overcrowding I had known in Germany. Suddenly it was not difficult to speak up. Most important: an excellent library where—amazingly—students were allowed in the stacks.

Also amazing to me was a whole circle of young writers, musicians, artists gathered around Keith. James Camp said "piffle-paffle" and "schnorkle-fookle." Or, when trying to convey some elusive point, lifted his hand exactly like

Rosmarie at Ann Arbor, 1963

In Paris at the Jabès's, about 1976: (top) Arlette Jabès, (middle row, from left) Raquel Levi, Joseph Guglielmi, Emmanuel Hocquard, Anne-Marie Albiach, Adolfo Fernandez-Zoïla, (front row) Rosmarie Waldrop, Thérèse Bonnelalbay, Mme. Fernandez-Zoïla, Edmond Jabès, (bottom) Keith Waldrop

the angel in Crivelli's *Annunciation.* Nelson Howe made beautiful sculptures and collages. Dallas Wiebe, alias Skyblue the Badass, leaned forward and declared, "Cleanliness is next to nothing." His poems gave no hint yet of the magnificent, adventurous prose he would come to write. X. J. Kennedy played an archetypal Père Ubu. Chris Longyear, mad genius and linguist, tried to save me from copying Keith's Kansas pronunciation. Jeanne Longyear did "save our marriage" by teaching me to drive.

And there was Yoko Sugiyama, who covered her mouth whenever she laughed. She was systematically reading American *women* writers—and made me aware how unquestioningly I had gobbled up the "canon."

GORDON MUMMA,

Keith's first friend in Ann Arbor, and Robert Ashley founded the "Once Festival." ("Once"

because they thought there would be no second.) The first festival performed mostly local composers (Mumma, Ashley, Roger Reynolds, George Cacciopo, and Don Scvarda, whose flute part I more or less murdered). But it quickly grew into an international avant-garde event where I first encountered Cage, Berio, and Merce Cunningham, an aleatory grammar, a decentering, out-of-phase syntax.

THE REST OF US

formed the "Pound Society," reading the *Cantos* out loud, the "Joyce Society," reading *Finnegans Wake,* and, most important, the "Wolgamot Society" with a "holy book": John Barton Wolgamot's *In Sara, Mencken, Christ and Beethoven, There Were Men and Women.* (For this story, see Keith Waldrop's autobiography.) There was the memorable Beatnik Hoax. Keith directed plays, Jarry's *Ubu Roi* or *Gopotty Rex,* with X. J. Kennedy in the title role, Grabbe's *Comedy, Satire, Irony and Deeper Meaning*, Paul Goodman's *Jonah*. We had a better time than graduate students do now, in this time of job anxiety, when the United States has more words for getting fired than the Inuit have for snow. We were afraid we might have to go to some godforsaken place, but were sure we would get *some* job.

"YOU'VE BECOME AMERICAN,"

Keith told me one morning. "You talked in your sleep, and it was English." It was true, I was thinking in English by this time, which made writing poems in German very artificial. I could not keep it up. If I could not be a poet, I decided, I would become a translator. At first I translated American and French poems into German, but except for a few by Creeley and Queneau found it difficult to get them published, difficult to establish contact with magazines across the ocean. I switched direction and began to translate Arp, some Expressionists, Surrealists, and more recent poets like Krolow, Heissenbüttel, Mon into English. After a while, I got up the courage to try writing poems in English. Keith encouraged these attempts and was midwife to my becoming an American poet.

A POETRY MAGAZINE OF HIS OWN

was Keith's dream. Printers' estimates were beyond our graduate student means. Keith decided we would buy a press and print it ourselves. I objected: "We don't know how." Keith: "We'll learn." To my German mind this meant apprenticing with a printer, difficult to reconcile with graduate school. But Keith was undaunted: "No, no, we'll just get a book."

We found a print shop going out of business and bought a small Chandler & Price for $100 (with all the trimmings). We did learn from books, from trial and error, and from some professional advice. *Burning Deck Magazine* was born.

The sound of the press, the smell of ink and solvents also took me back to my childhood. Behind the apartment house we lived in was a print shop. Next to it a bit of untended yard where I was allowed to play among slabs of limestone, still showing the brightly colored wine labels printed from them.

I like setting type and printing in spite of its drudgery and miss it now that most of our books are done offset. I love holding in my hands a book I have made—such a tangible counterpart to reading and writing.

Setting type by hand is so slow it seemed the invention of close reading. It also made me extremely aware of any excess "fat" in writing.

Another impulse toward leanness came from Robert Creeley's example. Our last year in Michigan (1963–64), Keith taught at Wayne State University in Detroit, replacing W. D. Snodgrass, while I, supposed to write my dissertation, became what the Russians call

A "HEROIC SLEEPER"

Keith left the house at 7 A.M., drove the hour to Detroit, taught three classes, was back at 3 P.M.—and got me out of bed. He felt very superior. Luckily the Wayne poetry festival he got to organize was in the evening! Creeley's reading was a revelation. He so clearly read the silence at the end of each line without, however, letting the tension of the grammatical arc drop. It brought home the crucial difference of verse: its refusal to fill up all available space. So that even if the words celebrate what *is*, each line acknowledges what is *not*. As Clark Coolidge puts it: "to create is to make a pact with nothingness."

Duncan, by contrast, overwhelmed and finally numbed me. He seemed an engine accelerating to get in as many poems as possible. In Ann Arbor, he read for two hours, announced an intermission—which did not come—and read another hour. After which he came to our house and talked for another three or four about anything from Presocratics to Rosicrucians. Meanwhile W. D. Snodgrass set up court in the bedroom, singing Elizabethan songs with theorbo accompaniment. That night I oscillated between the two "courts" of discourse and music, as my working has oscillated between wanting Duncan's "swarming of the bees" and following my natural bent for slowly digging up one word and then another from my "word hoard."

"WON'T THEY MISS TOO MUCH OF THE WESLEYAN EXPERIENCE?"

the president asked. The College of Letters (a Comparative Literature Program) was proposing a year abroad for its students. Except for the president's provincial attitude, I had no complaints about my first teaching job. I wrote little. I was still finishing my thesis on the distrust of language as theme and impulse toward innovation. It was the time of marches and sit-ins, the Civil Rights Movement, the beginnings of the Vietnam War protests. Photos of burning churches, of a white woman spitting at a black girl who walks through a school gate. I grieved over Martin Luther King's assassination, as I had not over Kennedy's, and buried what was left of my teenage illusions. But I was still shocked when, after the Kent State shooting, one of my students took the mike to say: "I'm joining the Marines. I'll be on the other side when I see you next." And again when, in the middle of all this, the student lecture committee wanted to invite the leader of the American Nazi Party. The faculty were appalled, especially the German Department. The students reveled in the controversy and played the free speech issue to the hilt. I was surprised at my own violent reaction, because *theoretically* I agreed that objectionable opinions have the right to be heard. We finally succeeded in nixing the invitation by arguing that the invitation (and speaker's fee!) constituted support.

What I liked most about Wesleyan was its "World Music Program." There were weekly "curry concerts," all-nighters of Indian music and food, Sunday afternoons of Japanese koto and shakuhachi and, a little less often, a gamelan orchestra and Javanese dancers. My narrow Western music horizon was blown wide.

MY FATHER DIED IN 1966

I returned to Germany for the first time in seven years, just barely in time.

I was in for a second shock when I opened my mouth. My little nieces laughed. I "talked funny." I had an American accent in my native language! I spoke nothing "right" any more. Even my speech marked my place between languages, between countries. My non-place.

A few years later, Keith got a job at Brown University. Keith had been a displaced person among the fields and cows of Connecticut. He needed a city, more precisely, a bookstore within walking distance. I commuted between Providence and Wesleyan, which would feed into the

poems of *The Road Is Everywhere; or, Stop This Body.*

THE MYSTICAL MARRIAGE OF AMY LOWELL AND ALEXANDER VON HUMBOLDT

In 1970–71 Keith and I each received a fellowship. We settled in Paris, though I spent part of the year in Munich, doing research on German poetry. There were many jokes on this joining of Amy Lowell and Alexander von Humboldt, in whose name we were brought there, but it was only twelve years later that I actually "married" these two figures in *A Form / Of Taking / It All,* a collage-prose on encounters with otherness. Among them the discovery/conquest of America and the new physics so disturbing to me because of the absence of images.

We lived on the rue des Saints Pères, in a somewhat damp apartment in an inner court. It was absolutely quiet except for a faint sound of printing presses which we at first thought we were hallucinating. We walked, bought books, read, wrote, saw innumerable films, made pilgrimages to Gertrude Stein's grave and her house in the rue de Fleurus, explored the wine, and walked, and walked.

Work was going well. We were happy to be alone with each other and did not try to meet anybody. In January 1971, George Tysh, who had been Keith's student at Wayne, found us. He had been working in a Paris gallery for some time. He arranged a poetry reading of David Rosenberg and the French Canadian Robert Hébert in our living room.

Claude Royet-Journoud and Anne-Marie Albiach were there. Claude noticed Edmond Jabès's *Livre des questions* in our bookcase and asked if we had just bought it. "No," Keith said, "we brought it along because Rosmarie has started translating it." At this Claude shot across the room:

"I MUST KISS YOU BECAUSE YOU ARE TRANSLATING JABES"

I had translated fifty pages and sent them, with a description of the whole project, to about twenty American publishers. All declined on the grounds that translations had always lost them money. I had brought the book along in case I got stuck in my own work.

Rosmarie and Keith Waldrop at the press, Providence, about 1981

That day happened to be the publication date of Anne-Marie Albiach's first book, *Etat.* When people had left we went around the corner to the "Drugstore" on Saint-Germain (the French idea of an American drugstore, complete with café and bookstore) and found a copy. We were overwhelmed by its intelligence, its energy, its sheer beauty. I later used the book's grammatical structure as a matrix for *When They Have Senses.* The discrepancy between French and English grammar made for a fruitful tension.

The next afternoon, Claude brought Edmond Jabès. I gave him what I had translated. He said he recognized himself in the rhythm. This was the beginning of a long translation project (fourteen volumes to date) and of a close friendship with Edmond and Arlette Jabès.

"SHALL WE ESCAPE ANALOGY"

Claude and Anne-Marie "lived" poetry with an intensity I had not found elsewhere. We shared many enthusiasms, among them Zukofsky (who at the time was barely read in the United States). We talked endlessly. It was rare that we caught the last metro, at 1 A.M. Most of the time we had to talk till the first metro of the morning, around 5.

Claude's first book, *Le Renversement,* had at its center the provocative line: *échapperons-nous à l'analogie*—without question mark. This clarified something I had been fumbling toward. I had begun writing the sequence "As If We Didn't Have to Talk." It avoided literal metaphors, but worked with an implicit equation of walk and talk, movement in space and in language, pushing metaphor out of the texture into the structure. What in Claude's case was a conscious reaction against Surrealism, may in mine have been a subliminal reaction against Imagism and Pound. But in both our cases, the raw esperience of war is no doubt the more crucial "cause" of this turn against images, even if we were children, even if it is impossible to pin down precisely. I also began to push at

THE BOUNDARIES OF THE SENTENCES,

sliding them together by letting the object of one sentence flip over into being the subject of the next:

> two pairs of eyes
> see
> two different initial
> questions too
> disappear . . .

I liked the flowing, quasi-unending sentence and how it played against the short lines that determine the rhythm. On one level, I was simply exacerbating the tension between sentence and line that is there in all verse.

Later I realized that my feminist concerns were surfacing in this very grammar. Who could have more interest in subverting a rigid subject-object relation than women, who have been treated as the object par excellence? Instead, these poems propose a grammar (a society?) in which subject and object functions are not fixed but reversible roles, where there is no hierarchy of main and subordinate clauses, but a fluid and constant alternation.

WHEN I ASKED EDMOND JABES QUESTIONS

he never answered directly. He would look at the paragraph and begin to talk about it, around it. He gave me additional context. More crucial yet, it allowed me additional glimpses of his way of thinking.

I asked him how he reconciled being an atheist with constantly writing about God. He said it was a word his culture had given him, a metaphor for nothingness, the infinite, silence, death, for all that calls us into question. For the ultimate otherness. This God, this unbeliever's God I could accept. "The very condition of His freedom: *not to be.*"

"With my husband, Keith, Claude Royet-Journoud, Roger Laporte," Paris, 1984

The year in Paris ended with a bang: Random House would publish my first book of poems, *The Aggressive Ways of the Casual Stranger*.

THE BOY STOOD ON THE BURNING DECK

The magazine *Burning Deck* had been intended to come out as a "quinterly," five times a year. Instead it came out four times in five years. Unable to keep to a regular schedule, we had changed to printing chapbooks. When the National Endowment for the Arts began to support independent publishing, Burning Deck was able to grow. Anthony Barnett's *Poem about Music* was our first "full length" book of poems, in 1974. The direction also changed or, rather, narrowed somewhat. Keith's is a "catholic," inclusive spirit containing multitudes. He conceived the magazine as a bridge between poetry camps. Considering the limited resources of a small press, I argued for a narrower focus, on innovative, "avant-garde" work. Which had always been what we were most interested in though, for both of us, poems still come before theories.

It had taken me a year to translate *The Book of Questions*; it took four to find a publisher. It might have taken even longer without Jan Miel championing it.

ISOGRAMMATICAL LINES MAP THE DISCOURSES OF THE WORLD. AGAINST THEIR AVERAGE, EXTREMES OF SENSE AND ABSENCE CREATE THE PLEASURE OF FRAGMENTS

I had already begun to write sequences rather than single poems, but it was Jabès's work that pushed me into thinking in terms of *books* (though there is also the example of Spicer). It was specifically Jabès's insistence on the book on the one hand (as the writer's only place, as Mallarmé's "spiritual instrument") and fragmentation on the other, that focused my own contradictory impulses toward flow and toward fragmentation.

Jabès, like the German Romantics, holds that the fragment is our only access to the infinite. I tend to think it is our way of apprehending anything. Our inclusive views are mosaics. And the shards catch light on the cut, the edges give off sparks. This is the case in Anne-Marie Albiach's *Etat*, where the fragmentation adds pressure, even violence. And I hope that it is happening in *When They Have Senses*. That the glimpses amount to more than their sum, that the breaks allow possibility to enter, as Blanchot says, and thought.

DAS IST DIE BERLINER LUFT LUFT LUFT

Three opera houses playing repertory: Keith's notion of paradise. One in West Berlin, two in the East. We crossed the border between East and West Berlin so often that the guards at Friedrichstrasse began to recognize us. "You go to the opera an awful lot." We decide to use Checkpoint Charlie for a while.

I was stunned to find the bookstores in East Berlin almost empty. If I saw a book of interest I must buy it immediately. By the next day it would be gone. What a contrast to the ostentatious shops on Kurfürstendamm with their unending supplies. And not just the bookstores. The poverty was evident everywhere. It was 1975, thirty years after the end of the war, and still whole streets were in ruins. Most strikingly, the Synagogue on Oranienburgerstrasse. A plaque explained it was left a ruin in remembrance of the events of the Kristallnacht.

(When I came again, in 1993, I did not recognize the building. It *had* been rebuilt, with a shiny gold dome. The "Wessie" solution. With a guard in front. The ruin had been the more eloquent monument. But at this time, monuments were out of favor, being toppled by the hundreds. I imagined a museum of monumental Soviet statues in an open field. Like the actual field full of old printing presses that rust away in the rain, in Taunton, Massachusetts. A surreal landscape. But what did happen to the statues? Keith wondered: how would a monumental Stalin look in our front yard?! But only succumbed to buying a small piece of The Wall and a Baby Lenin medal.)

Back in a medium of German, my mother's Northern variety, not the softer "Fränkisch" I had grown up with, memories flooded. I started a novel, *The Hanky of Pippin's Daughter*. It began with portraits of my parents, but quickly became a way of trying to understand, to explore, at least obliquely, the Nazi period, the shadow of the past—and the blurred borders

"Reading with Keith at the Lelong Gallery in front of John Coplans's 'Self-Portraits,'" New York, 1991

of fact, fabrication, tradition, experience, memory. Till the drive to know and tell touches the violence inherent in its own mechanism. I tried to use the structure of Wittgenstein's *Tractatus:* there were to be seven central sentences, with all the rest in a logical (?) relation to them. Johannes Bobrowski has done something like it in his great novel, *Levin's Mill,* but I could not do it. The novel went through many versions. I abandoned it several times. It took me eight years to complete—all 160 pages of it!

MY MOTHER

had already started the long backward loop out of the mirror. Though her body hung on till 1980. And she had already taken the distance I thought of: she did not recognize me any more.

THE YEARS IN PROVIDENCE

seem round, filling the whole space. Like whales, in smooth hipless motion. Simple time open

toward quiet, persistent love, friends, reading, writing. Black dots across the screen. To pinpoint events not as easy as in the times abroad, memories keyed to place.

I like the image in *Don Quixote* that compares translation to working on a tapestry: you sit *behind* the canvas, with a mess of threads and a pattern for each color. You follow out patterns, but you have no idea what image will appear on the other side. This holds for living as well. Step by single step. And for writing. I don't even have thoughts, I have methods that make language think, take over and me by the hand. Into sense or offense, syntax stretched across rules, relations of force, fluid the dip of the plumb line, the pull of eyes.

IN FOREIGN PARTS

again. Of speech. For Keith's 1984 sabbatical, Arlette Jabès had found us an apartment off the Place de la Bastille. That year we were well informed on all demonstrations because they either began or ended there. No matter what political persuasion, all banners proclaimed LA LIBERTE and against L'INFAMIE.

Arlette was having radiation treatments. She felt exhausted, she said, but seemed bubbling with life to me. Edmond seemed more tired. Eyes returning to his face as if from a distance.

Claude Royet-Journoud had chosen a Wittgenstein phrase for the title of his third book: *Objects Contain the Infinite.* I was translating *El, or the Last Book,* the seventh volume of Jabès's *Book of Questions,* which has a substantial epigraph from Wittgenstein's *Tractatus.* There were copies in German and in French in the libraries, but not the English translation, which I finally had sent from home. Then it sat on my table, irking me with my failure to use its structure.

Reading the *Tractatus* again, two things fascinated me: the problem of representation and the propositional sentence with its extreme closure. The latter in particular was a challenge because my poems had always worked toward opening the boundaries of the sentence, either by sliding sentences together or by fragmentation. True, I was tired of this "main-clause highway" and hankering for complex sentences. I love the conditional, even in the past: "If I had stayed in Germany . . . " I decided to take up the challenge. To accept the complete sentence (most of the time), but to do my best to subvert it from the inside, by sliding between frames of reference, especially pitting logic against the body. The body is, after all, our means to have a world—even to have logic.

I was also reading Kafka's *Description of a Struggle* and Mei-mei Berssenbrugge's *Heat Bird,* one of the Burning Deck books I am most proud of having published. Phrases from both books entered into the prose poems of *The Reproduction of Profiles.*

COLLAGE, THE SPLICE OF LIFE

is one of my main methods. No text has one single author in any case. The blank page is not blank. Whether we are conscious of it or not, we always write on top of a palimpsest. Like many writers, I have foregrounded this awareness of the palimpsest as a method: using, trans-forming, "translating" parts of other

works. It is not a question of linear "influence" and not just of tradition. It is a way of getting out of myself. Into what? An interaction, a dialog with language, with a whole net of earlier and concurrent texts. Relation. Between.

I once wrote: "I need a book to say I love you." The distance of another's words to say what touches me most. Or is it that it needs to remain masked? Hofmannsthal: "We must hide what is deep. Where? On the surface."

"ALL RESONANCE GROWS FROM CONSENT TO EMPTINESS"

This sentence from *The Reproduction of Profiles* kept surfacing in my mind even after the book was finished. I was not done with the emptiness at the center of flute or violin, at the center of the female body. This emptiness which is not empty, as the excluded middle between true and false is not as empty as the law of logic would have it. On the contrary, it is the locus of fertility. Hence my *Lawn of Excluded Middle.*

I was delighted to find this "negative capability" a commonplace in physics. The picture of the world drawn by classical physics con-

Rosmarie Waldrop and J. Laughlin, Providence, 1986

flicts with the picture drawn by quantum physics. I like A. S. Eddington's statement: we use classical physics on Monday, Wednesday, Friday, and quantum theory on Tuesday, Thursday, Saturday.

I have now for some years been working on a third volume, *Reluctant Gravities*. Am I trying to *prove* this is fertile ground?

A KEY INTO THE LANGUAGE OF AMERICA

My fascination with American Indians goes back to my childhood when I devoured the *Leatherstocking Tales* and, above all, Karl May's Kraut-Westerns. By the dozen. When I came to this country my reading got more serious, and some of it, like Franz Boas's *Keresan Texts* and Gene Weltfish's *The Lost Universe: The Way of Life of the Pawnee,* have spilled over into poems. But nothing had prepared me for Roger Williams's *A Key into the Language of America* of 1643. I turned to this book for a look at the Narragansett Indian language that I encountered in the place names of Rhode Island, for a bit more Indian subsoil under the American English. I found something much richer than a phrase book. As far as I know it is the first sympathetic presentation of Indian customs. Roger Williams recognized a culture where his contemporaries saw only savages. Which got him into trouble as it led him to question the European settlers' right to "unused" Indian land. Using Williams's book as a matrix allowed me to work out some of my own ambivalences as an immigrant: a "conqueror" of sorts, and yet irredeemably between cultures.

DOES THE BODY ALWAYS CONTAIN ITS OWN ABSENCE?

Montaigne thought of writing, studying, as an apprenticeship of death. Because it can draw our soul out of us and keep it busy outside the body. Or as Foucault put it: One writes to become someone other than one is. Nevertheless, I was totally unprepared for breast cancer. Or for Keith's gangrenous gall bladder four years later. I think of Tutuola's "man of parts reduced to head" and hope that it won't come to this, that one part each is all we have to give up.

Waldrop with (left) Mark McMorris and Lee Ann Brown of Tender Buttons Press on the publication day of Lawn of Excluded Middle, *Providence, 1993*

In January 1991, Edmond Jabès died, Keith's new book by his chair. In August 1992, Arlette followed him. Their absence has spread through my present as if in its marrow.

The years Keith and I have lived together are piled on the path to the shore. In splendid profusion. We walk on them, with the air cooling. Turning a "Noh" mask slightly downward is known as "clouding" because the mask takes on a melancholy aspect. "Light cannot be wrong." But the difference of shadow bespeaks other crossroads. Still, I circle like a moth until the blinding splendor will exceed the anxiety of wings.

December 1997

BIBLIOGRAPHY

Poetry:

(With Keith Waldrop) *Change of Address,* Burning Deck, 1968.

(With Keith Waldrop) *Letters from Rosmarie and Keith Waldrop,* Burning Deck, 1970.

The Aggressive Ways of the Casual Stranger, Random House, 1972.

(With Keith Waldrop) *Alice ffoster-Fallis: (an outline),* Burning Deck, 1972.

The Road Is Everywhere; or, Stop This Body, Open Places, 1978.

When They Have Senses, Burning Deck, 1980.

Nothing Has Changed, Awede, 1981.

Differences for Four Hands, Singing Horse, 1984.

Streets Enough to Welcome Snow, Station Hill, 1986.

The Reproduction of Profiles, New Directions, 1987.

Shorter American Memory, Paradigm, 1988.

Peculiar Motions, Kelsey St. Press, 1990.

Lawn of Excluded Middle, Tender Buttons, 1992.

A Key into the Language of America, New Directions, 1994.

Another Language: Selected Poems, Talisman House, 1997.

Well Well Reality, Post-Apollo, 1998.

Split Infinites, Singing Horse Press, 1998.

Reluctant Gravities, New Directions, forthcoming.

Fiction:

The Hanky of Pippin's Daughter, Station Hill, 1986.

A Form of Taking It All, Station Hill, 1990.

Nonfiction:

Against Language?: Dissatisfaction with Language as Theme and as Impulse towards Experiments in Twentieth Century Poetry, Mouton (The Hague), 1971.

The Ground Is the Only Figure, Impercipient Lecture Series, 1997.

Translator of:

Peter Weiss, *Bodies and Shadows,* Delacorte, 1969.

Edmond Jabès, *Elya* (also see below), Tree Books, 1973.

E. Jabès, *The Book of Questions,* Wesleyan University Press, Volume 1, 1976, Volume 2: *The Book of Yukel,* 1977, Volume 3: *Return to the Book,* 1977, Volume 4: *Yael,* 1983, Volume 5: *Elya,* 1983, Volume 6: *Aely,* 1984, Volume 7: *El, or the Last Book,* 1984, published together as *The Book of Questions: Complete Seven Volumes in Four Books,* 1984.

E. Jabès, *The Death of God,* Spectacular Diseases, 1979.

(With Harriet Watts) *The Vienna Group: Six Major Austrian Poets,* Station Hill, 1985.

Alain Veinstein, *Archaeology of the Mother,* by Waldrop and Tod Kabza, Spectacular Diseases, 1986.

Paul Celan, *Collected Prose,* Carcanet (Manchester, U.K.), 1986.

E. Jabès, *The Book of Dialogue,* Wesleyan University Press, 1987.

Emmanuel Hocquard, *Late Additions,* Spectacular Diseases, 1988.

E. Jabès, *The Book of Shares,* Chicago University Press, 1989.

E. Jabès, *The Book of Resemblances* (three volumes), Wesleyan University Press, 1990-92.

Jacques Roubaud, *Some Thing Black,* Dalkey Archive Press, 1990.

E. Jabès, *Intimations the Desert,* Wesleyan University Press, 1991.

E. Jabès, *From the Book to the Book: An Edmond Jabès Reader,* Wesleyan University Press, 1991.

Joseph Guglielmi, *Dawn,* Spectacular Diseases, 1991.

E. Jabès, *The Ineffaceable the Unperceived,* Wesleyan University Press, 1992.

Friederike Mayröcker, *Heiligenanstalt,* Morning Star (Edinburgh, Scotland), 1992.

E. Jabès, *The Book of Margins,* University of Chicago Press, 1993.

E. Jabès, *A Foreigner Carrying in the Crook of His Arm a Tiny Book,* Wesleyan University Press, 1993.

Elke Erb, *Mountains in Berlin,* Burning Deck, 1995.

Roubaud, *The Plurality of Worlds of Lewis,* Dalkey Archive Press, 1995.

"Berlin (plus) Portfolio," selected and translated by Waldrop, *Exact Change Yearbook,* 1 (1995): 61-90.

E. Jabès, *The Little Book of Unsuspected Subersion,* Stanford University Press, 1996.

Other:

Editor of poetry series for Burning Deck, 1968—.

Contributor of articles, poems, and translations to numerous periodicals and anthologies including *The Art of Translation: Voices from the Field, Conjunctions, Denver Quarterly, Lingo, New American Writing, O.blek, Postmodern American Poetry,* and *Twentieth Century Literature.*

Author of many chapbooks, including *Camp Printing,* 1970, *Light Travels* (with husband Keith Waldrop), 1992, and *Blindsight,* 1998.

Brenda Webster

1936-

From the beginning it seemed that I was going to be a detective or a writer of gothic novels. When I was five, I spent hours spying on our housekeeper, a woman with an enormous behind, to see if she had a tail curled under her corset. Later, I dictated my first story (about a girl spy) to my mother. My mother was an artist and was convinced that I was going to be one too. My father contented himself with imagining me growing up to be a beauty like the debutante sensation of the thirties, Brenda Fraser. I had doubts about both possibilities.

My parents were idealistic, glamorous, acculturated Jews—so glamorous that it was hard not to feel like an ugly duckling born into a family of swans. My father, Wolfgang Schwabacher, was a prominent entertainment lawyer. Dorothy Parker and her circle were social acquaintances, and his clients included Lillian Hellman, said to lie even when she said yes or no, and Erskine Caldwell, whose novel sparked an obscenity trial that was pure theatre. As a young man, my father had a bohemian side: he was engaged eight times and once popped up naked from under a table at a Marx Brothers party. My mother, Ethel Schwabacher, studied with Arshile Gorky and, after he hung himself, became his first biographer. Later, she was recognized as an important abstract expressionist in her own right, one of the very few women in the movement.

But in addition to her beauty and talent, my mother brought into the marriage a serious history of mental instability in her family. Her brother, reputedly a mathematical genius, was psychotic and her mother, while not obviously crazy, was frantic with anxiety. By the time I was born, in 1936, Grandma had been analyzed once and Mother twice. Mother didn't tell me about any of this (I didn't even know she had a brother), or about why she was so angry at my grandmother, but my childhood impulse to investigate the intimate details of people's lives was undoubtedly fueled more by

Brenda Webster, 1985

my sense that there were fascinatingly important things I wasn't supposed to know than by my budding vocation as a novelist and psychoanalytic critic.

Despite my mother's difficulties, in many respects I had a magical childhood. For as long as I can remember, our lives were divided between our New York apartment on Ninety-fourth and Park and our country place, an old farm outside of Princeton, where we went for Christmas and Easter and the long hot summers. The farm was a big one, two hundred acres set in softly rolling dairy country, surrounded by red barns and grazing cows. Everyone did what they liked there. Mother spent long hours in the fields sketching bulls and fruit trees while I lolled by the pool with my adored father. It was also the place where I made my first acquaintance with a psychoanalyst. Dr. Muriel Gardiner was a close family friend. She was also the unwitting model for Julia in the movie with Vanessa Redgrave. In 1940 she bought half of the farm from my father and moved in with her daughter, Connie, and her husband Joe, who had just gotten out of a French internment camp after heading the Austrian resistance in the war.

As a small child, I knew nothing about what Muriel did, or who she was, but I loved her because she spoke to me in a frank unself-conscious way. More important, she really listened when I talked to her, while my own mother was often distracted. Muriel took children's wishes and needs seriously. She didn't just talk liberation the way my parents seemed to, she practiced it with her daughter. Her method of child-rearing gave me some new ideas about what was possible for a girl.

Muriel's own life was fascinating. Early married and divorced, with a small child, she found herself at medical school in Vienna during the Nazi takeover. There she met Joe Buttinger and helped him in the Austrian underground. She didn't tell Connie that they were lovers or about the danger they were in, but Connie must have sensed the tension. She was in the midst of a war zone with a mother who was not only going to medical school and embarking on a helping profession but was actually saving people from death. Muriel continued to help people throughout the war, filling her house with refugees.

My ideal of what a girl could be was Muriel's daughter. Connie had green eyes and black hair that she cropped short as a boy's. Four years older than I, she was allowed to do pretty much what she wanted. She had not only stripped her room of furniture, including the bed, but she had filled it with rows of rat cages, except for a fenced-off portion of the floor which was covered with sand for turtles. Much of the time, she slept in the barn or in the woods, where she caught more exotic animals, like skunks.

I was allowed to run around and play freely, but my parents would never have allowed me to make a zoo of my room. And for social occasions, I was expected to wear a nice dress and patent leathers. I didn't realize at the time how extraordinary it was for Muriel to let her daughter grow up this way. Not only because Muriel was a woman but because she was training to be an analyst and analysis at that time favored clear divisions of sexual roles: men were active, women passive and envious. Muriel had been trained in Vienna by Ruth Mack Brunswick, one of Freud's inner circle (and a frequent visitor to the farm), but from the beginning she was a maverick. None of the women she knew, she once told me laughing, were like

Freud's ideal female—and she certainly wasn't raising Connie to be.

Connie didn't save people the way her mother had during the war, she saved rats and mice. But she was passionate as any patriot—and she had an enemy too: cats. One day—I must have been seven by then—I mistakenly let out some kittens that she had locked in the woodshed to be taken away by the hired man. She tracked them down, put them in a sack, then made me go with her to the barn and hold the sack while she smashed their heads with the blunt edge of an axe.

Connie was my model of fearless activity and, until the kitten episode, I really wanted to be like her. But what if being active meant you might kill? Wasn't it better to stick to being a girlie girl? I doubt if I thought of it that way at the time. I just ran crying to my mother—who had always said I played with Connie too much—and put my head in her lap.

For years I saw the murder scene in my dreams. And when I was about ten, I wrote it down, then again in high school—each time forgetting about it completely. When I started writing fiction again in my forties, after a long gap, my first story was about Connie. Afterwards, drawn mysteriously to some old papers in the cellar, I found I'd already written this story in college, twenty years before.

Though I wrote stories all through my childhood, I really wanted to be a painter like my mother. When I was ten, I asked her for an easel of my own. I was more aware of her painting the summer of 1946 because she had a show coming up in the fall at the Passedoit gallery in New York, the first show she'd had since my birth, and she was working hard. Mother's paintings of red and black bulls set against giant lilies had a lot to do with sex. Her mentor and friend Arshile Gorky had close connections with French surrealists such as André Breton. I didn't know the theory behind mother's art—the importance of symbolic forms, association of ideas, dream images—but I certainly sensed its vitality.

I decided to set up my new easel under the eaves in the barn where I could see the summer fields. Unlike my mother, I was a realist. I wanted things to look the way they were. My plan was to show the fields sloping gently backward towards the woods behind them and then to put in some horses. But my canvas was a disaster before I even got to the fig-

(Top) With Connie Buttinger, about 1942

ures—my fields resembled oblong swatches piled on top of each other under a strip of sky-blue. I consoled myself for my failure as an artist by redoubling the time I spent riding with my father. We went out every morning before it got hot. He had a gorgeous hunter, I had an old nag named Trigger. But it didn't matter. Just being with him was enough to make me forget my disappointment.

The other great influence on my life besides the farm, Muriel, and my parents was my school, Dalton, which was founded by Helen Parkhurst in the twenties. Dalton was based on the ideas of the philosopher John Dewey, the father of progressive education. His radical new teaching methods stressed individual growth and social awareness and emphasized the role of experience. "Learning by doing" was Dewey's principle and Dalton's catchphrase.

Dalton students were the children of intellectuals, artists, and professionals. From my parents' perspective it was the perfect school. It combined my mother's ideas about creativity and the evils of repression with my father's interest in community. My father served on the board along with other socially minded German Jews, including Stanley Isaacs, "the conscience of the New York City Council," and Ben Buttenweiser, a wealthy, liberal friend of Alger Hiss.

Apparently these mostly Jewish parents were content with Dalton's relativistic attitude towards religion. (My mother of course believed with Freud that religion was dangerous.) Mrs. Durham, the principal, had a statue of Buddha outside her door, and the school year was marked by a series of alternating pagan and Christian festivals. Interestingly, there was nothing Jewish. This probably reflected the way Judaism had been translated into social activism for many of our parents. Certainly it had for my father. He raised money for Jewish causes but happily celebrated Christmas. As a child, I remember him saying how good it was that Dalton not only taught children independent thinking but taught them about their social responsibilities.

I had gone to Dalton from the age of three and I always loved it. Unlike my German nurses, who prized docility, the Dalton teachers praised my energy and "creativity." By six I was reading and writing little stories that were printed in the Lower School paper. I never wanted to go home.

From the early grades we practiced Dewey's hands-on philosophy—blissfully ignorant that what we were doing went back to "Emile" and "Héloïse," Jean Jacques Rousseau's ideally educated children. Like Emile we did concrete things—planted seeds, milked cows, and made model volcanoes that really exploded. Later, we studied world history and, when there weren't texts in Indian or Asian history, our teachers wrote them. In line with progressive ideas we had no tests and no grades.

Flexibility and freedom were at a premium but sometimes spontaneity was overdone. To learn grammar we sat in a circle and imagined what part of speech we would have invented first if we were cave men. Would it have been an expletive ("Ugh") or a word to signal danger ("Look") or something on the order of "Me Tarzan, you Jane"? When I graduated from high school, I still couldn't diagram a sentence, but I had a freedom and playfulness with words that I might not have had under a more result-oriented system.

My progressive school created an environment that was nurturing and comfortable and where we were praised continually for our creative efforts. From the Dalton perspective, being an artist or writer seemed like the most enjoyable and rewarding thing a person could do. But at home I was getting a different message. My mother put the same high value on creativity and got deep satisfaction from her painting, but she also suffered a lot. I liked being free and "creative" but I began to wonder if creative work had too steep a price. Mother was hysterical with fear before her show at the Passedoit gallery, even though afterwards it seemed silly, the reviews were so good. Could being an artist drive you crazy?

The summer after sixth grade, in July 1948, there was a terrible example of what could happen to an artist. Arshile Gorky, Mother's friend and teacher since before I was born, hung himself in his glass house in Connecticut. Mother liked to tell me that as soon as she met him and saw his work, she recognized his genius just the way Gertrude Stein had heard a little bell go off in her head when she met Picasso. When he killed himself we were at the farm, and I have a vivid memory of my mother crying uncontrollably while my father tried to comfort her.

With her mother, Ethel Schwabacher,
at the farm, about 1938

The winter before he died I had driven to Connecticut with Mother to visit him. How black his long hair and moustache seemed against the snow. How big he seemed. How cold it was. I don't think I paid much attention to clothes but I noticed his coat had patches on the elbows and it seemed too short to cover his wrists. I was startled by the house itself. The huge glassed-in living room, the high roof, the sparse furnishings.

At some point, he began to lay paint on a canvas with a palette knife and I wondered at its thickness. He stood back looking at it, black hair over his forehead, black eyes like coals. Intent. His children, Maro and Natashya, must have been there, though I remember them only vaguely. I was more impressed by the white sheepskin rug placed next to my bed upstairs in just the right place for toes to snuggle into before crawling under the covers. It gave me a sense of being in a primitive enchanted forest with a woodcutter and his family. Gorky's wife, Agnes, was beautiful with long black hair and blue eyes. I dimly sensed that there was some trouble in the house but no one knew Agnes was thinking of leaving. On the contrary, Mother was planning to write a book with her about Gorky.

Mother kept saying that analysis could have helped him—it was clear she thought the mind doctors had great power. I had no way of judging back then, but the relation of art to madness and suicide stayed in my mind as a tantalizing puzzle whose solution could mean the difference between life and death.

My childhood came to an end three years later when my father—who had always had perfect health, boasting that he'd never even had a cavity—died of a heart attack. He was only fifty-two. I was fourteen. I couldn't cry, it was too unbelievable, but I started writing poetry and the poems—which were really love poems—gave me some relief from the pain of missing him.

I found a more mature voice in my poems than I had in my real life. My mother balanced on the edge of breakdown for months after my father's death, and some of my poems were to her, trying to give her courage. Then just when I thought she was beginning to feel better, her Gorky book was rejected by Lloyd Goodrich, director of the Whitney Museum, and she took an overdose of sleeping pills.

I was the one who found her. She was lying in her bed in a peach silk nightgown, her mouth slightly open, snoring slightly. When I shook her she didn't respond. I stared fascinated at the little violet veins in her lids. Then I saw the empty pill bottle and called emergency.

Unlike Gorky, she didn't succeed in killing herself. When she came home from the hospital she started going to Marianne Kris, the analyst she would see for the next thirty years. It was hard to recognize my beautiful, cosseted mother in the staring, suspicious stranger who came home from the hospital. She had nurses around the clock, and bars were put on the windows to keep her from jumping. She thought my brother and I were plotting against her and shrieked imprecations at us. But despite her distraught state, she immediately started to paint: abstract canvases filled with stark colors of black and red. A little later, she started working with glass, shattering it and gluing the sharp fragments onto pieces of wood to make collages. She played Gluck's *Orpheus* at top volume and sang along with it in a desperate voice, *"che faro senza Euridyce?"* Orpheus's lament for his dead wife still strikes a chill in me.

While Mother was still in the hospital, Betty Parsons, director of the famous gallery on Fifty-seventh Street, visited her and asked her to have a show in 1953. The names of Betty's artists read like a roster of who's who in abstract expressionism, including Mark Rothko, Jackson Pollack, and Hans Hoffman. Betty asking Mother to exhibit with her may have saved her life. Betty's gallery was the first to provide pure, large open spaces for the new, often large canvasses of abstract art. Mother, echoing what Betty had done with her gallery, stripped our living room of its bourgeois furniture and made it her studio. The dining room was converted into a neutral space for hanging paintings. Now that she was no longer a wife, she shed friends who didn't fit the new life she envisioned for herself as a woman without a husband (keeping only artists or close personal friends like Muriel).

She also decided to send me to a famous child analyst, a close friend of Muriel Gardiner. My problems with boys—mostly, how far to go—were too much for her to handle. After my father's first heart attack, his liberal sexual views had disappeared in a panic over what might happen to me if he died and couldn't watch

With her father, Wolf Schwabacher, Provincetown, 1941

over me. In his wish to protect me, he even brought me home a boyfriend, the son of someone in his office who he was sure would be afraid to touch me. Then suddenly, after my father died, I had a shrink who was urging me to talk about sex, describe sex, and have sex if I wanted to. My efforts to talk about my troubles with my mother seemed to bore her. At the same time Mother—whose own doctor endorsed sexual experimentation—gave me D. H. Lawrence's *Lady Chatterley's Lover,* for my birthday.

Though most of my mental energy was taken up with wondering if my mother was going to try to kill herself, I somehow managed to get through Dalton High School. In senior year, I became editor of our literary magazine, *The Blue Flag.* I had been writing stories—mostly about horses—since childhood, writing my first tolerably good one about a boy whose possessively jealous mother is glad when his beloved colt dies. Writing after my father died wasn't a luxury, it kept me from going crazy. The poetry that spilled out of me then was like condensed tears. But I was very far from having the idea of writing as a craft. It was a relief, a necessity, a lifesaver (as painting was for my mother), but not something I worked at over and over again until it perfectly expressed what I had to say. That idea came much later.

At my high school graduation in the spring of 1954, I stood with my classmates, in my white dress, reciting T. S. Eliot's "The Hollow Men," in chorus. "We are the hollow men, we are the stuffed men," we recited, "headpieces stuffed with straw." It seemed a very brave statement to make just then, on the eve of our departure. Afterwards we chanted Gerard Manly Hopkins. "How to keep beauty from vanishing away. . . ." The pessimism was heady stuff; but more than the content there was the way the alliterating words chimed against each other, the lovely mounting rhythm filling my mouth with pleasure. A sense that the crescendos of sound were what I wanted to make too.

When we got back from graduation my mother gave me a strange present—the secret of why she was so angry at my grandmother. Grandma, by the time I knew her, was an old lady with iron-gray hair, living with a companion in a dingy hotel downtown. She was always kind to me, gave me wonderful ornaments, boats with gold filigree sails, tiny dolls, and I never understood why my mother was so cold to her. Now I heard that when my grandfather—a Jewish lawyer from the South—died, Grandma had taken up with a German baron named Willy, who turned out to be a con man. After she married him, she signed over her fortune and he left her.

Money wasn't something my mother ever talked about any more than she had talked about her parents. Because my father had told me that his grandfather had fought with Lincoln, I always thought of the men in his family as heroic figures. In fact, after his father moved east from Alabama, he sold cigars in Newark. They were thoroughly middle-class. My mother's family, on the other hand, had been international bankers. The Oppenheimer family tree on the maternal side stretched back to the seventeenth century, when an ancestor financed the Kaiser's wars. In more recent incarnations, the Oppenheimers were diamond merchants and theatre owners. Mother, being a socialist and a believer in psychoanalysis, would have scorned their faith in money, but underneath she clearly cared about it too. "Grandma gave Willy my inheritance," mother said, her face contorted. "I begged her not to do it, but she did. It was terrible." She brought the subject up again when I was getting ready to leave for college, explaining that no matter how much you love a man, you must keep your bank accounts separate. Armed with this knowledge—which conflicted with everything she'd ever said about following your impulses—I packed my bags.

Swarthmore College was like a dose of strong medicine given to a patient already weakened by disease. I had gotten away from my mother and my shrink (and my boyfriend) to an incredibly beautiful and stimulating place but I was emotionally exhausted. After two years, I came home, transferred to Barnard, and, in 1956, at my mother's insistence, began psychoanalysis.

Dr. Kurt Eissler made a profound difference in the direction my life took. I started out analysis wanting to be a writer and ended up a fledgling psychoanalytic literary critic. He also managed to persuade me that I needed to fulfill my female destiny by getting married.

Eissler was part of the New York analytic community that had grown during the thirties and forties with an influx of refugees from Nazi Europe—the first wave of Freud's famous disciples. Eissler was a friend of my child analyst as well as of Muriel. When I started to see him, he was already well known as Freud's fervent champion. As founder of the Freud Archives—Janet Malcolm was later to write a series of articles for the *New Yorker* about his conflict with his young protégé Jeffrey Masson—he had boxes full of historic documents and records on his top shelves. I didn't know anything about the struggles within and around the movement, but it was impossible not to sense his commitment. If Freud was King Arthur, Eissler was Launcelot, a quixotic but fiercely loyal defender of the faith.

We decided right away that I would start my therapy with three times a week and lie on the couch. The main things he concentrated on in the sessions were my fights with my mother—I was having a difficult time at home—and my sex life. Being an orthodox Freudian, he tried hard to connect my high degree of anxiety with conflict over sex. I liked him better than I did my child analyst and it was rather fun to talk to him about sex. When our talk turned to other things, he confused me by his fixed and restrictive ideas about women's roles. Women should care first about their children. He insisted Mother should have spent more time with me, for instance, which would clearly not have made her a better mother. Deprived of her time at the easel, she might very well have been worse. Furthermore, no female could be a genius. Since Eissler's main interest was the psychology of genius—he had written on Goethe, whom he worshipped—this had a depressing effect on me. He consoled me with the idea that I had the opportunity of becoming the wife of a genius and spent a good deal of time gently probing to see if I had the endurance, say, of Mrs. Tolstoy.

Meanwhile, Barnard was a relief from the pressures of Swarthmore. I switched from philosophy to English and joined the Barnard magazine. Our year was a particularly good one for writers. The staff included Lynne Sharon Schwartz and Rosellen Brown. I also found my first mentor, Rosalie Colie, a brilliant woman, small and dark with flashing eyes, who taught the metaphysical poets and Milton. She had been a friend of my father's secretary, knew all about our tragedies, and was inclined to be nice to me. I was thrilled when, in a footnote in her book on paradox, she acknowledged my paper on *King Lear.*

But I was also confused. Was I supposed to develop my mind or train myself to be a sort of high-grade domestic as the wife of a genius? I tried to work it out in a story about work and love, called "The Garden and the Sea." At least that's what I thought it was about. A kind of meditation on the difficulties of being an artist and trying to love someone too. In my story, the heroine, a young painter who couldn't cope with either the demands of life or love, drowns herself by walking into the sea.

"I don't want you to send this out," Mother said, when I gave her the story to read. "It will lead to talk."

"But lots of people kill themselves," I said ingenuously, "like Virginia Woolf."

On the day after I showed her my story, I found her lying across her bed crying. When I touched her shoulder and asked her what was the matter, she turned away from me, pressing her face into the white spread. Finally, she sat up and let me get her a glass of water.

"My brother died," she said when I'd given her a sip. The flap of her dress jacket was turned back and the crimson silk inside made me think of blood.

"What?" I stammered stupidly. "What brother? You don't have a brother."

That's how I learned about my uncle John. He had been a brilliant mathematician as a young man, then inexplicably had gone crazy.

This discovery made me doubly curious about my mother's mysterious family. Since Eissler wouldn't reassure me that I hadn't inherited some genetic instability, I concluded that I had. There was some inherited weakness in the basic fabric that predisposed it to crazing—like a badly fired pot.

Despite his patriarchal ideas, Eissler encouraged my writing, just as he encouraged me when I took acting senior year with Mildred Dunock and thought briefly of a career on the stage. But after reading a story that he didn't like, he began to suggest that a career as an academic might fulfill my ambitions better than being a writer of fiction. Gradually, without being aware of it, I had begun to think in psychoanalytic terms when I read literature. I had the feeling that the standard New Critical approach wasn't getting to the heart of things. I thought I could get to a deeper truth by analyzing emotional meanings. At this point Eissler be-

Webster in Taos, after her first year at Swarthmore, 1955

came not only my therapist but my mentor, and we would take turns in my hours talking about what I had discovered in my readings of Yeats and what Eissler was finding out about Hamlet.

It was satisfyingly soothing to analyze texts. Yeats's haunting images distracted me from my ongoing fights with Mother. It was much easier to track images through texts than it was to find meaning in my puzzling life. But even so I wouldn't have thought of applying to graduate school at Columbia if my mentor, Professor Colie, hadn't recommended me for a Woodrow Wilson Fellowship. Because of my upbringing—none of the women in my family had ever worked for a living—I didn't think of graduate school as a path to a future profession; I simply wanted an excuse to keep on probing writers' secrets.

After about a year at Columbia, a friend of the family introduced me to a young history professor, Richard Webster. We were drawn to each other more by what we disliked—materialism, hypocrisy, and our difficult relationships with our mothers—than by affinities. He was a religious Jew and I was an atheist. But his mother had dated my father when she was at MIT and he was at Harvard Law, and there was a comforting sameness about our backgrounds. Though Richard wasn't a genius—Eissler had been enthralled by my previous suitor, who appeared to be a genius but turned out to be psychotic—Eissler was excited by the fact that Richard was a real intellectual and urged me to overcome my doubts about marriage. When I complained that Richard hadn't come to a poetry reading I gave at a coffee house on Morningside Heights, Eissler reminded me that the male was the breadwinner and that his career and interests were naturally the more important.

It seemed both dangerous and subversive to want too much for myself. That didn't mean I stopped wanting, but I began to stop seeing how much I was actually doing. Or I would find ways to rationalize it. For instance, I thought of my first novel—written during a summer holiday we spent in Italy for Richard's research—as an engagement gift. My past offered up to my future husband in what I hoped was an appealing form. The book, which I titled rather bleakly "The Bare Branch," was about a love affair I'd had in Vienna just before I met him, when my self-esteem was at an all-time low.

Richard wasn't placated by my suggestion that I was giving him something. He would come into our hotel bedroom, look over my shoulder, and mutter, "More of your unpleasant fantasies." Since I was secretly afraid my mind was some sort of sinkhole, I didn't contradict him. But when I finished the novel—which I wrote in one swoop without correcting a line—I sent it to a family friend who found me an agent in New York. She couldn't sell it—partly due to the antiromantic ending where the young lover begs the heroine not to make her marry him—but I had learned that whether people liked it or not, I wanted to keep writing.

I didn't think of my second novel as a gift to anyone. Married to Richard by this time, "Adam" came into being along with my pregnancy—a sort of parallel mode of being pregnant. I had had an abortion while I was at Swarthmore (two analysts had to certify that I was unbalanced) and felt duly guilty about it. Then, just before we went to Florence for Richard's sabbatical (in 1962-63), I had a miscarriage. I immediately got pregnant again but I was scared to death—afraid that my college abortion had done something awful to my insides and that I'd never be able to have a child. My novel, "Adam," rewrote the past in a more satisfactory manner. It was about a man in love with two women: a selfish, sexually predatory bitch and a plainer but creative and nurturing woman who gets pregnant and—unlike me at Swarthmore—decides to have the baby.

I wrote sitting at the dining room table in the run-down villa we had rented on Viale Michelangelo. When I looked up from my old Olivietti, I could see olive trees and white oxen ploughing just outside the back window. In the afternoons, I went shopping for exquisitely embroidered baby clothes. I still didn't think of myself as a writer—being pregnant seemed like a more legitimate occupation—it was simply something I did. A form of exploration. And since Richard clearly didn't like what I wrote, I kept pretty quiet about it.

I hadn't counted on what having a baby would do to me. It made me remember my mother standing at her easel singing while I wailed outside the door. She had been such a lousy nurturer, I was determined not to let my baby Lisa—with her astonishing peach fuzz hair and huge blue eyes—suffer any deprivation. I certainly wasn't going to let any work of mine stand in the way of caring for her. Being a wife and mother were the most important facts of my existence—the work was secondary. Almost overnight, I did more to diminish any sense of vocation than the reactionary forces of the fifties, my husband, and my analyst combined. I'd finished my novel before Lisa was born, but when people asked me what I did, I always said, "Wife and mother."

When I got back to Berkeley, I hoped that the woman analyst Dr. Eissler referred me to when I left New York might explain why I felt writing fiction was so dangerous for my baby. But Anya Maenchen—another of Freud's early disciples—turned out to be a disaster. Instead of relieving my anxieties, she made me feel even more shaky. "Why do you have to write books?" she would ask me repeatedly. "You might be just as happy working in your garden. Being a housewife can be very creative, you know."

Meanwhile, Christopher Lehmann-Haupt at Dial wrote my agent that he had turned "Adam" down: It had great humanity but was "too quiet and uncommercial to sell." And a senior editor at Viking suggested I rewrite, emphasizing the nice Jewish girl who has the baby and cutting out the selfish bitch. Since I had projected myself into both women and the male hero, I was appalled at the thought. I can't tell at this distance how I could have sharpened the book without sacrificing any of my characters, but it certainly would have benefitted from revision. It would have helped me to have been told by my agent, or someone else, that writing is 80 percent rewriting. I hadn't outlined, hadn't planned, I'd just written a few pages a day in my notebook and, at the end, typed it up. But in any case I'd probably learned something from the sheer act of writing the earlier novel, and this time my book aroused considerable interest. Lots of beginners are rejected. I could have rewritten. I could have tried a new novel. But my inner resistance was too strong.

Somehow writing a Ph.D. dissertation didn't conflict so much with my ideas of motherhood. Scholarship was less emotionally taxing and didn't seem to drain my vital juices. I was lucky I had it as an alternative outlet or, given my confusion and conflict, I might have stopped writing altogether.

My professors had their own ideas of what being female implied. When I passed my Ph.D. orals, the head of my committee said that my feminine charms made my faults appear virtues. Then the head of my committee told me that

the book I wanted to write on Yeats was too ambitious (ambition being reserved for males) and refused to pass my prospectus. My advisor, Thomas Flanagan, an Irishman with a wicked sense of humor, took me aside. "The problem isn't with your project, it's with your manner." My mistake, he said, was "to sit there like Goldilocks with a shit-eating smile on your face. Get tough!" Six months later, not having changed a word, I went back. This time, I dressed in black pants and a leather jacket and combed my hair down over my eyes. When they challenged me, I spoke back. "We release you in the custody of your advisor," the committee head announced, winking at Tom, as though I were some sort of lunatic. I'd gotten through.

I finished my dissertation the year the Arno overflowed its banks and caused such wholesale devastation in Florence. We had gone there so that Richard could research his book on Italy's entry into World War I. Our ramshackle villa on Viale Michelangelo was a block away from the river. When I went downstairs the morning of the flood, a green-brown river had replaced our street. Like my marriage, the water was deceptively calm. It was only when you looked more closely that you could see the wreckage from people's houses and the submerged cars, their roofs caved in by the force of the water.

It was a frightful year. I should have felt proud of the way I took care of everyone and managed to keep writing, but I was simply exhausted. After the water went down, Richard contracted a mysterious illness—probably from standing knee-deep in mud trying to save books—and he could barely move his legs. His joints were painfully inflamed. I piled us all into our Fiat, drove to Rome, and installed us in the pensione Villa Borghese across from the park. All four of us—I had a new baby, Michael, by now—were crammed in two rooms with no place for the children to play. As soon as one of them recovered from a bout of bronchitis, the other would get it. On well days, we went to the park. At night, when I lay in bed too tired to sleep, I thought of writing a novel about a woman whose monotonous routine is broken into by a flood; afterwards there would be a new life. But I found myself incapable of imagining what that new life would be. The only way I could imagine myself getting close to Richard was by becoming an orthodox Jewess and wearing a wig. I tried sketching out an ending where we were all happy in Jerusalem, but the phrases when they came at all were stiff and false.

It's a cliché that people in failing marriages often buy a new house or have another child. By the time Michael was a toddler, I was yearning to be pregnant again. I wanted a new baby with the urgency a freezing person would want to be near a hot stove: children were my only source of warmth. I was revising my dissertation into a book by then. I'd also gotten a part-time job at University Extension. The fact that it was a tenuous appointment that could be terminated at any time suited me. I was desperately afraid that if I threw myself into a career, I'd neglect the children. I kept working, but I tried not to notice how important it was to me. In that respect, getting pregnant again served as a perfect cover. I was energetically revising my Yeats book, but if anyone had asked me what I was doing, I would have said, being pregnant. More to the point, I was afraid to see myself as an ambitious, man-envying woman, hankering to see her works in print. I

was a nice, good, sweet, and—see, see my belly—very pregnant woman.

Despite my best efforts at being a good wife and mother, I was increasingly angry at Richard. When he stayed out at night (which he did several times a week), I sometimes imagined his car crashing on the bridge. I felt as if I was drowning. When I asked Dr. Maenchen if there was some way she could help me, she responded with a lecture on wifely tolerance. Then she reminded me of my hostility to men and my penis envy. "You're angry that he gets to do what he wants, and you have to stay home and take care of the children," she said, "but that's your job." Clearly to be "cured" meant continuing to do my female job without showing any signs that I was coming apart at the seams.

I undoubtedly should have found another, more empathetic therapist. But my mother's total dependence on her analyst and my childhood conditioning to treat one's analyst as a guru made it impossible to see the obvious. Instead of feeling that my analyst had failed, I felt as though I had. At the same time, I began to

With her children Lisa and Michael in the Borghese Gardens, Rome, after the flood, 1966

have my doubts about aspects of psychoanalytic theory—particularly Freud's ideas about women. I began to wonder—too timidly, I admit—why Maenchen repeatedly questioned my need to write. Didn't she have a profession herself? Didn't she give papers and go to conferences? Why then did she keep asking me mockingly why I always needed something more, why I was afraid "just to live"?

I decided that reading theory wasn't enough, I needed to see what went on in the analytic process from the other side of the couch. When my third child, Rebecca, was a few months old, I applied to the Psychoanalytic Institute for training. Maenchen said that the root of my writing was a dissatisfaction with myself. To me, it seemed as though my writing self was my best self, clearer, more certain, not afraid of risk. I thought that seeing creative people as patients might help me understand how creativity meshed with the rest of personality. What its relation was to sickness. Besides, I instinctively felt that becoming a lay analyst might equalize the power relation between me and Maenchen.

I was interviewed by several of the old-guard analysts with disastrous results. When a famous woman analyst who worked with disturbed children asked me how I could think of applying for an arduous course of study when I had "a suckling infant at home," I knew I was finished. (A friend told me that when she applied a few years later, she refused to answer questions they wouldn't have asked a male candidate.) A senior analyst called and explained that training would take too much time from my young family, and that I seemed to write books well enough without it. The pain of rejection was softened by the acceptance of my first scholarly article on Yeats by *American Imago*.

While unlucky with my analysts, I've always been lucky with my mentors. Estelle Weiss, one of the Institute's training analysts, offered to help me revise my Yeats book with a more sophisticated framework. She also told me that most of what they taught at the Institute was irrelevant. Estelle not only winnowed out the theoretical wheat from the chaff but she was funny. While telling me about pre-Oedipal phenomena, she would suddenly break into song, "Here we go searching for primal scenery / among California's mountain greenery."

My main problem was a sort of dreamy passivity—so was Yeats's, and at this point my work became part of a process of growth. I used it to understand things about myself at one remove. My curiosity about the way Yeats worked his way out of his passive stance gave me the energy to plow through reams of boring theoretical papers searching for clues. I began to see that his passivity was part of a defensive system that didn't work very well. As he grew older, he found better means of protecting himself. He invented concepts and images such as his Golden Bird, which he used to make himself stronger not just in his poetry but in his life. The revelation for me was that growth as an artist doesn't have to be at the expense of the lived life. That it might enhance the life.

But I wasn't ready to put my insight into practice. For every step I took forward, I seemed to take one backward as well. My book gained depth, but instead of becoming stronger myself, I became intensely anxious, worrying obsessively about my children. Every time one of them had a defeat at school or was home with a stomach ache, I felt as if it was my fault.

In an effort to figure out what was bothering me, I wrote a series of poems about my mother. In one she was painting my portrait as a child. I was standing on a green table naked, eating a tomato. As I was writing, the image transformed itself into an image of her skewering my smile on the tip of her brush and transferring it to her canvas, leaving me with a blank face. I thought at the time the poem was about my mother's coldness, her involvement with her art somehow negating me, and that my anxiety about my children was just another bout of guilt about my work. But now I think that what was frightening me was the idea of having my book accepted, of actually succeeding and being recognized. More important, having to recognize—because it would be public—that the self who wrote the book was the same one who mothered the children. It would blow my cover.

When Harold Bloom praised my book as one of the best books written on Yeats, and one of the only ones that made a sensible use of psychoanalytic principles, my husband scowled. When a reviewer in the *Times Literary Supplement* implied I was "an opinionated bitch," Richard smirked. I began to think of leaving him.

Instead I threw myself into work on my new project, Blake's prophecies. I think I purposely chose something more difficult than anything I had done before so that my energies would be fully engaged. While Blake's famous *Songs* are lucidly clear, his prophecies are murky in the extreme. Before I could interpret them, I had to learn how to read them. It was like working up Old Norse and took a corresponding amount of time. I was fascinated by the fact that most critics ignored the intense emotion in his texts, and that the psychoanalytic emphasis on Oedipal conflict and motives of love and jealousy was in many respects similar to Blake's own. In drawings for his late works, Blake literally depicted the staples of the Freudian worldview of the psyche: the primal scene, incest, the phallic woman. Moreover, the fact that Blake was tormented by rage and frustrated ambition helped me with my own frustrations. I could imagine how he felt, forced to illustrate the children's songs of a vastly inferior poet, while his own magnificently illustrated books were neglected or mocked by his contemporaries. When Richard mocked me, I read Blake's lines out loud to myself in the bathroom and cried.

Part of what I loved about doing this work was the feeling of power I got from noticing how other people had failed to see things: in analytic terms how they defended themselves against the full force of Blake's meaning. How Blake himself had to retreat from the force of his desires, turning in a short space from sexual revolutionary to Christian and eventually denying sex altogether. It made me feel calm and somewhat above it all to be able to create a framework that would make sense of all this. The pity of it was that while I was becoming expert at pointing out contradictions and defects of vision in others, I was oblivious to my own.

It's hard to look back and see how split I was: my brain was working at top form, but I was still as emotionally dependent as a child. Not at all the sort of person I'd want my daughters to imitate. Hardly the heroine of a nineties novel. But finally—after futile efforts to make my marriage work—something started to move. Like a storybook heroine, I met a powerful charismatic man. It was a *coup de foudre.* Looking at myself through his eyes, I began to see myself as not only intelligent but desirable. I suddenly saw what had been obvious to everyone around me, that I'd been unhappy, even abused. As a feminist I wish I'd come to this realization by myself. But at least I was ready

for it. I could, I suppose, have gone on, like Sleeping Beauty frozen in my glass coffin, for another twenty years. But my Prince Charming wasn't the real thing—or at least he was following quite a different storyline. When I mustered the courage to ask Richard for a separation, my life-changing lover turned tail and ran. It was 1979. I was forty-three.

It's tempting to see my life falling into a fictional shape. Idyllic childhood ended by my father's tragic death and my mother's suicide attempt; midlife, twenty years of wandering in the desert. Going through endless contortions so that I could keep doing what I loved without censoring myself, terrified that my work would somehow turn me into my mother or harm my children. Finally in middle age having it all come together: work, love, children.

When I see my life this way, the episode that brought a term to my wandering was another suicide attempt by my mother. She had taken a mixture of painkillers and sleeping pills and was in intensive care in a coma. My brother called to tell me how he had found her unconscious in the hall of her apartment. After a few days, he began to wonder if we should disconnect her from her life support system. The doctors were afraid that if she did wake up, she'd be a vegetable.

It is rare that life gives you a chance to replay traumatic incidents from the past. But I got one then. I flew to New York and went directly to the hospital, where I sat by Mother's bed for hours, talking to her. I told her what I was doing and how I'd left Richard, but mostly I told her how I wanted her to come back, that she just had to live. Eventually, when my voice was about to give out, her eyelids fluttered and she opened her eyes and looked at me. The nurses couldn't believe it.

When I was fifteen, on the awful day that I had found her asleep in her room, I'd felt helpless, frightened out of my mind. This time, I wasn't afraid for myself or horrified at what she had done. When she woke up, I felt it as a personal triumph. She'd heard me calling and answered. The next day, she lay propped up on her pillows, wires still running out of her, and I fed her Jello. She opened her mouth for it like a baby bird. Between spoonfuls she told me she had seen a mysterious woman and gone on a long journey. "I never refuse an angel," she whispered, eyes shining. "I know," I said. I could see that the Jello didn't mat-

The Webster children (from left), Michael, Lisa, and Rebecca, cleaning up the wedding banquet for their mother and Ira Lapidus, San Francisco, 1983

ter to her any more than the bag beside her bed that was slowly filling with her urine. She was already thinking how to paint her angel.

Macmillan wanted world rights to my Blake book. The book would ruffle some feathers, my editor said, but that was fine with him. It was an original work. He liked it. They were going to publish it with sixty illustrations from Blake's *Songs* and Prophetic Books. Besides that, the English edition of my Yeats book had done quite well, reviews had been generally good, and two anthologies of critical method were taking excerpts from it. In one, I was sandwiched between Harold Bloom and Jacques Derrida as an example of criticism based on psychoanalytic object relations.

I not only found my critical niche but I finally found a man who loved both me and my work, Ira Lapidus, a Berkeley professor, amateur photographer and musician, and Himalayan trekker. But as far as being an inde-

pendent woman, I wasn't yet home free. Though things were better than they'd ever been—I was actually having fun!—I couldn't seem to break my habit of returning to my analyst whenever troubles cropped up. Though Ira and I loved each other passionately, it was anything but easy to absorb him and his teenage son into a family of teenage and pre-teenage children. What I needed was some good practical advice. The best advice would probably have been to try trusting myself. What I got instead were Maenchen's biblical pronouncements about how a true female should act—not show anger, not confront things directly, back off, lie low. It made no sense that I kept listening to this stuff, but when you're emotionally dependent on someone, whether abusive spouse or analyst, it doesn't have to make sense. Again my work came to my aid, and I unwittingly found a rather ingenious way to gain the distance I needed and escape my dependence. I decided to write about Maenchen's professional sisters, the women analysts in Freud's inner circle.

My task, as I saw it, was a friendly one. Many feminists were down on analysis. I was going to find redeeming qualities in the women analysts (just the way I had hoped to find them in Maenchen) and then explain them to the feminists. If I'd realized that I really wanted to bring the whole analytic establishment crashing down so I could escape Maenchen's couch in the general conflagration, I probably wouldn't have been able to begin.

I was going to collaborate with a friend and we thought we should call our book *What Do Women Want?* When my friend got pregnant and lost interest, I decided to write a series of short pieces instead, starting with my mother's analyst in the twenties, Helene Deutsch. After my essay on Deutsch appeared in *Signs: Journal of Women in Culture and Society*, feminist women who had dismissed her told me they had gone back to take another look. I had convinced them, they said, that despite Deutsch's lip service to Freud's demeaning ideas about women, she had really encouraged her patients to develop their strengths. Someone even phoned me and asked, "Is this Brenda Webster, the feminist?"

"Yes," I said after a moment's thought. "I guess it is."

Though I wasn't aware of it, this was a turning point. By the time I started on my next essay, on Phyllis Greenacre, I decided that I

"Reading from my mother's journal at Elliot Bay Books," Seattle, 1993

didn't have to accept a theory that defined me or other women negatively. Greenacre interested me because of her writing on the creative process, but I was disappointed to find that she went further than Freud in downgrading women. She even invented a new concept called Penis Awe and asserted that women couldn't be artists without imagining they had a male organ! It began to get into my dim brain that the people who'd been "helping" me with my life worked on the basis of theories like these. When I interviewed my old analyst Dr. Eissler, he explained to me in all seriousness that women couldn't be geniuses because they had a limited quantity of eggs while men had an unlimited quantity of sperm. I put my Greenacre essay aside and wrote a spoof instead. That was it for me. It was the end of my career as a psychoanalytic critic and as a docile analysand: I quit.

I had started writing fiction again soon after I met Ira. Now stories came pouring out. Not surprisingly they were about my father, my early life, the farm, and Connie. It was as though the circle was coming round again—I couldn't relive it but I could, as it were, rewrite it, make sense of it. I learned more by writing my stories than I had in years of therapy.

Ira's love stimulated my writing fiction. My mother's death in 1984, the year after our marriage, was a catalyst of another sort. It made me want to get her work the recognition it deserved. I organized retrospective shows across the country, and spent part of the next six years editing the journals of Mother's old age with my friend, the poet Judith Emlyn Johnson. Reading what Mother had written about her art and her emotional pain made me understand her better than I ever had. I began to write short stories exploring my intense love and hate.

I worked over my short stories until I felt ready to try something longer. (The ability to rewrite was probably the most valuable thing I'd picked up in the years since my progressive education.) In 1993, my novel *Sins of the Mothers* came out with Baskerville, a small press in Texas. My edition of Mother's journal, *Hungry for Light,* appeared the same fall. At fifty-seven years old I was launched on a new career.

Before my mother died, I came closer to her, but the past still unrolled behind me in two separate strands. In one, Mother was the

With husband, Ira Lapidus, at Giverny, about 1986

gifted woman who taught me to love beauty and persevere in trying to create it, and in the other, she was the raving, cruel woman who often hurt me. I still hadn't brought the two together and laid them to rest.

When I read from her journal at Cody's, a Berkeley bookstore, with my commentary and slides of Mother's paintings, people cried—I was almost crying too. The paintings were beautiful and her words were not just inspiring but nourishing. Afterwards, someone asked me how I could have written a novel in which this eloquent, moving woman—because even though *Sins* is fiction everyone assumes she is the heroine's artist-mother—is portrayed as a monster of narcissism. Mother was split, I told her, and my feelings towards her are split too.

I wanted to bring the two sides of her together and see her whole. To do this, I decided to write a novel—which eventually became *Paradise Farm*—about her as a young artist. I'd start from where I could understand her imaginatively and try to figure out what made her the way she was later. What her own mother must have been like. What it was like growing up with a crazy brother. I began to think about how what we call a self is formed. What is it? What helps or hinders its growth? I imagined a spectrum of selves from the most rudimentary and damaged—an autistic child who can't even say the word "I"—to the most integrated, with my young artist heroine somewhere in the middle, like one of those countries with a highly developed north and an underdeveloped south. The polar opposite of the sick child

would be a healer, perhaps someone like Muriel. I had been thinking about Muriel since her daughter, Connie, had written me that Muriel had died suddenly of lung cancer. (I had instantly seen her talking animatedly, with her lip drawn back crookedly on one side, a cigarette in her mouth.)

I realized that I needed to write about Muriel because she wasn't just someone I loved. She was a model for life that I had had in front of my eyes but never used. Most people have areas that are unused or split off, but with Muriel, I had the sense of a personality vibrantly whole to its utmost boundaries, using every ounce of herself. I had rarely written about strong, loving people. Now I wanted to try. To set Muriel in a fictional context with my mother and my grandmother and my crazy uncle and, literally, see what she would do with them. Maybe I could find new ways of looking at them myself. A difficult family isn't fate. The great thing about being human is that you can re-create yourself, not by analyzing but by active imagining.

I don't remember who said that anyone who has had a childhood has enough material for a lifetime. It has certainly been the case with me. Every time I think I have exhausted the vein, I find it again. My current project, a memoir, was stimulated by watching my three adult children make their own experiments with balancing work and creative life. At first I thought simply of writing about my early years—as a sort of gift to my oldest grandchild. But it is something of a fantasy that my children or their children are interested in my work. I am mother or grandmother to them. They see me only grudgingly as a writer. Perhaps this isn't surprising since I often write about things that disturb them, or divulge family secrets. But it makes me sad—and is perhaps the only sad thing about becoming publicly a writer. I can't hide anymore, and I hate it when something I write makes them angry. So it seems that I haven't healed the split between being a mother and being a writer that tormented me so much throughout my marriage. Maybe it is unhealable.

When I started to write it in earnest, my memoir turned out to be about my family's relation to psychoanalysis and my place in the wider curve that contains not just the farm and my parents but issues of Jewish identity, social class, and modern art. One good thing about getting older is that you get a certain perspective. Though I feel, as I do after every book,

With grandchild Guillermo Webster,
Los Angeles, 1998

that I am written out, have gone as far as I could, I know by now that this is an illusion. Now I can already feel half-formed thoughts swirling around in my mental dark. When I pick up my pen again, I know they'll miraculously declare themselves, and one morning I'll be surprised at what I was thinking. Writing by now is part of the way I apprehend reality. As necessary as touching or seeing. And it isn't likely I'm going to stop it anytime soon.

BIBLIOGRAPHY

Fiction:

Sins of the Mothers, Baskerville, 1993.

Tattoo Bird (short stories), FictionNet, 1996.

Paradise Farm, SUNY Press, 1998.

Nonfiction:

Yeats: A Psychoanalytic Study, Stanford University Press, 1973; Macmillan (London), 1973.

Freud under Analysis, edited by Todd Dufresne, Jacob Aronson, Inc., 1977.

Blake's Prophetic Psychology, University of Georgia Press, 1983; Macmillan (London) 1983.

Hungry for Light: The Journal of Ethel Schwabacher, edited by Brenda Webster and Judith Emlyn Johnson, Indiana University Press, 1993

Also contributor to *Critical Paths: Blake and the Argument of Method,* edited by Dan Miller, Mark Bracher, and Donald Ault, Duke University Press, 1987; *Literary Theories in Praxis,* edited by Shirley Staton, University of Pennsylvania Press, 1987; *Mythopoesis: Literatura, Totalidad, Ideologia,* edited by Joan Ramon Resina, Anthopos, 1992; *William Blake* (New Casebooks), edited by David Punter, Macmillan, 1996; *Sideshow* (short stories), edited by Shelley Anderson, Marjorie Jacobs, and Kathe Stoltz, Somersault Press, 1995.

Translations from the Italian are included in *The Penguin Book of Women Poets, The Other Voice* (Norton), and *Women Poets of the World* (Macmillan). Contributor of short stories, essays, and reviews to magazines, journals, and papers, including *American Imago, Caprice, Chariton Review, Confrontation, Crazy Quilt, Fiction International, Hurricane Alice, San Francisco Chronicle, San Francisco Review of Books, Signs, Southern Lights, Thirteenth Moon, William and Mary Review, Women's Art Journal, Women's Review of Books,* and *Women's Studies.*

Cumulative Author List

CUMULATIVE AUTHOR LIST
Volumes 1-30

List is alphabetical, followed by the volume number in which autobiographical entries appear.

CUMULATIVE INDEX

The names of essayists who appear in the series are in boldface type. Subject references are followed by volume and page number(s). When a subject reference appears in more than one essay, names of the essayists are also provided.

INDEX